Windows® 8
ALL-IN-ONE
FOR
DUMMIES®

by Woody Leonhard

WILEY

John Wiley & Sons, Inc.

Windows® 8 All-in-One For Dummies®

Published by
John Wiley & Sons, Inc.
111 River Street
Hoboken, NJ 07030-5774
www.wiley.com

For general information on our other products and services, please contact our Customer Care Department within the U.S. at 877-762-2974, outside the U.S. at 317-572-3993, or fax 317-572-4002.

For technical support, please visit www.wiley.com/techsupport.

Wiley publishes in a variety of print and electronic formats and by print-on-demand. Some material included with standard print versions of this book may not be included in e-books or in print-on-demand. If this book refers to media such as a CD or DVD that is not included in the version you purchased, you may download this material at http://booksupport.wiley.com. For more information about Wiley products, visit www.wiley.com.

Library of Congress Control Number: 2012949004

ISBN 978-1-118-11920-4 (pbk); ISBN 978-1-118-22461-8 (ebk); ISBN 978-1-118-23799-1 (ebk); ISBN 978-1-118-26270-2 (ebk)

Manufactured in the United States of America

10 9 8 7 6 5 4 3 2 1

WILEY

About the Author

Curmudgeon, critic, and fiercely independent "Windows victim," **Woody Leonhard** has dished up the truth about Microsoft products since his first Windows book two decades ago. *Windows 8 All-In-One For Dummies,* his 40th and most ambitious computer book, takes on both sides of the Windows 8 interface, then branches out to cover the ways Windows interacts with all sorts of products — iPads to Google Apps, Facebook to Mac networks, VPNs to Android. Woody's unique reader-first approach ensures that you get the best advice about solving your problems — whether Microsoft likes it or not.

Woody is best known online as a Senior Contributing Editor for *Infoworld,* and Contributing Editor of *Windows Secrets Newsletter.* He also runs AskWoody. com, the web's leading source of news about Microsoft updates. He tweets frequently on tech topics from @woodyleonhard.

He's a Microsoft MVP, one of the first Microsoft Consulting Partners, and a charter member of the Microsoft Solutions Provider organization. He delights in being a constant thorn in Microsoft's side. Along with several coauthors and editors, Woody has won an unprecedented six Computer Press Association awards and two American Business Press awards.

Woody moved to Phuket, Thailand, in 2000, with his teenage son. His dad joined them in 2006. Woody married a southern Thai lady — yes, they met in Starbucks — and now have a toddler who keeps life running a mile a minute.

Dedication

And to Add and Andy, the lights of my life.

Author's Acknowledgments

I'm very lucky to have an outstanding editorial dream team at Wiley, with Becky Huehls in the thick of it, once again. This book is by far the thickest book I've ever written, covering a topic that's enormously complex, and Becky and crew led the charge to keep it accurate, timely, and directed squarely at the features Windows users need most.

Thanks, also, to Claudette Moore and Ann Jaroncyk at Moore Literary Agency, the best agents in the biz.

My thanks to Rob Oppenheim for his research on Windows search. As you can see in Book VI, Chapter 8, Windows search is a complex topic that's barely documented elsewhere — and much of the published documentation is wrong. Rob's show-me attitude brought many oddities to light.

I also want to thank the people at TechSmith for keeping their screen-capture program, Snagit, working through the Windows 8 versions. I've use Snagit for all the screen shots in all my books, going back as far as I can remember. Snagit is a workhorse — one of the most reliable pieces of software I've ever encountered.

Publisher's Acknowledgments

We're proud of this book; please send us your comments at http://dummies.custhelp.com. For other comments, please contact our Customer Care Department within the U.S. at 877-762-2974, outside the U.S. at 317-572-3993, or fax 317-572-4002.

Some of the people who helped bring this book to market include the following:

Acquisitions and Editorial

Sr. Project Editor: Rebecca Huehls

Acquisitions Editor: Amy Fandrei

Copy Editors: Jen Riggs, Debbye Butler

Technical Editor: Ryan Williams

Sr. Editorial Manager: Leah Michael

Editorial Assistant: Leslie Saxman

Sr. Editorial Assistant: Cherie Case

Cover Photo: © Veer/Blend Images Photography

Cartoons: Rich Tennant (www.the5thwave.com)

Composition Services

Project Coordinator: Katherine Crocker

Layout and Graphics: Carrie A. Cesavice, Jennifer Creasey, Corrie Niehaus

Proofreaders: John Greenough, Evelyn Wellborn

Indexer: BIM Indexing & Proofreading Services

Special Help: Jean Nelson

Publishing and Editorial for Technology Dummies

    Richard Swadley, Vice President and Executive Group Publisher

    Andy Cummings, Vice President and Publisher

    Mary Bednarek, Executive Acquisitions Director

    Mary C. Corder, Editorial Director

Publishing for Consumer Dummies

    Kathleen Nebenhaus, Vice President and Executive Publisher

Composition Services

    Debbie Stailey, Director of Composition Services

Contents at a Glance

Table of Contents

Introduction

*W*indows 8 shows two completely different personas: the traditional desktop and the tiled Start screen interface. The traditional Windows desktop resembles every Windows desktop you've seen over the past decade, give or take a bit. More than a billion people have used it. The tiled "immersive" persona, which Microsoft calls the Start screen (and in this book, I do, too), represents the future of Windows.

I think of the desktop as the staid, dependable, conservative Dr. Jekyll and the tiled Start screen as the dashing, new, outlandish, and occasionally inexplicable Mr. Hyde.

You may prefer Jekyll. You may prefer Hyde. You'll certainly find yourself, from time to time, jumping between the two, sometimes at the moment you least expect. But, armed with this book, you can make both places work the way you want.

Prefer the desktop? I show you how to change the Start screen so it'll help you get more out of the desktop. Prefer the showy tiles? I show you how to get a lot done — quite possibly almost everything you want a computer to do — without leaving the tiles behind.

This isn't the manual Microsoft forgot. This is the manual Microsoft wouldn't dare print. I won't feed you the Microsoft Party Line, or make excuses for pieces of Windows 8 that just don't work. My job is to take you through the most important parts of Windows, give you tips that may or may not involve Microsoft products, point out the rough spots, and guide you around the disasters. Frankly, there are some biggies.

I also look at using non-Microsoft products in a Windows way: iPads, Androids, Kindles, Gmail and Google Apps, Facebook, Twitter, Flickr, Dropbox, Firefox, Google Chrome, and iCloud. Even though Microsoft competes with just about every one of those products, each has a place in your computing arsenal and ties into Windows in important ways.

I'll save you more than enough money to pay for the book several times over, keep you from pulling out a whole shock of hair, lead you to dozens if not hundreds of "Aha!" moments, and keep you awake in the process. Guaranteed.

About This Book

Windows 8 All-in-One For Dummies takes you through the Land of the Dummies — with introductory material and stuff your grandmother could (and should!) understand — and then continues the journey into more advanced areas, where you can truly put Windows to work every day.

I start with the tiled Start screen, and for many of you, that's all you'll ever need. The Start screen coverage here is the best you'll find anywhere, because I don't assume that you know Windows, and I step you through everything you need to know both with a touch screen and a mouse.

Then I dig into the desktop and take you through all the important pieces.

I don't dwell on technical mumbo jumbo, and I keep the baffling jargon to a minimum. At the same time, though, I tackle the tough problems you're likely to encounter, show you the major road signs, and give you a lot of help where you need it the most.

Whether you want to get two or more e-mail accounts set up to work simultaneously, hook into your Facebook page, or publish photos of your Boykin Spaniel on the web, this is your book. Er, I should say ten books. I've broken out the topics into ten different minibooks, so you'll find it easy to hop around to a topic — and a level of coverage — that feels comfortable.

I didn't design this book to be read from front to back. It's a reference. Each chapter, and each of its sections, is meant to focus on solving a particular problem or describing a specific technique.

Windows 8 All-in-One For Dummies should be your reference of first resort, even before you consult Windows Help and Support. There's a big reason why: Windows Help was written by hundreds of people over the course of many, many years. Some of the material was written ages ago, and it's confusing as all get-out, but it's still in Windows Help for folks who are tackling tough "legacy" problems. Some of the Help file terminology is inconsistent and downright misleading, largely because the technology has changed so much since some of the articles were written. Finding help in Help frequently boggles my mind: If I don't already know the answer to a question, it's hard to figure out how to coax Help to help. Besides, if you're looking for help on connecting your iPad to your PC or downloading pictures from your Galaxy phone, Microsoft would rather sell you something different. The proverbial bottom line: I don't duplicate the material in Windows 8 Help and Support, but I point to it if I figure it can help you.

A word about Windows 8 versions. As we went to press, Microsoft was preparing a completely different kind of Windows, made for small, light, highly portable tablets known as "ARM architecture," because the computers innards are designed by a company called ARM. This book doesn't cover ARM computers, or the version of Windows called Windows RT (code-named WOA "Windows on ARM," get it?). While many of the interactions with the tiled Mr. Hyde side of Windows 8 are basically identical to those on Windows RT, there are many, many differences. Don't try to psych out Windows RT using the nostrums in this book.

Foolish Assumptions

I don't make many assumptions about you, dear reader, except to acknowledge that you're obviously intelligent, well-informed, discerning, and of impeccable taste. That's why you chose this book, eh?

Okay, okay. The least I can do is butter you up a bit. Here's the straight scoop: If you've never used Windows, bribe your neighbor (or, better, your neighbor's kids) to teach you how to do four things:

✦ Play a game with your fingers (if you have a touchscreen). Any of the games on the tiled side of Windows 8 will do. If your neighbor's kids don't have a different recommendation, try Cut the Rope.

✦ Start File Explorer.

✦ Get on the web.

✦ Put Windows to sleep. (Hint: nudge your finger or mouse in the upper right corner, choose Settings, then look for the Power icon.)

That covers it. If you can play a game, you know how to turn on your computer, log in if need be, touch and drag, and tap and hold. If you run File Explorer, you know how to click a taskbar icon. After you're on the web, well, it's a great starting point for almost anything. And, if you know that you need to use the Charms bar — that weird flyout on the right — you're well on your way to achieving Windows 8 Enlightenment.

And that begins with Book I, Chapter 1.

What You Don't Have to Read

Throughout this book, I've gone to great lengths to separate "optional" reading from "required" reading. If you want to find out more about a topic or solve a specific problem, follow along in the main part of the text. You can skip the sidebars as you go, unless one happens to catch your eye.

On the other hand, if you know a topic pretty well but want to make sure that you catch all the high points, read the paragraphs marked with icons and be sure that the information registers. If it doesn't, glance at the surrounding text.

Sidebars offer information above and beyond what you need to know for those who are curious about a specific topic — or who stand knee-deep in muck, searching for a way out.

How This Book Is Organized

Windows 8 All-in-One For Dummies contains ten minibooks, each of which gives a thorough airing of a specific topic. If you're looking for information on a specific Windows topic, check the headings in the Table of Contents or refer to the index.

By design, this book enables you to get as much (or as little) information as you need at any particular moment. Want to know how to e-mail a picture from your Facebook account to a friend? Look at Book III, Chapter 3. Want to change to a picture logon? Flip to Book II, Chapter 2. *Windows 8 All-in-One For Dummies* is a reference that you will reach for again and again whenever a new question about Windows comes up.

Here's a description of the ten minibooks and what they contain:

✦ **Book I, Starting Windows 8** takes you through the two very different faces of Windows 8. Whether you're just starting out, or you've been using Windows for decades, there's a whole lot of stuff that you've never seen before. This is where you start to earn your chops.

✦ **Book II, Personalizing Windows** runs you all around the Windows playing surface, pointing out what you can do, what you should do, and where you might fall into a rabbit hole. It shows you how to get your Lock screen and Logons working right, add new users, take advantage of cloud syncing of your Windows settings, and stay on top of your privacy. Yeah, even some of the stuff Microsoft doesn't want you to know about.

✦ **Book III, Navigating the Start Screen** goes through the whole nine yards. Mr. Hyde gets a thorough deconstruction, with every important Start screen setting fully explicated.

✦ **Book IV, Maximizing Tiled Windows 8 Apps,** introduces you to the latest and greatest programs from Microsoft. They're free, they're flashy, and they're oh-so-frustrating when they don't do what you want. See how to tame them into submission.

✦ **Book V, Connecting Online with Tiled Apps,** shows you all the important online apps both from Microsoft and from Microsoft's competitors. Whether you use Facebook, Twitter, Flickr, financial apps, news apps, or games, this is where you can find the real story.

✦ **Book VI, Working on the Desktop,** takes you on a very thorough tour of the desktop — the part of Windows you've probably seen before. You'll get advice on picking a web browser, setup instructions, and a bunch of important tips on browsing on the Internet. You'll also see my full Start screen makeover for people who really prefer to use the desktop.

✦ **Book VII, Controlling Your System** goes through the Control Panel and then covers many new and exciting Windows 8 capabilities, like the hard drives that heal themselves (and keep your system running even when a drive dies), setting up libraries, and sharing easily on a network. I also go through some school-of-hard-knocks tips on working with printers and other worse-than-senseless things.

✦ **Book VIII, Maintaining Windows 8** explains how to restore, refresh, and reset your computer, using tools that Microsoft touts, as well as the ones Windows hides. I also talk about how to use the key built-in Windows programs and tools, including how to keep independent historical file backups, so you'll never lose old data. It's easy.

✦ **Book IX, Securing Windows 8** goes way beyond the usual recommendations about Windows Defender and Firewall. I talk about the biggest security vulnerability on all Windows systems — the person behind the keyboard. And I step you through a couple of real-life takedowns of scammers, to show you how to take care of yourself.

✦ **Book X: Enhancing Windows 8** takes you to the outside world. How do you get your iPad to work with your PC? What you can do with an iPhone? Where do Android tablets and phones fit into the picture? This minibook explains all that. You also find out how to use Google Apps and Docs, Microsoft's largest online app competitor.

See. I told you this is a manual Microsoft wouldn't dare to publish.

Conventions

I try to keep typographical conventions to a minimum:

✦ The first time a buzzword appears in text, I *italicize* it and define it immediately. That makes it easier for you to glance back and reread the definition.

✦ Whenever I want you to type something, I put the letters or words in **bold**. For example: "Type **William Gates** in the Name text box." If you need to press more than one key at a time on the keyboard, I add a plus sign between the keys' names; for example, "Press **Ctrl+Alt+Delete** to initiate a Vulcan Mind Meld."

✦ I set off web addresses and e-mail addresses in `monospace`. For example, my e-mail address is `woody@AskWoody.com` (true fact), and my website is at `AskWoody.com` (another true fact). You may be accustomed to seeing web addresses (commonly known as URLs) spelled out in their entirety, such as `http://www.dummies.com`. Mercifully, some printed media drop the (completely superfluous) `http://` and the most progressive printed sources drop the `www`. That's the convention you see in this book: I write `dummies.com` instead of `http://www.dummies.com`. If you type `dummies.com` into your Web browser and it comes back with `http://ww9.redirect.dummies.com/index.asp?lang=en,source=ohmy`, don't be too surprised, okay? Computers talk funny.

There's one other convention, though, that I use all the time: I always, absolutely, adamantly include the filename extension — the period and (usually) three letters at the end of a filename, such as `.doc` or `.vbs` or `.exe` — when talking about a file. Yeah, I know Windows 8 hides filename extensions by default, but you can and should change that setting. Yeah, I realize that Bill G. himself made the decision to hide the extensions and that Steve B. and Steve S. won't back off. (At least, that's the rumor.)

I also know that, years ago, hundreds — probably thousands — of Microsoft employees passed along the ILOVEYOU virus, primarily because they couldn't see the filename extension that would've warned them that the file was a virus. Uh, bad decision, Bill.

Icons

Some of the points in *Windows 8 All-in-One For Dummies* merit your special attention. I set off those points with icons.

When I'm jumping up and down on one foot with an idea so absolutely cool that I can't stand it anymore, I stick a Tip icon in the margin. You can browse any chapter and hit its highest points by jumping from Tip to Tip.

When you see this icon, you get the real story about Windows 8 — not the stuff that the Microsoft marketing droids want you to hear — and my take on the best way to get Windows 8 to work for you. You find the same take on Microsoft, Windows, and more at my eponymous website, AskWoody.com.

You don't need to memorize the information marked with this icon, but you should try to remember that something special is lurking.

Achtung! Cuidado! Thar be tygers here! Anywhere that you see a Warning icon, you can be sure that I've been burnt — badly. Mind your fingers. These are really, really mean suckers.

Okay, so I'm a geek. I admit it. Sure, I love to poke fun at geeks. But I'm a modern, New Age, sensitive guy, in touch with my inner geekiness. Sometimes, I just can't help but let it out, ya know? That's where the Technical Stuff icon comes in. If you get all tied up in knots about techie-type stuff, pass these paragraphs by. (For the record, I managed to write this whole book without telling you that an IPv4 address consists of a unique 32-bit combination of network ID and host ID, expressed as a set of four decimal numbers with each octet separated by periods. See? I can restrain myself sometimes.)

Where to Go from Here

That's about it. It's time for you to crack this book open and have at it.

If you haven't yet told Windows 8 to show you filename extensions, flip to Book VI, Chapter 1. If you haven't yet set up the File History feature, go to Book VIII, Chapter 1.

Don't forget to bookmark my website: www.AskWoody.com. It keeps you up-to-date on all the Windows 8 news you need to know — including notes about this book, the latest Windows bugs and gaffes, patches that are worse than the problems they're supposed to fix, and much more — and you can submit your most pressing questions, for free consultation from The Woodmeister himself.

For updates specific to this book, point your browser to www.dummies. com/go/windows8aioupdates.

See ya! woody@AskWoody.com

Sometimes it's worth reading the Intro, eh?

Book I

Starting Windows 8

The 5th Wave   By Rich Tennant

"The odd thing is he always insists on using
the latest version of Windows."

Contents at a Glance

Chapter 1: Windows 8 4 N00bs

*D*on't sweat it. Everyone started out as *n00bs* (or *newbies*).

All those high-falutin' technical words you have to memorize, eh?

If you've never used an earlier version of Windows, you're in luck — you don't have to force your fingers to "forget" so much of what you've learned. Windows 8 is completely different from any Windows that has come before, and Windows 7 (or XP) users who try to apply their hard-gained knowledge frequently get very frustrated just trying to get to first base with Win8.

The easiest way to learn about the new tiled "immersive" interface formerly known as "Metro" is to forget everything you ever knew about Windows and be prepared to start again from scratch. Considering more than a billion people around the world have used Windows 7 and earlier, that's a whole lot of forgettin' goin' on.

So you're sitting in front of your computer and this thing called Windows 8 is staring at you. Except the screen (see Figure 1-1), which Microsoft calls the *lock screen*, doesn't say "Windows" much less "Windows 8." In fact, the screen doesn't say much of anything except the current date and time, with maybe a tiny icon or two that shows you whether your Internet connection is working, how many unopened e-mails await, or whether you should just take the day off because your holdings in AAPL stock soared again.

Figure 1-1:
The
Windows 8
lock screen.
Your picture
may differ,
but the
function
stays the
same.

You may be tempted to just sit and admire the gorgeous picture, whatever it may be, but if you use your finger or mouse to swipe up from the bottom, or press any key on an attached keyboard, you see the logon screen, possibly resembling the one in Figure 1-2. If more than one person is set up to use your computer, you see more than one name.

Figure 1-2:
The
Windows 8
logon
screen.

That's the logon screen, but it doesn't say "Logon" or "Welcome to Win8 Land" or "Howdy" or even "Sit down and get to work, Bucko." It has names and pictures only for people who can use the computer. Why do you have to click your name? What if your name isn't there? And why in the %$#@! can't you bypass all this garbage, log on, and get your e-mail?

Good for you. That's the right attitude.

Windows 8 ranks as the most sophisticated computer program ever made. It cost more money to develop and took more people to build than any previous computer program — ever. So why is it so blasted hard to use? Why doesn't it do what you want it to do the first time? For that matter, why do you need it at all?

Someday, I swear, you'll be able to pull a PC out of the box and plug it into the wall, turn it on, and get your e-mail — bang, bang, bang, just like that, in ten seconds flat. In the meantime, those stuck in the early 21st century have to make do with PCs that grow obsolete before you can unpack them, software that's so ornery you find yourself arguing with it, and Internet connections that surely involve turtles carrying bits on their backs.

If you aren't comfortable working with Windows and you still worry that you might break something if you click the wrong button, welcome to the club! In this chapter, I present a concise, school-of-hard-knocks overview of how all this hangs together, and what to look for when buying a Windows PC. It may help you understand why and how Windows has limitations. It also may help you communicate with the geeky rescue team that tries to bail you out, whether you rely on the store that sold you the PC, the smelly guy in the apartment downstairs, or your eight-year-old daughter's nerdy classmate.

Hardware and Software

At the most fundamental level, all computer stuff comes in one of two flavors: hardware or software. *Hardware* is anything you can touch — a computer screen, a mouse, a hard drive, a CD (remember those coasters with shiny sides?). *Software* is everything else: e-mail messages, that letter to your Aunt Martha, digital pictures of your last vacation, programs like Microsoft Office. If you shoot a bunch of pictures, the pictures themselves are just bits — software. But they're probably sitting on some sort of memory card inside your phone or camera. That card's hardware. Get the difference?

Windows 8 is software. You can't touch it. Your PC, on the other hand, is hardware. Kick the computer screen, and your toe hurts. Drop the big box on the floor, and it smashes into a gazillion pieces. That's hardware.

Chances are very good that one of the major PC manufacturers — Dell, Acer, HP, Lenovo, Toshiba, or ASUS, for example — or maybe even Microsoft, with its Surface line, made your hardware. Microsoft, and Microsoft alone, makes Windows 8.

When you bought your computer, you paid for a license to use one copy of Windows on the PC you bought. The PC manufacturer paid Microsoft a royalty so that it could sell you Windows along with your PC. You may think that you got Windows from, say, Dell — indeed, you may have to contact Dell for technical support on Windows questions — but, in fact, Windows came from Microsoft.

Windows on ARM — Windows RT

This book covers the whole Windows 8 experience — both the tiled interface and the old-fashioned Windows 7–style desktop. You only get the whole enchilada if you buy a PC that runs on the original Intel/AMD kind of hardware.

Microsoft has developed a different branch of Windows 8 known as Windows RT. The new Windows RT computers are generally small, light, and inexpensive, and will have a long battery life and amazing, touch-sensitive displays. In other words, they're everything the current Intel/AMD tablets aren't, and they're meant to be very similar to the iPad. Window RT computers don't run traditional Windows apps. With a few (Microsoft-controlled) exceptions, they run only on the tiled interface. They don't connect to corporate networks, don't have the security that Win8 packs, and don't have anywhere close to the same number of apps. Those are the machines Microsoft targets directly at the iPad.

If you have a Windows RT machine, Books I–V (and, to a lesser extent, IX and X) should help.

Most software these days, including Windows 8, asks you to agree to an End User License Agreement (EULA). When you first set up your PC, Windows asked you to click the I Accept button to accept a licensing agreement that's long enough to wrap around the Empire State Building. If you're curious about what agreement you accepted, a printed copy of the EULA may be in the box that your PC came in or in the CD packaging, if you bought Windows 8 separately from your computer.

Why Do PCs Have to Run Windows?

Here's the short answer: You don't have to run Windows on your PC.

The PC you have is a dumb box. (You needed me to tell you that, eh?) To get the dumb box to do anything worthwhile, you need a computer program that takes control of the PC and makes it do things, such as show web pages on the screen, respond to mouse clicks or taps, or print résumés. An *operating system* controls the dumb box and makes it do worthwhile things, in ways that mere humans can understand.

Without an operating system, the computer can sit in a corner and count to itself or put profound messages on the screen, such as `Non-system disk or disk error` or maybe `Insert system disk and press any key when ready`. If you want your computer to do more than that, though, you need an operating system.

Windows is not the only operating system in town. The other big contenders in the operating system game are Mac OS and Linux:

✦ **Mac OS:** Apple has made great strides running on Intel hardware, and if you don't already know how to use Windows or own a Windows computer, it makes a great deal of sense to consider buying an Apple computer and/or running Mac OS. Yes, you can build your own computer and run the Mac OS on it: Check out www.hackintosh.com. But, no, it isn't legal — the Mac OS End User License Agreement specifically forbids installation on a "non-Apple-branded computer" — and it's certainly not for the faint of heart.

✦ **Linux:** The big up-and-coming operating system, which has been up and coming for a couple of decades now, is Linux, which is pronounced *LIN-uchs*. It's a viable contender for netbooks (covered in more depth at the end of this chapter). If you expect to use your PC only to get on the Internet — to surf the web and send e-mail from the likes of your Gmail or Hotmail account — Linux can handle all that, and can do it with few of the headaches that remain as the hallmark of Windows. By using free programs like Libre Office (www.libreoffice.org) and online programs like Google Apps and Google Drive (drive.google.com), you can even cover the basics in word processing, spreadsheets, presentations, contact managers, calendars, and more. Linux may not support the huge array of hardware that Windows offers — but more than a few wags will tell you, with a wink, that Windows doesn't support that huge of an array, either.

In the tablet sphere, iOS and Android rule, with iOS for iPhones and iPads — all from Apple — and Android for phones and tablets from a bewildering number of manufacturers. Windows 8 doesn't exactly compete with any of them, although Microsoft's trying to take on the iPad with Windows RT (see sidebar).

What do other people choose? It's hard to measure the percentage of PCs running Windows versus Mac versus Linux. One company, Net Applications, specializes in inspecting the online records of big-name websites and tallying how many Windows computers hit those sites, compared to Apple and Linux. Although the numbers are changing quickly, in the U.S., Windows accounts for about 83 percent of all hits on major websites, Mac runs about 14 percent, and Linux kinda picks up the crumbs. (That's not counting mobile operating systems such as iOS and Android.) You can see the report for the first quarter of 2012 in Figure 1-3.

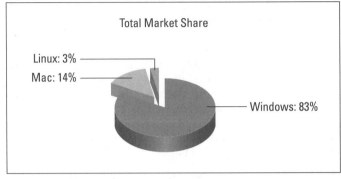

Total Market Share

Linux: 3%
Mac: 14%
Windows: 83%

Source: Net Applications

Figure 1-3: Web access by operating system, first quarter 2012, U.S. only.

Worldwide, Windows still accounts for 90 percent or more of all web hits. Windows is very big in China, and as of late 2011, more PCs are sold in China than in the U.S.

A Terminology Survival Kit

Some terms pop up so frequently that you'll find it worthwhile to memorize them, or at least understand where they come from. That way, you won't be caught flat-footed when your first-grader comes home and asks whether he can download a program from the Internet.

If you want to drive your techie friends nuts the next time you have a problem with your computer, tell them that the hassles occur when you're "running Microsoft." They won't have any idea whether you mean Windows, Word, Outlook, Hotmail, Messenger, Search, Defender, Media Center, or any of a gazillion other programs.

An *app* or a *program* is *software* (see the earlier "Hardware and Software" section in this chapter) that works on a computer. "App" is modern and cool; "program" is old and boring, "application" manages to hit both gongs, but they all mean the same thing.

Windows, the *operating system* (see the preceding section), is a program. So are computer games, Microsoft Office, Microsoft Word (the word processor part of Office), Internet Explorer (the web browser in Windows), Windows Media Player, those nasty viruses you've heard about, that screen saver with the oh-too-perfect fish bubbling and bumbling about, and others.

A special kind of program called a *driver* makes specific pieces of hardware work with the operating system. For example, your computer's printer has a driver, your monitor has a driver, your mouse has a driver, and Tiger Woods has a driver (several, actually, and he makes a living with them). Would that everyone were so talented.

Many drivers ship with Windows, even though Microsoft doesn't make them. The hardware manufacturer's responsible for making their hardware work with your Windows PC, and that includes building and fixing the drivers. (Yes, if Microsoft makes your computer, Microsoft's responsible for the drivers, too.) Sometimes you can get a driver from the manufacturer that works better than the one that ships with Windows.

When you stick an app or program on your computer — and set it up so that it works — you *install* the app or program (or driver).

When you crank up a program — that is, get it going on your computer — you can say you *started* it, *launched* it, *ran* it, or *executed* it. They all mean the same thing.

If the program quits the way it's supposed to, you can say it *stopped, finished, ended, exited,* or *terminated.* Again, all these terms mean the same thing. If the program stops with some sort of weird error message, you can say it *crashed, died, cratered, croaked, went belly up, jumped in the bit bucket,* or *GPFed* (tech-speak for "generated a General Protection Fault" — don't ask), or employ any of a dozen colorful but unprintable epithets. If the program just sits there and you can't get it to do anything, no matter how you click your mouse or poke the screen, you can say the program *froze, hung, stopped responding,* or *went into a loop.*

A *bug* is something that doesn't work right. (A bug is not a virus! Viruses work as intended far too often.) U.S. Navy Rear Admiral Grace Hopper — the intellectual guiding force behind the COBOL programming language and one of the pioneers in the history of computing — often repeated the story of a moth being found in a relay of an ancient Mark II computer. The moth was taped into the technician's logbook on September 9, 1947. (See Figure 1-4.)

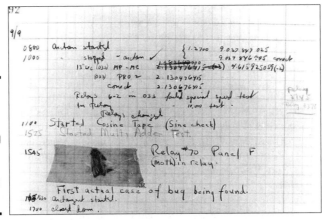

Figure 1-4: Admiral Grace Hopper's log of the "first actual case of bug being found."

Source: U.S. Navy, www.history.navy.mil/photos/pers-us/uspers-h/g-hoppr.htm

The people who invented all this terminology think of the Internet as being some great blob in the sky — it's *up,* as in "up in the sky." So if you send something from your computer to the Internet, you're *uploading.* If you take something off the Internet and put it on your computer, you're *downloading.*

When you put computers together, you *network* them, and if your network doesn't use wires, it's commonly called a *WiFi network.* At the heart of a network sits a box, commonly called a *hub,* or a *router,* that computers can plug into. If the hub has rabbit ears on top for wireless connections, it's usually called a *WiFi router.* (Little WiFi routers may not have antennae.) Yes, there are fine lines of distinction among all these terms. No, you don't need to worry about them.

There are two basic ways to hook up to the Internet: *wired* and *wireless.* Wired is easy: you plug it into a wall. Wireless falls into two categories: WiFi connections, as you'll find in many homes, coffee shops, airports, and some exceptionally enlightened cities' common areas; and cellular (mobile phone style) wireless connections.

Cellular Wireless Internet connections are usually identified with one of the "G" levels: 2G, 3G, 4G, or maybe even 5G.

Truth be told, all the "G" nomenclature has turned into marketing malarkey. One vendor will call something 3G, while another calls it 4G. A vendor may call the same service 4G today and 3G tomorrow. Yes, they can get away with that. The general rule of thumb is that 4G should be faster than 3G, but in specific instances, that may not be true. When shopping for a wireless Internet service, look for reliability, speed, and price. Nothing else matters — in particular, 4G isn't necessarily better than 3G.

If you plug your Internet connection into the wall, you probably have broadband, which may run via fiber (DSL or ADSL over the phone lines), cable (as in cable TV), or satellite. The fiber, DSL, cable, or satellite box is commonly called a *modem,* although it's really a *router.* Although fiber optic lines are inherently much faster than DSL or cable, individual results can be all over the lot. Ask your neighbors what they're using and then pick the best. If you don't like your current service, vote with your pocketbook.

Turning to the dark side of the force, Luke, the distinctions among *viruses, worms,* and *Trojans* grow blurrier every day. In general, they're programs that replicate and can be harmful, and the worst ones blend different approaches. *Spyware* gathers information about you and then phones home with all the juicy details. *Adware* gets in your face, all too frequently installing itself on your computer without your knowledge or consent. I tend to lump the two together and call them *scumware* or *crapware* or something a bit more descriptive and less printable.

If a bad guy (and they're almost always guys) manages to take over your computer without your knowledge, turning it into a zombie that spews spam by remote control, you're in a *botnet.* (And yes, the term *spam* comes from the immortal *Monty Python* routine that's set in a café serving Hormel's SPAM luncheon meat, the chorus bellowing "lovely Spam, wonderful Spam.") Check out Book IX for details about preventing scumware and the like from messing with you.

The most successful botnets employ *rootkits* — programs that run "underneath" Windows, evading detection because normal programs can't see them. The number of Windows 7 computers running rootkits is order of magnitudes less than the number of zombified XP computers. It looks like Windows 8 should drop the botnet count by another order of magnitude or more. But as long as Windows XP computers are out there, botnets will continue to be a major threat to everyone.

This section covers about 90 percent of the buzzwords you hear in common parlance. If you get stuck at a party where the bafflegab is flowing freely, don't hesitate to invent your own words. Nobody will ever know the difference.

What, Exactly, Is the Web?

Five years from now (although it may take ten), the operating system you use will be largely irrelevant, as will be the speed of your computer, the amount of memory you have, and the number of terabytes of storage that hum in the background. Microsoft will keep milking its cash cow, but the industry will move on. Individuals and businesses will stop shelling out big bucks for Windows and the iron to run it. Instead, the major push will be online. Rather than spend money on PCs that become obsolete the week after you purchase them, folks will spend money on big data pipes: It'll be less about me and more about us. Why? Because so much more is "out there" than "in here." Count on it.

But what is the Internet? This section answers this burning question (if you've asked it). If you don't necessarily wonder about the Internet's place in space and time just yet, you will . . . you will.

You know those stories about computer jocks who come up with great ideas, develop the ideas in their basements (or garages or dorm rooms), release their product to the public, change the world, and make a gazillion bucks?

This isn't one of them.

The Internet started in the mid-1960s as an academic exercise — primarily with the RAND Corporation, the Massachusetts Institute of Technology (MIT), and the National Physical Laboratory in England — and rapidly evolved into a military project, under the U.S. Department of Defense Advanced Research Project Agency (ARPA), designed to connect research groups working on ARPA projects.

By the end of the 1960s, ARPA had four computers hooked together — at UCLA, SRI (Stanford), UC Santa Barbara, and the University of Utah — using systems developed by BBN Technologies (then named Bolt Beranek and Newman, Inc.). By 1971, it had 18. I started using ARPANET in 1975. According to the website `http://internetworldstats.com`, by the end of 2011, the Internet had more than 2.2 billion users worldwide.

Today, so many computers are connected directly to the Internet (including all who run digital subscriber line [DSL] or cable modems) that the Internet's addressing system is running out of numbers, just as your local phone company is running out of telephone numbers. The current numbering system — named *IPv4* — can handle about 4 billion addresses. The next version, named *IPv6,* can handle this number of addresses:

340,000,000,000,000,000,000,000,000,000,000,000,000

That should last for a while, don'tcha think?

Ever wonder why you rarely see hard statistics about the Internet? I've found two big reasons:

✦ Defining terms related to the Internet is devilishly difficult these days. (What do you mean when you say "*X* number of computers are connected to the Internet"? Is that the number of computers up and running at any given moment? The number of different addresses that are active? The number that could be connected if everybody dialed up at the same time? The number of different computers that are connected in a typical day, or week, or month?)

✦ The other reason is that the Internet is growing so fast that any number you publish today will be meaningless tomorrow.

Getting inside the Internet

Some observers claim that the Internet works so well because it was designed to survive a nuclear attack. Not so. The people who built the Internet insist that they weren't nearly as concerned about nukes as they were about making communication among researchers reliable, even when a backhoe severed an underground phone line or one of the key computers ground to a halt.

As far as I'm concerned, the Internet works so well because the engineers who laid the groundwork were utter geniuses. Their original ideas from 45 years ago have been through the wringer a few times, but they're still pretty much intact. Here's what the engineers decided:

✦ **No single computer should be in charge.** All the big computers connected directly to the Internet are equal (although, admittedly, some are more equal than others). By and large, computers on the Internet move data around like kids playing hot potato — catch it, figure out where you're going to throw it, and let it fly quickly. They don't need to check with some übercomputer before doing their work; they just catch, look, and throw.

✦ **Break the data into fixed-size packets.** No matter how much data you're moving — an e-mail message that just says "Hi" or a full-color, life-size photograph of the Andromeda galaxy — the data is broken into packets. Each packet is routed to the appropriate computer. The receiving computer assembles all the packets and notifies the sending computer that everything came through okay.

✦ **Deliver each packet quickly.** If you want to send data from Computer A to Computer B, break the data into packets and route each packet to Computer B by using the fastest connection possible — even if that means some packets go through Bangor and others go through Bangkok.

Taken together, those three rules ensure that the Internet can take a lickin' and keep on tickin'. If a chipmunk eats through a telephone line, any big computer that's using the gnawed line can start rerouting packets over a different telephone line. If the Cumbersome Computer Company in Cupertino, California, loses power, computers that were sending packets through Cumbersome can switch to other connected computers. It all works quickly and reliably, although the techniques used internally by the Internet computers get a bit hairy at times.

Big computers are hooked together by high-speed communication lines: the *Internet backbone*. If you want to use the Internet from your business or your house, you have to connect to one of the big computers first. Companies that own the big computers — Internet service providers (ISPs) — get to charge you for the privilege of getting on the Internet through their big computers. The ISPs, in turn, pay the companies that own the cables (and satellites) that comprise the Internet backbone for a slice of the backbone.

If all this sounds like a big-fish-eats-smaller-fish-eats-smaller-fish arrangement, that's quite a good analogy.

It's backbone-breaking work, but somebody's gotta do it.

What is the World Wide Web?

People tend to confuse the World Wide Web with the Internet, which is a lot like confusing the dessert table with the buffet line. I'd be the first to admit that desserts are mighty darn important — life–critical, in fact, if the truth be told. But they aren't the same as the buffet line.

To get to the dessert table, you have to stand in the buffet line. To get to the web, you have to be running on the Internet. Make sense?

The World Wide Web owes its existence to Tim Berners-Lee and a few co-conspirators at a research institute named CERN in Geneva, Switzerland. In 1990, Berners-Lee demonstrated a way to store and link information on the Internet so that all you had to do was click to jump from one place — one web page — to another. Nowadays, nobody in his right mind can give a definitive count of the number of pages available, but Google has indexed more than 50 billion of them.

Like the Internet itself, the World Wide Web owes much of its success to the brilliance of the people who brought it to life. The following list describes the ground rules:

✦ Web pages, stored on the Internet, are identified by an address, such as `http://www.dummies.com`. The main part of the web page address — `dummies.com`, for example — is a *domain name*. With rare exceptions, you can open a web page by simply typing its domain name and pressing Enter. Spelling counts, and underscores (_) are treated differently from hyphens (-). Being close isn't good enough — there are just too many websites. As of this writing, DomainTools (`www.domaintools.com`) reports that about 140 million domain names end in `.com`, `.net`, `.org`, `.info`, `.biz`, or `.us`. That's just for the United States. Other countries have different naming conventions: `.co.uk`, for example, is the U.K. equivalent of `.com`.

✦ Web pages are written in the funny language HyperText Markup Language (HTML). HTML is sort of a programming language, sort of a formatting language, and sort of a floor wax, all rolled into one. Many products claim to make it easy for novices to create powerful, efficient HTML. Some of those products are getting close.

✦ To read a web page, you have to use a web browser. A *web browser* is a program that runs on your computer and is responsible for converting HTML into text that you can read and use. The majority of people who view web pages use Internet Explorer as their web browser, but more and more people (including me!) prefer Firefox (see `www.mozilla.org`) and/or Chrome, from Google (`http://chrome.google.com`). Unless you live under a rock in the Gobi Desert, you know that Internet Explorer is part of Windows 8. You may not know that Firefox and Chrome can run right alongside Internet Explorer, with absolutely no confusion between the two. In fact, they don't even interact — Firefox and Chrome were designed to operate completely independently, and they do very well playing all by themselves.

One unwritten rule for the World Wide Web: All web acronyms must be completely, utterly inscrutable. For example, a web address is a *Uniform Resource Locator*, or *URL*. (The techies I know pronounce URL "earl." Those who don't wear white lab coats tend to say "you are ell.") I describe the HTML acronym in the preceding list. On the web, a gorgeous, sunny, palm-lined beach with the scent of frangipani wafting through the air would no doubt be called SHS — Smelly Hot Sand. Sheeesh.

The best part of the web is how easily you can jump from one place to another — and how easily you can create web pages with *hot links* (also called *hyperlinks* or just *links*) that transport the viewer wherever the author intends. That's the *H* in HTML and the original reason for creating the web so many years ago.

Pay more to get a clean PC

I hate it when the computer I want comes loaded with all that nice, "free" crapware. I'd seriously consider paying more to get a clean computer.

You don't need an antivirus and Internet security program preinstalled on your new PC. It'll just open and beg for money next month. Windows 8 comes with Windows Defender, and it works great — for free.

Browser toolbars? Puh-lease.

You can choose your own Internet service provider. AOL? EarthLink? Who needs ya?

And trialware? Whether it's Quicken, Office, or any of a zillion other programs, if you have to pay for a preinstalled program in three months or six months, you don't want it.

If you're looking for a new computer but can't find an option to buy a PC without all the "extras," look elsewhere. The big PC companies are slowly getting a clue, but until they clean up their act, you may be better served buying from a smaller retailer, who hasn't yet pre-sold every bit that isn't nailed down. Or you can buy direct from Microsoft: Its Surface tablets are as clean as the driven snow. Pricey, perhaps. But blissfully clean. Microsoft Stores (if you can find one) sell new, clean computers from major manufacturers as part of Microsoft's "Signature PC" program. If you pay more, you get a dreck-free computer.

Who pays for all this stuff?

That's the $64 billion question, isn't it? The Internet is one of the true bargains of the 21st century. When you're online — for which you probably have to pay EarthLink, Comcast, Verizon, NetZero, Juno, Netscape, Qwest, your cable company, or another ISP a monthly fee — the Internet itself is free.

Internet Explorer is free, sorta, because it comes with Windows 8, no matter which version you buy. Firefox is free as a breeze — in fact, it's the poster child for open-source programs: Everything about the program, even the program code itself, is free. Google Chrome is free, too.

Most websites don't charge a cent. They pay for themselves in any of these ways:

- ✦ **Reduce a company's operating costs:** Banks and brokerage firms, for example, have websites that routinely handle customer inquiries at a fraction of the cost of H2H (er, human-to-human) interactions.

- ✦ **Increase a company's visibility:** The website gives you a good excuse to buy more of the company's products. That's why architectural firms show you pictures of their buildings and food companies post recipes.

- ✦ **Draw in new business:** Ask any real estate agent.

✦ **Contract advertising:** Google has made a fortune. A thousand fortunes.

✦ **Use bounty advertising:** Smaller sites run ads, most commonly from Google but in some cases, selected from a pool of advertisers. The advertiser pays a bounty for each person who clicks the ad and views its website — a *click-through*.

✦ **Use affiliate programs:** Smaller sites may also participate in a retailer's affiliate program. If a customer clicks through and orders something, the website that originated the transaction receives a percentage of the amount ordered. Amazon is well known for its affiliate program, but many others exist.

Some websites have an entrance fee. For example, if you want to read more than a few articles on *The New York Times* website, you have to part with some substantial coin — about $17 per month for the most basic option, the last time I looked. Guess that beats schlepping around a whole lotta paper.

Buying a Windows 8 Computer

Here's how it usually goes: You figure that you need to buy a new PC, so you spend a couple of weeks brushing up on the details — bits and bytes and kilobytes and megabytes and gigabytes — and comparison shopping. You end up at your local Computers Are Us shop, and the guy behind the counter convinces you that the absolutely best bargain you'll ever see is sitting right here, right now, and you'd better take it quick before somebody else nabs it.

Your eyes glaze over as you look at yet another spec sheet and try to figure out one last time whether a RAM is a ROM, how fast hard drive platters spin, and whether you need a SATA 3 Gbps, SATA 6 Gbps, or eSATA. In the end, you figure that the guy behind the counter must know what he's doing, so you plunk down your plastic and pray you got a good deal.

The next Sunday morning, you look in the paper and discover you could've bought twice as much machine for half as much money. The only thing you know for sure is that your PC is hopelessly out of date, and the next time you'll be smarter about the whole process.

If that describes your experiences, relax. It happens to everybody. Take solace in the fact that you bought twice as much machine for the same amount of money as the poor schmuck who went through the same process last month.

Here's everything you need to know about buying a Windows 8 PC:

✦ **Comparison shop via the Windows Experience Index.**

The Windows Experience Index is a tool that looks at your computer components and then spits out a number that tells you how wonderful your Windows experience will be. Although the Windows Experience Index (see Figure 1-5) has its faults, it's an easily accessible, relatively unbiased measure of performance that helps you accurately size up a new computer. See Book VIII, Chapter 4 for details.

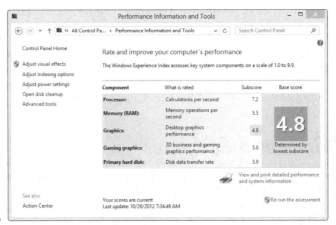

Figure 1-5: The Windows Experience Index gives you a simple, unbiased overview of a PC's performance.

✦ **Buy at least 2GB of memory.**

If you end up with 4GB or more (which you probably don't need, but it may be cheap), remember that you must run the 64-bit version of Windows 8 to handle it all. See Book I, Chapter 3 for a description of 64-bit.

✦ **If you're going to use the old-fashioned Windows 7–style desktop, get a high-quality monitor, a solid keyboard, and a mouse that feels comfortable.**

Corollary: Don't buy a computer online unless you know for a fact that your fingers will like the keyboard, your wrist will tolerate the mouse, and your eyes will fall in love with the monitor.

✦ **If you're going to use the tiled Start screen, get a screen that's at least 1366 x 768 pixels — the minimum size to support all the Start screen's features.** Although a touch-sensitive screen isn't a prerequisite for using the Start screen, believe me, you'll find it much, much easier to use the Start screen with your fingers than with your mouse.

There's no substitute for physically trying the hardware on a touch-sensitive Windows 8 computer. Hands come in all shapes and sizes, and fingers, too. What works for size XXL hands with ten thumbs (present company included) might not cut the mustard for svelte hands and fingers experienced at taking cotton swabs out of medicine bottles.

See the following section, "Inside a touch-sensitive tablet."

✦ **Go overboard with hard drives.**

In the best of all possible worlds, get a computer with a Solid State Drive (SSD) for the system drive (the C: drive) plus a large hard drive for storage. For the low-down on SSDs, hard drives, backups, and putting them all together, see the upcoming section, "Managing disks and drives."

How much hard drive space do you need? How long is a string? Unless you have an enormous collection of videos, movies, or songs, 1TB (= 1,024GB = 1,048,576MB = 1,073,741,824KB = 1,099,511,627,776 bytes, or characters of storage) should suffice. That's big enough to handle about 1,000 broadcast-quality movies. Consider that the printed collection of the U.S. Library of Congress runs about 10TB.

If you're getting a laptop or Ultrabook with an SSD drive, consider buying an external 1TB or larger drive at the same time. You'll use it.

✦ **Everything else they try to sell ya pales in comparison.**

If you want to spend more money, go for a faster Internet connection and a better chair. You need both items much more than you need a marginally faster, or bigger, computer.

Inside the big box

In this section, I give you just enough information about the inner workings of a desktop or laptop PC that you can figure out what you have to do with Windows. In the next section, I talk about touch-enabled tablets, the PCs that respond to touch. Details can change from week to week, but these are the basics.

The big box that your computer lives in is sometimes called a *CPU,* or *central processing unit* (see Figure 1-6). Right off the bat, you're bound to get confused, unless somebody clues you in on one important detail: The main computer chip inside that big box is also called a CPU. I prefer to call the big box "the PC" because of the naming ambiguity, but you've probably thought of a few better names.

Monitor   The "CPU"

Figure 1-6:
The
enduring,
traditional
big box.

Keyboard   Mouse

The big box contains many parts and pieces (and no small amount of dust and dirt), but the crucial, central element inside every PC is the motherboard. (You can see a picture of a motherboard here: http://www.gigabyte. us/fileupload/product/2/4139/5627_big.jpg).

You find the following items attached to the motherboard:

✦ **The processor, or CPU:** This gizmo does the main computing. It's probably from Intel or AMD. Different manufacturers rate their CPUs in different ways. If you want to compare performance, at least to a first approximation, look at the Windows Experience Index for processor performance (the top line in Figure 1-5).

✦ **Memory chips and places to put them:** Memory is measured in megabytes (1MB = 1,024KB = 1,048,576 characters) and gigabytes (1GB = 1,024MB). Although Windows 8 can run on a machine with 512MB (I've done it), Microsoft recommends a minimum of 1GB. Unless you have an exciting cornfield to watch grow while Windows 8 saunters along, aim for 2GB or more. Most computers allow you to add more memory to them, and boosting your computer's memory to 2GB from 1GB makes the machine much snappier, especially if you run memory hogs such as Office, InDesign, or Photoshop. If you leave Outlook open and work with it all day and run almost any other major program at the same time, 2GB isn't overkill.

+ **Video chipset:** Most motherboards include remarkably good built-in video. The easiest quick way to judge is with the Windows Experience Index: Look at the Graphics score and, to a lesser extent, the Gaming Graphics scores. (Hard core gamers will give more credence to the Gaming Graphics score, but paying for a higher Gaming score is just wasted money for most Windows users.) If you want more video oomph, you have to buy a video card and put it in a card slot. Advanced motherboards have multiple PCI card slots, to allow you to strap together two video cards and speed up video even more. For more information, see the "Screening "section in this chapter.

+ **Card slots (also known as expansion slots):** Laptops have very limited (if any) expansion slots on the motherboard. Desktops generally contain several expansion slots. Modern slots come in two flavors: PCI and PCI-Express (also known as PCIe or PCI-E). Most expansion cards use PCI, but very fast cards — including, notably, video cards — require PCIe. Of course, PCI cards don't fit in PCIe slots, and vice versa. To make things more confusing, PCIe comes in three sizes — literally, the size of the bracket and the number of bumps on the bottoms of the cards are different. The PCIe 1x is smallest, the relatively uncommon PCIe 4x is considerably larger, and PCIe 8x is a bit bigger still. PCIe 16x is just a little bit bigger than an old-fashioned PCI slot. Most video cards these days require a PCIe 16x slot.

If you're buying a monitor separately from the rest of the system, make sure the monitor takes video input in a form that your PC can produce. See the upcoming section, "Screening," for details.

+ **USB (Universal Serial Bus) cable:** This cable has a flat connector that plugs into your slots. Make sure you get plenty of USB slots — at least two, preferably four, or more. More details are in the section "Managing disks and drives," later in this chapter.

+ **Lots of other stuff:** You never have to play with this other stuff, unless you're very unlucky.

Here are a few upgrade dos and don'ts:

+ **Don't** let a salesperson talk you into eviscerating your PC and upgrading the CPU: i7 isn't that much faster than i5; a 3.0 GHz PC doesn't run a whole lot faster than a 2.4 GHz PC, and a dual-quad-core ChipDuoTrioQuattroQuinto stuck in an old motherboard doesn't run much faster than your original slowpoke.

+ When you hit 2GB in main memory, **don't** expect big performance improvements by adding more memory.

+ On the other hand, if you have an older video card, **do** consider upgrading it to a faster card, or to one with 512MB or more of on-board memory. They're cheap. Windows 8 will take good advantage of it.

+ Rather than nickel-and-dime yourself to death on little upgrades, **do** wait until you can afford a new PC, and give away your old one.

If you decide to add memory, have the company that sells you the memory install it. The process is simple, quick, and easy — if you know what you're doing. Having the dealer install the memory also puts the monkey on his back if a memory chip doesn't work or a bracket snaps.

Inside a touch-sensitive tablet

Although touch-sensitive tablets have been on the market for more than a decade, they didn't really take off until Apple introduced the iPad in 2010. Since the iPad went ballistic, every Windows hardware manufacturer has been clamoring to join the game. Even Microsoft has entered the computer-manufacturing fray with its line of innovative tablets known as Surface.

The old Windows tablets generally required a *stylus* (a special kind of pen), and they had very little software that took advantage of touch input. The iPad changed all that.

The result is a real hodge-podge of, basically, first generation Windows tablets. It really isn't fair comparing a full-featured Windows 8 tablet to an iPad: They're built for different situations, aimed at different markets. The Win8 tablet can do much more than an iPad, but at quite a price: The iPad wins hands-down in terms of weight, heat, battery life, and price. The screen on an iPad runs rings around Windows tablets; the camera's better; and on and on. But you can't run Windows applications on an iPad — at least, not without connecting to a Windows computer.

That may be a plus or a minus, depending on where you sit.

To further complicate matters, Microsoft offers different versions of Windows for traditional Intel/AMD processors, and for the far-more-svelte ARM processors. See the sidebar "Windows on ARM — Windows RT" earlier in this chapter.

As this book went to press, hardware manufacturers were stumbling all over each other trying to get fast, cool, light Windows 8 tablets to market.

If you're thinking about buying a Windows 8 tablet, keep these points in mind:

 ✦ **Make sure you understand the differences between an Intel/AMD tablet and an ARM tablet.** If you want to use the Windows 8 desktop — the one that looks like the Windows 7 desktop — you have to stick with Intel/AMD models (frequently called *x86/x64* or *32-bit/64-bit* tablets).

   This book specifically covers Intel/AMD tablets, but not ARM tablets.

 ✦ **Focus on weight and heat.** Touch-sensitive tablets are meant to be carried, not lugged around like a suitcase, and the last thing you need is a box so hot it burns a hole in your pants, or a fan so noisy you can't carry on a conversation.

 ✦ **The screen has to run at 1366 x 768 pixels or better.** The tiled interface doesn't work well at all on a smaller screen.

 ✦ **Get a Solid State Drive if you can afford it.** In addition to making the machine much, much faster, SSDs also save on weight and heat. Don't be overly concerned about the amount of storage on a tablet. Many people with Win8 tablets end up putting all their data in the cloud with, for example, SkyDrive, or Google Drive. See Book IV, Chapter 4.

 ✦ **Try before you buy.** The screen has to be sensitive to your big fingers, and look good, too. Not an easy combination.

 ✦ **Make sure you can return it.** If you have experience with a "real" keyboard and a mouse, you may find that you hate using a tablet to replicate the kinds of things you used to do with a laptop or desktop PC.

As the hardware market matures, you can expect to see many variations on the tablet theme. It ain't all cut and dried.

Screening

The computer monitor or screen — and LED, LCD, and plasma TVs — use technology that's quite different from old-fashioned television circuitry from your childhood. A traditional TV scans lines across the screen from left to right, with hundreds of them stacked on top of each other. Colors on each individual line vary all over the place. The almost infinitely variable color on an old-fashioned TV combined with a comparatively small number of lines makes for pleasant, but fuzzy, pictures.

By contrast (pun absolutely intended, of course), computer monitors, touch-sensitive tablet screens, and plasma, LED, and LCD TVs work with dots of light called *pixels.* Each pixel can have a different color, created by tiny, colored gizmos sitting next to each other. As a result, the picture displayed on computer monitors (and plasma and LCD TVs) is much sharper than on conventional TV tubes.

The more pixels you can cram on a screen — that is, the higher the screen resolution — the more information you can pack on the screen. That's important if you commonly have more than one word-processing document open at a time, for example. At a resolution of 800 x 600, two open Word documents placed side by side look big but fuzzy, like caterpillars viewed through a dirty magnifying glass. At 1280 x 1024, those same two documents look sharp, but the text may be so small that you have to squint to read it. If you move up to wide-screen territory — 1680 x 1050 or even 1920 x 1200 — with a good monitor, two documents side-by-side look stunning.

Apple's Retina Displays, at 2880 by 1800 pixels, simply blow away anything yet available for the PC. That will change, but it'll take years. Take a look at one and you'll see.

A special-purpose computer called a *graphics processor* (or *GPU*), stuck on your video card, or possibly integrated into the CPU, creates everything that's shown on your computer's screen. The GPU has to juggle all the pixels and all the colors, so if you're a gaming fan, the speed of the GPU's chip (and, to a lesser extent, the speed of the monitor) can make the difference between a zapped alien and a lost energy shield. If you want to experience Windows 8 in all its glory, you need a fast GPU with at least 512MB (and preferably 1GB or more) of its own memory.

Computer monitors and tablets are sold by size, measured diagonally, like TV sets. Just like with TV sets, the only way to pick a good computer screen over a run-of-the-mill one is to compare them side by side or to follow the recommendation of someone who has.

Managing disks and drives

Your PC's memory chips hold information only temporarily: Turn off the electricity, and the contents of main memory go bye-bye. If you want to reuse your work, keeping it around after the plug has been pulled, you have to save it, typically on a disk, or possibly in the *cloud* (which means you copy it to a location on the Internet).

The following list describes the most common types of disks and drives:

+ **Floppy disk:** The 1.44MB floppy disk drives that were ubiquitous on PCs for many years have bitten the dust. You have little reason to buy one nowadays. . . .

+ **SD/xD/CF card memory:** Many smaller computers, and even some tablets, have built-in SD card readers. You probably know Secure Digital (SD) cards best as the kind of memory used in digital cameras, or possibly phones (see Figure 1-7). Micro SD cards slip into hollowed-out cards that are shaped like, and function as, SD cards.

Figure 1-7:
A 128GB
SD card.
MicroSD
cards slip
into holders
shaped like
an SD card.

Compliments of SanDisk.

Even now, long after the demise of floppy disks, many desktop computer cases have drive bays built for them. Why not use the open spot for a multifunction card reader? That way, you can slip a memory card out of your digital camera (or your Dick Tracy wristwatch, for that matter) and transfer files at will. SD card, xD card, CompactFlash, memory stick — whatever you have — the multifunction readers cost a pittance and read almost everything, including minds.

✦ **Hard drive:** The technology's changing rapidly, with traditional hard disk drives (HDDs) now being augmented by *Solid State Drives* (SSDs) with no moving parts, and *hybrid drives* that bolt together a regular rotating drive with an SSD. Each technology has benefits and drawbacks. Yes, you can run a regular HDD drive as your `C:` drive, and it'll work fine. But SSD-goosed systems, on tablets, laptops, or desktops, run like greased lightning. For tips on installing an SSD and moving your files around, see Book VIII, Chapter 5.

The SSD wins as speed king. After you use an SSD as your main "system" (`C:`) drive, you'll never go back to a spinning platter, I guarantee. SSDs are great for the main drive, but they're awfully expensive for storing pictures, movies, and photos. They may someday supplant the old whirling dervish drive, but price and technical considerations (see the sidebar, "Solid State Drives have problems, too") assure that hard drives will be around for a long time. SSDs feature low power consumption and give off less heat. They have no moving parts, so they don't wear out like hard drives. And, if you drop a hard drive and a Solid State Drive off the Leaning Tower of Pisa, one of them may survive. Or maybe not.

Solid State Drives have problems, too

Although I love my SSD system drives and would never go back to rotating hard disk drives (HDDs), SSDs aren't perfect.

SSDs don't have any moving parts, and it looks like they're more reliable than HDDs. But when an HDD starts to go belly up, you can usually tell: whirring and gnashing, whining and groaning. Expiring SSDs don't give off any advanced warning signals. Or at least sounds.

When an HDD dies, you can frequently get the data back, although it can be expensive and time-consuming. When an SSD goes, you rarely get a second chance.

SSDs have to take care of a lot of internal bookkeeping, both for trimming unused space and for load balancing to guarantee uniform wear patterns. SSDs actually slow down after you've used them for a few weeks, months, or years. The speed decrease is usually associated with the bookkeeping programs kicking in over time.

Finally, the SSD's own software has to be ultra-reliable. SSDs don't lay down tracks sequentially like HDDs. They hopscotch all over the place, and the firmware inside the SSD needs to keep up.

Hybrid drives combine the benefits and problems of both HDDs and SSDs. Although HDDs have long had *caches* — chunks of memory that hold data before being written to the drive, and after it's read from the drive — hybrid drives have a full SSD to act as a buffer.

If you can stretch the budget, start with an SSD for the system drive, a big hard drive for storing photos, movies, and music, and get *another* drive (which can be inside your PC, outside attached with a USB cable, or even on a different PC on your network) to run File History (see Book VIII, Chapter 1).

If you want full on-the-fly protection against dying hard drives, you can get three hard drives — one SSD, and two hard drives, either inside the box or outside attached with USB or eSATA cables — and run Storage Spaces (see Book VII, Chapter 4).

✦ **CD, DVD, or Blu-ray drive:** Of course, these types of drives work with CDs, DVDs, and the Sony Blu-ray discs, which can be filled with data or contain music or movies. CDs hold about 700MB of data; DVDs hold 4GB, or six times as much as a CD. Dual-layer DVDs (which use two separate layers on top of the disc) hold about 8GB, and Blu-ray discs hold 50GB, or six times as much as a dual-layer DVD.

Unless you want to stick a high-definition movie on a single disc or play Blu-ray discs that you buy or rent in your local video store, 50GB of data on a single disc is overkill. Someday, the price of Blu-ray drives and discs will come down out of the stratosphere, but at least for now, most Windows 8 users will do quite well with a dual-layer DVD-RW drive. You can always use a dual-layer drive to record regular (single-layer) DVDs or CDs. If you're nervous about installing a new drive, add an external

USB version: Windows 8 loves external DVD drives, and it tolerates external Blu-ray drives.

✦ **USB drive or key drive:** Treat it like it's a lollipop. Half the size of a pack of gum and able to hold an entire PowerPoint presentation or two or six, plus a half dozen full-length movies, flash memory (also known as a jump drive, thumb drive, or memory stick) should be your first choice for external storage space or for copying files between computers. (See Figure 1-8.) You can even use USB drives on some DVD players and TV set-top boxes.

Figure 1-8:
A USB drive.

Compliments of SanDisk.

Pop one of these guys in a USB slot and suddenly Windows 8 knows it has another drive — except that this one's fast, portable, and incredibly easy to use. Go for the cheapest flash drives you can find: Most of the "features" on fancy key drives are just, uh, Windows dressing.

What about USB 3? Even though the technology's been around for a while, USB 3 hasn't taken the world by storm, although it seems to be picking up in popularity lately. If you have a hard drive that sits outside of your computer — an *external drive* — it'll run faster if it's tethered with a USB 3 cable. For most other outside devices, USB 3 is overkill, and USB 2 works just as well.

This list is by no means definitive: New storage options come out every day.

Making PC connections

Your PC connects to the outside world by using a bewildering variety of cables and connectors. I describe the most common in this list:

✦ **USB (Universal Serial Bus) cable:** This cable has a flat connector that plugs into your PC, known as *USB A* (see Figure 1-8). The other end is usually shaped like a D (called *USB B*), but smaller devices have tiny terminators (usually called *USB mini* and *USB micro,* each of which have two different shapes).

USB 2 connectors will work with any device, but hardware — such as a hard drive — that uses USB 3 will run much faster if you use a USB 3 cable and plug it into the back of your computer in a USB 3 port. USB 2 works with USB 3 devices, but you won't get the speed. Note that not all PCs have USB 3 ports!

USB is the connector of choice for just about any kind of hardware — printer, scanner, phone, camera, portable hard drive, and even the mouse. Apple iPhones and iPads use a USB connector on one side — to plug into your computers — but the other side is Apple-only, and doesn't look or act like any other connector.

If you run out of USB connections on the back of your PC, get a USB hub with a separate power supply and plug away.

✦ **LAN cable:** Also known as a CAT-5, CAT-6, or RJ-45 cable, it's the most common kind of network connector. It looks like an overweight telephone plug (see Figure 1-9). One end plugs into your PC, typically into a *network interface card* (or *NIC,* pronounced "nick"), a network connector on the motherboard. The other end plugs into your network's hub (see Figure 1-10) or switch or into a cable modem, DSL box, router, or other Internet connection–sharing device.

Figure 1-9: LAN connectors.

Courtesy of CablesToGo.com

Figure 1-10: A network hub.

Courtesy of CablesToGo.com

+ **Keyboard and mouse cable:** More and more mice and keyboards (even cordless mice and keyboards) come with USB connectors.

+ **DVI-D and HDMI connectors:** Although many older monitors still use legacy 15-pin HD15 VGA connectors, most monitors and video cards now use the DVI-D digital cable (see Figure 1-11). Given a choice, go with DVI-D: It's faster and capable of delivering a much better picture. Some video cards and many TVs also support the small HDMI connector (see Figure 1-12), which transmits both audio and video over one cable.

If you hope to hook up your new TV to your PC, make sure your PC can connect to the TV with the right kind of cable.

Figure 1-11:
DVI-D has largely supplanted the old VGA video adapter.

Courtesy of CablesToGo.com

Figure 1-12:
HDMI carries both audio and video signals.

Courtesy of CablesToGo.com

Old-fashioned serial (9-pin) and parallel (25-pin) cables and Centronics printer cables are growing as scarce as hen's teeth. Hey, the hen doesn't need them, either.

Futzing with video, sound, and multitudinous media

Unless you're using a tablet, chances are pretty good that you're running Windows 8 on a PC with at least a little oomph in the audio department. In the simplest case, you have to be concerned about four specific sound jacks (or groups of sound jacks) because each one does something different. Your machine may not have all four (are you feeling inadequate yet?), or it may look like a patch board at a Korn concert, but the basics are still the same.

Here's how the four key jacks are usually marked, although sometimes you have to root around in the documentation to find the details:

+ **Line In:** This stereo input jack is usually blue. It feeds a stereo audio signal — generally from an amplified source — into the PC. Use this jack to receive audio output into your computer from a cable box, TV set, radio, CD player, cassette player, electric guitar, or other audio–generating box.

+ **Mic In:** This jack is usually pink. It's for unamplified sources, like most microphones or some electric guitars. If you use a cheap microphone for Skype or another VoIP service that lets you talk long distance for free, and the mic doesn't have a USB connector, plug in the microphone here. In a pinch, you can plug any of the Line In devices into the Mic In jack — but you may hear only mono sound, not stereo, and you may have to turn the volume way down to avoid some ugly distortion when the amplifier inside your PC increases the strength of an already-amplified signal.

+ **Line Out:** A stereo output jack, usually lime green, which in many cases can be used for headphones or patched into powered speakers. If you don't have fancy output jacks (like the Sony-Philips SPDIF), this is the source for the highest-quality sound your computer can produce.

+ **Rear Surround Out:** Usually black, this jack isn't used often. It's intended to be used if you have independent, powered rear speakers. Most people with rear speakers use the Line Out connector and plug it into their home theater systems, which then drives the rear speakers; or they use the HDMI cable (see the preceding section) to hook up to their TVs. If your computer can produce full surround sound output, you'll get much better results using the black jack.

Laptops typically have just two jacks, pink for Mic In and lime for Line Out. If you have a headphone with a mic, that's the right combination. It's also common to plug powered external speakers into the lime jack.

Tablets may or may not have a Line Out jack. If you see a jack — particularly a lime green jack — chances are good you can plug headphones or earbuds into the jack and get decent quality sound.

Fancy sound cards can have full Dolby DTS or THX 5.1 output (that's left front, center front, right front, left surround, right surround, and a sub-woofer). The 7.1 configuration uses two back surround speakers. Front panel output — where your sound card connects to jacks on the front of your PC, possibly a panel in a hard drive bay — makes connections easy. With a sufficiently bottomless budget, you can make your living room sound precisely like the 08R runway at Honolulu International.

PC manufacturers love to extol the virtues of their advanced sound systems, but the simple fact is that you can hook up a rather plain-vanilla PC to a home stereo and get great sound. Just connect the Line Out jack on the back of your PC to the Aux In jack on your home stereo or entertainment center. *Voilà!*

Netbooks and Ultrabooks

I really fell in love with an ASUS netbook while working with Windows 7. But then along came the iPad, and at least 80 percent of the reason for using a netbook disappeared. Sales of *netbooks* — small, light, inexpensive laptops — have not fared well, and I don't see a comeback any time soon. Tablets just blow the doors off netbooks.

Ultrabooks are a slightly different story. Intel coined the term *Ultrabook* — actually, trademarked it — and set the specs. In order for a manufacturer to call their piece of iron an Ultrabook, it has to be less than 21mm thick, run for five hours on a battery charge, and resume from hibernation in seven seconds or less. In other words, they need to work a lot like an iPad.

Intel threw a $300 million marketing budget at Ultrabooks, but to date, they haven't sold well. Times change, though, and with the advent of Windows 8 on Ultrabooks, you may see a turnaround.

At least, that's what Intel hopes.

Chapter 2: Windows 8 for the Experienced

In This Chapter

↙ **Introducing what's new for XP, Vista, Windows 7 users**

↙ **Checking out the new interfaces**

↙ **Getting to know the new Windows**

↙ **Deciding whether you really need Windows 8**

*I*f you're among the billion-or-so souls on the planet who have been around the block with Windows 7, Vista, or Windows XP, you're in for a shock.

In fact, if you know your way around the Windows desktop, I can almost guarantee that you're going to hate Windows 8 the first time you see it.

And the second, third, and fourth times.

Hang in there, though. It gets better — especially if you take advantage of the tricks in Book VI, Chapter 3, which let you impose some sort of retro sanity on the tiled Start screen — the side of Windows formerly known as "Metro."

Windows 8 isn't made for the garden-variety Windows expert. You and I aren't exactly being ignored, but we're not at the top of the Win8 food chain. Scary as it sounds, that's probably a good decision. Whether it'll lead to Windows's demise is the 64 billion dollar question.

Microsoft is cutting you old salts loose for good reason: Money. People aren't generating enough revenue, and the future looks grim indeed. Microsoft made its basic decisions about moving to a touch-centric world before the first iPad was released. Microsoft's traditional PC market has sunk into a funk, and it appears to be on a slow ride into the sunset. Or it may just turn belly up and sink, anchored with mounds of iPhones, iPads, and MacBooks.

How did everyone get into this nice mess, Stan?

Microsoft's been making tablet software for 20 years, and it never did put a dent in the market. Never did "get it." Apple started selling tablet software in 2010, and it's selling a ton of it. Boy howdy. Now Microsoft's diving in to get a piece of the touch-enabled action.

There's a big difference in approaches. Apple started out with a telephone operating system, iOS, and grew it to become the world's best-selling tablet operating system. There's very little difference between iOS 6 on an iPhone and iOS 6 on an iPad: Applications written for one device usually work on the other, with a few obvious changes, such as screen size. On the other hand, Apple's computer operating system, OS X, is completely different. It's built and optimized for use with a Mac computer. Apple is slowly changing the programs, er, apps on both iOS and OS X so they resemble each other and work together. But the operating systems are fundamentally quite different (even though, yes, iOS did originally start with the Mac OS Darwin foundation).

When Windows 7 was finished, Steve Sinofsky and crew decided to take a fundamentally different tack. Instead of the good people at Microsoft growing their phone software "up,"

they decided to grow their computer operating system "down." (The fact that the phone software at that point drew nearly universal scorn could've been part of the reason.) Windows 8 is the result of that decision: There's a touch-friendly part and a mouse/keyboard-friendly part. The two aren't mutually exclusive: You can use your mouse on the new–fangled tiled Start screen and in the tiled full–screen apps; you can use your greasy thumb on a Legacy Windows app. But the approach is different, the design is different, and the intent is different.

Microsoft's on a roll. The next step is to extend Windows down even further, to the Windows Phone — which is in the throes of a gut-wrenching change. I call it a brain transplant: The old Windows CE core of the phone software gets replaced by the Windows "MinWin" kernel. Microsoft will be able to say that Windows covers all the bases, from lowly smartphone to gigantic workstations (and server farms, for that matter). The fact that the "Windows" running in each of the device classes is quite different kinda gets swept under the rug.

Windows president Steve Sinofsky puts it this way: "We started planning Windows 8 during the summer of 2009 (before Windows 7 shipped) . . . Why not just start over from scratch? Why not just remove all the desktop features and ship only the Metro experience? Why not 'convert' everything to Metro? The arguments for a 'clean slate' are well known, both for and against. We chose to take the approach of building a design without compromise. A design that truly affords you the best of the two worlds we see today."

The result is what you see — two completely different interfaces, the tiled Start screen (see Figure 2-1), which looks a lot like a Microsoft mobile phone screen, and the old-fashioned Windows 7 style desktop (see Figure 2-2), which looks and behaves a lot like Windows 7, with a few minor differences, but one crucial difference — there's no Start menu.

The tiled Start screen itself isn't bad. Play with it for five minutes — put your cursor or finger in each of the corners, click or tap and drag — and you can see what's happening. The problem is that Microsoft wants you to use this screen instead of the Start menu. In fact, Microsoft wants you to change over to this new style Start screen so much, that it's removed the Start menu completely.

As you'll soon see, moving between the tiled Start screen and Legacy desktop can be an intensely jarring experience.

Figure 2-1: Disconcerting to many grizzled Windows veterans, the new tiled Start screen greets you when you sign on to Windows 8.

Figure 2-2: The Windows 8 old-fashioned desktop works much like the Windows 7 desktop, but without a Start button or Start menu.

Every bit as jarring is that Microsoft now refers to the programs on the Windows desktop that you've known and loved for 20 years — the one shown in Figure 2-2 — as Legacy programs. *Legacy* is a Microsoft buzzword for, "Go away, kid. We don't want you anymore." Microsoft doesn't really have a name for the old, Windows 7–style desktop, except "desktop" — which draws no distinction with the place the new tiled apps live — so in this book I'll usually refer to the old-fashioned desktop as the "Windows 7 style" desktop or, imaginatively, the "old" desktop.

What you know — what your fingers know — is headed to the operating system old folk's home. Clearly, Microsoft will be focusing all its future development on the tiled style side of the fence, as the old desktop slowly fades into the sunset. If you're going to stay with Windows, it's time to get with the system and learn about this new tiled stuff.

Here's a quick guide to what's new — and what's still the same — with some down 'n' dirty help for deciding whether you truly need Windows 8.

What's New for the XP Crowd

Time to fess up. You can tell me. I won't rat you out.

If you're an experienced Windows XP user and you're looking at Windows 8, one of two things happened: Either your trusty old XP machine died and you *had* to get Win8 with a new PC, or a friend or family member conned you into looking into Win8, to provide tech support.

Am I right, or am I right?

If you're thinking of making the jump from XP to Win8, you have two big hurdles:

✦ Learning the tiled Start screen side of the force (which I outline in the next section, "What's New for Windows 7 and Vista Victims")

✦ Making the transition from XP to Windows 7 because the Win8 old-fashioned desktop works a lot like Windows 7

Are you sure you want to tackle the learning curve? Er, curves? See the nearby sidebar about switching to a Mac.

That said, if you didn't plunge into the Windows 7 or Vista madness, and instead sat back and waited for something better to come along, many improvements indeed await in Windows 8.

Wouldn't it be smarter to get a Mac?

Knowledgeable Windows XP users might find it easier — or at least more rewarding — to jump to a Mac, rather than upgrading to Windows 8. I know that's heretical. Microsoft will never speak to me again. But there's a lot to be said for making the switch.

Why? XP cognoscenti face a double whammy: learning Windows 7 (for the Win8 desktop) and learning how to deal with the tiled Start screen "immersive experience." If you don't mind paying the higher price — and, yes, Macs are more expensive than PCs, feature–for–feature — Macs have a distinct advantage in being able to work easily in the Apple ecosystem: iPads, iPhones, the App Store, iTunes, iCloud, and iTV all work together remarkably well. That's a big advantage held by Apple, where the software,

hardware, cloud support, and content all come from the same company. "It just works" may be overblown, but there's more than a nugget of truth in it.

Yes, Macs have a variant of the Blue Screen of Death. Yes, Macs do get viruses. Yes, Macs have all sorts of problems. Yes, you may have to stand in line at an Apple Store to get help — I guess there's a reason why Microsoft Stores seem so empty.

If you're thinking about switching sides, take a look at *Switching to a Mac For Dummies, Mac OS X Lion Edition,* by Arnold Reinhold. I bet you'll be surprised at the similarities between Mac OS X and Windows XP.

Improved performance

Windows 8 (and Windows 7 before it) actually places fewer demands on your PC's hardware. I know that's hard to believe, but as long as you have a fairly powerful video card, and 1GB or more of main memory, moving from XP to Win8 will make your PC run faster.

If you don't have a powerful video card, and you're running a desktop system, you can get one for less than $100, and extra memory costs a pittance. I've upgraded dozens of PCs from XP to Win8, and the performance improvement is quite noticeable. You laptop users aren't so lucky because laptop video's usually soldered in.

Better video

Windows 8 doesn't sport the Aero interface made popular in Vista and Win7, but some of the Aero improvements persist.

Hover your mouse in the lower-right corner of the old-fashioned desktop, and you see outlines of all open windows. That used to be called *Aero Peek*, before Microsoft decided to ban the term Aero, but it still works. The *Aero Snap* feature lets you drag a window to an edge of the screen and have it automatically resize to half-screen size — a boon to anyone with a wide screen. Sounds like a parlor trick, but it's a capability I use many times every day.

Windows 8's desktop shows you thumbnails of running programs when you hover your mouse over a program on the taskbar (see Figure 2-3).

Figure 2-3:
Three Internet Explorer tabs are open, so hovering your mouse over the IE icon in the taskbar shows three thumbnails.

Video efficiency is also substantially improved: If you have a video that drips and drops in XP, the same video running on the same hardware may go straight through in Windows 8.

Sizing up other improvements

The old Windows XP Media Center Edition was billed — and sold — as a separate operating system, almost exclusively available on new PCs. That always struck me as odd because Media Center is an application that runs on top of Windows just like, oh, Internet Explorer or Windows Media Player.

In Windows 8, Media Center is an extra-cost add-in to Windows 8 Pro only. You can buy it with the Add Features to Windows 8 program, which is in the Control Panel's System and Security category. Note that, if you're starting with the standard version of Windows 8, you have to pay for Windows 8 Pro, and then pay more for the Media Center upgrade. Media Center comes along free if you pay for an upgrade from XP, Vista, or Win7 to Windows 8 Pro.

Many other features — less sexy but every bit as useful — put Windows 8 head and shoulders above XP. The standout features include

✦ **The taskbar:** I know many XP users swear by the old Quick Launch toolbar, but the taskbar, once you get to know it, runs rings around its predecessor. Just one example is shown in Figure 2-3 earlier in this chapter.

✦ **A backup worthy of the name:** Backup was a cruel joke in Windows XP. Windows 7 did it better, but Windows 8 makes backup truly easy, particularly with File History (see Book VIII, Chapter 1).

✦ **A less infested notification area:** XP let any program and its brother put an icon in the notification area, near the system clock. Windows 8 severely limits the number of icons that appear and gives you a spot to click if you really want to see them all.

✦ **Second monitor support:** Although some video card manufacturers managed to jury-rig multiple monitor support into the Windows XP drivers, Windows 8 makes using multiple monitors one-click easy (see Book VI, Chapter 2).

✦ **Homegroups:** Windows 8, like Windows 7, lets you put together all the PCs in a trusted environment and share among them quite easily.

✦ **Easy wireless networking:** All sorts of traps and gotchas live in the Windows XP wireless programs. Windows 8 does it much, much better.

✦ **Search:** In Windows XP, searching for anything other than a filename involved an enormous kludge of an add-on that sucked up computer cycles and overwhelmed your machine. In Windows 8, search is baked in.

Although Windows 8 isn't the XP of your dreams, it's remarkably easy to use and has all sorts of compelling new features.

What's New for Windows 7 and Vista Victims

Anything that works with Windows 7 — and almost everything from Vista — will work in Windows 8. Programs, hardware, drivers, utilities, just about anything.

That's a remarkable achievement, particularly because your Legacy programs (there's that "L" word again) have to peacefully co-exist with the all-new tiled Start screen side of the fence.

Windows 8 does have a lot going for it, although it's become fashionable to diss it out of hand. Let me skip lightly through the major changes between Windows 7 and Windows 8.

Getting the hang of the tiled Start screen

By now you've no doubt seen the tiled Start screen (refer to Figure 2-1) and the old-fashioned desktop (refer to Figure 2-2). Microsoft has developed the tiled Start screen to be easily accessible with the mouse and the thumb, with two-dimensional tiles instead of fancy icons. All the programs, uh, excuse me, all the tiled Start screen apps, run full-screen; none of this re-sizing stuff, except for the tiled Snap capability, which lets you run two programs side-by-side in strictly cordoned off containers.

The biggest mental hurdle you'll have is reconciling that Dr. Jekyll/Mr. Hyde interface bifurcation (there, I said it politely) with the Windows desktop you've grown to know and love and hate. Here's my very quick take on how to conceptually integrate the two:

✦ Among the many ways to move from the tiled Start screen to the old-fashioned desktop and back, the easiest one, if you have a keyboard, is to press the Windows key. If you don't have a keyboard, tap the Start key on your tablet. Yes, your tablet has a Start key. Probably.

✦ Alt+Tab still works. Hold down the Alt key and press Tab to run through all running programs — tiled full-screen programs, desktop programs, all of them.

✦ Think of the Windows 7 style desktop as just another tiled app. In many ways the entire old-fashioned desktop — the whole thing, not individual programs running on it — behaves like one, single tiled app.

✦ The Start button is gone. Get over it.

✦ The Start menu is gone, but you can jury-rig the tiled Start screen so it sort of acts like a Start menu . . . if you don't think about it too much, squint your eyes hard and mumble an appropriate mantra.

The tiled part of Windows is new and different. Sometimes new and different is better. Sometimes it's just new and different. If you use the full-screen tiled apps for a while, you'll probably come up with a few things about them that you actually like.

What's new in the old-fashioned desktop

You'll notice many improvements to long-neglected portions of the Windows 7–style desktop. For example, if you copy more than one file at a time, Windows actually keeps you on top of all the copying in one window. Imagine that.

A new and much better *Task Manager* rolls in all the usage reporting that's been scattered in different corners of Windows (see Figure 2-4). The new Task Manager even gives you hooks to look at programs that start automatically, and stop them if you like. Some serious chops. See Book VIII, Chapter 5.

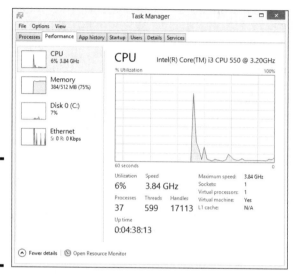

Figure 2-4:
The new and greatly improved Task Manager

File Explorer (formerly known as Windows Explorer) takes on a new face and loses some of its annoying bad habits. You may or may not like the new Explorer Ribbon (see Book VI, Chapter 1), but at least Windows 8 brings back the up arrow to move up one folder — a feature that last appeared in Windows XP. That one feature, all by itself, makes me feel good about the new File Explorer. Explorer also now offers native support for ISO files. About time.

Backup gets a major boost with an Apple Time Machine work-alike called *File History.* You may not realize it, but Windows 7 had the ability to restore previous versions of your data files. Windows 8 offers the same functionality, but in a much nicer package — so you're more likely to discover that it's there. See Book VIII, Chapter 1.

If you ever wanted to run a Virtual Machine inside Windows, Microsoft has made *Hyper-V* available, free. It's a rather esoteric capability that can come in very handy if you need to run two different copies of an operating system on one machine. You must be running a 64-bit version of Windows 8 Pro (or Enterprise), with at least 4GB of RAM. See Book VIII, Chapter 5.

What's New for All of Windows

Storage Spaces requires at least two available hard drives — not including the one you use to boot the PC. If you can afford the disk space, Windows 8 can give you a fully redundant, hot backup of everything, all the time. If a hard drive dies, you disconnect the dead one, slip in a new one, grab a cup of coffee, and you're back and running as if nothing happened. If you run out of disk space, stick another drive in the PC or attach it with a USB cable, and Windows figures it all out. It's a magical capability that debuted in Windows Home Server, now made more robust. See Book VII, Chapter 4.

Taking a cue from iPad . . . er, other tablets, Windows 8 also offers a one-stop "system restore" capability. Actually, it's two capabilities — *PC Reset* wipes everything off the machine and then re-installs Windows 8. *PC Refresh* goes through the same motions, but retains your data, apps from the Windows Store, and settings. Note that PC Refresh zaps out your Legacy desktop apps and doesn't put them back. See Book VIII, Chapter 2.

Internet Explorer 10, in both tiled (see Figure 2-5) and desktop versions (Figure 2-6) offers some new features and performance improvements, but Firefox and Chrome have strong points as well. The tiled IE10's most endearing trait is its insistence on running with no "chrome" showing, so the whole screen is just the web page. See Book IV, Chapter 1.

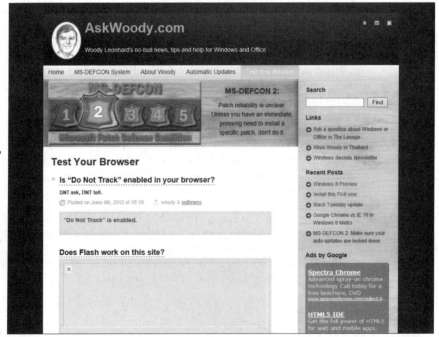

Figure 2-5: The tiled Internet Explorer 10 runs without showing any "wrapping" and doesn't always show Flash animations.

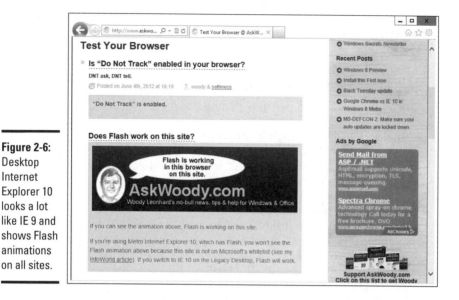

Figure 2-6:
Desktop
Internet
Explorer 10
looks a lot
like IE 9 and
shows Flash
animations
on all sites.

Power options have changed significantly. Again. The new options allow Windows to restart itself much faster than ever before. See Book VII, Chapter 1.

Security improvements

I'm told that Pliny the Elder once described the alarm system of ancient Rome by saying, "Even when the dogs sleep, the goose watches."

By that standard, Windows 8's been goosed.

Microsoft's somehow found a new backbone — or decided that it can fend off antitrust actions — and baked full antivirus, antispyware, antiscumstuff protection into Windows 8 itself.

Although the 'Softies resurrected an old name for the service — *Windows Defender* — the antivirus protection inside Windows 8 is second to none. And it's free.

Microsoft is also encouraging hardware manufacturers to use a boot-up process called *UEFI*, as a replacement to the decades-old BIOS. UEFI isn't exactly a Windows 8 feature, but it'll be a requirement for all PCs that carry the Windows 8 logo. UEFI can help protect you from rootkits by requiring digital signatures on any operating system that gets loaded. See Book IX, Chapter 3.

Banishing Adobe Reader from IE10 on the tiled side of the fence, and limiting Flash under tiled IE 10 to specific "white list" sites, should go a long way toward improving security, as well.

What's new in the cloud

Windows 8 has "cloud" written all over it.

Even if you never buy anything from the Windows Store, it's still poking around. All your tiled Start screen apps will get their updates from the Windows Store, just like that other company's apps and the Apple App Store. See Book III, Chapter 5.

Although the Windows Store is integral to the tiled side of things, Microsoft also promises to offer desktop programs through the Store, too. If you remember the old, much maligned Windows Marketplace, just hope Microsoft doesn't make the same mistakes. It remains to be seen whether the Windows Store can begin to live up to the App Store's reputation.

More intriguing, to me at least, is the expanded nature of *SkyDrive*. Microsoft's been offering free Internet-based storage space on SkyDrive since 2007. What started out as an online data warehouse has turned into an integral part of Windows 8, particularly for the tiled Start screen apps, which connect directly into SkyDrive. The browser-based interface has improved substantially, and the tiled SkyDrive app makes using SkyDrive much simpler. To add to its general popularity, Microsoft has made iPad and iPhone apps for SkyDrive as well. See Book IV, Chapter 4.

What you lose

Although Microsoft hasn't talked much about it, the fact is that all the old Windows Live programs are disappearing. Windows Live is, in fact, dead. Windows 8 killed it. If you use any of the Windows Live apps in Windows 7 (or Vista or XP, for that matter), your old Live apps will still be available, but it doesn't look like Microsoft's going to do much with them.

Why? The Windows 8 tiled apps cover many of the "Live" bases. Consider:

✦ **Windows Live ID** (formerly known as Microsoft Wallet, Microsoft Passport, .NET Passport, and Microsoft Passport Network), which now operates from the Windows Live Account site (confused yet?), will be rebranded Microsoft Your Account and referred to informally as "your *Microsoft Account.*"

✦ **Windows Live SkyDrive** has already turned into just plain *SkyDrive*. Parts of Ray Ozzie's Windows Live Mesh — formerly Live Mesh, Windows Live Sync, and Windows Live FolderShare — have been folded into SkyDrive, although Microsoft has squashed PC-to-PC sync; the only way to synchronize files is through the SkyDrive cloud. It appears as if Mesh has met its match.

✦ **Windows Live Mail** is missing in action. Expect Microsoft to push the new *Windows Store Mail* as a "core Windows communications app" even though its feature set, at time of this writing, is pathetic.

✦ **Windows Live Calendar** has turned into the *Windows Store Calendar*.

✦ **Windows Live Contacts** is now called *People*.

✦ **Windows Live Photo Gallery** morphed into *Photos* on the tiled Start screen.

✦ **Windows Live Messenger** sits perched in a particularly precarious position, with Lync on one side and Microsoft Skype on the other. Windows Live Messenger's been integrated in various degrees into all sorts of sites and apps, including Internet Explorer, Outlook.com, SkyDrive, Facebook, Myspace, LinkedIn, Windows Live Photo Ga... er, Photos, Bing, Xbox Live, Windows Phone, and Zune (which is also biting the dust). And Windows Live Messenger is available for iPhone and iPad from the Apple App Store. On the Win8 tiled Start screen, the Windows Live Messenger equivalent is called *Messaging,* but Messaging's ripe for inclusion in either Skype or Lync, or both.

It's not just the Live apps that are dying. Some of the old Windows programs — **Media Player** being a good example — are being supplanted, and will soon be overshadowed, by tiled apps.

Some people feel that losing both **Flash** and **Adobe Reader** (and other browser add-ins) in the tiled version of Internet Explorer 10 is a bad thing. I disagree strongly. Flash and Reader have brought on more pain and misery — and hijacked systems — than they're worth. Microsoft's own ActiveX technology, which won't run on the tiled IE10, is another malware magnet that deserves to die. You can run all those add-ins in the Legacy desktop version of IE10, if you absolutely must. The tiled IE10 will also run Flash on specific sites, but only if they're on a Microsoft-controlled white list of trustworthy sites.

Some other odd missing pieces include the following:

✦ **Gadgets'** time is gone. Microsoft tried to put "active" items on the Windows desktop for nearly a decade. Windows Vista brought active content — otherwise known as *gadgets* — to the Windows desktop. In Windows 8, Microsoft has killed off gadgets and replaced them with Start screen tiles.

+ **ClearType** doesn't run on the tiled applications' interface, at all. It's still on the old-fashioned desktop, but your tiled apps can't use it. That's one of the reasons why switching from tiled to Legacy is so jarring.

Note that this is different from Microsoft's ClearType HD technology, a marketing term for the monitors on Microsoft Surface tablets. I have no idea why Microsoft used the same term for both.

+ **Flip 3D** is gone. Little more than a parlor trick, and rarely used, the Windows Key+Tab used to show a 3D rendering of all running programs, and flip among them. Stick a fork in it.

Do You Need Windows 8?

Unless you have a touch-sensitive tablet, there's little compelling reason to leave Windows 7 and move to Windows 8.

The security improvements are nice, but Win7 and Microsoft Security Essentials (see *Windows 7 All-In-One For Dummies,* by yours truly) work quite well.

Win8 data backup is good, but Windows 7's Previous Versions does almost the same thing.

The Windows 8 tiled apps are getting better, while the Windows Live Essentials apps are entering a state of suspended animation. They're still fully functional.

SkyDrive's great, but you can access it from your web browser. Dropbox, Google Drive, and Amazon Cloud Drive offer good alternatives — free.

Bottom line: If you see something bright and shiny in Windows 8, by all means go for it. If you want to work with the new touch-friendly tiled style interface, it's certainly worth the plunge. But if you're using a mouse and keyboard and don't particularly want to try anything new, Windows 8 may not be a very good choice.

Wonder what they'll cook up for Windows 9?

Chapter 3: Which Version?

*I*f you haven't yet bought a copy of Windows, you can save yourself some headaches and more than a few bucks by buying the right version the first time. And, if you're struggling with the 32-bit versus 64-bit debate, illumination — and possibly some help — is at hand. It's hard to keep track of all the various versions without a scorecard. That's where this chapter comes in.

Although Windows 8 comes in many versions, you likely need to be concerned about only three — and one of them isn't really Windows. At least, it doesn't run Windows programs.

Microsoft used to have a simple, small set of SKUs (Stock Keeping Units — what you and I would call *versions*) for Windows. For example, Windows XP shipped with two versions: Windows XP Home Edition and Windows XP Professional. XP Professional included features that were needed to use XP in a company, on a large corporate network.

Then the proverbial hit the fan, and within two years, there was Windows XP Starter Edition, Media Center Edition, and Tablet PC Edition — which were all available only pre-installed on new systems. In theory. XP Professional was also released in two 64-bit versions, one for Itanium, and one for Itanium 2, which worked on alternate Tuesdays. Then there was the XP Professional x64 Edition . . . you get the idea. Vista didn't make things any clearer, and Windows 7 followed in Vista's dirty footsteps.

With Windows 8, everyone's been hoping that Microsoft would finally reduce the complexity and just bring, well, uh, Windows 8.

It didn't quite work out that way — in spite of what the salespeople will tell you.

Roll an 8 — Any 8

Windows 8 appears in five — count 'em, five — different versions. Three of those versions are available in 32-bit and 64-bit incarnations. That makes eight different versions of Windows to choose from. And if you want Windows Media Center, you only have two choices, and it'll cost you more.

Fortunately, most people need to concern themselves with only three versions, and you can probably quickly winnow the list to one. Contemplating the 32-bit conundrum may exercise a few extra gray cells, but with a little help, you can probably figure it out easily.

In a nutshell, the five Windows versions (and targeted customer bases) look like this:

✦ **Windows 8 for Emerging Markets,** which probably won't concern you if you're reading this in English. Tailored for specific countries and available only in specific languages, this is the version Microsoft will use to try to increase Windows sales in places where people just don't buy Windows. They borrow it. Permanently.

✦ **Windows RT,** quite possibly the worst name Microsoft has ever given any product, isn't really Windows because it won't run old-fashioned Windows programs and it doesn't have a real Windows 7 style desktop. Windows RT is Microsoft's iPad-wannabe, built on a completely new kind of computer, commonly called *ARM.* It contains the tiled interface, four customized Office-like apps (Word, Excel, PowerPoint, and OneNote), File Explorer, and Internet Explorer on an ersatz desktop.

Windows 8 All-In-One For Dummies doesn't cover Windows RT. The ARM version of Windows is a very different beast from the more traditional versions of Windows 8.

✦ **Windows 8** — the version you probably want — works great unless you specifically need one of the features in Windows 8 Pro. A big bonus for many of you: This version makes all the myriad Windows languages — 96 of them from Afrikaans to Yoruba — available to anyone with a normal, everyday copy of Windows, at no extra cost.

✦ **Windows 8 Pro** includes everything in Windows 8 plus the ability to attach the computer to a corporate domain network; the Encrypting File System and BitLocker (see the "Encrypting File System and BitLocker" sidebar, later in this chapter) for scrambling your hard drive's data; Hyper-V for running virtual machines; and the software necessary for your computer to act as a Remote Desktop host — the "puppet" in an RD session.

You also need Windows 8 Pro if you want to run Windows Media Center, which is an extra-cost add-on. Not many people run WMC any more, with the Xbox filling in and extending the missing feature set.

An added bonus: If you want to buy Windows on Microsoft hardware, the Microsoft Surface computers come with Windows 8 Pro and Windows RT (but not Windows 8 itself). Surface computers are capable, junk-free, innovative — and pricey.

✦ **Windows 8 Enterprise** is available only to companies that buy into Microsoft's Software Assurance program — the (expensive) volume licensing plan that buys licenses to every modern Windows version. Enterprise offers a handful of additional features, but they don't matter unless you're going to buy a handful of licenses or more.

Windows Vista and Windows 7 both had "Ultimate" versions, which included absolutely everything. Win8 doesn't work that way. If you want the whole enchilada, you have to pay for volume licensing and the Software Assurance program. And then you have to buy Windows Media Center.

Before you tear your hair out trying to determine whether you bought the right version, or which edition you should buy your great-aunt Ethel, rest assured that choosing the right version is much simpler than it first appears. Flip to "Narrowing the choices," later in this chapter. If you're considering buying a cheap version now and maybe upgrading later, I suggest that you first read "Buying the right version the first time" before you make up your mind.

Buying the right version the first time

What if you aim too low? What if you buy Windows 8 and decide later that you really want Windows 8 Professional? Be of good cheer. Switching versions ain't as tough as you think.

Microsoft chose the feature sets assigned to each Windows version with one specific goal in mind: Maximize Microsoft profits. That's why you find plenty of upgrade routes and plenty of opportunity to spend more money in the Add Features to Windows program (see Figure 3-1).

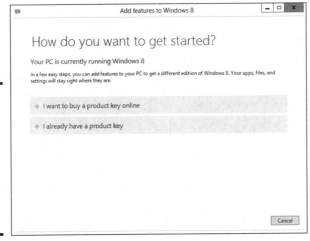

How do you want to get started?

Your PC is currently running Windows 8

In a few easy steps, you can add features to your PC to get a different edition of Windows 8. Your apps, files, and settings will stay right where they are.

→ I want to buy a product key online

→ I already have a product key

Cancel

Figure 3-1:
Add
Features to
Windows 8,
ready to
take your
shekels at
any time,
24/7.

All it takes is a credit card and a Windows Live ID to upgrade from Windows 8 to Windows 8 Professional, or to add Windows Media Center to Win8 Pro. No, you can't downgrade and get a refund. Bonus points for thinking about it, though.

Upgrading is easy and cheap, but not as cheap as buying the version you want the first time. That's also why it's important for your financial health to get the right version from the get-go.

Add Features to Windows 8 counts as pure gravy for Microsoft: Follow the upgrade steps, and Windows invites you to log on to the Internet, hand over your credit card number, and upgrade on the spot. You don't get a new box or a new CD. All you get is a new product key and a walk-through that installs the new version from media that's already in your possession. It's pure profit for the folks in Redmond. Smart.

Narrowing the choices

You can dismiss three Windows versions out of hand:

+ **Windows for Emerging Markets** probably isn't even available where you live.

+ **Windows RT** may be a good choice if you aren't the least bit interested in running older Windows programs, and you can live in a very touch-centric universe, with versions of Word, Excel, PowerPoint, and OneNote that are very different from the versions you use now. Windows RT is only available pre-installed on new computers.

✦ **Windows 8 Enterprise** is only an option if you want to pay through the nose for five or more Windows licenses, through the Software Assurance program. Microsoft may change its mind — either lower the price for small bunches of licenses and/or make the Enterprise version available to individuals — but as of this writing, Enterprise is out of the picture for most of you.

That leaves you with plain vanilla Windows 8, unless you have a crying need to do one of the following:

✦ **Connect to a corporate network.** If your company doesn't give you a copy of Windows 8 Enterprise, you need to spend the extra bucks and buy Windows 8 Pro.

✦ **Run Windows Media Center.** Not many people use Media Center to control their TVs anymore; the Xbox has become far more popular. But if you have a lot invested in your older Media Center, you may want to pay for it in Windows 8. Only Win8 Pro will run Media Center.

✦ **Play the role of the puppet — the** *host* **— in a Remote Desktop interaction.** If you're stuck with Remote Desktop, you have to buy Windows 8 Pro.

Note that you can use Remote Assistance, any time, on any Windows PC, any version. (See Book VII, Chapter 2.) This Win8 Pro restriction is specifically for Remote Desktop, which is commonly used inside companies, but not used that frequently in the real world.

Many businesspeople find that *LogMeIn,* a free alternative to Remote Desktop, does everything they need and that Remote Desktop amounts to overkill. LogMeIn lets you access and control your home or office PC from any place that has an Internet connection. Take a look at the website `http://logmein.com`.

✦ **Provide added security to protect your data from prying eyes or to keep your notebook's data safe even if it's stolen.** Start by determining whether you need Encrypting File System (EFS), BitLocker, or both (see the later sidebar "Encrypting File System and BitLocker"). Win8 Pro has EFS and BitLocker — with BitLocker To Go tossed in for a bit o' lagniappe.

✦ **Run Hyper-V.** Some people can benefit from running *virtual machines* inside Windows 8. If you absolutely have to get an old Windows XP program to cooperate, for example, running Hyper-V with a licensed copy of Windows XP may be the best choice. For most people, VMs are an interesting toy, but not much more.

Encrypting File System and BitLocker

Encrypting File System (EFS) is a method for encrypting individual files or groups of files on a hard drive. EFS starts after Windows boots: It runs as a program under Windows, which means it can leave traces of itself and the data that's being encrypted in temporary Windows places that may be sniffed by exploit programs. The Windows directory isn't encrypted by EFS, so bad guys (and girls!) who can get access to the directory can hammer it with brute-force password attacks. Widely available tools can crack EFS if the cracker can reboot the, uh, crackee's computer. Thus, for example, EFS can't protect the hard drive on a stolen laptop/notebook. Windows has supported EFS since the halcyon days of Windows 2000.

BitLocker was introduced in Vista and has been improved since. BitLocker runs *underneath* Windows: It starts before Windows starts. The Windows partition on a BitLocker-protected drive is completely encrypted, so bad guys who try to get to the file system can't find it.

EFS and BitLocker are complementary technologies: BitLocker provides coarse, all-or-nothing protection for an entire drive. EFS lets you scramble specific files or groups of files. Used together, they can be mighty hard to crack.

BitLocker To Go provides BitLocker-style protection to removable drives, including USB drives.

Windows 8 Pro is also an excellent choice if you're sold on the Microsoft Surface tablets. At least as of this writing, Microsoft only offers its own tablets in Windows RT and Windows 8 Pro versions.

In addition, you need Windows 8 Pro if you want to do an in-place upgrade from Windows 7 Pro or Ultimate, but in-place upgrades have their own quirks. See Book I, Chapter 4 for details.

Choosing 32-Bit versus 64-Bit

If you've settled on, oh, Windows 8 as your operating system of choice, you aren't off the hook yet. You need to decide whether you want the 32-bit flavor or the 64-bit flavor of Windows 8. (Similarly, Windows 8 Pro and Enterprise are available in a 32-bit model and a 64-bit model.)

Although the 32-bit and 64-bit flavors of Windows look and act the same on the surface, down in the bowels of Windows, they work quite differently. Which should you get? The question no doubt seems a bit esoteric, but just about every new PC nowadays uses the 64-bit version of Windows for good reasons:

✦ **Performance:** The 32-bit flavor of Windows — the flavor that everyone was using a few years ago and many use now — has a limit on the amount of memory that Windows can use. Give or take a nip here and a tuck there, 32-bit Windows machines can see, at most, 3.4 or 3.5 gigabytes (GB) of memory. You can stick 4GB of memory into your computer, but in the 32-bit world, anything beyond 3.5GB is simply out of reach. It just sits there, unused.

The 64-bit flavor of Windows opens your computer's memory, so Windows can see and use more than 4GB — much more, in fact. Whether you need access to all that additional memory is debatable at this point. Five years from now, chances are pretty good that 3.5GB will start to feel a bit constraining.

Although lots of technical mumbo jumbo is involved, the simple fact is that programs are getting too big and Windows as we know it is running out of room. Although Windows can fake it by shuffling data on and off your hard drive, doing so slows your computer significantly.

✦ **Security:** Security is one more good reason for running a 64-bit flavor of Windows. Microsoft enforced strict security constraints on drivers that support hardware in 64-bit machines — constraints that just couldn't be enforced in the older, more lax (and more compatible!) 32-bit environment.

And that leads to the primary problem with 64-bit Windows: drivers. Many, many people have older hardware that simply doesn't work in any 64-bit flavor of Windows. Their hardware isn't supported. Hardware manufacturers sometimes decide that it isn't worth the money to build a solid 64-bit savvy driver, to make the old hardware work with the new operating system. You, as a customer, get the short end of the stick.

Application programs are a different story altogether. The 64-bit version of Office 2010 is notorious for causing all sorts of headaches: You're better off running 32-bit Office 2010, even on a 64-bit system (yes, 32-bit programs run just fine on a 64-bit system, by and large). Some programs can't take advantage of the 64-bit breathing room. So all is not sweetness and light.

Now that you know the pros and cons, you have one more thing to take into consideration: What does your PC support? To run 64-bit Windows, your computer must support 64-bit operations. If you bought your computer any time after 2005 or so, you're fine — virtually all the PCs sold since then can handle 64-bit. But if you have an older PC, here's an easy way to see whether your current computer can handle 64 bits: Go to Steve Gibson's SecurAble site, at www.grc.com/securable.htm. Follow the instructions to download and run the SecurAble program. If your computer can handle 64-bit operations, SecurAble tells you.

If you have older hardware — printers, scanners, USB modems, and the like — that you want to use with your Windows computer, do yourself a favor and stick with 32-bit Windows. It's unlikely that you'll start feeling the constraints of 32 bits until your current PC is long past its prime. On the other hand, if you're starting out with completely new hardware and you plan to run your current PC for a long, long time, 64-bit Windows makes a lot of sense. You may end up cursing me when an obscure driver goes bump in the night. But in the long run, you'll be better prepared for the future.

Chapter 4: Upgrades and Clean Installs

In This Chapter

🖊 **Finding out whether you can upgrade that old bucket**

🖊 **Upgrading online to Windows 8**

🖊 **Installing Windows 8 from a DVD**

🖊 **Cleaning the gunk off a new PC**

🖊 **What to do if Windows dies**

_____

*I*f your current PC runs Windows 7, you can install Windows 8 over the top of the old system by using Microsoft's online upgrade. Indeed, if you bought a new Windows 7 PC after June 1, 2012, you probably already have a $14.99 upgrade certificate in hand.

As long as your copy of Windows 7 bears a "genuine" product key the whole process takes less than 30 minutes — much less if you have a fast Internet connection. ("Genuine" being a Microsoft term that means your copy of Windows has passed an online test and doesn't appear to be fake.)

I've been upgrading Windows machines since I moved from Windows 286 (a souped-up version of Windows 2.0) to Windows 3.0 on my trusty Gateway PC in 1990. All the upgrade took was five of those new-fangled high density (1.2MB) 5¼ inch floppies. Since then, I don't know how many systems I've upgraded over the years, how many times, but the count certainly runs more than a thousand. During all those upgrades, I've sworn and kicked and moaned about in-place upgrades. They never worked. Sooner or later, putting a new version of Windows on top of an old one, without wiping out the old version, led to heartache, yanks of pulled hair, and screams of anguish. This time, for the first time ever, I'm changing my tune. I talk about my near-religious conversion in this chapter.

Can your PC handle Windows 8? Probably. I talk about that in this chapter, too, along with details about running upgrades, both online and from the DVD–based System Builder edition, creating a backup DVD, and what to do if your PC dies.

I also sandwich in a few tips about getting the crap off new PCs — or how to avoid getting a junker altogether. It's shameful that Microsoft has to charge extra to get rid of PC manufacturer's junk, but that's how things shake out. Imagine how the fans would wail if Apple charged extra for clean, decrapified Macs.

If you're here because Windows 8 is misbehaving and you want to tear out its beating heart and stomp on it . . . you're in the wrong place. After Windows 8 is installed on your PC, it's very rare indeed that you have to install it again. Instead, look into resetting or restoring your PC, a topic I cover in Book VIII, Chapter 2.

Deciding Whether to Upgrade Your Old PC

If you're currently running Vista or Windows 7 on a PC, the answer is yes, you can almost certainly upgrade it to Windows 8 — and it'll probably run faster than Vista, at least.

Officially you can (not should, but *can*) upgrade if your PC has at least:

+ **1 GHz** or faster processor — an Intel or AMD processor. A different version of Windows, called Windows RT, runs on an entirely different class of processors — but you can only buy that version of Windows preinstalled on a new computer.

+ **1GB** of RAM memory for the 32-bit version, **2GB** for the 64-bit (see Book I, Chapter 3 for a discussion of "bittedness").

+ **16GB** (for 32-bit) to **64GB** (for 64-bit) of available hard drive space. Of course, that's just for Windows. If you want to install any programs or save any data, you're going to need a leeeeeetle bit more.

+ **DirectX 9** graphics card with WDDM 1.0 or higher driver. Every video card made in the past five years meets that requirement.

Here are the two additional requirements that are key to using the tile-based Start screen side of Windows 8:

+ **A touch-sensitive screen.** Yes, you can use a mouse in the tiled, immersive interface — lots of people do every day. But you won't appreciate tiled programs as much.

+ **A screen resolution of 1366 x 768.** In fact, you can run Windows 8 with a 1024 x 768 screen, but you can't do a tiled *snap* — put two tiled Windows Store apps side by side (see Book III, Chapter 1) — unless you have a screen that runs at least 1366 pixels wide and 768 pixels high. You can get a screen that's bigger, and it'll run everything.

The much more difficult question of whether you *should* upgrade launches me into a metaphysical discussion. Consider how the following apply to you:

✦ **If you have a touch-enabled PC,** there's absolutely no question you should upgrade to Windows 8. Touch on the Win8 tiled Start screen side is infinitely better than touch on Windows 7.

✦ **If you're using a mouse and keyboard and don't plan on getting a touchscreen,** you only need Windows 8 if you really need one of the new features I mention in Book I, Chapter 2, or if one of the Windows Store apps tickles your fancy. If the benefits there don't put a tingle down your spine, no, you don't need Windows 8.

Personally, I have a Windows 8 tablet, a generic beast I bought just as Windows 8 test versions became available. The beast works well though, and I'll keep running Windows 8 on it. I also have a test desktop system, dedicated to Windows 8 all the time.

On my main machine, which I talk about in *Windows 7 All-In-One For Dummies,* I'm going to stick with Windows 7. I know that'll raise eyebrows in some corners, but Win7 does everything I need to do for work.

The laptops and netbooks around the house and office will stay with Win7, by and large — although I may find a compelling reason to upgrade one or two of them so they can run Windows Store apps, even without a touchscreen.

I love my iPad, Android phone, and Kindle Fire. I also seriously covet my wife's iPhone. That's why I include a lot of information about those dern Appley and Googlie things in this book. I find them all useful, although my life is still seriously buried in Windows.

Frankly, as things stand right now, I'm not sure I'll ever buy another desktop machine, unless the one I have turns shiny side up. I'll always need a big screen and a keyboard built like a brick house to get my work done, but the machine I have now does everything I need just fine. When I need a new laptop, I'll look hard at the MacBook and the Chromebook.

Will I ever *buy* a Windows 8 machine? Could happen.

Choosing Your Upgrade Path

Here are the two ways to get a Windows 8 upgrade:

✦ **You can buy a Windows 8 upgrade key and download the upgrade from the Internet.** This is the way I recommend to almost everybody, as long as your current computer is running a "genuine" copy of Windows XP, Vista, or Windows 7 — and you have a decent Internet connection.

Note: You can make a backup bootable USB drive or DVD drive if you use the online installation method. Yes, Microsoft thought of that.

✦ **You can buy a Windows 8 DVD, called the System Builder Edition, in a box, through a process not unlike the one everybody used ten years ago.** If you already have a copy of Windows running on your computer, this approach is not only wasteful (just try recycling the DVD jewel case!), but it's also a pain in the neck because you have to futz with booting from the DVD, entering a product key, deciding which partitions to nuke, and then running Windows Activation.

But if you need to create a Win8 system from scratch — perhaps on a newly built computer, or inside a Virtual Machine, or for double-booting — the System Builder DVD fills the bill.

Whether you upgrade online or upgrade by booting from a DVD or USB drive, Windows 8 has certain restrictions:

✦ **When upgrading from Windows 7,** you can choose to keep your programs, some of your settings (desktop background and Internet Explorer favorites and history), and data (anything in your user folders, including Documents, Desktop, and Downloads). If you have anything stored outside of one of the user's libraries, don't count on it coming across. You may be pleasantly surprised, but it may not come through.

Of course, you should always, always, always back up all your data before you perform an upgrade.

✦ **When upgrading from Vista,** you can keep most of your settings as well as Windows logon accounts and files, but you have to re-install your programs. So, for example, if you have Office 2007 running on your Vista machine, you need to have the installation CD for Office 2007 in order to get your programs back after the upgrade.

✦ **When upgrading from Windows XP,** you can keep only your logon accounts and user files.

✦ **If you want to change from a 32-bit version of Windows to 64-bit Windows 8,** you will necessarily wipe out all of your old programs and settings, as is the case with an upgrade from XP.

I take you through the upgrading details, step by step, in the next two sections.

Upgrading to Windows 8 online

Unless you have a fake copy of Windows or your Internet connection's slower than a filibustered Senate, I strongly recommend that you buy the Windows 8 Online Upgrade. (The name may vary depending on where you live.) You can find it in your local computer store or online at, among other places, the Microsoft Store (www.microsoftstore.com) and just about anywhere software is sold.

If you run the online upgrade, as a bonus, you also get a no-hassle run of the compatibility checker, which can be a real godsend.

To upgrade using the web-based installer:

1. **Make sure you have a backup of everything that's important to you.**

The only way to "undo" any upgrade to Windows 8 is to wipe it out and start all over again.

2. **Start Internet Explorer (yes, I recommend using IE in this case), go to the website specified in your upgrade package, and follow the instructions to connect.**

The website's probably http://windows.microsoft.com/en-US/ windows-8/download, or some variation, but the location may change. Do whatever your instructions say.

3. **If you don't want spam — er, helpful updates and notices from Microsoft — leave the sign-up box empty and select the Download Windows 8 check box. If you see a notification that asks about running or saving the Upgrade Assistant program, click Run.**

No, you won't download all of Windows 8, in spite of what the button says. The Upgrade Assistant is a small (5MB) file that guides you through the installation.

The Upgrade Assistant runs a compatibility check and shows you a summary of the results, as shown in Figure 4-1.

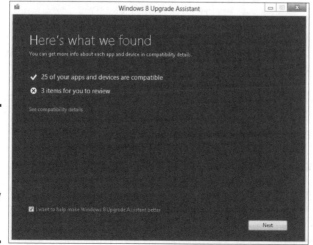

Figure 4-1:
With an online upgrade, you get a compatibility report up front.

4. **If the Upgrade Assistant report shows any items for you to review, click the See Compatibility Details link.**

   The Upgrade Assistant shows you a report like that in Figure 4-2, which displays common compatibility problems for anyone upgrading from Windows 7. These are the most common compatibility problems:

   - *Install an App to Play DVDs* is a common problem because Windows 8 can't play DVDs. Fortunately, solving the problem is as simple as installing the free VLC media player. See Book VI, Chapter 7.

   - *Secure Boot Isn't Compatible with Your PC* affects almost all PCs except some very recent ones that don't have Secure Boot compatibility. Although it's nice to have, Secure Boot isn't a show-stopper. See Book IX, Chapter 3.

   - *Your Screen Resolution Isn't Compatible with [tiled] Snap* is true on any PC that isn't configured at 1366 x 768 resolution or higher. If your video card and monitor run that high, you can change it after you upgrade. If they don't, you have to ask yourself whether tiled Snap is worth an upgrade. (*Hint:* It probably isn't.) See Book II, Chapter 1.

   In Figure 4-2, Windows also advises that I may have a problem with Apple not recognizing that my copy of iTunes is running on an authorized PC. A quick look at the iTunes online documentation shows how to re-authorize a new PC (or new operating system).

Figure 4-2:
Three of
the most
common
upgrade-
compatibility
sticking
points.

Make sure you understand the implications of the report. If there are any significant problems, it's much, much better to solve them now, rather than waiting until after you've upgraded to Windows 8.

5. **Take your time and when you're sure you can solve all the problems in the report, print it if you like, and then click Close.**

You return to the compatibility report (refer to Figure 4-1).

6. **Click Next.**

The installer may show you a product key.

7. **If you see a product key, take a picture of it with your phone.**

Or you can pull out a stylus and handy clay tablet, or try indelible ink on the palm of your hand. You probably won't need the key, but if you do, you'll be glad you have a copy.

8. **Click Next.**

The installer starts downloading a big file. On a typical ADSL connection, this might take 30 minutes; on a Google fiber line, oh, about 10 seconds.

When the download's done, the Install Windows 8 screen (see Figure 4-3) appears.

9. **Decide from the following options:**

- *To install now,* keep the Install Now button selected (it's selected by default).

- *To create a DVD or USB drive that can be used to install Windows 8 on this computer,* choose Install by Creating Media.

- *To put an installation program on your desktop to use later,* choose the last item, Install Later on this Computer.

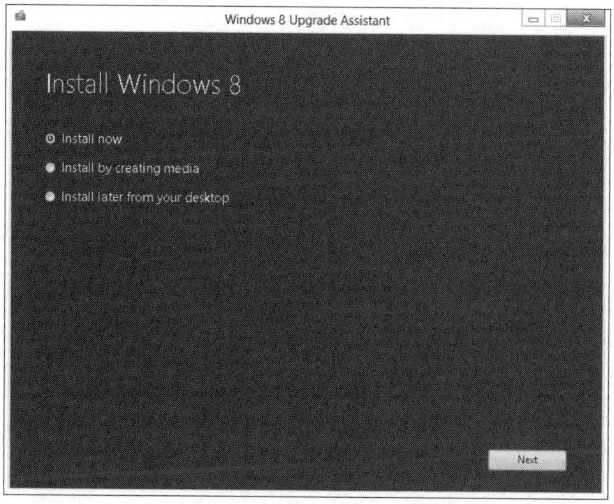

Figure 4-3:
Make sure everything's ready — you have backups and answered all the advisor questions — before you proceed.

Windows 8 Upgrade Assistant

Install Windows 8

○ Install now
● Install by creating media
● Install later from your desktop

Next

10. **Click Next.**

Most likely you chose Install Now in Step 9. If you did, Windows whirs for a while and then comes up with a Choose What to Keep dialog box. The choices (Windows Settings, Personal Files and Apps; Just Personal Files; Nothing) vary depending on which version of Windows you're upgrading from.

If you chose Install by Creating Media, the installer downloads the files necessary for installing Windows 8, helps you put them on a DVD or USB drive, and gives you a product key that will work on this particular PC. Continue with the steps in the next section, in order to install Windows.

11. **See Table 4-1 to help you choose what you want to keep, and then click Next.**

The upgrader makes a special compatibility pass to make sure you've been notified of all the possible problems. It may even ask you to uninstall programs (such as antivirus or firewalls) that may interfere with the upgrade. When everything's okay, you're prompted to restart your machine.

12. **Click Restart.**

Your old version of Windows shuts down and then comes up. You're asked whether you're ready to install Windows 8.

13. **Make sure Continue from Where I Left Off is selected and then click Next.**

The User Account Control challenge appears. You may have to provide the user name and password for an admin account on your Windows 7 computer.

14. **Click Yes.**

The installer, again, checks to make sure everything is okay. When it's done, the Ready to Download Windows screen, as shown in Figure 4-4, appears.

15. **Jot down the product key (you probably won't need it) and click or tap Next.**

Go have a latte . . . or two . . . or three. This installation can take 30 minutes or more. Don't touch your machine while Windows works.

You're ready to personalize your installation.

16. **Continue with the instructions in the next section, starting at Step 9.**

The online installer actually copies all the installation files into a hidden folder called ESD on your C: drive. You can just copy those files onto a DVD or USB, or any drive you like, and you'll have a Windows upgrade disk: Double-click the Setup.exe file, and the installer takes off.

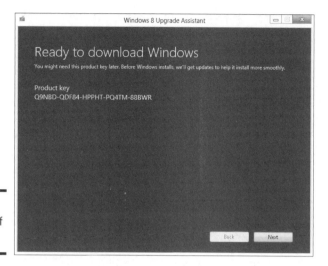

Figure 4-4:
The point of
no return.

Table 4-1	Choose What to Keep
This Choice . . .	*. . . Actually Means This*
Keep Windows Settings	Some of your Windows settings survive the upgrade: user accounts and passwords, your desktop background, Internet Explorer favorites and history, some File Explorer settings. Other Windows settings don't survive.
Keep Personal Files	Specifically means all the files in the Users folder. That includes the Documents, Pictures, Photos, Videos, and Desktop folders. But if you have data sitting in some other folder, stored outside Users, it may or may not make the transition, even if it's in one of your libraries.
Keep Apps	The upgrade process keeps all the application programs that are identified and understood by the upgrader. Microsoft has hundreds of thousands of programs and drivers on file — but it doesn't have every Windows program made. In addition, some programs (such as some system utilities) can't make it through the upgrade process. The problematic programs should be listed in the compatibility scan.
Nothing	A clean install. The upgrade routine moves several folders (Windows, Program Files, Program Files [x86], Users, and Program Data) to the windows.old folder, but all the originals are overwritten in the upgrade process. *Remember:* If you use a fingerprint reader or some other device that doesn't rely on passwords to log you in, make sure you have your password before you upgrade. The biometric data doesn't survive the upgrade.

Making an ISO file usable

Many people get a copy of Windows 8 in the form of a single file with the filename extension .iso. Microsoft MSDN and TechNet subscribers, for example, get ISO files. An *ISO file* is just a compressed version of a DVD image. You can turn an ISO file into a bootable DVD or USB drive by using a simple tool that Microsoft provides.

To perform the magic, download Microsoft's Windows 7 USB tool, which is located at (hold your breath) `http://microsoftstore.com/store/msstore/html/pbPage.Help_Win7_usbdvd_dwnTool`. Run the tool. Navigate to the ISO file, and then choose whether you want to burn a DVD or create a bootable USB drive. Four steps, and you're done.

Installing Win8 from a DVD or USB drive

If you're going to upgrade from Windows 7 to Windows 8, and want to keep your data and programs intact, I strongly urge you to perform the online upgrade I mention in the preceding section. As long as you stick to upgrading 32-bit Win7 to 32-bit Win8, or 64-bit Win7 to 64-bit Win8, the online installer works great.

On the other hand, if you want to wipe your computer and install Windows 8 from scratch, do that by booting from a DVD or USB drive and running a clean install. That's the process I describe in this section.

I can't emphasize enough that you must make full backups of *all* your data, write down *all* your passwords (unless they're stored online someplace like LastPass), get *all* your software installation CDs and DVDs, and make yet another backup just in case, before starting this process.

If you buy a shrink-wrapped copy of Windows 8, you get a DVD (or possibly a USB drive) that's ready to boot. If you have an ISO file, follow the instructions in the sidebar "Making an ISO file usable" to turn the file into a bootable DVD or USB drive.

With a bootable USB drive or DVD in hand, you may have to adjust your computer so that it boots from the USB or DVD.

Here's how to go through the whole process — and survive to tell the tale:

1. **With your old version of Windows running, insert the Windows installation disk in the DVD drive, or the installation USB in a USB port.**

2. **Choose Start⇨Shut Down to go through a full shutdown.**

Windows might offer to install itself while you're trying to shut down. If it does, click the Cancel button.

3. **Power off the PC, wait at least a full minute, and then turn on the power.**

   If the PC can start (or *boot*) from the DVD drive or USB drive, you see text on the screen that says something like `Press any key to boot from CD` or `Press Esc to choose boot device`.

4. **Press whatever key is recommended.**

   If the PC doesn't offer to boot from the DVD drive or USB stick, you have to look in your PC's documentation for the correct setting in your PC's BIOS. If you're not familiar with your PC's BIOS, go to the website for your PC manufacturer and search for the terms *change boot sequence.*

5. **When the PC boots, you may be asked if you want to go online to get the latest updates. If you do, choose Go Online to Install Updates Now and click Next.**

6. **In the Windows Setup screen, change the language if you wish, click Next, and then click Install Now.**

7. **When the installer prompts for the product key, enter it. When a license terms screen appears, accept it.**

   The Which Type dialog box, as shown in Figure 4-5, appears.

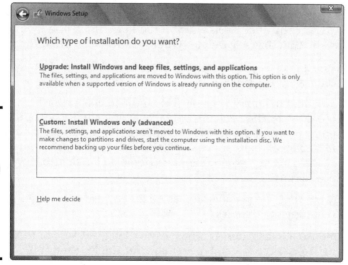

Figure 4-5:
Wipe
everything
and perform
a clean
install by
choosing
the Custom
option.

8. **To wipe everything and start fresh, click Custom Install Windows Only (Advanced).**

   The installer asks you where you want to install Windows, as shown in Figure 4-6.

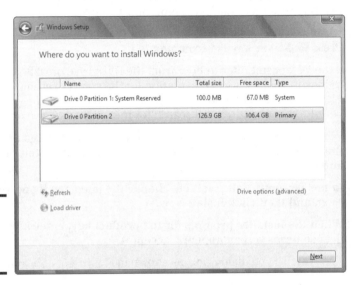

Name	Total size	Free space	Type
Drive 0 Partition 1: System Reserved	100.0 MB	67.0 MB	System
Drive 0 Partition 2	126.9 GB	106.4 GB	Primary

Figure 4-6:
Where
to install
Windows?

9. **If there is more than one entry in the upper box, choose Drive Options (Advanced), click each entry in the upper box, one by one, and click on the link that say Delete. When you're done, click Next.**

   Then go have another latte . . . or two . . . or three. Your computer restarts several times.

   If you had to jimmy your BIOS in Step 4 to make your PC boot from a DVD drive or USB, you might reach an odd situation where you see the setup screen again, and your computer just sits there waiting for you to start again. If that happens, pull the DVD or USB drive out of its slot, and manually restart your computer. The installer kicks back in again the second time.

   By the time the installer comes up for air, you're ready to personalize your copy of Windows.

10. **Choose a background color for the tiled Start screen (don't worry, it's easy to change later), type a name for the PC (better if you stick to letters and numbers, no spaces or weird characters), and click Next.**

    Windows asks about your initial settings, as shown in Figure 4-7.

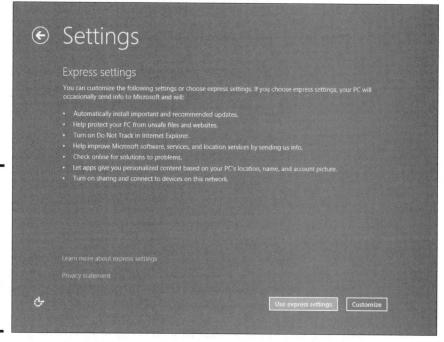

Figure 4-7:
I suggest
the
Customize
option.
It saves
having to
change bad
choices
later.

11. **If you trust Microsoft, choose Use Express Settings. If you're like me, choose Customize.**

If you choose Customize, the installer takes you through a series of questions. Here's what I do:

I turn on sharing. I have Windows Update notify, but don't download — yes, you have to install updates from time to time, but you don't need to follow Microsoft's schedule. If you don't see Notify but Don't Download among the offered options — Microsoft seems to vacillate on what it allows during setup — choose Don't Set Up Windows Update and see Book VIII, Chapter 3 for instructions on how to set it properly.

I automatically get new device drivers/apps (both set to On). I turn on both SmartScreen filters (see Book IX, Chapter 3). I turn off sending all the Microsoft info. I check online for solutions to problems (both set to On). I choose to send Do Not Track requests to websites that I visit (see Book VI, Chapter 6).

I don't send Microsoft any info "to help make Windows and apps better." I use Windows Error Reporting and IE Compatibility lists. I let apps use my name (set to On). And finally, I turn on Windows Location, which is a tough one. I usually turn it on, but you don't have to if you don't want Windows to track your location. The only real downsides are in the Windows Store apps Maps and Weather.

12. **If you just upgraded from Windows 7, provide your account's password. If you performed a clean install, don't let Windows bully you into using a Microsoft account. Enter the account name (and type!) you like.**

Personally, I use a clean Microsoft account, but you may feel differently.

In Book II, Chapter 4, you find an extensive discussion of the pros and cons of Microsoft accounts. Suffice it to say, there's no clear-cut "right" answer, but if you create a new, clean Microsoft account and use it exclusively for Windows 8, you won't be giving away too much of your privacy in exchange for the benefits of having a Microsoft account.

13. **Click Finish and stand back.**

The tiled Start screen appears, and you're done.

Cleaning the Gunk Off New PCs

On your new PC, did you get a free 60-day trial for Norton Internet Security with Symantec Live Update and the trial version of WinDVD and Roxio and Quicken — and oh! — this neat discount for EarthLink?

If you bought a new computer with Windows pre-installed, the manufacturer probably sold some desktop real estate to a software company or an Internet service provider (ISP).

Oh yeah, the AOLs and Nortons of the world compensate the Sonys and Dells and HPs for services, and space, rendered.

The last thing you need is yet another come-on to sign up for AOL or an antivirus program that begs you for money every week, or a fancy manufacturer-installed driver that just sits there and sucks up space.

Some manufacturers have wised up and started offering clean PCs, for a slight premium. Microsoft stores also sell Signature editions of popular PCs — *Signature* implies that the PCs have been divested of typical manufacturer junk. Believe me, it's worth the money to get the cleanest PC you possibly can.

The easiest way to get a clean PC? Install Windows 8 from Microsoft. Use any of the methods mentioned in the preceding section and, as long as you don't bring across old programs in an upgrade, your new computer will be clean as can be. Blissfully so.

If you have a PC with all that junk, here's what you can do to remove it:

✦ **Take it to a Microsoft store** (one of the brick-and-mortar ones), where you can pay $99 for someone to take the junk off a new PC.

✦ **Use a tool that removes most, if not all, the useless junk.** PC Decrapifier is a free, simple program that scans your machine and gets rid of most of the junk. As this book went to press, the Windows 8 version wasn't ready, so check at the developer's website, `www.pcdecrapifier.com`, to see whether it's Win8 safe.

What If the Wheels Fall Off?

So what should you do if Windows dies? Try this:

✦ **If Windows came bundled with a new PC,** scream bloody murder at the vendor who sold you the %$#@! thing. Don't put up with any talk about "it's a software problem; Microsoft is at fault." If you bought Windows with a new PC, the company that sold you the machine has full responsibility for making it work right. Period.

✦ **If you upgraded from Vista or Windows 7 to Windows 8 and didn't complete a custom (clean) install,** try that. You don't have much to lose, eh? Follow the instructions in the section, "Installing Win8 from a DVD or USB Drive," earlier in this chapter, and go for the Custom (Clean) Install.

✦ **If you completed a custom (clean) install and Windows still falls over and plays dead,** man, you have my sympathies. Check with your hardware manufacturer and make sure that you have the latest BIOS version installed. (Make sure to find an instruction book; changing the BIOS is remarkably easy, if you follow the instructions.) Visit the online newsgroups or drop by my lounge, at `http://lounge.windowssecrets.com`, to see whether anybody there can lend a hand. If all else fails, admit defeat and re-install your old operating system.

Life's too short.

Book II

Personalizing Windows

The 5th Wave   By Rich Tennant

AFTER INSTALLING WINDOWS 8 NED AND LORETTA SELECT THE COMPUTER'S BACKGROUND

© RICHTENNANT

"Oh — I like this background much better than the basement."

Contents at a Glance

Chapter 1: Getting around Windows

In This Chapter

- ✔ Dr. Jekyll, meet Mr. Hyde
- ✔ Navigating via your fingers or via a mouse
- ✔ Getting to know shortcuts
- ✔ Switching among apps
- ✔ Turning the dern thing off

*I*f you're an experienced Windows user, I can almost guarantee that you won't like Windows 8, until you have a chance to work with it for a while.

Even *after* you're used to it, there's at least a 50/50 chance you won't like it.

On the other hand, if you're new to Windows — or you just love your Windows Phone — you're going to appreciate that Windows doesn't force you to learn all that arcane stuff that's in the second half of this book.

Former Microsoft General Manager and Distinguished Engineer Hal Berenson said it best: "Consumers increasingly reject the old experiences in both their personal and work lives. For the 20-something and under crowd, the current Windows desktop experience is about as attractive as the thought of visiting a 19th century dentist."

Windows 8 is Microsoft's first step out of the 19th century dentist's office. It's long, long overdue.

I figure that 90 percent of the stuff that 80 percent of the people do with a computer, runs just fine on a tablet. So why put up with all the hassles of running Windows on a piece of iron that weighs more than your refrigerator, and breaks down twice as often? Maybe you're addicted to blue screens and frozen mice. Or maybe you're ready to leave it all behind and tap your way to something new.

In this chapter, I show you what's to like about the new Windows, how to get around if you're new to Windows, and if you're an experienced Windows hand, how to reconcile your old finger memory with the new interface. It isn't as hard as you think.

Really.

I also show you how to be input-agnostic — how to use either your fingers or your fork, er, mouse to get around the screen. And I give you a few not-at-all-obvious tips about how to get the most out of your consorting with the beast.

Windows' Jekyll and Hyde Personality

The way I look at it, almost all the people starting with Windows 8 start in one of four groups, with the largest percentage in the first group:

✦ Somewhat experienced at some version of Windows, and primarily comfortable with a mouse and keyboard. (More than a billion people have used Windows.)

✦ Experienced at Windows, but want to learn touch input.

✦ New to Windows, prefer to use touch.

✦ New to Windows, and want to visit the 19th century dentist's office to see what all the screaming's about.

If you fall into that final group, you need to learn to use the antique interface apparatus known as a mouse and keyboard. I'm reminded of Scotty on the Enterprise picking up a mouse and saying, "Computer! Computer! Hello computer . . ." When Scotty's reminded to use the keyboard, he says, "Keyboard. How quaint."

So this section offers a whirlwind tour of your new Windows 8 home that helps you start clicking and tapping your way around.

A tale of two homes

As you undoubtedly know by now, Windows 8 has two faces. They're designed to work together. You can be the judge of how well they live up to the design.

The first face you see when you start Windows is the tiled Start screen, as shown in Figure 1-1.

Tap or click, paper or plastic?

A lot of people have asked me whether I'm serious about tapping on a Windows machine. Yes, I am, and I hope you will be, too.

I tried the old stylus Windows interface, back when the luggable Windows tablets first appeared, in the Windows XP days. I hated it. I still hate it. I hated it so much that when I saw someone using an iPad, all I could think was, "Oh, that must suck." (Remember, "suck" is a technical term.)

An hour later, I tried an iPad, and all of a sudden using a finger was fine. More than fine, it was tremendous. When my then-18-month-old son spent a few hours playing on the iPad, then started using the interface like a virtuoso, I was hooked. The tap-and-swipe interface is astonishingly easy to learn, use, and remember.

Windows 8's tap interface isn't as elegant as the iPad's. Sorry, but it's true. The main difference is that Windows has to accommodate a lot of things that the iPad just doesn't do — right-click comes immediately to mind. But for many, many things that I do every day — web surfing, quickly checking e-mail, scrolling through Twitter, catching up on Facebook, reading the news, looking at the stock market, and on and on — the touch interface is vastly superior to a mouse and keyboard. At least, it is to me.

As I'm writing this book, I have three computers on my desk. One's a traditional desktop running Windows 7, the other's running Windows 8. The third one's a Win8 tablet with a portable keyboard. When I want to look up something quickly, guess which one I use?

**Book II
Chapter 1**

**Getting around
Windows**

Figure 1-1:
The tiled
Start
screen.

The Desktop tile

Surprisingly, as best I can tell, Microsoft doesn't really have a name for this screen. I call it the *Start screen* because it's identified in various places (not the least of which is on the screen itself) as "Start" and, uh, well, it's a screen. Microsoft used to call the style used here "Metro" but an apparent conflict with the name has led them to oblique reference to their tiled interface.

I think of Figure 1-1 as the Mr. Hyde face of Windows 8.

On the other hand, the old-fashioned Dr. Jekyll (was Jekyll a 19th century dentist?) looks like Figure 1-2.

The Dr. Jekyll version of Windows 8 looks almost exactly like the Windows 7 desktop, except it doesn't have a Start button, or Windows orb, in the lower-left corner. In fact, if I couldn't see the lower-left corner, I'd be very hard-pressed to tell the Windows 7 and Windows 8 desktops apart.

I call the screen in Figure 1-2 the *Windows 7 style* or *old-fashioned desktop.* Microsoft uses the term "legacy" to describe programs that run on the old-fashioned desktop — thus, for example, legacy Control Panel or legacy Office — but there doesn't seem to be a name for this desktop, either. I can't call it the "desktop" because the Start screen is a desktop, too, although it works quite differently. So I'll just settle for "old-fashioned" or "Windows 7 style."

Legacy, in Microsoft-ese means "something that it supports because it has to, but will drop it like a hot potato as soon as it can." That's an important lesson for you folks who have some experience with Windows. The Windows programs you know and have sworn at for years are now "legacy" programs — in official parlance.

Figure 1-2:
The old fashioned desktop.

Switching from the Start screen to the old-fashioned desktop and back

Get your computer going. Go ahead. I'll wait.

You're looking at the Start screen, right?

The very first question I get from new Windows 8 users is (more or less): "How do I get my desktop back?" The answer's easy. When you're in the Start screen, just click or tap the big Desktop tile.

The second question I hear, when people are looking at the Legacy desktop: "WTTffffftttt heck is my Start button?" Of course, as you probably know, the old-fashioned desktop has no Start button. Instead, you need to jump to the tiled Start screen. Returning to the Start screen is easy — just do one of the following:

+ **Click in the lower-left corner, where the Start button used to be.**

+ **Press the Windows key on your keyboard or tap the Windows button on your tablet computer.**

+ **Click the Start charm on the Charms bar.** The Charms bar is a small pane with a handful of icons, on the right (see Figure 1-3; more about charms in Book II, Chapter 3). You access it by swiping the right edge of the screen until the Charms bar appears: put your finger off the screen on the right side and drag it toward the center. The Start charm is in the middle.

If you can get from the old desktop to the Start screen by pressing the Windows key, you'd think that you could go the other way — get from the Start screen to the old desktop — by pressing the Windows key. Unfortunately, it doesn't work that way. There's a reason why, but it's a bit complicated. I talk about that reason in the section "Running, Switching, and Shutting Down Apps" later in this chapter.

To summarize, to get from the Start screen to the old-fashioned desktop, tap or click on the Desktop tile. To get from the old-fashioned desktop to the tiled Start screen, press the Windows button or tap the Windows key on your tablet, or click in the lower-left corner of the old fashioned desktop, where the Start button used to be.

It's visually perturbing: one second you're on the (old fashioned) Windows desktop; and the next second you're playing with telephone buttons. The old desktop Start menu's gone, and in its place is a big black hole. Believe me, the Start screen doesn't act anything like the venerable Start menu. But, from Microsoft's point of view, that's the point.

Now I take a look at many of the other navigation choices that are available to you, whether you eat with your hands or with a mouse.

Figure 1-3:
The Charms
bar on the
right side of
the screen.

The Start charm

Navigating around a Touchscreen

This section is all about navigating with your fingers on a touchscreen. In the
land of tiled Windows Store programs, the *one-finger swipe* (dragging your
finger across the touchscreen) is king.

Here's a guided tour of your PC, using only your fingers:

1. **Go to the Start screen, as shown in Figure 1-1.**

If you can't see the Start screen, press the Windows button on your
tablet (or press the Windows key on your keyboard, if you have an
attached keyboard).

2. **Swipe your finger up from the bottom.**

You see a stripe across the bottom with one icon on it, as shown in
Figure 1-4. That's the *App bar;* it has different icons that vary depending
on which tiled Windows Store app you're using. For example, if you're
looking at the Start screen, only one All Apps icon appears.

Figure 1-4:
The tiled App bar along the bottom varies depending on which app is running.

3. **Tap the All Apps icon at the bottom.**

You see an oddly organized, kind of grouped and alphabetized list of all the programs (or *apps*) on your computer, per Figure 1-5.

Because a swipe from the bottom got you here, you might imagine that a swipe from the bottom would take you back. Ha! What fools these mortals be. You'll discover, if you try it, that swiping from the bottom doesn't do bumpkiss.

Figure 1-5:
A list of all the programs on your computer, sort of categorized and alpha- betized.

4. **Pinch the screen and then unpinch the screen.**

   If you've never done a *pinch*, this is a good place to practice. Stretch two fingers out, put them on the screen, and pull your fingers together. Think of pinching a baby's butt. Gently.

   You see the same weird alphabetized list and groups, but instead of seeing all the apps, you just get the first letters — A, B, C, and so on. This view of all apps is uninteresting but can be useful if you group apps appropriately (see Book III, Chapter 1, where I talk about *semantic zoom*). Right now, I sent you here only for a good exercise in pinching that won't mess up anything.

   To reverse the action and *expand* (variously called *unpinch* or *spread*) the screen, stick two fingers together, touch the screen, and move them out. *Violà* — you're back to the screen in Figure 1-5.

5. **To get back to the Start screen, press the Windows button on your tablet (or press the Windows key on your attached keyboard).**

   Back on *terra firma*, per Figure 1-1.

6. **Tap the Internet Explorer tile.**

   IE appears, filling the screen.

7. **Swipe from the bottom, or from the top.**

   Either way, you get App bars on the top and bottom (see Figure 1-6).

   On the top, you see the *tab switcher*. The tab switcher lets you move among active tabs. The Plus sign lets you start a new tab. The ellipsis sign lets you start a new InPrivate browsing tab (see Book II, Chapter 5).

   The App bar on the bottom is called a *navigation bar*. The IE navigation bar has a place to type an address or search terms and icons to reload and pin a location to the Start screen.

8. **While you're still in Internet Explorer, swipe from the right.**

   The Charms bar appears, as shown in Figure 1-7.

Delete a tab   Start InPrivate browsing   Add a tab

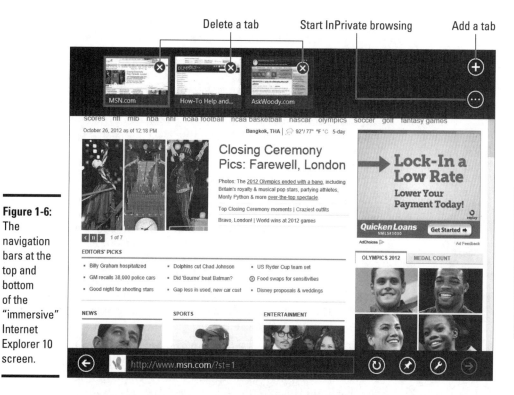

Figure 1-6:
The
navigation
bars at the
top and
bottom
of the
"immersive"
Internet
Explorer 10
screen.

Figure 1-7:
The
Windows
Charms bar
is available
anywhere in
Windows.

Charms bar is a strange name, and the execution is also, uh, strange. The basic idea is that the Charms bar gives you quick access to certain functions common in many applications and Windows. The Charms bar has links to the following functions:

- *Search* lets you search inside the application, or in Windows as a whole. If you're sitting in Internet Explorer, swipe from the right and tap the Search charm to bring up the Bing search engine. If you're in the tiled Windows 8 Mail app, the Search charm lets you search through your e-mail — or at least, the e-mail that's on your computer; Search in the Windows 8 tiled Finance app asks you to type a stock symbol; and so on.

The Charms bar is a good concept, but doesn't carry through to the old fashioned desktop. For example, if you're using File Explorer and right-swipe and choose the Search charm, you aren't put into Explorer search, you get tossed into the Start screen search.

- *Share,* in theory, lets you take items from one Windows 8 tiled app and put them in another. In practice, the inter-connections that you would expect may or may not exist — for example, you can't Share a contact from your People list in an email message. There are many more examples in Book IV.

- *Start* takes you to the Start screen, duplicating the function of the Windows button on your tablet. See "Switching from Start screen to the old–fashioned desktop and back," earlier in this chapter for details about this charm.

- *Devices* is a system-wide charm that lets you control your system's devices — printers, scanners, and so on — directly. For example, if you're looking at your Calendar, bringing up the Devices charm should let you print the current Calendar. (As of this writing, it doesn't, but that's pretty typical for the tiled Windows Store apps.)

- *Settings* brings up settings that are apropos for the app in particular, and for your system in general.

Details vary from application to application, but you get the general idea: When you're working with your thumbs in the tiled side of the fence, swipe from the bottom or the top or the right to get more options that are tailored for the program you're using.

I take a deep dive through the Charms bar in Book II, Chapter 3.

9. **Press the Windows button on your tablet (or press the Windows key on your attached keyboard) to go back to the Start screen.**

Take a breather.

Now that you've seen the basics of what the Start screen and tiled Windows 8 applications have to offer, you're ready take a look at the controls built into Windows 8 that let you switch programs. The controls work even when you're running a "legacy" program on the old fashioned desktop. In my experience, the controls frequently work when Windows *itself* has frozen — that's quite an accomplishment.

Follow these steps to switch Windows 8 tiled programs:

1. **Go to the Start screen, as shown in Figure 1-1.**

   If you can't see the Start screen, press the Windows button on your tablet (or press the Windows key if you have an attached keyboard).

2. **To start a few programs, tap Store, tap the Windows button to return to the Start screen, tap the Desktop tile, tap the Windows button again, and tap, oh, News.**

   That gives you some apps to work with.

3. **This step is tricky: Swipe from the left, but not very quickly, and not too far.**

   If you swipe the sweet spot, you see thumbnails of every running program, as shown in Figure 1-8. This part of the tiled interface is the *Switcher*.

   As you can see, Switcher treats the entire old fashioned desktop like it's one app, no matter how many programs are running on it simultaneously.

4. **Tap one of the Switcher apps.**

   Not unexpectedly, you switch to that app.

5. **Slide quickly from the left. Wash, rinse, repeat.**

   Windows switches you from app to app, going in the same sequence that appears in the Switcher pane.

6. **Sloooooowly drag from the left.**

   The new app appears in its own window, to the left of the main window, as shown in Figure 1-9. The new window takes up about one-fifth of the screen. Microsoft calls this *Snap* — I call it *Tiled Snap* so as not to confuse it with a legacy desktop feature called *Aero Snap.* (Yes, Aero is gone in Windows 8, but Aero Snap lives on.)

The entire old-fashioned desktop

Every running program

CHOOSING RYAN, ROMNEY
EASES BOTH LEFT AND RIGHT

IE WASHINGTON BUREAU 14 HOURS AGO

Vith his surprise decision to run with Rep. Paul D. Ryan,
ey has done something truly rare in today's politics: He
d both the left and the right.

Figure 1-8:
Switcher
shows
thumbnails
of every
running
program.

Note that you can Tiled Snap with the whole old fashioned desktop, as if it were just one running app, which, in a sense, it is.

7. Slowly drag the vertical bar between the snapped apps to the right.

You can also snap the apps so the small piece appears on the right, which can be helpful. Solitaire has the built-in intelligence to turn the deck of cards sideways, so you can play it while another app is snapped.

8. Press the Windows button on your tablet (or press the Windows key on your attached keyboard).

You're back to home base.

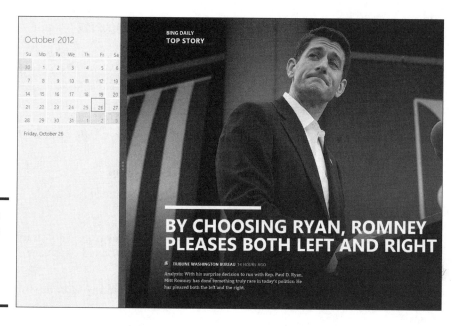

Figure 1-9:
Tiled Snap
lets you
place two
apps side-
by-side.

In some cases, you can replicate a right-click by tapping and holding your finger on the touchscreen. That is, if you ever encounter a situation where a right-click might've worked in Windows 7 and you don't have a mouse handy, try putting your finger on whatever you would've clicked and just leave your finger there for a while. Sometimes this brings up an option menu that's identical to the old right-click.

I talk about many variations on those themes in the remainder of this chapter.

Bringing up the Touch Keyboard

Sooner or later, if you're using your fingers, you'll need a keyboard. While earlier versions of Windows had on-screen keyboards — and those keyboards still exist in Windows 8 — the side of Win8 has its own Touch Keyboard.

You can always bring up the Touch Keyboard. To do so, swipe from the right to get the Charms bar and tap Settings. In the lower-right corner, you see a tile marked Keyboard. Tap it, and the keyboard appears.

The Win8 Touch Keyboard isn't just one keyboard. It's three: a regular Touch Keyboard, a split screen keyboard suitable for typing with just your thumbs, and a two-panel "writing" box that uses a stylus. To change keyboard types, tap on the keyboard tile in the lower-right corner.

Navigating with a Mouse and Keyboard

Microsoft has been very careful to ensure that anything you can do with a finger can also be done with a mouse. You have to make sure that you run your mouse properly, but the general gist goes like this:

1. **Go to the Start screen, as shown in Figure 1-1.**

   If you can't see the Start screen, press the Windows key on your keyboard.

2. **Right-click any blank spot on the desktop.**

   You see the App bar at the bottom, just like Figure 1-4.

3. **Click the All Apps icon at the bottom.**

   You see the oddly organized list of all your programs (refer to Figure 1-5). If you followed along with the finger-based exercises, you should see a pattern here.

4. **Click in the lower-right corner. There's a tiny icon down there — it looks like a minus sign. Trust me.**

   The effect is the same as pinching the screen with your fingers.

5. **To get back to the Start screen, press the Windows key on your keyboard.**

   Your screen should look, once again, like Figure 1-1.

6. **Click the Internet Explorer tile.**

   IE appears, full-screen.

7. **Right-click inside Internet Explorer.**

   You see the navigation bar at the bottom, and the tab switcher at the top, as shown in Figure 1-6.

   This is fairly common behavior in tiled Windows Store apps. On a touchscreen, you slide up from the bottom to get the lower App bar, and slide down from the top to get the upper App bar. When you're navigating with a mouse, right-click and both bars appear simultaneously.

8. **Hover your mouse in the upper-right or lower-right corners, and then move your mouse along the right edge.**

   The Charms bar appears (see Figure 1-7), first as a silhouette, and then as you move your mouse along the edge, with a solid background. The behavior of each of the charms — Search, Share, Start, Devices, and Settings — is exactly as you would expect, based on the description in Step 9 of the earlier "Navigating around a Touchscreen" section.

If you're on the old-fashioned desktop and hover your mouse in the lower-right corner, you trigger an old Windows behavior known as Show All: Windows creates outlines of all the open windows on your desktop. That's why I recommend that mousers generally hover in the upper-right corner to bring up the Charms bar. You won't see your screen go bananas if you stick to the upper-right corner.

9. Click in the lower-left corner to go back to the Start screen.

Usually if you aren't on the Start screen, clicking in the lower-left corner takes you back to it. Or you can get there by pressing the Windows key on your keyboard, or bringing up the Charms bar and choosing Start. You can also get there if you click your heels together three times and repeat, "There's no place like home."

10. Hover your mouse in the upper-left or lower-left corner, and then slowly drag your mouse along the left edge.

The Switcher appears with thumbnails of all running programs, as shown in Figure 1-8.

Again, it's important to note that the entire Windows desktop is treated as one app.

If you want to cycle through all running apps — both tiled and Legacy desktop apps, one at a time, hold down the Alt key and press Tab. You may be familiar with the Alt+Tab trick from Windows 7 or earlier. In Windows 8, the selection of running apps you see after pressing Alt+Tab includes all the running tiled full–screen apps.

11. To switch to a new app in the Switcher, click it. To set up a Tiled Snap arrangement (see Figure 1-9), slowly drag the app to the right.

12. Click in the lower-left corner to get back to the Start screen.

There's one more, very important mousing action you should memorize. To get to the *Power User Tasks menu* (I know, what a name, huh? Most people call it the WinX menu), right-click in the lower-left corner. You know, where the Start button should be. If you right-click in the lower left, you get the (impressive!) menu shown in Figure 1-10. You can see the same menu by holding down the Windows key and pressing X.

Figure 1-10:
The Power
User menu,
accessible
by right-
clicking in
the lower-
left corner,
or with the
Windows
key+X.

| Programs and Features |
| Power Options |
| Event Viewer |
| System |
| Device Manager |
| Disk Management |
| Computer Management |
| Command Prompt |
| Command Prompt (Admin) |
| Task Manager |
| Control Panel |
| File Explorer |
| Search |
| Run |
| Desktop |

Keying Keyboard Shortcuts

Windows 8 has about a hundred zillion — no, a googleplex — of keyboard shortcuts.

I don't use very many of them. They make my brain hurt.

Here are the keyboard shortcuts that everyone should know. They've been around for a long, long time:

✦ **Ctrl+C** copies whatever you've selected and puts it on the Clipboard. On a touchscreen, you can do the same thing in most applications by tapping and holding, and then choosing Copy.

✦ **Ctrl+X** does the same thing, but removes the selected items — a cut. Again, you can tap and hold, and Cut should appear in the menu.

✦ **Ctrl+V** pastes whatever is in the Clipboard to the current cursor location. Tap and hold usually works.

✦ **Ctrl+A** selects everything, although sometimes it's hard to tell what "everything" means — different applications handle Ctrl+A differently. Tap and hold usually works here, too.

✦ **Ctrl+Z** usually "undoes" whatever you just did. Few touch-enabled apps have a tap-and-hold alternative; you usually have to find Undo on a Ribbon or menu.

✦ When you're typing, **Ctrl+B**, **Ctrl+I**, and **Ctrl+U** usually flip your text over to Bold, Italic, or Underline, respectively. Hit the same key combination again, and you flip back to normal.

In addition to all the key combinations you may have encountered in Windows versions since the Dawn of 19th Century Dentistry, there's a healthy crop of new combinations. These are the important ones:

+ The **Windows Key** opens the Start screen or the last app. See the next section for details. In general, if you aren't looking at the Start screen, pressing the Windows Key will take you there.

+ **Alt+Tab** cycles through all running Windows programs, one by one — and each running Legacy desktop app is treated as a running program. (Windows key+Tab treats the entire desktop as one "app.")

+ **Ctrl+Alt+Del** — the old Vulcan three-finger salute — brings up a screen that lets you choose to lock your PC (flip to Book II, Chapter 2), switch the user (see Book II, Chapter 4), sign out, or run the new, much improved Task Manager (see Book VIII, Chapter 4).

+ **Just type** on the Start screen to begin a search of all your apps (see Figure 1-11).

Book II
Chapter 1

Getting around
Windows

Figure 1-11:
On the Start screen, start typing to search for Windows programs.

The following keyboard shortcuts may come in handy:

+ **Windows key+C** opens the Charms bar.

+ **Windows key+F** opens the Search charm, specifically to start searching for files.

+ **Windows key+X** opens the Power User menu (refer to Figure 1-10).

+ **Windows key+O** locks the screen rotation.

Working with the App Bar

You've already seen how tapping or clicking a tile runs the associated program. Not exactly surprising. But there's more to the story.

On the Start screen, you can select a tile and the App bar at the bottom appears. To select a tile with a mouse, right-click it. To select a tile with your finger, you have to drag it down just a little bit — nope, tap and hold doesn't work.

Once you've selected an individual tile, depending on which tile you've chosen, you may be offered the opportunity to open the program in a new window, change the size of a tile, or turn off automatic Live Tile updates.

Shutting Down Apps

Windows 8 has been designed to minimize battery drain, and a big part of the optimization involves curtailing programs that aren't actively running. There have to be a few exceptions — some legacy desktop programs, for example, have to keep working even when you're playing Solitaire. But most apps go into a quiet phase where they don't take up any battery time at all.

Sooner or later, Windows completely turns off idle apps. The exact timing and details seem to vary with the program and how many other apps are running, but in general, you don't need to worry about it.

Every once in a blue moon, though, you might want to turn off an app. If you have an app that may be crashing Windows, for example, you could give it the heave-ho and turn it off completely. If there are too many apps along the left side of your Switcher screen, you may want to kill one of them. To turn off — or *shut down* — a running tiled full–screen style app, do the following:

+ **On a touchscreen,** drag your finger slowly down from the top and keep dragging it all the way to the bottom of the screen.

+ **With a mouse,** hover your mouse up at the very top of the screen until it turns into a fist. Click and slowly drag the whole window down.

It probably won't surprise you too much to know that you can shut down the whole old fashioned desktop using that exact technique.

How Do You Turn This Thing Off?

"Jane! Stop this crazy thing! Help! JANE!"

George Jetson had the same problem.

Among the thousand ways to turn off Windows 8, none of them are obvious or intuitive. I recommend you bring up the Charms bar by swiping from the right or hovering your mouse in the upper-right corner. Tap or click Settings. At the bottom of the Settings pane, you see the Power button (see Figure 1-12). Tap or click Power and choose Shut Down.

Figure 1-12:
So *that's*
where they
hid the Off
button.

Chapter 2: Changing the Lock and Logon Screens

In This Chapter

✔ **Creating your own lock screen**

✔ **Putting apps on the lock screen**

✔ **Changing the way you log on**

✔ **Setting a picture password or PIN**

✔ **Avoiding logon altogether**

*W*indows presents three hurdles for you to clear before you can get down to work (or play, or whatever):

1. You have to get past the *lock screen.* That's a first-level hurdle so your computer doesn't accidentally get started, like the lock screen on a smartphone, say, or an iPad.

2. If there's more than one person — one *account* — set up on the computer, you have to choose which person will log on. I go into detail about setting up user accounts in Book II, Chapter 4.

3. If a password's associated with the account, you have to type it into the computer. Windows allows different kinds of passwords, which are particularly helpful if you're working on a touch-only tablet or a tiny screen like a telephone's. But the idea's the same: Unless you specifically set up an account without a password, you need to confirm your identity.

Only after clearing those three hurdles are you granted access to the Start screen and, from there, to everything Windows has to offer. In the sections that follow, you find out how you can customize the lock screen and the login methods to suit yourself.

Working with the Lock Screen

The very first time you start Windows, and any time you shut it down, restart, or let the machine go idle for long enough, you're greeted with the lock screen, such as the one in Figure 2-1.

Individualized lock screens

If you read the Microsoft help file, you may think that Windows keeps one lock screen for all users, but it doesn't. Instead, it has a lock screen for each individual user, and one more lock screen for the system as a whole.

If you're using the system and you lock it — say, tap your picture on the Start screen and choose Lock — Windows shows your personal lock screen, with the badges you've chosen. If you swipe or drag to lift that lock screen, you're immediately asked to provide your password. There's no intervening step to ask which user should log on.

If, instead of locking the system when you leave it, you tap your picture and choose Sign Out, Windows behaves quite differently. It shows the system's lock screen, with the system's badges. Your lock screen and badges are nowhere to be seen. If you drag or swipe to go through the lock screen, you're asked to choose which user will log on.

Bottom line: If you change your lock screen using the techniques in this chapter, you change only *your* lock screen. Windows' idea of a lock screen stays the same.

Figure 2-1:
The
Windows
lock screen.

You can get through the lock screen by doing any of the following:

✦ Swiping up with your finger

✦ Dragging up with your mouse

✦ Pressing any key on your keyboard

You aren't stuck with the lock screen Microsoft gives you. You can customize your picture and the little icons (or *badges*). The following sections explain how.

Using your own picture

Changing the picture for your lock screen is easy. (See the nearby sidebar "Individualized lock screens" for details about the difference between your lock screen and the system's lock screen.) Customizing the picture is a favorite trick at Windows demos, so you know it has to be easy, right? Here's how:

1. **On the Start screen, swipe from the right or hover your mouse in the upper-right corner to bring up the Charms bar, and then at the bottom, choose the Settings charm.**

2. **At the bottom of the Start Settings pane, tap or click the Change PC Settings link.**

The PC Settings screen, as shown in Figure 2-2, appears.

Book II
Chapter 2

Changing the Lock and Logon Screens

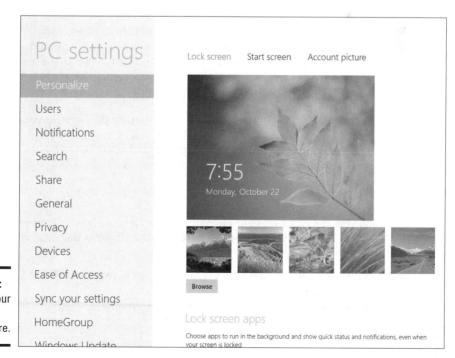

Figure 2-2:
Change your
own lock
screen here.

3. **Select Personalize on the left and Lock Screen on top. If you see a picture you like, tap or click it. If you want to look for your own picture, tap or click Browse.**

   If you tap or click Browse, Windows takes you to your Pictures library.

4. **Tap or click a picture and select Choose Picture.**

   You're done. There's no Apply or OK button to tap or click.

Test to make sure that your personal lock screen has been updated. The easiest way is to go to the Start screen (press the Windows key on the keyboard, or tap or click the Windows button on your PC), tap or click your picture in the upper-right corner, and choose Lock.

Adding and removing apps on the lock screen

Badges are the little icons that appear at the bottom of the lock screen. They exist to tell you something about your computer at a glance, without having to log on — how many e-mail messages are unread, whether your battery needs charging, and so on. Some badges just appear on the lock screen, no matter what you do. For example, if you have an Internet connection, a badge appears on the lock screen. If you're using a tablet or laptop, the battery status appears; nothing you can do about it.

Mostly, though, Windows lets you pick and choose quick status badges that are important to you. The question I most often hear about badges is, "Why not just choose them all?"

Good question. The programs that support the badges update their information periodically — every 15 minutes, in some cases. If you have a badge on your lock screen, the app that controls the badge has to wake up every so often, so it can retrieve the data and put it on the lock screen. Putting everything on the lock screen drains your computer's battery.

Corollary: If your computer has a short battery life, whittle your needs down as much as you can, and get rid of every quick status badge you don't absolutely need. But if your computer is plugged into the wall, put all the badges you like on the lock screen.

Here's how to pick and choose your quick status badges:

1. **On the Start screen, swipe from the right or hover your mouse in the upper-right corner to bring up the Charms bar, and then at the bottom, choose the Settings charm.**

2. **At the bottom of the Start Settings pane, tap or click the Change PC Settings link.**

   The PC Settings screen appears (refer to Figure 2-2).

3. **Select Personalize on the left and Lock Screen on top.**

   At the bottom of the screen are two rows of grayed-out icons.

   The first row of seven icons corresponds to seven badge quick status locations on the lock screen. They appear in order from left to right, starting in the approximate location you see in Figure 2-1. In theory (this doesn't always work), you can choose which badges appear, and where they appear, in order from left to right.

4. **Tap or click one of the icons, and then choose which display badge you want to appear in that slot on the lock screen (see Figure 2-3).**

   If you don't want any badge to appear in that slot, choose Don't Show Quick Status Here.

   Apps have to be specially designed to display the badge information on the lock screen. You're given a choice of all the apps that have registered with Windows as being capable of displaying a quick status badge on the lock screen. As you add more apps, some of them appear spontaneously on this list.

   If you choose Don't Show Quick Status Here, the gray icon gets a plus (+) sign, indicating that it isn't being used. No badge appears in the corresponding slot on the lock screen.

**Book II
Chapter 2**

**Changing the Lock
and Logon Screens**

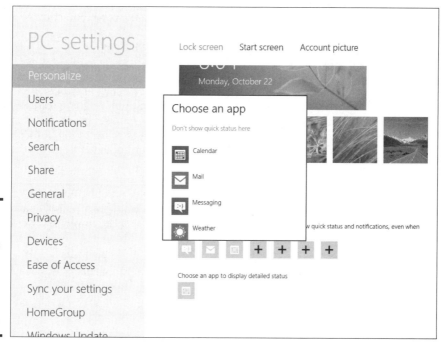

Figure 2-3:
Choose which app's badge appears in a particular slot on the lock screen.

5. **At the bottom of the page, you can choose which app(s) displays the extra-large detailed status, corresponding to the date and time in Figure 2-1.**

   The app has to be specially designed to display the large block of information shown in Figure 2-1.

   You're done. There's no Apply or OK button to tap or click.

Go back out to the lock screen — press the Windows key or button; tap or click your picture; choose Lock — and see whether you like the changes. If you don't like what you see or you're worried about unnecessarily draining your battery with all the fluff, start over at Step 1.

Logging In Uniquely

In this section, I step you through setting up picture passwords and PINs, and I give you a little hint about how you can bypass logon completely, if you aren't overly concerned about other people snooping around on your PC. Yes, it can be done, quite easily.

Using a picture password

If you follow the instructions in Book II, Chapter 4, set up an account, and the account has an everyday, ordinary password, you can use a picture password.

It's easy.

A *picture password* consists of two parts: First, you choose a picture — any picture — and then you tell Windows that you're going to draw on that picture in a particular way, such as taps, clicks, circles, and straight lines, with a finger or a mouse. The next time you want to log in to Windows, you can either type your password or you can repeat the series of clicks, taps, circles, and straight lines.

So, for example, you may have a picture of an old gold mill, as shown in Figure 2-4, and you may decide that you want your picture password to consist of tapping the higher roof peak, tapping the lower roof peak, and then drawing a circle around the door.

That picture password is simple, fast, and not easy to guess.

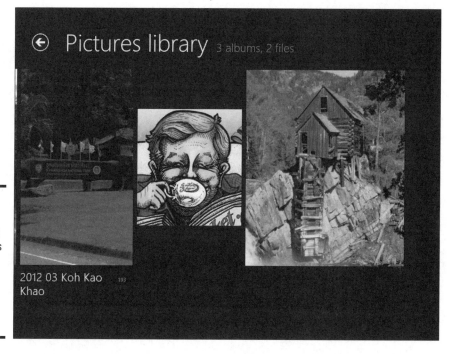

2012 03 Koh Kao   193
Khao

Figure 2-4:
Photo on
the right, in
my Pictures
library,
will make
a great
picture
password.

Everybody I know who has a chance to switch to a picture password loves it. Whether you're working with a mouse or a stubby finger, a few taps or slides are sooo much easier than trying to remember and type `a17LetterP@ssw0rd`.

Microsoft has a few suggestions for making your picture password hard to crack. These include the following:

✦ **Start with a picture that has a lot of interesting points.** If you have just one or two interesting locations in the photo, you don't have very many points to choose from.

✦ **Don't use just taps (or clicks).** Mix things up. Use a tap, a circle, and a line, for example, in any sequence you can easily remember.

✦ **Don't always move from left to right.** Lines can go right to left, or top to bottom. Circles can go clockwise or counterclockwise.

✦ **Don't let anybody watch you sign in.** Picture passwords are worse than keyboard passwords, in some respects, because the picture password appears on the screen as you're drawing it.

✦ **Clean your screen.** Really devious souls may be able to figure out that trail of oil and grime is from your repeated use of the same picture password. If you can't clean your screen and you're worried about somebody following the grime trail, put a couple of gratuitous smudges on the screen. I'm sure you can find a two year old who would be happy to oblige.

Here's how to change your account to use a picture password:

1. **On the Start screen, swipe from the right or hover your mouse in the upper-right corner to bring up the Charms bar, and then at the bottom, choose the Settings charm.**

2. **At the bottom of the Start Settings pane, tap or click the Change PC Settings link.**

   The PC Settings screen appears (refer to Figure 2-2)

3. **Select Users on the left.**

   The settings for your account, as shown in Figure 2-5, appear.

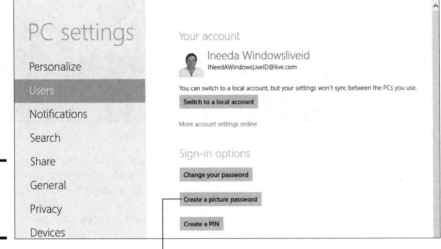

Figure 2-5:
Your
account's
settings.

Tap or click Create a Picture Password

4. **Under Sign-In Options, tap or click Create a Picture Password.**

   Windows asks you to verify your typed password.

   You must have a typed password — the password can't be blank — or Windows will just log you in without any password, either typed or picture.

5. **Type your password, and then tap or click OK.**

   Windows asks you to choose a picture.

6. **Tap or click Choose Picture, find a picture (remember, with ten or more interesting points), and tap or click Open.**

Your picture appears in a cropping bucket. The picture has to conform to an odd shape, or it won't fit on the logon screen.

7. **Slide the picture around to crop it the way you want it. Then tap or click Use This Picture.**

   Windows invites you to set up your gestures, as shown in Figure 2-6.

   Windows then asks you to repeat your gestures. This is where you get to see how sensitive the gesture-tracking method can be.

8. **Repeat the gestures. When you get them to match (which isn't necessarily easy!) tap or click Finish.**

   Your new picture password is ready.

9. **Go to the Start screen, tap your picture, choose Lock, and make sure you can replicate it.**

If you can't get the picture password to work, you can always use your regular typed password.

**Book II
Chapter 2**

**Changing the Lock
and Logon Screens**

Set up your gestures

Draw three gestures on your picture. You can use any combination of circles, straight lines, and taps.

Remember, the size, position, and direction of your gestures — and the order in which you make them — become part of your picture password.

1 2 3

Start over   Cancel

Figure 2-6:
Here's where you draw your three taps/ clicks, lines, and circles.

Creating a PIN

Everybody has PIN codes for ATM cards, telephones, just about everything.

Reusing PIN codes on multiple devices (and credit cards) is dangerous —
somebody looks over your shoulder, watches you type your Windows PIN,
and then lifts your wallet. They can have a good time, unless the PINs are
different. Word to the wise, eh?

Creating a PIN is easy:

1. **On the Start screen, swipe from the right or hover your mouse in
   the upper-right corner to bring up the Charms bar, and then at the
   bottom, choose the Settings charm.**

2. **At the bottom of the Start Settings pane, tap or click the Change PC
   Settings link.**

   The PC Settings screen appears (refer to Figure 2-2).

3. **Select Users on the left.**

   The settings for your account appear (refer to Figure 2-5).

4. **Tap or click Create a PIN.**

   Windows asks you to verify your password — it has to be your typed
   password; a picture password won't do.

5. **Type your password, and tap or click OK.**

   Windows gives you a chance to type your PIN, and then re-type it to confirm it. *Note:* The PIN must be four digits long.

6. **Type your PIN, confirm it, and tap or click Finish.**

   You can log on with your PIN.

Bypassing passwords and logon

So now you have three convenient ways to tell Windows your password: You
can type it, just like a normal password; you can click or tap on a picture; or
you can pretend it's a phone and enter four digits.

But what if you don't want a password? What if your computer is secure
enough — it's sitting in your house, it's in your safe deposit box, it's dangling
from a vine over a pot of boiling oil — and you just don't want to be bothered with typing or tapping a password?

As long as you have a Local account, it's easy. Just remove your password.
Turn it into a blank. Follow the steps in Book II, Chapter 4 to change your
password but leave the New Password field blank. (Shortcut: in Figure 2-5,
tap or click Change Your Password.)

Microsoft accounts can't have blank passwords. But Local accounts can.

If you have a blank password, when you click your username on the logon screen, Windows ushers you to the Start screen.

If there's only one user on the PC and that user has a blank password, just getting past the lock screen takes you to the Start screen.

Chapter 3: Working with Charms and Notifications

The new tiled Windows 8 interface brings two completely new solutions to Windows age-old problems.

The problems? Telling Windows what you want it to do, quickly and easily, and receiving messages from Windows about something you need to do. In the past, people have been treated to all sorts of warnings and bubbles and bleeps and blops.

The solutions? Charms and notifications. These two new features not only address the two aforementioned problems, but also set up Windows to accomplish both of those goals in a touch-friendly universe.

This chapter gives you a quick overview of the *Charms bar* — the quick and dirty way you can interact with the most exposed parts of Windows — and *notifications,* which are notices from Windows to you, delivered in a very specific way. Er, ways.

Bringing on the Charms

The desktop has its *Control Panel* — a central point to access all of the pain-inducing instruments every diabolical 19th century dentist might gleefully deploy. By contrast, the newer version of Windows has a simple bar with a charming name, the *Charms bar* (see Figure 3-1), and a significantly limited repertoire.

Figure 3-1:
The Charms
bar on the
right side of
the screen.

As long as the Charms bar is up, you see the system time and date, and the system badges that appear on the lock screen (for example, network status or battery charged — see Book II, Chapter 2) in a big black box on the lower left of the screen, which you can see in Figure 3-1.

Here's what you do to bring up the Charms bar, which you can do when you're on the Start screen, on the desktop, or inside any running program, any time:

✦ **On a touch-enabled screen,** slide a finger or thumb from the right toward the center of the screen.

✦ **With a mouse,** hover it in the upper-right or lower-right corner of the screen, and wait until you see a ghost outline of the charms. Then move your mouse along the right edge toward the middle of the screen. When the charms have fully materialized and the background has turned black, you're ready to click a charm.

Several of the charms lead to powerful programs inside Windows, others can take you interesting places, and a couple are just dullards. I go into great detail about the powerful charms (Search, Settings) in Book III, but here I just want to give you an overview and a bit of a teaser about what lies ahead for the interesting ones.

Search charm

The hardest thing to understand about the Search charm is its semblance to a chameleon: Search changes depending on where you are when you bring it up.

If you think of Search as being a global endeavor — something you perform over your entire PC — you miss the important nature of the Search charm. Although you can search your whole PC — just as Windows has done for ages — using the Search charm targets your search. For example

✦ When you're on the Start screen, Search looks for apps that match the name you type, although it also gives you a number of "hits" on settings and files (see Figure 3-2).

Book II
Chapter 3

If you just type when you're looking at the Start screen, Windows behaves as if you brought up the Search charm and runs a search on whatever you type.

✦ When you're in the Mail app, Search looks for text in your messages. The Search charm works similarly in the People, Photos, and Video apps.

Working with
Charms and
Notifications

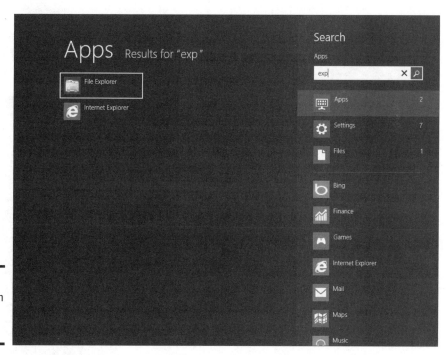

Figure 3-2:
Search from
the Start
screen.

✦ When you're in the Store app, Search offers all sorts of helpful tips on how to spend your money (see Figure 3-3). Same with Music, although Music search also searches through music you already own.

✦ While you're using the tiled, full-screen version of Internet Explorer, Search brings up your default search engine and does a regular search. But while you're using the desktop version of Internet Explorer, the Search charm just does a regular desktop search — of your machine, not the web.

✦ When you're on the desktop, no matter what applications you may be running, bringing up the Search charm runs a search in exactly the same way as searching on the Start screen.

There are many, many nuances.

For example, if you run Search on the Start screen and choose Settings on the right, Search shows you results for searching specific kinds of Windows programs and settings. Choose Files and you see all the files on your system that match the search criteria, including, unexpectedly, music files. But if you choose Store, Internet Explorer, or any other entry below Files, Windows actually starts the indicated app and then runs the search again.

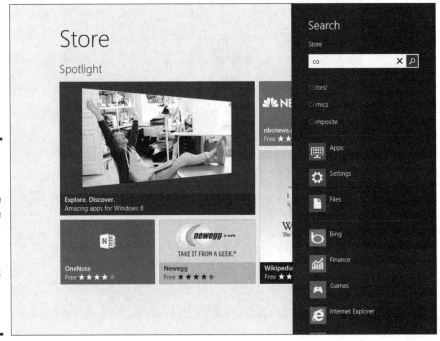

Figure 3-3:
Use the Search charm while you're in the Windows Store, and it helps you find all sorts of ways to spend your money.

What's a Share Contract?

In older versions of Windows, and on the desktop, items — files, pictures, text, formatted text, and so on — moved through the Clipboard, or by drag-and-drop. If you built a Windows app that needed to send or receive data from another program, you built hooks into the program that worked with dragging and dropping, or worked through the Clipboard.

The tiled side of Windows 8, on the other hand, requires apps that are going to share things to work through a *Share Contract*. The Share Contract is much more flexible than the old Clipboard; for example, an app can share not only the text in a web page, but also the URL of the web page and a thumbnail picture.

Both participants in a Share Contract — the app sending the stuff and the app receiving the stuff — have to accept the same contract. That way, they're both working from the same playbook on how the data's sent, and how it's interpreted when it arrives.

Windows 8 handles the contracts invisibly and on the fly.

Say you build a web browser that can send information about a specific page in a particular way — say, it sends a title, abstract, link, and thumbnail image, all arranged according to a very strict set of rules. You call the rule — the Share Contract — oh, *WoodysFancyBrowserShare*. When your browser's installed on a Windows system, the installer sends a message to Windows that says, "I can send data in WoodysFancyBrowserShare format."

Now say you build an e-mail package and you want it to be able to accept those fancy links from the web browser, the ones built to the WoodysFancyBrowserShare rules. When your e-mail package is installed on the system, the installer sends a message to Windows that says, "I can receive data in WoodysFancyBrowserShare format."

One day, somebody is using the browser, and she clicks the Share charm. Windows looks up all the Share Contracts that the browser can understand, and then looks in its tables to see which apps can take shared data in that particular format. Lo and behold, the browser can send data in WoodysFancyBrowserShare format, and the e-mail package can accept data in WoodysFancyBrowserShare format. Bingo. The Share application, on the right side of the screen, puts up an icon for the e-mail package.

If the user clicks that icon, Windows notifies the browser and the e-mail package that data's coming over using the WoodysFancyBrowserShare format, and then transfers the data from the browser to the e-mail package.

Contracts are much, much more flexible than the old Clipboard. They're also potentially more secure. But they're supported only on the tiled side, not on the old-fashioned desktop.

I go into more detail about the Search charm in Book III, Chapter 2. And I explore the complex search language built into Windows — which you can use from the Search charm — in Book VI, Chapter 8.

Several oddities in Search are hard to explain. For example, if you search the Store for recipes, you will *not* get a match for the Allrecipes app. But if you search for rope, you *will* get a hit on the Cut the Rope game. These mysteries and many more are explained in Book III, Chapter 2, and some (difficult) solutions appear in Book VI, Chapter 8.

Share charm

Over on the desktop side of the fence, it's easy to copy stuff: The (largely fictitious) Clipboard acts as intermediary if you copy, cut, and paste; clicking and dragging copies or moves files, pictures, or text; and you can even embed some documents inside other documents with a click and drag.

Not so on the tiled side of the Windows 8 fence. There's no desktop-style Clipboard (beyond very rudimentary cut and paste), no intermediary to handle that translation from one application to another, and no way to drag and drop from here to there. Even if you get two apps running side by side with a Tiled Snap, the two apps don't communicate and you can't move stuff from one app to the other.

That's why Microsoft had to invent this new approach to sharing and the *Share Contract,* which I explain in the sidebar, "What's a Share Contract?"

The general approach to sharing goes like this: Select something, bring up the Share charm, and choose which app you want to share it with. The prototypical example: Choose a picture in the Photos app, bring up Share, and attach the photo to a Mail message.

Sharing is also a pivotal capability of the SkyDrive app. That's how you move stuff into the *cloud* (that is, into and out of your online storage in SkyDrive) while you're working in a tiled Windows 8 app.

As you install more applications on your computer, you'll find more and more ways that you can use the Share charm. Who knows? Maybe someday Microsoft will build a Share app for the desktop's Clipboard.

Start charm

The Start charm, right in the middle of the Charms bar, behaves precisely the same way as pressing the Windows button on your PC (if you have one) or pressing the Windows key on your keyboard (if you have one).

Tap or click the Start charm and you cycle between the Start screen and the last app that you were using. If the last app you used was on the desktop, you get the entire desktop back in the state it was in when you left.

Devices charm

People are just beginning to see how much can be done with the Devices charm. I expect that, over the next few years, hardware manufacturers are going to come up with amazing capabilities.

The Devices charm is where hardware meets the new tiled software.

If you want to run with two monitors, bring up the Devices charm and connect them.

If you want to print something in Internet Explorer, the Devices charm has entries for all the printers that are accessible from your PC. Click a printer and you see the Print dialog box like the one in Figure 3-4.

Want to connect to a projector? If Windows can figure out how to connect to the projector, the Devices pane has an icon for project connections, too.

That said, the Devices charm on the desktop isn't very useful at all. Even if you have, say, Internet Explorer running full-screen, the Devices charm doesn't give you any options. If you want to print from IE 10 on the desktop, you have to choose Tools⇨Print.

Book II
Chapter 3

Working with
Charms and
Notifications

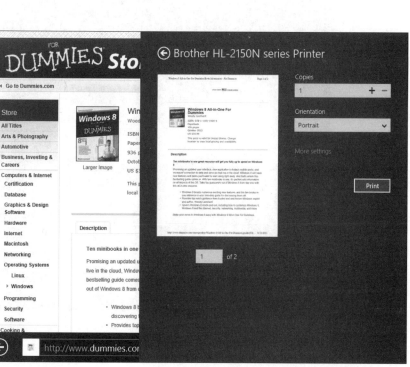

Figure 3-4:
While in the tiled, full–screen Internet Explorer, the Devices charm brings up a list of printers.

Settings charm

The Settings charm is where Alice fell down the rabbit hole.

Seriously, the Settings charm leads you to a myriad of screens that may or may not hold the settings you seek.

The most important detail about the Settings charm? It's different on the Start screen, as opposed to the desktop:

✦ **If you bring up the Settings charm from the Start screen,** you have access to a limited number of settings, as shown in Figure 3-5. Choosing Change PC Settings at the bottom gets you to many options, but they're only a small fraction of the number of settings in the desktop Control Panel.

✦ **If you bring up the Settings charm from the desktop,** you're given the keys to the city. As shown in Figure 3-6, you gain access to the full Windows Control Panel, right there on the top.

Figure 3-5: The limited selection available from the Start screen.

Figure 3-6:
The desktop
options may
not look so
impressive,
but they're
very
capable.

Every tiled Windows 8 application has its own settings — Internet Explorer, for example, gives you options on the Settings charm to delete browsing history. In the desktop version of IE, you need to tap or click Tools, inside the browser.

In general, settings for tiled apps are accessible through the Settings charm. Settings for desktop programs are typically inside the program — although there are exceptions. It's very confusing.

Setting and Responding to Notifications

The desktop side of Windows allows all sorts of notifications: blinking task-bar tiles, balloon messages over the system time (in the lower-right corner, dire-looking icons in the system notification area, near the system time), or dialog boxes that appear out of nowhere. However, the tiled full–screen side is very conservative, and in my opinion, much more effective because of it.

These new notifications — the things that can happen when Windows or one of the tiled, full–screen apps wants your attention — fall into three broad categories:

+ They can put rectangular notices, usually gray, in the upper-right edge of your screen, with a few lines of text. Typically the notifications say things like `Tap or choose what happens when you insert a USB drive,` or `Turn sharing on or off.`

These notifications are *toaster notifications* (or sometimes just *toast*), and they're a core part of Windows on the tiled side of Windows 8. It's a fabulous name because they pop up, just like toast, but on its side.

+ They can show toaster notifications on the lock screen. This is considered direr than simply showing the notifications on tiled apps or the desktop. Why? Because the apps that create lock screen notifications may need to run, even when Windows is sleeping. And that leads to battery drainage.

+ They can play sounds. Don't get me started.

Windows lets you disable all notifications rather easily, or you can pick and choose which apps can send notifications, and which just have to stifle their utterances.

Here's how to disable all notifications:

1. **Swipe from the right or hover your mouse in the upper-right corner to bring up the Charms bar, and then at the bottom, choose the Settings charm.**

The Settings pane, as shown in Figure 3-7, appears.

2. **At the bottom of the Settings pane, tap or click the Notifications icon.**

From there you can hide all notifications, of all kinds — noisy ones, flashy ones, drab "you're toast" notifications, whatever — for 1, 3, or 8 hours.

Windows also lets you disable specific kinds of notifications (I'm a big fan of turning off notification sounds), or notifications from select apps.

If you want to permanently disable notifications from just one application — say, you aren't a big fan of Messaging, and you definitely don't want to see its notifications — here's how to do it:

1. **Swipe from the right or hover your mouse in the upper-right corner to bring up the Charms bar, and then at the bottom, choose the Settings charm.**

2. **At the bottom of the Start Settings pane, tap or click the Change PC Settings link.**

The PC Settings screen, as shown in Figure 3-8, appears.

Figure 3-7:
Disable all
notifications
here.

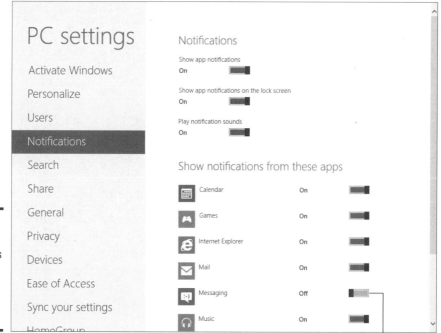

Figure 3-8:
Silence
notifications
from one
or more
Windows
apps here.

Turn off Messaging notifications

3. Select Notifications on the left.

4. Switch off the specific kind of notification that you don't want to see or, if you only want to silence a particular app, switch it off at the bottom.

   You're done. There's no Apply or OK button to tap or click.

Chapter 4: Controlling Users

In This Chapter

- ✓ Choosing an account type
- ✓ The pros and cons of Microsoft accounts
- ✓ Adding a new user
- ✓ Changing accounts
- ✓ Switching between users

Microsoft reports that 70 percent of all Windows PCs have just one user account. That's a startling figure. It means that 70 percent of all Windows PCs run at the most permissive security level, all the time. It means that, on 70 percent of all Windows PCs, little Billy can install Internet Antivirus 2009 — a notorious piece of scumware — and have it bring down the whole family with a couple of simple clicks. "Sorry, Dad, but it's an anti-virus program and it said that we really need to install it, and it's just $49.95 for a three-month subscription. I thought you said that antivirus was good. They wouldn't lie about stuff like that, would they?"

Although it's undoubtedly true that many PCs are each used by just one person, I think it's highly likely that people don't set up multiple user accounts on their PCs because they're intimidated. Not to worry. I take you through the ins and outs.

Even if you're the only person who ever uses your PC, you might want to create a second account — another user, as it were — even if the second user is just you. (As Pogo said, "We have met the enemy and he is us.") Then again, you might not. And therein lies this chapter's story.

If you're running Windows 8 Pro or Enterprise and your PC is connected to a big corporate network (in the parlance, a *domain*), you have little or no control over who can log on to your computer and what a logged-on user can do after she's on the machine. That's a Good Thing, at least in theory: Your company's network administrator gets to worry about all the security issues, relieving you of the hassles of figuring out whether the guy down the hall should be able to look at payroll records or the company Christmas card list. But it can also be a pain in the neck, especially if you have to install a program, like, right now, and you don't have a user account with sufficient capabilities. If your computer is attached to a domain, your only choice is to convince (or bribe) the network admin to let you in.

The nostrums in this chapter apply only to PCs that are connected to small networks or to standalone PCs. If you're on a big network, you must pay homage to the network gods. Pizza, beer, and a smile can help.

Windows 8 has two separate locations that control user accounts. If you only want to do some simple stuff — create a new account, change the password, or switch to a picture password, say — you can do it all on the touch-friendly tiled side of Windows 8. On the other hand, if you want to do something more challenging — change the account type or set the User Account Control trigger levels — you have to work with the old-fashioned Windows 7–style desktop's Control Panel. I show you how to use both in this chapter.

User Account Control is a security topic, only tangentially related to user accounts. I talk about it in Book IX, Chapter 3.

Why You Need Separate User Accounts

Windows assumes that, sooner or later, more than one person will want to work on your PC. All sorts of problems crop up when several people share a PC. I set up my screen just right, with all my icons right where I can find them, and then my son comes along and plasters the desktop with a shot of Alpha Centauri. He puts together a killer teen Media Player playlist and "accidentally" deletes my Grateful Dead playlist in the process.

It's worse than sharing a TV remote.

Windows helps keep peace in the family — and in the office — by requiring people to log on. The process of *logging on* (also called *signing on*) lets Windows keep track of each person's settings: You tell Windows who you are, and Windows lets you play in your own sandbox.

Having personal settings that are activated whenever you log on to Windows doesn't create heavy-duty security. Unless your PC is a slave to a big Active Directory domain network, your settings can get clobbered and your files deleted, if someone else with access to your computer or your network tries hard enough. But as long as you're reasonably careful and follow the advice in this chapter, Windows security works surprisingly well.

If someone else can put his hands on your computer, it isn't your computer any more. That can be a real problem if someone swipes your laptop, if the cleaning staff uses your PC after hours, or if a snoop breaks into your study. Unless you use BitLocker (in Windows 8 Pro), anybody who can restart your PC can look at, modify, or delete your files or stick a virus on the PC. How? In many cases, a miscreant can bypass Windows directly and start your PC with another operating system. With Windows out of the picture, compromising a PC doesn't take much work.

Choosing Account Types

When dealing with user accounts, you bump into one existential fact of Windows life over and over again: The type of account you use puts severe limitations on what you can do.

Unless you're hooked up to a big corporate network, user accounts can generally be divided into two groups: the haves and the have-nots. (Users attached to corporate domains are assigned accounts that can exist anywhere on the have-to-have-not spectrum.) The have accounts are *administrator* accounts. The have-nots are *standard* accounts. That's it. "Standard." Kinda makes your toes curl just to think about it.

What's a standard account?

A person running with a standard account can do only, uh, standard tasks:

✦ Run programs that are installed on the computer, including programs on key drives.

✦ Use hardware that's installed on the computer.

✦ Create, view, save, modify and use documents, pictures, and sounds in the Documents, Pictures or Music folders as well as in the PC's Public folders.

✦ If your computer is part of a Homegroup (see Book VII, Chapter 5), a standard user can also create, view, save, modify and use any files in the Public folders of computers that are part of your Homegroup. A standard user can also access any shared folders on other computers in the Homegroup.

✦ Change his password or switch back and forth between requiring and not requiring a password for his account. He can also add a picture or PIN password.

✦ Switch between a Local account and a Microsoft account. I talk about both in the next section of this chapter.

✦ Change the picture that appears next to his name on the Welcome screen and the Start screen, change the desktop wallpaper, resize the Windows toolbar, add items to the old-fashioned desktop toolbar and Start screen, and make other small changes that don't affect other user accounts.

In most cases, a standard user can change system-wide settings, install programs, and the like, but only if he can provide the username and password of an administrator account.

If you're running with a standard account, you can't even change the time on the clock. It's quite limited.

What's an administrator account?

People using administrator accounts can change almost anything, any-where, at any time. (Certain folders remain off limits, even to administra-tor accounts, and you have to jump through some difficult hoops to work around the restrictions.) People using administrator accounts can even change other Local accounts' passwords — a good thing to remember if you ever forget your password.

If you start Windows with a standard account and you accidentally run a virus, a worm, or some other piece of bad computer code, the damage is usually limited: The malware can delete files in your `Documents` folder, and probably in the `Public` folders, but that's about the extent of the damage. Usually. Unless it's exceedingly clever, the virus can't install itself into the computer, so it can't run repeatedly, and it may not be able to replicate. Poor virus.

Someone with an administrator account can get into all the files owned by other users: If you thought that attaching a password to your account and putting a top-secret spreadsheet in your `Documents` folder would keep it away from prying eyes, you're in for a rude surprise. Anybody who can get into your machine with an administrator account can look at it. Standard users, on the other hand, are effectively limited to looking only at their own files.

Choosing between standard or administrator accounts

The first account on a new PC is always an administrator account. If you bought your PC with Windows pre-installed, the account that you have — the one you probably set up shortly after you took the computer out of the box — is an administrator account. If you installed Windows on a PC, the account you set up during the installation is an administrator account.

When you create new accounts, on the other hand, they always start out as standard accounts. That's as it should be.

Administrator accounts and standard accounts aren't set in concrete. In fact, Windows helps you shape-shift between the two as circumstances dictated:

✦ If you're using a standard account and try to do something that requires an administrator account, Windows prompts you to provide an adminis-trator account's name and password (see Figure 4-1).

Figure 4-1:
Windows
asks
permission
before
performing
administra-
tive actions.

If the person using the standard account selects an administrator account without a password, simply clicking the Yes button allows the program to run.

✦ Even if you're using an administrator account, Windows normally runs as though you had a standard account, in some cases adding an extra hurdle when you try to run a program that can make substantial changes to your PC — and *substantial* is quite a subjective term. You have to clear the same kind of hurdle if you try to access folders that aren't explicitly shared (see Figure 4-2). That extra hurdle helps prevent destructive programs from sneaking into your computer and running with your administrator account, doing their damage without your knowledge or permission.

Figure 4-2:
Windows
lays down
a challenge
before you
dive into
another
user's
folder.

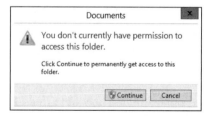

Most experts recommend that you use a standard account for daily activities and switch to an administrator account only when you need to install software or hardware or access files outside the usual shared areas. Most experts ignore their own advice: It's the old do-as-I-say-not-as-I-do syndrome.

I used to recommend that people follow the lead of the do-as-I-say crowd and simply set up every knowledgeable user with an administrator account. Times change, and Windows has changed: It's rare that you actually need an administrator account to accomplish just about anything in "normal" day-to-day use. (One exception: You can add new users only if you're using an administrator account.) For that reason, I've come to the conclusion that you should save that one administrator account for a rainy day, and set up standard accounts for yourself and anyone else who uses the PC. Run with a standard account, and I bet you almost never notice the difference.

What's Good and Bad about Microsoft Accounts

In addition to administrator and standard accounts, Microsoft also has another pair of account types, *Microsoft accounts* and *Local accounts.* You can have an administrator account that's a Microsoft account, or a standard account that's a Microsoft account, or an administrator account that's a local account, and so on.

The basic differentiation goes like this:

✦ **Microsoft accounts** are registered with Microsoft. Most people use their `@hotmail.com` or `@live.com` or `outlook.com` e-mail addresses, but in fact, you can register any e-mail address at all as a Microsoft account (details in Chapter 5 of this minibook). Microsoft accounts must have a password.

When you log on to Windows 8 with a Microsoft account, Windows goes out to Microsoft's computer in the clouds and verifies your password, then pulls down many of your major Windows settings (background, Start screen tile layout, and Internet Explorer favorites) and transfers them to the PC you just logged on to. If you change, say, your background, the next time you log on to Windows 8 — from any machine, anywhere in the world — you see the new background. More than that, if the Microsoft account is set up to do so, you can get immediate access to all your music, e-mail, SkyDrive storage, and other Windows features without logging in again.

✦ **Local accounts** are regular, old-fashioned accounts that exist only on this PC. They don't save or retrieve your settings from Microsoft's computers. Local accounts may or may not have a password.

On a single PC, administrator accounts can add new users, delete existing users, or change the password of any Local account on the computer. They can't change the password of any Microsoft accounts.

As you might imagine, privacy is among the several considerations for both kinds of accounts. I go into the details in Book II, Chapter 5.

Adding Users

After you log on to an administrator account, you can add more users quite easily. Here's how:

1. **On the Start screen, swipe from the right or hover your mouse in the upper-right corner (or type Windows Key + C) to bring up the Charms bar. At the bottom, choose the Settings charm.**

2. **At the bottom of the Start Settings pane, tap or click the Change PC Settings link and then select Users on the left.**

   The PC Settings screen appears, as shown in Figure 4-3.

3. **Under Other Users, choose Add a User.**

   You see the challenging Add a User dialog box, as shown in Figure 4-4.

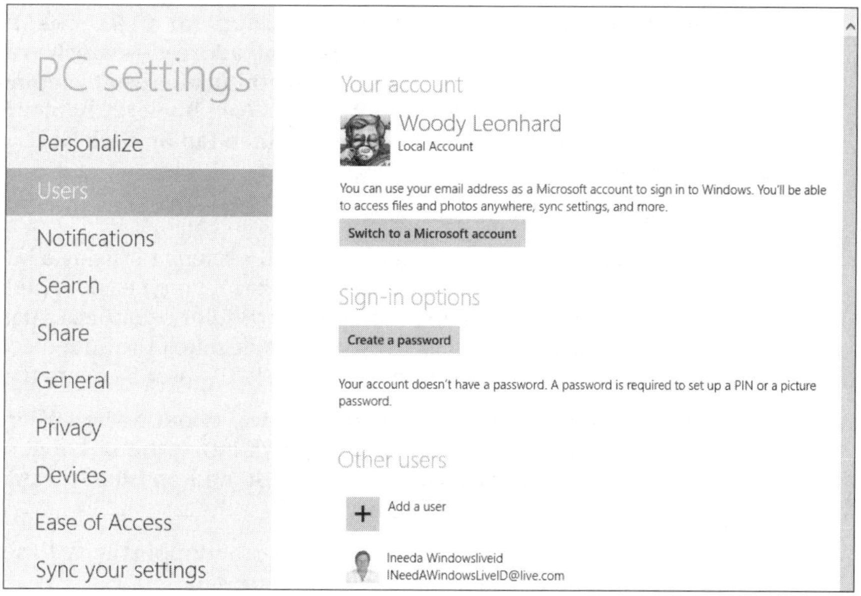

Book II Chapter 4

Controlling Users

PC settings

Personalize

Users

Notifications

Search

Share

General

Privacy

Devices

Ease of Access

Sync your settings

Your account

Woody Leonhard
Local Account

You can use your email address as a Microsoft account to sign in to Windows. You'll be able to access files and photos anywhere, sync settings, and more.

Switch to a Microsoft account

Sign-in options

Create a password

Your account doesn't have a password. A password is required to set up a PIN or a picture password.

Other users

+ Add a user

Ineeda Windowsliveid
INeedAWindowsLiveID@live.com

Figure 4-3: The PC Settings Users options.

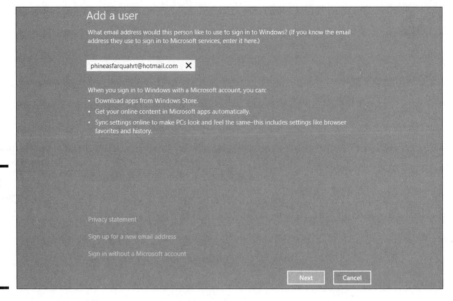

Figure 4-4:
Microsoft
really
wants you
to set up a
Microsoft
account.

4. **If you already have a Microsoft account (or an @hotmail.com or @live.com or @outlook.com e-mail address — which are automatically Microsoft accounts), and you don't mind Microsoft keeping information about when you log in to Windows (see Book II Chapter 5), type the address in the box at the top and then tap or click Next. Then skip to Step 7.**

   Windows sets up your account.

   Don't get me wrong. There are good reasons for using a Microsoft account — a Microsoft account makes it much easier and faster to retrieve your mail and calendar entries, for example, bypassing individual account logins. Only you can decide if the added convenience is worth the decreased privacy. Book II, Chapter 5 covers the details.

5. **On the other hand, if you're skeptical about using a Microsoft account, waaaaaay down at the bottom, click or tap the link that says "Take your Microsoft account and shove it, and no I don't want this user to sign in with a Microsoft account."**

   Windows helpfully gives you yet another opportunity to set up a Microsoft account, as shown in Figure 4-5.

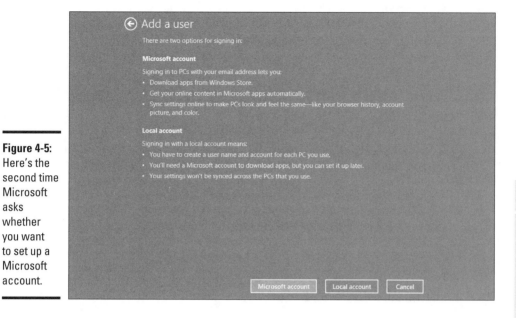

Figure 4-5:
Here's the
second time
Microsoft
asks
whether
you want
to set up a
Microsoft
account.

6. **At the bottom, click or tap the Local Account box. Sheesh.**

Windows (finally!) asks you about a Local account name and password.
See Figure 4-6.

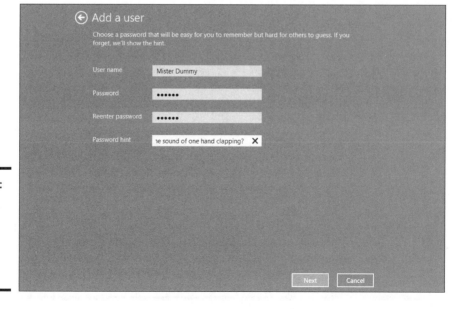

Figure 4-6:
Now you
get to the
"adding
a new
account"
part.

7. **Type a name for the new account.**

   You can give a new account just about any name you like: first name, last name, nickname, titles, abbreviations . . . No sweat, as long as you don't use the characters / \ [ ] " ; : | < > + = , ? or *.

8. **(Optional) Type a password twice and then add a password hint.**

   If you leave these fields blank, the user can log on directly by simply tapping or clicking the account name on the logon screen.

   Note that the password hint can be seen by anybody on the computer, so avoid that NSFW (Not Suitable For Work) hint you were thinking about.

9. **Click or tap Next; then click or tap Finish.**

   You're done. Rocket science. You have a new standard account and its name now appears on the Welcome screen.

If you want to turn the new account into an administrator account, follow the steps in the section, "Changing Accounts," later in this chapter. To add an account picture for the logon screen and Start screen, flip to Book III, Chapter 1.

This topic is more than a bit confusing, but you aren't allowed to create a new account named Administrator. There's a good reason why Windows prevents you from making a new account with that name: You already have one. Even though Windows goes to great lengths to hide the account named Administrator, it's there, and you may encounter it one night when you're exploring a blind alley. For now, don't worry about the ambiguous name and the ghostly appearance. Just refrain from trying to create a new account named Administrator.

Enabling the Guest Account

The *Guest* account is a special standard account that comes in handy if many people need to use a computer but you don't want any of them to be able to get at important information — or run potentially destructive programs. To make the Guest account available on your computer, follow these steps:

1. **Bring up the Control Panel by going to the Start screen, typing** con, **and then, on the left, tapping or clicking Control Panel.**

   If it's too hard to type, you can also bring up the Control Panel with your fingers: Tap on the Desktop tile, swipe from the right, choose the Settings charm, and then at the top choose Control Panel.

2. **In the upper right, under User Accounts and Family Safety, click or tap the Add or Remove User Accounts link.**

   The Manage Accounts dialog box appears, with the Guest account turned off, as shown in Figure 4-7.

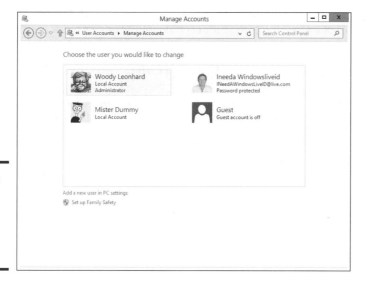

Book II
Chapter 4

Controlling Users

Figure 4-7:
The Guest account is turned off until you turn it on.

3. **Click or tap the Guest account icon and then select Turn On.**

   From that point, Windows shows Guest as an account on the Welcome screen. It behaves just like any other standard account.

If you only have a few people who sporadically use your PC, set up standard accounts for each of them. That way, your PC can save their settings and make them available the next time each person logs on. But if you have more than a handful of guests, enable the Guest account and have them all use the Guest account.

Don't enable the Guest account unless you need it. One more account is just one more potential hole for a slobbering cretin virus writer to exploit.

If you ever encounter instructions on the Internet that show you how to get rid of the Guest account, ignore them. The Guest account, which exists on every Windows PC, is used for all sorts of behind-the-scenes stuff. You need the Guest account lurking in the background, even if you don't enable it and it isn't visible on the Logon screen — no matter what those self-appointed experts might say.

Changing Accounts

If you have an administrator account, you can reach in and change every detail of every single account on the computer — except one.

Changing other users' settings

If you can't already see the Manage Accounts window (refer to Figure 4-7), log on to Windows with an administrator account and follow the steps in the preceding section, "Enabling the Guest Account," to bring up the Manage Accounts dialog box.

In the Manage Accounts dialog box, click the account you want to change. Windows immediately presents you with several options (see Figure 4-8).

Figure 4-8:
Maintain
another
user's
account.

Here's what the options entail:

+ **Change the Account Name:** This option appears only for Local accounts. (It'd be kind of difficult if Windows let you change someone's Microsoft account, eh?) Selecting this option modifies the name displayed on the Logon screen and at the top of the Start screen while leaving all other settings intact. Use this option if you want to change only the name on the account — for example, if Little Bill wants to be called Sir William.

+ **Create/Change/Remove a Password:** Again, this appears only for Local accounts. If you create a password for the chosen user, Windows requires a password to crank up that user account. You can't get past the Logon screen (using that account) without it. This setting is weird because you can change it for other people: You can force Bill to use a password when none was required before, you can change Bill's password, or you can even delete the password.

If you change someone's password, do her a big favor and tell her how to create a Password Reset Disk. See Book VI, Chapter 4.

Passwords are cAse SenSitive — you must enter the password, with uppercase and lowercase letters, precisely the way it was originally typed. If you can't get the computer to recognize your password, make sure that the Caps Lock setting is off. That's the number one source of logon frustration.

Much has been written about the importance of choosing a secure password, mixing upper- and lowercase letters with punctuation marks, ensuring that you have a long password, blah blah blah. I have only two admonitions: First, don't write your password on a yellow sticky note attached to your monitor; second, don't use the easily guessed passwords that the Conficker worm employed to crack millions of systems (see Table 4-1, at the end of this list). Good advice from a friend: Create a simple sentence you can remember, and swap out some letters for numbers (`G00dGr1efSteve`) or think of a sentence and only use the first letters! (`toasaoutfl!`)

✦ **Set Up Family Safety:** This link takes you to a stunted set of controls for limiting the times a user can use the computer, turn off games, or block specific programs. Your kids probably know how to bypass it already.

✦ **Change the Account Type:** You can use this option to change accounts from administrator to standard and back again. The implications are somewhat complex; I talk about them in the section "Choosing Account Types," earlier in this chapter.

✦ **Delete the Account:** Deep-six the account, if you're that bold (or mad, in all senses of the term). Windows offers to keep copies of the deleted account's `Documents` folder and desktop, but warns you quite sternly and correctly that if you snuff the account, you rip out all the e-mail messages, Internet Favorites, and other settings that belong to the user — definitely not a good way to make friends. Oh. And you can't delete your own account, of course.

Table 4-1

The Most Frequently Used Passwords*

000	0000	00000	0000000	00000000	0987654321
111	1111	11111	111111	1111111	1111111
123	123123	12321	123321	1234	12345
123456	1234567	12345678	123456789	1234567890	1234abcd
1234qwer	123abc	123asd	123qwe	1q2w3e	222
2222	22222	222222	2222222	22222222	321
333	3333	33333	333333	3333333	33333333
4321	444	4444	44444	444444	4444444
4444444	54321	555	5555	55555	555555
5555555	55555555	55555555	666	6666	66666
666666	666666	6666666	7654321	777	7777
77777	777777	7777777	7777777	87654321	888
8888	88888	888888	8888888	88888888	987654321
999	9999	99999	999999	9999999	9999999
a1b2c3	aaa	aaaa	aaaaa	abc123	academia
access	account	Admin	admin	admin1	admin12
admin123	adminadmin	administrator	anything	asddsa	asdfgh
asdsa	asdzxc	backup	boss123	business	campus
changeme	cluster	codename	codeword	coffee	computer

controller	cookie	customer	database	default	desktop
domain	example	exchange	explorer	file	files
foo	foobar	foofoo	forever	freedom	f**k
games	home	home123	ihavenopass	Internet	internet
intranet	job	killer	letitbe	letmein	login
Login	lotus	love123	manager	market	money
monitor	mypass	mypassword	mypc123	nimda	nobody
nopass	nopassword	nothing	office	oracle	owner
pass	pass1	pass12	pass123	passwd	password
Password	password1	password12	password123	private	public
pw123	q1w2e3	qazwsx	qazwsxedc	qqq	qqqq
qqqqq	qwe123	qweasd	qweasdzxc	qweewq	qwerty
qwewq	root	root123	rootroot	sample	secret
secure	security	server	shadow	share	sql
student	super	superuser	supervisor	system	temp
temp123	temporary	temptemp	test	test123	testtest
unknown	web	windows	work	work123	xxx
xxxxx	xxxxxx	zxccxz	zxcvb	zxcvbn	zxcxz
zzz	zzz	zzzzz			

* From the Conficker worm, Bowdlerized with an asterisk (*) as a fig leaf

Book II
Chapter 4

Controlling Users

Changing your own settings

Changing your own account is just a little different from changing other users' accounts. Follow these steps:

1. **Bring up the Control Panel.**

   To do so, go to the Start screen, type **con**, and then, on the left, tap or click Control Panel.

2. **In the upper right, under User Accounts and Family Safety, click or tap the Add or Remove User Accounts link.**

   The Manage Accounts dialog box displays (refer to Figure 4-7).

3. **Click or tap your own username.**

   The Change an Account dialog box appears.

   Most of the options for your own account mirror those of other users' accounts, as described in the preceding section. If you have the only administrator account on the PC, you can't delete your own account and you can't turn yourself into a standard user. Makes sense: Every PC must have at least one user with an administrator account. If Windows lost all its administrators, no one would be around to add users or change existing ones, much less to install programs or hardware, right?

Switching Users

Windows allows you to have more than one person logged on to a PC simultaneously. That's convenient if, say, you're working on the family PC and checking Billy's homework when you hear the cat screaming bloody murder in the kitchen and your wife wants to put digital pictures from the family vacation on SkyDrive while you run off to check the microwave.

The ability to have more than one user logged on to a PC simultaneously is *Fast User Switching,* and it has advantages and disadvantages:

✦ **On the plus side:** Fast User Switching lets you keep all your programs going while somebody else pops onto the machine for a quick jaunt on the keyboard. When she's done, she can log off, and you can pick up precisely where you left off before you got bumped.

✦ **On the minus side:** All idle programs left sitting around by the inactive ("bumped") user can bog things down for the active user, although the effect isn't drastic. You can avoid the overhead by logging off before the new user logs on.

To switch users, go to the Start screen, click or tap on your picture, and choose either the name of the user you want to switch to, or Sign Out. If you choose the latter, you're taken to the sign in screen, where you can choose from any user on the computer.

Chapter 5: Microsoft Account: To Sync or Not to Sync?

In This Chapter

✔ Getting the lowdown on a Microsoft account

✔ Figuring out whether you even want a Microsoft account

✔ Getting a Microsoft account without spilling the beans

✔ Care and feeding of your Microsoft account

✔ Cutting back on syncing through a Windows account

Microsoft has been trying to get people to sign up for company-branded accounts for a long, long time.

In 1997, Microsoft bought Hotmail and took over the issuance of `@hotmail.com` e-mail addresses. Even though Hotmail's gone through a bunch of name changes — MSN Hotmail, Windows Live Hotmail, among others — the original `@hotmail.com` e-mail addresses work, and have worked, through thick and thin.

Then came *Microsoft Wallet,* a short-lived attempt to get consumers to put their credit card information online and trust Microsoft to take care of it. Microsoft scrubbed that idea and, in 2000, replaced it with *Microsoft Passport.*

Here's what tech commentator Joel Spolsky had to say about Microsoft Passport, in his Joel on Software blog:

> "Am I the only one who is terrified about Microsoft Passport? It seems to me like a fairly blatant attempt to build the world's largest, richest consumer database, and then make fabulous profits mining it. It's a terrifying threat to everyone's personal privacy and it will make today's "cookies" seem positively tame by comparison. The scariest thing is that Microsoft is advertising Passport as if it were a *benefit* to consumers, and people seem to be falling for it!"

Everything old is new again. More than a decade later, Microsoft is trying to do the same thing, but this time they're dangling a much bigger carrot, and they will undoubtedly garner a much larger audience.

Microsoft Passport became .NET Passport, and then Microsoft Passport Network. When Microsoft started branding everything as "Live," the same username became a Windows Live ID.

Fifteen years after its inception, that old @hotmail.com ID still works the same as it ever did — except now it's called a *Microsoft account.* If you picked up an @live.com ID along the way, it's now a Microsoft account as well.

In this chapter, I show you exactly what's involved with a Microsoft account, show you why it can be useful, explore the dark underbelly of Microsoft account-ability, and give you a trick for acquiring a Microsoft account that won't compromise much of anything.

What, Exactly, Is a Microsoft Account?

Now that Microsoft has finally settled on a name for its ID — at least, this month — permit me to dispel some of the myths about Microsoft accounts.

If you have an e-mail address that ends with @hotmail.com or @live.com, that e-mail address is, *ipso facto,* a Microsoft account. The same is true for Hotmail and Live accounts in any country, such as @hotmail.co.uk. You don't have to use your Microsoft account. Ever. But you do have one.

Many people don't realize that *any* e-mail address can be a Microsoft account. You need only to register that e-mail address with Microsoft — I show you how in the section "Setting Up a Microsoft Account" later in this chapter.

In the context of Windows 8, the Microsoft account takes on a new dimension. When you set up an account to log in to Windows, it can either be a Microsoft account, or a *Local account.* The key differences:

✦ Microsoft accounts are always e-mail addresses, and they have to be registered with Microsoft. As I explain in Book II, Chapter 4, when you log on to Windows with a Microsoft account, Windows automatically syncs some settings — Windows settings like your picture and back-grounds, Internet Explorer history and favorites, and others — so if you change something on one machine, and log on with the same Microsoft account on another, the changes go with you.

In addition, a Microsoft account gives you something of a one-stop log in to Internet-based Microsoft services. For example, if you have a SkyDrive account, logging in to Windows with a Microsoft account automatically hitches you up to your SkyDrive files.

✦ Local accounts can be just about any name or combination of characters. If you sign in with a Local account, Microsoft doesn't try (indeed,
can't) sync anything on different machines. Sign in with a Local account,
and you have to sign in to your SkyDrive account separately. Windows
will remember your settings — your backgrounds, passwords, favorites
and the like — but they won't be moved to other PCs when you log on.

So, for example, `phineasfarquahrt@hotmail.com` is a Microsoft account.
Because it's an `@hotmail.com` Hotmail e-mail address, it's already registered
with Microsoft. I can create a user on a Windows 8 machine with the name
`phineasfarquahrt@hotmail.com`, and Windows will recognize that as a
Microsoft account.

On the other hand, I can set up an account on a Windows PC that's called,
oh, *Woody Leonhard*. It's a Local account. Because Microsoft accounts have
to be e-mail addresses (you see why in the section "Setting Up a Microsoft
Account"), the Woody Leonhard account has to be a Local account.

When you set up a brand-new Windows PC, you have to enter an account,
and it can be either a Windows account or a Local account. Microsoft stacks
the deck and makes you tap or click all over heaven's half acre to avoid using
a Microsoft account (see Book I, Chapter 4). When you add a new account,
Microsoft nudges you to use a Microsoft account, but will begrudgingly accept
a Local account (see Book II, Chapter 4).

Deciding Whether You Want a Microsoft Account

If Microsoft tracks a Microsoft account, you may ask, why in the world would
I want to sign on to Windows 8 with a Microsoft account?

Good question, grasshopper.

Signing on to Windows 8 with a Microsoft account brings a host of benefits.
In particular:

✦ **Most of your Windows settings will travel with you.** Your user picture,
desktop, Internet Explorer favorites, and other similar settings will find
you no matter which PC you log on to.

I find this helpful in some ways, and annoying in others. For example,
I have a big screen Windows desktop, and a little Windows tablet. If I
set the screen for the desktop, it looks horrible on the tablet, and
vice-versa.

✦ **Your tiled full–screen apps — the ones that came with Windows 8, or you downloaded from the Windows Store — revert to their last state.** So if you're on a killer winning streak with Solitaire, that'll go with you to any PC you log on to. Your tiled full–screen Internet Explorer open tabs travel. Settings for the Windows 8 Finance app travel. Even apps *that Microsoft doesn't make* should have their settings moved from machine to machine.

✦ **Sign-in credentials for programs and websites travel.** If you rely on Internet Explorer to keep sites' logon credentials, those will find you if you switch machines.

✦ **You will be automatically signed in to Windows 8 apps and services** that use the Microsoft account (or Windows Live ID).

Don't be overly cynical. In some sense, Microsoft dangles these carrots to convince you to sign up for, and use, a Microsoft account. But in another sense, the simple fact is that none of these features would be possible if it weren't for some sort of ID that's maintained by Microsoft.

Personally, I use a Microsoft account on my main machine, although I employ a little trick, which I describe in the next section.

That's the carrot. Here's the stick. If you sign in with a Microsoft account, Microsoft has a record of every time you've signed on, to every PC you use with that account. More than that, when you crank up Internet Explorer, you're logged in with your Microsoft account — which means that Microsoft can, at least theoretically, keep records about all your browsing (except, presumably, InPrivate browsing). Bing gets to jot down your Microsoft account every time you search through it. Microsoft gets detailed data on any music you view in the Windows 8 tiled Music app. Your stock interests are logged in the Windows 8 tiled Finance app, even the weather you request ends up in Microsoft's giant database.

Perhaps it's true that you have no privacy and should get over it. Fact is that most people don't care. But I do, and I suggest that you do, too.

Setting Up a Microsoft Account

Just to make life a little more complicated, shortly before Microsoft released Windows 8, it suddenly decided to kill off the name "Hotmail" and replace it with "Outlook.com." I talk about the reasons why — basically, Hotmail was losing market share, and Microsoft needed to get it back — in Book X Chapter 3.

What if my Hotmail/Outlook.com account is hijacked?

So you set up a Hotmail account or Outlook. com for logging on to your Windows PC, and all of a sudden the account gets hijacked. Some cretin gets into the account online and changes the password. The next time you try to log in to your Windows PC, what happens?

It's not far-fetched: I get complaints almost every day from people who have been locked out of their Hotmail/Outlook.com accounts.

If you use a Hotmail ID Windows Live account or Outlook.com account for your Microsoft account and your Hotmail/Outlook.com account gets hijacked and the password changed, Windows 8 lets you log on to your PC, but when you do, you get the notice `You're signed in to this PC with your old password. Sign in again with your current password, or reset it.` If you then try to reset your password, you can't — clicking or tapping the Reset link doesn't do anything.

Until you can come up with your Hotmail/ Outlook.com account's password, you're put in a reduced functionality mode that's very similar to logging on with a Local account. As long as you can remember your old password — the last one you used to log on to this machine — you can continue to log on in Local account mode. But ultimately you're going to want your Windows logon account back!

To get your account back, you need to contact the people at Microsoft and convince them that you're the rightful owner. If you set up your Hotmail/Outlook.com account recently, chances are at least fair that you have an alternate e-mail address or phone number designated for just such an emergency. Microsoft started asking for that specific information on sign-up a couple of years ago. Go to `http://account.live.com/resetpassword.aspx` and have a Microsoft rep contact you.

For purposes of this chapter, a Hotmail account or an Outlook.com account, a Live.com account, Xbox LIVE account, SkyDrive account, MSN account, Microsoft Passport account, Zune account, or a Windows Phone account) are all interchangeable: they're e-mail addresses that have already been automatically signed up as Microsoft accounts. I tend to refer to them collectively as Hotmail accounts because, well, most Microsoft accounts have been Hotmail accounts for the past two decades or so. Old habits die hard.

If you don't have a Microsoft account, the way I see it, you have three choices for setting one up:

✦ **You can use an existing e-mail address**. But if you do that, Microsoft will be able to put that e-mail address in its database, and it can cross-reference the address to many things you do with Windows 8. (Can you tell my tinfoil hat is showing?)

✦ **You can use (or set up) a Hotmail/Live/Xbox/SkyDrive/Windows Phone/Outlook.com account.** If you already have one, Microsoft tracks it already — Microsoft knows when you receive and send e-mail, and it can actively look at the contents of your e-mail. But that's true of any online e-mail program, including Gmail and Yahoo! Mail. Using a Hotmail/Outlook.com account to log on to Windows 8, though, means that Microsoft can track additional information and associate it with your Hotmail/Outlook.com account — the times you log in to Windows, locations, and so on — as described earlier in this section. You may be okay with that, or you may not want Microsoft to be able to track that kind of additional information.

✦ **You can create a completely bogus new Hotmail/Outlook.com account, and only use it to log in to Windows 8.** It's free and easy, and if you use it wisely, nobody will ever know the difference. The only downsides: If you use Hotmail/Outlook.com, you have to retrieve your mail (sent to your existing Hotmail/Outlook.com account) using the Internet, not the Windows 8 tiled Mail app; your existing Hotmail/Outlook.com contacts won't get carried over into the tiled People automatically; and the tiled Windows 8 Messenger will only work with your new, bogus ID.

I love to use bogus Outlook.com accounts. I keep in mind that every time I use Internet Explorer, having signed in to Windows with a Microsoft account, that Microsoft will dump all my browsing history in its coffers.

So, of course, I use the Firefox or Chrome browser when I want to use the Internet. Google keeps Chrome data, but it doesn't have Microsoft's database of logged in Windows 8 users, and Firefox isn't beholden to anybody.

Setting up a Hotmail/Outlook.com account

Here's how to set up a new Hotmail/Outlook.com account:

1. **Using your favorite web browser, go to** `http://outlook.com`.

The main screen asks whether you have a Microsoft account.

2. **Tap or click Sign Up or Sign Up Now.**

You see the sign-up form, as shown in Figure 5-1.

3. **Fill out the form. Be creative.**

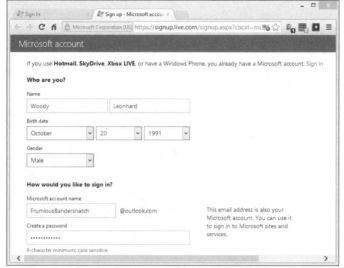

Book II
Chapter 5

Microsoft Account:
To Sync or Not
to Sync?

Figure 5-1:
Sign up
for an
anonymous
Hotmail/
Outlook.com
ID.

Even though the form says your phone number is required, in my experiments, it wasn't required at all — an alternate e-mail address suffices.

That alternate e-mail address is useful if your Microsoft account gets hijacked. You can contact Microsoft and have them send account reset information to that address. You don't need to monitor the address constantly, but if you can retrieve e-mail from that alternate e-mail address, it can help get your new account back.

If you decide to tap or click the link and provide answers to security questions to make a password reset easier, make sure you keep the answers stored away some place safe.

Microsoft's headquarters in Redmond has the zip code 98052.

4. **Type in the CAPTCHA codes, if you can figure them out, deselect the Send Me Mail check box, and then tap or click I Accept.**

   Hotmail/Outlook.com whirrs for a minute or so, and then shows you the Hotmail/Outlook.com welcome screen, as shown in Figure 5-2. That's it.

Figure 5-2:
Your new
Microsoft
account (*née*
Windows
Live ID,
Hotmail
account,
MSN
account,
Outlook.com
account,
Xbox Live
account) is
alive and
working.

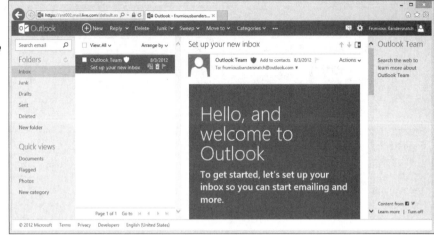

You can now use your new Hotmail account as a Windows logon ID. You can use it for e-mail, Messenger . . . just about anything.

Making any e-mail address a Microsoft account

There's an extra loop in turning any e-mail address into a Microsoft account, but the procedure's quite simple, as long as you can retrieve e-mail sent to the address. Here's how:

1. **Using your favorite web browser, go to** `http://signup.live.com.`

You see the sign-up form, per Figure 5-3.

2. **In the Microsoft Account Name box, type an e-mail address that you can access — it can be a Gmail address, a Yahoo! Mail address, or any other e-mail address, no problem.**

3. **Fill out the rest of the form. Fancifully, if you wish.**

If you don't want to give Microsoft your phone number, select and answer one of their security questions. Note, though, that giving Microsoft your phone number allows them to SMS you a reset password, if you require one, instead of relying on a question — one that a hijacker may be able to figure out.

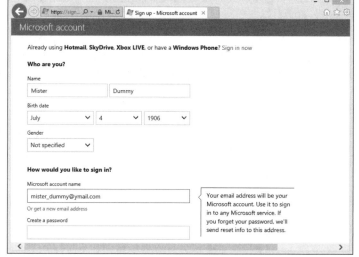

Figure 5-3:
You can
use any
valid e-mail
address as
a Microsoft
account.

4. **Type in the CAPTCHA code, and tap or click I Accept.**

Note that the password you provide here is for your Microsoft account.
It is NOT your e-mail password. The password you enter here will be the
password you need to use in order to log on to Windows 8, or any website that requires a Microsoft account.

Within a minute or two, the e-mail address in the application form
receives a message that says

```
This e-mail address was used to start setting up a
Windows Live ID. To finish setting it up, we need
you to confirm that this e-mail address belongs to
you. Click this link to confirm your account:
```

If you don't see the message, check your Junk folder.

5. **Tap or click the link in the message to confirm your e-mail address.**

You end up on a Hotmail welcome screen (refer to Figure 5-2).

Taking Care of Your Microsoft Account

If you ever want to change any of the details in your Microsoft account, it's
easy — if you know where to go.

For reasons only understood by Microsoft, to maintain your Microsoft account, go to `http://account.live.com`. Sign in, and you see full account information, as shown in Figure 5-4.

To change any of the information for your account, or the password, tap or click the related link below the item you want to change.

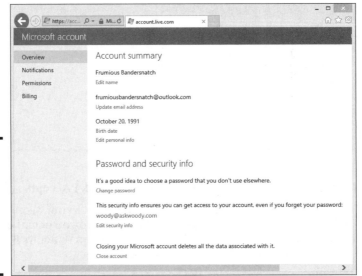

Figure 5-4: Microsoft account maintenance, accessible from the Live site.

Controlling Sync

If you don't specifically change anything, logging on to Windows with a Microsoft account syncs a number of settings across all the PCs that you use.

You can tell Microsoft that you don't want to sync specific items. Here's how:

1. **On the Start screen, swipe from the right or hover your mouse in the upper-right corner to bring up the Charms bar. At the bottom, choose the Settings charm.**

2. **At the bottom of the Start Settings pane, tap or click the Change PC Settings link. Select Sync Your Settings on the left.**

    The PC Settings screen appears, as shown in Figure 5-5.

3. **If you see the admonition at the top, or on one of the settings, To Help Protect Your Personal Info, tap or click Confirm This PC.**

   You're taken to Internet Explorer, where you have to supply your password and tap or click Confirm next to the current PC in the list.

   Confirming your PC gives Microsoft permission to sync Sign-In info for tiled Windows 8 apps, websites, networks, and even the Homegroup password.

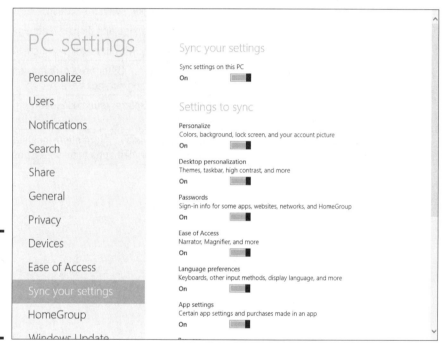

Figure 5-5:
Control
the way
Microsoft
accounts
sync here.

4. **Following the list in Table 5-1, choose whether you want to sync specific items.**

   Sync happens only when you log on with the same Microsoft account on two different PCs.

   You're done. No need to tap or click OK or Apply. The changes take effect with your next logon.

Table 5-1	Sync Settings
Setting	*What It Controls*
Sync Settings on This PC	An overall "off" switch. If you don't want to sync anything, turn this off.
Personalize	Your user picture, Start screen color, and background.
Desktop Personalization	Pinned Taskbar items and desktop themes.
Ease of Access	Features that can help if you have difficulty seeing the screen or working with the mouse.
Language Preferences	Keyboard language and display language.
App Settings	Tiled apps only. May not work with non-Microsoft apps.
Browser Settings	Internet Explorer. Other browsers may or may not support adjusting settings here.
Other Windows Settings	State of File Explorer (such as whether the Ribbon appears).
Passwords	Potentially sensitive information, including logon credentials for tiled apps and some websites.

Chapter 6: Privacy Control

In This Chapter

✔ **Finding out why privacy *is* important**

✔ **Discovering the complicated web of shared data**

✔ **Blocking location tracking**

✔ **Lessening the intrusion on your privacy**

"**T**he best minds of my generation are thinking about how to make people click ads. That sucks."

— Jeff Hammerbacher, early Facebook employee

When you work with "free" services — search engines like Google and Bing; social networks like Facebook, Pinterest, and LinkedIn; online storage services like SkyDrive and Google Drive; free e-mail services like Gmail and Hotmail/Outlook.com or Yahoo! Mail; and on and on — these services may not charge you anything, but they're hardly free. You pay with your identity. Every time you go to one of those sites, or use one of those products, you leave a trail that companies are eager to exploit, primarily for advertising.

There's a reason why you might buy something on, say, Alibaba, and then find ads for Alibaba appearing on all sorts of websites. One of the big advertising conglomerates has your number. Maybe just your IP address. Maybe a planted cookie. But they've connected enough dots to know that, whatever site you happen to be on at the moment, you once bought something on Alibaba.

Now, even when you log on to Windows 8, if you opt to use a Microsoft account, you leave another footprint in the sand. (I talk about Microsoft accounts in Book II, Chapter 5.)

This isn't horrible. Necessarily. It isn't illegal. In most cases, anyway. The advertisers view it as a chance to direct advertising at you that's likely to generate a response. In some respects, it's like a billboard for a cold Pepsi on a hot freeway, or an ad for beer on Super Bowl Sunday.

In other respects, though, logging your activity online is something quite different.

I talk about privacy in general in Book IX, Chapter 1, and the browser Do Not Track flag (which may or may not do what you think it should do) in Book VI, Chapter 6. In this chapter, I want to give you an overview of privacy settings — and some privacy shenanigans — specifically inside Windows.

Why You Should Be Concerned

As time goes by, people are becoming more and more aware of how their privacy is being eroded by using the Internet. Some people aren't particularly concerned. Others get paranoid to the point of chopping off their clicking fingers. Chances are pretty good you're somewhere between the two poles.

Windows 8 users need to understand that this version of Windows, *much* more than any version of Windows before, pulls in data from all over the web. Every time you elect to connect to a service — Facebook, Flickr, whatever — you're connecting the dots for Microsoft's data-collection routines. And if you use a Microsoft account, Microsoft's dot connector gets to run into overtime.

I'm not implying that Microsoft is trying to steal your data, or somehow use your identity for illegal purposes. It isn't. At this point, Microsoft mostly wants to identify your buying patterns, and your interests, so it can serve you ads that you will click, for products that you will buy. That's where the money is.

Although Google freely admits that it scans your inbound and outbound Gmail e-mail, all the better to generate ads that you will click, Microsoft (as of early 2012, anyway) insists that it doesn't. But Microsoft *does* scan Hotmail/Outlook.com mail and tiled Mail app messages that you receive with Windows 8 — for spam detection, if nothing else. Whether MS will start keeping track of detailed information about your messages in the future is very hard to say.

Here's how the services stack up, when it comes to privacy (or the lack thereof):

✦ **Google:** Without a doubt, Google has the largest collection of data. You leave tracks on the Google databases every time you use Google to search for a website. (That's true of every search engine, not just Google, but Google has 70 percent or more of the search engine market.) You also hand Google web-surfing information if you sign in to your Chrome browser (so it can keep track of your bookmarks for you) or if you sign in to Google itself (for example, to use iGoogle or Google Drive).

Google also owns *Doubleclick,* the best-known third-party cookie generator on the web. Any time you go to a site with a Doubleclick ad — most popular sites have them — a little log about your visit finds its way into Google's database.

✦ **Facebook:** Although Facebook may not have the largest collection of data, it's the most detailed. People who sign up for Facebook tend to give away a lot of information. When you connect your Microsoft account in Windows 8 to Facebook, all the data that you allow to be shared on Facebook is accessible to Microsoft. That's why it's important to lock down your Facebook account (see Book V, Chapter 1).

Every time you go to a website with a Facebook Like icon, that fact is tucked away in Facebook's databases. If you're logged on to Facebook at the time you hit a site with a Like icon, your Facebook ID is transmitted, along with an indication of which site you're looking at, to the Facebook databases. As of this writing, Microsoft can't get into the Facebook database — which is truly one of the crown jewels of the Facebook empire — although it can pull a list of your Friends, if you allow it.

✦ **Microsoft:** Microsoft's Internet access database may not be as big as Google's, or as detailed as Facebook's, but the 'Softies are trying to get there fast. One of the ways they're catching up is by encouraging you to use a Microsoft account. The other is to create all these connections to other data-collecting agencies inside Windows 8, including Facebook and Yahoo! (through Flickr). Then there's Bing, which logs what you're looking at just like Google search.

Windows 8 is light-years ahead of earlier versions of Windows when it comes to harvesting your data. Or perhaps I should say it's light-years behind earlier versions of Windows when it comes to protecting your privacy. Same, same.

For an ongoing, authoritative discussion of privacy issues, look at the Electronic Frontier Foundation's Defending Your Rights in the Digital World page at `www.eff.org/issues/privacy`.

Knowing What Connections Windows Prefers

If you use Windows, you're not on a level playing field. Microsoft plays favorites with some online companies and shuns others as much as it possibly can.

Cases in point:

✦ **Microsoft owns part of Facebook.** You see Facebook everywhere in Windows. There's a reason why: Microsoft owns a 1.6-percent share (at the time of this writing, anyway).

If you link your Windows 8 system to Facebook, Windows pulls all your contact data from Facebook. If, in addition, you're signed in with a Windows account, all that contact data from Facebook becomes available in the Microsoft cloud.

It isn't clear whether Microsoft and Facebook share any other data about individual users. But that's certainly a possibility, if not now, at some point in the undefined future.

✦ **Microsoft doesn't play well with Google.** Windows has some hooks into Google, but invariably they exist in order to pull your personal information out of Google (for example, Contacts) and put it in Microsoft's databases. When you see a ready-made connector in Windows 8's Mail app to add a Gmail account — so you can retrieve your Gmail messages in Microsoft's tiled Mail app — there's an ulterior motive.

✦ **Microsoft would love to import your data from LinkedIn or Twitter.** If you connect to either from inside Windows, all your contacts come across.

✦ **Microsoft gives lip service to Apple.** There's no love lost between the companies. Microsoft still makes software for Mac and iPad platforms (for example, OneNote runs on the iPad, and Office has been on the Mac for longer than it's been on Windows!). Apple still makes software for Windows (such as iTunes, Safari, and QuickTime). But they're both fiercely guarding their own turf. Don't expect to see any sharing of user information.

✦ **Microsoft once tried to buy Yahoo!, which owns Flickr.** Although that possibility seems less likely now than it did in 2008 and again in 2011, it comes up from time to time. Microsoft has hired a boatload of talented people from Yahoo!. The net result is that Flickr is welcome in Windows 8.

And of course, you know that Microsoft also owns Skype, Hotmail/Outlook.com, and SkyDrive, right?

Your information — aggregated, personally identifiable, vaguely anonymous, or whatever — can be drawn from any of those sources and mashed up with the data that Microsoft has in its databases. No wonder data mining is a big topic on the Redmond campus.

Controlling Location Tracking

For the first time in any version of Windows, this version has *location tracking*. You have to tell Windows and specific applications that it's okay to track your location, but if you do, those apps — and Windows itself — know where you are.

Location tracking isn't a bad technology. Like any technology, it can be used for good or not-so-good purposes, and your opinion about what's good may differ from others'. That's what makes a horse race. And a lawsuit or two.

Location tracking isn't just one technology. It's several.

If your PC has a *GPS* chip (see Figure 6-1) — they're common in tablets, but unusual in notebooks and rare in desktops — and the GPS is turned on, and you've authorized a Windows app to see your location, the app can identify your PC's location within a few feet.

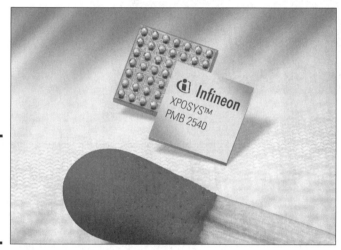

Figure 6-1:
GPS chips
are smaller
than the
head of a
match.

Source: Infineon

GPS is a satellite-based method for pinpointing your location. Currently two different commercial satellite clusters are commonly used — GPS (United States, 2 dozen satellites) and GLONASS (Russia, 3 dozen satellites). They travel in a geosynchronous orbit around the earth (see Figure 6-2). The GPS chip locates four or more satellites and calculates your location based on the distance to each.

If your Windows PC doesn't have a GPS chip, or it isn't turned on, but you do allow Windows apps to track your location, the best Windows can do is to approximate where your Internet connection is coming from, based on your IP address. And in many cases, that can be miles away from where you're actually sitting. (See the sidebar in Book VI, Chapter 5 for a description of IP addresses.)

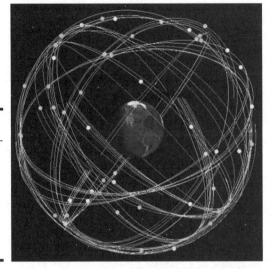

Figure 6-2:
Geosynchronous orbits ensure that a GPS chip can almost always find four satellites.

Source: Colorado Center for Astrodynamics Research

How Apple's location tracking rankled

In April 2011, two researchers — Alasdair Allan and Pete Warden — found that iPads and iPhones with GPS systems were keeping track of location and time data, inside the devices, even if the user explicitly disallowed location tracking. They discovered a log file inside every iPad and iPhone running iOS 4 that included detailed information about location and time since 2010.

They also found that the file was being backed up when the iPhone or iPad was backed up, and the data inside the file wasn't encrypted or protected in any way, and a copy was kept on any computer you synced with the iPhone or iPad.

When confronted with the discovery, Apple at first denied it, and then said that "Apple is not tracking the location of your iPhone. Apple has never done so and has no plans to ever do so" — effectively confirming the researchers' discoveries. As details emerged, Apple claimed it was storing the information to make the location programs work better, but it wasn't being used in, or passed to, any location tracking programs.

In May 2011, Apple released iOS 4.3.3, which no longer kept the data. But by then a series of lawsuits and a class action suit followed in the U.S. In Korea, the Communications Commission fined Apple about $3,000 for their transgressions. As I write this, the U.S. case is making its way through the courts.

Location tracking in tablets is a relatively new phenomenon, and it's bound to have some bugs. With a little luck, the bugs — and gaffes — won't be as bad as Apple's.

Tracking your shots

Any time you put a GPS system and a camera together, you have the potential for a lot of embarrassment. Why? Many GPS-enabled cameras — including notably the ones in many phones and tablets — brand the photo with a very precise location. If you snap a shot from your tablet and upload it to Facebook, Flickr, or any of a thousand photo-friendly sites, the photo may have your exact location embedded in the file, for anyone to see.

Law enforcement has used this approach to find suspects; the U.S. military warns active duty personnel to turn off their GPSs to avoid disclosing locations; and even some anonymous celebrities have been outed by their cameras and phones. Be careful.

When you start a Windows 8 app that wants to use your location — the tiled Weather app being a good, innocuous example — you see a message like the one in Figure 6-3.

Figure 6-3:
Windows 8's
Weather
app wants
to know
whether it
can use your
location.

If you've already turned on location services, each time you add another app that wants to use your location, you see a notification that says, "Can *[Windows 8 app]* use your location?" You can respond either Allow or Block. The following sections explain how you can control location tracking in Windows 8.

Blocking all location tracking

To keep Windows from using your location in *any* app — even if you've already turned on location use in some apps — follow these steps:

1. **Swipe from the right or hover your mouse in the upper-right corner to bring up the Charms bar. At the bottom, choose the Settings charm.**

2. **At the bottom of the Start Settings pane, tap or click the Change PC Settings link and then select Privacy on the left.**

   The PC Settings screen appears, as shown in Figure 6-4.

3. **To turn off location tracking — even if you've already given your permission to various and sundry applications to track your location — set Let Apps Use My Location to OFF.**

   That's all it takes.

Blocking location tracking in an app

If you've given an app permission to use your location, but want to turn it off, without throwing the big OFF switch described in the preceding steps, here's how to do it:

1. **Bring up the app you want to throttle.**

   In this example, I start the Windows 8 Weather app.

2. **Swipe from the right or hover your mouse in the upper-right corner to bring up the Charms bar. At the bottom, choose the Settings charm.**

3. **Select Permissions.**

   Depending on the app, you see a screen like the one in Figure 6-5.

4. **Under Privacy/Allow this App to Access Your, slide the Location slider to Off.**

   The app loses its permission.

Figure 6-4:
The location tracking master shut-off switch is at the top.

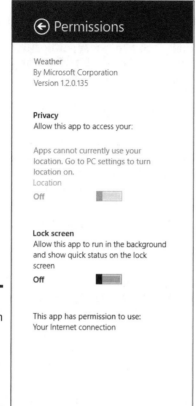

Figure 6-5:
You can turn
off location
tracking for
individual
apps, as
well.

Some apps keep a history of your locations, or searches that may pertain to your location. If you want to verify that's been deleted, too, bring up the Charms bar, choose the Settings charm, and select Settings. If the app saves history files, you see a choice to Clear History and/or a slider that allows you to turn off Search History.

Minimizing Privacy Intrusion

Although it's true that using Windows 8 exposes you to many more privacy concerns than any previous version of Windows, you can reduce the amount of data kept about you by following a few simple rules:

✦ **If you want to log on to Windows using a Microsoft account — and there are many good reasons for doing so — consider setting up a Microsoft account that you use only for logging on to Windows (and possibly for SkyDrive).** See Book II, Chapter 5 for details.

✦ **Don't use the Windows 8 apps for Mail, People, Calendar, Messaging, or SkyDrive.** If you have a Hotmail/Outlook.com or Gmail account, don't access them through Windows 8 Mail, go to your browser, and log on to Hotmail/Outlook.com or Gmail. If you keep a separate Microsoft account for logging on to Windows only, use the web interface for SkyDrive — by going through SkyDrive. Run your Contacts, Calendar, and Messaging through Hotmail/Outlook.com or Gmail as well. It isn't as snazzy as using the Windows 8 tiled apps, but it works just as well. Even better, in many cases.

Also, as noted earlier in this chapter, be very aware of the fact that both Google (Gmail) and Microsoft (Hotmail/Outlook.com) scan every inbound message. Google has no qualms about saying it scans inbound and outbound messages for text that will improve its aim with advertising. Microsoft swears it doesn't.

Personally, I still use Outlook. Nothing tracked, nothing trackable.

✦ **Don't connect the Windows 8 Photos app to SkyDrive, Facebook, or Flickr.**

✦ **Always use "private" browsing.** In Internet Explorer it's called *InPrivate;* Firefox calls it *Incognito;* Chrome says *Private Browsing.* Turning on this mode keeps your browser from leaving cookies around, and it wipes out download lists, caches, browser history, forms, and passwords.

Realize, though, that your browser still leaves crumbs wherever it goes: If you use Google to look up something, for example, Google still has a record of your IP address and what you typed.

"Private" browsing isn't the same thing as Do Not Track. In fact, as of this writing, Do Not Track is just a request that you make to the websites that you visit, asking them to refrain from keeping track of you and your information. For details, see Book VI, Chapter 6.

✦ **Don't opt in for Microsoft's Consumer Experience Improvement Program.** (CEIP is the method Microsoft uses to watch what you're doing, and send information back for their analysis about what you tried and how you tried it.) Yes, I know that Microsoft swears it doesn't keep any personally identifiable information from the CEIP. But "personally identifiable" is a squishy topic, and it's simpler to just not go there.

There really is a trade-off between privacy and ease of use: All the apps mentioned in this chapter require a piece of your privacy in order to function. Only you can make the decision about how much of your privacy you want to give up, in exchange for nifty new features. Just be aware of what you're doing, before you do it.

Book III

Navigating the Start Screen

Contents at a Glance

Chapter 1: Controlling the Start Screen

In This Chapter

✔ **Stop worrying and start loving that tiled Start screen**

✔ **Changing tiles and the background on the Start screen**

✔ **Making the Start screen yours**

✔ **Behind the scenes with Tiled Snap**

*1*f you're an experienced Windows user, chances are good the first time you saw the Start screen, you wondered who put an iPad on it. However, if you're an experienced iPad user, chances are good the first time you worked with the Start screen, you went screaming for your iPad.

The Start screen — the first screen you see in Windows when you get past the login, and the screen you'll come back to over and over again — defines and anchors Windows. Like it or not.

As much as I like to kvetch about Start, the screen's, uh, starting to grow on me. More than a few times I've strayed back to a Windows 7 machine and found myself wondering why pressing the Windows key doesn't bring up Start.

My advice, if you're Start–adverse, is to give it a real workout for a month or two. I don't expect you'll end up singing hosannas about Microsoft's new interface. But I do expect you'll learn to live with it — and, like me, you may even miss it when you go back to Windows 7. That goes double if you can use the tiled interface on a touch-friendly tablet.

In this chapter, I take you through the Start screen, from beginning to end. Some of the material in this chapter overlaps discussions in Book VI, particularly in Chapter 3. That's okay. Book VI, Chapter 3 focuses specifically on changing the Start screen so it feeds into the desktop as easily as possible, and it's very mouse-centric. In this chapter, I look at the larger picture, and explain ways to modify the Start screen that may help even if you intend to shun the old-fashioned desktop and spend most of your time on the tiled side of the Windows street. In this chapter, I also have a more touch-friendly slant, just in case you're thinking of abandoning that giant rodent perched on your desk, and putting your screen in a more recumbent position.

Hey, if you can get your thumb and all your pinkies on the screen simultaneously, touch has the mouse beat five to one.

Touring the Start Screen

The very first screen you see when you start Windows, the Start screen (see Figure 1-1), is designed to be at the center of your Windows universe. Don't let the fact that it's intentionally made to look like a smartphone screen deter you in the least.

You've probably sworn at the Start screen a few times already, but if you can keep a civil tongue, permit me to expound a bit:

✦ *Tiles* (the squares on the screen) appear in two sizes, *smaller* and *larger* (rocket science). Most tiles that come from Microsoft are *live tiles*, with *active content* (latest news, stock prices, date, temperature, email messages) that changes the face of the tile.

✦ Tiles are bunched into *groups*, which may or may not have *group names*.

✦ The Start screen has a *background color* (the color below the tiles) and a *background design* (a pattern below the tiles) — the latter of which is confusingly called just *Background*. If you can't see the background design, don't worry. Sometimes it takes a microscope. Sometimes the background design is *no design*. Did I say something about rocket science?

✦ In the upper-right corner, you see either your Windows username or (if you're logged on with a Microsoft account) your full name. For a description of the Microsoft account and the pros and cons of using one, see Book II, Chapter 5.

Figure 1-1:
The Start
screen.

The most important tip for using the Start screen? How to bring it up. Windows packs at least a half-dozen ways to get to the Start screen, but the two simplest are

✦ If your PC has a Windows button on it, press the button.

✦ Otherwise, press the Windows key on your keyboard.

You can go straight to the Start screen quickly in two more ways, depending on where your hands are located. (I know, I know, they're at the end of your arms. Wiseacre. You know what I mean.) Try this:

✦ **Tappers,** if it's too hard to press the Windows key, swipe from the right and choose the middle charm, which is Start.

✦ **Mousers**, if your hand is already on the mouse, swing down to the lower-left corner of the screen and click.

Now that you have the lay of the land, take a minute to explore the edges of the Start screen. That's where the action is.

Here's how to walk around the fringe. Think of these steps as a Microsoft demo, without the hard sell:

1. **Start a few programs.**

a. *Tap or click, oh, Calendar.*

b. *Go back to the Start screen, tap or click Travel, and go back to the Start screen.*

c. *Tap or click Weather, and then go back to the Start screen.*

d. *Get the desktop going, too — tap or click Desktop, and then go back to the Start screen.*

That gives you a few *programs* (er, *apps* — they mean exactly the same thing) to bounce around.

2a. **If you're using your finger, swipe slowly on the left edge and keep your finger pressed down.**

2b. **If you have a mouse, hover in the upper-left corner.**

Windows shows you a thumbnail of the last program you ran, as shown in Figure 1-2.

The desktop counts as one program. Even if you have ten programs running on the desktop, there's only one thumbnail for them all.

You can bring up the last-run program by either clicking the thumbnail, or slowly sliding farther out from the left, toward the center of the screen. This maneuver is *pulling,* and it can take a while to get used to it. Some screens respond better than others, and the grease on your fingers can make a difference.

**Book III
Chapter 1**

**Controlling the
Start Screen**

Figure 1-2:
A thumbnail of the last-run program appears in the upper left when you use a mouse.

If you drag an app to the right and it *snaps* into place beside the running app, drag the dotted line between the apps to the left. That gets rid of the split screen. I look at *Tiled Snap* — the ability to display two running programs side by side — in the last section in this chapter.

3a. **If you're using your finger, pull slowly from the left, and when the thumbnail appears, pull back just a bit.**

This, too, is a difficult gesture with your finger(s), and it's highly dependent on the touch sensitivity of your tablet. If you can't get this gesture to work with a finger, try your thumb; if you can't get it to work with your thumb, press and hold down the Windows button on your tablet. One way or another, you get to the right place.

3b. **With your mouse hovering in the upper-left corner, slide it down the left edge of the screen but don't click.**

Windows rolls out a black carpet and puts thumbnails of all the other currently running programs on the left edge, as shown in Figure 1-3. The thumbnails and carpet are dubbed the *Switcher*.

Some subtleties are at work. If you're looking at the Start screen when you slide your mouse along the left edge, there's no thumbnail for the Start screen (as is the case in Figure 1-3). That's what you'd expect. But if you slide on the left side while looking at any other app, a thumbnail for the Start screen appears at the bottom of the list. That makes it easy to get to the Start screen — it's always on the bottom. But that also explains the behavior you see in the next step.

If you have a keyboard handy, there's a much better way to look at program thumbnails and cycle through them. Hold down the Alt key and press Tab. If you've used earlier versions of Windows, you may know that's the old CoolSwitch (see Figure 1-4), which has been switching Windows apps, er, programs, since Windows 3.0. Works like a charm, er, champ in Windows 8.

Figure 1-3:
Slide
down the
left to see
thumbnails
of all
running
programs.

The CoolSwitch has one distinct advantage over the slide-mouse-down-the-left approach: It treats each running desktop program as a separate program. If you slide on the left, the desktop as a whole appears as a single program.

4a. **Use your finger or thumb to pull from the bottom-left edge of the screen toward the right. If you can get the black carpet thumbnail Switcher to appear, pull back just a touch to lock it in place.**

4b. **Hover your mouse in the lower-left corner and for added excitement, slide the mouse up on the left side of the screen.**

If you're looking at the Start screen when you hover your mouse in the lower left, you see a thumbnail for the last app that ran. In every other instance, when you hover the mouse in the lower-left corner, a thumbnail for the Start screen appears, as shown in Figure 1-5.

If you hover in the lower left, slide your mouse up the left side, or if you can get your screen to cooperate with the analogous pull and pullback gesture, you see the same black carpet and thumbnails of running programs — the Switcher — that you see in Figure 1-3.

5. **With a mouse, right-click in the lower-left corner of the screen.**

The *Advanced System menu* or *WinX menu* (so-called because you can bring up the same menu from the keyboard by holding down the Windows key and tapping X) appears, as shown in Figure 1-6.

Figure 1-6:
The
Advanced
System
menu
(or WinX
menu) gives
you quick
access
to many
system
functions,
notably
including
many
Control
Panel
applets.

Programs and Features
Power Options
Event Viewer
System
Device Manager
Disk Management
Computer Management
Command Prompt
Command Prompt (Admin)

Task Manager
Control Panel
File Explorer
Search
Run

Desktop

6a. **If you're using your pinkies, swipe in from the right side of the screen.**

6b. **If you're using a mouse, hover in the upper-right corner and then move your mouse down the right side of the screen.**

In either case, you see another black carpet with the five so-called Windows charms icons: Search, Share, Start, Devices, and Settings, as shown in Figure 1-7.

Figure 1-7:
Windows
charms
appear on
the right
side of the
screen.

When you use a mouse, hovering in the upper right brings up silhou-ettes of the charms (I call them *ghost charms,* but never mind), which solidify only when you move your mouse down on the right.

As soon as the black carpet appears, Windows also shows you the time and date, and the current status of all the notification icons that appear on the lock screen (see Book II, Chapter 2).

As I mention in Book II, Chapter 1, the Start charm takes you to the Start screen. I talk about the other charms in detail in Book III, Chapters 2 (Search), 3 (Share), and 4 (Settings and Devices).

7a. **Flip into Semantic Zoom by pinching the Start screen with your fin-gers and move back out by unpinching it.**

7b. **Perform the following with a mouse:**

a. *Click the tiny, tiny icon that looks like a minus sign, in the lower right corner of your Start screen.*

Your Start screen transmogrifies with Semantic Zoom.

b. *Click an unoccupied piece of the Start screen to go back to regular zoom.*

I talk about Semantic Zoom in the section "Organizing Your Start screen" later in this chapter.

That concludes this portion of the ongoing Windows 8 tile demo. Please fasten your seatbelt and return your seat back to the fully upright position.

The Start screen has one more action you can perform — bring up the App bar. You can bring up the App bar in any tiled application by sliding down from the top with your finger or up from the bottom, or right-clicking it. Unfortunately, the App bar on the Start screen doesn't do much: The App bar has one, solitary icon mysteriously labeled All Apps. Click the icon, and Windows behaves as if you brought up the Search charm.

Changing Tiles on the Start Screen

You can click and drag tiles anyplace you like on the Start screen. Drag a tile way off to the right, and you start a new group. Install a new program, and its tile magically appears in the rightmost group on the Start screen.

You can change every tile, too. The actions available depend on what the creator of the tile permits. Here's how to mangle a tile:

1. **If you're using your fingers, slide the tile down just slightly and then let go. If you have a mouse, right-click the tile you want to change.**

A check mark appears in the upper-right corner of the tile and an App bar for the tile appears at the bottom, as shown in Figure 1-8.

The Mail tile is selected

Figure 1-8:
Control tiles
individually.

2. **See Table 1-1 to determine which action(s) you want to take and then select the desired action.**

3. **To get rid of the App bar, tap or click on any blank spot on the Start screen.**

   You immediately revert back to the Start screen in its original form, plus or minus the actions you've taken.

Table 1-1	Tile Actions
Tile Action Name	*What the Action Does*
Larger/Smaller	Makes the tile icon larger (twice as wide) or smaller (half as wide). These are the only two sizes.
Unpin from Start	Removes the tile from the Start screen. Doesn't affect the app itself. If you later change your mind, see the section "Organizing Your Start screen" for details on how to bring back the tile.
Pin to Taskbar	Puts an icon for the app on the desktop's taskbar (see Book VI, Chapter 2).

(continued)

Table 1-1 *(continued)*

Tile Action Name	What the Action Does
Uninstall	Removes all vestiges of the program, using the desktop Control Panel's Remove Programs.
Open New Window	Runs the program in a new window on the desktop.
Run as Administrator	Prompts for an administrator account password, and then runs the program in elevated mode.
Turn Live Tile Off/On	Stops/starts the animation that's displayed on the tile. Stopping the active content can help reduce battery drain, but the big benefit is stifling obnoxious flickering tiles — of which there are many.
Open File Location	Starts File Explorer and goes to the folder that contains the program.

Changing the Start Screen Background

Changing the color and pattern of the Start screen background couldn't be simpler — if you know where to look. Here's how:

1. **Swipe from the right or hover your mouse in the upper-right corner to bring up the Charms bar, and then at the bottom, choose the Settings charm.**

2. **At the bottom of the Settings pane, tap or click the Change PC Settings link, select Personalize on the left (as shown in Figure 1-9), and then at the top on the right, select Start Screen.**

The Start Screen Settings screen appears.

3. **Select a background pattern from the Choose a Background collection.**

Yes, I know they're hard to see. Squint.

4. **Slide the Change Background Color slider to a color you can live with.**

Note how the *highlight color* — the color that the Start screen uses to highlight things that you've chosen — changes as the background color changes.

5. **When you're done, use your favorite method to go back to the Start screen.**

The changes take effect immediately; you don't need to click OK or Apply.

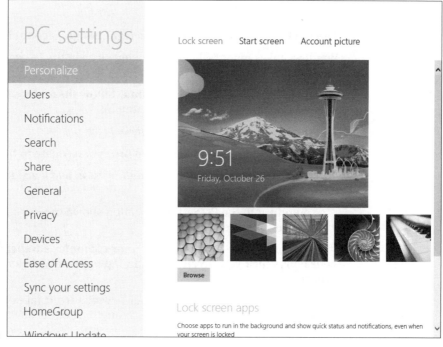

Figure 1-9:
Change the
Start screen
background
here.

You *can* change the Start screen to colors that aren't on Microsoft's palette. You can dig into the Registry if you're handy with hex editors. But if you'd rather work through an intermediary, try the Windows 8 Start Tweaker from Ruanmei. To find the latest version, go to `www.deviantart.com` and search for *Windows 8 Start Tweaker*.

Organizing Your Start Screen

The beauty of the Start screen is that, within strictly defined limits, you can customize it like crazy. As long as you're happy working with the basic building blocks — small tiles, large tiles, and groups — you can slice and dice 'til the cows come home.

The hard part about corralling the Start screen is figuring out what works best for you.

Changing your picture

I start with an easy change to the Start screen: changing the picture in the upper-right corner.

Here's how to change your picture:

1. **Tap or click your name and then select Change Account Picture.**

   Windows takes you to a familiar-looking place in the PC Settings hierarchy, as shown in Figure 1-10.

2. **If you already have a picture in mind, follow these steps (if you'd rather take a picture, continue to Step 3):**

   a. *Choose Browse and navigate to the picture.*

      You may need to choose Files, in order to navigate to the location.

   b. *When you find the picture you want, select it, and then tap or click Choose Image.*

      You return to the PC Settings location shown in Figure 1-10, with your new picture in place.

3. **If you'd rather take a picture with your computer's webcam, comb your hair, pluck your eyebrows, and tap or click Webcam (in that order).**

   In any case, however you create your new picture, it takes effect immediately — no need to click OK or anything of the sort.

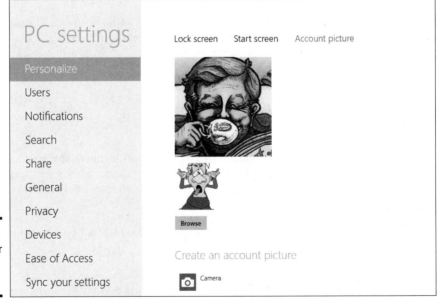

Figure 1-10:
Change your
picture in
PC Settings.

Want a weird picture? Don't have an avatar-generating source, like the Xbox? Try re-using an avatar that somebody's posted on the Internet. Here's the easy way:

1. **In your favorite web browser, search for *avatars* and then switch to the image-viewing mode in your search engine where you find tons and tons of them.**

I found a picture I like in the Wikimedia Commons library on the web (see Figure 1-11).

2. **Let's take a screen shot. When you find the picture you want, make sure the whole picture appears on the screen. Then hold down the Windows key and press Print Screen.**

Windows puts a copy of the screen shot in your Pictures library.

3. **On the Start screen, tap or click the Desktop tile. Over on the desktop, on the Taskbar at the bottom, tap or click the File Explorer icon — the one that looks like a bunch of file folders. Then go to your Pictures library, and select the screen shot you just made (it will have a name like** `Screenshot (1).png`**).**

4a. **With your fingers, tap the Home tab at the top, tap the Open icon in the Open section of the Explorer Ribbon, and choose Paint.**

Book III
Chapter 1

**Controlling the
Start Screen**

Figure 1-11: The avatar from AJ Gonzalez that I want to grab.

4b. **With a mouse, right-click the picture and choose Open With⇨Paint.**

You need to crop your picture, to take away all of the stuff in the screen shot except the avatar. Windows Paint is more than up to the task.

5. **Tap or click the Select icon on the Ribbon, and then draw a rectangle around the picture you want to use for your Start screen.**

If you don't get the rectangle the way you like the first time, don't worry. Start over and try Step 5 again. When you start again, your old rectangle disappears.

6. **When you have the picture framed properly, tap or click the Crop icon on the Paint Ribbon.**

Your cropped picture takes over the whole Paint area.

7. **Tap or click the Save icon — the tiny icon that looks like a floppy disk (eh, what's THAT?) at the very top of the screen — and save the cropped picture in your Pictures library.**

8. **On the Start screen (press the Windows key on the keyboard, or the Windows button on your computer to bring it up), tap or click your name, and then choose Change Account Picture.**

9. **Tap or click Browse, and then choose Files⇨Pictures⇨Screenshots. Find your cropped picture, select it, and tap or click Choose Image.**

There you go. You've just successfully perpetrated identity theft on a defenseless avatar.

Adding apps to the Start screen

The Start screen starts out with a bunch of tiles that may or may not run the programs you want to run. When you install new programs, their tiles get unceremoniously deposited in a blob on the rightmost group on your screen. You can delete individual tiles using the procedure I describe in the section "Changing Tiles on the Start screen" earlier in this chapter.

Now you might be wondering, "How do I put tiles *I want* on the Start screen?" Good question. Glad you asked it.

In the preceding section, I show you how to use Microsoft Paint — an old stalwart, not very capable but stable as a rock — to crop a picture. Microsoft Paint doesn't appear on any tiles. Let me show you how to create a new tile that runs a program, using Paint as an example. Here's how:

1. **Find the program.**

That's the hardest part of this whole process, if you don't know the name of the program. Fortunately, you do: Paint.

2a. **If you have a keyboard, go to the Start screen and type** paint.

2b. **If you don't have a keyboard, swipe from the right to bring up the charms; tap or click the Search charm; tap inside the Apps search box (the white box); and in the Windows onscreen keyboard that appears, type** paint.

Your screen looks like the one in Figure 1-12.

3a. **Slide the Paint tile down and then release it.**

3b. **With a mouse, right-click the Paint tile, just underneath Apps.**

The App bar, as shown in Figure 1-13, appears.

Figure 1-12: Looking for Paint in all the wrong places — in this case, on a tablet, using the onscreen keyboard.

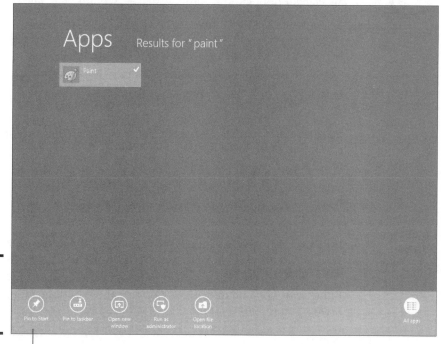

Figure 1-13: Options for the Paint program.

The Pin to Start option

4. **At the bottom left, tap or click Pin to Start.**

   A tile for the Paint program appears on your Start screen in the right-most group, which you can verify by flipping over to the Start screen.

Organizing with Semantic Zoom

After you have most of your programs present and accounted for on the Start screen, you're ready to sort them into groups and assign names to those groups. Follow these steps:

1. **Tap and drag (or click and drag) your tiles so similar tiles are in the same group.**

   For example, if you use Mail, Messaging, People, and Calendar all day long, put them in the same group. If you have Office installed, move the important Office tiles into a group, and either delete the Office tiles you never use or move them into a separate group. (I describe the process in more detail in Book VI, Chapter 3.)

   Don't worry just yet if the groups are in the wrong sequence: There are easy ways to move entire groups. Just concentrate on getting your similar tiles into the same group.

   If you have programs that you look at constantly because they have important information — stock market results, your music playlist, Messenger notifications, or new Mail — keep them in one or two groups.

   If you need to create a new group, drag a tile all the way over to the right. You see a faint vertical bar, which indicates that a new group has just been formed. Drop the tile to the right of the bar.

2. **Switch to Semantic Zoom, where it's easy to rearrange groups.**

   If you use a touch screen, pinch the screen.

   If you have a mouse, click way, way down in the lower-right corner of the Start screen. (There's a tiny icon that looks like a minus sign down there just waiting for you to find it.)

   With a click or a pinch, you end up in a zoomed-out view of the Start screen that Microsoft dubs *Semantic Zoom.* (See Figure 1-14.)

   While in Semantic Zoom, you can't move tiles around or create new groups. But you can slice and dice the groups you have.

3. **If you want to give a group a name (which I recommend, especially if you have a lot of tiles), slide the group down and then release it, or right-click the group.**

   Either way, you end up with an App bar at the bottom with an icon that invites you to Name Group.

Figure 1-14:
The
Semantic
Zoom view
of your Start
screen.

4. **Tap or click Name Group, type in a name for the group, and then tap or click Name.**

   The name appears above the group.

5. **When you're done rearranging and naming groups, tap or click any empty place on the Start screen.**

   Sit back and enjoy your newly organized Start screen. (See Figure 1-15.)

If you use the old-fashioned desktop more than the tiled side of Windows, I have a series of recommended steps for turning your Start screen into a lean, mean, not-quite-as-good-as-a-Win7-Start-menu machine, in Book VI Chapter 3.

Don't hesitate to go back and change the tiles and groups around. It's easy, and you can fine-tune it to your heart's content.

Figure 1-15: Start screen with tiles and groups rearranged, and names on top.

Working with Tiled Snap

Windows has a new, odd way of running two — and only two — programs side by side. I call it *Tiled snap* to distinguish it from *Aero Snap* (also known as *Windows Snap*). The easiest way to explain the difference, I think, is to show you what they look like.

Aero Snap has been around for several years; it involves snapping a desktop program to either the left or the right side of the desktop screen, by clicking and dragging the program's window to the left or right edge of the screen. After an old-fashioned Windows "legacy" program has been Windows Snapped, it takes up exactly half of the screen. The resized window behaves just like any other window on the old-fashioned desktop: It can be resized, moved, maximized to take up the whole screen, and so on. Figure 1-16 shows an old-fashioned Windows program that's been snapped to the right half of the screen.

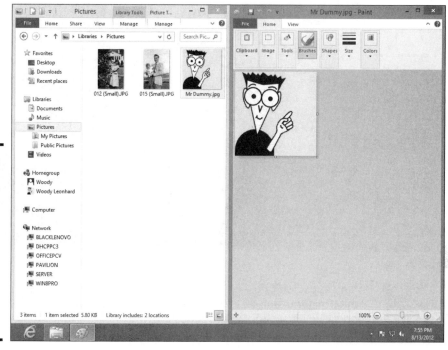

Figure 1-16:
Aero Snap is a quick way to resize an old-fashioned Windows program so it takes up half the screen.

Tiled snap is similar to Aero Snap, but more rigid:

✦ **Minimum screen size:** If your display is 1366 x 768 pixels or more, you can Tile snap two tiled full–screen apps. (Remember that the entire old-fashioned Windows desktop counts as one app.)

✦ **Specifically sized containers:** The two apps appear in defined containers, one of which is 320 pixels wide, and as tall as the screen. The other app occupies the rest of the screen, less a narrow 22-pixel vertical band that separates the two apps. Visually, it looks like Figure 1-17.

Those numbers are far from random, by the way. On a 1366 x 768 screen — the minimum size that will run Tiled snap — one of the apps takes up 320 x 768 pixels, which is a common phone app size. The other occupies 1024 x 768 pixels, which you probably recognize as a common Windows app size.

✦ **No interactivity:** Whereas apps snapped on the old-fashioned desktop can interact with each other — you can click and drag files or text from one to the other, for example — the two apps in a Tiled snap arrangement *cannot.* There's no interaction between them, other than through the Share charm.

Figure 1-17:
Two snapped tiled apps — read the Bing News while you watch your stocks (time delayed) on Bing Finance.

Many apps don't do well in a small space, although some may surprise you. Solitaire, for example, turns the card deck on its side — and the gameplay is good! The Music app, which looks horrible full screen, retreats into a reasonably usable playlist view if you Tile snap it.

Here are the many ways to Tile snap a tiled app:

✦ Swipe or drag from the left side of the screen to bring up the most recently-run program, and slowly drag it to the right. When the Tiled snap vertical bar appears, release the thumbnail. The thumbnail's program gets Tile snapped on the left.

✦ Bring up the running program thumbnails, in the black carpet Switcher I describe in the section "Touring the Start screen" at the beginning of this chapter. There are many ways to show the Switcher. Tap or click one of the thumbnails, and slowly drag the thumbnail to the right. When the Tiled snap vertical bar appears, release the thumbnail.

✦ With a mouse, click at the very top of a tiled app, or at the very top of the desktop. Slowly pull the top down toward the middle of the screen. When the app turns into a big thumbnail, drag it to the left or right, and then release. The app gets snapped next to the last-running program. You can do the same thing with your finger, swiping down slowly from the top.

✦ Bring up the running program thumbnails, in the black carpet Switcher described earlier. Right-click the thumbnail you want to Tile snap, and choose either Snap Left or Snap Right.

✦ If you have a keyboard, when you're running a tiled app or when you're working on the desktop, press down the Windows key and tap the period. The current app (or the desktop) gets snapped to the right.

To close out this section on Tiled snap, here are a few handy tips:

✦ You can't Tile snap the Start screen.

✦ When you Tile snap the desktop into one of the small spaces, individual programs running on the desktop have their own thumbnails on the snapped screen. See Figure 1-18.

✦ You can make the apps switch sides (so the wide one is on the left or on the right) by dragging the vertical separating bar. If you drag the vertical separating bar all the way to the edge of the screen, the snapped app disappears and the main app takes over the whole screen.

That's the whole shtick.

Figure 1-18:
The Tile snapped desktop shows each running program in its own small thumbnail.

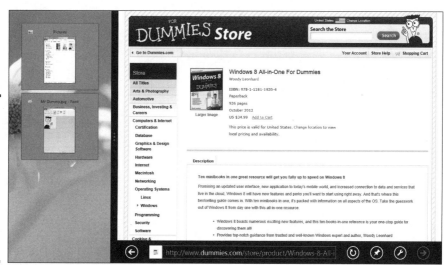

Chapter 2: Searching in and with the Start Screen

In This Chapter

✔ The Start screen Search shtick

✔ Using the touch keyboard

✔ Searching for programs, settings, and files, tile style

✔ Removing apps from search

Microsoft designed search on the tiled side of the Windows 8 fence to run quickly and easily, and in a way that finds most of what needs to be found, with minimal hassle. Unfortunately, the way most people use Search on the tiled side misses things in ways that mystify.

In this chapter, I talk about search with training wheels: The simple tiled way of doing things, with simple searches — realizing that sometimes the searches don't produce reasonable results. What do I mean by "reasonable"? Good question. If you go into the Windows Store, for example, and search for the term recipes, you will never find the Allrecipes app. If you search your files for the term invoice, you will never find a file named CustomerInvoice123.xlsx. In this chapter, the beginning course, I won't be overly concerned about those anomalies.

If you want to wade through the advanced course, I talk about the real search options in Book VI, Chapter 8. While it's true that you can use advanced search techniques in the Start screen's Search app, it's also true that you can't focus Start screen Searches on specific folders or drives. If you want to do a "real" search on a large number of files, you really need to be working over on the old-fashioned desktop.

The oddest thing about Start screen Search? If you have a keyboard, you can start your search by simply typing while you're looking at the Start screen. There's no box to type into, no hint that typing will trigger a search. But it does.

General Approaches to Searching

Microsoft, through its Customer Experience Improvement Program (CEIP), keeps an enormous amount of data about the way people use Windows. The folks who designed Windows 8 pondered mightily over the telemetry that they received from Windows 7, and relied on it heavily to make design decisions for Windows 8. (I call it "steering a boat by its wake," but never mind.)

Microsoft discovered that 67 percent of all searches performed on the Start menu in Windows 7 were to find and launch programs. Searches for files accounted for 22 percent and Control Panel program searches came in at 9 percent.

Those are astounding numbers. Between everyday apps and system apps (er, Control Panel programs), 76 percent of all the searches in the old Start menu simply sought programs — and almost all the rest were looking for files. That's why the Start screen is heavily biased toward looking for programs and, one click away, system programs.

Keep that in mind as you step through this little experiment:

1. **Press the Windows key on the keyboard or the Windows button on your tablet to go to the Start screen.**

2. **Do one of the following:**

   If you have a keyboard, just type **no**.

   If you don't have a keyboard, swipe from the right to bring up the Charms bar, tap the Search charm at the top, tap inside the Apps search box, and use the touch keyboard to type **no**.

   Windows immediately starts searching for programs that start with, or contain, the characters *no*. See Figure 2-1.

   I have a detailed explanation of the touch keyboard in Book II, Chapter 1.

3. **On the right, tap or click the entry Settings to see Windows settings that match your search criteria.**

You see a very lengthy list (see Figure 2-2) of links to Settings locations and then Control Panel programs that start with the letters *no*. Here's the key point: either the name of the location or program starts with *no*, or the letters *no* appear after a space in the name. I have a more detailed explanation in the section "Searching for Programs/Apps" later in this chapter.

Figure 2-1:
Searching
for
programs
that start
with, or
contain, the
characters
no is very
simple and
fast.

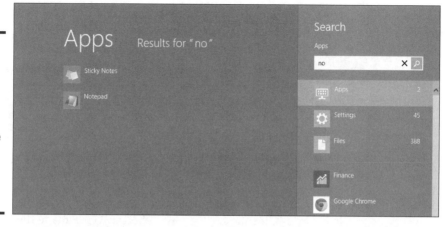

Figure 2-2:
A hodge-
podge of
results with
system
connections.

**Book III
Chapter 2**

Searching in and
with the Start
Screen

4. **Tap or click Files to see a list of files that match your search.**

If you have any files at all on your computer, you undoubtedly see
a swarm of files; I have 389 matches in Figure 2-3. Why? Because *no*
matches all sorts of things: song titles, data inside files, pictures with the
hidden tag `Orientation: Normal`, and on and on.

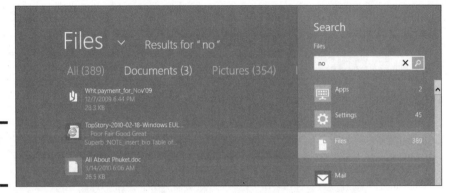

Figure 2-3:
Files that
match *no*.

In Figure 2-3, the file `All About Phuket.docx` made the search list because it's based on the template `Normal.dotx`, and the template name is part of the hidden metadata buried inside the file. *no* matches `Normal.dotx`. Cool. Search really does go out and look for *everything*.

5. **Tap or click any search result to either see the setting or open the file, depending on what you tapped or clicked.**

You can search in many tiled Windows 8 apps by just clicking the app, there on the right. I talk about the apps you can search at the end of the chapter. For now, go back to the Start screen.

Searching for Programs/Apps

If you know that you're looking for a program (er, an app), or you think that you're looking for a program, keep in mind that you need to know the program name, or at least part of the program name.

With that caveat, here's how easy it is to search for an app:

1. **Press the Windows key on the keyboard or the Windows button on your tablet to go to the Start screen.**

2. **Do one of the following:**

   If you have a keyboard, type the first few letters of the name of the program.

   If you don't have a keyboard, swipe from the right to bring up the Charms bar, tap the Search charm at the top, tap inside the Apps search box, and use the touch keyboard to type the first few letters of the program name.

   Windows immediately starts searching for programs that start with the characters you type. Mostly. Sort of.

To better understand your search results, it helps to know that Windows looks at the names of all the programs, and it tries to match the characters you type with the beginning letters of the program names, or the beginning letters of each of the words in the program's name. Confused? Here, follow an example:

1. **Type** win **to search for a program.**

Windows finds all the programs with names that start with *win,* as shown in Figure 2-4.

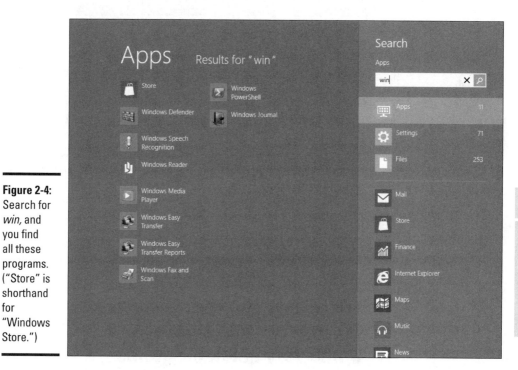

Figure 2-4: Search for *win,* and you find all these programs. ("Store" is shorthand for "Windows Store.")

2. **Hit Backspace a few times and then search for** *in.*

If Windows were searching for all the apps with the characters *in* in their names, you'd see a long list like the one in Figure 2-4. But that isn't what Windows actually searches for. It looks for full words in the program names that start with *in.* So, for example, searching on *in* draws hits for *In*ternet Explorer and Math *In*put Panel, but it doesn't get a match on W*in*dows Media Player. See Figure 2-5.

Figure 2-5:
Search looks only for matches on the first characters of full words in the programs' names.

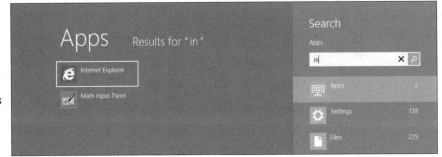

Windows search results are based on the first characters of a program name but *program names are inconsistent.* For example, there's a Windows system program called Windows PowerShell. Because there's no space between *Power* and *Shell* in *PowerShell,* if you search for *shell,* you won't find the program. Similarly, you'll never find Microsoft OneNote by searching for *note,* or Microsoft InfoPath by searching for *path.*

If you're accustomed to search using most programs on most computers, you would expect that searching for *no* would match anything with the letters *no* in the name. That isn't the case with Start screen Search. The letters *no* must appear either at the beginning of the name, or after a space in the middle of the name.

Now you see why the search term *recipes* doesn't match *Allrecipes,* but the search term *rope* matches *Cut the Rope.* Bizarre, but true — and the source of endless confusion for people who are looking for recipe apps in the Windows Store.

Some very quick programs

Want to launch the Calculator quickly? Press the Windows key, type **calc**, and press Enter. That's all it takes. In fact, if you're looking at the Start screen, you don't even need to press the Windows key.

Want to launch Word, Excel, Paint, Notepad, Help, or WordPad? Hit the Windows key, type the name, and press Enter. It's really that easy.

When you install new programs, many of them will also be accessible quickly. Experiment with them a bit. When you start typing the name, you see a list of programs that match the name. As soon as the program you want moves to the top of the list, press Enter and Windows runs it.

Searching for Settings

Windows has a plethora of settings — not just the settings you can see with the Settings charm, but zillions of system programs, dialog boxes, check boxes, Action Center notifications, and on and on. The Control Panel on the desktop functions as a command center for settings, warnings, and other kinds of reports. I talk about Control Panel in Book VII, Chapter 1. But it's only part of the search story.

Microsoft would have a hard time calling all the aforementioned things "Control Panel programs, system programs, administrative tools, dialog boxes, status reports, and all the internal stuff you never want to touch," so it settled on the term *Settings*.

Just keep in mind that when you search for settings, you're searching for a whole lot more than the settings you can get to from the Settings charm.

Permit me to step you through an example:

1. **Press the Windows key on the keyboard or the Windows button on your tablet to go to the Start screen.**

2. **Do one of the following:**

If you have a keyboard, type the first few letters of the setting. When the search screen appears looking for an app, tap or click the Settings line on the right. (If you want to take the ready-fire-aim approach, press Windows key+W to bring up the search screen, with Settings already selected.)

If you don't have a keyboard, swipe from the right to bring up the Charms bar, tap the Search charm at the top, tap Settings on the right, tap inside the Settings search box, and use the touch keyboard to type the first few letters of the setting name.

In Figure 2-6, I search for settings that have to do with *network*.

Note how the Settings items appear on the left, and a motley assortment of programs, troubleshooters, Control Panel applets, Help topics, and anything else that might contain the term *network* appear on the right.

**Book III
Chapter 2**

Searching in and with the Start Screen

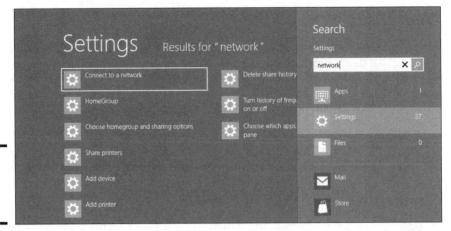

Figure 2-6:
Search for
network
settings.

Searching for Files

The most important advice for searching for files: If you're looking for
a particular kind of file — a Word document, an Excel spreadsheet, or a
graphic file that you created with some program — go into the program
and search from there. So, crank up Word, Excel, or the graphics program
and then use the program to perform the search.

Two big reasons why:

✦ **Unless you change something, the application automatically limits the
kind of files being sought**. For example, if you go into Word and search
by choosing File➪Open, Word returns only Word documents. If you
know what kind of file you want, searching with the program that creates that type of file makes it easier to zero in on what you seek.

✦ **Most applications limit the search to the current folder and its subfolders**. So if you know you're looking for an Excel spreadsheet in the
\Invoices folder, Excel can do a much better job than Start screen
Search. How? In Excel, choose File➪Open. Navigate to the \Invoices
folder. Then type your search criteria in the search box. The search
goes faster, and the list of files you have to rummage through is much
smaller.

You'll almost always find that Start screen Search gives you too many files to
sift through — many of them irrelevant — compared to working with the app.

If I didn't scare you off, here's a quick introduction to using Start screen Search for files. I look at simple searches; they can get much more complex, as I describe at the end of this section.

Here's how to run a file search from the Start screen:

1. **Press the Windows key on the keyboard or the Windows button on your tablet to go to the Start screen.**

2. **Do one of the following:**

If you have a keyboard, type the first few letters of the file's name. When the search screen appears looking for an app, tap or click the Files line on the right. (If you want to go straight to file search, press Windows key+F to bring up the search screen, with Files already selected.)

If you don't have a keyboard, swipe from the right to bring up the Charms bar, tap the Search charm at the top, tap Files on the right, tap inside the Files search box, and use the touch keyboard to type the first few letters of the file's name.

In Figure 2-7, I search for files that start with the characters *all*.

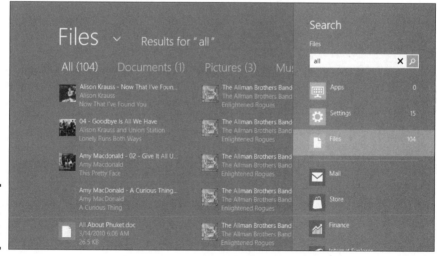

Figure 2-7:
A search for files with *all*.

Book III
Chapter 2

Searching in and
with the Start
Screen

Note that you get matches not only on the filenames, but also on the file contents and on other *metadata,* such as tags on pictures, descriptions for certain kinds of files, and much more.

Hover your mouse over any of the matching files for a ToolTip with a great deal of information — file size, date, location, and much more.

3. **At the top, choose what kinds of files you want to look at.**

Depending on the results of your search, that may include Documents, Pictures, Music, or any of several other categories.

Just as in the search for programs, the text you type has to match the start of a filename, or the start of a separate word inside a filename. It can also match a whole word inside the document, or the beginning of a whole word inside a document.

So, for example, if you search for *dum,* you get hits on the filenames `dummies.doc` and `My Dumb Mistake.jpg` (note the spaces) and the search will also match an Excel spreadsheet with a cell that contains the word *dummer.*

But searching for *dum* does not generate a match on files named `SomeDumbThing.rtf` (no spaces) or a PDF document that contains the word *datadump.*

Searching for Other Tiled Things

It probably won't come as any surprise that you can search in any of the apps listed on the right side of the Search screen, as shown in Figure 2-7. In general, here's what happens:

1. You bring up the search screen, type your search terms, and then tap or click the app.

   If you want to try a few different approaches to search, you can also

   • Bring up the search screen, tap or click the app, and then type your search terms.

   • Go to the app, use the Search charm to bring up the search screen, and then type your search terms.

   Here's the interesting part. The app itself returns the search results. That's a huge change from how Windows worked before. Search is done with a *contract* programming technique, and the contract controls what the app can search for and how it returns the results.

2. The app puts the results on the screen in a way that makes sense for the app. You choose the result you like, and the app takes over from there.

Here are the more commonly searched tiled apps:

✦ **Store** searches for the name of an item in the Windows Store, or a tag. For example, searching for *game* brings up the game, Cut the Rope.

✦ **Internet Explorer** brings up the tiled full–screen IE with the search term entered in the default search engine (probably Bing, unless you've jumped through some extraordinary hoops to change it to Google).

✦ **Maps and Weather** search for the location you type in the search box.

✦ **Finance** looks for a stock based on what you typed in the search box.

✦ **People**, **Mail**, **Photos, and Video** search for items with the typed name, or for a tag that matches.

✦ **Music**, on the other hand, goes out and tries to get you to buy an album.

✦ **Xbox Live** similarly looks at your collection, and also prompts you to spend some money.

Removing Apps from the Search List

Any program you install can "register" its ability to perform a search with Windows. When the program installer properly registers itself, the program appears in the list on the right of the search screen (refer to Figure 2-7). The list can get mighty bloated, mighty fast. If you never search for stocks, can't imagine searching for an Xbox Live game, and/or don't want to use Internet Explorer's mainline to the Bing search engine, why keep them on the list?

Follow this easy way to remove programs from the right side of the search list:

1. **Swipe from the right or hover your mouse in the upper-right corner to bring up the Charms bar, and then at the bottom, choose the Settings charm.**

2. **At the bottom of the Settings pane, tap or click the Change PC Settings link and then select Search on the left.**

The Search Settings screen, as shown in Figure 2-8, appears.

3. **For any app that you want to remove from the right side of the search screen, set the slider to Off.**

The change takes effect immediately.

Book III
Chapter 2

Searching in and
with the Start
Screen

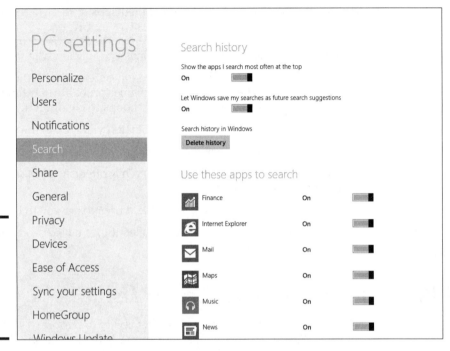

Figure 2-8:
Remove
apps from
the right
side of the
search
screen.

Chapter 3: Sharing Among Tiled Apps

In This Chapter

✔ Sharing with the Share charm

✔ Working through a share

✔ Knowing what can be shared

✔ Controlling which tiled apps are allowed to share

The tiled side of Windows doesn't have much of a Clipboard — and no drag 'n' drop.

If you've used Windows before, that statement should stop you dead in your tracks. The Windows Clipboard — which works just fine on the old-fashioned desktop side of Windows 8 — is the primary means for moving data around. You can copy just about anything to the Clipboard and then paste it just about anywhere: Text can go from a browser to a Word document; numbers can go from an e-mail to a spreadsheet; pictures can be copied and pasted into different folders — or into documents, messages, spreadsheets, or even different pictures.

Old-fashioned desktop select-and-drag works, too, in many situations, but in every version of Windows since the primordial ooze, the Clipboard has always done the lion's share of the work.

When you walk on the tiled side of the fence, you don't copy or paste, cut, drag, or empty the Clipboard. You *share.*

Like Start screen search, which I discuss in Chapter 2 of this minibook, sharing among tiled apps is actually performed through *contracts,* or technical agreements among the apps about what they have to offer and what they will accept. In many ways, sharing is much more advanced than copying to the Clipboard. But it's also more restrictive because apps have to specifically be built to create and fulfill the contracts — which can be much more complex than simple Clipboard copying.

Sharing the Easy Way

Windows 8's sharing goes way beyond the old cut and paste. Let me show you what I mean.

In older versions of Windows, and the desktop of the current version of Windows, you can copy the web address of a site and paste it into, say, an e-mail message. The pasted address is just text, something that starts with `http://`. Depending on which e-mail program you use, the address may appear with an underline signifying it's *hot,* as shown in Figure 3-1.

Figure 3-1:
A copied hot link in an Outlook mail message.

> **Internet Explorer 9 may stop responding if DFX Audio Enhancer is installed:**
>
> Sent: Sat 23/06/2012 9:57 PM
> To: woody Leonhard
>
> Internet Explorer 9 may stop responding if DFX Audio Enhancer is installed:
> http://support.microsoft.com/kb/2727797/en-us?sd=rss&spid=15672

When someone receives your e-mail, he can see the link and, if he's curious, click it and have Outlook automatically bring up the default web browser and go to the location mentioned in the hot link.

That's so 20th century, don't you think? Over on the tiled side of the fence, life's in a faster lane.

The tiled, full–screen version of Internet Explorer has many sharing contracts (see the "What's a sharing contract?" sidebar). One of those contracts says, in effect, "the tiled Internet Explorer can hand you a hot link for the current location, a picture, and some text from the page."

What's a sharing contract?

When a programmer writes a tiled app that can share, she has to set up the app's installer so it notifies Windows not only that the app can send or receive data, but also tell Windows what kind of data can be sent or received.

For example, the Windows 8 Photos app can send out a picture. One of the sharing contracts Photos supports simply sends a picture. If there's another tiled app that wants a picture,

the contracts match, and Photos can share a picture with the second app.

Think about it for a second, and you realize how complex that sharing contract could be. For example, maybe Photos will only share particular kinds of photo files, and not others. The contract has to spell out specifically what kinds of pictures can be provided — and the receiving tiled app better be able to handle all the different kinds.

The Windows 8 Mail app also has a contract that says, in effect, "Win8 Mail can accept a hot link, a picture, and some text." Of course, Mail can accept all kinds of things. One of the contracts it supports is this one, which is designed specifically to accept shared data from a web browser.

Here's how to share a web page through Windows 8's Mail app:

1. **Fire up the tiled version of Internet Explorer.**

   Sharing only works on the tiled side — the desktop version of Internet Explorer can't share.

2. **Navigate to a web page that you want to e-mail to a friend.**

3. **Bring up the Charms bar by swiping from the right, hovering your mouse in the upper-right corner of the screen, or holding down the Windows key and pressing C. Then tap or click the Share Charm.**

   Windows looks through the list of apps that can accept shared stuff, and zeroes in on apps that can handle the kind of contract that Internet Explorer can provide. Mail just happens to be one of those apps, as shown in Figure 3-2.

4. **Choose Mail.**

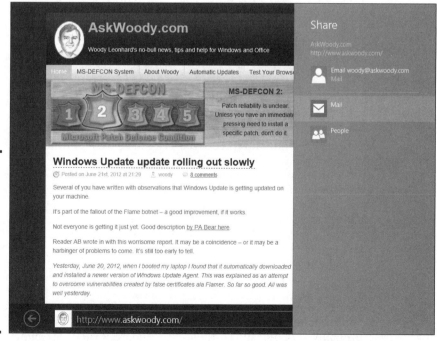

Figure 3-2: Internet Explorer has sharing contracts that match with the Windows 8 Mail and People apps.

Windows starts Mail, creates a new message, and copies the information — using the contract — from the browser into the message.

5. **Fill in the addressee, type in any additional information you like, and tap or click the Send icon in the upper right.**

The message that gets sent out looks like what you see in Figure 3-3.

Figure 3-3: Windows 8 Mail gets a web page name, picture, link and text — and an ad for Windows 8, of course.

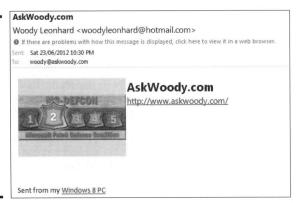

> **AskWoody.com**
>
> Woody Leonhard <woodyleonhard@hotmail.com>
>
> ⓘ If there are problems with how this message is displayed, click here to view it in a web browser.
>
> Sent: Sat 23/06/2012 10:30 PM
>
> To: woody@askwoody.com
>
> **AskWoody.com**
> http://www.askwoody.com/
>
> Sent from my Windows 8 PC

Compare Figures 3-1 and 3-3. That's the difference between copy and paste, and a tiled app share, respectively. In the old-fashioned method, you have to do all of the copying and heavy lifting, and the result isn't anything to write home about. But sharing with tiled apps, there's a very significant amount of data that's sent for you — and you don't need to lift more than a finger or two.

On the other hand . . . sharing among tiled apps isn't quite so simple, eh? Both the program that sends the data — the *source* — and the app that receives the data — the *target* — have to agree exactly on what kind of data is being sent, and how it goes across. That's why contracts are so important.

Over on the old-fashioned desktop, you have to select something, and then copy or cut it to the Clipboard. Here on the tiled side, in many cases, you don't really need to select anything. For example, if you're playing a game and there's a Share charm that works with the game, the people who made the game may decide that what you share is your current list of top scores. If you're in Internet Explorer, looking at a website, and share, IE is smart enough to know that you don't want to share anything specific on the website — you just want to share a link to it, and a picture.

As this book went to press, there were very few source/target pairs of tiled apps that agreed to work under the same contracts. That's going to change, probably very quickly. Fortunately, standard formats are in place for many different kinds of data — contacts, for example, or formatted text — that will help make the formulation of contracts more uniform.

Stepping Through a Photo Share

Understand how sharing basically hangs together? Good. In this section, try a simple sharing task — sending a photo in an e-mail message.

Here's how to share a photo in an e-mail:

1. Go to the Start screen (press the Windows key on the keyboard or the Windows button on your tablet), and then tap or click the Photos app.

The Windows 8 Photos app appears.

2. Select one of your Photos.

See Book IV, Chapter 3 if you can't find any photos. If you want to see the whole sequence go by in slow motion, choose a high definition photo — a large file.

You need to tap or click the photo. It appears in the middle of the screen.

3. Swipe from the right or hover your mouse in the upper-right corner to bring up the Charms bar and then choose the Share charm, which is the second charm.

Windows gives you a choice of all the tiled apps that can accept data from the Photos app. In this case, only Mail can accept a shared picture from Photos. See Figure 3-4.

4. Choose the Mail app.

**Book III
Chapter 3**

**Sharing Among
Tiled Apps**

Figure 3-4:
Only the
Mail app
has a
contract
that
matches
with Photos.

Mail starts a new e-mail message and copies a thumbnail of the picture into the message. See Figure 3-5.

5. **Fill in the message and tap or click the Send button on the upper-right.**

   Make sure you get a To: address, and add a subject if you like. The usual e-mail stuff.

   After Mail starts to send the message, you return to the Photos app.

6. **If you chose a small photo, it's probably sent in seconds. But if you sent a large photo, you might want to make sure it goes out. To check, go back to the Charms bar and choose Share again. Tap or click the Check Sharing Progress link at the bottom.**

   The Charms bar shows you the status of the message while Mail puts it together and then ships it out.

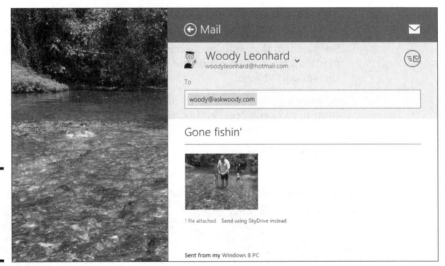

Figure 3-5: The message is ready to be filled out.

That's how sharing works.

What Can You Share?

As of this writing, you can share very little. The steps in the preceding section show you how to share a photo in an e-mail message.

If you go into Internet Explorer, navigate to a page, then use the Share charm to put the page in an email message, you get the kind of message shown in Figure 3-3.

If you start Internet Explorer and select text on a web page *before* you share, you can use the Share charm to share that text in an e-mail message, as shown in Figure 3-6.

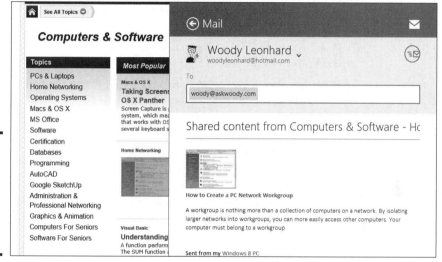

Figure 3-6: Selected text on a web page gets shared in a Mail message.

Controlling Share

Sharing depends on contracts that work behind the scenes in an app to control what information one app can share with another app. The contract on a tiled app that wants to send data has to match the contract on another tiled app that wants to receive data. Windows works behind the scenes to match the contracts, pairing sending and receiving apps.

If you like, you can tell Windows that you don't want it to allow sharing with specific tiled apps.

Also, Windows maintains a list of the most commonly shared apps. For any specific contract, Windows counts how many times you use that contract to share with a tiled app, and it modifies the list of apps it shows you based on how much you use the apps. For example, if you bring up the Share charm in the Photos app and you choose to share your photo with the Mail app, Windows starts putting Mail at the top of the shared list.

You can control what appears at the top of the Share list, too. Here's how:

1. **Swipe from the right or hover your mouse in the upper-right corner to bring up the Charms bar, and then at the bottom, choose the Settings charm.**

2. **At the bottom of the Settings pane, tap or click the Change PC Settings link and then select Share on the left.**

   The Share Settings screen, as shown in Figure 3-7, appears.

3. **(Optional) If you don't want Windows to show you a list of the tiled apps that you use to share most frequently, turn off the feature.**

   Similarly, you can clear the list or adjust the number of items in the list. Presumably you'd do that to be able to see more of the available apps at the bottom of the list.

   Windows shows you a list of the apps that can accept the correct contract. You won't see the same apps listed every time you bring up the Charms bar, because not every app can handle the same sharing contracts.

4. **To disable sharing with a specific app — don't allow it to send data or receive data — set the appropriate slider to Off.**

   You might want to disable a tiled app if you find yourself mistakenly using it in place of an app that you really want to use. You might also want to disable an app if the list of apps that appears in the Charms bar gets too long.

Figure 3-7:
Control
Share
settings
here.

This kind of contract sharing is just starting. As developers make more and more apps for the tiled part of Windows, the amount of sharing available — and the usefulness of that sharing — will increase dramatically.

Chapter 4: Settings, Settings, More Settings, and Devices

In This Chapter

✔ Using common settings

✔ Diving into the Settings page

✔ How Settings works in the apps

✔ Taking control of your devices

*W*indows has settings. Boy howdy, does it have settings.

The desktop's Control Panel — long the bastion of Windows settings, through many generations of Windows — controls the lion's share of settings on a Windows PC. The new Settings charm controls several hundred settings. And — get this — there's only a little bit of overlap between the two.

Although the Settings charm controls only a very small percentage of all the settings in Windows, the settings you find via the Settings charm are key to using the tiled side of Windows, and the tiled apps properly. They also have an impact on the old-fashioned desktop side of the fence, too.

In this chapter, I talk about the settings that you can access with the Settings charm from the tiled Start screen. If you can't find the setting you want here, flip to Book VII, Chapter 1.

Using the Settings Charm

No matter where you are in Windows, the Settings charm gives you immediate access to six common settings, plus a hook to get into more settings. Here's how to use the charm:

1. **Swipe from the right or hover your mouse in the upper-right corner (or hold down the Windows key and press I) to bring up the Charms bar, and then at the bottom, choose the Settings charm.**

You see the Settings pane, with six icons at the bottom. See Figure 4-1. Table 4-1 describes what each icon does.

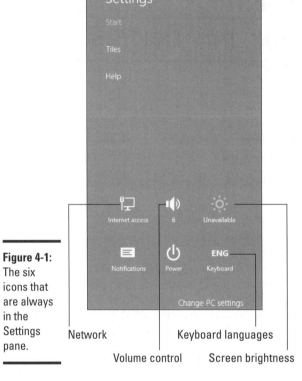

Figure 4-1:
The six icons that are always in the Settings pane.

Network
Volume control

Keyboard languages
Screen brightness

2. **Choose one of the following: any icon, one of the options at the top (which vary depending on where you're located inside Windows), or Change PC Settings at the bottom.**

3. **To close the Settings pane, tap or click anywhere outside the pane.**

Table 4-1	Actions for the Settings Pane Icons
Icon	*Action*
Network	Verify your network connection, connect to a different network, switch to Airplane mode, turn sharing on or off (right-click the connection; see Book VII, Chapter 5). Tap and hold, or right-click the specific connection to see how much data you've used since you last reset the counter.
Volume	Set the overall system volume.
Brightness	Sliding scale, not available on desktop PCs.
Notifications	Master switch that turns notifications on or off for all the apps that can produce notifications (see Book II, Chapter 3)

Icon	Action
Power	Sleep, Shut Down, Restart (if you have updates waiting, the options change to Update and Shut Down, and Update and Restart). Some people recommend that you turn off your PC through this icon. I figure it's easier to use the account picture.
Language	Change the way keystrokes are interpreted (to use keyboards in different languages) but without changing date or time formats.

Some mobile broadband providers have applications that notify you when you're reaching your monthly data cap. The notifications appear as *toaster* fly-ins from the right of the screen, or as live tiles on the Windows logon screen or Start screen. If your service provider has such an app, it's well worth seeking.

Changing PC Settings

At the bottom of the Settings pane is the Change PC Settings link. Tap or click it, and the PC Settings page, as shown in Figure 4-2, appears.

Book III
Chapter 4

Settings, Settings,
More Settings, and
Devices

Figure 4-2: The treasure trove of Start screen-based settings.

The PC Settings page is a remarkable collection of settings, arranged in a way that's infinitely more accessible than the old-fashioned desktop Control Panel. On the left, you see these categories:

✦ **Personalize:** From here, you can change the lock screen, which appears whenever your PC resumes from Sleep (see Book II, Chapter 2); the Start screen (see Book III, Chapter 1); or your account picture (see Book III, Chapter 1).

✦ **Users:** Find options that enable you to add a new standard user (you have to use the Control Panel to add administrators, as I explain in Book II, Chapter 4), change your password or switch to a picture or PIN password (flip to Book II, Chapter 4), or switch between a Microsoft account and a Local account (see Book II, Chapter 5).

✦ **Notifications:** Turns notifications (which appear on your lock screen and also occasionally toaster-style from the right) on and off, both overall and for individual tiled apps. See Book II, Chapter 3.

✦ **Search:** Lets you clear your search history and choose which apps appear when you perform a search on the tiled side of Windows 8. See Book III, Chapter 2.

✦ **Share:** Helps you control which tiled apps appear at the top of the Share pane. Also lets you turn off specific apps for sending or receiving data. Details are in Book III, Chapter 3.

✦ **General:** This is the "all other" category that includes your time zone, switching between apps, how to use the touch keyboard (see Book II, Chapter 1), or turn spelling correction on or off. A link to the language center whisks you to the area of the Control Panel where you can add different styles of keyboards or change your default date and time layout and shorthand.

Remarkably, this section also includes (be careful!) links to refresh or reinstall Windows on your PC. Don't accidentally choose one of these, okay? Details in Book VIII, Chapter 2.

✦ **Privacy:** There's a global switch for location reporting, a name and account picture switch, and a slider that lets you send web addresses accessed by tiled apps to the Windows Store. I talk about all those — including why nobody in their right mind would send web history to the Windows Store — in Book II, Chapter 6.

✦ **Devices:** Presents one location where you can add new devices (such as printers or scanners) to your PC, or get rid of old ones. I talk about devices in the final section of this chapter.

✦ **Wireless:** If you're connected to the Internet over a wireless connection (so-called *mobile broadband,* 3G, or 4G, or something-or-another-G),

Wireless appears as one of your options. Here you can turn Airplane mode on or off, and choose between running on your mobile account or running on Wi-Fi (which, if you can get a signal and log on, is almost always cheaper and faster, but probably less secure).

Given a choice, Windows is designed to always use a Wi-Fi connection (like the wireless connection in your house or at a coffee shop) over a mobile broadband connection (the one that can rack up data usage charges on your mobile phone bill). Windows is also smart enough to detect when you've connected to a Wi-Fi network and disconnect you from mobile broadband, saving both money and battery power.

✦ **Ease of Access:** Microsoft has long had commendable aids for people who need help seeing, hearing, or working with Windows. All the settings are here.

✦ **Sync Your Settings:** If you log in to Windows using a Microsoft account and confirm that the PC you're using is a "trusted" PC, this section lets you control precisely what's being synced as you move from PC to PC, logging in with your Microsoft account along the way. In many situations, you likely don't want to sync everything — maybe not sync *anything*. Details are in Book II, Chapter 5.

✦ **HomeGroup:** This is the central control for HomeGroup settings (which are duplicated in the desktop Control Panel). If your PC is eligible to participate in a HomeGroup, this is where you can tell Windows what, precisely, should be shared in the HomeGroup. It's also an easy place to find the HomeGroup password, if you need it. Full details can be found in Book VII, Chapter 5.

✦ **Windows Update:** An abbreviated form of the Automatic Update settings found in the Control Panel. See my contrarian opinion about Windows Automatic Update in Book VIII, Chapter 3.

All in all, it's a well-thought-out subset of the settings that you might want to use, particularly if you spend most of your time on the tiled side of Windows.

Book III
Chapter 4

Settings, Settings,
More Settings, and
Devices

Searching for settings

If you use the Search charm, as I describe in Book III, Chapter 2, and search for *Settings,* you see an absolute flood of options: the App Settings that I talk about in this chapter, yes, but also all the matching Legacy Control Panel entries, Action Center troubleshooters, Help entries, and much more. Realize that running a search on Settings is far, far more complex than using the Settings charm to stay within the simple, staid confines of the tiled Settings.

Touring the Start Screen Settings

The Settings charm (like all the charms except the Start charm) changes depending on where you are and what app you're using. Here's a brief rundown of what the charm does in the different apps:

✦ **If you're on the desktop and you bring up the Settings charm,** you get a direct link into the desktop Control Panel (see the top of Figure 4-3). The other two entries — Personalization and PC Info — are just links to the corresponding piece of the Control Panel.

Figure 4-3:
The desktop's Settings pane.

✦ **If you bring up the Settings charm while you're in Windows 8's tiled Mail, Calendar, or People,** you can add e-mail accounts or control permissions for the tiled app (to use your webcam and microphone, and to run in the background even if the PC is locked). I talk about those tiled apps in Book IV, Chapter 2.

✦ **From Windows 8's Messaging app,** you can set permissions for the webcam and microphone, and notifications, both on the desktop and on the lock screen. See Book IV, Chapter 5.

✦ **The Settings charm in the Windows 8 Photos app controls a small set of details,** including shuffling photos on the Photos tile in the Start screen, and the accounts/sources of your photos (SkyDrive, Facebook, or Flickr). See Book IV, Chapter 3.

✦ **By contrast, the Settings charms in Xbox Music and Xbox Video** primarily concern themselves with all the wonderful ways you can spend more money with Microsoft.

✦ **In the tiled, full–screen Internet Explorer,** the Settings charm offers a tiny subset of all the settings that are available in the desktop IE version. For example, you can clear your browsing history, turn off the physical location sensing, set zoom to make text bigger or smaller, and change the encoding method for non-Latin characters.

Here are a few more minor settings:

✦ **Weather,** in the Settings charm, lets you switch between Fahrenheit and Celsius.

✦ **Solitaire** lets you choose between Draw 3 and Draw 1, and turn off the sound.

Doing the Devices Charm

Most people go to the Start screen, bring up the Devices charm, see one entry — to add a second screen — and figure the Devices charm is broken. See Figure 4-4. (Your computer may show one or two more devices, depending on what hardware you have installed.)

Devices

Start

There's nothing to send right now.

Second screen

Figure 4-4:
The Devices
charm may
underwhelm
at first.

Not so.

Like all the other charms, the Devices charm shows only items that pertain to the location you're sitting in at any particular moment. If you can see only the Add a Second Screen option, it just happens that the only device-related action your PC can take while you're looking at the Start screen is to connect a second screen.

If you bring up a tiled app — say, the tiled, full–screen Internet Explorer — you're likely to see many more devices accessible to the app. In the case of IE, you can access all your printing devices: printers and other sorta-printer-like things, possibly including OneNote and Microsoft's XPS Document writer (don't ask, it isn't worth your effort trying to figure out XPS). You can see a typical overblown list in Figure 4-5.

Figure 4-5:
A list of devices (including many phantom printers, long deceased) appears on the tiled full–screen Internet Explorer's Devices pane.

The tiled Internet Explorer is designed to work with the Devices list to print a web page. Similarly, Windows 8's Photos app works with Devices to print photos. The precise procedure isn't exactly obvious from any descriptions that I've seen, but here's how to print a picture in Photos:

1. **Open the tiled Photos app. Navigate to the photo you want to print and select it (tap or click it).**

2. **Swipe from the right or hover your mouse in the upper-right corner of the screen (or hold down the Windows key and press I).**

   The black carpet and the Charms bar appear.

3. **Choose the Devices charm.**

   You see an abbreviated list of recently available printers, plus a few odds 'n ends, as shown in Figure 4-6.

4. **Choose the device you want to use to print.**

   Windows shows you the print options screen, which can vary depending on the printer. Figure 4-7 shows a sample.

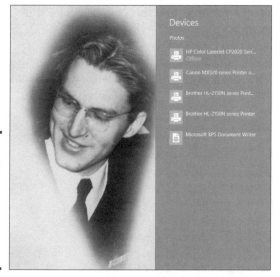

Figure 4-6:
The Devices pane for the Win8 Photos app, showing the available printers.

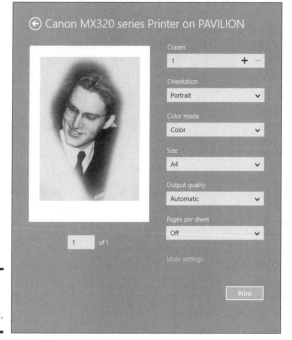

Figure 4-7:
A typical print screen.

5. Make any changes you like, and then tap or click Print.

The entire page prints.

As of this writing, with a few small exceptions — for example, setting up a second screen — the Devices charm doesn't work with *anything* on the old-fashioned desktop.

Chapter 5: Taking Control of the Windows Store

In This Chapter

✔ **Getting the lowdown on Windows Store apps**

✔ **Exploring the Windows Store**

✔ **Updating your Store accounts and preferences**

*I*f you're familiar with buying programs in the Apple App Store, you already know about 90 percent of what you'll find in the Windows Store.

Microsoft's Windows Store launched simultaneously with the release of Windows 8. The Windows Store is a big, extensible, very usable source of new programs for the tiled side of your Windows computer. There are even apps that run on the desktop side, too.

Apps make or break any computer these days, and Microsoft knows it. That's why you find an enormous breadth of apps in the Windows Store — it's good for you, and good for Microsoft, over and above the 30-percent commission Microsoft makes on every sale.

The only way you can get apps for the tiled side of Windows is to download and install the app from Windows Store. While large companies can put tiled apps on their Windows devices (using a technique known as *sideloading*), normal people like you and me have to go through the Windows Store: the alpha and omega of tiled, new style Windows 8 apps.

Checking Out What a Tiled App Can Do

The longer Windows Store is available, the more apps you'll find there. The apps do all sorts of things, but each app also has to meet a set of requirements before Microsoft will offer the app in the Windows Store.

Here's a short version of what you can expect from any app you buy (or download) via the Windows Store:

✦ **You can get both tiled-style apps (which run on the tiled side of Windows) and legacy-style apps (which run on the old-fashioned desktop) from the Windows Store.**

If you want a new program for the desktop, you may be able to find it in the Windows Store, or you may be able to get it through all the old sources — shrink-wrapped boxes, monster download sites — to find and install what you want.

But if you want a new tiled program, you have to get it through Windows Store. (Unless you have a big company; see the sidebar "Bypassing the Windows Store restrictions.")

✦ **Tiled apps can be updated only through the Windows Store.** If your apps are set to update automatically — the default — when an update is available, the Store tile on the Start screen shows a number, indicating how many apps have updates available. See "Adjusting Your Store Accounts and Preferences" later in this chapter.

✦ **Apps that use any Internet-based services have to request permission from the user before retrieving, or sending, personal data.**

✦ **The app has to be usable on up to five computers at a time.** For example, if you buy the latest high-tech version of Angry Birds, you can run that same version of Angry Birds on up to five Windows 8 devices — computers, tablets — at no additional cost.

✦ **Microsoft won't accept apps with a rating over ESRB** *Mature* **(which is to say "adult content").**

✦ **Apps can (thankfully) put only one tile on the Start screen.**

✦ **Apps must start in five seconds or less, and resume in two seconds or less.** Microsoft wants apps to be speedy, not sluggish, and thus requires developers to make sure their apps meet this requirement.

In addition to the basic requirements for any app, you're also likely to find that the following is true of most apps:

✦ **Microsoft's tools help developers create trial versions of their apps, so you can try before you buy.** The trial versions can be limited in many ways — for example, they work only on a certain number of pictures, messages, or files or only for a week or a month — before demanding payment. That's all part of the plan.

Where try-before-you-buy has a long and checkered history on the desktop, it's baked into many Windows Store apps. Microsoft is very strict about requiring the developer to explain precisely what has been limited, and what happens if you fork over the filthy lucre.

✦ **If an app breaks, you can complain to Microsoft, but the support responsibility lies 100 percent with the developer.** Although Microsoft acts as an agent in the distribution and sale of apps, Microsoft doesn't actually buy or sell or warrant anything at all. Even the license for using the tiled-style program goes between seller and buyer, with Microsoft out of the loop.

✦ **Many apps attempt to get you to buy more — more levels, more features, more content.** Microsoft has that covered, just like Apple: Orders generated by the app have to go through Windows Store. Only Microsoft can fulfill the orders. Ka-ching.

Don't confuse the Windows Store — which hooks directly into the tiled part of Windows — with the Microsoft Store, which has both Internet and meatspace manifestations. Brick-and-mortar Microsoft stores are popping up all over the place (another bright idea borrowed from Apple). The online Microsoft Store, www.microsoftstore.com, serves as an online extension of the physical Microsoft stores. In the online Microsoft Store, you can buy the new Microsoft-sourced Windows RT and Windows 8 Pro Surface computers, applications that run on the desktop, as well as competitors' computers, Xboxes, headphones, mice, phones — in short, everything you would find at a Microsoft store.

Bypassing the Windows Store restrictions

Microsoft runs the Windows Store as a business — a tightly held business — and for that reason, it restricts what can be bought in the Windows Store. Microsoft can reject an application submitted to the Windows Store for a huge variety of reasons.

Here's the key point you need to understand about the Windows Store: With two exceptions, the Windows Store is the *only place* you can get programs that will run on the tiled side of Windows.

The exceptions:

✔ Big companies can bypass the restriction and put their own programs on Windows machines using a technique called *sideloading*. At least in theory, sideloading can be accomplished only on machines that are locked into a corporate network.

✔ If you *jailbreak* your PC, you may be able to put any tiled apps you like on your

computer — Microsoft's censors no longer apply. On the other hand, jailbreaking your computer voids every warrantee in existence, and automatically disqualifies you from Microsoft support.

Unlocking (which may or may not be accompanied by jailbreaking) allows you to switch carriers, if you bought your PC from a carrier who's locked in their services. Some carriers in the US, for example, may offer a discounted price for your tablet in exchange for a multi-year internet contract. If you unlock the computer, you may (or may not) be able to hook it up to a different network. All sorts of penalties may apply.

I don't recommend that you jailbreak your PC. But if you find an app that you really want, and Microsoft won't let it into the Windows Store, jailbreaking may be your only option. Google is your friend.

Browsing the Windows Store

When you're ready to venture into the Windows Store for tiled apps, tap or click the Store tile, and you see something like Figure 5-1.

Figure 5-1:
The
Windows
Store.

Moving around in the Windows Store is a little funky. The following tips can help you move around and find what you're looking for:

✦ **To order an app,** tap or click the app's tile. The Store takes you directly to the ordering screen for the app. For example, if you tap or click on the tile for the Kindle app, you see the ordering page in Figure 5-2.

Each of the three tabs at the top — Overview, Details, and Reviews — contains information that you may find important, depending on the app. At the very least, you can vent your spleen on the Reviews page if the app doesn't live up to your expectations.

The star rating shouldn't impress you — it's the accumulated wisdom of all the people who've bothered to rate the app. But the supported languages section, if there is one, may be of interest — and the permissions list is detailed and thorough.

✦ **To view apps by group,** tap or click the text heading for each group. For example, in Figure 5-1, if you scroll to the right, then tap or click Games, you see the mass shown in Figure 5-3.

✦ **To sort the list of apps in a group,** tap or click a subcategory. In the case of Games, you can choose from the subcategories shown in Figure 5-3, or sort the list based on age *(newest),* the highest customer-assigned rating, or price. There's also a Sort by Noteworthy option, which seems to be tied to how well the game is doing in the marketplace.

If instead of tapping or clicking Games, you choose the All Stars tile, you get a list very similar to the one sorted by customer-assigned rating.

Figure 5-2:
The app ordering page for the Kindle app.

Figure 5-3:
Tiled games, showing the sub-categories available.

What? A Kindle app on Windows?

Hard to believe, but Amazon and Microsoft have cooperated long enough to put a Kindle app on the tiled part of Windows.

The Kindle app takes the approach that many third-party apps mimic: As soon as you install the app, you need to sign in with your username and password. Don't be confused: Amazon (the purveyors of Kindle) isn't looking for your Microsoft account, or your Local account. Amazon's looking for your Amazon Kindle account.

After you sign in to the Kindle app with your Kindle account, all the Kindle books you've bought from Amazon are immediately available. Yes, inside Windows. As of this writing, the app had lots of minor problems — scrolling is cumbersome, the library is hard to view — and you can't go to the Kindle Store from inside the app, you get flipped over to your browser. Still, it's an amazing accomplishment organizationally, if not technically.

If you choose the Free tile, you get precisely the same list as the one in the main Windows Store listing (see Figure 5-1), if you choose Free as the price.

+ **To see more of the categories at one time,** use semantic zoom: with a touch-sensitive screen, "pinch"; with a mouse, click the small icon in the lower right that looks like a minus sign. Other than semantic zoom, though, there's nothing you can do to rearrange the tiles in the store. What you see is what Microsoft wants to sell.

Searching the Windows Store

The Search charm enables you to search the Store app. Here's how searching works in the Windows Store:

1. **On the Start screen, tap or click the Store tile to bring up the Store app.**

   If you can't find a tile for the Store app, go to the Start screen and type **store**.

2. **Swipe from the right to bring up the Charms bar or hover your mouse in the upper-right corner.**

3. **Choose the Search charm on top, and then type whatever you want to search for.**

   Search in the Shop app is limited to searching on the names of the apps — you can't type *game*, for example, and bring up a list of all games.

Adjusting Your Store Accounts and Preferences

In the Windows Store app, you can adjust a limited number of settings for your accounts and preferences, as follows:

1. **Tap or click the Windows Store app from the Start screen.**

2. **Swipe from the right to bring up the Charms bar or hover your mouse in the upper-right corner. Tap or click the Settings charm.**

   You see the Settings pane shown in Figure 5-4.

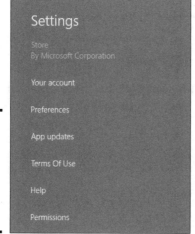

Figure 5-4: The first three settings contain important information.

3. **Choose Your Account.**

   Windows shows you the Windows Store Your Account page, as shown in Figure 5-5.

   You can change these settings:

   • *Change User* lets you switch to a different Microsoft account. That's useful if you're using an anonymous Microsoft account, but want to buy something in the Windows Store — switch your account over, buy whatever you want, download it, then switch back to your anonymous account. (I talk about anonymous Microsoft accounts in Book II, Chapter 4.)

   • *Payment and Billing Info* if you don't already have a credit card associated with your current Microsoft account, you can add it here. Having Windows ask for your password when buying an app makes it more difficult for your three year old to run up at $1,000 bill.

- *Your PCs* shows the five PCs that are permitted to share the apps that you buy. You can remove a PC here.

  The PCs are associated with your Microsoft account. If you log on to a different computer, using the same Microsoft account, you can download and install any tiled apps you've already bought on that different computer. The name of the new PC is added to this list. See the "Which apps do I own?" sidebar.

4. **Swipe from the right to bring up the Charms bar or hover your mouse in the upper-right corner. Tap or click the Settings charm. Choose Preferences.**

   Windows shows you the Store Preferences page, which makes it easier to find apps that support limited accessibility; it also lets you extend your searches to other languages.

5. **Swipe from the right to bring up the Charms bar or hover your mouse in the upper-right corner. Tap or click the Settings charm. Choose App Updates.**

   Windows shows you the Store App Updates page, as shown in Figure 5-6.

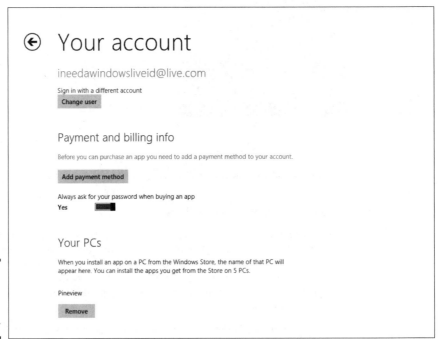

Figure 5-5:
Set your
shopping
preferences.

Which apps do I own?

If you're wondering which apps you own, there's an easy way to find out. Make sure you're logged on with whichever Microsoft account you're using to download apps; start the Store app and swipe down from the top of the screen or right-click in the middle of the screen. You see a navigation bar at the top, with a link that says Your Apps.

Click the link, and the Store app retrieves a list of all the computers that have apps installed that you ordered with your Microsoft account.

It gets complicated because one PC can have two different accounts that bought the same tiled app. It would behoove you to look at the Your Apps list from time to time and see if you can remove a PC, to free up one of the five licenses for a different PC.

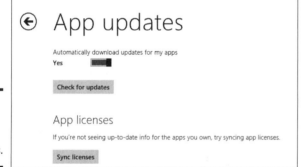

Figure 5-6:
Set your
update
preferences.

In this case, *automatic* means that Windows downloads the updates, but doesn't install them until you give your permission.

Unlike Windows updates — where I don't trust Microsoft for a moment, and recommend that you carefully control which updates are applied and when (see Book VIII, Chapter 3) — app updates are relatively innocuous. Unless and until Microsoft conclusively demonstrates that it can't update tiled apps properly, I suggest that you go ahead and let the apps update automatically.

6. **When you're done, tap the Windows button on your tablet or click the lower-left corner to go back to the Start screen.**

Chapter 6: How Do I Turn Off This Thing?

In This Chapter

✔ **Turning off your PC and apps**

✔ **Understanding the Windows sleep state**

✔ **Discovering Connected Standby**

*I*f you've been using Windows for a while, you know that — perhaps surprisingly — *sleep* is a very, very complex topic. Over the years Windows has had different forms of hibernating, sleeping, suspending, standing by, and shutting down. The only thing Microsoft hasn't tried is snoring.

In Windows 7, 57 percent of desktop PC users and 45 percent of laptop users shut down their PCs instead of putting them to sleep. Folks who shut down their PCs cite reasons running the gamut from reducing electricity consumption to improving battery life. They also found that their systems, once restarted, ran better: The old cobwebs got cleared out with a restart.

Until now, there's never been a good substitute for turning off your computer: Hibernate or standby in older versions of Windows doesn't clean your system and get everything restarted. Restarting cleaned and refreshed everything, but it took f-o-r-e-v-e-r to get back and going again.

This version of Windows has a better way.

In this chapter, you find out where to find the settings to turn off Windows 8, and I talk about the new, improved version of Windows sleep that's probably running on your PC right now. I also talk about killing off individual tiled apps, in case you want to stop one.

Turning Off Your PC

So how do you turn off your PC?

Short answer: You don't need to. Windows is smart enough to retreat to a zero-power consumption state, and you don't need to lift a finger. Unless you change your power settings, your PC will go into zero-power sleep when it's been idle for 30 minutes (15 minutes on a tablet or notebook that isn't plugged into the wall).

Now that Microsoft has finally fixed sleep, rebooting is necessary only if your machine locks up — and when that happens, you probably won't be able to reboot using anything other than the power switch. If your machine isn't locked up, here's the easiest way to shut down, reboot, or tell your computer to go to sleep:

1. **Swipe from the right to bring up the Charms bar, hover your mouse in the upper-right corner, or hold down the Windows key on your keyboard and press C.**

2. **Choose the Settings charm, at the bottom.**

   You see the Settings pane, as shown in Figure 6-1.

3. **At the bottom, tap or click Power, and then choose whether you want to Sleep, Shut Down, or Restart.**

   A Restart is precisely the same thing as a Shut Down, followed by a boot.

Figure 6-1:
This is where you can turn off your PC — if you really want to.

If you want to know more about why sleep is so improved in Windows 8, see the next section. If you want to adjust how much time passes before Windows falls asleep, see "Adjusting sleep settings" later in this chapter.

Understanding the new windows sleep state

Microsoft has experimented with so many variations of sleeping over the years, it's nice to know that sleep finally works right in Windows 8.

When your PC goes to sleep, here's what happens:

✦ Windows asks each running program to shut itself down. Each app either responds by shutting down immediately, or asks for a little extra time.

✦ Each of the user sessions is closed.

✦ Windows shuts down its own internal programs (services) and device drivers.

✦ Windows hibernates the *kernel* session — the part of Windows that runs closest to the hardware — by taking a snapshot of the core programs' status and putting an exact copy on the hard drive. The data goes into a `hiberfil.sys` file.

✦ Windows tells the computer to turn off the power.

That's very different from the old-fashioned hibernate and standby, where Windows used to wait for everything, including the kernel session, to finish, before shutting off the power.

When Windows wakes up, it doesn't have to pull all the system programs in from a disk and get them going. Instead, it relies on the hibernated kernel session. Here's how the restart goes:

✦ Power goes on, and the system boots. If UEFI works (UEFI, the *Unified Extensible Firmware Interface*, runs before Windows gets loaded, much like BIOS; see Book IX, Chapter 3), the system verifies that it has a digitally signed copy of Windows, and runs the Windows loader.

✦ The Windows loader starts any device drivers it needs to start Windows and then pulls in the hibernated kernel session.

✦ Here's a crucial part: Windows starts the device drivers and system programs (services) *from scratch.* They're all loaded fresh.

✦ The logon screen appears, and you can log on.

✦ Windows initializes the Start screen, and you can see it.

By starting the device drivers and system programs all over again, you get a fresh copy of Windows, and the whole process runs very quickly.

Microsoft is convinced — and based on what I've seen, I agree — that this method of shutting down and restarting Windows is much superior to any method previously available.

What is Connected Standby?

Think of your phone. It's on all the time, but it isn't really on. Mostly, it's just sitting around waiting for you to punch a button, or for someone to call the phone or send an SMS.

That's *Connected Standby.*

Windows implements Connected Standby, but only on tablets that support it. As of this writing, that means system-on-a-chip computers. Although that designation includes Windows RT computers (which I don't explicitly cover in this book), Intel and AMD are in the process of bringing out system-on-a-chip computers that will support Connected Standby.

The beauty of Connected Standby is that it allows you to keep your tablet running for an inordinate number of hours with just one charge — while keeping the whole fleet going just in case you get an important tweet or Messenger message.

Connected Standby is a worthwhile feature if you like to leave your tablet on, just in case somebody tries to get in touch.

That's why you'll find the Hibernate option buried deep inside one Legacy Control Panel dialog box (choose Hardware and Sound⇨Power Options⇨ Change Plan Settings⇨Change Advanced Power Settings), but in the rest of Windows, including all of the tiled part of Windows, your only options are to Shut Down, Sleep, or Restart.

Adjusting sleep settings

If you really, really want to micro-manage your machine, here's how you can change when your computer goes to sleep:

1. **Press the Windows key on the keyboard or tap the Windows button on your tablet to go to the Start screen.**

2. **Do one of the following:**

   If you have a keyboard, type **power**.

   If you don't have a keyboard, swipe from the right to bring up the Charms bar, tap the Search charm at the top, tap inside the Apps search box, and use the touch keyboard to type **power**.

3. **On the right, tap or click Settings.**

   Windows shows you all the Settings — primarily Legacy Control Panel applications — that contain *power*.

4. **On the left, tap or click Change When the Computer Sleeps.**

   The Control Panel's Edit Plan Settings dialog box, as shown in Figure 6-2, appears.

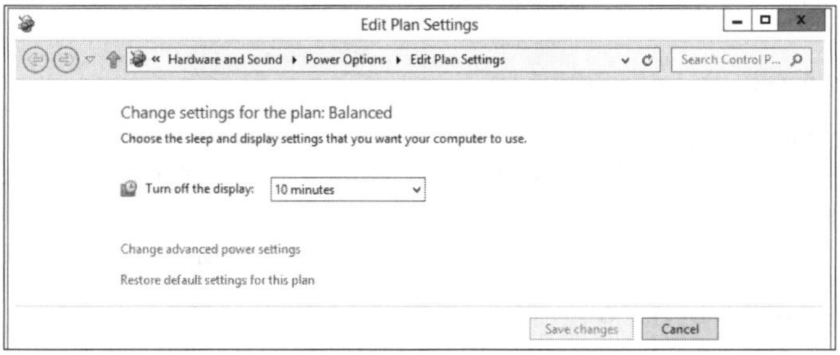

Figure 6-2:
The Edit
Plan
Settings
dialog box.

Edit Plan Settings	‒ ☐ ✕

« Hardware and Sound ▸ Power Options ▸ Edit Plan Settings ˅ ⟳   Search Control P... 🔎

Change settings for the plan: Balanced
Choose the sleep and display settings that you want your computer to use.

🖥 Turn off the display: [10 minutes ˅]

Change advanced power settings

Restore default settings for this plan

Save changes   Cancel

5. **Change the entries as necessary.**

   Keep in mind that sleep consumes almost no power, depending on the computer doing the sleeping.

6. **Tap or click Save Changes.**

   Your new settings take effect.

Turning Off Individual Apps

Windows has largely done away with the need for turning off the PC — it'll take care of itself and rejuvenate the whole machine when you wake it from sleep mode.

So, too, with killing individual apps. You don't need to do it.

Windows doesn't bother to turn off tiled apps unless they've been sitting idle for ten minutes or so. There's just no advantage to turning off a well-behaved app that isn't being used. The resting app isn't consuming any computing power, so why not let it be?

The answer: if you have a hundred apps going at the same time, you might want to kill a few.

Case in point: Sometimes my toddler son starts running many dozens of tiled apps. When that happens, on very rare occasion, one of the apps acts up — The Farmer in the Dell doesn't make any sound, or one of his books freezes. It's a bit disconcerting to have a duck dancing with no music or quacks. Elmo isn't quite the same.

When something strange happens to my tiled apps and a myriad of apps are all running at the same time, the obvious solution is to kill some apps.

Here's how to turn off a tiled app:

1. **Navigate to the app.**

   Finding the app can be challenging. You can use the app picker (swipe in from the left, or hover your mouse in the upper-left corner and slide down). You might also want to use the Alt+Tab CoolSwitch.

   Remember that these steps work only with tiled apps.

2. **Do one of the following:**

   If you use a touchscreen, slowly swipe down from the top, and continue swiping all the way to the bottom of the screen.

   The app turns into a smaller window and then drops "poof" off the bottom.

   If you have a mouse, hover your mouse at the very top of the screen — the cursor turns into a little hand — and then click and slowly drag down to the bottom of the screen.

   Similarly, the app turns into a smaller window and disappears at the bottom of the screen.

Book IV

Maximizing Tiled Windows 8 Apps

The 5th Wave   By Rich Tennant

UBER-USER DWAYNE GRANTZ CHALKS
UP BEFORE PUTTING WINDOWS 8
THROUGH ITS PACES.

Contents at a Glance

Chapter 1: The Tiled Internet Explorer

In This Chapter

✔ **Exploring the two faces of IE**

✔ **Navigating the tiled version of Internet Explorer**

✔ **Flipping to the desktop IE**

✔ **Sorting your settings**

✔ **Choosing your default browser**

✔ **Getting the lowdown on Flash and HTML5**

After spending many years playing catch-up ball with Firefox and, more recently, Google's Chrome browser, Internet Explorer has blazed new ground with the tiled, full–screen version of Internet Explorer. The desktop version of Internet Explorer mostly re-works the same-old same-old, with a few notable improvements. Tiled IE, on the other hand, changes the game entirely. New playing field. New goal posts. And a new chance to shed the accumulated garbage of the past decade or more.

I talk about the desktop version of IE in Book VI, Chapter 6. If you're just interested in running a browser on the desktop, that's where you should look. I refer to that chapter frequently in this chapter because tiled IE can't yet stand on its own two legs — some things can't be done in tiled IE; they have to be done in desktop IE.

Your web browser is the single most important piece of software you use every day — even more important than Windows. This chapter helps you get to know it well.

In this chapter I also talk very briefly about the tiled version of Google's Chrome browser. As of this writing, Chrome is going through some enormous changes — it's still a moving target. From what I've seen to date, I prefer Chrome to IE on the tiled side of the Windows fence.

The browser market is changing rapidly — the pace of change has never been faster. As always, I keep up with the changes, and help point you to new developments, on my website, www.askwoody.com.

Introducing the Two Faces of IE

Microsoft insists that there's just one Internet Explorer in Windows 8, but it has two faces — a traditional interface, similar to the one you've probably seen many times before; and a tiled style interface that fits right in with the tiled, full-screen Windows 8 experience, as shown in Figure 1-1.

In some respects, the difference is a matter of semantics, but I don't see the dichotomy that way. Tiled IE and desktop IE share a *rendering engine* — the piece of IE that pulls everything off a web page and turns it into something that you can read. The settings are shared with both faces of IE — that's a necessity because tiled IE has very few settings available for you to change. But as you'll see over and over again, the two browsers work very, very differently.

In general use, you'll probably gravitate to one version of IE or the other. If you spend most of your web time on a touch tablet, tiled IE most likely fits the way you work. If there's a mouse and keyboard available, I bet you end up with the desktop IE, more often than not.

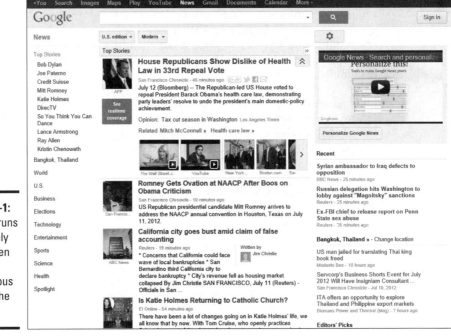

Figure 1-1:
Tiled IE runs absolutely full screen with no extraneous stuff in the way.

It isn't a clear-cut decision though. Each browser has advantages.

The desktop version of IE

+ **Puts the most important browsing information in your face.** You can tell, at a glance, what tabs you have open and which website you're on. Putting favorite sites on their own navigation bar is easy. You can pin sites to your Windows taskbar.

+ **Keeps all your IE settings.** Just tap or click the gear icon for tools, or the star icon to set Favorites. For example, setting the home page for desktop IE is easy; I talk about it in Book VI, Chapter 6. But you *can't* set a home page inside tiled IE.

+ **Lets you run all those plugins, programs, and toolbars you've always run.** These plugins include Microsoft Silverlight, Microsoft ActiveX, Adobe Flash, Adobe Reader (so you can see PDFs just as if they were web pages), LastPass or AI RoboForm for storing and managing passwords, Bing Weather, ad blockers, Java blockers, and — oh, lest I forget! — the Yahoo! Toolbar.

The tiled version of IE, on the other hand, has real advantages, too:

+ **The whole screen is devoted to the content of just one web page.** No extras — such as the address bar, tabs, or menus — are floating around. If you're running on a big screen, the extras probably aren't a big deal. But if you're on a little screen (such as a tablet), the extraneous stuff can take up a lot of valuable screen real estate.

+ **With very few exceptions, it doesn't allow plugins or add-in programs, extensions, toolbars, or anything that might gum up the works.** Yes, that means you can't use Microsoft Silverlight, Microsoft ActiveX controls, the Java Runtime Environment (which Microsoft used to distribute as part of Windows), the Internet Explorer Developer Toolbar or the Bing Toolbar, (er, Bing Bar), or the MSN Toolbar. In fact, you can't even use *Microsoft* add-ins, plugins, or toolbars, much less those from other companies like Ask or Yahoo!.

    In addition, tiled IE won't play Flash animations on any site unless that site has been vetted by Microsoft and added to a list of "allowed" sites. I have details about that whitelist in the last section in this chapter, "Exploring IE under the Hood: Flash and HTML5."

    By getting rid of all the junk (including many pieces of flotsam created, distributed and promoted by Microsoft), tiled IE is considerably faster, more uniform, easier on the battery, and much more secure than any other version of IE, ever.

Although tiled IE charges out into this brave new world of plugged plugins and kneecapped toolbars, the desktop version of IE just sails right along, as if nothing had happened.

To see what that means in the real world, compare Figure 1-2, which shows a speed test page on the DSLReports.com website as viewed in tiled IE 10, to Figure 1-3, which shows precisely the same page viewed in the desktop version of IE 10.

For now, just know that Flash is a likely culprit if your favorite sites aren't displaying in tiled IE the way you expect. As you explore the tiled IE interface in this chapter, I show you how to flip to desktop IE for help.

Figure 1-2:
The DSLReports speed test page as viewed in tiled IE 10 (with Flash disabled).

Figure 1-3:
The same DSLReports speed test page as viewed from the desktop version of IE 10 (with Flash enabled).

Navigating the Tiled Internet Explorer

When you click the Internet Explorer tile on the Start screen, tiled Internet Explorer usually appears without any navigational aids (refer to Figure 1-1). But a swipe from the top or bottom, or a right-click just about anywhere, brings up navigational aids in panes at the top and bottom, as shown in Figure 1-4. In this section, you figure out how to navigate with the address bar and other basic tools at the bottom. After you visit a few sites, check out how to move around with the recently visited sites at the top.

Open web pages
(similar to tabs)

Open In Private tab   Open a new tab

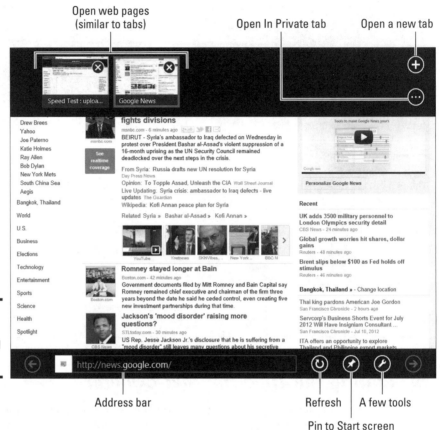

Figure 1-4:
Tiled IE's
navigational
aids.

Address bar

Refresh   A few tools

Pin to Start screen

Surfing with the address bar and navigation buttons

At the bottom of the navigation panel, you see:

✦ **Backward and forward buttons,** which work much like the analogous buttons in IE on the desktop side of the fence.

✦ **The address bar,** which serves multiple purposes. You can type an address here, and IE travels to the indicated location. You can use the common shortcuts (for example, type **dummies**, press Ctrl+Enter, and IE goes to `http://www.dummies.com`) to reduce the amount of typing. The address bar in tiled IE is also your ticket to the following:

• *Searching your browsing history and favorites:* When you type any word(s) into the address bar, tiled IE searches for it in your browsing history and in your desktop IE favorites. Bizarrely, this is the only place in tiled IE where you can access your favorites. I talk about favorites in Book VI, Chapter 6.

- *Searching the web:* If you type a word(s) in the address bar and press Enter, tiled IE uses the default search engine to look up what you've typed. It performs precisely the same way as bringing up the Search charm (swipe from the right or hover in the upper-right corner) and typing the search terms in the search box.

✦ **The circular-arrow Refresh button,** which you tap or click to have IE reload the screen.

I don't know of any way to force a cache reset in tiled IE — no equivalent to the Ctrl+F5 in the other version of IE.

✦ **The Pin to Start menu button,** which you tap or click and IE offers to put a shortcut to the current website on your Start screen, as shown in Figure 1-5.

Figure 1-5: Add a tile for the current web page to the Start screen.

✦ **A very stunted Page Tools icon,** with only three entries.

- *The Get App for This Site option* doesn't seem to work.

- *Find on Page* is the only way I know (besides pressing Ctrl+F) to perform a search on the contents of the current page.

- *View on the Desktop* is a very helpful shortcut that takes the current web page and displays it inside the desktop IE version. If you can't get a page to display properly, try choosing this entry to see whether the big IE can handle it correctly. More details in the section, "Flipping to the desktop IE" later in this chapter.

Worth repeating: Bringing up the Search charm does *not* search the contents of the current page. It goes out to your search engine and looks for other web pages. If you want to look for text on the current page, you can use Ctrl+F. Or you can swipe to bring up the navigation pane and on the lower pane, tap or click the wrench icon; then choose Find on Page.

Tapping Tiled IE's recently visited sites

When you swipe from the top or bottom or right-click the tiled IE interface, at the top, you see up to ten thumbnails of the pages you most recently visited: They're roughly analogous to tabs in other browsers. Tap or click a thumbnail, and tiled IE dutifully flips over to the tapped page.

The pane on the top only holds ten thumbnails — a maximum of ten tabs. If you venture to an eleventh page, tiled IE unceremoniously dumps one of the thumbnails. There doesn't appear to be any logic to which one gets dumped.

If you want to switch to a different recently visited site, you have to drag from the top or bottom of the tiled IE screen to bring up the thumbnail list again.

The app switcher, which slides out from the left side of the screen, doesn't enable you to switch among the website thumbnails. When you drag from the left side of the screen to access the switcher, Windows treats IE as one, single app, and has only one entry in the app switcher (on the left side of the screen) for IE.

Here are a few more tricks to navigating around using the thumbnails:

✦ **Delete a thumbnail:** If you tap or click a thumbnail's X, the thumbnail goes away — basically analogous to removing the tab. Close all the thumbnails, and you end up with a solitary blank page.

✦ **Open a new window:** If you tap or click the + sign on the upper pane in the upper-right corner (see Figure 1-4), tiled IE opens a new tab (er, window) and brings up a pane on the bottom that invites you to choose one of your most frequently visited sites, or a pinned site, as shown in Figure 1-6. In this case, a *pinned* site is one pinned to the Start screen by tiled IE only. (You can also pin sites to the taskbar, as I explain in Book VI, Chapter 2, but you won't see websites pinned to the desktop taskbar here.)

If you tap or click inside the address bar, tiled IE brings up tiles for sites that you visit frequently, as shown in Figure 1-6.

✦ **Browse in InPrivate mode:** As I describe in Book VI, Chapter 6, *InPrivate mode* lets you surf to web sites without leaving any telltale traces on your PC — no cookies, no history, and no temporary files. To move into InPrivate mode, tap or click the Tab Tools button — the one with the three dots — to start a new InPrivate browsing session. The Tab Tools button also enables you to get rid of all the tabs except the current one.

InPrivate in tiled IE works just like InPrivate in the desktop version of IE — see Book VI, Chapter 6. You can tell that you're in an InPrivate tab because *InPrivate* appears against a blue background both in the tab list at the top, and to the left of the address in the navigation pane at the bottom.

Figure 1-6:
Tiled IE
invites you
to type
a site's
address, or
choose from
frequently
visited or
pinned sites.

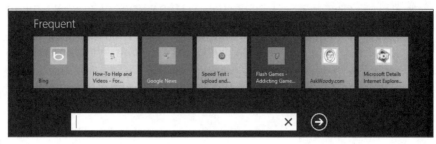

Navigating with Flip Ahead

Flip Ahead is an Internet Explorer option that works in tiled IE and the desktop version. It's designed primarily to give you a consistent way to "flip ahead" in websites with multiple pages. For example, if you're reading a long newspaper blog, it might be broken into many pages. Frequently, product reviews and web-based slide shows have multiple pages that you flip through, one by one.

With Flip Ahead, you can slide your finger on the page, much as you would flip the pages of an electronic book, to advance from one page to the next. It's not exactly earth shattering, but if you're navigating with your fingers and you don't want to hunt around for Next buttons, it's a reasonably good — and accurate — approach.

The pages aren't preloaded, so Flip Ahead doesn't speed up your browsing. You still have to wait for pages to load, while staring at a screen that says Next page. But Flip Ahead does give you one simple way to move from page to page.

The downside? You agree to send Microsoft data on the pages you view, so it can improve the feature.

Flipping to the desktop IE

If you use tiled IE and bump into a site that just doesn't look right, chances are at least 50/50 that Flash has been disabled for the site. Just compare Figures 1-2 and 1-3, and you see what I mean.

**Book IV
Chapter 1**

The Tiled Internet
Explorer

Fortunately you can easily check whether you're missing something, uh, by design — just switch to the desktop version of Internet Explorer. Here's how:

✦ **If you're running on thumbs,** swipe from the top or bottom, and in the bottom navigation pane, tap Page Tools⇨View on the Desktop.

✦ **If you have a mouse,** right-click in the middle of the tiled IE screen, and in the bottom navigation pane, choose Page Tools⇨View on the Desktop.

In either case, you're flipped over to the desktop, IE pops up — actually, Windows starts a new instance of IE — the web address you're currently viewing gets filled in, and in a fraction of a second (because the page is already downloaded), you get a second opinion on the site's appearance.

Sharing and Printing Web Pages

The Charms bar is your ticket to sharing and printing web pages in tiled IE:

✦ **The Share charm** lets you send an e-mail to one of the people on your People list, with a synopsis of the website, a picture, and a link, like the one shown in Figure 1-7.

Figure 1-7: Share a website through an e-mail, and this is what the recipient sees.

If you have a Twitter or Facebook account linked to your Windows login account, Share also lets you send a tweet about a particular website, or post a link on your Facebook Wall.

✦ **The Devices charm** enables you to print a copy of the web page.

    The print connection doesn't work very well on some printers: You end up with chopped-off pages, or many basically blank pages.

Sorting Out Your Settings

Legacy Internet Explorer has many, many settings that affect tiled IE, but you can't access them from tiled IE. Something as simple as the tiled IE home page can't be set in tiled IE — but it can be set over on the desktop. In tiled IE, you get the Settings charm, and that's pretty much it. This section explains how the charm settings work and points you to a few settings in desktop IE that are important to the way tiled IE works.

Charming tiled IE settings

The Settings charm brings up a few options, as shown in Figure 1-8. Here's how they work:

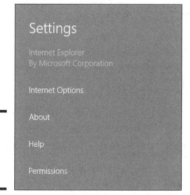

Figure 1-8:
The tiled
IE Settings
charm.

  ✦ **Internet Options** lets you delete your browsing history, turns on/off reporting your physical location to websites, applies a zoom to text on all pages, and lets you turn on/off the Flip Ahead feature (see the earlier section, "Navigating with Flip Ahead"). Also, if IE isn't correctly interpreting the language on the page you're viewing, you can manually switch encoding, so Burmese, for example, looks like Burmese instead of a bunch of nonsense boxy characters.

  ✦ **About** tells you the current version number of IE.

✦ **Help** flips you to a website with answers to frequently asked questions about IE.

✦ **Permissions** lets you determine whether IE can show toaster sliding notifications on the Start screen and desktop (see Book VI, Chapter 2).

Changing your default search engine

As far as I can tell, there's no easy way to change the default search engine. But there is a hard way, at least as of this writing. Don't blame me if Microsoft changes it. If you want to switch to using Google as your default search engine, follow these steps:

1. **Go to** `http://iegallery.com/en-US/Addons/Details/813` **(using either version of IE) and tap or click the Add to Internet Explorer button.**

That's the shortcut to the Google search engine add-on for Internet Explorer.

2. **Select the Make This My Default Search Provider check box.**

Settings and whitelists for Adobe/Flash

Only specific websites are allowed to play their Flash animations inside tiled IE. To make sure you can see as many Flash sites as possible, make sure Windows updates its *whitelist,* or the list of allowed websites, for Adobe Flash. Here's how:

1. **Go to** `http://get.adobe.com/flashplayer` **and then flip Internet Explorer to the desktop.**

See the earlier section, "Flipping to the desktop IE" for details.

2a. **If you have a keyboard, press the Alt key on your keyboard to bring up the IE menu/command bar.**

2b. **If you don't have a keyboard, tap and hold or click a blank part of the top of the IE window, and then select Command Bar.**

3. **Tap or choose Tools⇨Compatibility View Settings.**

The Compatibility View Settings dialog box appears, as shown in Figure 1-9.

4. **Make sure the Download Updated Compatibility Lists from Microsoft check box is selected. Then click Close.**

As Adobe mentions, this ensures your tiled IE Flash whitelist is updated regularly.

Figure 1-9:
Make
sure IE's
getting its
compatibility
view (read:
Flash
whitelist)
updates.

Managing passwords

I don't use tiled IE on a daily basis, specifically because it doesn't accept plugins. In particular, I'm not sure I could survive without LastPass or RoboForm (see Book IX, Chapter 4) to keep all my site passwords sorted. Perhaps someday LastPass or RoboForm will figure out a way to hook into tiled IE, but at this point, the prognosis is dismal.

If you need even *one* plugin, tiled IE is out for anything except casual browsing.

An alternative to LastPass is the Microsoft Credential Manager, which Microsoft has been improving for the past ten years or so. Microsoft has a series of tutorials on Credential Manager, directed at Windows 7 users, starting at `http://windows.microsoft.com/en-US/windows7/What-is-Credential-Manager`. If you really want to cut the cord and go with tiled IE, that's your only choice for password management.

Choosing and Setting a Default Browser

As this book goes to press, plans for a Windows 8 version Firefox that works on both the traditional desktop and the tiled side of Win8 were still shrouded in secrecy, but the tiled version of Google Chrome is out, and I think it's a winner. See the sidebar "Why I prefer tiled Chrome over tiled IE."

Don't take this chapter's coverage of tiled IE, exclusively, as an endorsement of IE over Firefox and Google. It isn't. It's an in-depth discussion of the best ways to use tiled IE, not a comparative review.

Why I prefer tiled Chrome over tiled IE

Google is infamous for changing its browsers rapidly, so anything I write about Chrome now may change in a month or two. But I've seen Google's beta test version of the Chrome browser for the tiled side of Windows 8, and I'm a believer.

In its current form, tiled Chrome breaks all the Microsoft tiled design rules: There are tabs on the top of the screen, just where the browser gods intended, as well as an address bar and icons for all the things you normally want to do with a browser. Google doesn't force you to run over to the desktop version of Chrome to set a home page, or change your default search engine, as is the case with IE. In Chrome, it's all right there and easily accessible from the tiled side of the Windows fence.

Chrome also runs Flash on any site. There's no IE-style whitelist. Although I may change my tune if tiled Chrome's Flash starts sprouting security problems, from what I can tell right now, it's darn near cracker-proof.

For anyone who's ever used a browser — any browser, on any computer — tiled Chrome works the way you would expect. I can't say the same for tiled IE's swipe-here, click-there, and flip-over if you hit a problem approach. More than that, Chrome doesn't have those arbitrary tiled IE restrictions: Chrome lets you have more than ten tabs, your bookmarks are available on the tiled side, and it's easy to change search engines.

I do all my tiled browsing in Chrome and most of my desktop browsing in Chrome, as well. Most of the Internet screen shots you see in this book were done with Chrome. There's a reason why.

Firefox may well come out with a compelling competitor as well. Stay tuned.

Setting the default Windows browser

Back in the Halcyon days of Windows, setting a default browser meant you chose among Internet Explorer, Chrome, or Firefox (or possibly Opera or Safari, and so on) and made that browser your default.

Life isn't so simple now. A behind-the-scenes interdependency between the tiled browser and the desktop browser gets in the way of having complete freedom of browser choice. Until somebody figures out how to sever the ties, the restrictions work like this:

✦ You can choose any browser — Internet Explorer, Chrome, Firefox, probably others — as your Windows default browser. The default browser behaves on the desktop precisely the way you would expect (details in Book VII, Chapter 1).

✦ After you choose a Windows default browser, the tiled version of that browser is *the only browser* allowed to run on the tiled side of Windows 8.

So, for example, if you choose Chrome as your default browser, Internet Explorer won't run at all on the tiled side — you can only use Chrome for browsing on the tiled side of the fence. If you choose IE as your default, IE runs on both the old-fashioned desktop and the tiled part of Win8, and Chrome will run on the desktop, but Chrome won't work as a tiled app.

Setting the default IE browser

As if setting a default Windows browser weren't complicated enough, Internet Explorer gives you yet another option. If IE is your default Windows browser, you can also choose which *flavor* of the browser should be the default: the tiled version, or the desktop version.

If you don't change the default, here's what happens:

✦ When you tap or click a link in a Windows 8 Mail message, or inside one of the other tiled apps, the site appears inside the tiled version of IE.

✦ When you tap or click a tile on the Start screen, the site opens in whichever browser you used to create the tile.

✦ When you tap or click a link inside an Outlook or Windows Live Mail message, or inside any other legacy program, the site appears inside the desktop version of IE.

No matter what you do, if you tap or click a link inside tiled IE, you get a new page inside tiled IE, and the same is true for the desktop version.

If you don't like those defaults, you can change them. Here's how:

1. **Fire up the desktop version of IE.**

   If you're in tiled IE, swipe from the bottom, tap the wrench icon, and then tap View on the Desktop.

2. **Inside desktop IE, tap or click the gear icon in the upper-right corner, and then tap or click the Programs tab.**

   The Internet Properties dialog box appears, as shown in Figure 1-10.

3. **In the drop-down box at the top, choose either Always in Internet Explorer or Always in Internet Explorer on the Desktop:**

   • *Let Internet Explorer Decide:* This is the default behavior, described earlier.

   • *Always in Internet Explorer:* Forces all links to open in the tiled version of IE, even if they come from an Office app on the desktop.

   • *Always in Internet Explorer on the Desktop:* This has the opposite effect.

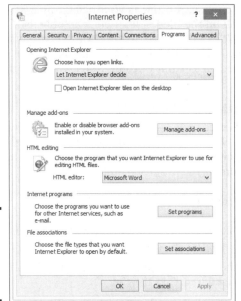

Figure 1-10:
Change IE's
default web
browser
here.

4. **If you want all of the tiles on the Start screen with links to IE to use the desktop version of IE, select the box marked Open Internet Explorer Tiles on the Desktop.**

5. **Tap or click OK.**

   Your new choice takes effect immediately.

Exploring IE under the Hood: Flash and HTML5

Around the time Windows 7 shipped in 2009, almost all the "moving" stuff you saw on web pages was done with *Flash* — a product originally released in 1996 by Macromedia, which was bought by Adobe in 2005. Adobe gives away the Flash Player, but charges developers for the tools necessary to build Flash applications.

By all estimates, several billion Flash-enabled devices are in use around the world. Yes, that means more computers are running Flash *than there are PCs* in the world. Flash runs on all sorts of devices — just about everything except the iPhone and iPad. Apple nixed Flash support in those devices because Flash drains devices' battery life and poses security risks. Adobe Flash, along with Adobe Reader, have become the two largest sources of PC infections in recent years.

HTML5 is different. It isn't a proprietary product, like Flash. HTML5 is a set of specifications being put together by an international committee.

Programmers can use the specifications instead of Flash to build things on web pages that move. Actually that's a bit of an understatement, somewhat akin to saying that a Ferrari can get you to the office in the morning. You get the idea.

The hitch is that the HTML5 committee is moving slowly, so browser manufacturers add support for new HTML5 features as they can. But no browser can support all the HTML5 yet because the details about how certain features work aren't nailed down yet.

Both the tiled version of IE and desktop IE support HTML5 equally well — they share the same "rendering engine" which converts HTML5 commands into drawings on the screen. A great deal of debate is ongoing about whether IE, Chrome, Firefox, or Safari does a better job of handling HTML5.

The net result: Flash is on its way out, and HTML5 is on its way in. Although some industry observers may disagree with that simplistic assessment, I think that's how the industry will go. This will take several years of transition, where some web pages still use Flash. But sooner or later, just about every web page with animation will move to HTML5 and a sister technology known inscrutably as H.264 format.

Here's why that's important to you: For the near term, if you want to be able to see moving things on some web pages, you're going to need Flash. Most of the major websites have already adjusted — YouTube, for example, can tell if you don't have Flash and will almost always switch to H.264 format, so you can see your videos. But there are still some hold-outs, a few sites where you really need Flash to see everything.

The iPad doesn't have Flash. The iPhone doesn't have Flash. But Windows 8's tiled Internet Explorer does. Sometimes.

Flash doesn't always work in Internet Explorer, because tiled Internet Explorer doesn't accept plugins. The Flash Player is a plugin. But tiled Internet Explorer runs Flash. How can that be?

Shortly before Microsoft shipped Windows 8, the 'Softies announced that it had reached an agreement with Adobe, wherein Flash would be built into, and become part of, Internet Explorer.

In one respect, that's not really a big deal — Google's Chrome has had Flash Player capabilities built into the browser for years. But in other respects, it's a very big deal:

✦ Tiled IE can, at least in theory, play Flash videos, a feature that's forbidden to the iPad. That extends the useful life of Flash, and takes some of the heat off web designers for converting quickly to HTML5.

✦ Because the Flash player is actually built into Internet Explorer, Microsoft can (at least in theory) program a cage around it to increase security, decrease power consumption, and better behave itself.

✦ Surprisingly, Microsoft doesn't have access to, or control over, the Flash program code. Adobe updates the Flash Player, and Microsoft distributes those updates through its usual Windows Update mechanism.

The desktop version of IE runs Flash, no problem. But Microsoft's more circumspect with tiled IE. MS allows only specific websites to play their Flash animations inside tiled IE. That's why you can see Flash on some sites, and not on others.

Microsoft maintains a list of blessed sites — the so-called IE Compatibility View list — on the web at `http://iecvlist.microsoft.com/ie10/201205/iecompatviewlist.xml`. If you ever wonder why Flash won't play when you're using tiled IE on a specific site, you can check that list to see whether the site's been added.

A website set up at `www.askwoody.com/testdntflash` tests your browser's ability to show Flash, and checks for the Do Not Track flag, which I describe in Book VI, Chapter 6. (See Figure 1-11.) If you're curious about how tiled IE handles Flash, that's a good place to start.

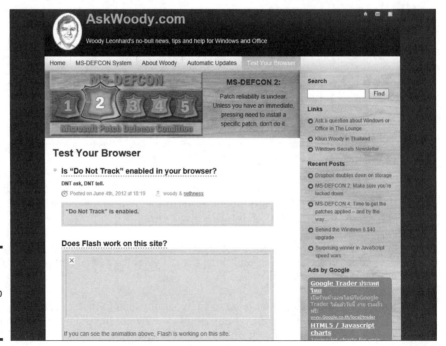

Figure 1-11:
Test tiled
IE's ability to
show Flash
animations.

And for those sites that use other plugin technologies? The writing's on the wall. As late as 2011, Microsoft promoted Silverlight as its great new web animation alternative. Now, Microsoft doesn't support Silverlight in tiled IE. Boom. Silverlight programmers are livid. Microsoft raised a whole generation of programmers on ActiveX plugins. Those are going away in tiled IE, too. Just be happy you aren't an ActiveX programmer.

Chapter 2: Windows 8 Mail, People, and Calendar Apps

In This Chapter

✔ **How the new Win8 communication apps hang together**

✔ **Choosing a Mail, Contacts, and Calendar app**

✔ **Navigating Win8's tiled Mail**

✔ **Placing all your contacts in Win8 People**

✔ **Avoiding duplicates and other Win8 Calendar problems**

*T*he Windows communication apps — Mail, Calendar, People, and to a lesser extent, Messaging — form the core of Microsoft's Windows 8 tiled app assault.

On the one hand, they're free — or, I should say, no additional cost when you buy a Windows computer. So you can't really expect too much out of them. On the other hand, they're competing against other free communication apps — I won't mention the iPad by name — so there's a lot of pressure to deliver solid apps that people will want to use.

The communication apps in Win8 don't quite deliver the breadth and depth of features and ease of use that will draw people to using them — at least as this book goes to press. However, by necessity, this chapter is a snapshot in time. You can bet that some of the features in Mail will have improved by the time you read this, simply because Mail at this point is so incapable it's embarrassing.

Improvements to the apps will arrive via the app update feature built into Windows 8. Because of the way Windows is built, Microsoft can update the communication apps — indeed, any of the Win8 apps — with minimal fuss: Microsoft simply posts the update to the Windows Store. You go to the Store, perhaps drawn by the number on the Store tile that tells you updates are available. A few minutes later, you have a new version of the Mail app.

In this chapter, I talk about the three Windows 8 communication apps that are joined at the hip and elbow: Mail for handling your e-mail; People for consolidating your contacts; and Calendar for bringing together any calendars you may have on various services.

I discuss the tiled Windows 8 Messaging app in Book IV, Chapter 5 because Messaging is rapidly being absorbed into all sorts of Microsoft products — Mail, Hotmail/Outlook.com, and the vestiges of the old Windows Live line — and it's rapidly going to be replaced, merged, or somehow adapted to peacefully coexist with Microsoft Skype. Messaging is a communications horse of an entirely different color.

Choosing a Mail/Contacts/Calendar app

Life is full of difficult choices, and I swear Microsoft sits behind about half of them. For me, anyway.

Before you jump into the communication wallow, think about how you want to handle your mail, contacts, and calendar.

Comparing e-mail programs

Mail has its benefits, but it may not best suit your needs.

Complicating the situation: Mail isn't an either/or choice. For example, you can set up Hotmail/Outlook.com or Gmail accounts, and then use either Mail to work with the accounts or the Internet-based interfaces at `www.hotmail.com` and `www.gmail.com`. In fact, you can jump back and forth between working online at the sites, and working on your Windows computer.

Mail functions as a gathering point: It pulls in mail from Hotmail/Outlook.com, for example, and sends out mail through Hotmail/Outlook.com. It pulls in and sends out mail through Gmail. But when it's working right, Mail doesn't destroy the mail: All your messages are still sitting there waiting for you in Hotmail/Outlook.com or Gmail. Although there are some subtleties, in most cases, you can use Mail in the morning, switch over to Gmail or Hotmail/Outlook.com when you get to the office, and go back to Mail when you get home — and never miss a thing.

As currently configured, Mail can pull in mail from Hotmail/Outlook.com, Gmail, or Exchange Server (a typical situation at a large office) as well as IMAP (a method supported by some Internet service providers). It seems likely that Mail will soon add support for regular e-mail accounts (so-called POP3 e-mail) and Yahoo! Mail — possibly by the time you read this.

That's the short story. Permit me to throw some complicating factors at you.

You can add your Hotmail/Outlook.com account to Gmail, or add your Gmail account to Hotmail/Outlook.com. In fact, you can add just about any e-mail account to either Hotmail/Outlook.com or Gmail. If you're thinking about moving to Mail just because it can pull in mail from multiple accounts, realize that Gmail (see Book X, Chapter 3) and Hotmail/Outlook.com (see Book X, Chapter 4) can do the same thing.

The main benefit to using Mail, over Hotmail/Outlook.com or Gmail, is that Mail stores your most recent messages on your computer. If you can't get to the Internet, you can't download new messages or send responses, but at least you can look at your most recent messages.

Some people prefer the Mail interface over Gmail or Hotmail/Outlook.com. Personally, I prefer Gmail, but decide for yourself. *De gustibus* and all that. Moreover, the interfaces change all the time, so if you haven't looked in the last year or so, it'd be worth the effort to fire up your web browser and have a look-see.

Hotmail/Outlook.com and Gmail are superior to Mail in these respects:

✦ Hotmail/Outlook.com and Gmail have all your mail, all the time. If you look for something old, you may or may not find it with Mail — by default, Mail only holds your mail from the past two weeks, and it doesn't automatically reach out to Hotmail/Outlook.com or Gmail to run searches.

✦ Gmail and Hotmail/Outlook.com pack a lot more information on the screen. Although Mail has been tuned for touch, with big blocks set aside to make an all-thumbs approach feasible and lots of white space, Hotmail/Outlook.com and Gmail are still much more mouse-friendly.

But wait! I've only looked at Mail, Hotmail/Outlook.com, and Gmail. Many, many more options are in the mail game. To-wit:

✦ **Microsoft Outlook:** Bundled with Office since pterodactyls powered PCs, Outlook has an enormous number of options — many of them confusing, most of them never used — but it's also the only app that can handle hundreds of thousands of messages. Or at least, that's what I keep telling myself. Outlook's the Rolls Royce of the e-mail biz, with all the positive and negative connotations.

   In fact, among the many, many different versions of Outlook, each has its own foibles. Many people settled on Outlook 2007 because that's the last version without the Office Ribbon.

✦ **The Outlook Web App:** It isn't really Outlook, but Microsoft marketing wants you to believe that it is. It's part of Exchange Server (or Office 365), so companies with big iron can let their employees access their mail without using Outlook.

✦ **Windows Live Mail:** It's still alive and kicking, although it's going through a name change. For people who don't want to jump into the tiled side of Windows 8 with both feet (and fingers) — particularly those who feel more comfortable working with a mouse and an information-dense screen — it's a respectable, free alternative, and it works great with Windows 8. See Book VI, Chapter 5.

✦ **Free, open source, inexpensive alternatives:** These include Mozilla Thunderbird, SeaMonkey, Eudora, and many more that have enthusiastic fan bases.

✦ **Your Internet service provider (ISP):** It may well have its own e-mail package. My experience with ISP-provided free e-mail hasn't been very positive, but the service can come in very handy if I'm on the road and need to take a peek. mail2web (`www.mail2web.com`) also lets you get into just about any mailbox, from just about anywhere — if you know the password.

The iPad Mail app has many of the problems that Mail exhibits, but it has a host of advantages, including most notably, the ability to merge inboxes, so you don't have to flip between accounts to read all your incoming messages. Truth be told, I use the iPad Mail app when I'm on the road and don't expect anything important to arrive by e-mail. Most of the time, though, I'm still stuck on and in Outlook.

. . . and that's just the Mail app!

Comparing calendar apps

Calendars can also be handled by a bewildering array of packages and sites. Among the hundreds of competing Calendar apps, each has a unique twist. The highlights:

✦ **Google Calendar** is highly regarded for being powerful and easy to use. It's also reasonably well integrated into the other Google Apps, er, Google Drive, although you can use it — and share calendars with other people — without setting foot in any other Google app. See Book X, Chapter 3 for details. (`http://calendar.google.com`)

✦ **Hotmail/Outlook.com Calendar**, on the other hand, lives inside Hotmail/Outlook.com. It's reasonably powerful and integrated, and you can share the calendar with your contacts or other people.

✦ **Outlook** also does calendars, ten ways from Tuesday, with so many options it'll bring a tear to your eye. Or maybe that tear is from tearing out your hair.

If you want to schedule one conference room in an office with a hundred people, all of whom use Outlook, the Outlook Calendar is definitely the way to go. If you want to keep track of your flight departure times, Aunt Martha's birthday, and the kids' football games, any of the Calendar apps will work fine.

The biggest problem with the Windows 8 Calendar? It doesn't sync with Outlook. A friend of mine runs Google Calendar Sync on his Windows 8 PC, to sync his Outlook calendar with his Google Calendar. From there, Calendar syncs with Google Calendar.

Checking out contact apps

Finally, the Contact managers, er, People programs. Windows has had Contact managers for so long I can't even remember when I saw the first one. The web is packed with Contact managers. If you have a Skype account, you have contacts. If you have a mobile phone, you have contacts. If you run any Messenger, you have contacts. Facebook. Pinterest. LinkedIn. Google+. And on and on — they all have contact lists, and many of them will eagerly import contacts from other sources. So, too, with the Windows 8 People app.

The biggest downside to the People app? It doesn't sync with Outlook.

Choosing the right package

So how do you choose a Mail/Contacts (People)/Calendar program? Tough question, but let me give you a few hints:

+ The Win8 communication apps — Mail, Calendar, and People — work well enough if your demands aren't great.

   But if you have an iPad, consider using it instead. Until Microsoft improves its basic tiled apps, the iPad clearly offers superior Mail handling, and arguably better Contacts and Calendar.

+ Online services — specifically Hotmail/Outlook.com and Gmail — have many more usable features than either Win8 Mail or iPad Mail. As long as you can rely on your Internet connection, look at both of them before settling on a specific Mail/Contacts/Calendar program.

   Realize, though, that if you have your own e-mail domain name (such as, woody@askwoody.com), getting it flipped over to Gmail isn't easy. If you use a provider's domain name (such as littlenel12345@comcast.com), you have to change your e-mail address.

   A good compromise is to use either Gmail or Hotmail/Outlook.com most of the time, but hook up either iPad Mail or Win8 Mail (or both!) to the

Gmail or Hotmail/Outlook.com account, so you can grab your iPad when you're headed out the door.

✦ If you don't feel comfortable storing your mail in the cloud, or you don't want to go through the hassle of converting your e-mail account, try Windows Live Mail (see Book VI, Chapter 5).

✦ Ancient dinosaurs (present company included) will probably keep using Outlook until its bits rot away. It's ponderous and painful, the embodiment of 19th century dentist's office chic. But it works.

Sometimes, better the devil ye ken.

Drilling Down on Windows 8 Mail

Tap or click the Start menu's Mail tile, and you see the Mail screen. This section walks you through the different parts of this screen, explains how to add an e-mail account to Mail, and how to search your e-mail. At the end of this section, I talk about the features Mail is missing as this book goes to press but that might appear as Microsoft releases updates for the Mail app.

Microsoft allows you to use Mail, Calendar, People, and Messaging if you supply a Microsoft account. Full stop. If you don't have a Microsoft account and you want to use one of those apps, follow the steps on the screen and see the instructions in Book II, Chapter 4 to get one. If you used a Local account to sign in to Windows (see Book II, Chapter 4) — one that isn't known to Microsoft — you're prompted to provide a Microsoft account, as shown in Figure 2-1.

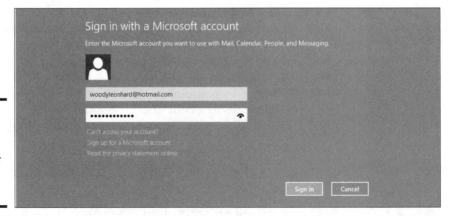

Figure 2-1:
Provide a
Microsoft
account, or
you won't
get in.

Navigating the Windows 8 Mail screen

If you signed in to Windows or the Mail app with a Microsoft account that's also a Hotmail/Outlook.com ID (@hotmail.com or @live.com or @outlook. com), Mail reaches out to your Hotmail/Outlook.com account and pulls the last two weeks' worth of messages. The result is something like that shown in Figure 2-2.

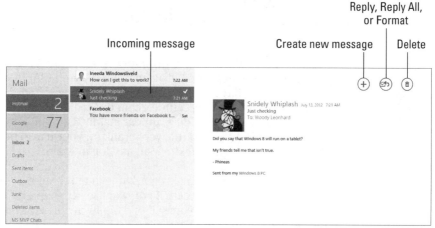

Incoming message   Create new message   Reply, Reply All, or Format   Delete

Figure 2-2:
Windows 8
Mail pulls
your recent
Hotmail/
Outlook.com
messages
and gets
you started.

If you only see two columns, instead of the standard three, check your screen resolution. If the resolution is less than 1366 x 768, you see only two columns, and navigating the Mail maze becomes much more of a slide-and-click hassle.

Mail's standard layout takes three columns:

✦ The left column lists your accounts on top, and the folders associated with the selected account below. In Figure 2-2, I have two accounts, a Hotmail/Outlook.com account and a Gmail account. Because the Hotmail/Outlook.com account is selected, the Inbox, Drafts, Sent Items, Outbox, Junk, Deleted Items and MS MVP Chats folders are all the ones associated with the Hotmail/Outlook.com account. If I tap or click the Gmail account, the contents of the lower folders change to reflect my Gmail account.

✦ The middle column lists all the messages in the selected folder. If you don't specifically select a folder, Mail selects the Inbox for you.

✦ The right column shows you the selected message and has the buttons that let you quickly react to the message.

If you swipe from the bottom or top, or right-click in the body of Mail, the additional tools appear (see Figure 2-3).

**Book IV
Chapter 2**

Windows 8 Mail,
People, and
Calendar Apps

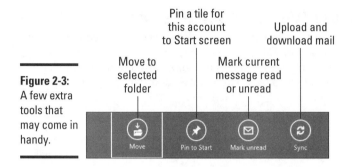

Pin a tile for
this account
to Start screen

Upload and
download mail

Move to
selected
folder

Mark current
message read
or unread

Figure 2-3:
A few extra
tools that
may come in
handy.

If you noticed the Move icon, you probably asked yourself, "How do I create a new folder to move stuff into?" The answer: You don't. At least, as of this writing, Mail doesn't have any capability for adding new folders. You can create new folders in Hotmail/Outlook.com or Gmail (or even in Outlook using Exchange) and those folders appear inside Mail. But in order to get new folders, you have to go to the web, crank up your e-mail program, add the folders, and then come back to Mail and log in again.

The Pin to Start icon is also quite remarkable in that it allows you to pin a Mail account to the Start screen. If you want to bring up Mail with that account pre-selected (saving yourself one tap in the process), you can place a tile for the account on your Start screen.

Adding a new account

As I write this, Mail can accept only four kinds of accounts: IMAP (which is a fairly common "normal" mail account type), Hotmail/Outlook.com, Gmail, and Exchange Server. It doesn't connect to POP3 accounts, which are the most common ones on the Internet. On the bright side, you can add any number of different Hotmail/Outlook.com, Gmail, or Exchange Server accounts.

Chances are very good that, by the time you read this, you will also be able to add standard POP3 or IMAP mail accounts. Yahoo! Mail might get a nod, too. The basic procedures for adding a standard e-mail account parallel the methods for Hotmail/Outlook.com and Gmail.

To add a new account:

1. **From the Mail app, swipe from the right edge of the screen or hover your mouse in the upper-right corner, and choose the Settings charm.**

2. **Tap or click Accounts; then tap or click Add an Account.**

    The Add an Account list appears, as shown in Figure 2-4.

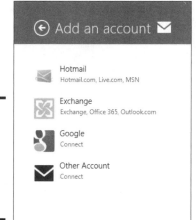

Figure 2-4:
Add a new
e-mail
account
to the tiled
Windows 8
Mail app.

3. **Tap or click the account type that you want to add.**

The Other Account entry is for adding e-mail accounts that can be accessed using IMAP. If in doubt, contact your e-mail provider to see if they support IMAP.

When you add an e-mail account, you're also adding the contacts from that account, which go in your People app, and the calendar(s) attached to that account, which go in the Calendar app. It's an all-or-nothing proposition.

4. **Enter your e-mail ID, password, and any ancillary information that may be required. Tap or click Connect.**

Mail is probably smart enough to look up or find any other information it needs, but you might have to provide something from your e-mail provider.

When Mail comes back, your new account appears on the left.

If you want to change the details about your account — in particular, if you don't particularly want to see the name Hotmail, Outlook, or Gmail as an account name — bring up the Settings charm, click or tap Accounts, and then tap or click the account you wish to change. The Account Details pane appears, as shown in Figure 2-5. In the top box, you can type a name that will appear in the first column of the Mail main page. You can also choose when to download new messages and how far back you want the messages to go.

Book IV
Chapter 2

Windows 8 Mail,
People, and
Calendar Apps

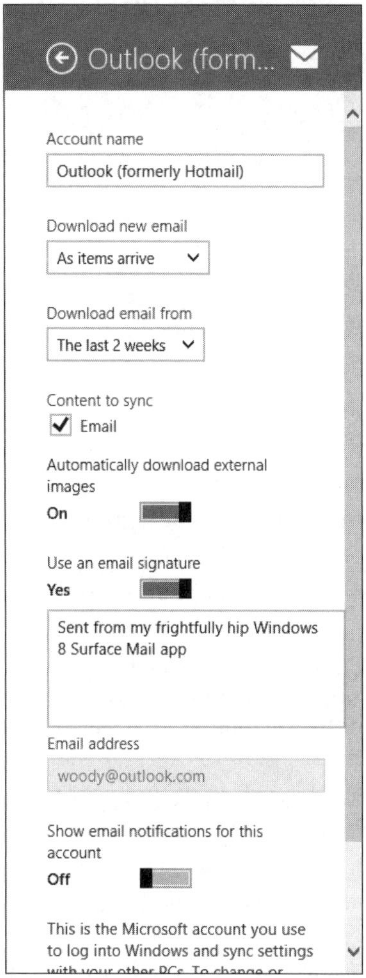

Account name

Outlook (formerly Hotmail)

Download new email

As items arrive

Download email from

The last 2 weeks

Content to sync

☑ Email

Automatically download external images

On

Use an email signature

Yes

Sent from my frightfully hip Windows 8 Surface Mail app

Email address

woody@outlook.com

Show email notifications for this account

Off

This is the Microsoft account you use to log into Windows and sync settings with your other PCs. To change or

Figure 2-5:
Change details of an account.

Creating a new message

When you reply to a message, Mail sets up a typical reply (or a reply to all) in a two-column screen, as shown in Figure 2-6. Similarly if you tap or click the + icon in the upper right, Mail starts a new, blank message. Whether you reply or start a new message, your message is all set up and ready to go — just start typing.

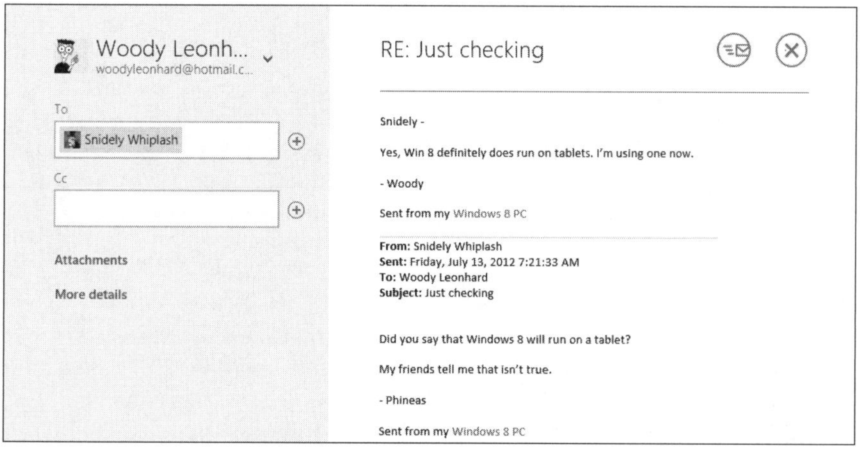

Figure 2-6:
When you
reply to a
message,
or compose
a new
message,
Mail gives
you these
options.

Woody Leonh... ⌄
woodyleonhard@hotmail.c...

RE: Just checking

To
Snidely Whiplash   ⊕

Cc
                               ⊕

Attachments

More details

Snidely -

Yes, Win 8 definitely does run on tablets. I'm using one now.

- Woody

Sent from my Windows 8 PC

From: Snidely Whiplash
Sent: Friday, July 13, 2012 7:21:33 AM
To: Woody Leonhard
Subject: Just checking

Did you say that Windows 8 will run on a tablet?

My friends tell me that isn't true.

- Phineas

Sent from my Windows 8 PC

Here's a quick tour of the features available to you as you create your e-mail message:

+ **Format the text:** The new text you type appears in Calibri 11-point type. If you want to format the text, just select the text, and you see the formatting options in Figure 2-7.

  Those who have a keyboard and know how to use it will be pleased to know that many of the old formatting keyboard shortcuts still work. Here are the most commonly used shortcuts:

  - *Ctrl+B* toggles bold on and off.

  - *Ctrl+I* toggles italic on and off.

  - *Ctrl+U* toggles underline on and off.

  - *Ctrl+Z* undoes the last action.

  - *Ctrl+Y* redoes the last undone action.

+ **Insert emoticons, smiley faces, bulleted or numbered lists:** You can bring up the formatting options shown in Figure 2-7 — which includes emoticons, undo, redo, and bulleted and numbered lists — by simply swiping from the top or bottom, or by right-clicking inside the message. There's even an emoticon that looks like Steve Sinofsky with glasses.

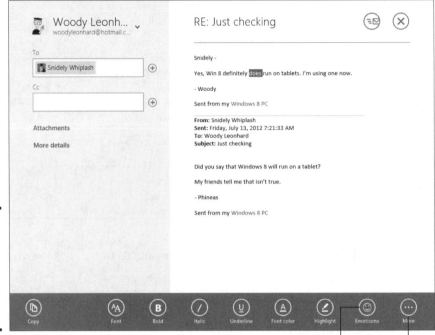

Figure 2-7:
Select
the text;
then apply
formatting
in the usual
way.

More than 100
smiley faces &
emoticons

Insert bulleted
or numbered
list, undo, or
redo

+ **Add an attachment:** In the first column, the Attachments link jumps to the file picker and starts in the Pictures library. You can move around to all your files, choose whichever file(s) you like, and then tap or click Attach. The file(s) are attached to your message.

Alternatively, if you start in the Photos app, navigate to the picture you want and bring up the Share charm (swipe from the right, or hover your mouse in the upper-right corner and then choose Share). This way, you can take advantage of larger images to find the pic you want. If you go this route to share a picture, Mail starts a new message.

+ **Add a BCC or message priority indicator:** In the first column, the More Details link lets you add a *blind carbon copy (BCC)* that sends a copy to someone without alerting any of the other recipients, and sets the mail priority to High, Normal, or Low.

Tap or click the Send icon in the upper-right corner, and the message is queued in the Outbox, ready to send the next time Mail syncs for new message.

If at any time you don't want to continue, tap or click the X button in the upper right, and choose either Delete or Save Draft. If you save the draft, a copy appears in the Drafts folder.

Searching for e-mail in Windows 8 Mail

Searching for mail is relatively easy, if you remember two very important details:

+ **Navigate to the folder that you want to search before you actually perform the search.** If you search while you're looking at your Inbox, for example, you won't find anything in your Sent Items folder. In fact, Mail won't even download the messages in your Sent Items folder unless you select it.

+ **Use the Search charm.** Yes, Mail is a typical tiled Windows 8 app. All tiled Win8 apps are supposed to use the Search charm.

To search for e-mail messages:

1. **Tap or click the folder you want to search, slide from the right (or hover your mouse in the upper-right corner), and choose the Search charm.**

2. **Type your search term; then press Enter or tap the magnifying glass icon.**

Mail may or may not search all your mail — Microsoft hasn't released details on exactly which messages are searched, but the search appears to be limited to the number of messages shown on the screen — two weeks' worth. To find older messages in your search, fire up your browser, hop over to Gmail or Hotmail/Outlook.com and search directly.

MIA in Windows 8 Mail

By the time you read this, Mail may have mended its wayward ways. But as it stands now, Mail just misses the boat in many important respects:

+ **The Inbox automatically shows all graphics, triggering web beacons.** Many e-mail programs are smart enough to wait for permission before they show you graphics that originate from the web. The reason is to stop *web beacons* — graphics that, when opened, will tip off the sender that you actually viewed the e-mail. It's a spammer's technique, and one that Mail should be smart enough to handle.

+ **Spam handling is nonexistent.** There's no way to mark a message as spam or to block (or *whitelist*) a sender or sender's e-mail domain.

+ **There's no conversation view.** One of the nicest features in Gmail (and Hotmail/Outlook.com) is the ability to tell Gmail that you want to see your messages grouped by conversation.

+ **You can't see a message's header.** This is an important ability if you want to find out who really sent a message.

+ **You can't import old mail** from, for example, Microsoft Outlook.

Hundreds of additional features that are common to almost any e-mail program are missing in Mail: As of this writing, you can't even create a new folder in Mail, for heaven's sake. It will be interesting to see how quickly or whether Microsoft fixes any or all the shortcomings.

Putting All Your Contacts in the Win8 People App

If you set up Mail with a Hotmail/Outlook.com, Gmail, or Exchange Server account, all the contacts belonging to that account have already been imported into People. If you set up more than one Hotmail/Outlook.com account, for example, all the contacts in both accounts have been merged and placed in People.

But you aren't even halfway done yet.

Adding accounts to Win8 People

Before you start pulling all your contacts from Hotmail/Outlook.com, Gmail, Exchange Server, Facebook, Google, LinkedIn, and Twitter, realize that there are side effects, not just in establishing Microsoft-controlled links with outside applications, but even inside the core Win8 communication apps.

Before you add an account to People, be aware of the effects that adding that account has in other tiled apps. Here's how connecting the following accounts with People impacts other tiled apps:

+ **Facebook account:** Brings your friends to the People list. In addition, adds your Facebook photos to the Photos app, and lists your friends' status updates in the What's New section of People.

+ **Google account:** Brings in your Gmail contacts but not your Google+ contacts. In addition, adds your Gmail account to the Mail app. (Apparently Microsoft hasn't dug into the Google+ social networking mill yet.)

+ **Hotmail/Outlook.com account:** Brings in your Hotmail/Outlook.com (and Windows Live) contacts. In addition, adds your contacts' Windows Live status updates to the People What's New page.

What? You didn't know that you and your contacts (er, People) *have* Windows Live status updates? Sure you, and they, do! Microsoft tried to get into the Facebook business years ago, and added the almost-never-used "Share something new" option at the top of the Windows Live landing page — the page that used to greet most people when they first logged in to Hotmail. With the ascendancy of Outlook.com, that page has gone away, but vestiges of "Share something new" persist. If your, uh, People are verbose enough to actually type something in the "Share something new" box, it'll get shared in your People app. Sharing is good, right?

+ **LinkedIn account:** Brings only your LinkedIn connections.

+ **Exchange Server account:** Stirs up all of the Exchange stuff — contacts, mail, and calendar entries.

+ **Twitter account:** Adds the folks you follow on Twitter to your contacts. In addition, their tweets are siphoned into the People What's New page.

Now that you understand the implications, you're ready to add accounts. Here's how to add many/most/all your contacts (you get to choose how many accounts to connect) to the People app:

1. **Bring up the People app from the Start screen by tapping or clicking the People tile.**

   If you've added only a single e-mail address to Mail, you may see an Add People to Your Contact List window on the left.

2a. *If the Add People to Your Contact List window appears,* **tap or click the Add More Accounts link.**

2b. *If the window doesn't appear,* **slide from the right or hover your mouse in the upper-right of the screen, choose Settings⇨Accounts⇨ Add an Account.**

   However you get there, the Add an Account pane appears on the right, as shown in Figure 2-8.

3. **If you have Facebook, Google, Hotmail/Outlook.com, LinkedIn, Twitter, or Exchange Server accounts, think carefully about which ones you want to add to People.**

   If you have old information in one or more of those accounts, you might want to think carefully about whether including the contacts in your People list will be more of a pain than it's worth. Modifying existing contacts, er, people is intensely time-consuming: You have to tap or click each contact one by one, review the information about the contact, and modify accordingly. While People tries to identify duplicate entries — the same people coming from two different sources — and merge the data, it's not real good at resolving differences.

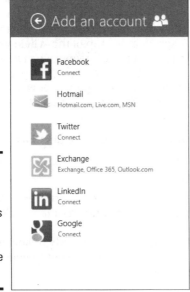

Figure 2-8:
Merge
contacts
from various
accounts
into your
Win8 People
app.

4. **One by one, tap or click accounts that you want to add, and provide login ID's and passwords.**

In some cases, you have to go to the account's site to verify your identity before People can import your contacts.

When you finish, your contacts appear in the People app.

5. **As you import each set of contacts, take a few minutes to review the combined list.**

You're bound to find many duplicates, and a lot of mismatched data. Hang in there and do the best you can.

No, there's no way (at least at this moment) to directly import Outlook, Windows Live Mail, or Windows contacts into People. (Windows Contacts come from the little-used Windows Contacts program in Vista and Windows 7, or from the Windows Address Book in Windows 95, 98 and 2000.) You can, however, sync Outlook contacts with Gmail and bring them into People through Gmail. Look for the GO Contact Sync Mod program at `http://sourceforge.net/projects/googlesyncmod/files`.

Navigating the Windows 8 People app

The People app has four different personas. You can see three of them at the top of the page in Figure 2-9. The fourth appears when you tap or click one of your people.

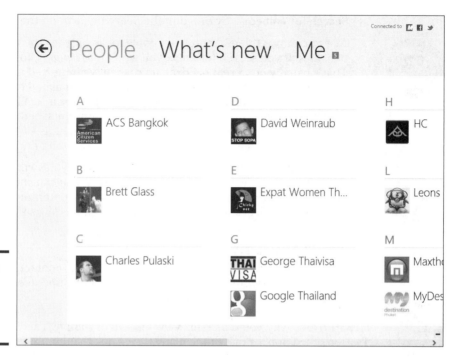

Figure 2-9:
The Win8
People
app main
screen.

The following sections introduce you to the three different tabs, each leading to their own screens, and what they offer.

The People screen

The People screen shows you a tile for each contact (uh, *people*?) in People. The people don't need to be people, if you know what I mean. They can be businesses, organizations, or just about anything else you might put in a contact list (refer to Figure 2-9). Here are a few tips to help you find the person you're looking for:

✦ **Entries are arranged alphabetically** by first name, or by whatever text appears first in the business name. At this point, there's no way to change that. If you want to skip to a particular letter and you have a keyboard, just type the letter.

✦ **You can "semantic zoom" out** to see blocks for A, B, C, and so on. To zoom out, pinch the screen or click on the tiny "minus sign" icon in the lower right of the screen. Tap or click on an A, B, or C block, and your People list opens up at that letter.

✦ **Search for someone by opening the Search charm on the right.**

Just to confuse things: Search in People looks only for the beginning of names. If you search for *umm,* you won't find *Dummy,* for example. That's usually not a real big deal, unless you've imported names where both the first and last name have been magically mashed together and stuck in the First Name field. As I write this, Twitter is a guilty party — everything I bring in from Twitter has both names mashed into the First Name field. If your contact's name has been mashed to *MisterDummy* (with no space), and you search for *Dummy,* you won't find it. Gotcha.

✦ **Display only people who are currently online.** If you swipe from the top or bottom, or right-click the People screen, you can show only the people who are currently identified as *online* — a determination that apparently stems from their Hotmail/Outlook.com /Messaging status.

The What's New screen

The What's New screen includes a tile for each of your contacts that come from Facebook or Twitter, and shows Facebook status updates and tweets from each. Check out how it looks in Figure 2-10.

I have no idea why you'd use this view instead of running Facebook's or Twitter's tiled app, or one of the many tiled Apps that combine the two.

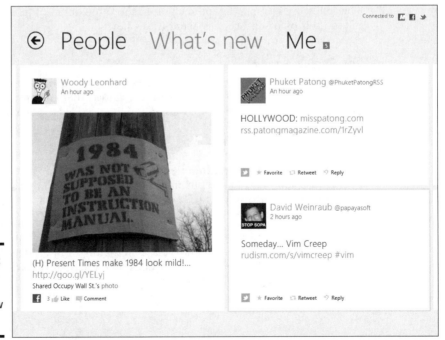

Figure 2-10: Windows 8 People's What's New page.

Here are a few tips for working in this view:

✦ **Refresh tweets and status updates:** Swipe from the bottom or top, or right-click the What's New page, and you can refresh the tweets and status updates. Although People refreshes from time to time, if you don't refresh, the stuff you're looking at is probably stale.

✦ **See all the ways to contact someone at once.** Tap or click an individual tile in the People or What's New list, and you see contact information and the What's New listing for the contact, as shown in Figure 2-11. With an individual tile showing, you can tap or click in the obvious places to send a Facebook message, Like, comment, re-tweet, or run a Twitter reply. To dance with the devil in the pale moonlight, you need a Joker account (just kidding).

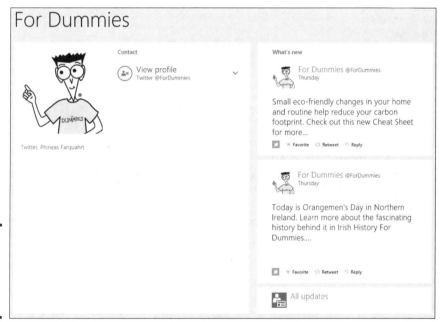

Figure 2-11: The contact tile for someone familiar.

The Me screen

The Me screen shows you you. Imagine that. You get your login picture, a link to your public Facebook profile, a list of your Facebook status updates and tweets, and the same photos that appear in your Photos app. See Figure 2-12. Definitely a narcissistic adventure.

What's new

Ineeda Windowsliveid
Thursday

RT @dangoodin001: Hackers expose
453,000 credentials allegedly taken from
Yahoo service, possibly Yahoo Voice:
is.gd/tG5pk3

Photos

Profile Pictur

Ineeda Windowsliveid

View profile
Facebook

★ Favorite   ⤺ Reply

All updates

Figure 2-12:
That's me,
me, me . . .
and a little
bit of me (or
at least my
retina).

Editing a contact

If you want to change the information associated with a People person — a
contact — here's how to do it:

1. **Inside People, tap or click a contact's tile.**

   The contact details appear (refer to Figure 2-11).

2. **Swipe from the top or bottom, or right-click the desktop to bring up
   the App bar at the bottom. On the right, tap or click the Edit icon.**

   The Edit Contact Info pane appears, as shown in Figure 2-13. (Extra
   points if you noticed how People switched from using the term *People* or
   Person to *Contact.*)

3. **Change the information you want to change.**

   See the next section for a list of the different data fields.

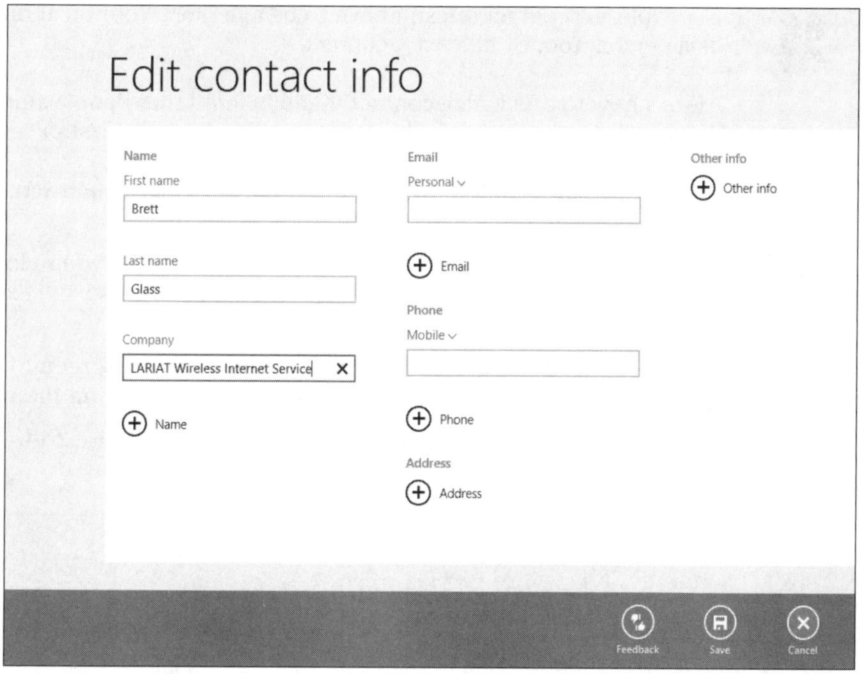

Edit contact info

Name
First name

Brett

Last name

Glass

Company

LARIAT Wireless Internet Service ✕

➕ Name

Email
Personal ⌄

➕ Email

Phone
Mobile ⌄

➕ Phone

Address

➕ Address

Other info

➕ Other info

Feedback   Save   Cancel

Figure 2-13:
Change the
contact's
information
here.

4. Tap or click Save.

If your contact suddenly disappears, there's a reason why! If you
changed the name, and the new name matches the name of a contact
that's already in your People list, People consolidates the two contacts,
throws away the picture for one of them, and presents you with the
merged result.

A word to the wise: If People threw away one of your contacts, it'd be a
very good idea to look at the details of the surviving contact, and make sure
they're accurate.

Adding people in Windows 8 People

Adding a new contact in People isn't difficult, if you can keep in mind one
oddity: You add *accounts* via the Charm bar's Settings charm, on the right
side of the screen, but to add a *contact,* you use the App bar at the bottom of
the screen.

**Book IV
Chapter 2**

**Windows 8 Mail,
People, and
Calendar Apps**

A people, er, contact doesn't have to be a person. Your local Animal Shelter is a person, too. Or at least a contact.

Here's how to add a new contact. Keep in mind that People alphabetizes by the first name, or by the company name if there is no first or last name.

1. **Start People and go to the People screen — the main screen (refer to Figure 2-9).**

   Actually, you *could* try to add a new contact while you're looking at the Me screen, but that would probably lead to some sort of existential dilemma, so I won't go there.

2. **Swipe from the top or bottom, or right-click the screen to bring up the App bar at the bottom. Tap or click the New icon on the right.**

   The New Contact screen appears, as shown in Figure 2-14.

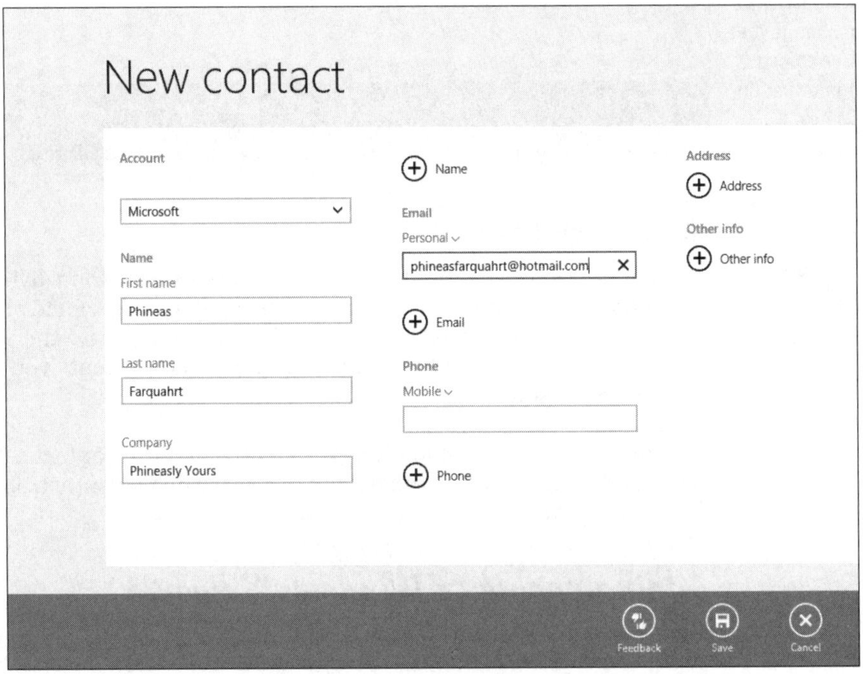

New contact

Account	⊕ Name	**Address**
		⊕ Address
Microsoft ⌄	**Email**	
	Personal ⌄	**Other info**
Name	phineasfarquahrt@hotmail.com ✕	⊕ Other info
First name		
Phineas	⊕ Email	
Last name	**Phone**	
Farquahrt	Mobile ⌄	
Company		
Phineasly Yours	⊕ Phone	

⟳ Feedback   🖫 Save   ✕ Cancel

Figure 2-14: Add a new contact.

3. **At the top, under Account, choose the e-mail provider that you want to sync this new contact to.**

   You can choose from any account that's been identified to the Mail app. When you add a contact to that account, People goes to the account and puts the person in your contact list for that account. So, for example, if I add Phineas Fahrquahrt to my `SnidelyWhiplashed@hotmail.com` account, as soon as I'm done, Windows 8's People app will log on to my `SnidelyWhiplashed@hotmail.com` account and add poor Phineas to my contact list.

4. **Type a first and last name, keeping in mind that People alphabetizes by the first name.**

   For additional name options — phonetic names, middle names, nicknames, title, or suffix — you can tap or click the Name button.

5. **If you have an e-mail address for the contact, choose what kind of e-mail address — Personal, Work, or Other — and type the address in the box.**

6. **Similarly, if you have a phone number, choose the type — Home, Home 2, Work, Work 2, Pager, Work Fax, Home Fax — and type it in the indicated box.**

7. **If you want to add an address, tap or click the Address button and choose among Home, Work, and Other address.**

8. **Type as you feel inclined for Other Info, such as Job Title, Significant Other, Website, and Notes.**

9. **In the App bar at the bottom, tap or click Save.**

   It takes a few seconds — you can actually see People going to your mail account and updating it — but you come back to the People screen.

Avoiding Windows 8 Calendar App Collisions

The first time you bring up the Calendar app, you may think that you're seeing double. Or triple. In Figure 2-15, you can see what I mean.

Don't panic.

The reason for the duplication? Assuming you have two or more accounts into Mail or People, the calendars associated with those accounts came along for the ride, and any appointment that appears in both calendars shows up as two stripes on the consolidated calendar.

Figure 2-15:
The first
time in Win8
Calendar
may make
your head
spin.

Fortunately, it's easy to see what's going on, and to get rid of the duplicates. Or at least some of the duplicates. Maybe. Here's how to re-organize your Calendar:

1. **From the Start screen, tap or click the Calendar tile to start it.**

   If this is the first time you've looked at the Calendar app, it may look like the one in Figure 2-15.

2. **Swipe from the right, or hover your mouse in the upper-right corner, choose the Settings charm, and then tap or click Options.**

   The color-coded Options pane appears, as shown in Figure 2-16.

3. **See whether two or more of your calendars have a source that overlaps. If so, turn off one of the interfering calendars.**

   For example, in Figure 2-16, I have two Hotmail/Outlook.com accounts, both of which have the U.S. Holidays calendar turned on. That's why the holidays are double entries on the main calendar.

   By simply turning off one of the U.S. Holidays calendars, the main calendar goes back to looking somewhat normal, as shown see in Figure 2-17.

Figure 2-16:
Set
calendar
colors and
eliminate
some
duplicates
here.

4. **Go through the calendars, one by one, and set the color coding for each calendar component to something your eyes can tolerate.**

5. **When you're done, simply tap or click outside the Options pane.**

If you swipe from the top or bottom, or right-click the calendar, the App bar appears, as shown in Figure 2-18.

Figure 2-17:
Getting rid of the second U.S. Holidays calendar cuts down the clutter.

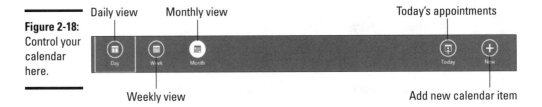

Figure 2-18:
Control your calendar here.

Daily view   Monthly view   Today's appointments

Weekly view   Add new calendar item

Adding Calendar Items

To add a new appointment, or other calendar item, tap or click the New icon in the lower-right corner. Calendar shows you the Details pane, as shown in Figure 2-19.

Most of the entries are self-explanatory, except

✦ **You must choose a calendar — actually, an e-mail account — which will be synchronized with this appointment.** As soon as you enter the appointment, Calendar logs on to the indicated account and adds the appointment to the account's calendar.

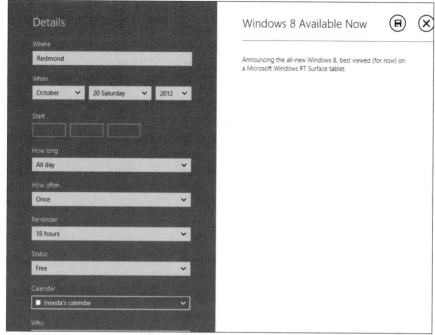

Figure 2-19:
Create
a new
appointment
or calendar
entry.

+ **You may optionally specify e-mail addresses in the Who box.** If you put valid e-mail address(es) in the Who box, Calendar automatically generates an e-mail message and sends it to the recipient, asking the recipient to confirm the appointment. When you finish the appointment, in the upper right-corner, tap or click Save or Send, depending on whether you're setting the appointment or sending invitations.

At this moment, the How Often box is very simple, inviting you to repeat the appointment every day, weekday, or week at the same time; or once a month or once a year on the same date. Presumably you'll see more advanced controls sooner or later.

Struggling with Calendar shortcomings

The Calendar app is a just-barely-passable calendaring program. It doesn't have any of the goodies you would expect from more advanced calendaring apps — notably, Google Calendar.

You can view the calendar by Day — actually, Today and Tomorrow (and, if you have a wide enough screen, one more day). You can also a Week or Month by using the app bar at the bottom: Right-click on the calendar, or swipe from the top or bottom. But there's no way to jump to a specific day, week, or month; to look in the future or the past, you have to scroll, scroll, scroll your date gently down the stream.

You can set an alert for any given appointment — it appears as a toast notification, rolling in from the right — but there's no additional notification, and no way to "snooze" the notification.

On the plus side, you can have Calendar notifications placed on your lock screen. The notifications list individual appointments for the current day. See Book II, Chapter 2 for details.

Chapter 3: The Windows 8 Photos App

In This Chapter

✓ Taking a tour of the tiled Photos app

✓ Adding photos in various ways

✓ Pinning your photos

*W*indows 8's tiled Photos app is meant to be a pleasing, full-screen way to look at your picture collection. If your expectations go a little bit outside that box, you're going to be very disappointed.

In this chapter, you find an introduction to what Photos can and can't do. A quick tour shows you how to navigate around the Photos app. Then I explain how to connect Photos to other photo-friendly locales on the web, such as Facebook and Flickr, and how to import images from your camera (or phone) with Photos.

Discovering What Windows 8's Photos App Can Do

Photos has a very simple layout for viewing your photos. Here's what you get:

✦ A central place to view photos from several sources — your computer, your SkyDrive account, Facebook, and Flickr — that keeps each photo source separate

✦ Help searching for a photo

✦ A way to show your photos organized by date

✦ A single location that brings together photos on your PC with photos you may have in your accounts on SkyDrive, Facebook, and Flickr.

The next section, "Touring Photos," explains the photo sources and how to search or change the display of your photos. The section "Adding Photos" later in this chapter explains how to connect Photos with the web.

If you want to fuss over your photos in Photos, fuhgeddaboutit. Windows 8's Photos app doesn't offer any editing capability, navigating physical locations on the hard drive is daunting, and moving photos and videos in and out of different locations is a massive pain in the neck. For that kind of support — which you get from just about any photo program worth its salt — you need to turn to the likes Photoshop or Photoshop Elements, iPhoto (available on the Mac and iPad), Paint Shop, Picasa, or Windows Photo Gallery (see Book VI, Chapter 5).

Touring Photos

To take a walk around the Photos app:

1. **From the Start screen, tap or click the Photos tile.**

The main screen of the Photos app appears, as shown in Figure 3-1.

Figure 3-1: The Photos app can consolidate picture files from several sources.

The following may appear, depending on where you store your photos:

- *If you have pictures or videos in your Windows Pictures library,* you see a picture in the Pictures Library tile on the left. The Pictures library includes your \Pictures folder and the computer's \Public\Pictures folder, although you can add other folders. See Book VII, Chapter 3 for more about the Windows Pictures library.

- *If you're connected to SkyDrive and your SkyDrive has files in its Pictures folder,* you see a picture in the SkyDrive Photos tile. See Book IV, Chapter 4 for more about SkyDrive.

- *If you're connected to Facebook — perhaps while working in the Windows 8 People app — and you have any photos in your albums,* they appear in the Facebook Photos tile.

- *If you're connected to other computers that actively share content,* your photos may or may not appear in the Devices tile. This tile can use the Fetch feature in SkyDrive to reach out to other computers and retrieve photos, whether those photos are in your SkyDrive folder or not. I talk about the SkyDrive program (available only on the desktop) and Fetch in Book IV, Chapter 4.

- *If you have a Flickr account, and you've already connected to it,* your current Photo Stream may appear in the Flickr tile. The only way to see photos you've uploaded to Flickr in Windows 8 Photos is by connecting to Flickr inside Photos. See "Adding Photos" later in this chapter.

2. **Tap or click the Pictures Library tile.**

   The Win8 Photos app shows you the folders inside your Pictures library, with a representative pic for each. In addition, you see all the pictures and videos that aren't inside folders, as shown in Figure 3-2. If you don't have any photos in your Pictures library, see "Adding Photos" later in this chapter for help. (Microsoft probably left a sample photo or two for you, though.)

3. **If you have a folder inside the Pictures library, tap or click the folder.**

   The contents of that folder and any other folders inside it appear inside the Pictures library. Open those folders to reveal more folders within — *ad infinitum.*

   In fact, the folder hierarchy looks a lot like the folders inside your Pictures library, with one big exception: Any folders inside your Pictures library that don't physically reside on your computer aren't included. See the sidebar, "Seeing videos and network attached folders" for more details.

   The Photos app, like all tiled Win8 apps, supports search using the Search charm.

Book IV
Chapter 3

The Windows 8
Photos App

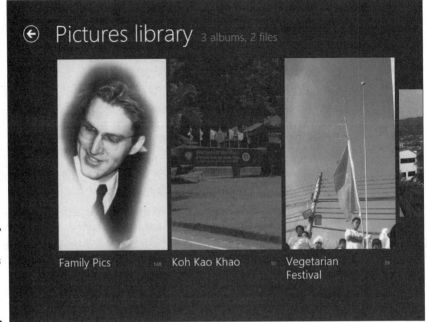

4. **To perform your own search, swipe from the right or hover your mouse in the upper-right corner and choose the Search charm. Type your search term in the box and tap or click the magnifying glass.**

   Your results should look like Figure 3-3. Keep in mind that Photos search is subject to all the bizarre behavior of Windows 8 search in general, which I dissect in Book III, Chapter 2.

   You can perform a search covering all your Photos — in which case you should bring up the Search charm while looking at the main Photos screen, shown in Figure 3-1 — or you can navigate to a specific folder and search that folder.

5. **To browse your Pictures library photos by date, tap or click the left arrow in the upper-left corner, and make your way back to the main screen (Figure 3-1). Tap or click the Pictures library, as shown in Figure 3-2. Right-click or swipe from the top or bottom.**

   An App bar appears at the bottom.

6. **Choose Browse by date.**

   Photos groups your Pictures library photos by month, then shows you large tiles for each month, as in Figure 3-4. You can click on each large tile and look at all the photos for that month.

7. **To get back to the main Photos screen (Figure 3-1), in the upper-left corner, tap or click the back arrow repeatedly.**

Figure 3-3:
Like all
Windows 8
tiled apps,
search
takes place
through
the Search
charm.

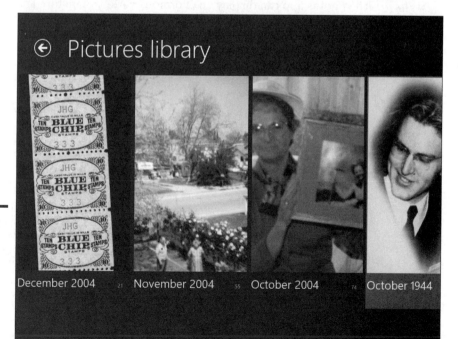

Figure 3-4:
Photos
can group
photos
in your
Pictures
library by
month.

**Book IV
Chapter 3**

**The Windows 8
Photos App**

Seeing videos and network-attached folders

In Photos, you see some videos and photos, but not others. The reason has to do with the nuances of how Photos works behind the scenes to show you images. The following points may clear up a few mysteries for you:

✔ **Photos shows all the picture or video files in your Windows Pictures library.** Although Photos does show videos, the videos need to be in your Pictures library (not your Videos library) in order to appear in Photos. Your video files in the Windows Video library don't appear in Photos at all — odd, but true. This is a good place to note that the Windows 8 Video app isn't anything at all like the Windows 8 Photos app: Video shows a tiny slice of your videos wedged in between mountains of marketing, trying to get you to rent or buy movies. For more on the tiled Video app, flip to Book IV, Chapter 6.

✔ **But . . . if you have a network-attached folder in your Windows Pictures library, Photos won't look at it.** That means you can't put a bunch of photos on a Windows Home Server, a network attached server, or even a different PC in your home network and have the pictures appear in Photos — even if you add the folder to your Pictures library. Worse, Photos can't even see photos inside your HomeGroup. Book VII, Chapter 3 explains how to put network folders in your Libraries.

The Photos app can display an enormous variety of picture and video formats, including AVI, BMP, GIF, JPG, MOV, MP4, MPEG, MPG, PCX, PNG, many kinds of RAW (high quality photos), TIF, WMF, and WMV files. That covers most picture and movie formats you're likely to encounter.

Adding Photos

You can add pictures to your collection in Photos in four ways:

✦ **Connect with SkyDrive, Facebook, or Flickr:** If you already have an account with the service in question, connecting Photos with that service is easy. If you don't have an account with the service, signing up for one takes only minutes.

If you have a Microsoft account (either a @Hotmail.com or @Live.com or @Outlook.com e-mail address, or another email address that you've registered with Microsoft), you already have a SkyDrive account. All you need to do is copy pictures into your SkyDrive folder, and Photos takes care of the rest. Book II, Chapter 5 explains how Microsoft accounts work in detail. Book IV, Chapter 4 gives you tips on using SkyDrive.

You can find introductions to Facebook in Book V, Chapter 1, and Flickr in Book V, Chapter 3. Those chapters discuss what you need to know about setting up an account with each of these services, enabling privacy, and putting pictures where you can use them.

✦ **Use the Fetch feature in SkyDrive:** This pulls pictures into the Devices tile. It's a bit complicated, but Fetch lets you go out to other computers using SkyDrive and retrieve files from those other computers. That's quite different from connecting to SkyDrive itself and pulling in the photos already stored on SkyDrive. See Book IV, Chapter 4 for details.

✦ **Use the Photos Import app:** You can import pictures from a camera or any removable device, including a USB drive, SD card, or even a big honking external hard drive. See "Importing pictures from a camera or external drive" for details.

✦ **Add pictures to your Pictures library:** I call this the old-fashioned way, and it's how I add pictures to the Photos app (in addition to SkyDrive). Simply flip over to the desktop and use File Explorer to stick photos in your Pictures library (see Book VII, Chapter 3).

Connecting Photos to SkyDrive

If you have a Microsoft account, you already have a SkyDrive account, although you might not yet have any pictures in your SkyDrive folder.

Putting pictures in your SkyDrive folder is easy, using the tiled SkyDrive app, which I discuss in Book IV Chapter 4. After you've installed the SkyDrive program on your PC (discussed in the same chapter), you can also click and drag photos or pictures into your SkyDrive folder, using File Explorer. The files are automatically uploaded to your SkyDrive account in the, uh, sky. Nothing to it.

You can put any kind of picture or video in any of the SkyDrive folders, and Photos will find it.

Connecting to Facebook or Flickr

Do you have blank tiles on your main Photos page, as in Figure 3-1? If you see a See Your Albums tile or two, you can connect Facebook, or Flickr to Photos, so Photos can suck in pics that you've uploaded to the service, and display your images via the main Photos screen.

The only hitch? To connect the Win8 Photos app to an online service, you have to sign up for a Microsoft account, so Microsoft can track your Facebook or Flickr account and remember your password for you. If you're concerned about the privacy implications of your different online accounts tracking your whereabouts on the Internet, flip to Book II, Chapter 5, where I explain the privacy ramifications of your Microsoft account.

If you have already set up your Microsoft account, and couldn't care less if Microsoft sees and keeps a copy of your Facebook or Flickr password, you're ready to connect Photos to the online services of your choice.

Here's how to connect Photos to Facebook:

1. **Make sure you already have a Microsoft account, and make sure that you have a Facebook account and that you know the login ID and password for it.**

   I talk about setting up (and, perhaps more importantly, locking down) a Facebook account in Book V, Chapter 1. Flickr accounts are covered in Book V, Chapter 3.

2. **On the Start screen, tap or click the Photos tile.**

   Your Photos main screen appears, something like Figure 3-5.

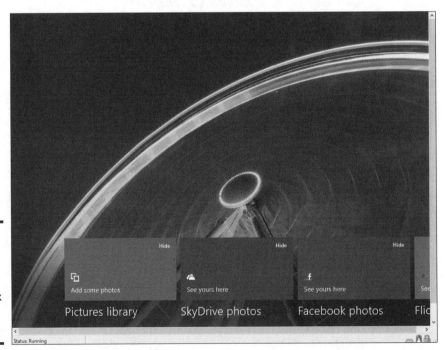

3. **Tap or click the Facebook Photos tile.**

   If you didn't log in to Windows with a Microsoft account, Photos forces you to provide a Windows account and password at this point, and then shows you the sign-up pane in Figure 3-6. If you did log in to Windows with a Microsoft account, you go straight to the sign-up pane.

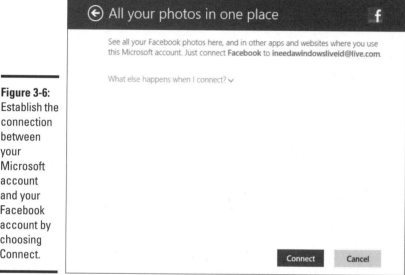

Figure 3-6: Establish the connection between your Microsoft account and your Facebook account by choosing Connect.

4. **Tap or click Connect.**

   Facebook shows you the login screen shown in Figure 3-7. It's important to remember (and more than a little confusing) that this pane is looking for a *Facebook* account, not a Microsoft account.

5. **Fill in your Facebook username (which is an email address — that's Facebook's rule) and your password; then tap or click Log In.**

   If you got your Facebook username and password right, a You're Ready to Go pane appears.

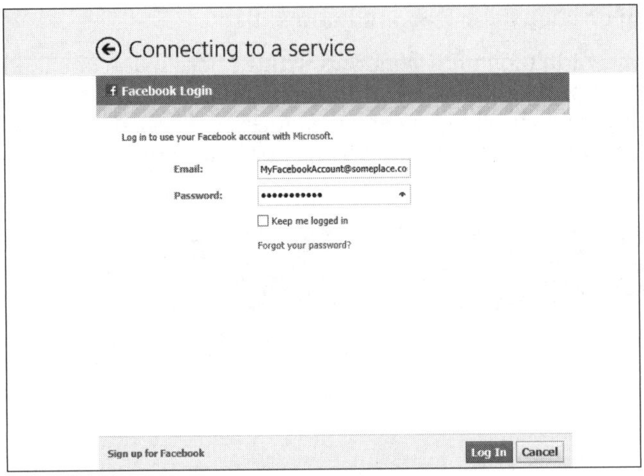

Figure 3-7:
Log in to
Facebook
using your
Facebook
account.

6. **On the You're Ready to Go pane, tap or click Done.**

   In fact, you aren't quite ready to go. Photos takes a while — sometimes
   a very long while — to download your most recent photos. Facebook
   then sends a `You've connected to the Photos app` message to
   your Microsoft account e-mail address. After Facebook and Photos have
   duked it out and finished the cross-loading, you also see a picture in the
   Facebook tile, as shown in Figure 3-8.

Connecting Photos to Flickr is similar, but you have to sign on with a Flickr
account (which is actually a Yahoo! account, although Flickr will let you sign
in with a Facebook or Google account). The sign-in confirmation screen,
shown in Figure 3-9, is a little funky. But it works. On the confirmation
screen, you have to tap or click the button that says OK, I'll Authorize It.

When you connect to Flickr, Photos brings in your Flickr *photo stream* —
that's a Flickr term — which is a well defined set of photos that you (usually) have uploaded recently. See Book V Chapter 3 for more about photo
streams.

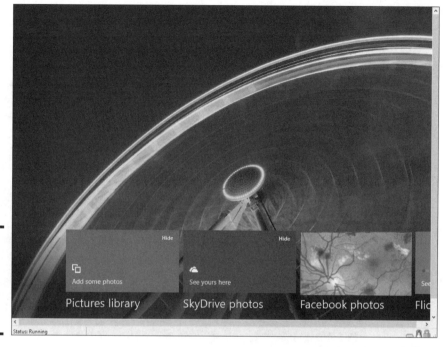

Figure 3-8:
Facebook
is set up
and feeding
photos to
Photos.

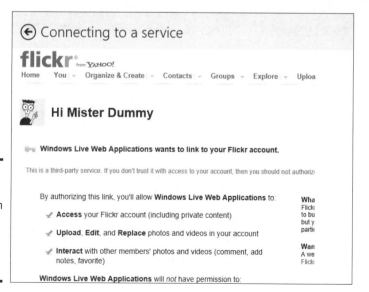

Figure 3-9:
The sign-up
confirmation
pane from
Flickr is a
bit hard to
read.

If you have a Facebook and Flickr account, and you've moved pictures into your SkyDrive drive account, your Photos main page should look something like Figure 3-10.

Pictures library   SkyDrive photos   Facebook photos   Flic

Status: Running

Figure 3-10:
A fully
connected
Photos app.

Importing pictures from a camera or external drive

The Win8 Photos app has a very, very limited picture import capability. You're much better off using Windows Photo Gallery (flip to Book VI, Chapter 5) or any of the many photo apps.

If you really want to use Photos to import pictures from your phone, camera, USB drive, SD card, or just about any external hard drive, here's how to do it:

1. **Tap or click the Photos tile on the Start screen.**

The main Photos page appears (refer to Figure 3-1).

2. **Plug in your phone, camera, USB drive, SD card, or external hard drive to your computer.**

Windows probably shows you a toaster notification. Depending on what kind of camera you attached, you may get a generic notification that says something like, `Removable Disk (X:) / Tap to Choose What Happens with Removable Drives.` (*X* is the drive letter.) Or you may get a more specific notification, like the one in Figure 3-11.

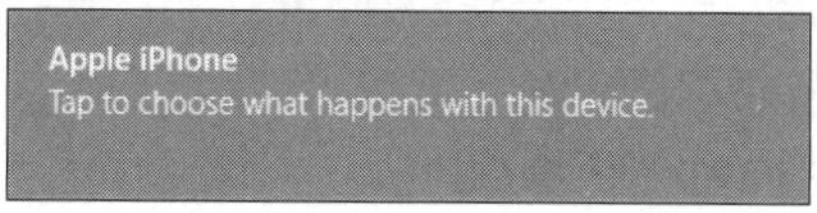

Figure 3-11:
Attaching an
iPhone to a
Windows 8
computer.

Apple iPhone
Tap to choose what happens with this device.

3. **Tap or click the notification.**

A dialog box appears, as shown in Figure 3-12.

If the notification appears and then disappears too fast, just unplug the device and plug it back in again, but this time have your mouse or finger ready to pounce while the dern little thing is on the screen.

Figure 3-12:
Windows
gives you
a chance
to do all
sorts of
things with
an inserted
camera,
phone or
drive.

Apple iPhone

Choose what to do with this device.

 Import photos and videos
Photos

 Open device to view files
Windows Explorer

 Take no action

4. **If you're feeling very brave, and the option is offered, you can tap or click Import Photos and Videos. If everything works properly and the import starts, skip down to Step 9a. (If everything goes to Hades in a handbasket, start all over at Step 1.)**

If you aren't feeling so lucky (remember Dirty Harry?), choose Open Folder to View Files and continue to Step 5.

Windows flips to the desktop and opens the drive.

5. **Note the drive letter that appears on the File Explorer location bar next to Removable Disk, and then go back to Photos.**

To return to Photos, you may need to tap the Windows button on the tablet or press the Windows key on the keyboard. Then tap or click the Photos tile.

6. **Swipe up from the bottom of the screen or right-click the screen.**

The App bar appears at the bottom.

7. **Tap or click the Import icon on the right.**

Photos responds with a Choose a Device to Import From pane, which contains a list of external devices, many of which probably don't exist (see Figure 3-13).

Figure 3-13: This is why you need to know the drive letter.

Choose a device to import from

If you don't see your device listed, make sure your device is turned on and connected to your PC.

Removable Disk (G:)

Removable Disk (E:)

Removable Disk (H:)

Removable Disk (D:)

Removable Disk (F:)

Removable Disk (I:)

8. **Tap or click the drive letter that corresponds to the device you plugged in to the computer.**

The Photos app scans the phone, camera, or drive and then shows you all the pictures that it found, as shown in Figure 3-14.

Figure 3-14:
A visual list
of all the
pictures that
were found.

9a. ***If you want to import all the pictures,*** **leave them selected.**

9b. ***If you want to select individual pictures to import,*** **tap or click
Clear Selection and then select the pictures you want to go into your
machine.**

Photos does *not* delete any pictures that it finds. They're still on your
camera or external drive, gathering dust — or at least taking up space —
until you go in with a real tool, such as File Explorer, and delete them.

10. **Type the name of a folder that you want to create to hold the pictures.**

This folder is actually placed in your \Pictures folder, if you need to find
it in the future. Because the folder is in your \Pictures folder, the folder
appears as a separate folder in the Photos Pictures library list (refer to
Figure 3-2).

11. **When you're happy with the selection, and with the folder location,
tap or click Import.**

The Win8 Photos app dutifully imports the pictures — without deleting
them on your camera or external drive — and sticks them in the indicated folder, tells you you're done, and then offers to open the album.

12. **(Optional) Tap or click Open Album.**

The Photos Pictures library list appears, with the imported folder open
(see Figure 3-15).

**Book IV
Chapter 3**

**The Windows 8
Photos App**

2012-06-30 Pictures library 14 files

Figure 3-15:
A newly
imported
folder
of shots
from my
Samsung
phone.

Pinning Photos within the Photos App

Although you can't pin multiple photos to the Start screen (as you can with, say, the Win8 People app), you can pick your favorite photo to appear as the

✦ **App tile:** The tile for the Photos app on the Start screen.

✦ **App background:** The background on the Photos main screen (refer to Figure 3-1).

✦ **Lock screen:** The background on your lock screen. You don't see your lock screen very often — in fact, many people never see their lock screen — but you can set a picture for it. (The lock screen appears only if you manually lock your account, as opposed to signing out or restarting.) Book II, Chapter 2 explains the lock screen in detail.

To pin a specific picture, tap or click the picture; swipe from the top or bottom, or right-click to bring up the app bar at the bottom; and then tap or click the Set As icon on the left. You can then choose one of the three options listed.

Chapter 4: Using SkyDrive in Windows 8

In This Chapter

✔ **Introducing SkyDrive**

✔ **Using the tiled SkyDrive app**

✔ **Working with SkyDrive on your desktop**

✔ **Running SkyDrive on the Internet**

✔ **Working with Fetch**

*S*tart with the basics: The Windows 8 tiled SkyDrive app doesn't do justice to SkyDrive, Microsoft's online storage service that enables you to keep files on the web and synchronize them among several devices.

To get any real use out of SkyDrive — beyond very simple interactions — you have to flip over to the desktop and run the SkyDrive application. And you won't really see it all put together until you get on SkyDrive using your web browser.

In this chapter, I show you the limited things you can do with Microsoft's tiled SkyDrive app. But I also show you the rest of the story, by jumping over to the desktop side of things and then digging directly into SkyDrive with a web browser.

Microsoft will undoubtedly bring more capabilities to the tiled SkyDrive app, probably dribbling out improvements over time. Slowly you'll see the SkyDrive app add some of the features that are already accessible from the desktop or the web.

You're lucky. You don't have to wait — because this chapter shows you where to look for the more robust SkyDrive features on the desktop. SkyDrive is up and running, and it doesn't cost you a cent.

SkyDrive has many competitors — Dropbox, Google Drive (see Book X, Chapter 3), the Apple iCloud (which isn't quite the same, although you can get to it through a web browser), the Amazon Cloud Drive, Facebook storage,

SugarSync, Box, SpiderOak, and cloud storage and sharing from many smaller companies. (*Cloud* is another word for the web or the Internet.) These competitors all have advantages and disadvantages — and the feature list changes from week to week. I talk about the tradeoffs in Book X, Chapter 3.

In this chapter, I show you just about everything you need to know to make SkyDrive work for you and in Windows 8.

What Is SkyDrive?

SkyDrive is an Internet-based storage platform offered for free by Microsoft to anyone with a Microsoft account. Think of it as a hard drive in the cloud, which you can share, with a few extra benefits thrown in. One of the primary benefits: SkyDrive hooks into Windows 8 pretty easily.

As of this writing, if you have a Microsoft account (see Book II, Chapter 4), you already have 7GB of free storage set aside. Microsoft, of course, wants you to buy more storage, but you're under no obligation to do so. The free storage is there whether you use your Microsoft account to log on to Windows, even if you never use SkyDrive. In fact, if you have a Microsoft account, you're all signed up for SkyDrive.

Here's the SkyDrive shtick:

✦ SkyDrive does what all the other cloud storage services do — it gives you a place to put your files on the Internet. You need to log on to SkyDrive with your Microsoft account (or, equivalently, log on to Windows with your Microsoft account) to access your data.

✦ If you log on to a different Windows 8 computer using the same Microsoft account, you have access to all your SkyDrive data through the tiled SkyDrive app.

✦ The tiled SkyDrive app offers a very clumsy process for copying files from your computer into SkyDrive (see Figure 4-1). The tiled SkyDrive app also lets you move files in the other direction, from SkyDrive storage onto your local hard drive, but navigating around your hard drive by using the tiled interface is clunky at best.

✦ You can log on to SkyDrive at www.skydrive.com and see all your data (see Figure 4-2). Working through your favorite web browser, you can also copy or move files into SkyDrive, or delete or rename files inside SkyDrive.

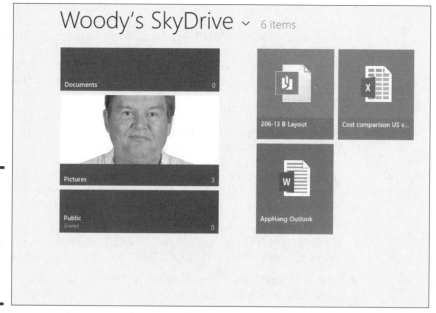

Figure 4-1:
Microsoft's tiled SkyDrive app doesn't do much, but it looks nice.

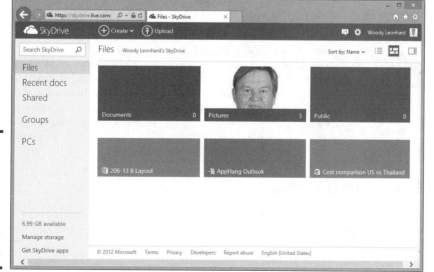

Figure 4-2:
Using SkyDrive through a web browser opens many possibilities.

✦ You can share files or folders that are stored in SkyDrive by sending or posting a link to the file or folder to whomever you wish. So, for example, if you want Aunt Martha to be able to see the folder full of pictures of Little Billy, SkyDrive will create a link for you that you can e-mail to Aunt Martha. You can also specify that a file or folder is *Public,* so that anyone can see it. See the section "Running SkyDrive on the Web," later in this chapter.

✦ To work with the SkyDrive platform on the desktop or a mobile device, you can download and install a SkyDrive program — SkyDrive for Windows, SkyDrive for Mac, SkyDrive for iPhone, iPad, or Android. This program is compatible with Windows Vista, Win7, Win8, OS X Lion, iOS (for the iPad and iPhone), Android, and Windows Phone. The program lets you use many of SkyDrive's capabilities. See the section "Installing SkyDrive: The legacy program," later in this chapter.

The Windows desktop SkyDrive program is *not* the same thing as the tiled SkyDrive app. The two apps/programs offer you two different ways of interacting with the SkyDrive platform. A web browser offers a third way.

✦ After you install the downloadable SkyDrive program on your desktop and/or mobile device, SkyDrive syncs data among computers, phones, and/or tablets. If you change a SkyDrive file on your iPad, for example, when you save it, the modified file is put in your SkyDrive storage area on the Internet. From there, the new file is "pushed" to all other computers with access to the file. Ditto for Android devices.

✦ SkyDrive has a unique Fetch feature that allows you to access other computers that are logged in to SkyDrive with the same Windows account. Fetch can come in very handy if, for example, you forget that important spreadsheet while you're on the road. As long as your home computer is logged on to SkyDrive with your Windows account, you can log on to SkyDrive from another computer, use the same Windows account, and retrieve the spreadsheet. See the "Fetching" section later in this chapter for details.

Using the Windows 8 Tiled SkyDrive

Microsoft's tiled SkyDrive app leaves much to be desired, but it's not a bad place to get your feet wet. Follow these steps to access SkyDrive via the tiled SkyDrive app:

1. **On the Start screen, tap or click the SkyDrive tile.**

The tile is tiny and blue, with billowy white clouds above the front car of a Japanese Shinkansen bullet train, which is undergoing a Lorentz contraction. I think that's what the designers intended.

If you haven't already logged on with a Microsoft account — either your Windows login ID is a Microsoft account, or you logged on to one of the other tiled apps with a Microsoft account — Windows asks you to sign in with a Microsoft account.

2. **If you aren't logged in automatically, log in using your Microsoft account.**

   In Book II, Chapter 4, I offer advice about the pros and cons of using a Microsoft account. A Microsoft account is the price of admission for SkyDrive. So no Microsoft account, no SkyDrive. Makes sense, actually.

   If you've never used SkyDrive, the Windows 8 tiled SkyDrive app shows you the screen in Figure 4-3.

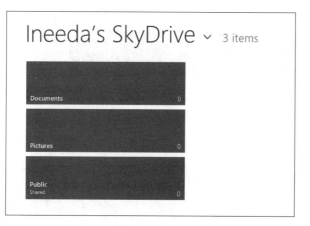

Figure 4-3:
A fresh, new SkyDrive account looks like this from the tiled interface.

The three folders — Documents, Pictures, and Public — in your online SkyDrive folder appear by default. Those are the three folders that Microsoft sets up for you in the cloud. From the screen shown in Figure 4-3, you can add a file to any of the folders, and after you've added files, you can delete files or download any of them to your computer. If you put a file in the Documents or Pictures folders, only you have access (unless you change permissions). However, anyone can see files you add to your Public folder.

If you use only the tiled SkyDrive app, you can't rename folders or change them so they're shared with other people. However, those actions are easy to do after you install SkyDrive for Windows on your desktop. It's also easy to modify folders using any web browser, on any computer (yes, even an Android phone or Chromebook) by going to www.skydrive.com and logging in with your Microsoft account.

Here's how to work with files in SkyDrive when you access SkyDrive via the tiled SkyDrive app:

✦ **Add a file:** Swipe from the top or bottom, or right-click in the middle of the screen. When the App bar appears, as shown in Figure 4-4, tap or click the Upload icon. After the file picker appears, as shown in Figure 4-5, hunt around your hard drive until you find a file; then tap or click the file and in the lower-right corner, tap or click Add to SkyDrive. The file is copied into your SkyDrive folder.

Check whether SkyDrive in the cloud has changed

Add file

Select all files and folders in SkyDrive folder

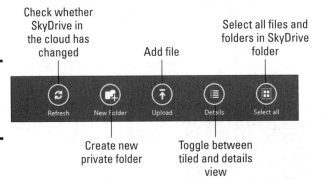

Figure 4-4: The tiled SkyDrive App bar.

Create new private folder

Toggle between tiled and details view

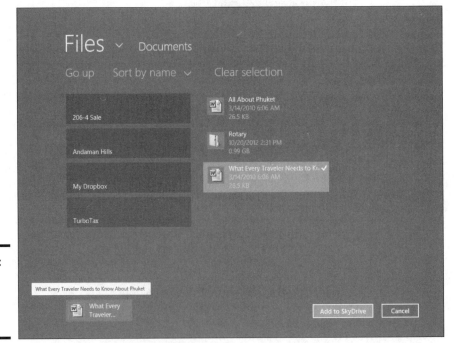

Figure 4-5: Choose a file to go into SkyDrive.

✦ **Delete a file:** Tap or click the file; swipe from the top or bottom, or right-click the file; and choose Manage⟳Delete.

✦ **Download a file to your computer:** Tap or click the file, swipe from the top or bottom, or right-click the file. Choose Manage⟳Save Local.

Running SkyDrive on Your Desktop

If you want to use SkyDrive (as opposed to just playing with it in the tiled Windows 8 SkyDrive app), you need to install the SkyDrive program on your computer. The SkyDrive program runs on the Windows desktop, not on the tiled side of Windows, so don't be overly concerned when Windows flips over.

Installing SkyDrive: The legacy program

Here's how to install the SkyDrive program:

1. **Go to** www.skydrive.com **with any browser and then log in with your Microsoft account.**

If you've never used SkyDrive, a SkyDrive screen like the one in Figure 4-6 appears.

Tap or click Download

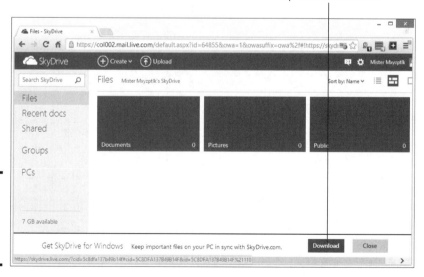

Figure 4-6:
An
untouched
SkyDrive
account.

2. **Tap or click the Download link at the bottom.**

   Microsoft *really* wants you to install the app.

   SkyDrive responds with a download link. See Figure 4-7.

3. **Tap or click the Download button.**

   Depending on which browser you're using, you probably have to tap or click several times to get the installer to run. If you didn't start on the Windows desktop, the installer flips over to the desktop and you're greeted with the Welcome to SkyDrive screen, as shown in Figure 4-8.

4. **Tap or click Get Started; sign in with your Microsoft account again, and tap or click Sign In.**

   The SkyDrive installer asks your permission to put the SkyDrive folder — the one destined to be synchronized to the cloud and to any of your other connected computers — in a reasonable location.

5. **Tap or click Next.**

   The SkyDrive installer asks whether you want to turn on Fetch. (See the "Fetching" section later in this chapter.) Fetch is a very useful feature, although some people are concerned about the security implications. I generally recommend that you turn it on and try it for a bit. If Fetch gives you the heebie-jeebies (that's a technical term), it's easy to turn off.

Tap or click Download

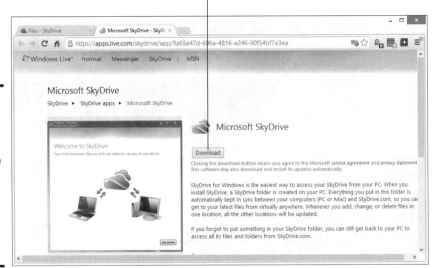

Figure 4-7:
The SkyDrive app is a prerequisite for getting SkyDrive to sync your data to multiple machines.

Figure 4-8:
Install the
SkyDrive
app from
here.

6. **Unless you're very concerned about your PC's security, select the Make Files on This PC Available to Me on My Other Machines check box, and then tap or click Done.**

   The installer whirrs and clicks a few times, does a handstand and polishes its nails, and when it's done, File Explorer opens to a new SkyDrive folder, as shown in Figure 4-9. SkyDrive is also added to your Favorites list in File Explorer.

Acts like a folder but stores contents on the Internet

Figure 4-9:
SkyDrive,
your new
automatically synchronized
folder.

**Book IV
Chapter 4**

**Using SkyDrive
in Windows 8**

Using the SkyDrive program on the desktop

The SkyDrive program is a rather unusual desktop program. You never need to start or stop it. The SkyDrive program just runs — fingers never leave the hands (if you'll pardon my W.C. Fields impression). In fact, most people who use SkyDrive to store their data never bother with the legacy desktop program. They cut straight to the SkyDrive folder in File Explorer and treat it as if it were any other folder.

Even though Microsoft urges you to "install" the SkyDrive "program," in fact, all you really need to know is that you have a magical new folder sitting there in File Explorer that stores its data on the Internet — and you can let other people look at or change the data, if you like.

To recap:

- ✦ The SkyDrive folder sits inside File Explorer (see Figure 4-9) and acts in many respects as if it were a regular, everyday folder. It isn't, of course, because the contents of the folder don't sit on your hard drive. They're up on Microsoft's servers, somewhere in the cloud.

- ✦ You can also access all the data that's stored on SkyDrive by logging in to www.skydrive.com with your Microsoft account.

- ✦ And as if that weren't confusing enough, there's the tiled SkyDrive app, which gives you just a few ways to access your SkyDrive data in the cloud.

With me still?

Anything you can do to files anywhere, you can do inside the SkyDrive folder — as long as you use File Explorer. For example:

- ✦ You can edit files, rename them, copy or move vast numbers of them. The SkyDrive folder in File Explorer is by far the easiest way to put data into SkyDrive and take it out.

- ✦ You can add subfolders inside the SkyDrive folder, rename them, delete them, move files around, and drag and drop files and folders in and out of the SkyDrive folder to your heart's content.

- ✦ You can change file properties (with a long tap or right-click).

- ✦ You can print files from SkyDrive just as you would any other file in File Explorer.

What makes the SkyDrive folder in File Explorer unique is that when you drag files into the SkyDrive folder, those files are copied into the cloud. If you have other computers connected to SkyDrive with the same Microsoft account, the SkyDrive folders on all those other computers are synchronized automatically — as long as the computers are connected to the Internet — and you needn't do a thing.

So if you have other computers (or tablets or phones) that you want to sync with your computer, now would be a good time to go to those other computers and follow the steps in "Installing SkyDrive: The legacy program" to install whichever version of the SkyDrive program is compatible with your devices. Remember that a SkyDrive program is available for Windows (Vista, Windows 7, and Windows 8 only), Windows Phone 7 or later, Mac OS X, and iOS (for iPad and iPhone). There's also a browser for Android phones and tablets.

Running SkyDrive on the Web

By far the most options and the best controls for SkyDrive are on the web. The option I use most? Sharing.

To share a file that's sitting in your SkyDrive folder:

1. **Go to** www.skydrive.com **with your favorite browser and then sign in with your Microsoft account.**

Your SkyDrive data appears as big boxy tiles on a web page, as shown in Figure 4-2. To make the whole thing more accessible, at least with a mouse and keyboard, click or tap the icon immediately to the right of the Sort by Name line. That brings you into Details View, shown in Figure 4-10.

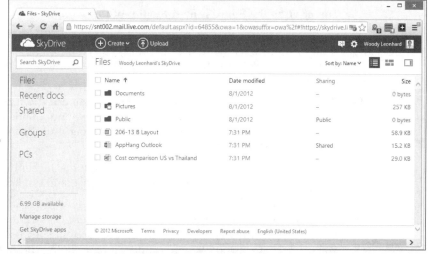

Figure 4-10: Details view is the easiest way to work with SkyDrive.

2. **Find the file or folder you want to share, and then select the box to the left of its name.**

Selecting the box is important. Don't click the file. If you click the file, you'll probably open it — not the end of the world, but it's easier to share without opening.

If the file or folder is already shared, the word "Shared" appears in the Sharing column (refer to Figure 4-10). Click the Shared text and a list of who can see the file or folder appears on the right, as in Figure 4-11.

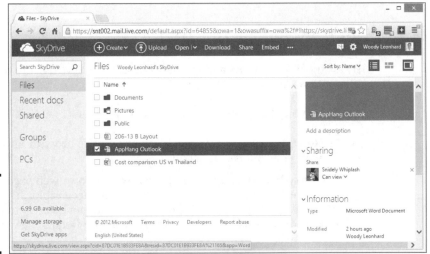

Figure 4-11:
Sharing lists appear on the right.

3. **Tap or click the Share link at the top of the screen.**

SkyDrive assumes that you not only want to share the file, but you also want to send an e-mail to the person(s) you're sharing the file with. The e-mail has a link to the file or folder. The Send a Link screen appears, as shown in Figure 4-12.

4a. **If you want to send a message to someone and put the link to the shared file/folder in the message, fill out the Send a Link screen: Type e-mail address(es) in the To box, add whatever note you like, and then tap or click Share. Go to Step 5.**

If you deselect both of the boxes at the bottom of the Send a Link screen, the person receiving the e-mail message and the link can only view, and not edit, the file.

If you select the box at the bottom, the recipient of the e-mail message has to log on with a Microsoft account that matches the e-mail address you sent. That's a good way to reduce the possibility that the person who receives the email will pass along the link.

4b. **If you don't want to send an e-mail, or you don't want to share the file (folder) with specific e-mail addresses, tap or click the Get a Link option on the left.**

SkyDrive shows you the rather ambiguous Get a Link screen, shown in Figure 4-13. Although the options seem straightforward, they aren't.

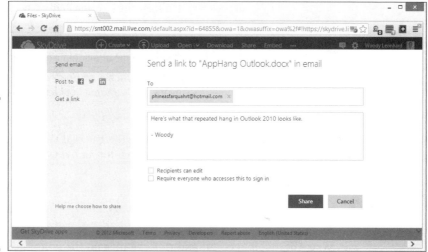

Figure 4-12:
You can e-mail a link to someone, so they can see a file in your SkyDrive folder.

Figure 4-13:
Create links with the appropriate restrictions.

5. **Consult Table 4-1 and tap or click the correct button for your situation.**

A link appears. Send that link to somebody, and when they click it, their web browser will open with the file you've selected, giving the person who clicked the link editing permissions indicated in Table 4-1.

6. **Make sure you copy the link provided by SkyDrive.**

You can use the link any way you wish.

**Book IV
Chapter 4**

**Using SkyDrive
in Windows 8**

Table 4-1	Get a Link Options
This Option	*Really Means This*
View Only	SkyDrive gives you a link to your file or folder. Anybody who has that link can view, but not change, the file or folder. This setting doesn't lock out other people: If someone can guess the link, they're in like Flynn. Similarly if you give the link to someone, and she gives it to someone else, the third party can see the file or folder.
View and Edit	Like View Only, except anybody who gets into the file or folder can change or delete the file or anything in the folder.
Public	Makes the contents searchable, so Google or Bing may pick it up someday. Anyone can view, but not change, the file or folder.

SkyDrive has many more capabilities. See the tutorial at `http://windows.microsoft.com/en-US/skydrive/home` for an overview.

Fetching

The SkyDrive Fetch feature lets you go into any computer that's logged on with your Microsoft account and retrieve files on the computer.

Say you're going on a business trip. Before you leave, you log on to your Windows 8 computer using a Microsoft account. While you're driving through a corn field in Kansas, you suddenly realize that you left your favorite picture of a scarecrow back on the computer at home. You whip out your iPad, use its 3G connection to go to `www.skydrive.com`, log on with the same Microsoft account, and with a few clicks, you can reach into your home computer and retrieve the picture. In fact, you can fetch any file you want.

For security verification, you need to be able to access a secondary verification channel; for example, if you have a phone registered with your Microsoft account, you may get an SMS with a code that lets you get into the computer.

To pull out a file with Fetch:

1. **Make sure the computer that contains your desired file meets the following criteria:**

- The computer is turned on. Fetch will usually "wake up" a sleeping Windows 8 computer, but if the computer's turned off, there's nothing you can do about it from a cornfield in Kansas.

- You must be logged onto that computer with a Microsoft account.

  You also need to know this computer's name, which is assigned when you set up Windows. I talk about assigning a computer name in Book I, Chapter 4.

  That's all you need to do, before you set out on that road trip.

2. **When you want to fetch a file from the waiting computer, fire up a browser — any browser — and go to** www.skydrive.com. **Log in with your Microsoft account.**

   The SkyDrive main page appears, as shown in Figure 4-14. Under the PCs heading on the left, note the names of other computers that are connected with the same Microsoft account.

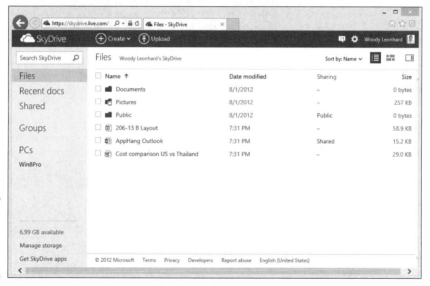

Figure 4-14:
The SkyDrive main page.

3. **In the lower-left corner, tap or click the name of the computer that you want to connect to.**

   In this case, I click Win8Pro.

   SkyDrive comes back with a representation of all the folders and libraries on your computer, as shown in Figure 4-15.

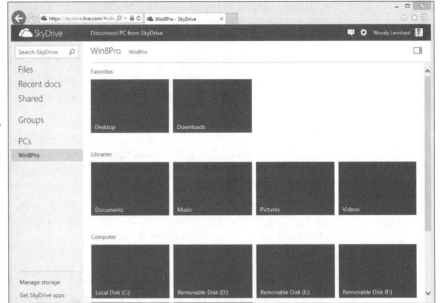

Figure 4-15:
You can see
all the files,
folders, and
libraries,
even hidden
files and
system
files, on the
connected
computer.

4. **Navigate to the file you want to retrieve, and then tap or click it.**

   Fetch selects it and shows it, as shown in Figure 4-16.

Figure 4-16:
One file
has been
chosen.

5. **Tap and hold or right-click the picture and choose Upload to SkyDrive.**

   Fetch asks where you want to put the file on SkyDrive.

6. **Choose an appropriate folder on SkyDrive, or create a new folder (click or tap the New Folder button); then tap or click Upload.**

   Fetch dutifully copies the file from the computer you're connected to into your SkyDrive folder.

   From that point, you can copy the file anywhere you like.

A couple of important disclaimers:

✦ The computer you're fetching from must have the SkyDrive program installed.

✦ Mac users (indeed any computer with a browser) can fetch files from PCs that have the SkyDrive program installed. But you can't use Fetch to retrieve files from a Mac. You can only use Fetch to retrieve files from a Windows PC.

✦ SkyDrive only retrieves files. It doesn't let you control the other computer, as you can with Remote Desktop Services or (my favorite) LogMeIn. If you're after a forgotten file, Fetch is great. If you're trying to trouble-shoot a cantankerous computer, you're out of luck.

Chapter 5: The Windows 8 Messaging App

In This Chapter

✔ **Introducing the tiled Messaging app**

✔ **Finding friends**

✔ **Chatting with friends**

✔ **Pretending you're offline**

*I*nstant messaging (IM) in the Microsoft milieu has gone through zillions of changes — not in the product itself, which hasn't changed all that much, but in the way it's been presented, marketed, and tucked into all sorts of strange parts of the Microsoft empire.

When Windows XP ruled the roost, there was Windows Messenger, MSN Messenger, and .NET Messenger, all from Microsoft, each with its own foibles and bumbles. Some versions of some Microsoft IM programs wouldn't even talk to others.

With Vista and through Windows 7, some sanity returned to Microsoft's instant messaging mess: Exactly one offering existed, and it had a funny name — Windows Live Messenger.

Now everything's new and improved, and there's *Messaging,* as in the *Windows 8 tiled Messaging app.* Messaging is based on the same underlying Messenger engine — in Messaging, you can message people running Windows Live Messenger, and vice versa — but it has a funny new face. Several, in fact.

This chapter touches on the high points of Messaging. I step you through establishing contact with other people running Messenger, in one of its many variants, and give a few pointers about using the tiled Messaging app.

And then I tell you how to shut off Messaging. That's probably the part you were looking for, right?

It's a noisy, pushy, cacophonous world.

Getting Started with the Windows 8 Messaging App

To start using the Messaging app, all you really need is a Microsoft account.

But before you jump into the deep end, I set the stage a bit by explaining the technical differences between Messaging, text (or SMS) messages, and Skype messages. These different types of messaging are becoming more and more intertwined, so a basic understanding of each type will help you get your, uh, message to your intended recipient.

The differences between MS Messaging and SMS

Some people are confused about *Microsoft Messenger* (which encompasses the Messaging app I examine in this chapter, the web-based Microsoft Messenger services, and Windows Live Messenger in its many forms) and how it relates to SMSing on a phone.

SMS stands for short message service, and SMS messages are more commonly known as text messages. I refer to text messages by their more technical name here (SMS) to help you differentiate between Windows 8's Messaging and SMSing.

On the surface Win8 Messaging and SMSing are similar, but the innards are quite different:

✦ Microsoft runs the plumbing that ties Messenger together. All the Messenger traffic goes over the Internet through Microsoft's computers.

✦ Your phone company runs the plumbing that delivers SMSs (text messages) to your phone. SMSs go over the normal voice phone network.

✦ Traditionally, SMSs were sent from mobile phone to mobile phone. That's changing. For example, you can now send and receive SMSs from Internet-based services like Gmail and Hotmail/Outlook.com to a phone. If you're connected to Exchange Server, it does wonders routing SMSs as well.

✦ Traditionally, people using Messenger had to be connected directly to the Internet. That's changing, too, as clever people find ways to cross over between the networks automatically.

As the technology changes, the distinctions between Microsoft Messenger and SMSing really boil down to this: If you want to use Microsoft Messenger to send or receive messages, you have to run one of the Microsoft Messaging programs.

You can send an SMS message to someone, and you don't really know whether he picked it up on his phone or Gmail.

The differences between MS Messaging and Skype

Microsoft Messaging and Skype (which is owned by Microsoft) grew up on two completely different continents. The technology behind each is radically different, and the marketing of each is totally independent. In fact, many people are surprised to find out that Skype is a 100-percent Microsoft owned company. You certainly wouldn't know it by looking at any of Skype's website or reading material.

That said, Skype and Microsoft Messaging are converging at a breakneck pace. Consider the following:

✦ Microsoft Messaging grew up as a text capability, but now encompasses voice and video. Microsoft Messaging has extensive connections with Windows users.

✦ Skype grew up as a voice capability, but now encompasses text and video. Skype has extensive connections with local telephone companies.

✦ Both services run on the Internet, using Microsoft's servers. But they run in completely different ways, using incompatible technologies.

✦ Skype has put a huge dent in long-distance telephone revenue. Microsoft Messaging threatens to do the same with the insanely profitable SMS business. Telephone companies don't like it but can't do much about it.

A lot of money is to be made in bringing together Microsoft Messaging and Skype. You can safely assume that an army of Microsoft programmers are working on the problem.

Whom you can message

If you set up Messaging correctly, you can communicate with people who are logged on to any of these Messenger programs:

✦ Windows Live Messenger running on Windows XP, Vista, Windows 7, Windows Phone, Xbox 360, Blackberry, or Zune HD

✦ Windows Live Messenger running on iOS (for iPhone and iPad) or Mac OS X

✦ Yahoo! Messenger

✦ Facebook Chat

Among the hundred different messaging networks, a few of them talk to the others. Nowadays most messaging takes place over the Microsoft Messaging network, Apple iChat (which doesn't work on Windows computers), Gmail Chat, Yahoo! Messenger, Skype (the texting part) and, remarkably, AOL Instant Messenger. Tencent is the dominant messaging program in China.

Understanding online status indicators

The mechanism for transmitting a message goes something like this: When you log in to Windows with a Microsoft account, Microsoft servers store a record of the Internet (IP) address you're using to log in. Anyone on your Messaging friends list (that is, people in your Windows 8 People app who have been approved for Messaging) sees that you're online, and their computer receives a copy of your IP address.

If one of your Messaging friends tries to send you a message, it doesn't go through Microsoft servers. Instead, it goes directly to your computer.

That explains why it can take a while for the Online status to reflect what's actually happening: Microsoft servers keep track of all the people who are online, but the messaging actually takes place between computers, with the servers out of the loop.

With the exception of Microsoft Messaging and Yahoo! Messenger, none of those messaging networks communicate with each other.

Messaging, as you know it, is dying — or maybe it's more accurate to say that it's spreading out and losing its identity as a separate program. Google+ has video circles. Facebook Chat draws a lot of people. Microsoft Messaging has become part and parcel of Hotmail/Outlook.com. Gmail has an embedded messaging program. All these developments point toward a future in which chat, all by itself, is kind of a ho-hum feature. You're certainly going to see less emphasis placed on Microsoft Messaging and more emphasis on social networking within Microsoft products.

The days of Messaging, as a separate program, are numbered.

How Messaging works

At its heart, Microsoft Messaging — in fact, any traditional messenger program — is pretty simple. Here's how a typical interaction goes:

1. You install a messenger program, and send chat invitations to people you may (or may not!) know.

   With Windows 8, the messenger program's already built in — the Messaging app — and you're connected to the Microsoft Messaging system as soon as you sign in to Windows with a Microsoft account.

2. The people that you notify send confirmation that they want to chat with you. They may send chat invitations to you, which you can accept, decline, or ignore.

Typically, the person sending the invitation never knows whether she was declined or ignored, but she receives notification if she was accepted.

Be aware: If you set up a connection to a Facebook account — usually through the Win8 tiled People app, but sometimes through the Win8 tiled Photos app — any of the people on your Facebook friends list are automatically approved for Messaging. That may or may not be what you are expecting. Microsoft's excuse/explanation is that you can chat with those Facebook people when you're using Facebook, so why not while using the Windows 8 tiled Messaging app?

3. If you already have contacts set up with some other version of Messenger that predates the Windows 8 Messaging app — perhaps an earlier version of Windows Messenger, or you've used Messenger through the Windows Live website — the Messenger-approved contacts are added to your Windows 8 People list.

People who accept your invitations, or those who are added through Facebook or an old Messenger contact, are *Messenger* or *Messaging friends*. The terminology is, uh, unevenly applied, but the fact remains: You can only have a Microsoft Messaging conversation with people who have, either directly or indirectly, accepted an invitation to chat.

4. Somebody sends you a message, and it appears on your Messaging tile.

5. When you ask Messaging to start a new conversation, it flips over to the People app.

6. The People app runs out to Microsoft servers and asks which of your Messaging friends are online.

7. You choose from the people listed as Online and begin your chat.

Microsoft servers check from time to time to make sure you're still around. In general, they keep your address on file until you log off of Windows.

Fishing for Messaging Friends

Ready to get started with the Windows 8 tiled Messaging app? First, you need to find some friends. You need to send invitations to people and see whether they respond. You may already have some Messaging friends if:

✦ You're working with a Microsoft account that already has Messenger friends (in the Windows Live, Hotmail, Outlook.com or Messenger websites, friends are called *Messenger Contacts* or sometimes *friends*).

✦ You've imported Facebook friends (with whom you can automatically chat).

Here's how to invite friends to chat with Messaging:

1. **Tap or click the Messaging tile on the Start screen.**

Chances are good that your screen looks like the one in Figure 5-1.

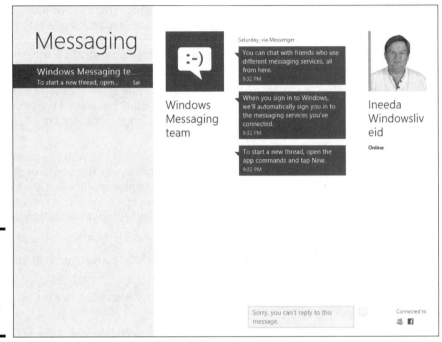

Figure 5-1:
The
Windows 8
Messaging
app's home
screen.

2. **Swipe from the top or bottom, or right-click the screen, to bring up the App bar.**

You see the options listed in Figure 5-2.

Figure 5-2:
Control
messaging
from down
here.

3. **On the left, tap or click Invite; then tap or click Add a Friend.**

Messaging flips over to your default browser and sends you to the Windows People Add Friends to Messenger site, shown in Figure 5-3.

Figure 5-3:
Add
Messaging
friends
by diving
through the
Add People
website.

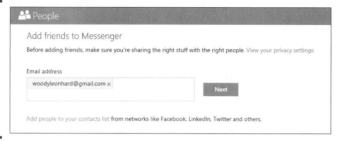

4. **In the Email Address box, type the e-mail address of whomever you wish to invite to become a Messaging friend. Tap or click Next.**

   A copy of the message that will be sent to initiate the invitation appears, as shown in Figure 5-4. No, you can't change the message.

   It's always bothered me that this message doesn't have more detail — what's involved in being "friends," for example. You might want to give your potential friend a heads-up e-mail and explain that in order to be able to chat with you over Microsoft Messaging, she has to accept your offer to become a friend. You might also warn her that if she accepts the offer, the fact that you and she have become friends is posted to all your other friends — and hers, too.

Figure 5-4:
The
contents
of the
outbound
message,
inviting
someone
to be your
friend.

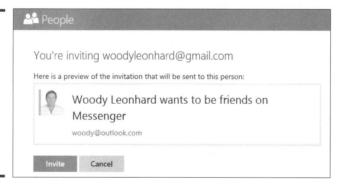

5. **Tap or click Invite.**

   The Add People website tells you that the message has been sent. All you can do now is wait. In my experience, the invitation can go out in an hour or less, but the person receiving the message has to respond.

If you're impatient, you can swipe from the top or bottom, or right-click in the middle of the Messaging main screen, and choose Invite⇨View Invites. Doing so puts you back in your default browser and points you to a web page that tells you the status of all your open invitations.

When your invitee receives the invitation message, she must tap or click the View Invitation link. If the person you invite doesn't have a Microsoft account, she can sign up for one. No Microsoft account, no Microsoft Messaging, eh? After signing on to the Windows website, your invitee must tap or click to accept the invitation.

At that point — after the invitee has accepted the invitation — you can start chatting.

No, you aren't notified when the invitation has been accepted. You just have to kind of guess and hope.

Running a Windows 8 Messaging Chat

You can initiate a Messaging session in several ways. For example, you can tap or click a picture in the Windows 8 People app, and then (if you've chosen a Messaging friend) tap or click Send Message.

More frequently, though, if you want to message with someone, you go through the Messaging app. Here's how:

1. **Tap or click the Messaging tile on the Start screen to start the Messaging app.**

   The main page appears (refer to Figure 5-1).

2a. *If the person you want to chat with is on the left,* **skip to Step 4a or 4b.**

2b. *If the person is not on the left,* **swipe from the top or bottom, or right-click the main page and in the lower-right corner, choose New.**

   Tapping New throws you into the People app, where you see all your Messaging friends who are online.

3. **Tap or click the person you want to chat with, and at the bottom of the screen, tap or click Select.**

   The Messaging main screen appears with your chosen Messaging friend highlighted on the left, as shown in Figure 5-5.

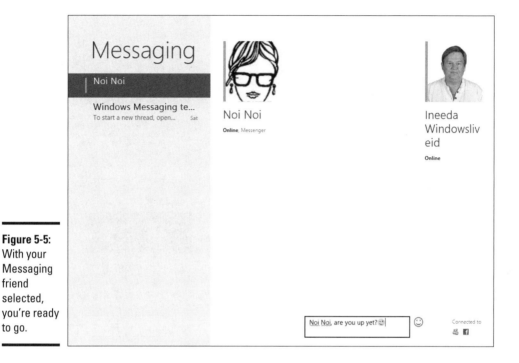

Figure 5-5:
With your
Messaging
friend
selected,
you're ready
to go.

4a. *If you have a keyboard,* **type your message.**

4b. *If you don't have a keyboard,* **tap in the Type a Message box at the bottom and then type.**

A few quick hints:

- *If you press Enter, you send the message.* To put a line break in your message without sending it, press Shift+Enter.

- *You can use all the usual keys,* such as the arrow keys, Delete, Ctrl+C to copy, Ctrl+V to paste, and so on.

- *For smiley faces,* you can type the old-fashioned symbols (such as :) or :D) and they're converted automatically to color pictures. But you can also tap or click the smiley face to the right of the text box and choose from a big bunch of smileys, or even use the vast array of (black and white) smiley faces on the tap-screen keyboard.

5. **When you're done, press Enter.**

Your message is sent to the recipient, and appears in the running dialogue in the middle of the page, as shown in Figure 5-6.

**Book IV
Chapter 5**

**The Windows 8
Messaging App**

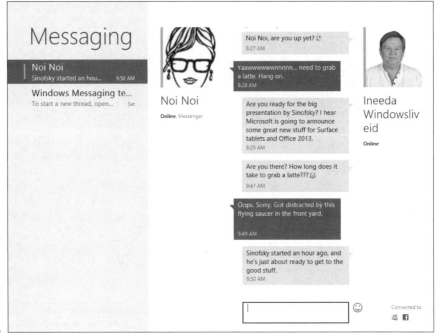

Figure 5-6:
The full con-
versation
appears in
the middle.

And yes, you can send another message before the recipient responds to the first one.

But you won't make many friends that way.

You can switch among your Messaging friends by tapping or clicking their names in the left pane.

Using Messaging Effectively

You have very few options in the Windows 8 tiled Messaging app. There are many more capabilities in the online, web-based program. Just sign in to Hotmail/Outlook.com, and a world of Messenger options awaits.

The one Messaging option I find myself using all the time is to appear offline. If you're tired of your friends — real and erstwhile — trying to start a chat, you can simply tell Microsoft Messaging that you've hung up the phone and walked away.

Here's how to appear offline:

1. **Tap or click the Messaging app on the Start screen.**

The main page appears, which may have a lot of conversations on it (refer to Figure 5-6).

2. **Swipe from the top or bottom, or right-click in the main part of the screen.**

The Messaging App bar appears.

3. **On the left, tap or click the Status icon and choose Invisible.**

That's it. Anybody who's on your Messaging friends list and looks to see whether you're around discovers that you're just gone.

Chapter 6: Xbox Music and Video

In This Chapter

✔ Pitching you Xbox Music and Video

✔ Playing music with Xbox Music

✔ Playing videos with Xbox Video

✔ Managing your playlists

✔ Playing music where you want

*M*icrosoft calls the Windows 8 tiled music app Xbox Music for two reasons:

✦ **To associate its wildly successful Xbox with its aging and sagging Windows platform:** A lot of effort has been expended to make the Windows 8 version of its music player look and behave just like the Microsoft Xbox music player.

✦ **To make money:** That surprises you, yes? In the music and video sphere, Microsoft makes more money by convincing you to buy music and videos — and sign up for expensive Xbox services — with the expectation that the music, videos, and services work on both Windows and the Xbox.

It's a good marketing move.

Ultimately, the Xbox Music app (on the Xbox) and the Windows 8 Music app might look alike, but they don't work the same way: They're completely different systems, running on totally different hardware, with utterly different foundations.

On the other hand, if you buy music or videos from Microsoft, the Xbox and Windows can keep track of your music and videos and play them for you, and many efforts are under way to bridge the gap between Windows and Xbox.

Your job is to figure out what's best for you, and that ain't easy. Unless, of course, you have an unlimited pocketbook and don't mind telling the butler to fetch the latest movie on Hulu. Perhaps the maid can prop up the footrest and bring a box of popcorn while he's at it.

What about Xbox LIVE?

It's a simple, incontrovertible fact of Xbox life: If you have an Xbox and expect to use it for anything except simple everybody-sit-at-the-console games, you have to shell out the $60 a year or so for Xbox LIVE Gold.

I'm not just talking about competing against other players online, which is what Xbox LIVE Gold was originally invented to facilitate. If you wanted to shoot aliens with your friends' help and they weren't sitting in the same room with you, buying Xbox LIVE Gold let you connect with them so you could gang up on the bad guys.

But Xbox LIVE Gold has evolved beyond those humble beginnings. Now you need Xbox LIVE Gold for all these features, too:

✔ Using your Xbox console to do anything with your TV

✔ Letting your Windows 8 apps run media through your Xbox

✔ Running Hulu Plus, Netflix, or MLB (Yes, you have to pay Hulu, Netflix, or MLB.TV *and* pay for Xbox LIVE Gold.)

I know; it doesn't make sense. You don't have to pay Apple to run Netflix — you can buy Netflix from inside the Apple TV app. You don't have to pay Roku to run Hulu Plus. You don't have to pay Sony to run Amazon Instant Video on the PlayStation 3. Why do you have to pay Microsoft to run the for-pay services?

When you calculate the cost of buying an Xbox, make sure you include that extra $60 a year for Xbox LIVE Gold because that may influence your buying decision. Heck, a Roku XD costs less than a one-year Xbox LIVE Gold subscription.

Why You Might Want Xbox Music or Video

In some specific situations, Xbox Music and Xbox Video make sense. For example:

✦ **If you subscribe to Xbox Music (formerly the Zune Music Pass),** the Xbox Music app is a good place to visit all the music you can play. At $9.99 per month, the Xbox Music subscription service is pricey, but there's a lot of depth, with 30 million songs on file.

✦ **If you really, really like the big, colorful advertising or if you're looking to spend a little loose change on an album or video,** the Windows 8 apps will definitely give you what you're looking for.

✦ **If you want to stream music or videos directly to your Xbox,** the Windows 8 Xbox Music or Xbox Video app lets you control the streaming. Just be aware that you have to pay for Xbox LIVE Gold (an additional $60 per year and up; see the nearby "What about Xbox LIVE?" sidebar).

The Xbox Music app and the Xbox Video app are basically the same app. They work almost identically — pretty typical for media-playing apps.

The two big differences between Xbox Music and Xbox Video are

✦ Xbox Music looks in your Music library for music files, whereas Xbox Video looks in your Video library for video files. (See the discussion of libraries in Book VII, Chapter 3.)

✦ Xbox Music lets you purchase music from Microsoft. Xbox Video works the movie side of the street for Microsoft. They're both hucksters at heart.

The number one thing you need to know about Xbox Music and Xbox Video is that they're *horrible* players, if you're playing music that you own. Not just bad, but positively *wretched*. In subsequent sections, I show you why.

If you want to manage and play your music or videos, install VLC on the old-fashioned desktop. VLC is a high-quality, barebones player that makes it easy to manage and play your music and videos — all your videos, including DVD movies — and it doesn't cost a cent. Easy to install and use, too, although it ain't beautiful. See the sidebar in Book VI, Chapter 7 for details.

Playing Your Music with Xbox Music

If you've never used the Xbox Music app, now's a good time to give it a try. Follow these steps:

1. **On the Start screen, tap or click the Xbox Music tile.**

Something like the screen in Figure 6-1 appears, displaying the Xbox Music app.

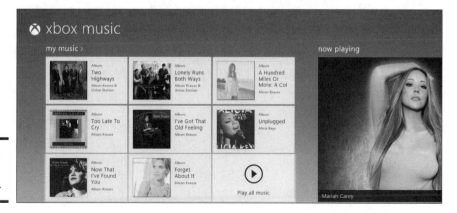

Figure 6-1:
The Xbox
Music app.

Book IV
Chapter 6

Xbox Music and
Video

2. **If you're asked to sign on to Xbox LIVE, ignore it for now.**

   If you have any music in your Music library, it appears on the left, under the My Music heading, probably in a rather jumbled state. (I talk about putting music in your Music library in Book VI Chapter 7, and about Libraries in general in Book VII Chapter 3.) Depending on your screen resolution, Xbox Music probably shows eight of the albums in your music collection — then fills out the rest of the app (which scrolls and scrolls and scrolls to the right) with stuff that's for sale. Oh goody!

   If you don't have any music on your computer yet, Xbox Music starts by showing you album covers for albums that you can buy from the Windows Store.

3. **Scroll to the right to see what Microsoft wants to sell you.**

   What you see in the Xbox Music screen (Figure 6-2) is a gigantic sales opportunity: Microsoft wants you to buy the music on offer. The interface makes a tiny concession that you might actually have some music already on your computer in the Music library that you want to play. For that odd possibility, your music is visible on the left, to the left of the gorgeous CD artwork that engulfs the app, urging you to open your pocket.

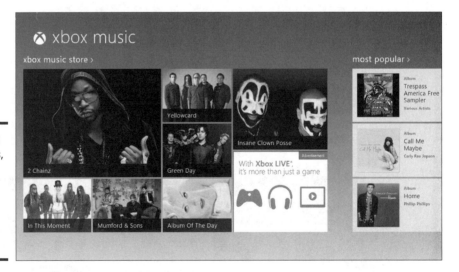

Figure 6-2:
All the tiles, except the ones at the very beginning, are advertisements.

4. **If you have any music already on your PC, on the left (refer to Figure 6-1), tap or click one of the album tiles and see how the controls work.**

When you play an album, it looks like Figure 6-3. The Play, Add to Now Playing, and Artist Details controls appear on the left. If you right-click or swipe from the top or bottom, you see the App Bar, with additional controls to Add to Playlist, Delete, Shuffle, Repeat, Skip to the Previous song, or Play.

Figure 6-3: Playing an album you already own in Xbox Music.

The volume control isn't inside the Xbox Music app, silly user. You find the volume control on the Charms bar. To change the volume, slide from the right or hover your mouse in the upper-right corner, and then choose the Settings charm. At the bottom, slide the volume control up or down.

You can't change the graphic that's shown when you play music. At least as of this writing, Microsoft shows the album cover for the main pane then grays-out the background. Xbox Music, though, has an extensive library of ancillary information.

5. **Click or tap on the album cover (at the bottom of Figure 6-3) to bring up a wealth of information about the artist(s), as shown in Figure 6-4.**

**Book IV
Chapter 6**

Xbox Music and Video

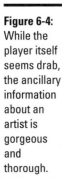

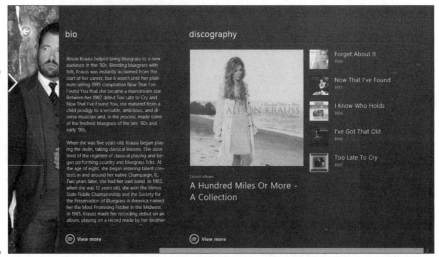

Figure 6-4:
While the
player itself
seems drab,
the ancillary
information
about an
artist is
gorgeous
and
thorough.

6. **To see your whole music collection, tap or click the left arrow in the upper-left corner, and then tap or click the My Music heading.**

   The slightly modified Excel spreadsheet appears, as shown in Figure 6-5. Actually, your music appears in a list ordered by the date that you put the music file in your Music library.

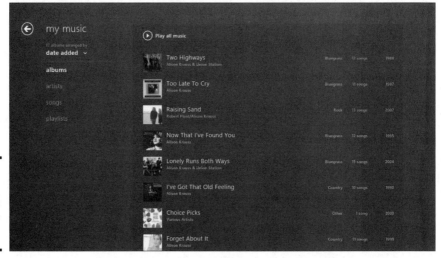

Figure 6-5:
Your music
displays in a
very lengthy
list.

7. **Sort a few ways.**

   For example, instead of showing Songs by Date Added, tap or click the entry at the upper left and then choose A to Z, Album, Genre, or Artist.

   The list is long and cumbersome.

8. **On the left, tap or click Artists to have Xbox Music show you the songs grouped by artist.**

9. **In the upper-left corner, tap or click the left arrow to go back to the main Xbox Music screen.**

   You see a different, random assortment of eight album covers in the My Music section. The number may differ depending on your screen resolution, but Xbox Music only shows a tiny fraction of the albums in your collection.

When you're back in the main part of the app, you can tap or click an album cover and, depending on the album, listen to a 30-second preview of most album songs, with an option to buy.

I won't bore you with a guided tour of the rest of the app. The meager controls (Shuffle, Repeat, Previous, Pause, and Next) are shown in Figure 6-3. That's almost all there is to it, unless you want to buy something from Microsoft.

Viewing Your Videos with Xbox Video

Promise me you won't get bored.

The Xbox Video app works almost exactly like the Music app. Here's a quick recap:

1. **Tap or click the Xbox Video tile.**

   You see an app that really wants you to buy or rent a movie. Way over on the left, your videos appear — assuming you have videos in the Windows Video library. See Figure 6-6.

   Many people store videos from their phones and cameras inside the Pictures library. That's a good place to put them — the Windows 8 tiled Pictures app, Windows Media Player, and VLC will find them there. But the Xbox Video app doesn't look through the Pictures library.

Figure 6-6:
The Xbox Video app shows some of your videos but mostly wants to sell, sell, sell.

2. **Tap or click the My Videos link at the upper left. You may have to scroll, scroll, scroll to get there.**

A scrollable list of tiles appears, as shown in Figure 6-7.

Choose to show only movies, TV, or other

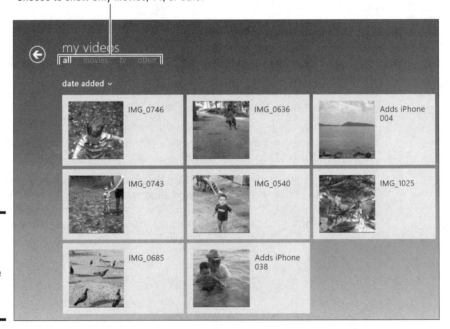

Figure 6-7:
Videos appear as a scrollable group of tiles.

3. **In the Date Added drop-down list, choose a sort option such as A to Z or Duration.**

4. **Tap or double-click a video to play it. When you're done, tap or click the back arrow in the upper-left corner to return to the movie tiles (Figure 6-7) and tap or click again to go back to the main Xbox Video page (Figure 6-6).**

5. **Out on the main page, to buy a movie, or play a trailer on your computer or Xbox, tap or click it.**

   The movie trailers are identical to what you see on www.rotten tomatoes.com, except Rotten Tomatoes usually has several trailers for each new release.

Plans are afoot to have the Xbox Video app supply you with movie show times, and even let you buy tickets online. However, those features weren't available as this book went to press.

Managing Playlists

The Xbox Music app has a rudimentary playlist capability. A *playlist* is just a list of songs that the app is supposed to play in order. I have a detailed discussion of playlists, such as how to create and maintain them, in Book VI, Chapter 7.

Remarkably, any playlist that you create in a different app, such as Windows Media Player or VLC, works great in the Xbox Music app. You just have to make sure you put the *WPL file* — the file that contains the playlist — in your Music library.

Unfortunately, the Xbox Video app doesn't support playlists. If you have kids in the household, you know how useful video playlists can be. Oh well. YouTube still lets you create and maintain video playlists.

You can create a playlist in the Xbox Music app in several ways. Here's the easiest:

1. **In the Xbox Music app, tap or click the My Music link in the upper-left corner.**

   A list of songs appears (refer to Figure 6-5).

2. **On the left, tap or click Playlists.**

3. **Tap or click the plus sign.**

   A small box invites you to type a name for the playlist.

4. **Type a name for your new playlist and tap or click Save.**

   The playlist appears on the screen, as in Figure 6-8, but there are no instructions or any indication of how to add songs to the playlist.

Figure 6-8:
A new but very empty playlist.

5. **On the left, tap or click Songs; then pick the songs you want in the playlist, one by one, by either tapping or right-clicking the song.**

   The App bar appears at the bottom of the screen, as in Figure 6-9.

6. **On the bottom left, tap or click Add to** *Name of Playlist You Just Created.*

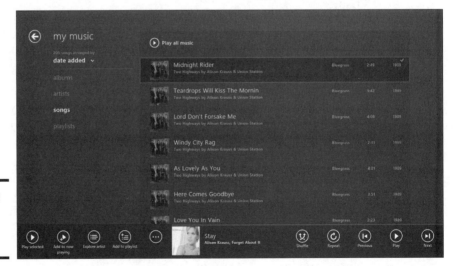

Figure 6-9:
Adding a song to a playlist.

You can also create a new playlist and add the song to it, by tapping or clicking the Add to Playlist icon in the App bar, and choosing to put the song in a new playlist.

When you play a playlist, you can remove an individual song from the playlist by tapping or right-clicking on it and, in the App bar, choosing Delete.

Turning Off the Tiled Apps as Default Media Players

One last little trick. This bugs the bewilickers out of me.

I'm rifling through a bunch of songs (or movies or other media) on the desktop side of Windows, and absent-mindedly tap or double-click a song. Windows doesn't play the song in Windows Media Player. Noooooh. It flips to Xbox Music and plays the song there. Bah! Humbug! That's the last place I want to play a song.

I think the best solution to this problem is to install VLC (see the sidebar in Book VI, Chapter 7), and have it handle all your media files, which is an option during the installation. If you prefer Windows Media Player, you can tell Windows that Media Player should handle your media instead.

To keep your double-clicked music from playing in the Xbox Music app, follow these steps:

1. **On the desktop side of the fence, in File Explorer, find a music file.**

You can probably start in your Music library. You definitely want to make this change for MP3 files, but if you use other music file formats (OGGs, for example), repeat these steps for each file type.

2. **Right-click or tap and hold on the music file, and then choose Open With⇨Choose Default Program.**

Windows shows you the options in Figure 6-10.

Figure 6-10: Keep Xbox Music (identified here as just "Music") away from your MP3 files!

3. **Choose Windows Media Player, or if you have a better music file player, choose More Options and find the player you want.**

From that point on, every time you tap or double-click an MP3 file (or OGG, or whatever you've chosen), Windows doesn't send you off to Xbox Music gaga land.

Score one for the good guys.

Book V

Connecting Online with Tiled Apps

Contents at a Glance

Chapter 1: Getting Started with Facebook

In This Chapter

✔ **Establishing a Facebook account**

✔ **Nailing down your settings**

✔ **Building your Timeline**

✔ **Locking down your Facebook info**

✔ **Connecting to Windows**

*I*f you don't yet have a Facebook account, about a billion people are ahead of you.

I have friends who figure Facebook is some sort of fad that's going away soon. They'd rather be drawn and quartered than put anything on Facebook. "You lose your privacy," they say, "I don't see any need for it."

Of course, many of them said the same thing about mobile phones a decade ago. ATMs. Online banking. Two decades before that they lambasted the newfangled color television stuff — it'll never catch on, you know? Mimeographs. Eight-track tapes. Wringer washing machines. Vinyl records.

Facebook's become an important part of the daily routine of hundreds of millions of people, and it claims just less than one billion registered users. It's been credited with starting revolutions. It's certainly a good source of news — almost as good as Twitter (see Book V, Chapter 2) — if you choose your sources carefully.

Facebook has fundamentally changed the way hundreds of millions of families interact, more so than any other invention since the telephone. It's altered the way people work. Businesses. Schools. Hospitals. Governments. Charities.

Facebook has even eaten into e-mail, for heaven's sake. E-mail usage has gone down the past couple of years because Facebook's one-to-many nature reduces the need for e-mail messages. To me, that's incredible. I grew up with e-mail — sent my first e-mail message in 1977 — and it boggles my mind that so many people prefer Facebook to e-mail. But that's how it is.

I'm tempted to stand up and bellow a chorus from Bob Dylan's "The Times They Are A-Changin'."

You can ignore Facebook, if you want to, but some day your kids or grand-kids or the young whippersnappers in the nursing home are going to ask why dad or grandpa or Uncle Fuddyduddy doesn't get off his duff and get with the system. It's the same argument people had with Luddites about typewritten letters and faxes a couple decades ago.

Besides, Facebook ties directly into Windows, if you let it. The hooks can be useful. And that's the reason for this chapter.

In this chapter, I only brush the surface of the capabilities available to Facebook users. You find a bit of depth about the Timeline because it's hard to find information about it. And I hit the privacy/security part hard because that's where you need to concentrate your efforts when you're just starting out.

As you get more adept at Facebook, you'll figure out about tagging photos; sharing things that have been posted to your home page or your Timeline; subscribing; setting up groups; chatting and video calling; setting up your own fan (or business, group, or charity) pages; posting events; searching; GPS location-based features; setting up your own lists — and much more. If Facebook intrigues you, I suggest you pick up a copy of *Facebook For Dummies,* 4th Edition by Carolyn Abram. For a deeper look at the side of Facebook that's tailored for businesses, charities, and groups (including that knitting circle or bridge club), look at *Social Media Marketing All-In-One For Dummies,* by Jan Zimmerman and Doug Sahlin.

Signing Up for a Facebook Account

If you don't yet have a Facebook account, I suggest you sign up. Don't worry, nobody's going to steal your identity or mine your personal data. Yet. And Facebook's absolutely free — and will be free to use, although some features may cost something someday.

There's one cardinal rule about Facebook, which I call the *prime directive:* Don't put anything on or in Facebook — *anything* — that you don't want to appear in tomorrow morning's news. Or your ex-spouse's attorney's office. Or your boss's inbox. Or your kid's school class. Privacy begins at home, eh?

Now that you have the right attitude, all you need is a working e-mail address, and as long as you state that you're more than 13 years old, you can have a Facebook account in minutes. Here's how:

1. **Use your favorite browser to go to** www.facebook.com.

    The Sign Up page, as shown in Figure 1-1, appears.

2. **Fill in your name and e-mail address (it must be a good one that you can get to because a confirmation e-mail goes to that address), give your new account a password, and make sure your birthday indicates that you're older than 13.**

    This is *not* the way to set up an account for a celebrity, band, business charitable organization, or knitting group. In all those cases, you need to set up an individual account first — follow the instructions here — and then after your individual account is ready, you add a *fan page* to your individual account. I know it's complicated, but Facebook works that way. Even Coca-Cola's page is attached to an individual — presumably either Mr. Coca or Ms. Cola signed up, and then created a page for Coca-Cola afterward.

There's no reason to give personally identifiable information in this sign-up sheet. Facebook may balk if you try to sign up as Mark Zuckerberg, but it (probably) won't have any problem with Marcus Zuckerbergus (although, now that I've mentioned it, the name may be added to Facebook's blacklist). And if you figure your birthday is your business, the Internet Police aren't going to come knocking. The one item that has to be valid, though, is the e-mail address — which can come from a free site, such as Hotmail/Outlook.com or Gmail.

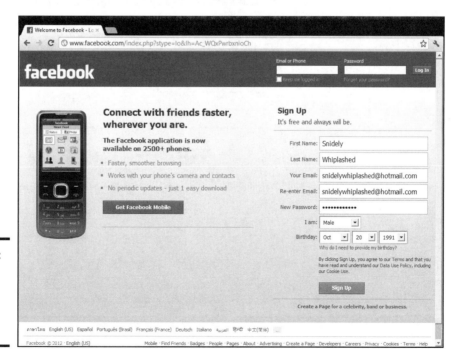

Figure 1-1:
Signing up for a Facebook account is easy.

3. **Tap or click Sign Up.**

   Facebook sends a confirmation e-mail to the address you specified and, at the same time, brings up a page that tries to get you to suck in contact data from other services, such as Hotmail/Outlook.com (see Figure 1-2).

   You don't have to bring in your contacts from elsewhere. Even if you decide to hook up with, for example, Hotmail/Outlook.com in the future, it's easy.

4. **Divulge the minimum amount possible and, in the lower-right corner, tap or click Skip This Step.**

   Facebook asks you to provide your high school and college/university info.

5. **Tap or click Skip in the lower-right corner, or register the fact that you went to Ridgemont High and Animal House University.**

   Facebook asks you to provide a profile picture.

6. **Upload an appropriate picture (see Figure 1-3), and then tap or click Save and Continue.**

7. **When the confirmation e-mail from Facebook arrives, tap or click the link and complete the confirmation.**

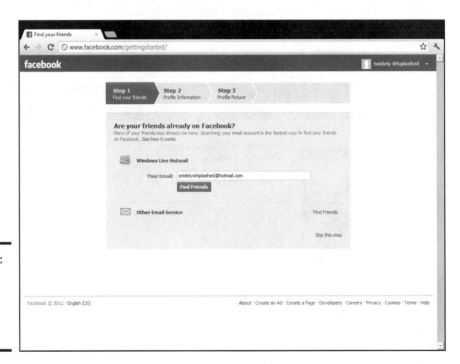

Figure 1-2:
Facebook starts by fishing for your contacts.

Figure 1-3:
Extra points
for creativity
in your
picture.

Robert Couse-Baker, from Flickr, www.flickr.com/photos/29233640@N07/6111053892

8. **Sign in with the e-mail address and password you just used.**

Congratulations. You now have a Facebook account, and it looks something like Figure 1-4.

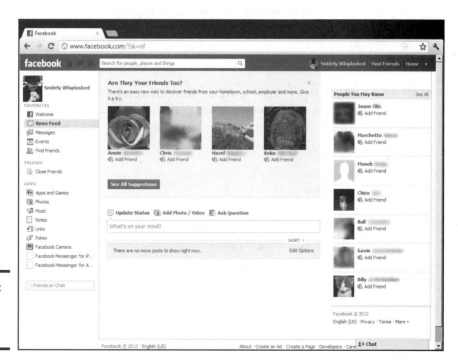

Figure 1-4:
A fresh
Facebook
account.

What, exactly, is a friend?

Most people new to Facebook think that "friends" are, well, friends. Not so.

On Facebook, a *friend* is someone you're willing to interact with. If you're interested in interacting with somebody who has a Facebook account — let her see what you've posted (typed in the What's on Your Mind box), look at your *Timeline* (a historic bulletin board), or look at the pictures you've posted on Facebook — you send a *friend request*. The person who receives the friend request decides whether she wants to accept the request, decline it, or just sit on it.

Many of my Facebook friends are people I've never met, and don't really know. They are, however, people I trust enough to allow them to look at my vacation pictures, say, and people who are interesting enough that I want to take a look at what they post on their sites. If the concept of a friend is a bit overwhelming at this point, don't worry about it. Find two or three people you know who have Facebook accounts, send friend requests to them, and watch what happens when they respond.

Get your feet wet with the concept before you start friending everything with two legs. Or four. You can always add new friends (or delete them — *unfriend* them — for that matter), but it's easier to start out slow while you're getting the hang of it. Too many friends at first can be overwhelming.

From this point on, any time you go to Facebook, it asks you to log in (or sign in). Use the same e-mail address and password, and you're in like Flynn.

Next, set up some basic settings and get your security locked down.

Choosing basic Facebook settings

Before you try to figure out what you're doing — a process that will take several days — step through setting up the rest of your Facebook account.

Here's what you do:

1. **Bring up your home page by tapping or clicking Home in the upper-right corner.**

   You see a home page like the one in Figure 1-5.

2. **In the upper-right corner of your home page, tap or click your name.**

   After you tap or click your name, Facebook either brings up your profile page or your Timeline page (Figure 1-6), depending on whether your account was set up under the old or new rules.

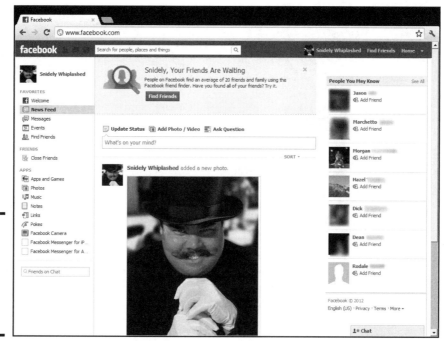

Figure 1-5:
Your home page, the main page you go to when you log in.

If your page doesn't look anything at all like the page in Figure 1-6 — if it doesn't start out by saying, "Welcome to Your Timeline," chances are good that you got stuck with a profile page, instead of a Timeline. As this book went to press, the switch to Timeline was an on-again, off-again endeavor. If you don't have a Timeline, see the nearby "Switching from profile to Timeline" sidebar.

In this section, I talk about making good choices for security. In the later section "Building a Great Timeline," I talk about gussying it up.

Switching from profile to Timeline

Facebook is gradually switching everyone from profile pages to Timeline pages. Although many long for the profile page, there are advantages to a Timeline. I suggest that you just switch over to a Timeline page and forget about going back.

Switching to a Timeline page is not difficult, but it takes several steps. I take you through them at the beginning of the section "Building a Great Timeline" later in this chapter.

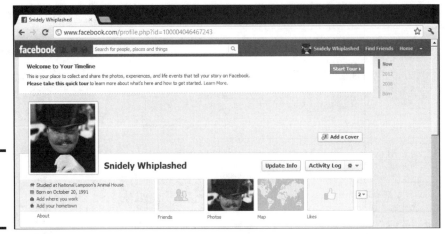

Figure 1-6:
The
Timeline
page.

3. **On the left, under the box that lists your school and birthdate, tap or click the About link.**

   The About page appears, as shown in Figure 1-7.

Limit who can see the entry

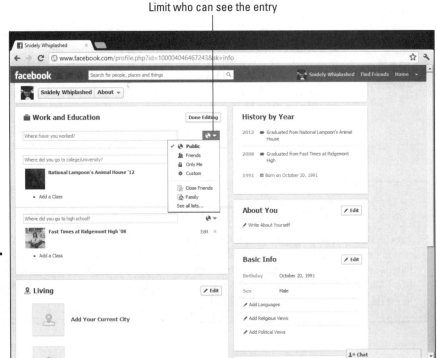

Figure 1-7:
Create the
profile that
you want
people to
see.

What businesses can see about you

Many people starting out with Facebook are worried that businesses — particularly businesses that pay to advertise on Facebook — can see all your personal information.

Sorry. As much as I love a good conspiracy theory, it just isn't true.

Anybody who controls a business page can see the profiles of people who have visited the page, and the people who have clicked the Like button on the page. So, for example, if you go to the Ford page (which is a very good one, by the way), Ford will know that one more female between 25 and 34 years old visited the page. Ford will also get one more visitor tallied by city, country, and major language. If you arrived at the page by clicking a Facebook ad, that fact is also counted. But that's it.

When a business pays for an ad, it chooses the demographics ("only show ads to males 18 to 24 living in Los Angeles") but there's no lingering information about who got served an ad, and no way to tie you, specifically, into a click on an ad. Facebook has that information. The advertiser does not.

Facebook guards your information jealously. It doesn't sell your info to businesses or give it away, unless you specifically permit an app to pull the data from Facebook. That's why Windows asks your permission before retrieving Facebook data — Facebook won't let Microsoft pull the data unless you specifically allow it.

4. **Keep in mind the prime directive (don't put anything on or in Facebook —** *anything* **— that you don't want to appear in tomorrow morning's news) and fill in the details sparingly.**

See the sidebar "What businesses can see about you."

As you get more adept at Facebook, and figure out how to lock down your account, you may want to add more information to your profile. Cool, as long as you understand the consequences. For now, put in the minimum you feel comfortable about disclosing to the world at large.

5. **To change an item, tap or click the Edit box to the right of the text box.**

Each line you can enter — from your schools and marital status to your religious views — has a drop-down choice to limit access to that information. See Figure 1-7.

Access limitations are based on your lists. For example, if you identify Snidely Whiplashed as a member of your family, Snidely can look at any items you've set to be visible to Family. Any friends who aren't on your Family list can't see the item.

For now, while you're still getting your feet wet, be very circumspect in what information you provide, *even if you limit access to the information to specific lists.* Give yourself awhile to get more friends. You can always update your profile.

What other people can see about you

Ever since the FTC slapped Facebook's hands, repeatedly, for privacy problems — and Facebook submitted to a 20-year ongoing audit by the U.S. Federal Trade Commission starting in November 2011 — Facebook has been quite forthcoming about its privacy policies.

Lots and lots of rumors circulate about what people can and can't see, so let me set the record straight.

If you look at someone's Timeline (or profile), the person you're snooping, er, looking up, doesn't have any way to tell that you've looked. In fact, there's no way to tell how many times people have looked at a Timeline. There are lots of Facebook scams that offer to give you a list of who's visited your Timeline. They're just that — scams. It can't be done.

Although the ubiquitous Facebook Like button sits on millions and millions of sites, Facebook doesn't give the people who run those sites any information at all about you. None. On the other hand, sites with the Like button allow Facebook to set third-party cookies on those sites. Facebook can trace your IP address (see the sidebar in Book VI, Chapter 5) as you go from site to site with the Like button. But the site itself doesn't get any information from Facebook.

6. **Work your way down the list of profile categories — Work and Education, Living, Relationships, History, About You, Basic Info, and so on. Don't enter anything unless you have an absolutely overwhelming desire to identify yourself as a Radical Vegan Parsee.**

    Even then, resist the urge. Some day your boss — or your son — may read this.

7. **When you're done, in the upper-right corner, tap or click Home.**

    You return to your home page (refer to Figure 1-5).

Interpreting the Facebook interface lingo

Now that you've taken the whirlwind tour, permit me to throw some terminology at you. Facebook used to be simple; it isn't anymore. In order to work with Facebook, you need to figure out the names of things and what the different pieces are supposed to do. The really complicated part? Names have changed over the years, and you're bound to run into old names for new things — and vice versa.

Here's my handy translator:

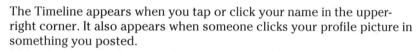
✦ **Home page (used to be the News Feed)** is primarily about your friends. The important stuff is in the middle — there are navigation aids on the left, and basically uninteresting things (including ads) on the right. When you type something in the What's on Your Mind box, it's added to the top of the list, as well as at the top of your Timeline. When your friends type something in their What's on Your Mind box, that gets added to your home page, too. When you add photos or videos, thumbnails of the photos go at the top of the list in the middle of the home page. Ditto for your friends' photos.

When you tap or click Home in the upper-right corner, you go to the home page. When you sign on to Facebook, you go to the home page.

✦ **Profile page (sometimes called the Info page)** — now basically obsolete — contains details about you. It's been supplanted by . . .

✦ **Timeline (replaces the old Wall and the old profile page)** is all about you. There's a big picture at the top, dubbed a cover, with your profile picture appearing to the left. Then there are all the settings you've made visible, followed by almost all the posts you've made over the years, in reverse-chronological order. I talk about the Timeline in the "Building a Great Timeline" section later in this chapter.

When you type something in the What's on Your Mind box, it's added to the top of the Timeline list, as well as at the top of your home page. Your friends can also post on your Timeline — in effect, leaving you a note.

The Timeline appears when you tap or click your name in the upper-right corner. It also appears when someone clicks your profile picture in something you posted.

✦ **News Ticker** is one of the uninteresting things that appears on the right side of your home page, toward the top. It's a scrolling jumble of things that your friends are doing. If you just joined Facebook and can't see the News Ticker, don't worry about it. You'll see it sooner or later.

Choosing basic Facebook security settings

One last, important checkpoint before you start exploring. I strongly suggest that you make three simple security changes. And I take advantage of the spelunking to look at one more part of Facebook's infrastructure.

Follow these steps:

1. **In the upper-right corner, to the right of the Home, tap or click the down arrow and choose Account Settings.**

The General Account Settings page appears, as shown in Figure 1-8.

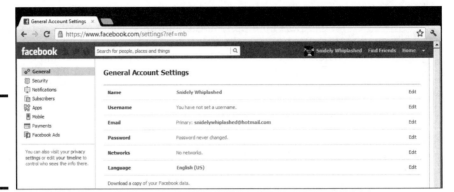

Figure 1-8:
Security
central,
Facebook
style.

2. **(Optional) To change your password, tap or click Edit on the Password line.**

   You probably don't want to change your password just yet, but when you do, this is where you change it. The directives for choosing a secure password in Book II, Chapter 4 applies to your Facebook password, too.

3. **On the left of the page, tap or click Security.**

   The Security Settings page appears, as shown in Figure 1-9.

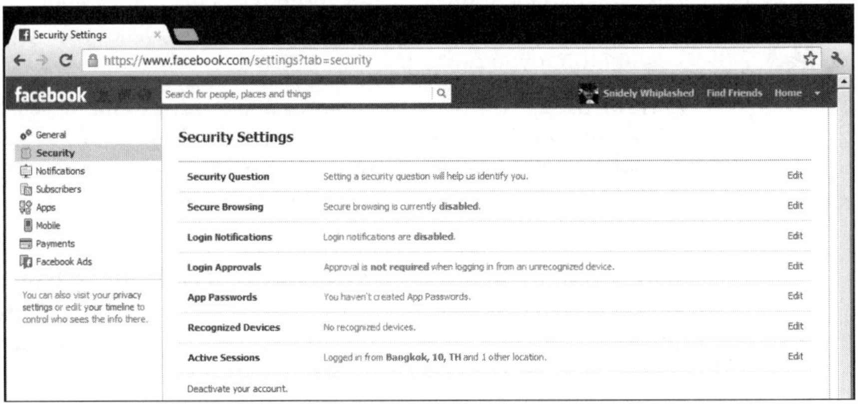

Figure 1-9:
Important
security
settings are
here.

4. **To the right of the Security Question line, tap or click Edit.**

   Facebook presents you with a pre-ordained list of security questions, as shown in Figure 1-10.

Figure 1-10:
You have to
pick one of
the security
questions
offered by
Facebook —
you can't
make up
your own.

5. **Pick a security question in the Security Question box, type the answer, type your password to confirm it, and tap or click Save Changes.**

   The answer is case-sensitive: `Newyork` is not the same thing as `New York`.

6. **To the right of the Secure Browsing line, tap or click Edit, select the Browse Facebook on a Secure Connection (https:) When Possible check box, and then tap or click Save Changes.**

   That ensures you always work over a secure connection, after you log in to Facebook. That's particularly important if you ever access Facebook over a WiFi connection that can be snooped — the kind you might find in a coffee shop or airport.

7. **Tap or click Home to return to your home page.**

   Now that security's set, time to look at the Timeline.

Building a Great Timeline

As this book went to press, Facebook had slowed its Timeline rollout, perhaps in response to complaints from customers who don't like it — of which there are more than a few. I like it. I suggest you get it.

If you tap or click your name and see an old-fashioned classic profile page one that doesn't say "Welcome to Your Timeline," as shown in Figure 1-6), you may — *may* — be able to upgrade to a Timeline page by going through these steps:

1. **Log on to Facebook. Then go to the Timeline page at** `www.facebook.com/about/timeline`**. At the top of the page, just under the video, tap or click the green Get Timeline button.**

If you can't see a green Get Timeline button, chances are good you've already been changed over to Timeline — although it's also possible that you forgot to log in to Facebook before you started.

If you click the Get Timeline button, Timeline is enabled for your account. It's that simple.

2. **In the upper right of your Facebook page, tap or click your name.**

   A blank Timeline page appears, as shown in Figure 1-11.

Timeline navigator

Your profile picture   Welcome to Your Timeline tour

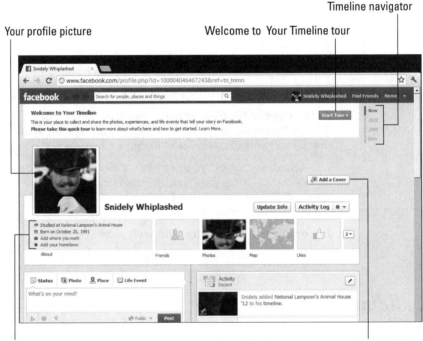

Figure 1-11:
Your
Timeline,
ready for
primping
and vetting.

Profile information   Put a big wide picture on your Timeline

The Timeline is where people usually go when they want to learn about you. If somebody clicks your picture in a post elsewhere in Facebook, he's sent to your Timeline.

Follow these steps to personalize your Timeline:

1. **Bring up your Timeline by tapping or clicking your name, in the upper-right corner of the Facebook screen.**

Depending on how much you've done to your Timeline, it looks like the one in Figure 1-11.

2. **Tap or click the Add a Cover button.**

   Facebook takes you through the steps of either uploading a new photo or choosing from one that you've already uploaded.

3. **After you choose or upload a photo, tap or click it to drag the part you want to see into the fixed-size frame. Then tap or click Save.**

   If you don't have a suitable photo already, pre-fab Facebook cover photos are all over the Internet. Just be careful when you go out looking: Any website that has you click and log on to Facebook in order to deliver the photo may be gathering your Facebook login ID in the process. It's much safer to simply download the photo to your hard drive and then upload it yourself to Facebook.

   The Facebook cover photo is 850 pixels wide x 315 pixels tall. Facebook will actually accept any picture as long as it's at least 720 pixels wide. When you drag the uploaded picture to fit it into the fixed-sized frame, you're telling Facebook how to crop the picture to make it fit into the 315 x 850 pixel box. For best results, use a photo-manipulation program — or even Windows Paint (Book VII, Chapter 6) — to get the photo just right before you upload it.

4. **To change your *profile picture* — the little picture on the left that also appears on anything that you post, tap it or hover your mouse and choose Edit Profile Picture.**

   Remember that your profile picture gets squeezed down most of the time, so a highly detailed photo usually doesn't work very well.

5. **When you're done editing your profile information, tap or click your name in the upper-right corner to go back to the Timeline.**

   By now the layout of the Timeline is a little more comfortable, but now it's time to change the contents of the Timeline itself.

6. **Find an item in the Timeline that you don't want other people to see, and then hover your mouse over the item (or tap on it) while watching the upper-right corner.**

   Two icons appear: one to highlight the item (which turns it into a double-width block), and the other to edit or remove the item.

7. **Tap or click Edit or Remove.**

   Facebook gives you the options shown in Figure 1-12.

Figure 1-12:
The options
available
for every
item in your
Timeline.

8. **To remove the item from your Timeline, tap or click Hide from Timeline.**

   The item disappears immediately, replaced by a placeholder that only you can see. If you ever want to bring back the deleted item, tap or click Undo.

   If you've been using Facebook for a long time, your Timeline may go on and on and on. But I bet there's no chance you have your baby picture pinned.

9. **To add something to your Timeline that goes waaaaaay back (I'm talking years or decades, not centuries), tap or click the Life Event link, just above the What's on Your Mind box.**

   Facebook lets you identify the event, as shown in Figure 1-13.

10. **Choose the life event, and then follow the instructions to give a date, choose or upload a picture, and provide more details about the event. When you're done, tap or click Save.**

    The item attaches itself to the appropriate place on your Timeline — even if it predates your joining Facebook.

Figure 1-13:
You can add
items to the
Timeline and
mark them
as a specific
life event.
Previous
lives don't
count.

Before you make your mind up irrevocably that Facebook is (a) the
greatest family-catching-up tool ever invented, (b) an unconscionable
invasion of your privacy, or (c) both, look at your Timeline the way
other people see it.

11. **To do so, go up to your cover photo. On the right, tap or click the gear
icon and choose View As . . .**

Facebook shows you the way your Timeline looks to the general public,
with a couple of additional boxes at the top (see Figure 1-14).

Figure 1-14:
Looking
at your
Timeline
from other
people's
perspective.

12. **Confirm that your Timeline isn't too over-the-top to the general public: To see how a specific individual will experience it, type her name in the Enter a Friend's Name box in the upper left.**

    You'll either come away from the experience convinced that you need to lock down your account even more — or you may figure that, heh, this is pretty cool.

13. **When you're done, click the Back to Timeline box in the upper right.**

    It's your account. Take control over it.

Locking Down Your Facebook Info

Once upon a time, Facebook privacy settings were useless. Comical. Scary. Foreboding. Not so now.

In November 2011, the U.S. Federal Trade Commission came to an agreement with Facebook, where control over privacy became a key feature, privacy warnings became mandatory, and Facebook agreed to regular privacy audits over the next 20 years.

In earlier sections in this chapter, I show you how to play with Facebook a bit and see your Timeline the way other people see it. After you do all that, take these seven steps to lock down your privacy settings:

1. **Log on to Facebook, click the down arrow next to Home, and choose Privacy Settings.**

    The general Privacy Settings page appears, as shown in Figure 1-15.

2. **Read about how you can control the privacy of each item you post.**

    You can decide for each item that you put on Facebook, at the time you post it, whether the item (message, photo, whatever) should be visible to Everybody, Family, Friends, Close Friends, people located in or near some town, people who graduated from the same university you went to, and so on. There's a lot of flexibility, and it's easy to get to, every time you make a post.

3. **Consider how much privacy you want on default posts.**

    Default posts are posts in which you don't want to mess around with the fine details in Step 2, or the posts you make when you're using an app that doesn't support the fine details.

    If you want maximum flexibility, tap or click the Custom button and then choose your recipients, block lists, location, and so on.

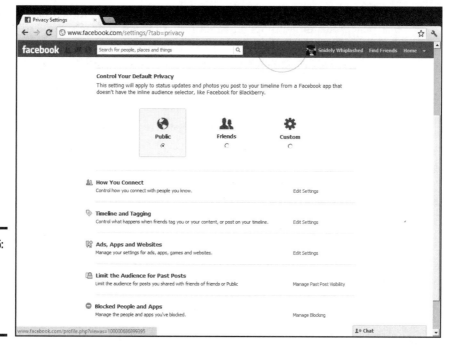

Figure 1-15:
A good
place to
start for
privacy
settings.

4. **Under the How You Connect heading, tap or click Edit Settings and then consider the following questions:**

   • Do you want to keep your personal information searchable? If so, do you want to let people search for you using your e-mail address or phone number?

   • Who can send you friend requests?

   • Who can send you messages?

5. **When you're finished, tap or click Done.**

6. **In Timeline and Tagging, think about who you want to see your timeline and who can post new items to it.**

   You can also choose to review posts tagged with your name, before they go on your Timeline (recommended), or to review tags that have been put on your Timeline before they're visible (also recommended).

   Facebook has a scary feature that tags uploaded photos with your name if the Facebook face recognition program identifies you. Unless you change the setting in this part of the Privacy options, that automatic tagging occurs only on photos uploaded by your friends. You can turn off that feature here, if face recognition gives you the heebie jeebies.

7. **In Ads, Apps and Websites, turn off all those apps that are following your movements on Facebook by tapping or clicking Edit Settings on the right, follow the instructions to remove specific apps, or them all.**

   Facebook shows you all the apps that can get at your profile; see Figure 1-16.

Figure 1-16:
Tap or click Edit Settings under Apps You Use to see a complete list of all the apps that can get into your profile.

I found one app — RockMelt Beta — that I allowed a long time ago. Heaven knows why. Before I cut it off at the knees, RockMelt Beta had my permission to use my e-mail address — in other words, I gave RockMelt Beta my e-mail address — and post on Facebook on my behalf. In other words, RockMelt Beta could update my status or make mean posts without my knowledge or permission. *Mea culpa.* I did it. I must've clicked something in a weaker (or more harried) moment. So I turned it off: On the Apps You Use list, tap or click Edit Settings, then on the right, next to RockMelt, tap or click X. That cuts off RockMelt: I can't use it anymore because it requires access to Facebook. So be it.

One really important part of this report: It shows you when the linked apps have accessed your account. So, for example, I can tell that TripAdvisor (which I have linked to Facebook — I log on to TripAdvisor with my Facebook ID) and Rotten Tomatoes looked at my profile recently.

In the same location, you can also control specifically which information is shared with apps — your name, your friends list, your birthday, photos, current city, and so on. Tap or click Edit Settings under the heading Apps You Use; then tap or click each app to see and edit the details.

8. **At the bottom of Figure 1-15, under Blocked People and Apps, consider whether you want to limit the people who can view your past posts, or if you want to block specific people and apps.**

If you decide to use this setting, don't forget that you've blocked specific people (or apps) getting at specific pieces of information. Like most manual, one-by-one security methods, maintaining the list can be a pain in the neck.

As you can see, Facebook's privacy settings are extensive and more than a little hard to understand. For basic privacy, judicious use of the privacy drop-down list when you post — limiting posts to friends or family, for example — gives you a lot of control. Tie that in with dropping any apps you don't use, and Facebook doesn't sap your privacy as badly as it once did. Go through all the settings and you can fine-tune it to your heart's content.

Downloading your Facebook data

Apps aren't allowed to download all your Facebook data. But you can.

Log in to Facebook. Tap or click the down arrow to the right of Home, and choose Account Settings. At the bottom of the General Account Settings page that appears (see Figure 1-8), tap or click the Download a Copy of Your Facebook Data link. Tap or click the Start My Archive button. Twice.

Then go have a latte. When you get back, check your e-mail. You — eventually — receive a message from Facebook that says

your download has been generated. Tap or click the indicated link to retrieve the download, and you go back to the General Account Settings page (getting vertigo yet?). Tap or click the Download a Copy link again. Enter your Facebook password, tap or click Continue, tap or click Download Archive, pick a location, and your browser downloads the zipped file. Finally.

Navigate to the `index.html` file and open it to see all your Facebook stuff.

Connecting to Windows

On the tiled side of Windows 8, Facebook ties into the Windows 8 Photos app (see Book IV, Chapter 3) and Messaging app (see Book IV, Chapter 5).

For example, in tiled Windows Photos app, there's a box at the bottom of the app that you can use to tie your Windows logon account (either a Microsoft account or a Local account) to your Facebook account (see Figure 1-17).

If you connect Photos to Facebook, all of your Facebook photos get pulled into the Windows 8 Photos app. Cool. If you connect Messaging to Facebook, you can use the Messaging app to post your Facebook status updates. Cool again.

Figure 1-17:
The tiled Win8 Photos app invites you to connect to Facebook.

But there's a downside. If you connect to Facebook through either the Photos or Messaging app, your Facebook friends get absorbed into the People app. From there, you can get to your Facebook friends through the Mail, People, and Calendar apps. If you have a lot of Facebook friends who aren't, uh, really your friends, the infusion of hundreds of Facebook faces into your People list may prove overwhelming. Or underwhelming. More than that, if your Facebook contacts don't match up with your other contacts — say, on LinkedIn — removing duplicates and clearing up differences can be enormously time consuming.

Moral of the story: If you don't want your Facebook friends cluttering your Mail address book, don't connect to Facebook from Photos or Messages! If you don't want your Facebook posts and photos to appear in the tiled Windows 8 People app, don't connect to Facebook in Messaging.

Many apps in the Windows Store tie into Facebook; a new one seems to appear every week. Which one is best? Hard to say, but next week the answer may be different from this week.

I keep up on the latest Windows 8 apps for Facebook at www.askwoody.com. Drop by if you have a question.

Book V
Chapter 1

Getting Started with Facebook

Chapter 2: Getting Started with Twitter

In This Chapter

- ✔ The idea behind Twitter
- ✔ Setting up your Twitter account
- ✔ Beginning to tweet
- ✔ Hooking Twitter into Windows

*T*he revolution will not be televised. It will be tweeted.

In July 2006, an amazing array of developers and entrepreneurs — originally intent on building a podcasting platform called Odeo — unleashed Twitter on an unsuspecting world. Five years on, Twitter has been credited with helping to overthrow totalitarian countries, spread fear and mayhem, aid and abet leaks of embarrassing government documents, shed light on official dirty dealings, establish a rallying point for the Occupy disenfranchised, and let everyone know what Lady Gaga had for breakfast.

That's quite an accomplishment. As of April 2012, Twitter had 140 million registered users, who send an average of 340 million tweets per day — up about 40 percent from September 2011, more than doubling in size every year.

I use Twitter all day, every day. I've used it to keep on top of important fast-breaking news; notify people around the world, quell tsunami fears; talk with other writers in the computer business; keep tabs on political organizations important to me; track down leaked builds of Windows 8; and point people to my favorite funny videos.

Just about every tech writer you can name is on Twitter. Every major news outlet is on Twitter — and breaking news spills out over Twitter much sooner than even the newspaper wire services. The Royal Society. The Wellcome Trust. Lots of people who are on the ground, relaying news as it happens, use Twitter. And did I mention Justin Bieber?

In short, Twitter's a mixed bag — but an interesting one.

Twitter's fast, easy, and free. It works with every web browser. It works with almost every telephone and tablet. It ties into the Windows 8 tiled apps. It's short, concise, sometimes vapid, but frequently illuminating and witty.

And every single piece of it is limited to 140 characters.

Understanding Twitter

When I try to explain Twitter to people who've never used it, I usually start by talking about mobile phone messaging — SMS. A message on Twitter — a *tweet* (see Figure 2-1) — is a lot like an SMS message.

Figure 2-1:
A typical tweet from an atypical source.

> **Dalai Lama** @DalaiLama   2h
> Through constant training we can enhance our positive attitudes and thoughts and reduce their opposing negative attitudes.
> Expand

Twitter is a very simple one-to-many form of communication, kind of like SMSing all the people who have agreed, in advance, that they want to receive your SMSs.

You usually send an SMS message to one person. If you have a business, you may send the same, identical SMS message to many people all at once. Now imagine a world in which

✦ You have an ID, not unlike a phone number, and you can send any messages *(tweets)* that you like, any time you want. The messages are limited to 140 characters — short and sweet.

✦ You get to choose whose SMSs you're going to receive. In Twitter parlance, you can *follow* anybody. If you get tired of reading their tweets, it's easy to *unfollow* them as well.

That's the whole shtick. Twitter has lots of bells and whistles — location tracking, if you turn it on, for example — but at its heart, Twitter is all about sending messages and wisely choosing whose messages you receive.

If you follow someone who posts a tweet, you see the tweet when you log on to Twitter. If you keep Twitter running on your PC, phone, or tablet, as I do, the tweet appears in your Twitter window. If you tweet, the people who follow you can see it.

In fact, *anybody* can see *every* tweet — a fact that's proved highly embarrassing to an amazingly large number of people. (Twitter has a Protected Tweets feature that lets you manually approve every person who's permitted to receive your tweets. But, in general, when you let it all hang out on Twitter, it's all hung out, eh?)

In addition, when you send a tweet, you can identify keywords in the tweet by using the # character in front of the keyword, creating a *hashtag*. See Figure 2-2.

Figure 2-2:
Two sample
tweets with
hashtags.

You can tell Twitter that, in addition to the tweets from people you follow, you also want to see all tweets that contain specific hashtags. For example, if you ask to see all the tweets with the hashtag #ForDummies, Twitter delivers to your web page or Twitter reader every tweet where the author of the tweet specifically typed the characters #ForDummies.

Twitter (and other sites, such as www.trendsmap.com) keep track of all the hashtags in all the tweets. It posts lists of the most popular hashtags, so you can watch what's really popular. Thus, hashtags are not only a way to make it easier for people to find your tweets, they're also a way to publicize your cause — and many good causes have risen to the top of the hashtag heaps. Some odd ones, too, such as Lady Gaga kissing Marge Simpson, but I digress.

In fact, Twitter now keeps tracks of every phrase that's tweeted and compiles its trending lists from the raw tweets, with or without hashtags. You really don't need to use hashtags any more. But you see them all the time in tweets, #knowwhatImean?

The power of Twitter — outside of gossip and teenage angst — lies in choosing those you follow carefully. If they, in turn, receive information from reliable sources and then re-tweet the results, you'll have a steady stream of useful information, each in 140-character capsules.

#FollowFriday

Ever since the dawn of the Twitterverse, people have been using one very strange hashtag, `#followfriday` or sometimes `#ff` for a very specific purpose: It's to show the people who are following them which twitterers are worth following. Something like an endorsement newsletter in 140 characters, `#ff` recommendations frequently point you to people who have interesting, timely, or important things to say.

Or maybe not.

You can do it, too. Every Friday, look at the people who send you interesting stuff, create a tweet that starts out `#FollowFriday`, and then list the usernames. Don't forget to tweet `#FollowFriday @woodyleonhard` at some point.

For example, during the Egyptian political crisis in January, 2011, which saw the downfall of President Hosni Mubarak, Twitter played a pivotal (if controversial) role in aiding communication among protestors. One of the government's first acts was to shut down access to Twitter and Facebook. The protestors found ways around the government's shutdown.

There's a fascinating re-creation of the tweeting and re-tweeting that followed the January 25 start of demonstrations in Cairo. Data about tweets with the hashtag `#jan25` was assembled by the University of Turin, the ISI Foundation, and a research institute at Indiana University, to come up with the graph you see in Figure 2-3.

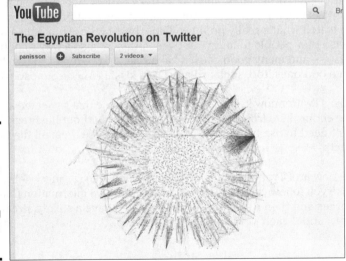

Figure 2-3:
The inter-
connections
among
Twitter
users during
the Egyptian
uprising.

Photo courtesy of `http://youtu.be/2guKJfvq4uI`

That's how a one-to-many social network like Twitter works. If there's an important tweet (or even an unimportant, but popular one), it jumps from person to person.

My Twitter ID for computer-related news is @woodyleonhard, and you're welcome to follow me any time you like.

Setting Up a Twitter Account

Starting a new account at Twitter couldn't be easier. Here's what you do:

1. **Fire up your favorite web browser and go to** www.twitter.com.

   You see the Sign Up box, as shown in Figure 2-4.

2. **Enter a full name, a valid e-mail account (you need to be able to retrieve e-mail sent to the account), and a password; then tap or click Sign Up for Twitter.**

   Twitter creates a sign-up sheet, together with a suggested username, and shows them to you, as shown in Figure 2-5.

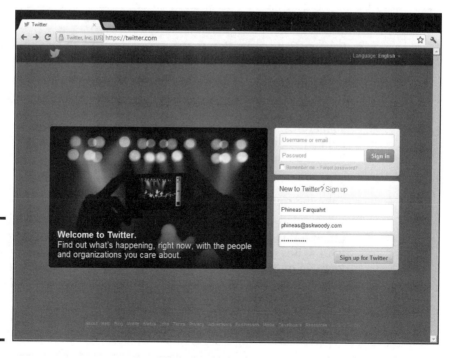

Figure 2-4: All you need to sign up for Twitter is a valid e-mail address.

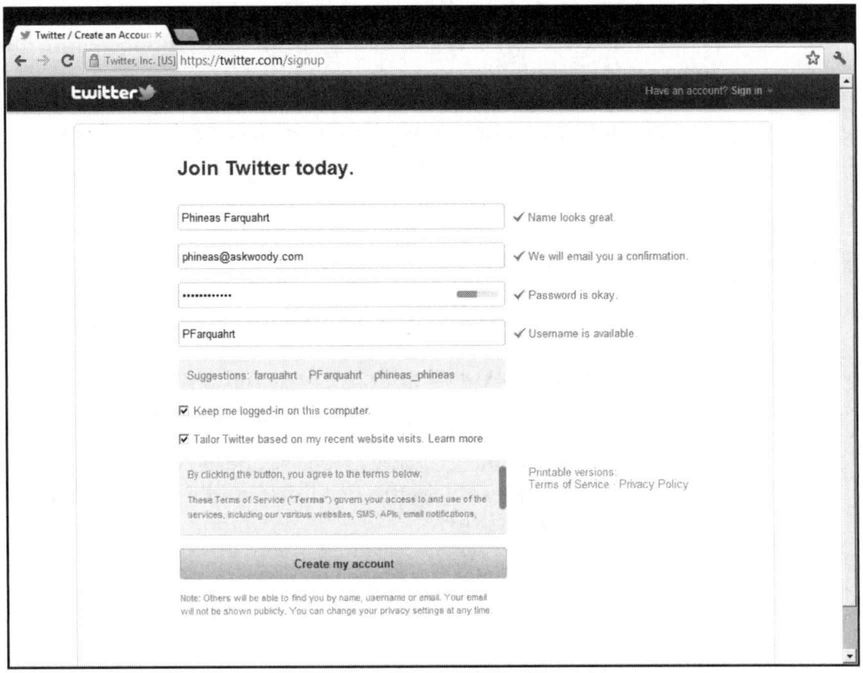

Figure 2-5:
Pay
particular
attention
to the
username.

3. **Pay particular attention to the username, and when you're ready, tap or click Create My Account.**

   Usernames are key because you want a name that will be easy for people to remember. Capitalization doesn't matter — MisterDummy is the same as MiStErDuMmY — but some characters are confusing. Be wary of the similarities between a number 0 and letter O; the letters I and l, and the number 1. And in particular, avoid ambiguous punctuation like underlines and hyphens.

   Twitter creates your account and then steps you through a brief tutorial.

4. **Take the tutorial!**

5. **When the tutorial asks you to start by following five people, think about following @woodyleonhard, @ForDummies, @AndyRathbone who writes the original *Windows For Dummies*, @windowsblog to keep up on the Microsoft Party Line, @windowssecrets to follow the newsletter, and some of the major news services — @BBCWorld perhaps, or @BreakingNews.**

   Or try a couple of the most-followed people on Twitter, @ladygaga or @justinbieber. They both have more than 20 million followers.

6. **Don't go overboard just yet. When you're done, tap or click Done.**

Most normal people have Twitter send them an e-mail message when someone follows them. (I'm sure Lady Gaga has long since opted out.) The message includes your name and Twitter account name. If you happen to follow somebody you know, that e-mail message may be enough incentive to have him start following you; it's a good way to get a following kick-started.

7. **Twitter tries to get you to sign up for five more, well-known people. If you aren't up for it, at the bottom, tap or click the Skip This Step link.**

8. **When Twitter offers to scan your Gmail, Yahoo! Mail, Hotmail/ Outlook.com, and/or AOL Mail accounts, to try to find contacts who are also tweeters, tap or click Skip This Step, too.**

9. **Upload a photo and describe yourself, as shown in Figure 2-6.**

Figure 2-6:
Upload a picture — an avatar. It doesn't have to be you.

The Internet is full of images. Go find a good one.

You may be tempted to bypass typing your bio. Give it some thought, if there's something unique about you that you want the world to know — if you're an expert on 18th century Tibetan bronzes, adding that to your bio may help someone else who's interested in bronzes find you. Your bio's accessible to anybody (unless it's protected), so don't put anything in there that you don't want to be widely known.

10. **In the e-mail message you receive, tap or click the link and you're done.**

Twitter advises that your account has been confirmed, and you're ready to roll, as shown in Figure 2-7.

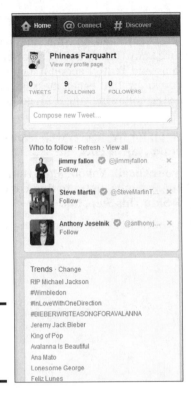

Figure 2-7:
Twitter is
ready for
you.

At first, you probably just want to watch and see what others are tweeting to give you a sense of how tweeting is done. Create a practice tweet or two, and see how the whole thing hangs together.

Tweeting for Beginners

On the surface, Twitter's easy and fun. Below the surface, Twitter's a remarkably adept application with lots of capabilities.

Beware hacking

Before I dig in to the more interesting parts of Twitter, permit me to give you just one warning.

There are unscrupulous people on Twitter, just as anywhere else. If you get a tweet from someone with a gorgeous picture who's trying to convince you to sign up for something or hand over your password, just ignore him and he'll go away. If you get a tweet saying, "Somebody is writing bad things about you" or "Want to see a funny photo of you?" or "Find out who's been looking at your bio," ignore her.

Better, yet, report her as a spammer. Tap or click the spammer's picture. That takes you to the spammer's profile page. In the upper right, tap or click the down arrow that's next to the little silhouette of a man and choose Report @spammersID for spam.

If your Twitter account has been hacked — somebody talked you into clicking something that gets into your account or someone guessed your password — don't feel too bad about it. Fox News was hacked in July 2011. Mark Ruffalo (who plays The Hulk in *The Avengers*) got hacked in May 2012. Justin Bieber's account was hacked — with almost 20 million followers. Ashton Kutcher. *The Huffington Post. USA Today.* Senator Chuck Grassley. Brett Favre. Miley Cyrus. If your account's been taken over, see the Twitter instructions at `http://support.twitter.com/articles/31796#su`.

Using the @ sign and Reply

You see the @ sign everywhere on Twitter. In fact, I used it when listing the people you might want to follow. The @ sign is a universal indication that "what follows is an account name."

But it goes deeper than that.

If you put an @ sign at the beginning of a tweet, the only people who will automatically receive copies of the tweet must match *both* criteria:

✦ They must follow you.

✦ They must follow the person whose username follows the @.

So, for example, if you tweet this:

`@woodyleonhard You're one big dummy!`

The only people who will automatically receive a copy of the tweet are people who follow you *and* follow `@woodyleonhard`.

There's a reason why Twitter works this way. If somebody follows you and follows the person you're @ responding to, he can see the whole conversation. But anybody who follows only one of you sees only half of the conversation.

If you want to send the message to everyone who follows you and to one specific person, put a character — any character or characters — *in front of* their name. For example, any of these tweets will go to all your followers, plus it'll go to @woodyleonhard:

```
.@woodyleonhard You're one big dummy!
> @woodyleonhard You're one big dummy!
You're one big dummy @woodyleonhard!
```

Now that you know how the @ sign works, you're ready to understand how Reply works.

In the Twitter viewer on the Internet there's a Reply option for a tweet. In Figure 2-8, on the Twitter website, a Reply link appears when you hover over the message.

Figure 2-8: Reply to a tweet.

Woody Leonhard @PhuketPC   21 Jun
Report: Microsoft to outsource Windows Surface tablets to a major
iPad/iPhone supplier. InfoWorld Tech Watch is.gd/C3X2vQ
Expand ← Reply ⇄ Retweet ★ Favorite

If you tap or click that Reply link, Twitter starts a new message with an @ sign followed by the sender's username. If you reply to the message in Figure 2-8, Twitter on the web creates a new tweet that starts: @woodyleonhard.

If you type a body to that message and click Tweet, the message goes only to people who are following *both* you and @woodyleonhard.

A reply is *not* a private or hidden message. It's completely out in the open. Anybody who searches for your username or @woodyleonhard will see the message in its entirety.

Re-tweeting for fun and profit

If you receive a tweet and want to send it to all the people who follow you, the polite way to do so is with a *re-tweet,* or *RT* for short. In order to give credit to the person who sent you the tweet, include her username in the re-tweet.

In Figure 2-8, one of the options is Retweet. Tap or click the Retweet link, and the Twitter program builds a new tweet that copies the original tweet, puts an RT on it, and adds the originator's username. Like this:

```
RT @woodyleonhard Windows 8 rocks!
```

By re-tweeting a tweet precisely, you pass the information on to your followers, yet preserve the attribution. If you want to modify the tweet (perhaps trim it down, in order to add a comment), use the modified tweet (MT) tag. Like this:

```
I think he's overly exuberant, and I wouldn't want to say it
    myself, but // MT @woodyleonhard Win8 rocks!
```

Hooking Twitter into Windows

I intentionally wrote this chapter to get you going on Twitter using the web directly. It's something of a lowest common denominator for Twitter access.

Do I actually *use* the web interface? Heavens no!

There are dozens of programs — many of them free, or very cheap — that run rings around the Twitter web interface. The names change every week, and the feature sets almost as quickly.

There's a very rudimentary Twitter client built into Microsoft's Windows 8 tiled People app (see Book IV, Chapter 2). But if you're serious about using Twitter — particularly if you have more than one Twitter account, or use both Twitter and Facebook — there are much better alternatives.

As of this moment, the major choice in the Twitter app wars is between running a Windows 8 tiled app for Twitter (and Facebook), or running a desktop app.

I use TweetDeck (www.tweetdeck.com, see Figure 2-9), which helps me keep track of Twitter accounts for international and local use. Twitter actually bought TweetDeck in May 2011, and has been extending its capabilities ever since. As of this writing, TweetDeck runs only on the desktop, and it's free, but I expect Twitter will have a Windows 8 tiled app out very soon.

Figure 2-9:
TweetDeck makes multiple Twitter accounts easy.

Some of my friends swear by MetroTwit, which has the added advantage of looking like a Metro app, tiles and all. Look for it in the Windows Store.

All the serious Twitter apps have support for several key features:

✦ **Automatic URL shortening**, so `http://www.somethingoranother.com/this/and/that.php` ends up looking like `http://is.gd/12345` — an important trick when you're limited to 140 characters.

✦ **Multiple Twitter (and sometimes Facebook) accounts** so people who keep their business and personal accounts separate can manage both simultaneously.

✦ **Picture attachments** with automatically generated links to picture sites. The best Twitter apps let you drag and drop pictures onto your tweets, and take care of all the details.

✦ **Sophisticated search functions** so you can display not only your tweets, and the tweets of those you follow, but also tweets on topics that interest you, such as `#19thcenturydentistoffices`.

If you find yourself using Twitter much at all, take the time to get a Windows Twitter app. And don't forget to download a Twitter app for your phone and iPad, too.

Chapter 3: Getting Started with Flickr and Pinterest

In This Chapter

✔ **Signing up and navigating Flickr**

✔ **Using Pinterest**

*A*lthough Flickr and Pinterest revolve around posting pictures on the Internet, they're actually quite different.

Flickr, as shown in Figure 3-1, is a great place to put your picture collection, so the pics are easy to organize and share with friends and family. If you're a serious photographer and want to get your pictures noticed and published — and you don't care about making money with them — Flickr has great features and community.

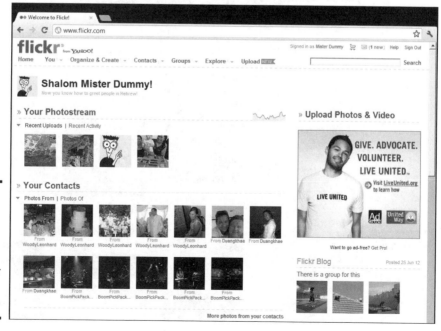

Figure 3-1: Flickr revolves around photos and sharing your photos with your friends.

Flickr was created in 2004, and bought by Yahoo! in 2005. One of the few Yahoo! acquisitions that hasn't gone into a downward spiral, Flickr now has more than 50 million registered users, with more than 6 billion pictures online.

Pinterest, by contrast, is a young upstart, which only opened its doors (and web pages) in 2010. It's been growing exponentially. In January, 2012, Pinterest overtook LinkedIn (see Book V, Chapter 4), YouTube, and Google+ for the total number of referrals to other sites. Pinterest (see Figure 3-2) is a visual bookmarking site that enables you to post a linked picture to a virtual board. You can use it to save and organize links you find around the web and share them with others.

The main difference between Flickr and Pinterest? Flickr is for your images, and Pinterest is a place for other people's images. In the pre-digital world, Flickr would be a photo album, and Pinterest would be an idea folder of pages photocopied or ripped out of magazines.

As of this writing, Flickr has direct ties into Microsoft's official tiled Windows 8 apps. In particular, the Windows 8 Photos app lets you pull in your pictures on Flickr, and your contacts, as well.

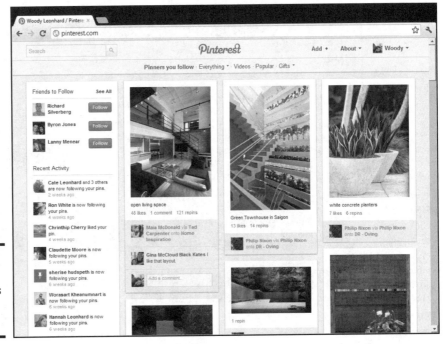

Figure 3-2:
Pinterest emphasizes the social side.

Pinterest, on the other hand, isn't tied directly into Microsoft's tiled apps. Yet. But a quick glance at the Windows Store will show you that there are tons and tons of Pinterest-friendly apps floating around.

I include Pinterest in this chapter because I think it's likely that Microsoft will forge Windows links to Pinterest in the near future. Only time will tell.

Using Flickr with Windows 8

To use Flickr with the Windows 8 Photos app, you need a Flickr account. The following sections show you how to get an account and get started organizing and sharing your photos.

Signing up for Flickr

If you have a Yahoo! ID (say, for Yahoo! Mail, Ymail, or Rocketmail), you're already signed up.

If you have a Facebook account or a Google ID (perhaps for Gmail, Google+, or Chrome), you can use one of those IDs to log in to Flickr, too.

If you don't have any of those IDs — or you don't particularly want Flickr to know about your Facebook or Google accounts — signing up for a free Flickr account is a snap. Here's how:

1. **Go to** www.flickr.com, **and tap or click one of the many links to Sign Up Now.**

   Flickr takes you to a screen that urges you to sign on with your Yahoo!, Facebook, or Google ID. If you don't want to use — or don't have — any of those, tap or click the Create New Account box.

   The sign-up page appears, as shown in Figure 3-3.

2. **Tap or click Create Account.**

   You don't need to provide an e-mail address.

   Yahoo advises that it sent a confirmation e-mail — it went to your new Yahoo! Mail address. You can log on to http://yahoomail.com if you like and look at it.

3. **Tap or click Continue, type a Flickr screen name (no problem using punctuation or spaces), and choose Create My Account.**

   Flickr takes you to the Getting Started page, as shown in Figure 3-4.

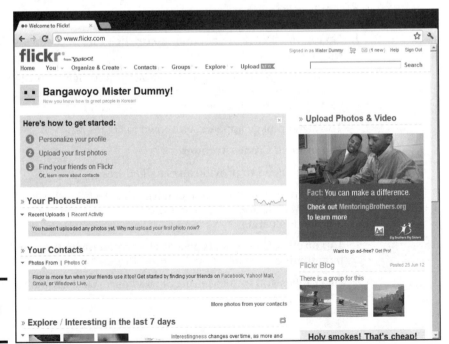

Figure 3-3:
The Flickr
sign-up
page.
Creativity
counts.

Figure 3-4:
Get started
here.

4. **Follow the links to fill out your profile and upload photos.**

   Flickr will gladly import your contacts from Facebook, Yahoo! Mail, Gmail, or Hotmail. I suggest you refrain from consolidating contact lists for now. Wait and see whether you really want to do it in the future.

Getting around Flickr

Flickr is a huge place.

Try this guided tour for a few tips on how to get around:

1. **Log on to Flickr and tap or click the You link.**

   Flickr shows your *photostream,* the pictures you uploaded recently, in chronological order. See Figure 3-5. There's nothing particularly magical about a photostream: It's just a much cooler way of saying, "all the photos that you've uploaded to Flickr."

2. **If you haven't uploaded any photos to Flickr yet, tap or click the Upload link at the top, and then drag and drop photos onto the screen (or follow the directions to navigate to photos that you want to upload).**

The photostream

Organize photos into sets

View photos by date taken or uploaded

Shows the most recent photos first

A photo set

Figure 3-5:
Your photo-
stream —
main page.

Flickr has apps for the iPhone and iPad, as well as Android phones and tablets, and Windows Phones. If you take any pictures at all on your phone or tablet, get the Flickr app. It'll make uploading the pictures infinitely easier than transferring them to your PC and then uploading.

3. **On the top, tap or click Organize & Create.**

   Flickr presents you a remarkably simple drag-and-drop interface that lets you organize your photos into groups, or *sets*. The sets appear on the right side of your home page.

4. **Drag a few photos onto the main screen and create a set.**

5. **At the top, tap or click Add to Set, then New Set. Type a name for your set, and tap or click Save.**

6. **In the upper-right corner, tap or click Your Photostream.**

   When you return to your main page, the set appears on the right.

7. **Tap or click the Archives link.**

   Flickr shows you two lists (see Figure 3-6): One is arranged by the date the photo was taken (using the EXIF data your camera put inside your picture), and the other lists when the photo was uploaded to Flickr.

8. **Tap or click the Your Photostream link, to the right of your user picture.**

   You return to the home page.

Figure 3-6:
You have two ways to find photos chronologically.

There are many things to see and do in Flickr. Try searching for something that interests you, via the box in the upper-right corner. Enjoy!

Sharing and licensing your photos

If you want to allow people to use your photos, enable the Creative Commons permission for your account. Here's how:

1. **At the top of your main Flickr page, tap or click the down arrow next to You and choose Your Account.**

   Flickr shows you general information about your account.

2. **Tap or click the Privacy & Permissions tab.**

3. **Scroll down to the Defaults for New Uploads section. On the What License Will Your Content Have line, choose Edit.**

4. **See Table 3-1, choose a licensing level that you feel comfortable with, and then tap or click the Set Default License button.**

   This licensing setting becomes the default for all new photos you upload.

Table 3-1	Creative Commons Licensing Choices
License	*What It Means*
None	You don't grant any license to anyone, for any reason. The pictures or videos are yours and yours alone. This is the default setting.
Attribution-NonCommercial-ShareAlike	Others may remix, tweak, and build upon your work non-commercially, as long as they credit you and license their new creations under the same terms.
Attribution-NonCommercial	Others may remix, tweak, and build upon your work non-commercially, and although their new works must also acknowledge you and be non-commercial, they don't have to license their derivative works on the same terms.
Attribution-NonCommercial-NoDerivs	Others may share your work, but they can't change them in any way, and they must credit you. They can't use the work commercially.
Attribution	Others can distribute, remix, tweak, or build upon your work in any way they like, as long as they credit you.
Attribution-ShareAlike	Others can remix, tweak, or build upon your work, but they must license their new creations under identical terms.
Attribution-NoDerivs	Others can distribute your work, even commercially, as long as it's distributed without any changes, and you are credited.

If you just want to share photos, such as an album of the newest member of the family or your high school reunion, with people you know, it's easy, if you know the trick.

1. **Follow the instructions in the preceding section, "Getting around Flickr" to create a set. In the set, add photos you want to be restricted to people you know.**

   The set appears on the right side of your Photostream page, per Figure 3-5.

2. **Under the name of the set, tap or click the Edit Set link.**

   Flickr shows you the whole set, as shown in Figure 3-7.

3. **Tap or click Batch Edit, and then choose Change Permissions.**

   Flickr brings up a dialog box that lets you limit viewing to your family or friends (or both).

4. **Choose the group you want to allow, and then tap or click Change Permissions.**

   That's all it takes.

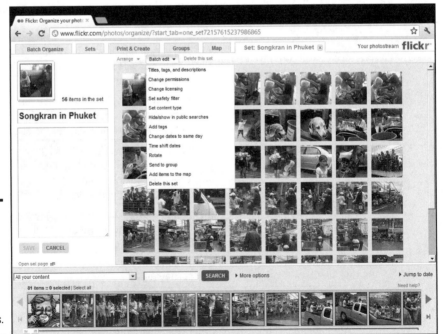

Figure 3-7:
Make a set accessible just to a group by choosing Change Permissions.

You might want to scurry back to your Photostream page and make sure that your friends and family are properly identified. To do that, tap or click Contacts and then tap or click Contact List. Each individual's Friend/Family status appears on the right of the list.

Flickr has a very active user community, with an amazing array of artists who help a lot of regular old everyday snapshooters like me. Keep up on the Flickr blog at http://blog.flickr.net.

Connecting Flickr with Windows 8 is quite straightforward, as long as you're using a Microsoft account (see Book II, Chapter 2) — Windows requires a Microsoft account so Microsoft can log you back in to Flickr automatically the next time you sign on to Windows. To set up the connection, go to the Photos app and, at the bottom, tap or click Flickr. You have to provide your Flickr account name and password. It takes a while, but all your Flickr pictures become available through the Photos app, and all your Flickr Contacts are pulled into the Windows 8 tiled People app. From that point, you can use the Flickr Contacts to create Windows 8 tiled Mail e-mail (if you have an e-mail address for your contacts) or run through Messaging.

Pinning with Pinterest

To use Pinterest with Windows 8, you need to sign up for a Pinterest account first. You can use the details in Book III, Chapter 5 to search for and add an app that enables you to connect Windows with Pinterest from the Start screen. Or if Pinterest becomes baked into Windows 8 at some point down the road, you may see a tile ready and waiting for you by default, perhaps inside the Windows 8 tiled Photos app. The following sections explain how to sign up for Pinterest and offer a brief tour of the features you can use to pin items from around the web.

Signing up for Pinterest

As this book went to press, Pinterest was limiting new users on its site. Be patient. It may take a few days before you're invited to join.

Here's how to get started:

1. **Go to** www.pinterest.com, **tap or click the Request an Invite button, fill in your e-mail address, and watch your e-mail.**

   Depending on the volume, it may take two or three days to get an invitation.

2. **When you receive the sign-up invitation in your e-mail inbox, click the link to sign up.**

   You can use your Facebook or Twitter account to sign in to Pinterest. Having a Facebook or Twitter account won't get you an invitation any faster, but it will make signing up simpler.

   If you consider using one of those accounts, Pinterest can connect the dots between your Pinterest usage and either your Facebook or Twitter activities. That isn't horrible, but it is something you should think about. If you use your Facebook or Twitter account to sign up, then, by default, Pinterest posts your pins to your Facebook and Twitter feeds, which most people don't want. Disconnect the cross-posting by going into Pinterest, tapping or clicking your name in the upper right and choosing Settings from the menu that appears. Scroll down to the Facebook and Twitter settings and move the slider to Off.

3. **In the image test that Pinterest shows you, tap or click the pictures that draw your attention, or topics that interest you: Travel, Food, Science, Technology, whatever.**

   Based on the pictures you've chosen, Pinterest sets you up to *follow* specific people. Following in Pinterest, like following in Twitter, doesn't require any confirmation from the person you're following. It just means that you want to see what the person pins.

Getting around Pinterest

When you first log in to Pinterest, you see what the people you follow have been pinning, as shown in Figure 3-8.

Each *pin* includes an image, so you can visually scan what's there. Often, a brief note below the image explains more about the web page that the image came from or links to. Scroll down the page to see more and more images. Tap or click an image to follow the link. Hover over an item, and you have the option to Repin, Like, or Comment on any of those items if you so choose. You find out more on repinning, liking, commenting in a moment. First, it helps to know about boards.

So what are boards? Pinterest presents you with some suggested pinboards (see Figure 3-9.) *Pinboards* are just categories, or groups, or sets of pictures. They're free-form — they are what you put in them.

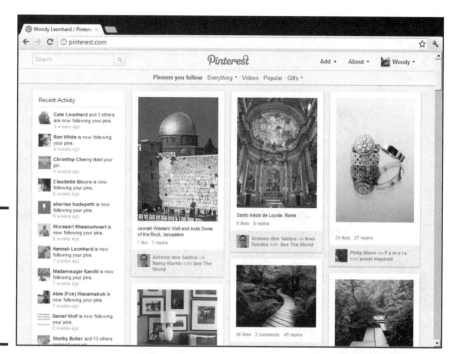

Figure 3-8:
Pinterest
assembles
an ever-
changing
array of
interesting
pics.

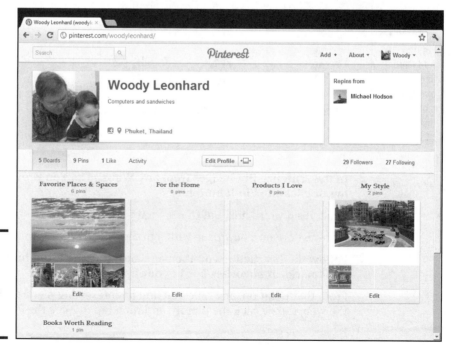

Figure 3-9:
Pinboards
are just
collections
that you
create.

Pinterest has several dozen predefined pinboards. You can (and should) use the ones you feel are appropriate for you, but don't feel completely constrained — create your own if you need one for, oh, Extraterrestrial Encounters, or Furniture I Want for the Living Room.

To add pinboards of your own, tap or click Add and choose Create a Board. To see your boards, tap or click the drop-down list next to your name in the upper right and choose Boards from the menu that appears.

Many people just repin items they see on Pinterest. But most people keep an eye out when they're on the web, and pin items from all sorts of places. Here's how to pin items from around the web:

1. If you want to be able to pin items from your current browser onto your Pinterest pinboards, in the upper-right corner, tap or click Add+.

This does not work with the tiled version of Internet Explorer. It will, however, work with the desktop version of IE, or with Chrome in either tiled or desktop flavors.

The Add dialog box appears, as shown in Figure 3-10.

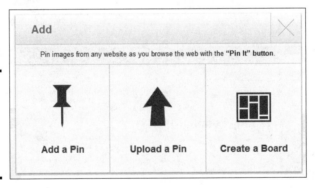

Figure 3-10: Add new items to one of your pinboards this way.

2. In the sentence Pin Images from any Website as You Browse the Web, tap or click the Pin It button.

Yeah, it's a weird link, but that's what you need to do.

Pinterest opens a new page with a draggable Pin It button.

3. Follow the instructions on the page and drag the Pin It button to the Bookmarks or Favorites bar in your browser.

From that point on, any time you find an interesting picture while surfing the web, tap or click the picture and then tap or click the Pin It button.

It's considered good Pinterest etiquette to link to the item's source. So if your favorite blog links to an artichoke recipe, pin a picture from the site that originally published the recipe, not one from the blog.

When you get back to your Pinterest main page, tap lightly or hover your mouse on one of the pictures that you particularly like. Three buttons appear (see Figure 3-11):

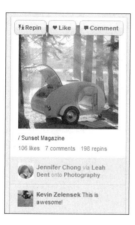

Figure 3-11: Three actions you can take on any pictures on your main page.

✦ **Repin** puts the picture in one of your pinboards — you get to choose which one. When the picture goes in your pinboard, all the people following you see the picture. See how that works?

✦ **Like** (if it isn't your picture) or **Edit** (if it is) lets you add your like to the picture. Increasing the Like number gives the picture preference in organizing other people's home pages; it also increases the chances someone else will click the picture and take a closer look at it.

✦ **Comment** allows you to comment on the picture. Your comment appears on other people's home pages.

After you watch for a while, you'll likely see that somebody is pinning stuff that really clicks with your interests. (Or, uh, taps with your interests, I guess.) When you find somebody who's pinning stuff you like, tap or click her name and see what pinboards she maintains. If you see more pinboards that you like, follow those, too.

Businesses use Pinterest, too. That's completely legit. If you're in the mood to go shopping, tap or click the Gifts link toward the top and choose a price range. You'll find lots and lots of options — nice illustrations, too.

Chapter 4: Getting Started with LinkedIn

In This Chapter

✔ Getting signed up for LinkedIn

✔ Hooking LinkedIn into Windows

✔ Using LinkedIn for fun and profit

In some ways, LinkedIn resembles Facebook — keeping up with people and expanding connections are grist for the mill. But in other ways, LinkedIn is completely different — LinkedIn is focused on business relationships, which LinkedIn calls *connections*.

You can use your LinkedIn connections to showcase products, look for a job, advertise a job, scout new business opportunities, find temporary help, keep up to date on companies that interest you — for any reason — or just replace your old Rolodex (does anybody still use a Rolodex?) or that tattered box of business cards on your desk.

With more than 150 million subscribers — half of whom are in the U.S. — LinkedIn has more than reached critical mass. Many business people consider it a key part of their existence.

And now, LinkedIn — at least part of it — is coming to Windows 8.

Signing Up for LinkedIn

Don't have a LinkedIn account? Got a few minutes?

Here's how to get started:

1. **Fire up your favorite browser and go to** www.linkedin.com.

   You see a sign-up page like the one in Figure 4-1.

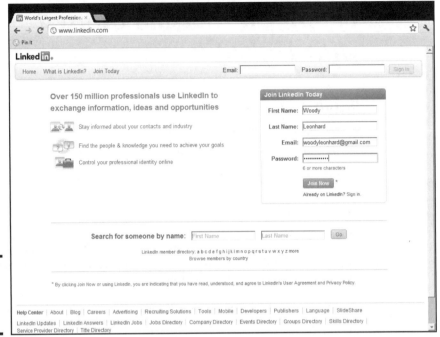

Figure 4-1:
Signing up
for LinkedIn
is easy.

If you want to sign up with your Facebook account, you can, but remember that doing so will add another note to Facebook and LinkedIn's databases, connecting one with the other.

2. **If you want to start a new account, fill in the blanks and tap or click Join Now.**

   Make sure you use a real e-mail address: LinkedIn uses it to verify your account.

   The first profile page appears, as shown in Figure 4-2, which asks the first of a series of questions that can be tricky to answer. In particular, if you're looking for a job, and you already *have* a job, advertising that fact is probably not politically correct.

My strong suggestion is that, if you have a job, declare that you're Employed *even if you're looking for a new job.* Why? Because your boss's boss may be on LinkedIn. (Of course, she may be looking for a new job, too, but I digress.)

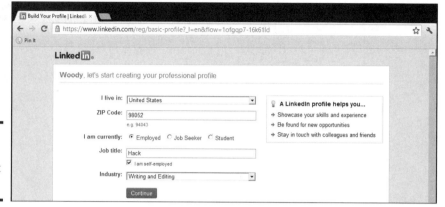

Figure 4-2:
Looks
simple but it
isn't.

3. **Fill out the boxes — extra points for a creative job title; Master of the Universe is a bit overworked — and tap or click Create My Profile.**

   LinkedIn says that it wants to Find Colleagues and Friends on LinkedIn.

4. **Unless you really want to spam your e-mail contacts, tap or click Skip This Step. If LinkedIn persists and asks you to sign on to your e-mail system (such as Hotmail/Outlook.com), choose Send a Confirmation Email Instead. If LinkedIn asks a *third time* (no, I'm not making this up) if you want to connect to your e-mail system, just ignore it.**

   LinkedIn sends you a message a few minutes later. The message includes a link.

5. **Tap or click the link in your e-mail message, provide your e-mail address and password, type the CAPTCHA code to prove that you're human, and sign in *again*.**

   You're confirmed.

6. **Tap or click Skip This Step to avoid broadcasting to Facebook and Twitter that you just set up a LinkedIn profile.**

   LinkedIn gives you an opportunity to spend money on a Premium account (see Figure 4-3). If you really want to see the details of everyone who's looked at your profile, you might want to consider Premium (the Free accounts can look at the last five viewers), or if you want to look at details about the people you're stalking, er, seeking (job and education history, recommendations and groups), pay for the Premium package.

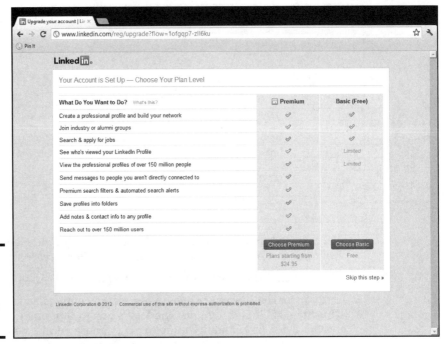

Figure 4-3:
For most people, Premium is overkill.

7. Choose a Premium or Basic account.

I chose Basic.

8. Step through a professional version of 20 guided questions. If you don't want to list anything, tap or click Skip This Step, but if you think it may help you connect with the right people, by all means, enter your job and education history.

The Skills question is another tricky one, particularly if you're looking for a job. Puffery here can come back to bite you, but being passive isn't good, either. If you're going to be looking for a job, put items in here that you would put on your résumé. Assume that people who want to interview you will see it before you arrive.

LinkedIn takes you to your main page, which looks more or less like Figure 4-4.

9. If LinkedIn asks you *again* whether you want to log on to your online e-mail accounts (it'll probably also ask whether LinkedIn can scan your Outlook, Apple Mail, or other mail program contacts), ignore it.

10. At the top, tap or click the Profile link.

LinkedIn shows you your profile, per Figure 4-5.

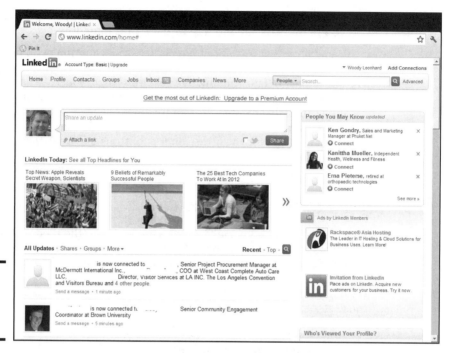

Figure 4-4:
The initial
LinkedIn
main page.

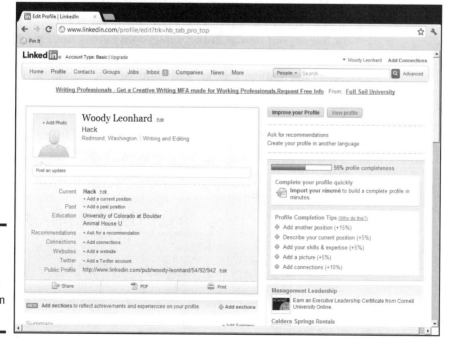

Figure 4-5:
It's a good
idea to get
your profile
right early in
the game.

11. **Update any items you want to flog on an unsuspecting world. When you're done, at the top, tap or click the Home link.**

Remember that just about anybody can see anything you post.

The social part of LinkedIn involves establishing *contacts* — connections with people you know, or know of. To start filling in your Contacts list, tap or click the Contacts link at the top of the home page, and add people based on their e-mail addresses. You can also find people you know based on others' connections. Look for the little Connect buttons and links throughout the LinkedIn interface.

Hooking LinkedIn into Windows

LinkedIn, like Facebook and Twitter, can hook into the tiled Windows 8 People app. If you decide to connect your Windows computer with LinkedIn, all your LinkedIn contacts get sucked into the Windows 8 People list.

Getting your LinkedIn contacts into Windows 8 couldn't be easier. Follow these steps:

1. **Start the People app by going to the Windows 8 Start screen and tapping or clicking the People tile.**

The People screen appears, as shown in Figure 4-6.

2. **If you don't have an Add People pane on the left, swipe from the right or hover your mouse in the upper-right corner until the Charms bar appears.**

3. **Select the Settings charm at the bottom and then at the top, tap or click Accounts.**

The People Accounts pane appears on the right.

4. **Tap or click Add an Account, and then choose LinkedIn.**

The People app brings up the Stay in Touch With Your LinkedIn Friends dialog box.

5. **Tap or click Connect.**

Windows reaches out to LinkedIn, which tosses up a gatekeeper screen like the one in Figure 4-7.

Figure 4-6:
All your
contacts
appear
here.

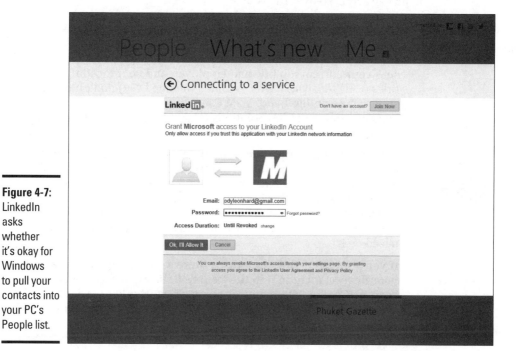

Figure 4-7:
LinkedIn
asks
whether
it's okay for
Windows
to pull your
contacts into
your PC's
People list.

6. **If you're okay with making the connection, type the e-mail address and password that you used to sign up for LinkedIn; then tap or click OK, I'll Allow It.**

   Realize that your LinkedIn contacts will be merged into your Windows People collection, which means that they'll be available from the Windows 8 tiled Mail app and the Messaging app.

   At the same time, realize that the People app may or may not be able to identify which contacts are duplicated: It may take a while for you to get all of the duplicates removed, and update the remaining People contacts with the latest information.

   If you don't want to make the connection, tap or click Cancel.

   It takes a minute or two (or longer if you have a lot of connections) for Windows to pull them down to your PC.

7. **Tap or click Done.**

   You return to the Windows 8 People app.

Using LinkedIn for Fun and Profit

Using LinkedIn with Windows is both an art and a science. Here are a few hints I've acquired over the years:

- ✦ **Use your current job title to your advantage.** I'm not sure why, but LinkedIn seems to show your current job title almost everywhere. Anytime someone hovers his mouse over your picture, for example, he sees your current job title and employer, and your location. Stock job titles (CEO, Analyst, Writer — that's the one I use) don't have much sizzle. On the other hand, M2M Executive with Expertise in the Rapid Implementation of CRM Solutions (M.S., Ph.D., O.B.E.) certainly draws attention.

- ✦ **Put a different, professional picture on your LinkedIn account.** Don't recycle your Facebook pic — you know, the one your friend took when you were completely plastered at the going-away party? Definitely a no-no in this arena. By all means, wear a suit and tie if you feel more comfortable that way, but casual is okay, too. Just remember that the people you want to impress will look at that mug and make decisions based on it.

- ✦ **If you graduated with honors, or there's something of note about your degree, include it in the Degree field.** Showing a college degree, such as B.A. Phi Beta Kappa or Summa Cum Laude or M.S. E.E., makes a greater impression than just listing your degree. People will see it.

✦ **Ask for recommendations, but don't use the stock request form.** Recommendations can make a difference in all sorts of situations, so don't be bashful about asking your friends to refer you. But when you do, take a few extra minutes and write a personal request message.

✦ **Start slowly.** Take a few days to get a feel for LinkedIn before you invite everyone to become a Connection. Look around and see how other people set up their profiles. Get a feel for what's acceptable and what's overly pushy. Only when you have your bearings are you really ready to add all those old e-mail contacts to your Connections list. And when you start building your Connections list, go slowly — just a handful of people a day.

Remember six degrees of separation?

After you have a few Connections put together, tap or click Contacts and then Network Statistics (see Figure 4-8).

Social networking works. Even if you don't use LinkedIn very much, having it available "just in case" — just in case you're looking for a new job, or for an expert in a particular field — is well worth the effort.

Figure 4-8: Even if you're only moderately well connected, you can have millions of people three hops away.

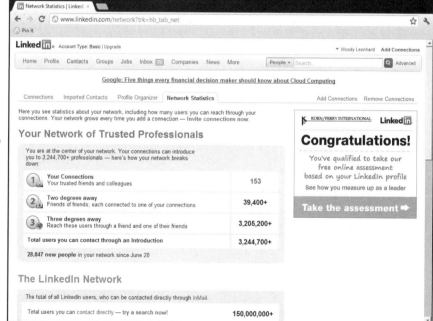

Chapter 5: Bing News, Finance, Travel, and Sports

In This Chapter

✔ Finding the Bing in everything

✔ Getting a different slant on the news

✔ Pinning finance for profit and fun

✔ Taking your tablet with you while you travel

✔ Working with the Sports app

*A*lthough the tiles may be scattered hither and yon on your Start screen, four of the key Microsoft tiled apps are really just portals to viewing stuff that's being fed by Microsoft Bing.

Bing News delivers a very visual take on the latest news, with short articles that aren't very touch-friendly. In this chapter, I show you how to personalize Bing News — there are several key options — but I also compare and contrast the Bing approach with the iPad Bing approach and the Web Bing approach. I also toss in a bit of Flipboard, which may suit your fancy better than all the others.

In a similar vein, *Bing Finance* delivers colorful, picture-filled news reports and lots and lots of charts which, once again, aren't very touch-friendly. In this chapter, I show you how to focus on stocks that concern you, track interest rates and other economic indicators, and explore a few other features, all the while repeating to myself that Microsoft wasn't willing to spend the bucks to deliver real-time stock quotes.

I like *Bing Travel*, and in this chapter, I show you why. The photos, in particular, are stunning. (Wonder how they'd look on a retina display?) Unfortunately, much of the material is seriously out of date, but that's why you have other travel apps, yes?

My friends tell me that *Bing Sports* is the greatest thing since live-streaming football games. (And those friends tend to think of "football" as what Americans call "soccer.") Although it's likely that other sporting outlets will have their own Windows 8 tiled apps sooner or later, Microsoft's Bing Sports packs a lot of information — and gorgeous pictures — into a compact frame.

Recognizing the Bing in Everyone

All four Microsoft Bing apps follow the same format:

✦ **A huge, high definition photo on the front page gets pushed onto the app's Start screen tile.** Bing Travel is the only exception; it has a huge photo on the splash screen, but other photos get pushed to the Start tile.

✦ **Tiles for articles come in various sizes.** (Bing Finance leads with a market graph, followed by the articles.) The individual articles obviously aren't written for touch-enabled devices. You can't even resize the text in them.

✦ **Each app has numerous customization options from stocks worth watching to favored news topics.** Slide from the top or right-click the desktop to bring up these options.

✦ **The source of all the information inside the apps is Microsoft's Bing.** And Bing is culled and maintained by a human team inside Microsoft. The team may or may not bring items to the limelight that interest you.

The Microsoft Bing apps are just shells: They rely on their connection to Microsoft's computers to come up with their content and perform their magic. That isn't necessarily bad. But it does contribute to a sort of blandness that you won't find if you go out on the web and find information in other ways.

Contrariwise, you aren't going to see too many Bing articles about three-fingered aliens attacking dorms in Nantucket. Sometimes it's good to have a content filter.

Reading the News with Bing

The Bing News app includes some remarkable customization options, making it one of the most advanced Windows 8 tiled apps available to date.

Getting around Bing News

At its heart, Bing News is a wire-service aggregator, with a disproportionate representation of news stories sent by Reuters and the Associated Press (AP). As you scan through the news stories, you can see where they came from.

Let me take you on a guided tour:

1. **Look at the News tile on the Start screen.**

   If you've used the News app at all while connected to the Internet, you see a picture that slides up and down, revolving with a one-sentence news description that actually matches the picture. See Figure 5-1.

   If you've never used the News app, it's just a blank tile with the text News.

Figure 5-1:
The News
Start screen
tile.

2. **Tap or click the Bing News tile.**

   The Bing Daily appears with a full-screen high definition photo associated with a top story. See Figure 5-2.

Figure 5-2:
The Bing
Daily News
top story
appears as
a full-screen
picture.

3. **Tap or click the story.**

   (Actually, you have to tap or click the text at the bottom of the picture, but close enough.)

   Most stories run 500 to 1,000 words, typical for a print tabloid, and vastly superior to a typical radio or TV news blurb, but stunted for a "serious news" paper.

   If you're using a tablet, you immediately realize that the text can't be pinched. The text size you see is what you get. But you can swipe to go from page to page. If you have a mouse, the scroll wheel doesn't move the story up and down; it moves the story left to right.

4. **Tap or click the left arrow next to the story's title; then scroll through the categories offered in the Bing News app.**

   Depending on your location, you probably see three or four stories each in these categories: U.S., World, Technology, Business, Entertainment, Politics, Sports, and Health.

   You can also pinch, or click the small minus sign in the lower-right corner, for a Semantic Zoom that shows you the sections, as shown in Figure 5-3.

5. **In your favorite web browser, go to** www.bing.com/news.

   Note the tabs at the top of the page in Figure 5-4. They're almost identical to the sections in the Bing app.

Figure 5-3:
A Semantic Zoom pinch brings up colorful pictures for each of the Bing News Daily's nine sections.

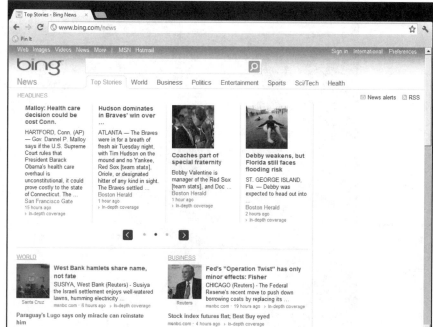

Figure 5-4:
The Bing
News
website
mirrors the
Bing News
app —
except the
web app has
more news,
faster.

The overlap in categories emphasizes that the Bing News app is just a
re-packaging of the Bing News site — but there's more to it than that.
Two concerns:

- The website packs a lot more information onto your screen, at the
  expense of those huge high def photos. Where the Windows 8 tiled
  app shows just one top story, the website shows six or more.

- In weeks of testing, I didn't see *any* breaking stories on the Bing News
  app until long after they appeared on the Bing News website. Usually,
  hot news items don't appear on the app until 12 hours or more after
  the news stories appeared on the Bing News site. Although the website's stories get updated frequently, they rarely seem to be updated
  on the Bing News app.

6a. ***Grab your iPad, if you have one,*** **install the Bing for iPad app (yep,
it's in the Apple App Store) and look at Bing News from the iPad point
of view. See Figure 5-5.**

6b. ***If you don't have an iPad,*** **skip to Step 8.**

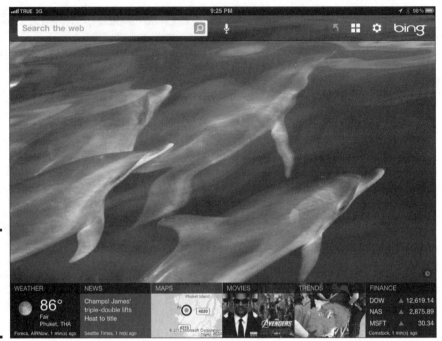

Figure 5-5:
Bing — yes,
the same
Bing — as
seen from
an iPad.

Bing for iPad looks a little different, but it has several of the same categories. Tap the Weather tile and you get an hourly and a ten-day forecast, just like the Bing Weather app. Tap the Finance tile and you can put your choice of three stocks or indices on the screen.

7. On the iPad, tap the News tile at the bottom.

You get a full array of news stories (see Figure 5-6). Bing puts 24 stories on the screen, compared to the handful on the tiled Bing News app. The pictures aren't as nice, but the categories are similar, and it's much easier to find a news story on the iPad.

8. Think about what you want from a news source.

Although tiled Bing News has beautiful pictures, it has very few stories, the stories are dated, and they're harder to find. The web version of Bing News is okay, and the iPad version is considerably better. But, frankly, I wouldn't waste my time on any of them.

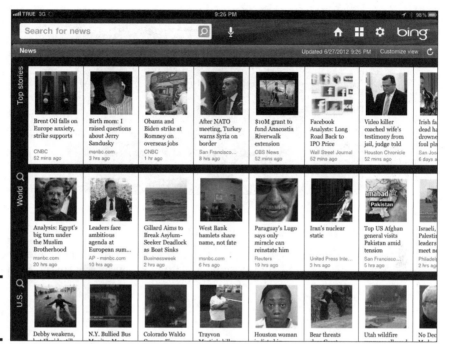

Figure 5-6:
Bing News
on the iPad.

I like Flipboard (www.flipboard.com) for the iPad, iPhone, Android, and — by the time you read this — probably for Windows 8's tiled side, as well. Flipboard has a wider variety of sources than Bing News, its interface is much better, and it feels more like a news magazine and less like a tablet-size billboard. And it's free.

Customizing Bing News

In the preceding section I stepped you through Bing Daily, which is the primary way of looking at Bing News. You may be surprised to discover that Bing News has other features, which might actually prove useful.

Here's how to get to the rest of the story:

1. **Bring up the Bing News app; then swipe from the top or bottom, or right-click the app.**

Four icons, as shown in Figure 5-7, appear. Each icon represents a different way of sorting the news feeds. You can customize the news that you see by picking a sorting method and setting sort criteria.

Figure 5-7:
Bing News
can present
news four
ways.

2. **Tap or click the My News icon.**

Bing News takes you into the My News view, which in most cases is oh-so-helpfully pre-populated with news about Microsoft. See Figure 5-8.

Figure 5-8:
My News
lets you set
the filters for
a different
view on the
news.

3. **Tap or click the plus sign below the Add a Section heading.**

   Bing News asks you to enter a news topic. Give it a try.

4. **Type a topic, such as** Dummies, **and then tap or click Add.**

   My News shows you three or four stories, as shown in Figure 5-9.

5. **Tap or click one of the articles.**

   Unlike Bing News Daily, the articles accessible from My News aren't touch-friendly at all: The pages scroll from top to bottom, they don't swipe from left to right, and they're covered with ads. (And the text doesn't resize or re-flow in either Bing News Daily or My News.)

   Why isn't My News very touchy? Because you're viewing the news site's web page using the tiled version of Internet Explorer. All the "wrapping" has been cut off so you can't move around, but you're definitely in tiled IE. How can you tell? If you go to a news site that isn't on Microsoft's Flash whitelist (see Book IV, Chapter 1), and the site has a Flash animation, you see warnings that say videos can't be viewed because you don't have the correct version of the Flash player. It's a bogus error message, but you're still stuck. The only way to view the Flash animation is to flip over to the desktop version of IE and try to find the same page — which could be challenging.

Figure 5-9: My News uses the same basic layout as Bing News Daily, but you supply the filters.

In some cases, the My News part of Bing News tells you that the article you chose can't be viewed in the Bing News app and offers to send you off to your default browser. From there, you have to find your way back into My News, to pick up where you left off.

6. Tap or click the left arrow next to My News, then swipe or right-click the Bing News page to bring up the icons in Figure 5-7. Tap or click Trends.

In the Trends section, Bing comes up with a list of topics that are *trending* — things felt to be popular, using techniques or inspirations unknown — and churns out stories, following a format very similar to My News.

7. Tap or click the left arrow next to Trends, then swipe or right-click the Bing News page to bring up the icons in Figure 5-7. Tap or click Sources.

Bing News brings up a list of all the news sources that it aggregates, as shown in Figure 5-10.

Figure 5-10: You can see the latest news feeds from more than a hundred sources.

8. **Tap or click a news source.**

   A list of the most recent news stories from the source appears.

9. **Tap on a story that you want to see.**

   Once again you're tossed into a wrapperless version of the tiled IE, where you can't pinch the text to make it larger, and where bogus `You need to have the Adobe Flash Player to view this content` messages abound.

Moral of the story? Use a different news aggregator. There are many.

Or just work with a news site on the web — I use `http://news.google.com` all the time.

Pinning Finance for Fun and Profit

Unlike the Bing News app, the Bing Finance app doesn't have any glaring usability problems.

Well, okay, you can't pinch to make the text look bigger. And the stock market quotes are delayed. It's heavy on the U.S. stock exchanges and very light outside the United States. But other than that, Bing Finance is reasonably usable, and it can even pin (delayed) stock market quotes to your Start screen.

Here's a quick run-through:

1. **On the Start screen, tap or click the Finance tile.**

   Like the Bing News app, the Bing Finance app opens with a gorgeous, high definition photo, as shown in Figure 5-11.

   You can also see the major U.S. index ticker at the bottom of the picture, with quotes delayed by 15 minutes.

2. **Tap or click the lead story, or one of the other stories.**

   You see a presentation identical to the one in the Bing News app.

   Pages can't be pinched to resize the text, but you can swipe to move pages. As in News, most of the stories are from Reuters, although there are a few from Benzinga.

Figure 5-11:
Bing
Finance
splashes a
gorgeous
photo, all
the better to
populate the
Finance tile
on the Start
screen.

3. **Tap or click the left arrow next to the story headline, and go back to the main screen. Scroll to the right.**

   Here's what you see:

   - *A very capable, interactive graph of the major U.S. indices:* DJIA, S&P 500, NASDAQ, and Russell 2000, with Day/Month/Week/Year tiles on the bottom. Tapping or hovering your mouse on a specific date or time brings up the index value, in blue, on the left.

   - *More News:* Shows just what it says — more news stories.

   - *A Watchlist of specific stocks:* See Step 4.

   - *Gainers, Losers, and Most Active:* By default, these are based on the NASDAQ. If you want to see Gainers, Losers, and Most Active for NYSE or Amex, tap or click the Market Movers headline. If you tap or click an individual stock, Bing Finance brings up full charts and news for the stock.

   - *Currencies, Commodities, Bonds, and ETFs (Exchange Traded Funds):* You start with a summary. For more details, tap or click the topic that interests you. For example, tapping or clicking Currencies brings up a conversion matrix for many major currencies and a currency converter (see Figure 5-12). Tapping or clicking Bonds brings up a chart of U.S. debt yield curves.

   - *Current nationwide average mortgage, savings, and credit card rates:* Tap or click the Rates heading for auto loan rates, savings rates, and much more.

   - *Fund Picks:* Highlights the top U.S.-registered fund performers in several categories. Tap or click the Fund Picks link, and you can slice and dice U.S. funds a hundred ways.

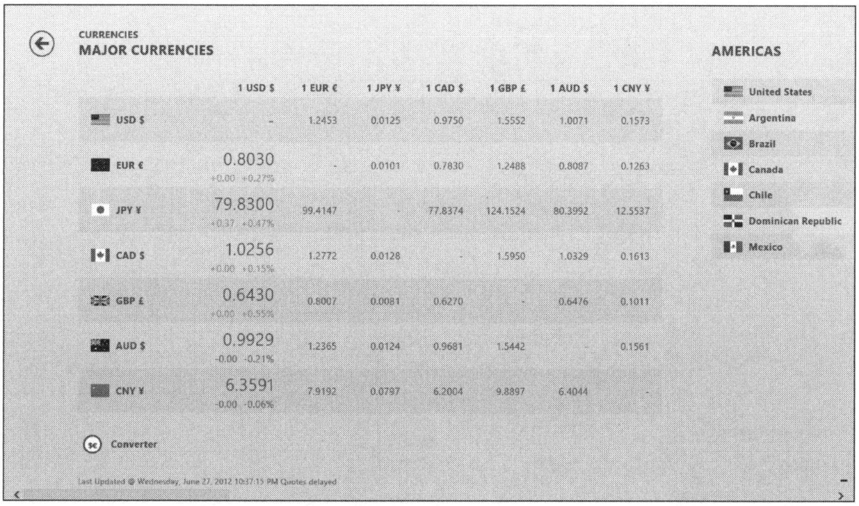

Figure 5-12:
Currency
conversion
inside
the Bing
Finance
app.

4. **Tap or click the left arrow next to the Currencies header, and then scroll to the Watchlist.**

   The Watchlist includes stocks, funds, and commodities — basically anything with a symbol — that you want to watch.

5. **At the bottom of the list, tap or click the plus sign.**

   Bing Finance prompts you to add a company name or stock symbol to the Watchlist.

6. **(Optional) Add a company name or stock symbol, or just tap or click Close.**

7. **Slide the tile down just a bit, until a check mark appears in the upper-right corner, or right-click one of the stocks on the Watchlist.**

   The App bar appears on the bottom, as shown in Figure 5-13.

8. **(Optional) To pin a tile for the stock to the Start screen, which shows the time delayed current price of the stock, tap or click Pin in the bottom-left corner.**

   The stock price appears on a Start screen tile, and it's updated throughout the day.

Figure 5-13:
Pin an
individual
stock to
the Start
screen.

You can pin just about **anything** — an individual stock, an index, an exchange, or a fund list — to the Start screen using the same action.

One final part worth exploring is the Bing Finance app's App bar. Swipe from the top or bottom, or right-click an empty space inside the app, and you see the icons shown in Figure 5-14.

Here's where the icons lead:

✦ **Watchlist** goes to your Watchlist, which I discuss earlier in this chapter.

✦ **News** shows an expanded news feed, which starts with a handful of news articles shown on the main page.

Figure 5-14:
A wide
array of
options for
financial
analysis.

✦ **Rates** goes to the Rates section — mortgages, home equity, auto loans, money markets, CDs, credit cards — just as if you had tapped or clicked the Rates heading on the main page.

✦ **Currencies** brings up the exchange rates matrix (refer to Figure 5-12).

✦ **World Market** shows a snapshot of the leading market indices in 11 countries worldwide, as shown in Figure 5-15. An indicator shows whether the markets are open.

✦ **Best of Web** takes you to a list of a hundred financial websites, not unlike the Sources page in Bing News (refer to Figure 5-10). If you tap or click a site, your default browser opens at the site's home page. It's up to you to find your way back.

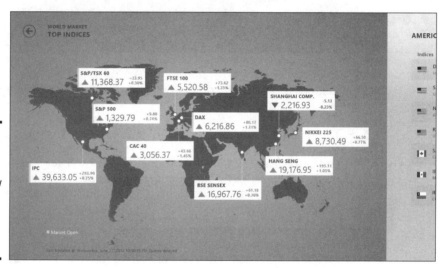

Figure 5-15:
The World Market map shows a few of the major market indices worldwide.

Traveling with Your Tablet

The Bing Travel app uses the same basic layout, with a much greater emphasis on pictures. See Figure 5-16.

I don't know how the app picks a pic to put on the Start screen tile, but invariably, they're gorgeous.

Figure 5-16:
Stunningly
gorgeous
photos in
the Bing
Travel app.

The main page, like all the other apps' main pages, has a big photo, with smaller photos to the right:

✦ **Tap or click the main photo,** and you see a brief overview about the location, with a static map, exchange rate, current temperature, photos, and more. Tap or click the introduction, and you get a more detailed travel guide, usually from Frommer's (although the source is likely to change by the time you read this, because Microsoft arch-rival Google bought Frommer's).

✦ **The Featured Destinations tiles** behave similarly, except some of the travel guides are quite detailed — five pages long or more, with hotel reviews, restaurant recommendations, and What to See lists. Tap or click the Featured Destinations heading to display the Destinations page, with hundreds of places to explore (see Figure 5-17).

✦ **Panoramas** shows 360-degree stitches of locations in several cities. Most seem to be from `www.360cities.net`. The website has a much larger selection.

✦ **The Articles section** carries a mixed bag of airline flight magazine-quality sketches interspersed with some real jewels, such as the culinary musings of *Bizarre Foods* guy Andrew Zimmern. Almost all the articles are attributed to Bing Travel, or licensed from Tribune Media Services.

Figure 5-17:
Destinations
pack
amazing
photos with
sometimes
excellent
commentary.

If you're looking for some place in particular, don't forget the Search charm!
Swipe from the right or hover your mouse in the upper-right corner, choose
Search, and type the name of your favorite destination.

The Bing Travel app comes complete with — you guessed it — plenty of
opportunities to book flights and hotel rooms, and otherwise part with your
hard-earned cash. If you feel in the mood to part with some samolians, swipe
from the top or bottom, or right-click in the middle of the page to bring up
the icons shown in Figure 5-18.

Figure 5-18:
More oppor-
tunities to
spend.

Here's where the icons lead:

+ **Destinations** brings up the tiles of destinations (refer to Figure 5-17).

+ **Flights** puts you into a flight search from KAYAK.com (www.kayak.com).
No doubt you've run flight searches before; this one's not significantly
different. I got a big kick out of the offered routing of a flight from Phuket
to Auckland via Guangzhou.

✦ **Hotels** sets you in a hotel search, again powered by KAYAK.com. There's very little ancillary information — certainly nothing like the comprehensive reviews on TripAdvisor (`www.tripadvisor.com`), for example, or the extensive price listings on LateStays.com (`www.latestays.com`).

✦ **Best of Web** (like its namesake in the Bing Financial app, and the Sources page in Bing News; refer to Figure 5-10) lists dozens of travel websites. If you tap or click a site, your default browser opens at the site's home page. Ironically, you gotta find your own way back to the app.

If you think of the Bing Travel app as a gazetteer, as opposed to a serious destination research site like `www.wikitravel.com` or `www.fodors.com`, you won't be disappointed.

Sports Fans Everywhere, Take Note

Of the four Bing-driven apps, Bing Sports consistently receives the highest accolades.

Like the others, when you open the app you see a gorgeous (well, given the subject matter, maybe not exactly gorgeous, but certainly well crafted) high-resolution photo (see Figure 5-19).

Scroll to the right, and you see news tiles, which behave just like similar tiles in the other apps.

Figure 5-19: Like the other Bing apps, Sports starts with a biiiig picture.

Scroll a bit farther, and you see two different sections:

✦ **Schedule** shows you the current schedule for all the teams in your favorite leagues. You can choose from NFL, NBA, MLB, NHL, Golf, Formula 1, Premier League, and La Liga. The selection changes with your location, and I'm told that AFL (that's Ozzie football to you sissy Yanks) and maybe even Rugby (give blood — play ruggers) are on the horizon.

✦ **Favorite Teams** lets you specify exactly which teams you want to follow.

Here's the chest buster: Tap or click one of the team tiles, and you see an enormous array of information about the team: a high definition photo-backed top story, news stories, played games and results, a roster of players with an enormous array of statistics — just about everything you could imagine about the team. See Figure 5-20.

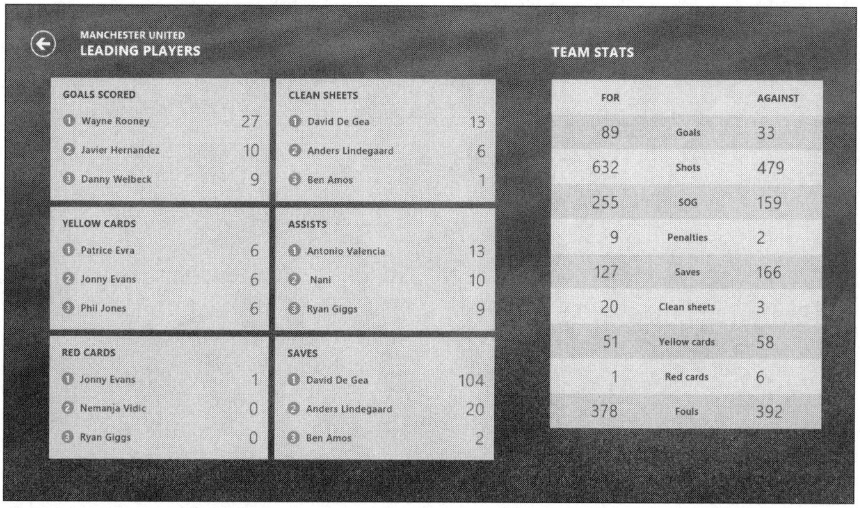

Figure 5-20:
Each team gets an enormous collection of statistics.

If you tap or click a game, Bing Sports brings up the Fox Sports listing for the game. Yes, Fox has listings for European matches as well as MLB GameTrax and all the others.

Swipe from the top or bottom, or right-click the main page, and you see the array of icons in Figure 5-21.

Figure 5-21:
Direct
access to
all the major
leagues.

From the icons, you can fly directly to the league that interests you or, as in the other Bing apps, look for references in the Best of Web section.

Chapter 6: Games, Games, and Games!

In This Chapter

✔ Searching for games

✔ Cutting the Rope with style

✔ Tapping Pirates Love Daisies

✔ Starting with Sudoku

✔ Beating Birzzle

The Windows store offers tons of games. Many of them, including some free ones, are well worth trying.

If you're looking for old Windows standbys like Minesweeper and Solitaire, they're here, too — but they're all gussied up, fabulously more playable, and very touch friendly, unlike their elder counterparts. In fact, the free, touch savvy Minesweeper and Solitaire may be enough to convince you to buy a touch tablet. No joke.

Unfortunately, the old Windows 7 cheats don't work any more, but the eye candy should more than compensate.

In this chapter, I talk about a sampling of games — free games — that you can download from the Windows store, and play directly on just about any Windows 8 computer. You don't need a monster graphics card, $600 joystick, or the reflexes of a trained fighter pilot to play.

Well, alright, it helps to have the reflexes of a trained fighter pilot. But that's okay. You can limp along, just like me.

One thing all these games have in common is that there really are strategies to help you win. Take a few minutes to read about the idiosyncrasies of the games, and you might find yourself jumping a few extra levels, or plucking off a couple of rats.

The free games that come with Windows 8 run quite a gamut. The poster child of the bunch, Cut the Rope, runs on iPads and iPhones, but the game action on Windows 8 is faster — primarily because the whole game was rewritten (with Microsoft's help) in HTML5. You can read all about the technical dexterity on the U.K. Team blog for the Microsoft Developer Network, http://blogs.msdn.com/b/ukmsdn.

If you're looking for Xbox games, you're in the wrong place. The Xbox ecosystem has some overlap with Windows 8, but by and large, Xbox gaming exists at a completely different level of complexity. If you're looking for an intro to that world, check out *Xbox 360 For Dummies* by Brian Johnson and Duncan Mackenzie.

Searching the Store for Games

Want to see what games will run on the tiled side of Windows 8? Head to the Windows store. Here's how:

1. On the Start screen, tap or click Store.

The Windows store appears.

2. Scroll a bit to the right, and at the top, tap or click Games.

An enormous array of tiles for games appears, as shown in Figure 6-1.

Figure 6-1: Games offered at the Windows store.

You can start searching based on Microsoft's assigned noteworthy rating, but I prefer to look at the list based on ratings from actual customers.

3. **At the top, tap or click the drop-down box and choose Sort By Highest Rating.**

   Choosing games is a black art, all by itself, but if you see a game that looks interesting, check it out.

4. **Tap or click any interesting game.**

   The Windows store shows you a complete description of the game and presents you with an opportunity to install the app, as shown in Figure 6-2.

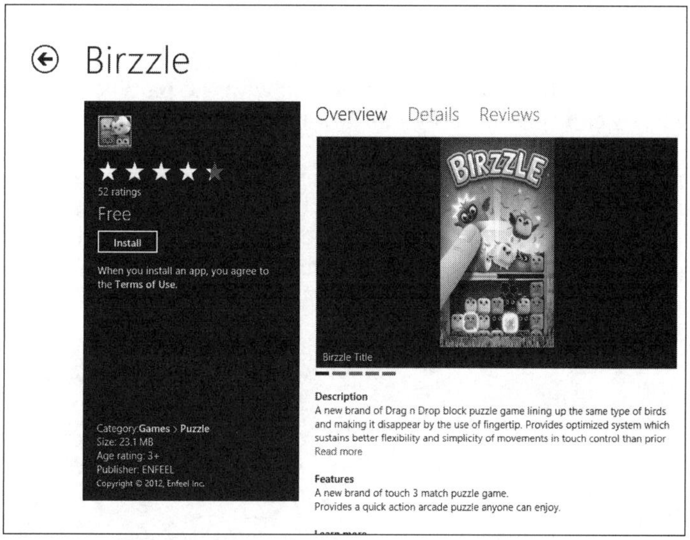

Figure 6-2:
If it tickles
your fancy,
install it.

⊛ Birzzle

Overview   Details   Reviews

★ ★ ★ ★ ☆
52 ratings
Free

[Install]

When you install an app, you agree to the **Terms of Use**.

Birzzle Title

Category: **Games** > Puzzle
Size: 23.1 MB
Age rating: 3+
Publisher: ENFEEL
Copyright © 2012, Enfeel Inc.

Description
A new brand of Drag n Drop block puzzle game lining up the same type of birds and making it disappear by the use of fingertip. Provides optimized system which sustains better flexibility and simplicity of movements in touch control than prior
Read more

Features
A new brand of touch 3 match puzzle game.
Provides a quick action arcade puzzle anyone can enjoy.

5. **To install the app, make sure you're willing to pay the price, and then tap or click Install.**

6. **If there's a charge, verify your billing details and/or provide a password.**

   While it's downloading, you see a notification at the top of the Windows store screen. When your app has finished downloading, it appears as a tile on your Start screen.

Installing games is easy. Beating them is anything but.

Cutting the Rope with Style

Everybody knows Angry Birds.

Cut the Rope isn't Angry Birds. The physics is a little more complex, and the variations are trickier. That said, it's every bit as addictive as its feathered counterpart. And there aren't any ^%$#@! pigs.

Many people don't realize it, but Cut the Rope was invented in Russia, in 2010. It became very successful on the iPad and iPhone, with more than one million copies sold in the Apple App Store *in the first nine days.*

Microsoft picked it up as a demo for its HTML5 browser experiments, then ported it hook, line, and sinking candy monster to the tiled side of Windows 8. No doubt the 'Softies hope that some of that App Store magic rubs off on Windows 8 players.

There are both free and paid versions, with the paid versions running more levels — and considerably more challenge.

The back story isn't terribly complex: You need to get a piece of candy into the mouth of the adorable monster Om Nom, and collect points along the way. The action is based on pendulum swings, anchored by ropes, where you get to decide when to, uh, cut the rope. See Figure 6-3.

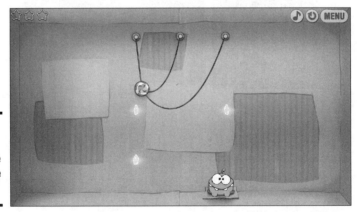

Figure 6-3:
Cut the
Rope to give
Om Nom the
candy.

Things get considerably more complicated when you encounter bubbles: When a piece of candy hits a bubble, it's absorbed into the bubble, and the bubble and candy rise together. Bellows push the candy and bubbles around. Spikes and electricity can pop the bubbles. With each new level, you see different layouts and accoutrement.

Scoring is pretty intuitive: You get points for touching stars with candy, and the faster you go, the more points you get.

Advancing levels isn't intuitive at all. You start in the Cardboard Box, which has nine levels, but only one is unlocked; that's the one you have to play.

Each level holds three stars. Collect at least one star and feed Om Nom, and the next level gets unlocked. See Figure 6-4.

Figure 6-4:
Collect at least one star and feed the monster, and you can go on to the next level.

Collect enough stars in the Cardboard Box, and you're allowed to progress to the Fabric Box. Get enough stars there, and you can go on to the Toy Box. And from there . . . you get to pay for the next levels.

You might think that your progress through the game is measured by points. It isn't. The trick is in the stars.

Here are a few more tricks:

✦ Don't get hung up on finishing a level. If you get frustrated, remember that you only need to catch one star and feed Om Nom, and you're granted access to the next level.

✦ If you're in an impossible position (believe me, it happens a lot), just cut the candy free or click the circle-arrow in the upper-right corner to start the level all over again (see Figure 6-4).

✦ If you encounter blue dotted circles with slider bars, think about moving the slider bar — and thus the circle — before you start cutting ropes.

Throw ol' Om Nom a bone.

Tapping Pirates Love Daisies

Another big Microsoft score for the Windows 8 platform, and another early port to HTML5, Pirates Love Daisies (see Figure 6-5) is a thoroughly modern rendition of a class of games called Tower Defense.

Figure 6-5:
Pirates Love Daisies, a considerably less-gory variation on Plants vs. Zombies.

Microsoft convinced Flash programming guru Grant Skinner to try his hand at an HTML5 game. Just like Cut the Rope, it was an attempt on Microsoft's part to demonstrate that HTML5 had the moxie to carry along a real-world game. The result is a fun and playable game that isn't overly sophisticated, and doesn't rely on zombies.

The back story reverberates with pre-teen swashbucklers: "Davy Jones is sending his scurvy minions to steal your most valuable possessions: your daisies. Only your stalwart crew can stop them before they take all your fragrant flowers to the murky depths. Hire new crew members and place them strategically to prevent the creeps from nabbing your daisies and returning to the water from whence they came."

In other words, shoot the crawling things before they take your daisies and crawl back in "the water from whence they came." I think "from whence" is a pirate phrase or something. Garrr.

When you bring up the main screen (see Figure 6-6), tap or click Help to get a general overview.

Figure 6-6:
Bright and colorful pirates with perfect hair.

The key thing to realize about Pirates Love Daisies is that your sole point of interaction is in placing one of the characters in a specific location on the map. You don't fire the guns, or swash the buckles. The characters do that all by themselves — no clicking required.

When you have enough gold stored (accumulated by killing the creepy critters), tap or click one of the characters, then tap or click at the base of one of the picks that appears. The character is transported to the location you click, and starts fighting all by himself.

A simple strategy for dealing with the first level: Put a lot of pirates at the entrance to the bridge. Then put more pirates next to the daisy field, to fend off flying critters.

Starting with Sudoku

If you've ever tried to finish a really hard Sudoku, you know it can be quite a challenge.

The Windows 8 Sudoku game starts by asking whether you want an Easy, Normal, or Hard game (see Figure 6-7). One guess which one I usually pick.

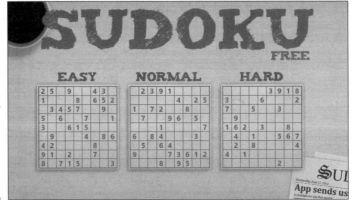

Figure 6-7:
When it
says *hard,*
it means
haaaaaaard.

Sudoku has a fascinating history. Apparently, the first puzzles of this type to appear in print were published in *Dell Magazines,* starting in 1979. They were known as Number Place. It appears as if they were created by a 74-year-old retired architect named Howard Garns, from Connersville, Indiana.

These puzzles first appeared in Japan in the *Monthly Nikolist* paper, starting in April 1984. The name *Sudoku* is an abbreviation of a lengthy Japanese name that means, roughly, "the digits are limited to one occurrence."

The object of Sudoku is to arrange the digits from 1 to 9 in a 9 x 9 grid, so that each column and each row has one of each digit. To make things a bit more complex, each of the nine 3 x 3 blocks must also have all the digits from 1 to 9.

You're presented with a grid, pre-filled with some numbers. Your challenge is to come up with an arrangement of digits that fits all the rules.

The game play in this app is a bit confusing. First, tap or click an empty square. A box appears around the square. Then, tap or click one of the digits. To clear a square, tap or click it, then tap or click the blank "number" below the 9.

If you put a number on the grid, and the number already exists in the same row or column, you goofed and the number appears in red. If there are no immediate conflicts, the number appears in white.

The Internet has about two hundred billion free Sudoku grids.

Beating Birzzle

Birzzle is the last game I cover in this chapter. I know that's an unlikely name, but it's a fascinating free game. I love it. Birzzle, made by a Korean company, started out on the iPad in 2011. I know, it's a common refrain. But it carries across nicely to Windows 8.

Actually, Birzzle isn't one game; it's two.

The first, Birzzle classic (see Figure 6-8), is a very fast-action drag-and-drop block matching game — get three of the same birds together and bzzzzzz–zap! They disappear in a puff of feathers. More birds fall down from the top.

Figure 6-8:
Birzzle
moves very,
very fast.

When a trio (or more) of birds is about to explode, they start vibrating. Pour on more birds, and they're taken out in the conflagration. Power Birds are also part of the mix — I think Power Birds are associated with larger explosions, but it's hard to tell. If you can get a Power Bird lined up with similar colored birds, the whole bunch can blast holes up, down, and sideways. Just keep dragging birds as fast as you can.

The second game, Birzzle Ice Break (see Figure 6-9) has more frenzied action, but in a slightly different way: Birds come diving out of a chute, and you control where they land. There are flying eggs, fuzzy Power Birds, ice blocks, and hourglasses thrown in for distraction.

Figure 6-9:
Birzzle Ice
Break, one
very cool
game.

Of course, the company that makes Birzzle wants you to buy its more
advanced game, Panorama. If it's even half as good as Classic and Ice Break,
it has to be a winner.

Book VI

Working on the Desktop

The 5th Wave   By Rich Tennant

"The funny thing is he's spent 9 hours organizing his computer desktop."

Contents at a Glance

Chapter 1: Running the Desktop from Start to Finish

In This Chapter

✔ **Re-introducing the hot spots and corners**

✔ **Discovering Aero Snap**

✔ **Navigating**

✔ **Working with File Explorer, files, and folders**

✔ **Viewing**

✔ **Sharing folders**

✔ **Touching on the taskbar**

✔ **Recycling**

✔ **Creating shortcuts**

*T*his chapter explains how to find your way around the windows on the desktop — the part of Windows 8 that isn't controlled by the tiled Start screen (and, thus, isn't really cool). If you're an old hand at Windows, you know most of this stuff — such as mousing and interacting with dialog boxes — but Windows 8 puts a whole new slant on things, whether you're touch-enabled or not.

This chapter also shows you the Windows 8 way to move around your files and folders, navigate the taskbar, create shortcuts, and more.

Most of all, you need to understand that Windows 8 has almost everything that was in Windows 7 — you just need to find it. In most cases, the new tiled, immersive stuff kind of floats alongside the old-fashioned Windows 7 desktop. By and large, if you're comfortable with the desktop — whether from years of experience, because you need to do the kinds of things that are best adapted to a keyboard and mouse, or just because you don't like the touchy tiles — you can spend most of your time on the desktop.

If you've used an earlier version of Windows, and spent any time at all with Windows 8, you're probably wondering where Microsoft hid all the programs that used to sit on the Start menu. In the Windows 8 scheme of things, you have to know how to find those programs and stick them someplace usable. I have complete instructions for finding your long-lost programs, and pinning them either to the tiled Start screen or the desktop Toolbar, in Book VI, Chapter 3.

If you're looking for a tour of the Windows 8 desktop interface, read on.

Getting Around

Your PC is a big place, and you can get lost easily. Microsoft has spent hundreds of millions of dollars to make sure that Windows 8 points you in the right direction and keeps you on track through all sorts of activities.

Amazingly, some of it actually works.

Knowing the desktop's hot spots

In Book II, Chapter 1, I talk about getting around Windows, both with your fingers and with a mouse and keyboard.

I won't dwell on what's come before, but I do want to give you a quick refresher on navigating the desktop using just the mouse and keyboard. For most people who use Windows to get "real work" done (definitions vary, *mutatis mutandis*), the mouse and keyboard — and increasingly the microphone — are the tools of choice.

Here are the crucial key combinations for navigation. It would be worth your while to memorize the following keystrokes (I find myself using these all the time):

✦ Tap the **Windows key** to cycle between the tiled Start screen and the last app that you were using. If the last app you used was on the desktop, you get your entire desktop back in the state it was in when you left.

✦ **Alt+Tab** invokes the Cool Switch.

If you don't want to hunt around for the mouse — or if your mouse has suddenly gone out to lunch — Windows 8 has the Cool Switch feature, which lets you switch among running programs while (insert your best W.C. Fields impression here) your fingers never leave your hands . . . er, your fingers never leave the keyboard. Wink, wink. Just hold down Alt and press Tab. When you see the program you want, release Alt. Bam!

✦ **Windows Key+C** brings up the Charms bar on the right, the current time and date, and the major notification icons that appear on your logon screen.

When you're looking at the desktop, the four corners are hot. In particular, here's what you see when you hover your mouse in each corner:

✦ **Upper left:** A thumbnail of the last app you ran appears. (By "app" I mean either one of the tiled, immersive apps, or the entire old-fashioned desktop, which counts as one "app.") Slide the mouse down the left and you get the Running Apps Bar, shown in Figure 1-1.

You can click any thumbnail to flip over to that program, or click and drag the thumbnail to the right, to set up the rigid, tiled Snap, which I describe in Book III, Chapter 1.

✦ **Upper right:** The Charms bar appears. Move your mouse down, into the Charms bar, and the background turns black, solidifying the Charms, as shown in Figure 1-2. Turning the Charms bar black also brings up the current time.

You may find yourself using the Charms Search function while on the desktop, but probably won't use the other Charms after you've tricked out your desktop with the customizations in Book VI, Chapter 3.

✦ **Lower right:** The Charms bar appears here, too, but strangely, all your desktop windows also turn into silhouettes (an old Vista trick known as *Aero Peek*). So you can see your Charms but not your windows. Give it a try, and you'll see what I mean.

Figure 1-1:
The Running
Apps Bar
on the left
has one
thumbnail
for each
app that's
currently
running;
the desktop
counts as
one app.

✦ **Lower left:** A thumbnail of the tiled Start screen appears. Click it if you prefer this method of switching back to the tiled Start screen, over pressing the Windows key.

Also awaiting if you *right*-click in the lower-left corner is a cool set of shortcuts called the Power User Menu, shown in Figure 1-3. You see the same menu if you press Windows Key + X.

Of course, Windows 8 has zillions of key shortcuts, clicks, taps, and combinations thereof, but these are the ones I use the most.

Figure 1-2:
The Charms bar has limited usefulness if you spend most of your time on the desktop, although Search comes in handy.

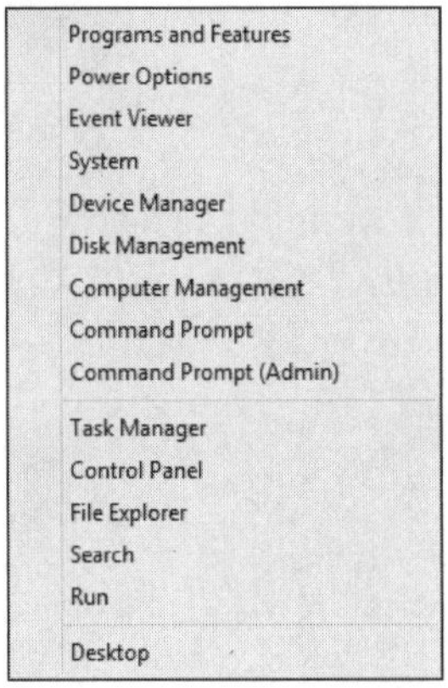

Search
Share
Start
Devices
Settings

Figure 1-3:
The Power User Menu appears if you right-click in the lower-left corner.

Programs and Features
Power Options
Event Viewer
System
Device Manager
Disk Management
Computer Management
Command Prompt
Command Prompt (Admin)

Task Manager
Control Panel
File Explorer
Search
Run

Desktop

Snapping windows into place

Windows 8, like Windows 7, includes several "gesture" features that can save you a lot of time. Foremost among them is Aero Snap, a Windows 8 feature that's been inherited from Windows 7, and works great.

On the desktop, Aero Snap is an easy way to place windows side by side, by using a mouse or your finger:

1. **Click the title bar of a window and drag the window a-a-all the way to the left side of the screen.**

   As soon as the mouse (finger) hits the edge of the screen, Windows 8 resizes the window so that it occupies the left half of the screen and docks the window on the far left side.

2. **Repeat Step 1, but drag a different window to the right side of the screen.**

   That makes it two-drag easy to put a Word document and a spreadsheet side by side, or a web page and File Explorer side by side, as shown in Figure 1-4.With the two windows side by side, you can easily click and drag between them and resize, minimize, maximize, and do all the other things Windows does with windows.

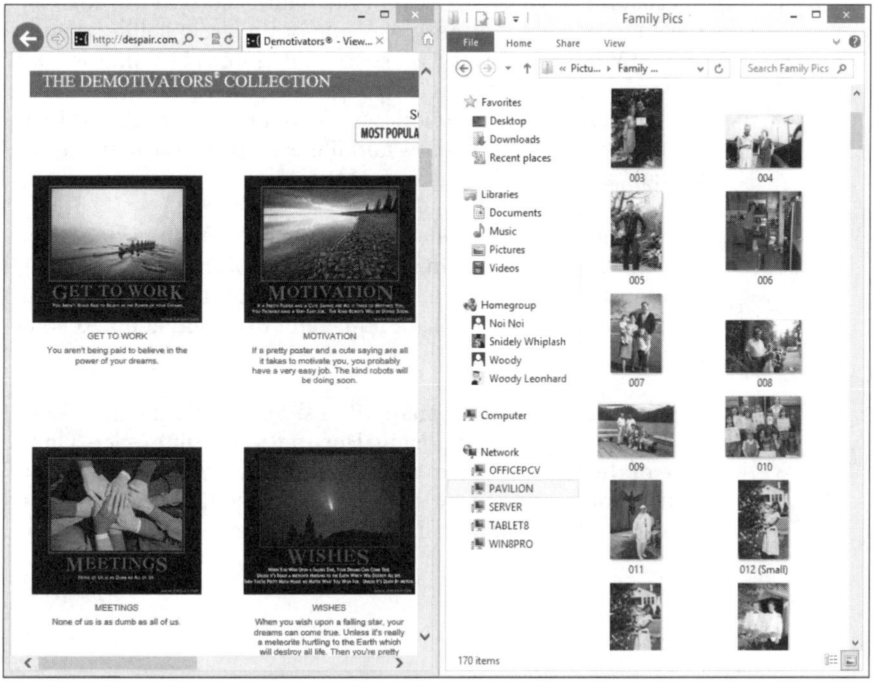

Figure 1-4: Two drags and you can have Windows arrange two programs side by side on the old-fashioned desktop.

Aero Snap isn't the only desktop gesture. Check out these window tricks:

✦ If you drag a window to the top of the screen, it's maximized, so it occupies the whole screen. (Yeah, I know: You always did that by double-clicking the title bar.)

✦ This only works if you have a mouse: click a window's title bar and shake it, all other windows on the screen move out of the way: They minimize themselves on the toolbar.

If you have "rodentophobia," you can also do the mouse tricks explained in this section by pressing the following key combinations:

✦ Aero Snap left: ⊞+←

✦ Aero Snap right: ⊞+→

✦ Maximize: ⊞+↑

There's another snap in Windows 8, and it only works on the tiled side of the fence. Most of the time, Microsoft calls this other snap, confusingly, "Snap." I call the tiled way of snapping "Tiled Snap." Not exactly rocket science, but it gets the point across.

Microsoft is trying to get rid of the name "Aero." For those of you who were raised to believe that Aero was one of the great selling points and big benefits of Windows 7, well, Microsoft killed Aero in Windows 8. The old Aero you may remember — see-through window outlines, "X" boxes that light up, cool 3D effects around windows — are all gone, replaced by the tiled vision of regimented straight lines and lifeless boxes. Little pieces of Aero live on, though, and Aero Snap is one of them.

Tiled Snap is a rather lame way of putting two apps side-by-side on the screen. As you can see in Figure 1-5, one of the "apps" can be the whole Windows 7 style desktop. You can't drag stuff between the two Tiled Snapped apps, can't resize them, can't do much at all. Read all about it in Book III, Chapter 1.

Are you thinking, "Aero snap, tiled snap, what's the difference?" The snap terminology can be confusing. Here's the big difference: On the desktop side of the fence, the two Aero Snapped windows can interact. You can drag things from one window to another. On the tiled side, the Tiled Snapped programs don't interact at all. Each lives in its own little Windows world.

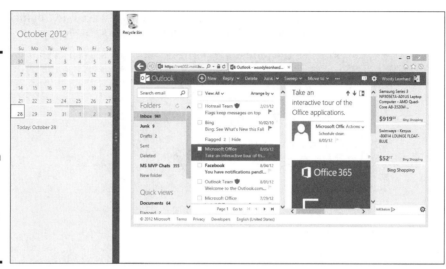

Figure 1-5:
Tiled Snap lets you put a tiled app and the desktop next to each other, or two tiled apps side-by-side, but there's no interaction.

Changing the mouse

If you're left-handed, you can interchange the actions of the left and right mouse buttons. That is, you can tell Windows that it should treat the left mouse button as though it were the right button and treat the right button as though it were the left. The swap comes in handy for some left-handers, but most southpaws I know (including my no. 1 son) prefer to keep the buttons as is because it's easier to use other computers if your fingers are trained for the standard setting.

The Windows ClickLock feature can come in handy if you have trouble holding down the left mouse button and moving the mouse at the same time — a common problem for notebook users who have fewer than three hands. When Windows uses ClickLock, you hold down the mouse button for a while (you can tell Windows exactly how long) and Windows locks the mouse button so that you can concentrate on moving the mouse without having to hold down the button.

To switch left and right mouse buttons or turn on ClickLock, follow these steps:

1. **Right-click in the lower-left corner to bring up the Power User Menu (refer to Figure 1-3) and choose Control Panel.**

You can also search for "Mouse Settings" from the Start screen.

2. **In Control Panel, click the link for Hardware and Sound, then, under Devices and Printers, click the link that says Mouse.**

   You see the Mouse Properties dialog box shown in Figure 1-6.

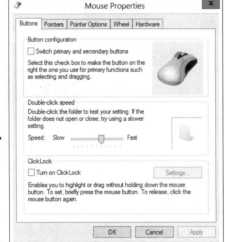

Figure 1-6:
Reverse
the left and
right mouse
buttons with
one click.

3. **If you want to switch the functions of the left and right mouse buttons, select the Switch Primary and Secondary Buttons check box.**

   Note that the function of the right and left buttons changes immediately, so you may have to *right-click* to deselect the box!

4. **If you want to turn on ClickLock, check the Turn On ClickLock box and immediately click the Settings button.**

   You can then click the Settings button to adjust the length of time you need to hold down the mouse button for ClickLock to kick in.

5. **Click OK.**

   The changes take place immediately.

Exploring Files and Folders

"What's a file?" Man, I wish I had a nickel for every time I've been asked that question.

A file is a, uh, thing. Yeah, that's it. A thing. A thing that has stuff inside it. Why don't you ask me an easier question, like "What is a paragraph?" or "What is the meaning of life, the universe, and everything?"

Seriously, though, this section answers your questions about the basics of the Windows 8 interface: basic terms, basic navigation techniques, basic ways to organize the 76 items you've saved to the desktop, and more.

Nailing the basic terminology

A *file* is a fundamental chunk of stuff. Like most fundamental chunks of stuff (say, protons or Congressional districts), any attempt at a definitive definition gets in the way of understanding the thing itself. Suffice it to say that a Word document is a file. An Excel workbook is a file. That photograph your cousin e-mailed you the other day is a file. Every track on the latest Gotye album is a file, but so is every track on every audio CD ever made. De Backer isn't that special.

Filenames and folder names can be very long, but they can't contain the following characters:

/ \ : * ? " < > |

Files can be huge. They can be tiny. They can even be empty, but don't short-circuit any gray cells on that observation.

Folders hold files and other folders. Folders can be empty. A single folder can hold millions — yes, quite literally millions — of files and other folders.

Book VI
Chapter 1

Running the Desktop from Start to Finish

Keeping folders organized

If you set folders up correctly, they can help you keep track of things. If you toss your files around higgledy-piggledy, no system of folders in the world can help. Unfortunately, folders have a fundamental problem. Permit me to illustrate.

Say you own a sandwich shop. You take a photograph of the shop. Where do you stick the photo? Which folder should you use? The answer: There's no single good answer. You could put the photo in with all your other "shop" stuff — documents and invoices and payroll records and menus. You could stick the photo in the Pictures folder, which Windows automatically provides. You could put it in the Public or Public Documents or Public Pictures folder so that other people using your PC, or other folks

connected to your network, can see the photo of the shop. You could create a folder named Photos and file away the picture chronologically (that's what I do), or you could even create a folder named Shop inside the Photos folder and stick the picture in \Photos\Shop.

This where-to-file-it-and-where-to-find-it conundrum stands as one of the hairiest problems in all of Windows, and until Windows 7, you had only piecemeal help in keeping things organized. Now, using Windows 8 libraries, and a Search function that (finally!) works the way you would expect, you stand a fighting chance of finding that long-lost file, especially if you're diligent in assigning tags to pictures and videos. See Book VII, Chapter 3 for all the details about working with libraries.

If you're going to get any work done with those files and folders, you have to interact with *File Explorer,* formerly known as Windows Explorer, the slow-beating heart of the user experience (or, the way Windows interacts with people). Gad. When you want to work with Windows, such as ask it where it stuck your wedding pictures, show it how to mangle your files, or tell it (literally) where to go, you usually use File Explorer.

If you click the icon at the bottom of the desktop, the one that looks like a file folder, you get tossed into File Explorer, with Explorer set up to look at your libraries. File Explorer comes up looking like Figure 1-7.

Figure 1-7: File Explorer in its native state.

See the first line of text in the windows, the line that says "File, Home, Share, View"? If you click any of those, Explorer brings up an icon-laden strip that offers various options. That's the File Explorer **Ribbon.** You can turn it on full-time by clicking the down-wedge icon in the upper-right corner. That brings up the Ribbon shown in Figure 1-8.

Some people hate the Ribbon, some people love it. I, personally, turn it off when I'm jumping in and out of File Explorer to get some work done — copying files, say, or moving or renaming. But if I need to do something that I don't usually do, and I need a little help, I turn the Ribbon on. That makes me a pariah in some geeky circles; real geeks don't use Ribbons, or so I'm told. So be it. Sometimes I'm a dummy, just like everybody else.

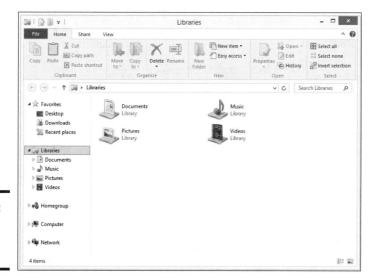

Figure 1-8:
The File
Explorer
Ribbon.

Navigating

As you can see in Figure 1-9, File Explorer arrives chock full of options, many of which have to do with getting around. File Explorer helps you get around in the following ways:

✦ **Click a folder to see the folders and files inside that folder.** On the left side of the File Explorer window (refer to Figure 1-9), you can click a real folder (such as Desktop or Downloads); a shortcut you dragged to the Favorites list on the left (InfoWorld Tech Watch, for example); one of the Windows libraries, including the predefined Documents, Music, Pictures, or Videos; other computers in your Homegroup; other drives on your computer; or other computers on the network.

✦ **Use the "cookie crumb" navigation bar or the up arrow to move around.** At the top of the File Explorer window (refer to Figure 1-9), you can click the wedges to select from available folders, or click the up arrow to move "up" one level in the folder hierarchy.

✦ **Details appear below.** If you click a file or folder once in the big area on the right, details for the file or folder appear in the Details box at the bottom of the File Explorer window. If you double-click a folder on the right, the folder becomes the current folder, which means you can see its contents. If you double-click a document, it opens. (For example, if you double-click a Word document, Windows fires up Word and has it start with that document open and ready for work.)

Pick a folder to move directly to it

Move up one level

Large Icon view

Click the wedges to move along folders

Search all visible files and folders

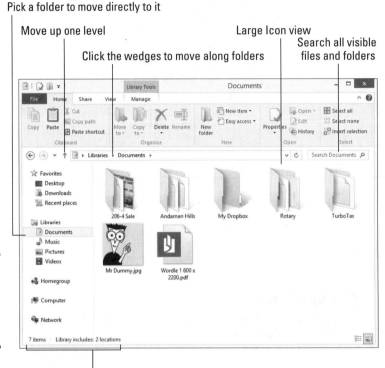

Figure 1-9:
File Explorer helps you move around.

Details about selected file or folder

✦ **Almost all the actions you might want to perform on files or folders show up in the Ribbon at the top.** You may have to click the tabs to move from Home to Share to View to Manage. Many of the actions you might want to perform are accessible by right-clicking the file or folder. Some people find it easier to use the Ribbon; others prefer a right-click.

✦ **Open as many copies of File Explorer as you like.** That can be very helpful if you're scatterbrained like I am . . . I mean if you like to multi-task and you want to look in several places at once. Simply tap and hold or right-click the File Explorer icon down on the taskbar, choose File Explorer, and a totally independent copy of File Explorer appears, ready for your finagling.

Viewing details and filename extensions

Large Icons view (refer to Figure 1-9) is, at once, visually impressive and cumbersome. If you grow tired of scrolling (and scrolling and scrolling) through those icons, down in the lower-right corner, click the icon that looks like dots and dashes. You see the succinct list shown in Figure 1-10.

Select Details view   Show filename extensions

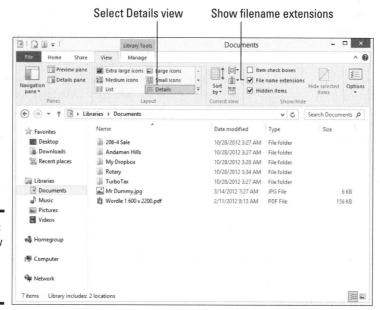

Book VI
Chapter 1

Running the Desktop from Start to Finish

Figure 1-10:
Details view has more meat, less sizzle.

Windows offers several picturesque views — dubbed Extra Large Icons, Large Icons, Medium Icons, Small Icons, and Infinitesimal Eyestraining Icons (okay, I got carried away a bit) that can come in handy if you're looking through a bunch of pictures. In most other cases, though, the icons only get in the way. Besides, if you're looking at a lot of pictures, you're probably going to want to use the Windows Photo Gallery program (Book VI, Chapter 5), put them on Flickr (Book V, Chapter 3) or maybe even delve into the tiled Photos app (see Book IV, Chapter 3).

In Details view, you can sort the list of files by clicking on one of the column headings (Name or Date Modified, for example). You can right-click one of the column headings and choose More to change what the view shows (get rid of Type, for example, and replace it with Tags).

Showing filename extensions

If you're looking at the Documents library on your computer and you can't see the period and three- or four-letter suffixes of the filenames (such as `.doc`, `,.xls`, `.jpg`, and `.html`) that are visible in Figure 1-10, don't panic! You need to tell Windows to show them — electronically knock Windows upside the head, if you will.

In my opinion, every single Windows user should force Windows to show full filenames, including the (usually three- or four-letter) extension at the end of the name. I've been fighting Microsoft on this topic for many years. Forgive me if I get a little, uh, steamed — yeah, that's the polite way to put it — but *everybody* needs to be able to see filename extensions. It's the only way to know what will happen when you double-click a file. It's the only way to rename a file without getting yourself all tied up in knots. More than anything, you need to see the extensions for security.

Microsoft has a tutorial (`windows.micro soft.com/en-US/windows-vista/ Recognizing-dangerous-file- types`) on recognizing malware based on — you guessed it — the filename extensions that most Windows users can't see *because Microsoft hides them* by default. Get with the system, have Windows show you filename extensions, and, while you're at it, have Windows show you hidden files as well. You're old enough to take off the training wheels.

It's easy. Click the icon down on the Taskbar that looks like a file folder. When File Explorer comes up, click the View tab and you see the Ribbon shown in Figure 1-10. On the right, check the boxes marked File Name Extensions and Hidden Items.

Previewing

File Explorer's View tab has a button on the left that lets you turn on the Preview pane: It's a strip along the right side of the window that, in many cases, shows a preview of the file you selected. See Figure 1-11.

Some people love the preview feature. Others hate it. A definite speed hit is associated with previewing: You may find yourself twiddling your thumbs as Windows gets its previews going. The best solution is to turn off the preview unless you absolutely need it. And use the right tool for the job: If you're previewing a lot of picture files and don't need to drag them anywhere, use Windows Photo Gallery, Flickr, or fire up the tiled Photos app from the Start screen.

Click the Preview Pane button...   ...to open the pane

Figure 1-11:
The File
Preview
pane on
the right
previews
some files'
contents.

Creating files and folders

Usually, you create new files and folders when you're using a program. You make new Word documents when you're using Word, say, or come up with a new folder to hold all your offshore banking spreadsheets when you're using Excel. Programs usually have the tools for making new files and folders tucked away in the File⇨Save and File⇨Save As dialog boxes. Click around a bit and you'll find them.

File Explorer context tabs

When you tap or click certain kinds of folders or files, File Explorer gains a sort of "super tab" above the usual Home, Share, View tabs. Officially they're known as *context tabs* because they change — appear and disappear — depending on the context of what you're viewing.

In Figure 1-11, for example, I select a picture file that's inside of the Documents Library. File

Explorer helpfully offers two context tabs: one for pictures and the other for Libraries. Click the super tab, and you see an array of actions that are appropriate for the specific kind of file, or the specific location, that you've chosen — rotating pictures, say, or setting a display icon for a Library.

You can also quite easily create a new file or folder directly in an existing folder without going through the hassle of cranking up a 900-pound gorilla of a program. Follow these steps:

1. **In File Explorer, move to the location where you want to put the new file or folder.**

For example, if you want to stick the new folder Revisionist Techno Grunge in your Music folder, click the Music link under Libraries.

2. **Tap or click the Home tab.**

You see the Home Ribbon, shown in Figure 1-12.

3. **Choose New Item and select what kind of item you want.**

If you want a new folder, choose Folder.

Windows creates the new file or folder and leaves it with the name highlighted so that you can rename it by simply typing.

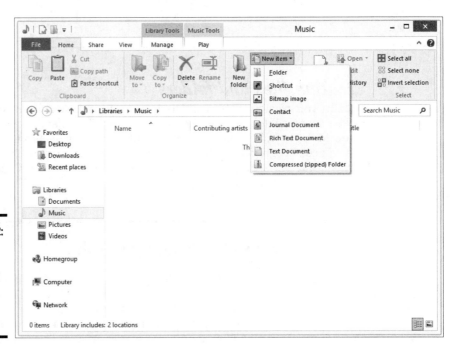

Figure 1-12:
Create a new file or folder from the New Item drop-down list.

Copy Path and Paste Shortcut

The File Explorer Home Ribbon has two new functions that haven't been part of the standard Explorer fare in earlier versions of Windows.

Select an item and click Copy Path to put the full, qualified filename in the clipboard. For example, if you select the file `Mr Dummy.jpg` in your Documents folder, then click

Copy Path, the clipboard will contain the string `"C:\Users\<name>\Documents\Mr Dummy.jpg"` (including the quotes).

Similarly, Paste Shortcut pastes the shortcut currently stored in the clipboard into the current folder.

Copying, moving, and modifying files and folders

As long as you have permission (see the section "Sharing Folders in the Public Folder," later in this chapter), modifying files and folders (renaming, deleting, moving, or copying them) is easy if you use the Home Ribbon.

Here's how to copy or move one or more files or folders:

1. **To bring up File Explorer on the desktop, click the folder icon down on the Taskbar (or if you're looking at the Start screen, click the tile for File Explorer).**

2. **When File Explorer is up, click the Home tab.**

   That brings up the Home Ribbon (refer to Figure 1-12).

3. **Navigate to the location of the file(s) and/or folder(s) you want to move or copy.**

   If you want to move or copy folders or files from more than one location, repeat Steps 3 through 6, gathering folders and files like flowers in May.

4. **Select the folder(s) or file(s) that you want to move or copy.**

   You can use the usual Windows selection tricks:

   - Select a single file or folder by clicking or tapping it.

   - Hold down the Ctrl key to select multiple items that aren't next to each other. (If you're tapping, tap one, then the next, then the next.)

   - Hold down the Shift key to select a group of contiguous items (ones that are next to each other). Just click the first item, hold down the Shift key, and click the last item.

   - You can even "lasso" items by drawing a box around the stuff you want to select.

5. **On the Home Ribbon, click the Copy To or Move To icon.**

Your screen should look like Figure 1-13.

Choose where to copy selected files

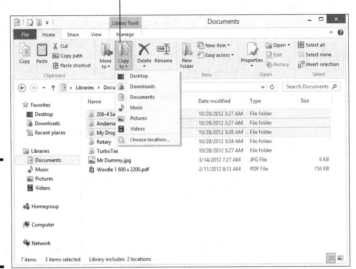

Figure 1-13:
Easy way
to copy or
move with
the Home
Ribbon.

6. **If the destination location you want is on the list, select it. Otherwise, at the bottom select Choose Location.**

Choose Location brings up a Copy Items or Move Items dialog box that lets you select where you want to copy or move the folders and files.

The preceding steps explain the simplest way to move or copy. This isn't the fastest way, though. If you want fast (and most people do after they've copied or moved a couple hundred files), and you have a keyboard, all you need to remember is the most-commonly used key combinations in Windows:

✦ Select the files or folders and press Ctrl+C to copy them (which is to say, hold down the Ctrl key, then press the C key).

✦ Select the files or folders and press Ctrl+X to "cut" them.

✦ Go to the place you want to hold the files or folders and press Ctrl+V to paste them. If you Ctrl+C copied the files, you'll have two copies, one in the original location. If you Ctrl+X "cut" the files, they'll be moved to the destination, and deleted from the original location.

Similarly, if you have a mouse, you can right-click a file or group of files or folders, and choose Copy or Cut, then move to the destination, right-click, and choose Paste.

If you have a file that needs to be organized in a few different ways on your computer and/or home network, don't copy and paste to several different locations. Instead, save the file in the best location and use libraries to create a single place where you can find files that are saved throughout your system or network. Libraries might sound complicated, but I think you'll be happy you checked them out. Book VII, Chapter 3 has all the details about libraries.

Handling copy and paste conflicts

Before Windows starts copying or moving files, it compares the filenames of the files you're copying with the names of the files (and folders) in the destination folder. If you're trying to copy a file named `Mxyzptlk.xlsx` into a folder that already has a file named `Mxyzptlk.xlsx`, then Windows has a problem. You may have a problem, too. Hard to say.

If Windows hits a duplicated filename, it tosses up the Replace or Skip Files dialog box shown in Figure 1-14, with the following options:

Book VI
Chapter 1

Running the
Desktop from Start
to Finish

Figure 1-14: Windows needs you to tell it what you want to do with files that have the same filename.

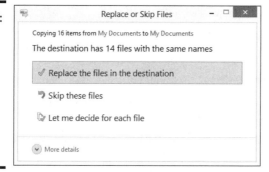

* **Replace the Files in the Destination Folder:** Choose this and your old files are overwritten with the new ones with matching names.

* **Skip These Files:** The old files remain intact. Or you can choose Behind Door Number Three, Monte, and pick and choose which files get bumped.

* **Choose the Files to Keep in the Destination Folder:** This option opens a File Conflicts dialog box like the one in Figure 1-15. Yes, files can have conflicts, too. Windows doesn't ask you to resolve conflicting folder names: It will create new folders or add to existing folders without being directed. But you do have to pick which individual files you want to keep, and which to leave behind.

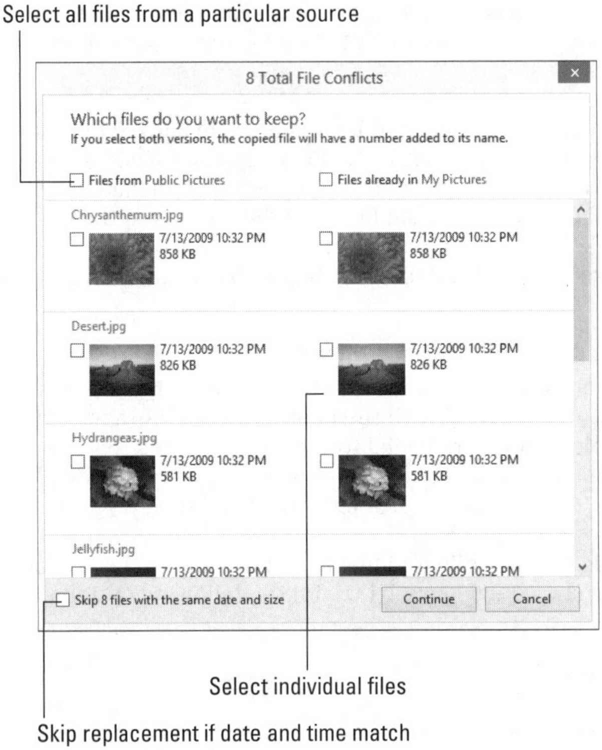

Select all files from a particular source

8 Total File Conflicts ×

Which files do you want to keep?
If you select both versions, the copied file will have a number added to its name.

☐ Files from Public Pictures   ☐ Files already in My Pictures

Chrysanthemum.jpg

☐ [image] 7/13/2009 10:32 PM   ☐ [image] 7/13/2009 10:32 PM
         858 KB   858 KB

Desert.jpg

☐ [image] 7/13/2009 10:32 PM   ☐ [image] 7/13/2009 10:32 PM
         826 KB   826 KB

Hydrangeas.jpg

☐ [image] 7/13/2009 10:32 PM   ☐ [image] 7/13/2009 10:32 PM
         581 KB   581 KB

Jellyfish.jpg

☐ ▬▬▬ 7/13/2009 10:32 PM   ☐ ▬▬▬ 7/13/2009 10:32 PM

☐ Skip 8 files with the same date and size   [Continue] [Cancel]

Figure 1-15:
Resolving
the conflicts
by hand;
choose
which files
you want.

Select individual files

Skip replacement if date and time match

In the File Conflicts dialog box, you can:

- Check a box at the top to choose all the files from the source location, or from the destination location.

- Check a box next to each individual file you want to keep. The unchecked files are discarded.

✦ Check the box next to each file in the match-up (for example, in Figure 1-15, if you check the box next to the frog on the left *and* the one on the right). If you elect to keep both, Windows puts a (1), including the parentheses, on the end of the name of the file from the source location.

✦ Check the box at the bottom to skip files with the same date and time. If you have files with the same name, but different dates/times, Windows copies the files across and puts a (1) (or (2), or (3), and so forth) at the end of the copied file's name.

Piloting the new copy manager

Windows 8 has a new copy manager that helps you keep track of longer copy (and move) jobs. The copy manager is mostly eye candy, but it does have one important function: It lets you pause or cancel a specific copy (or move).

That's an important capability because, as you'll soon discover, if you try to run two copies/moves on the same device, both slow down to a crawl. The effect is particularly noticeable on hard drives, where the heads have to dance the Texas Two Step to keep up, and on USB drives and other devices with limited bandwidth. Simply pausing one of the copy/move jobs will speed the other one up enormously.

Here's how the copy manager works:

1. **When you have a copy/move in progress, you see a progress indicator dialog box. Click the More Details link at the bottom.**

You see the Running Actions dialog box shown in Figure 1-16.

2. **To pause a particular copy/move activity, click the double-hash Pause icon. To cancel it completely, click the X.**

Cancel a copy or move

Pause a copy or move

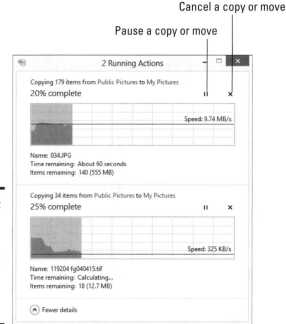

Figure 1-16:
When a copy or move is in progress, you can see the full details.

Bringing files back with File History

Did you accidentally copy over a worthwhile file? Don't worry, it happens all the time: You copy a spreadsheet from one location to another, for example, and in the process clobber the good version of the spreadsheet, replacing it with a week-old dud.

If you have File History turned on, recovering a copied-over, moved, or "permanently deleted" file is reasonably easy. See Book VIII, Chapter 1.

Deleting and renaming files

Deleting or renaming a file is very easy, with the Home Ribbon (refer to Figure 1-13). Just select the files or folders that you want to delete and tap or click the Delete icon, which is just to the right of the Copy icon.

Or you can just hit the Del key. Or right-click and choose Delete.

If you use the Delete icon, you have two choices: Recycle and Permanently Delete. When you Recycle, you don't actually delete anything: You just send it to the Recycle Bin, which I discuss in the section called "Recycling," later in this chapter.

Even if you Permanently Delete a file or folder, guess what: It's still on your hard drive, and anyone who can get on your computer can probably bring it back using an "undelete" utility such as Recuva. See my discussion of Recuva in Book X, Chapter 5.

Sharing Folders in the Public Folder

Sharing is good, right? Your mom taught you to share, didn't she? Everything you need to know about sharing you learned in kindergarten — like how you can share your favorite crayon with your best friend and get back a gnarled blob of stunted wax, covered in mysterious goo.

Windows supports two very different ways for sharing files and folders:

✦ **Move the files or folders that you want to share into the \Public folder.** The \Public folder is kind of a big cookie jar for everybody who uses your PC: Put a file or folder in the \Public folder so that all the other people who use your computer can get at it. The \Public folder is available to other people in your Homegroup, if you have one, but you have little control over who, specifically, can get at the files and folders.

(Homegroups make it easier to set up sharing among Windows computers on a network; see Book VII, Chapter 5 for details.)

✦ **Share individual files or folders, without moving them anywhere.**
When you share a file or folder, you can tell Windows to share the folder with everyone in your Homegroup, with other users who log on to your computer, or you can specify exactly who can access the file or folder and whether they can just look at it or change or delete it. This detailed level of permissions is beyond the scope of this chapter, but I do cover it in Book VII, Chapter 5, along with Homegroups.

This section focuses on sharing folders and files via the \Public folder.

You might think that simply moving a file or folder to the \Public folder would make it, well, public. At least to a first approximation, that's exactly how things work.

Any file or folder that you put in the \Public folder, or any folder inside the \Public folder, can be viewed, changed, or deleted by anybody who's using your computer, regardless of which kind of account she may have and whether she is required to log on to your computer. In addition, anybody who can get into your computer through the network will have unlimited access. The \Public folder is (if you'll pardon a rather stretched analogy) a big cookie jar, open to everybody who is in the kitchen.

For more details, and important information about public networks and big-company domains, check out *Networking All-In-One For Dummies,* by Doug Lowe.

Say you have an album in your \Music folder that you want to be available to everybody who has access to your computer, either by logging on to your computer with a different account, or by being attached to your Homegroup. The easiest way to share that folder or album is by moving it to your \Public\ Music folder. (You could put it in your SkyDrive folder, covered in Book IV, Chapter 4, but then you have to manage permissions for who can get into it and when.) Here's how to move a file into one of the Public folders:

1. **Start File Explorer.**

   If you're on the desktop, tap or click the icon down on the Taskbar that looks like a file folder. If you're on the Start screen, click the tile for the desktop, then choose File Explorer.

2. **Navigate to the folder or file that you want to put in one of your Public folders.**

   In Figure 1-17, I navigate to my Music folder, where I have a folder called Eriko Ishihara.

Figure 1-17:
Sharing a
file or folder
by moving it
into one of
the libraries'
\Public
folders is
as easy as
a click and
drag, if you
know where
to drag it.

3. **Here's the tricky part. Click the wedge-shaped icon to the left of the
   Library where you want to put the file or folder.**

   You see a list of all the folders currently in the Library. In Figure 1-17,
   the \Public\Music folder is called Public Music. Rocket science.

4. **Click and drag the file or folder from its current location into the
   appropriate folder.**

   In Figure 1-17, I drag the Eriko Ishihara Collection folder from my Music
   folder to the Public Music folder. From that point, anybody who has
   access to my Public Music folder can play the songs on the album.

Files and folders in the \Public folder may also be accessible to other computers connected to your network, workgroup, or domain, depending on
various network settings. See Book VII, Chapter 5, and *Networking All-In-One
For Dummies* for specific examples.

You can move other files and folders into the \Public folder by using File
Explorer the old-fashioned way. Navigate to the folder, Ctrl+X or right-click it
and choose Cut, and then go to the appropriate Public folder using the trick
with the wedges to the left of the library name. Paste the file or folder using
the Ribbon, Ctrl+V, or right-click Paste, as fits your proclivities.

Touching on the Taskbar

Windows sports a highly customizable, if not a bit ugly, taskbar at the bottom of the screen, shown in Figure 1-18. I go into detail in Book II, Chapter 2.

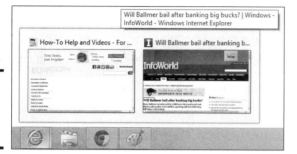

Figure 1-18: The Windows 8 taskbar.

The taskbar takes on new importance in Windows 8 because there's no Start menu on which to pin your hopes (or your programs or folders, much less your dreams). If you want to stay inside the desktop without venturing to the Start screen, you better get used to pinning things on the taskbar.

Keep these points in mind when considering the taskbar:

✦ **Hover your mouse over an icon to see what the program's running**. For example, in Figure 1-18, I hover my mouse over the Internet Explorer icon and see that I have two tabs open. I can click either thumbnail to bring up the appropriate tab.

✦ **Right-click an icon or tap and hold, and you see the application's Jump List.** The Jump List may show an application's most recently opened documents. It may show a browser's history list. Implementation of Jump Lists has been spotty, but it's bound to improve with the Taskbar's newfound importance.

If you click an icon, the program opens, as you would expect. But if you want to open a second copy of a program — say, another copy of Firefox — you can't just click the icon. You have to right-click and choose the application's name.

✦ **You can move the icons on the taskbar** by simply clicking and dragging.

The Windows taskbar has many tricks up its sleeve, but it has one capability that you may need, if screen real estate is at a premium. (Hey, you folks with 30-inch monitors need not apply, okay?)

The taskbar has an Auto-Hide feature that shrinks the taskbar to a thin line until you bump the mouse pointer way down at the bottom of the screen. As soon as the mouse pointer hits bottom, the taskbar pops up. Here's how to teach the taskbar to auto-hide:

1. **Right-click an empty part of the taskbar.**

2. **Choose Properties.**

The Taskbar tab should be visible.

3. **Select the Auto-Hide the Taskbar check box and then click OK.**

The taskbar holds many surprises. See Book II, Chapter 2.

Recycling

When you delete a file, it doesn't go to that Big Bit Bucket in the Sky. An intermediate step exists between deletion and the Big Bit Bucket. It's called purgatory. Oops. Wait a sec. Wrong book. (*Existentialism For Dummies,* anybody?) Let me try that again. Ahem.

The step between deletion and the Big Bit Bucket is the Recycle Bin.

When you delete a file or folder from your hard drive — whether by selecting the file or folder in File Explorer and pressing Delete, using the File Explorer Home Ribbon's Delete button, or by right-clicking and choosing Delete — Windows doesn't actually delete anything. It marks the file or folder as being deleted but, other than that, doesn't touch it.

Files and folders on key drives, SD cards, and network drives don't go into limbo when they're deleted. The Recycle Bin doesn't work on key drives, SD cards, or drives attached to other computers on your network. That said, if you accidentally wipe out the data on your key drive or camera memory card, there is hope. See my discussion of the program called Recuva in Book X, Chapter 5.

To rummage around in the Recycle Bin, and possibly bring a file back to life, follow these steps:

1. **Double-click the Recycle Bin icon on the Windows desktop.**

File Explorer opens to the Recycle Bin, shown in Figure 1-19.

2. **To restore a file or folder, select the file or folder and then click the Restore the Selected Items icon.**

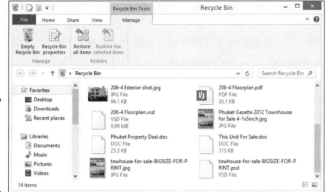

Figure 1-19:
Restore
files one at
a time or *en
masse.*

If you can't find what you want in the Recycle Bin, follow the steps in
Book VIII, Chapter 1 to see whether you can dig something out of the
Windows File History feature. If you don't have File History running, right
now is a good time to start.

To reclaim the space that the files and folders in the Recycle Bin are using,
click the Empty the Recycle Bin icon. Windows asks whether you really, truly
want to get rid of those files permanently. If you say Yes, they're gone . . .
except Recuva may be able to bring them back.

Creating Shortcuts

Sometimes life is easier with shortcuts. (As long as the shortcuts work,
anyway.) So, too, in the world of Windows, where shortcuts point to things
that can be started. You may set up a shortcut to the Calculator, say, and
put it on your desktop. Double-click the shortcut and the Calculator starts,
the same way as if you had gone out to the Start screen, typed `calc` and
pressed Enter.

You can set up shortcuts that point to the following items:

✦ **Programs** of any kind

✦ **Web addresses,** such as `www.dummies.com`

✦ **Documents, spreadsheets, databases, PowerPoint presentations, and
anything else** that can be started in File Explorer by double-clicking it

✦ Specific **chunks of text** (called *scraps*) inside documents, spreadsheets,
databases, and presentations, for example

✦ **Folders** (including the weird folders inside digital cameras, the Fonts folder, and others that you may not think of)

✦ **Drives** (hard drives, CD drives, and key drives, for example)

✦ **Other computers on your network, and drives and folders on those computers,** as long they're shared

✦ **Printers** (including printers attached to other computers on your network), **scanners, cameras, and other pieces of hardware**

✦ **Network connections, interface cards, and the like**

You have many different ways to create shortcuts.

Say that you use the Windows Calculator all the time, and you want to put a shortcut to the Windows Calculator on your desktop. Here's an easy way to do it:

1. **Hit the Windows key (or on a tablet, tap the Windows button) to flip over to the tiled Start screen.**

Yes, I promised that I wouldn't use the Start screen in this chapter, but this really is the easiest way to set up the shortcut. Trust me. (You can also hover your mouse in the upper-right corner, and choose Search from the Charms bar.)

2. **Immediately type** calc.

Windows finds the Calculator for you and shows it on the tiled Start screen, as shown in Figure 1-20.

3. **Right-click Calculator.**

Windows brings up the Apps bar, at the bottom of Figure 1-20.

4. **Click the icon in the Apps bar to Open File Location.**

Windows transports you to the desktop, and lands inside the Windows Accessories folder, as shown in Figure 1-21.

5. **Right-click Calculator and choose Create Shortcut.**

Windows says it can't create a Shortcut here, but would you like to put one on the desktop?

6. **Click Yes.**

A shortcut to the Calculator appears on your desktop.

Windows places an icon of the Windows Calculator on your desktop. The icon has an arrow, a kind of visual hint that the icon exists as a shortcut to the Calculator. Anytime you double-click the Windows Calculator shortcut on your desktop, the Calculator comes to life.

Figure 1-20:
The search
results
when you
type in **calc**.

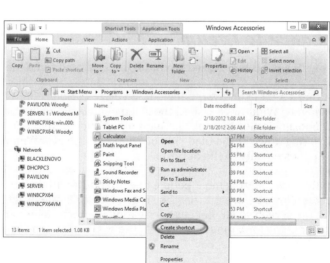

Figure 1-21:
Going
straight to
where the
Calculator
lives.

Once you have a shortcut on your desktop, it's easy to put an icon for the shortcut down on the taskbar. Just right-click the shortcut and choose Pin to Taskbar.

You can use a similar procedure for setting up shortcuts to any file, folder, program, or document on your computer or on any networked computer.

I find the File Explorer Home Ribbon confusing when it comes to shortcuts, which is why I didn't show that method here. If you really want to use the Ribbon, you can select the Calculator, then copy it (using Ctrl+C or right-click then copy). Move to whatever folder you want to hold the shortcut, and click Paste Shortcut. The complicated part is that you have to copy the whole program before it'll work; copying the path, for example, isn't sufficient.

Believe it or not, Windows thrives on shortcuts. They're everywhere, lurking just beneath the surface. For example, every single icon on the taskbar is a shortcut. As you may have noticed, the programs that you find when you run a search on the tiled Start screen are frequently shortcuts. Most of the Start screen is based on shortcuts, although they're hidden where you can't reach them. So don't be afraid to experiment with shortcuts. In the worst-case scenario, you can always delete them. Doing so gets rid of the shortcut but doesn't touch the original file.

Sleep: Perchance to Dream

Windows 8 has been designed so that it doesn't need to be turned off.

Okay, that's a bit of an overstatement. If you're curious about the details, I explain how Windows 8 visited the sleep clinic and finally fixed its long-term snoozing issues in Book III, Chapter 6. Although that chapter focuses on powering down in the tiled side of Windows, the new Windows sleep state applies equally to the desktop.

The only power setting most people need to fiddle with is the length of time Windows allows before it turns the screen black. On the desktop, that's tied in with the screen saver, because activating a screen saver may keep the computer going for a long time. Here's the easy way to adjust your screen blackout time:

1. **Right-click any empty part of the desktop and choose Personalize.**

   Windows brings up the Personalization dialog box.

2. **In the lower-right corner, choose Screen Saver.**

   You see the Screen Saver Settings dialog box, which I discuss in Book VI, Chapter 2.

3. **In the lower-left corner, click the link to Change Power Settings.**

   Windows shows the Power Options dialog box, shown in Figure 1-22.

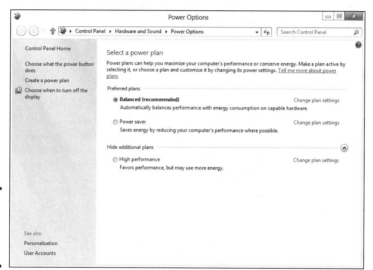

**Book VI
Chapter 1**

**Running the
Desktop from Start
to Finish**

Figure 1-22:
Set the
power
options.

4. **Choose one of the power options.**

   The only substantial difference between Balanced and Power Saver, on a desktop computer, is the length of time Windows waits before turning the screen black: With the Balanced plan, it goes out in ten minutes; with the Power Saver plan, it goes out in five minutes. They both spin down the hard drive after 20 minutes.

   If you want to look at the details, click one of the links to Change Plan Settings.

5. **"X" out of the Power Options dialog box.**

   Your changes take effect immediately.

Although Microsoft has published voluminous details about the power down and power up sequences, including the new sleep state, I haven't seen any details about how long it takes before your PC actually goes to sleep. In theory, that shouldn't matter too much, because the wake-ups are so fast.

Microsoft recently published some recommendations that I found fascinating. To truly conserve energy with a desktop computer, be aggressive with the monitor idle time (no longer than two minutes), and make sure that you don't have a screen saver enabled. If you want to conserve energy with a notebook or netbook, your top priority is to reduce the screen brightness!

I talk about power conservation and the many paths to greenness in *Green Home Computing For Dummies*, which I co-wrote with the publisher's own Katherine Murray. (Hi, Kathy!) It's packed with important information for anybody with a PC and a conscience.

Chapter 2: Personalizing the Desktop

In This Chapter

✔ Tricking out your taskbar

✔ Taking control of each desktop level

✔ Traipsing through themes

✔ Controlling the notification area

*I*t's your desktop. Do with it what you will.

You might think it'd be easy for a computer to slap windows on the screen, but it isn't. In fact, the Windows desktop uses six separate layers to produce that window, er, vista. However, you can take control of every layer. I show you how in this chapter.

Most importantly, in this chapter, I show you the quibbles and quirks of the Windows 8 taskbar. Now that the old Windows Start Menu has gone the way of the do-do, the taskbar takes on new importance as the most accessible way to control programs on the desktop. The taskbar occupies a key piece of real estate.

I also include a discussion of desktop background, themes, and screen savers. Pretty cool stuff.

Recognizing Desktop Levels

The Windows desktop — that is, the collection of stuff you see on your computer screen — consists of six layers (see Figure 2-1, which shows four of the six layers).

For a quick change of pace, desktop themes change five of the six layers, all at once. I talk about desktop themes in the section "Using Desktop Themes," later in this chapter.

Background color

A working
window

Icon

Desktop picture

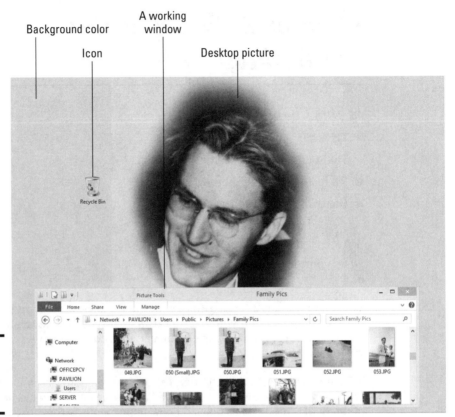

Figure 2-1:
The
Windows 8
desktop.

These six layers control how Windows dishes up your desktop:

✦ **Level 1:** At the bottom, the Windows desktop has a *base color,* which is
a solid color that you see only if you don't have a desktop background
picture or if your chosen desktop picture doesn't fill the entire screen.
Most people never see their Windows base color because the desktop
background (often a picture) usually covers it up. I tell you how to set
the base color and all the other Windows colors — for dialog boxes, the
taskbar, the works — in the next section of this chapter.

✦ **Level 2:** Above the base color lives the Windows *desktop background.*
(Microsoft used to call it *wallpaper,* and you see that name frequently.)
In Figure 2-1, my dad's photo appears as the desktop background. It isn't
stretched to fit the full screen, which is why you can see the base color.

The people who sold you your computer may have placed some sort of
dorky ad on the desktop. I tell you how to get rid of the ad and replace
it with a picture you want in the section "Picking a Background," later in
this chapter.

✦ **Level 3:** Windows puts all its desktop icons on top of the desktop background layer and underneath everything else. Bone-stock Windows 8 includes only one icon, the Recycle Bin. If you bought a PC with Windows preinstalled, the manufacturer probably put lots of additional icons on the desktop. You can easily get rid of them. I tell you how in the section "Controlling Icons," later in this chapter.

✦ **Level 4:** Above the icons you find (finally!) the program windows. These are the windows in which the likes of Word, File Explorer, and Media Player all run.

The old-fashioned window design — rounded corners, an affinity for blue, and transparency in wide window borders — came to be known as "Aero." Now Aero is out of style, and flat, boxy, minimalist tile-like outlines are in.

✦ **Level 5:** Then you have the mouse, which lives on the layer above the program windows. The mouse shares its level with the odd Windows Notification — specifically, toaster notifications can slide onto the screen in the upper right corner, as the need occurs. They appear above the program windows.

✦ **Level 6:** At the top of the desktop food chain sits the screen saver. It kicks in only if you tell Windows that you want it to appear when your computer sits idle for a spell. I talk about that beast in the section "Selecting Screen Savers," later in this chapter.

If you have more than one user on your PC, each user can customize every single part of the six layers to suit her tastes, and Windows remembers every setting, bringing it back when the respective user logs on. Much better than getting a life, isn't it?

Setting Color Schemes on the Desktop

Windows ships with 16 prebuilt designer color schemes. "Automatic" (which has a propensity to sky blue) is the scheme of choice. You can change to a different designer scheme or invent one all your own. To change color schemes, follow these steps:

1. **Right-click any empty part of the Windows desktop and choose Personalize.**

The Personalize dialog box appears.

2. **At the bottom, click the link that says Window Color.**

Windows opens the Color and Appearance dialog box (see Figure 2-2).

Figure 2-2:
The 16
designer
color
schemes —
and a nearly
infinite array
of alterna-
tives —
appear
here.

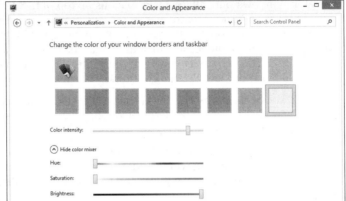

3. **Choose the window color scheme that suits your fancy.**

The "Automatic" color setting, in the upper-left corner, takes its cues from the background image.

4. **Click Save Changes.**

Your chosen window color scheme takes effect immediately.

Picking a Background

There's nothing particularly magical about the desktop background. In fact, Windows can put any picture on your desktop — big one, little one, ugly one — even a picture stolen straight off the web. If you have more than one picture you fancy, Windows can put together a running slide show. And if you have two monitors, side-by-side, Windows can put separate pictures on each. Here's how to personalize your desktop background:

1. **Right-click any empty part of the desktop and choose Personalize.**

The Personalization dialog box appears, as shown in Figure 2-3.

If you want to use one of the built-in combinations of the Windows desktop background, window color, sound scheme, and screen saver, you can simply choose among the offered themes. Scroll down in the box on the top and choose the one you like.

The Synced Theme (if you have one or more) that appears in the top part of this dialog box comes from other Windows 8 PCs, where you've logged on with the same Microsoft account ID.

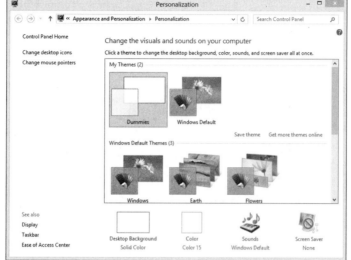

Figure 2-3:
Change your
desktop
background
here.

**Book VI
Chapter 2**

**Personalizing
the Desktop**

The Get More Themes Online link takes you to a Microsoft website that
has a huge variety of themes, which will work on both Windows 7 and
Windows 8. There are some truly astounding themes for two-monitor
Windows 8 setups, with half of the background showing in one screen,
and half in the other. The Nightfall & Starlight Panoramic theme is one
of those gorgeous two-monitor themes. See the section "Using Desktop
Themes," later in this chapter.

2. **At the bottom, click the Desktop Background link.**

   Remember, this is just the desktop. Nothing here changes the tiles or
   the background on the Start screen.

   Windows shows you the Desktop Background dialog box, shown in
   Figure 2-4.

3. **Select the Picture Location drop-down box and choose from many
   different wallpapers that ship with Windows. You can also click the
   Browse button and choose any picture you like.**

   If you hover your mouse over a picture, Windows shows you a description of the picture, and a check box appears in the upper-left corner. If
   you select the check box, Windows adds that particular picture to its
   background slide show. You can put dozens, hundreds, or even thousands of pictures in your slide show collection. And, at the bottom of the
   screen, you can change the speed of the slide show.

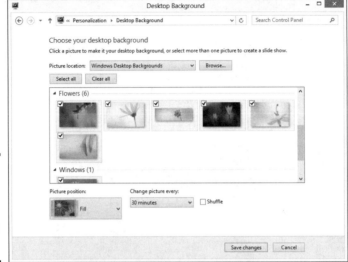

Figure 2-4:
Pick a
wallpaper
or a
collection of
wallpapers.

Keep in mind that cycling through desktop backgrounds quickly can create noticeable delays in your daily activities. Notebook and netbook owners should avoid setting the delay to high levels because of the additional, completely unnecessary, battery drain.

The Solid Colors category changes the base color of the desktop (see the section "Recognizing Desktop Levels," earlier in this chapter). The base color is what shows through if your desktop background doesn't fill the whole screen.

4. **If your picture is too big or too small to fit on the screen, you can tell Windows how to shoehorn it into the available space.**

   Use the drop-down Picture Position list at the bottom of the Desktop Background dialog box.

   Details are in Table 2-1.

5. **Click the Save Changes button, and then the X button to close the Personalization dialog.**

   Your desktop slide show begins immediately.

Windows lets you right-click a picture — a JPG or GIF file, regardless of whether you're using File Explorer or Internet Explorer or even Firefox — and choose Set As Desktop Background (in File Explorer or Firefox) or Set As Background (in Internet Explorer). When you do so, Windows makes a copy of the picture and puts it in the C:\Users\username\AppData\Roaming\Microsoft folder and then sets the picture as your background.

Table 2-1	Picture Position Settings
Setting	*What It Means*
Fill	Windows expands the picture to fit the entire screen and then crops the edges. The picture doesn't appear distorted, but the sides or top and bottom may get cut off.
Fit	The screen is letterboxed. Windows makes the picture as big as possible within the confines of the screen, and then shows the base color in stripes along the top and bottom (or left and right). No distortion occurs, and you see the entire picture, but you also see ugly strips on two edges.
Stretch	The picture is stretched to fit the screen. Expect distortions.
Tile	The picture is repeated as many times as necessary to fill the screen. If it's too large to fit on the screen, you see the Fill options.
Center	This one is the same as the Fit setting except that the letterboxing goes on all four sides.

Controlling Icons

Straight out of the box, the Windows desktop ships with exactly one icon: the Recycle Bin. Microsoft found that most people appreciate a clean desktop, devoid of icons — but it also found that hiding the Recycle Bin confused the living daylights out of most everyone. So Microsoft compromised by making the desktop squeaky clean except for the Recycle Bin: Tiles on one side and a Recycle Bin on the other. Who could ask for more?

If you bought a PC with Windows preloaded, you probably have so many icons on the desktop that you can't see straight. That desktop real estate is expensive, and the manufacturers receive a pretty penny for dangling the right icons in your face. Know what? You can delete all of them, without feeling the least bit guilty. The worst you'll do is delete a shortcut to a manufacturer's tech support program, and if you need to get to the program, the tech support rep can tell you how to find it.

Windows gives you several simple tools for arranging icons on your desktop. If you right-click any empty part of the desktop, you see that you can:

✦ **Sort:** Choose Sort By and then choose an option to sort icons by name, size, or type (folders, documents, and shortcuts, for example) or by the date on which the icon was last modified.

✦ **Arrange:** Choose View⇨Auto Arrange Icons. That is, have Windows arrange them in an orderly fashion, with the first icon in the upper-left corner, the second one directly below the first one, the third one below it, and so on.

✦ **Align to a grid:** Choose View⇨Align Icons to Grid. If you don't want to have icons arranged automatically, at least you can choose Align Icons to Grid so that you can see all the icons without one appearing directly on top of the other.

✦ **Hide:** You can even choose View⇨Show Desktop Icons to deselect the Show Desktop Icons option. Your icons disappear — but that kinda defeats the purpose of icons, doesn't it?

✦ **Delete:** In general, you can remove an icon from the Windows desktop by right-clicking it and choosing Delete or by clicking it once and pressing the Delete key.

The appearance of some icons is hard wired: If you put a Word document on your desktop, for example, the document inherits the icon — the picture — of its associated application, Word. The same goes for Excel worksheets, text documents, and recorded audio files. Icons for pictures look like the picture, more or less, if you squint hard.

Icons for shortcuts, however, you can change at will. (I talk about shortcuts in Book VI, Chapter 1.) Follow these steps to change an icon — that is, the picture — on a shortcut:

1. **Right-click the shortcut and choose Properties.**

2. **In the Properties dialog box, click the Change Icon button.**

3. **Pick an icon from the offered list, or click the Browse button and go looking for icons.**

Windows abounds with icons. See Table 2-2 for some likely hunting grounds.

4. **Click the OK button twice.**

Windows changes the icon permanently (or at least until you change it again).

Table 2-2	Places to Look for Icons
Contents	*File*
Windows 8, 7, and Vista icons	`C:\Windows\system32\imageres.dll`
Everything	`C:\Windows\System32\shell32.dll`
Computers	`C:\Windows\explorer.ex`
Household	`C:\Windows\System32\pifmgr.dll`
Folders	`C:\Windows\System32\syncui.dll`
Old programs	`C:\Windows\System32\moricons.dll` (Quattro Pro, anybody?)

Lots and lots of icons are available on the Internet. Use your favorite search engine to search for the term *free Windows icons*.

Selecting Screen Savers

Windows screen savers are absolutely, totally, utterly, 100 percent for fun. Ten or 15 years ago, screen savers served a real purpose: They kept monitors from "burning in" the phosphors in frequently used parts of the screen. Nowadays, monitors aren't nearly as prone to burn-in (or burnout — as can be the case with humans!), and saving screens rates right up there with manufacturing buggy whips on the obsolescence scale. Flat-panel LCD monitors don't have phosphors, so there's nothing to burn.

Now that Windows itself can run a slide show of desktop backgrounds, the demand for screen savers has taken a big hit. Screen savers delay the countdown for turning off the display, so you'll use a little more electricity with them than without them, but otherwise they're basically harmless.

Follow these steps to select a screen saver:

1. **Right-click any empty part of the desktop and choose Personalize. In the lower-right corner of the screen, click the Screen Saver link.**

Windows shows you the Screen Saver Settings dialog box (see Figure 2-5).

Figure 2-5:
Choose and configure a desktop screen saver here.

2. **Choose a screen saver from the Screen Saver drop-down list. Click the Preview button and take the screen saver for a test drive.**

   Don't like it? Jiggle your mouse, or tap on the screen, to return to the Screen Saver Settings dialog and pick another one, or click the Settings button to make adjustments to the current screen saver.

3. **Choose the number of minutes you want to wait before the screen saver kicks in.**

   Note that the screen saver will kick in after the given number of minutes of inactivity, whether you're looking at the desktop or the tiled Start screen.

4. **Select or deselect the On Resume, Display Logon Screen check box.**

   This setting can be a bit confusing. Basically, it controls what happens when the computer "wakes up" after the screen saver kicks in:

   • *When the On Resume, Display Logon Screen check box is selected:* When there's some activity on the PC, Windows reverts to the Windows lock screen. If the user who was logged on has an account that requires a password, she must reenter her password to get back into Windows. (I talk about passwords in the section on changing user settings in Book II, Chapter 2.)

   • *When the On Resume, Display Logon Screen check box is deselected:* When there's some activity on the PC, Windows returns to the state it was in when the screen saver started: either the tiled app or desktop. The user who was logged on remains logged on.

5. **When you're happy with your screen saver settings, click the OK button.**

   The screen saver kicks in whenever a sufficient length of time passes with no activity on the desktop.

To get rid of your current screen saver, right-click an empty spot on the desktop, choose Personalize, click the Screen Saver link at the bottom of the dialog box that appears, and select None in the Screen Saver drop-down list. Click the OK button, and your screen will never be saved again.

If you want to download screen savers from the Internet, be aware of one painful fact: The overwhelming majority of "free" screen savers you find on the web carry spyware, adware, and various kinds of scumware, which are installed when you install the screen saver. While Windows 8 does a reasonably good job of protecting your PC (see SmartScreen, Book IX, Chapter 3), don't let your guard down, and don't agree to install anything that seems even the least bit dicey.

Using Desktop Themes

Windows desktop themes incorporate many settings in one easy-to-choose package. The themes revolve around specific topics that frequently (and refreshingly) have nothing to do with Windows (say, cars with carapaces, cavorting carnivores, or carnal caruncles). A theme includes five of the six desktop levels I discuss earlier in this chapter plus a few extra goodies: a base color for the desktop, a background, settings for fonts and colors of the working windows, pictures for the reserved Windows icons (Recycle Bin and Documents, for example), a set of mouse pointers, and a screen saver. A theme can also include a set of custom sounds associated with various Windows events.

To bring in a new theme, follow these steps:

1. **Right-click any open spot on the desktop and choose Personalize.**

    Windows shows you the Personalization dialog box.

2. **On the right, click the Get More Themes Online link.**

    Windows opens the Microsoft Windows Themes home page, shown in Figure 2-6. At least as of this writing, it contains free themes that work well with Windows 7 and Windows 8, along with a host of other Windows-centric items.

    As this book went to press, Microsoft started adding some amazing dual-monitor themes. If you have two monitors installed on your PC, and both have the same resolution setting, the backgrounds take up the full panorama of both monitors. Even if you don't have two matched monitors attached to one PC, the themes show the "middle part" of the two pictures. Quite spectacular.

**Book VI
Chapter 2**

**Personalizing
the Desktop**

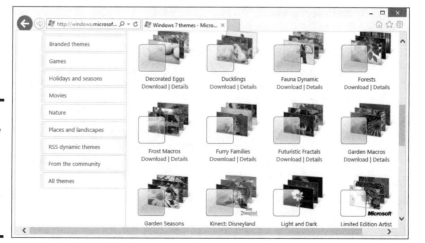

Figure 2-6:
Adding new themes is easy, if you use Microsoft's download page.

3. **If you can find a theme you like, click the Download link underneath it. In Firefox, tell the downloader that you want to open the file by using the `themepackfile` program. In Internet Explorer, just click Open, then Allow if prompted.**

   The themepackfile program adds the downloaded theme you selected to the My Themes collection. After the new theme has been downloaded, you're sent back to the Personalization dialog box.

4. **Choose the theme you downloaded. Then click "X" out of the Personalization dialog.**

After you switch themes, the old background, icon pictures, mouse pointers, and screen savers all remain on your PC. The new theme doesn't delete them, but if you want to get any of them back, you have to go through the customization steps you followed earlier.

Zillions of Windows desktop themes are available on the web, many of them quite good, and most of them can work with Windows 8. My comment in the screen saver section of this chapter applies here in spades: Watch out for scumware. To be on the safe side, visit wincustomize.com or themeworld.com for thousands of free themes. Remember that Windows 7 themes work just fine on the Windows 8 desktop.

Seeing Your Desktop Clearly

The best, biggest monitor in the world "don't mean jack" if you can't see the text on the screen. Windows contains a handful of utilities and settings that can help you whump your monitor upside the head and improve its appearance.

With apologies to Billy Crystal, sometimes it *is* more important to look good than to feel good.

Setting the screen resolution

I don't know how many people ask me how to fix this new monitor they just bought. The screen doesn't look right. Must be that %$#@! Windows, yes? The old monitor looked just fine.

Nine times out of ten, when somebody tells me that a new monitor doesn't look right, I ask whether the person adjusted the screen resolution. Invariably, the answer is no. So here's the quick course: the answer to one of the questions I hear most.

If you plug in a new monitor (or put together a new computer) and the screen looks fuzzy, the most likely culprit entails a mismatch between the resolution your computer expects and the resolution your monitor wants. To a first approximation, a screen resolution is just the number of dots that appear on the screen, usually expressed as two numbers: 1920 x 1080, for example. Every flat-panel screen has exactly one resolution that looks right and a zillion other resolutions that make things look like you fused your monitor with the end of a Coke bottle.

Setting the screen resolution is easy:

1. **Right-click any empty place on the desktop and choose Screen Resolution.**

Book VI
Chapter 2

You see the Screen Resolution dialog box, shown in Figure 2-7. (If you have more than one monitor, or certain kinds of video cards, you might see multiple monitors in the top box.)

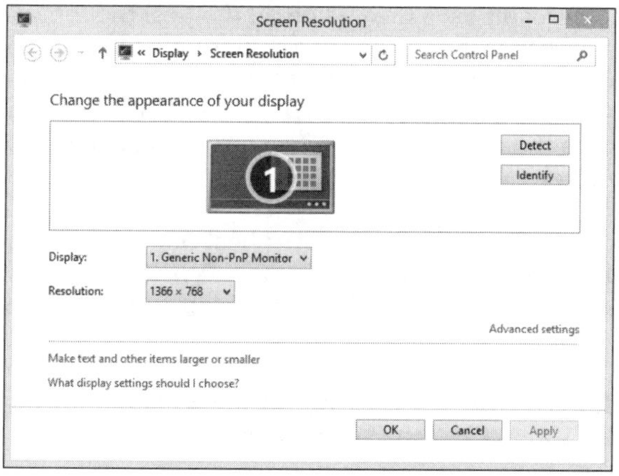

Figure 2-7:
Tell
Windows
which
screen
resolution
works best
on your
monitor.

2. **Click in the Resolution drop-down list and pick the resolution you want.**

That's the easy part.

The hard part? Figuring out which resolution your monitor likes: its *native resolution.* Some monitors have the resolution printed on a sticker that might still adhere to the front. (Goo Gone works wonders.) All monitors have their native resolutions listed in the manual. (You do have your monitor's manual, yes? No, I don't either.)

If you don't know your monitor's native resolution, Google is your friend. Go to www.google.com and type **native resolution** followed by your monitor's model number, which you can (almost) always find engraved in the bezel or stuck on the side. For example, typing **native resolution U3011** immediately finds the native resolution for a Dell U3011 monitor.

Activating and adjusting ClearType

Misbehaving text can make your monitor look fuzzy, too.

ClearType, the proprietary Microsoft method of sharpening the appearance of text on a screen, has been a fix-up fixture of Windows for many years, since Windows XP. Simply put, ClearType gets the sharpest text possible out of just about every monitor made in the past ten years. (Industry icon Steve Gibson has an excellent description of ClearType and its supremacy on LCD displays at grc.com/cleartype.htm.)

 In Windows 8, Microsoft uses ClearType on the desktop, but not on the tiled Start screen, the Charms bar, or in any of the tiled apps, whether they're made by Microsoft or not. It isn't available inside the tiled Internet Explorer, either. ClearType just isn't an option. Why? The theory goes that making type look good on the tiled side of the fence isn't important enough to weigh down the computer.

You can adjust ClearType so that it works best on your monitor, under your lighting conditions. Just remember that ClearType doesn't change anything inside the tiled part of Windows: It's the desktop only. Here's how to run the ClearType Text Tuner:

1. **Right-click in the lower-left corner of the screen, to bring up the Power User Menu. Choose Control Panel.**

    That puts you on the desktop, inside Windows Control Panel.

2. **On the right, click Appearance and Personalization.**

    You see the Appearance and Personalization dialog box.

3. **At the bottom, under Fonts, click the link to Adjust ClearType text.**

    Windows brings up the ClearType Text Tuner, shown in Figure 2-8.

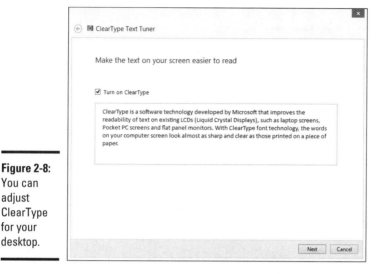

Figure 2-8:
You can
adjust
ClearType
for your
desktop.

4. **Ignore the comment about "Pocket PC screens," check the box marked Turn On ClearType, click Next, and go through the calibration steps.**

"Pocket PC" is the old name for Personal Digital Assistants that run the Windows Mobile Classic operating system, which is an operating system that has almost nothing in common with Windows itself. Microsoft dropped the name in 2007, shifting to Windows Mobile, which became Windows Phone, then Windows Phone 8. Wonder how long it'll take them to update this screen?

Showing larger fonts

If your eyes aren't what they used to be (mine never were), you might want to tell Windows to increase the size of text and other items on the screen. It's just enough boost to help, particularly if you're at an Internet cafe and forgot your glasses.

To adjust the size of fonts (actually, everything), follow Steps 1 and 2 in the preceding section to bring up the Appearance and Personalization dialog box. Under the Display icon, click the Make Text and Other Items Larger or Smaller link. You see the choices shown in Figure 2-9.

Programs running on the desktop generally won't recognize your preference for larger text; the Start screen or tiled style apps won't, either.

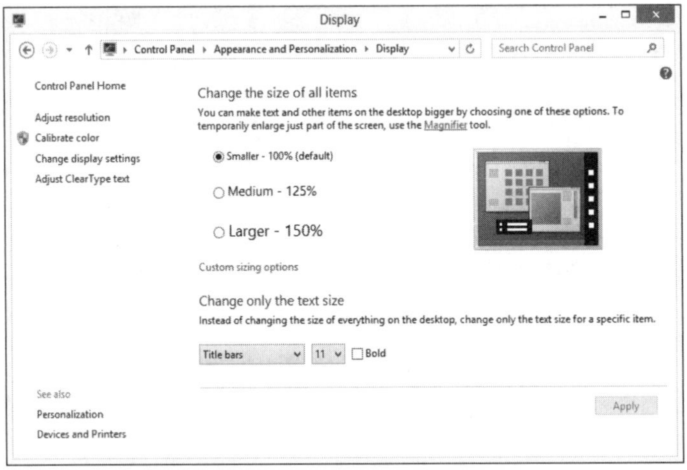

Figure 2-9:
Windows
itself has a
setting that
resembles
the "zoom"
you find
in many
programs.

The Display window shows:

> Change the size of all items
>
> You can make text and other items on the desktop bigger by choosing one of these options. To temporarily enlarge just part of the screen, use the *Magnifier* tool.
>
> ● Smaller - 100% (default)
> ○ Medium - 125%
> ○ Larger - 150%
>
> Custom sizing options
>
> Change only the text size
>
> Instead of changing the size of everything on the desktop, change only the text size for a specific item.
>
> Title bars   11   □ Bold

Using magnification

If you need more "zoom" than the font enlarger can offer, click the Magnifier link (refer to Figure 2-9; the link is in the first paragraph), and the Windows Magnifier appears. The Magnifier lets you zoom the entire screen by a factor of 200, 300, or 400 — or as high as you like.

Note that magnifying doesn't increase the quality or resolution of text or pictures. It makes them bigger, not finer. That CSI "David, can you make the picture sharper?" thing doesn't work with Windows. Sorry, Grissom.

If these nostrums don't do the job, you should take advantage of the Windows high-contrast themes. They use color to make text, in particular, stand out. High-contrast themes are available from the Themes list (refer to Figure 2-3) and are described in the section "Using Desktop Themes," earlier in this chapter.

Tricking Out the Taskbar

Microsoft developers working on the Windows 7 taskbar gave it a secret internal project name: the Superbar. Although one might debate how much of the Super in the bar arrived compliments of Mac OS, there's no doubt that the Windows 8 taskbar is a key tool for anyone who uses the desktop. In fact, with the demise of the old Start menu, the taskbar and shortcut icons on the desktop are your only ways of getting at programs, without slipping into the Start screen.

The next chapter covers slicing and dicing the Start screen to support your desktop inclinations. This section shows you how to take full advantage of the taskbar's capabilities.

The Windows Super, uh, taskbar, appears at the bottom of the screen, as in Figure 2-10.

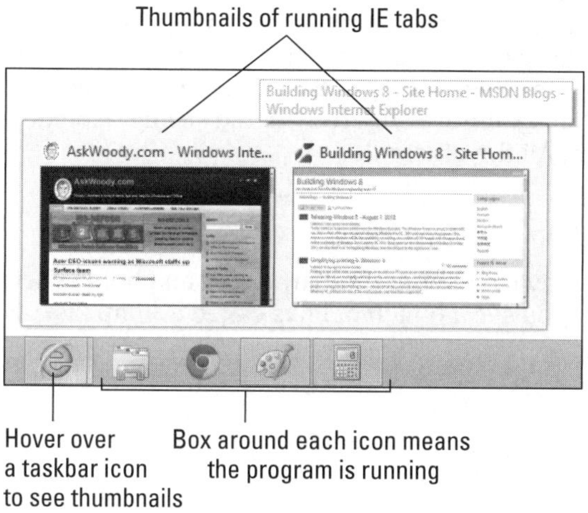

Thumbnails of running IE tabs

Figure 2-10:
The taskbar
juggles
many
different
tasks.

Hover over   Box around each icon means
a taskbar icon   the program is running
to see thumbnails

If you hover your mouse over an icon and the icon is associated with a program that's running, you see thumbnails of all the copies of the program. For example, in Figure 2-10, Internet Explorer 10 is running and two tabs are open. Hover your mouse over the IE icon and you can click on a thumbnail to bring up the specific tab.

Anatomy of the taskbar

The taskbar consists of two different kinds of icons:

✦ **Icons that have been pinned there:** Windows ships with two icons on the taskbar, one for Internet Explorer and one for File Explorer. You can see them on the left in Figure 2-10. If you install a program and tell the installer to put an icon on the taskbar, an icon for the program appears on the taskbar. You can also pin programs of your choice on the taskbar.

Some older programs have installers that offer to attach themselves to the Quick Launch Toolbar. It's a Windows XP era thing. If you agree to put the icon on the Quick Launch Toolbar, the icon for the program actually gets put on the far-more-upscale taskbar.

◆ **Icons associated with running desktop programs:** Every time a program starts, an icon for the program appears on the taskbar. If you run three copies of the program, only one icon shows up. When the program stops, the icon disappears. Tiled apps don't appear on the taskbar at all.

In general, you can't differentiate between the pinned icons and the ones that are just coming along for the ride, except by noting which ones are on the right (the running programs) and which ones are on the left (the pinned programs). You can, however, tell which icons represent running programs: Windows puts a little box around the icon for any running program. If you have more than one copy of the program running, you see more than one line on the right. It's subtle. In Figure 2-10, the second icon doesn't have a running program. All the others do.

Jumping

If you right-click any icon in the taskbar, or tap and hold, whether the icon is pinned or not, you see a bunch of links called a Jump List, as shown in Figure 2-11.

Figure 2-11: The Jump List in Internet Explorer.

The contents of the Jump List vary depending on the program that's running, but the bottom pane of every Jump List contains the name of the program and the entry Unpin This Program from Taskbar (or conversely, Pin This Program to the Taskbar, if the program isn't pinned).

Jump Lists were new in Windows 7, and they haven't taken off universally. Implementation of Jump Lists ranges from downright obsessive (such as Internet Explorer 10) to completely lackadaisical (including most applications that aren't made by Microsoft).

Here are the Jump List basics:

✦ **Jump Lists may show your recently opened file history.** For example, the WordPad Jump List (see Figure 2-12) shows you the same Recent Documents list that appears inside WordPad. The currently open document(s) appear at the top of the list.

Figure 2-12:
WordPad's
Jump List
shows
recently
opened
documents.

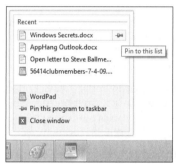

✦ **It's generally easy to pin an item to the Jump List.** When you pin an item, it sticks to a program's Jump List whether or not that item is open. To pin an item, run your mouse out to the right of the item you want to pin and click the stick pin. That puts the item in a separate pane at the top of the Jump List. In Figure 2-12, if I click the pin next to `Window Secrets.docx`, that document gets pinned to the top of the list. In the future, if I want to open `Windows Secrets.docx`, I just right-click the WordPad icon and select the document.

The Jump List has one not-so-obvious use. It lets you open a second copy of the same program. Say you want to copy a handful of albums from the music library to your thumbdrive on `F:`. You start by clicking the File Explorer icon in the taskbar, then on the left, click the Music Library. Cool.

You could do the copy-and-paste thang — select an album, press Ctrl+C to copy, use the list on the left of File Explorer to navigate to F:, and then press Ctrl+V to paste. But if you're going to copy many albums, it's much faster and easier to open a second copy of File Explorer, and navigate to F: in that second window. Then you can click and drag albums from the Music folder to the F: folder.

To open a second copy of a running program (File Explorer, in this example), you have two choices:

✦ Hold down the Shift key and click the icon.

✦ Right-click the icon (or tap and hold) and choose the program's name.

In either case, Windows starts a fresh copy of the program.

Changing the taskbar

The taskbar rates as one of the few parts of Windows that are highly malleable. You can modify it till the cows come home:

✦ **Pin any program** on the taskbar by right-clicking the program (see the next chapter of this minibook for a tricky way to find many programs) and choosing Pin This Program to Taskbar. Yes, you can right-click the icon of a running program on the taskbar.

✦ **Move a pinned icon** by clicking and dragging it. Easy. You know — the way it's supposed to be. You can even drag an icon that isn't pinned into the middle of the pinned icons. When the program associated with the icon stops, the icon disappears and all pinned icons move back into place.

✦ **Unpin any pinned program** by right-clicking it and choosing Unpin This Program from Taskbar. Rocket science.

Unfortunately, you can't turn individual documents or folders into icons on the taskbar. But you can pin a folder to the File Explorer Jump List, and you can pin a document to the Jump List for whichever application is associated with the document. For example, you can pin a song to the Jump List for Windows Media Player.

Here's how to pin a folder or document to its associated icon on the taskbar:

1. **Navigate to the folder or document that you want to pin.**

   You can use File Explorer to go to the file or folder, or you can make a shortcut to the file or folder.

2. **Drag the folder or document (or shortcut) to the taskbar.**

   Windows tells you where it will pin the folder, document, or shortcut, as shown in Figure 2-13. For example, if you are dragging a .docx file, Windows will let you pin it to WordPad, Word, File Explorer, or any program that can open a .docx file.

3. **Release the Mouse button.**

   That's all it takes.

Figure 2-13:
Drag a file
or folder
to pin it to
a taskbar
icon.

A little-known side-effect: If you pin a file to a program on the taskbar, the program itself also gets pinned to the taskbar, if it wasn't already.

Making your own little toolbars

You can turn your own folder into a toolbar, which sits on the taskbar. It's a cool tool if you frequently need to navigate around a hornet's nest of folders and don't want to do the navigating from inside a specific program (such as Word or Excel). Instead, you can put a pop-up menu — a new toolbar, in Windows parlance — on the taskbar. This toolbar whisks you directly to a folder, and from that point, subfolders turn into submenus. You can navigate through the folder maze to individual files.

The terminology here is confusing because the custom pop-up toolbar you create sits on top of the Windows taskbar. Your folder doesn't show up as an icon; it appears on the right side of the taskbar with the name of the folder. When you click the name of the folder, you see a navigable list of all subfolders and documents. Confused? Take a look at Figure 2-14. When you create your own toolbar, the entries on the toolbar match the underlying folder structure.

Figure 2-14:
The toolbar
entries
match the
underlying
folder
structure.

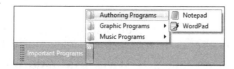

To create the file structure you see, I put a folder on my desktop called Important Programs. I put three folders inside that folder, called Authoring Programs, Graphic Programs, and Music Programs. In the Authoring Programs folder, I put shortcuts to Notepad and WordPad.

After I pinned the Important Programs folder to the taskbar, clicking on the double-right wedges to the right of the name of the folder brings up a pop-up list of subfolders. Clicking on one of the subfolders brings up a list of files in the subfolder.

Making your own toolbars is a reasonable way to create your own Start Menu substitute. I prefer using the tiled Start screen, as I show in the next chapter. But keep these toolbars in mind if you want certain items to be a click away without switching to the tiled side of the force.

To put a new toolbar on the Windows taskbar:

1. **Right-click any unused part of the taskbar and choose Toolbars⇨New Toolbar.**

You see the New Toolbar — Choose a Folder dialog box, shown in Figure 2-15.

Figure 2-15: Choose the root folder to place on the taskbar.

2. **Navigate to the folder you want as the root of the pop-up menu, click it once, and click Select Folder.**

The contents of this folder appear on your new toolbar. Figure 2-14 shows the result of my placing the Important Programs folder on my taskbar.

3. **If you want to relocate the toolbar, make sure the taskbar is unlocked (right-click an empty part of it and deselect the Lock the Taskbar option). Then click and drag your new toolbar wherever you want.**

If you play with the toolbar, you see that Windows restricts the placement and sizing of the toolbar quite drastically. It also has a habit of dragging out subfolders and files.

4. **When you're happy with the result, right-click an unused spot on the taskbar and select the Lock the Taskbar check box.**

Try using the new toolbar and see if you get used to it.

If you change your mind and want to get rid of the new toolbar, right-click an open place on the taskbar, choose Toolbars, and deselect the option that mentions the new toolbar.

Working with the taskbar

I've discovered a few tricks with the taskbar that you may find worthwhile:

✦ When you hover your mouse over an icon, you see thumbnails of the running copies of the program (refer to Figure 2-10). Normally, the thumbnails disappear when you move the mouse, but if you click the icon once, the thumbnails stay until you click somewhere else.

✦ Sometimes you want to shut down all (or most) running programs, and you don't want Windows to do it for you. It's easy to see what's running, by looking at the boxes around the icons (refer to Figure 2-10). To close down all instances of a particular program, right-click its icon and choose Close Window or Close All Windows.

Sometimes, if a program is frozen and won't shut itself down, forcing the matter through the taskbar is the easiest way to dislodge it.

The terminology is a bit screwy here. Normally, you would choose "Exit the program" or "Choose File⇨Exit" or "Click the red X" or some such. When you're working with the taskbar, you say "Close all windows." Different words, same meaning.

✦ This doesn't work for all programs, but for some (including Word), if you hold down the Ctrl key and click the Taskbar icon, the program will open with the most recently viewed document open.

If you drag your mouse to the lower-right corner and then click, Windows minimizes all open windows. Click again, and Windows brings back all minimized windows. You can also right-click and choose Peek at Desktop or Show Desktop.

Controlling the Notification Area

Windows gives you some specific control over the contents of the *notification area* — the glob of icons down near the clock that used to be known as the system tray.

Windows ships with a small handful of visible notification icons — for the Action Center, the Network Center, and the master audio volume control slider. That's it. If you see any additional icons, your computer's manufacturer probably put them there. When you install a new program that has an icon for the notification area, the icon is placed in the box that you can see when you click the up arrow at the left edge of the icons.

If you're tired of seeing a useless icon in the notification area — or if you know that you want to see an icon all the time — you can take control. Here's how:

1. Click the up arrow at the left edge of the icons.

You see all the notification icons available for you. If you don't see an up arrow, congratulations! You don't have any notification icons gumming up the works.

If you see an icon in the box that you absolutely must have visible all the time, simply click and drag it into the notification area, near the clock. If you later change your mind, you can click and drag the icon back from the notification area into the box.

2. Choose Customize.

Windows shows you the Notification Area Icons Zapper box. That's what I call it, anyway (see Figure 2-16).

Figure 2-16:
Control notification area icons here.

3. **Find the icon you want to zap and, in the drop-down list, choose Hide Icon and Notifications (to turn off the beast completely) or Only Show Notifications (shows the balloon warnings but doesn't show the icon).**

4. **Click OK.**

   The icon changes its wayward ways immediately.

Windows has some fairly sophisticated notification methods these days, much more usable than the old notification area icons. In particular, there are notifications on the lock screen, and "toaster" notifications that appear floating on the upper right side of the screen, just like a piece of toast popping out.

I talk about those other, tile-like notifications, in Book VIII, Chapter 4.

Book VI
Chapter 2

Personalizing
the Desktop

Chapter 3: Start Screen Mods for Desktop Users

In This Chapter

✓ Installing new programs and dealing with their tiles

✓ Getting rid of the Start screen chaff

✓ Finding and adding programs to the Start screen

✓ Organizing the Start screen for a lean, mean desktop

✓ Alternatives to the Start screen

*W*hen the Windows 8 design team took a look at how people were using the Windows Start menu, the team decided the Start menu wasn't being used as originally intended. Windows has changed, programs have changed, and users have changed. The design team felt they could do a better job by turning the menus into a field of tiles, going from cascading menus featuring dull straight text to the colorful but not hierarchical "live" tiles of the Start screen interface.

You may agree; you may disagree. The fact is that the Start screen is malleable enough that you can turn it into just about anything you want — except for cascading menus. In Windows 8, Start doesn't have cascading menus: all the tiles sit on the Start screen, and you have to scroll to find them.

I'm a desktop user, and I'm not afraid to say it. If you're like me, I bet you'll like this chapter. Here, I show you how I use all the tools at hand to make the Start screen launch programs on the desktop, so the new Start screen works kind of like the old Start menu. I concentrate on using the mouse and keyboard — not the touch interface — and look hard at how to bring back the programs you might've used in previous versions of Windows.

This chapter's approach is different from all the other chapters in this book. While the rest of the book offers references, such as jump in here, jump out there, this chapter's designed as a tutorial, a step-by-step guide to modifying your Start screen so it helps you get work done on the desktop.

In Figure 3-1, you can see the Start screen that I, uh, started with. By the end of the chapter, you'll see how it's morphed into something considerably less of a what-can-we-buy-from-Microsoft oriented experience, and considerably more of a get-some-work-done tool.

I change my Start screen so I can start the programs I frequently need quickly, can find programs that I occasionally want with a little bit of hunting, and relegate most of the rest of the stuff to the back of the bus — or at least the far outer reaches of the Start screen. Along the way, I show you how to do the following:

✦ Organize tiles that appear when you install new programs

✦ Sort through the tiles you need and those you don't

✦ Add tiles for the programs you want

✦ Organize the tiles into groups

Figure 3-1:
A bone stock Start screen. Let's build it from here.

Installing New Programs and Dealing with Their Tiles

When you install a new program in Windows 8, the installer throws a bunch of tiles up on the Start screen. They're disjointed and unorganized, and can be a massive pain to sort through.

To illustrate the point, I take my fresh, clean version of the Start screen (refer to Figure 3-1) and install the following, using only default settings:

✦ Office Professional Plus 2010

✦ 7Zip

✦ Secunia PSI, the software version checker (see Book X, Chapter 5)

✦ Google Chrome — and I made it the default web browser (see Book IV Chapter 1)

The left half of the Start screen remains exactly like Figure 3-1. Figure 3-2 shows the right half of the resulting Start screen. The programs' installers have thrown loose tiles onto the Start screen, with Windows lumping them all on the right side.

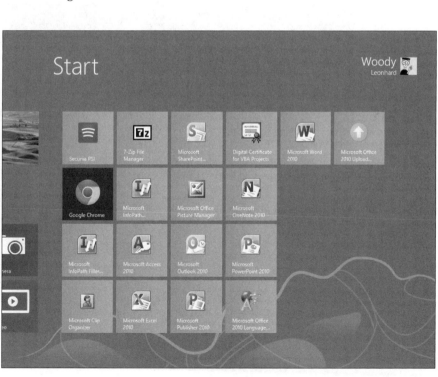

Figure 3-2:
The sorry state of the Start screen after installing Office 2010, Secunia PSI, 7Zip, and Chrome.

See that vertical blank area to the left of the Secunia PSI and Google Chrome tiles? That's a group separator: on the left is one group, on the right another. At this point the groups don't mean anything — they're just the places where Windows arbitrarily dropped tiles — but we're about to change that.

The general approach of whipping this mess into shape is to click and drag tiles into groups that make sense, and then use the pinch (or click in the lower-right corner) to assign names to the groups. Start with putting a few tiles in their proper places.

One cold, hard fact about the Start screen: When you bring up the Start screen, you can only see a handful of tiles. There are (almost) always more tiles than will fit on the screen. A Start screen blivet, if you will. If you aren't careful, every time you go to click an often-used tile, you may have to scroll and scroll and scroll to find it. Moral of the story: Put your frequently used tiles on the left, where they're easy to find.

Thus my first iteration is to move tiles for programs that I use all the time to the left. This first-stage result is in Figure 3-3.

Figure 3-3:
First step in the sorting: Start moving programs that you use commonly toward the left, so they're easier to find when you first see the Start screen.

Note that the Windows Store holds updates to all your basic tiled apps: The updates are free, but they come through the Windows Store. So you may end up using the Store more frequently than you might otherwise think — and it may be worthwhile moving the Store tile to the left, where it's easier to find.

Before you get to fine-tuning the tiles, go through the next section to make sure you have all the tiles you need.

Finding and Adding Programs to the Start Screen

Before I start grouping the tiles and making them a bit more accessible, and generally prettify the Start screen, I need to bring back many of the programs that used to be on the Windows Start menu — you know, the old stalwarts such as Notepad, Paint, and Calculator, that you might use once or twice a week, or even once or twice a day.

Here's an easy way to do it, using (forgive me) Search on the Start screen:

1. **Starting at the Start screen (refer to Figure 3-1 if you have changed anything), type the name of the program you seek.**

I start with Notepad, which just about everybody uses once in a while, and type **notepad**.

Windows Search kicks in and shows you the Notepad program, er, app, as in Figure 3-4.

2. **When your desired program is visible, tap and hold it, or right click it.**

You see the App bar at the bottom, which gives you several choices.

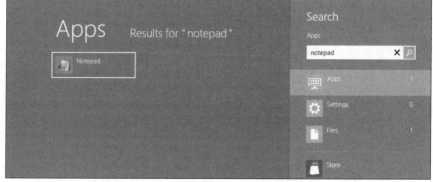

Figure 3-4: Finding the Notepad app, the easy way.

3. **Choose Pin to Start.**

   The program's tile is tossed on the Start screen, into the group on the right.

   You could also choose to pin your program to the desktop's taskbar by choosing Pin to Taskbar. Note that the two choices aren't mutually exclusive: You can have a program on the Start screen and on the desktop taskbar at the same time. For details about customizing your taskbar, see Book VI, Chapter 2.

Windows is loaded with "legacy" programs that deserve to be considered for inclusion either on the taskbar or on the Start screen. This is the easy way to put them on either or both: Use the Search function from the Start screen, right-click the program, and choose where you want an icon or tile to appear.

When I'm trying to decide whether to put a legacy program on the Start screen and/or the desktop taskbar, I keep three things in mind:

✦ When I'm working on the desktop, it's a whole lot easier to run a program from the taskbar than it is from the Start screen. That's why I put programs that tie in to the desktop — the Snipping Tool being an obvious example, because it only works on the desktop — on the taskbar.

✦ When I'm working on the tiled side of the fence, it's a little bit easier to click or tap a tile and flip over to run the program on the desktop. That's why I put the Calculator on the Start screen: If I need to calculate something while in, say, the Bing Finance app, it's easier to find it on the tiled Start screen side.

✦ The most constraining fact of all: There's a very limited amount of space on the desktop taskbar, and endless vistas of space on the Start screen. So if there's a program I use once in a blue moon, such as the Character Map, I'll stick it on the Start screen. That way I can find it if I go looking for it, but it won't get in the way most of the time.

   You might wonder why I put Character Map on the Start screen at all. That's easy. If it isn't on the Start screen, I'll either forget that it exists, or I'll forget the name and spend a lot of time trying to find it. That kind of "discoverability" is something that the old Windows Start menu had in spades. With the demise of the old Windows Start menu, the only other option is to stick a tile on the Start screen, and hope that I bump into it at the right time.

See Table 3-1 — quite possibly the most important table in this book — for details on what programs you should consider for inclusion on the Start screen, and on the desktop taskbar.

Table 3-1	Legacy Programs to Consider for the Start Screen and Desktop Taskbar	
Type This in Search	*Where I Pin It*	*Why*
Calculator	Start Screen and Taskbar	I use it all the time.
Character Map	Start screen	Very helpful for inserting odd characters.
Command Prompt	Start screen	Also on the Power User Menu, but I forget.
Control Panel	Taskbar	I use this one all the time.
Default Programs	Start screen	Accessible from the Control Panel, but it's easier to find here.
Magnifier	Start screen	Hard to find otherwise.
Math Input Panel	Start screen	Obscure, but a lifesaver if you work with equations.
Media Player	Start screen	I tend to use VLC to play media files, but if you use Media Player frequently on the desktop, put it on the taskbar, too.
Notepad	Start screen and Taskbar	Another ancient program I use all the time.
On-Screen Keyboard	Start screen	Just in case you need a keyboard on the desktop.
Paint	Taskbar	Although I usually use Paint.net.
Run	Start screen	It's hard to use because in many cases you have to know the exact name of the file, but I put it on the Start screen anyway; also appears on the Power User Menu.
Snipping Tool	Taskbar	It's one of the most useful Windows tools.
Sticky Notes	Start screen	I don't use them very often, but if I really need one, I know where to look — on the Start screen.
Task Manager	Taskbar	Microsoft's new and greatly improved Task Manager (see Book VIII, Chapter 5); also on the Power User Menu.
Windows Easy Transfer	Start screen	Particularly useful when setting up new machines.
Windows PowerShell	Start screen	A real power user's product.
WordPad	Start screen	I don't use it very often, but sometimes it comes in handy.

Now, finally, I have all the pieces in place to assemble a genuinely useful Start screen for desktop aficionados. The pieces are just all jumbled together, as you can see in Figure 3-5.

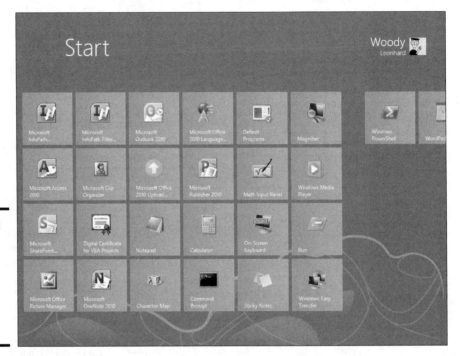

Figure 3-5:
The mass
of tiles on
the Start
screen,
waiting
to be
organized.

Sorting through the Default Tiles

So now you have a basic idea of how to move tiles around, and where to dredge up tiles for important programs — such as Calculator and Notepad — that otherwise wouldn't have any. At least they're important to me, and if you have much experience at all with older versions of Windows, I bet they're important to you, too.

Before I show you how I rearrange the tiles to best suit me — and hopefully give you a few useful ideas for your situation at the same time — there's one more group of tiles you should consider: The tiles that originally came on your Start screen.

Generally, you can do one of four things with the original Start screen tiles:

✦ You can drag the important ones toward the left, so they're easier to find when you land on the Start screen.

✦ You can drag the less important (even the downright useless) original tiles to the right, so they don't get in the way of tiles that you use all the time. Stick them out in the back forty, as it were, so you can find them if you need them, but keep them out of the way of your normal day-to-day use.

✦ You can make some tiles bigger (double-sized rectangle) or smaller (single-sized square). To do so, right-click the tile or nudge it down with your finger, and then at the bottom, choose Larger or Smaller.

✦ You can delete the tile entirely — remove it from the Start screen. I rarely recommend doing so, because a wayward tile waaaaay off on the right doesn't take up real estate or mindshare — and some day you may wish you had the tile back.

Here are the tiles that ship on the Start screen, and what I generally do with them. Your preferences may differ, of course:

✦ **Mail:** I use Gmail, so this one gets dragged to the right. If your e-mail needs aren't particularly voluminous, the tiled Windows 8 Mail app may be a good solution. See Book IV, Chapter 2. If you're going to use it, keep it on the left. Otherwise, make it smaller and drag it to the right.

✦ **People:** Tough call. I like the way it aggregates my contacts from various places, so I keep this one on the left. The photos on the Larger tile some-time remind me of contacts I haven't thought about in months, so I keep the tile big. Your mileage may vary.

✦ **Messaging:** No way. If I want to use MSN Mess . . . er, Windows 8 Messenger, I'll log on to Outlook.com. Make the tile smaller and drag it to the right.

✦ **Desktop:** Yeah, I use this one all the time. After some experimentation, I drag it to the lower-left corner. It's easier to find down there, I think.

✦ **Calendar:** I tend to use the Google Calendar, but it's convenient to have the date displayed on the Start screen. This tile is a painless way to do it. Because I don't maintain appointments in the tiled Windows 8 Calendar app, there's no particular advantage to having a large tile. (The large tile shows you a day's appointments.) So I make the tile smaller and keep it visible. Book IV, Chapter 2 introduces what the Win8 Calendar can do.

+ **Photos:** The tiled Windows 8 Photos app isn't much of an app, but it does cycle through many of my photos nicely, which makes the large tile a welcome addition to my Start screen.

+ **Video:** It's just a front for Microsoft marketing. Turn the tile smaller and drag it right.

+ **Weather:** Although I use this tile to get a glimpse of what the real world's doing while I toil away inside, the picture of the sun, or storm clouds, doesn't do much for me, so I right-click the icon and choose Smaller.

+ **Internet Explorer:** I generally use Chrome for my default browser, so I drag the Internet Explorer tile way off to the right.

+ **Store:** Can be useful, especially for updates, but I don't hang out there. I keep it on the left.

+ **Maps:** This one's handy, but I prefer Google Maps. I drag it to the right.

+ **SkyDrive:** I access SkyDrive through the desktop — the tiled Win8 SkyDrive app doesn't really do anything. If Microsoft ever improves this Win8 app it might be worth keeping. For now, I drag the tile to the right.

+ **Music:** I prefer listening to Pandora, so don't have much need for Microsoft's Win8 Music app. You may feel differently, though, especially if you've bought music through Microsoft's store. Drag the Music tile to the right if you don't need it.

+ **Camera:** I keep this on the left only on PCs with built-in cameras. Why? The desktop apps are a pain in the neck, but this one's pretty simple. If you don't have a built-in camera, drag this to the right.

+ **News:** I keep this tile where I can see it, in the off chance that it'll flash a news headline that I don't pick up earlier on some other media — notably Twitter (see Book V, Chapter 2). I turn it smaller and keep it to the left where I can see it.

+ **Finance:** Much like the News tile, I put this one where I can keep my eye on it, just in case, but I turn it smaller. I don't bother pinning individual stocks from the Bing Finance app to the Start screen because the quotes are delayed.

+ **Travel:** Yeah, I confess, I like the pretty pics. It goes to the left.

+ **Bing:** Generally useless "trending news" tile deserves to be dragged kicking and screaming to the right.

+ **Sports and Travel:** They're gorgeous tiles with pretty pictures, but if I want to see great sports or travel photography, I'll go on the web. These get dragged off to the right.

Organizing the Start Screen for a Lean, Mean Desktop

Now to bring a little order to the tile chaos. Remember that I'm building the Start screen specifically to help me use the old-fashioned Windows desktop as effectively as I can. I click and drag the tiles into these groups:

✦ **Core Desktop Apps** — Word, Excel, PowerPoint, Google Chrome, 7Zip (which is very handy for putting together password protected zip files; see Book X Chapter 5). I also stick the Calendar tile in the upper left corner, so I can see the date easily. See Figure 3-6.

✦ **Useful tiled Windows 8 apps** — yes, some of you will chide me for an oxymoron, but it's true. These are apps that serve a useful purpose (or at least serve up some nice eye candy) whenever I'm on the Start screen. See Figure 3-7.

Figure 3-6:
The most used desktop programs go on the far left, so I can get to them quickly if I find myself in the Start screen.

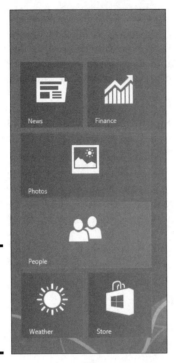

Figure 3-7:
The next group, tiled apps that serve a purpose.

✦ **Utilities** — the next bunch of programs (Secunia PSI, Notepad, Calculator, Internet Explorer, Windows Media Player) come in handy from time to time.

✦ **The dregs** — programs that I want to keep on the Start screen because I may use them once in a while, but I don't use them frequently enough for them to occupy an important spot.

Finally, clicking the minus sign semantic zoom icon in the lower-right corner, I gave the groups names. As I discuss in Book III, Chapter 1, assigning a name to a group is as easy as right-clicking, choosing Name Group, and typing in a name. The semantic zoomed final looks like Figure 3-8.

The net result is a Start menu (see Figure 3-9) that really does help me use the desktop. It ain't pretty, but it works well.

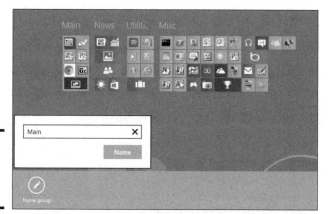

Figure 3-8:
Grouping
and naming
for speed.

Figure 3-9:
My desktop-
friendly
Start
screen. This
week.

And my desktop taskbar — created while stepping through Table 3-1 in this chapter — works just great. See Figure 3-10.

Figure 3-10:
My no-
nonsense
desktop
taskbar.

One of the nicest features of the Start screen? You can change it easily, any time. Just click and drag tiles to wherever you want them.

Chapter 4: Maintaining Your System

In This Chapter

✔ Understanding Refresh, Restart, and restore points, and older names

✔ Creating a Password Reset Disk

✔ Maintaining hard drives and SSDs

✔ Zipping and compressing

Windows is a computer program, not a Cracker Jack toy, and it will have problems. The trick lies in making sure that *you* don't have problems, too.

Windows is notorious for crashing and freezing, making it impossible to start the computer, or garbling things so badly that you'd think the screen went through a garbage disposal. Microsoft has poured a lot of time, effort, and money into teaching Windows how to heal itself. You can take advantage of all that work — if you know where to find it.

All of Book VIII is devoted to the topic of how to keep Windows alive and well. In this chapter, I introduce you to the basic ideas, and get you started with some of the parts of Windows that you can use in many different ways. If you log on to Windows with a local account (as opposed to a Microsoft account, which is always an e-mail address), I also want to cajole you into creating a Password Reset Disk, which may well save your tail some day.

You're welcome.

What's the Difference Between Restore, System Repair, Recovery Mode, Refresh, and Restart?

The terminology stinks. Bear with me.

Windows 8 has three very different technologies for pulling you out of a tough spot. I liken them to the Wayback Machine, a brain transplant, and global thermonuclear war.

✦ Like Rocky and Bullwinkle's WABAC Machine (thank you, Mr. Peabody), setting and using restore points provides a relatively simple way to switch your PC's internal settings to an earlier, and presumably happier state, should something go awry.

Restore points aren't intended to restore earlier versions of files that you work with — that's the function of File History (sometimes called "the Windows version of the Mac's Time Machine). I talk about File History extensively in Book VIII, Chapter 1.

✦ Sometimes, the problem doesn't lie with the settings. Sometimes Windows system files get messed up (the technical term is "borked"). In those cases, Microsoft has a program called **Refresh** that scans and fixes all the system files, without changing your settings, removing any installed programs, or blasting your data.

In previous versions of Windows, you might've used a System Repair disk, or booted into Safe Mode and hacked away at a `cmd.exe` command line, or used Recovery Mode from an installation DVD, or tried a dozen different incantations to bring Windows back from the dead. Having lived through many a late night with them, I can certainly sympathize. Those methods still work, by and large, but Microsoft has made it difficult to get them going, and doesn't recommend using them.

In my experience, Windows 8 Refresh works almost all the time. It's light years ahead of System Repair, Safe Mode, and Recovery Mode, and should be your fixit method of first resort. If Refresh doesn't work, you're in a world of hurt. Search online for instructions on manually booting into Safe Mode, and running a recovery. Good luck.

✦ If a Refresh doesn't work, and you don't mind losing all your data and installed programs, or if you want to wipe your computer clean before you sell it or give it away, the program you want to run is **Reset.**

Most of the time, you run a Restore when your computer starts acting flakey. You run a Reset to wipe the whole system when you're going to sell your PC. But either or both — or using restore points — may be offered as options when your computer won't boot right. I go into detail on restore points, Refresh, and Reset in Book VIII, Chapter 2.

Using a Password Reset Disk

If someone forgets his or her password, a Password Reset Disk is what saves the day by enabling you to reset a password you otherwise wouldn't be able to access.

What is Safe Mode?

Safe Mode used to be the gateway into the Windows inner workings: In earlier versions of Windows, if something went wrong, you booted into a very limited version of Windows — one that let you diagnose problems, and install minimalist drivers, but not much more.

Safe Mode still exists in Windows 8, but it isn't used as much as it once was. Microsoft really has improved things to the point where Safe Mode isn't nearly as important as it used to be. Running a Refresh, in particular, will do just about everything people used to do in Safe Mode, but without the hands-on nitty-gritty.

If you still want to get into Safe Mode, hover your mouse in the upper-right corner or swipe from the right, choose Settings, then Change

PC Settings. Choose General, and under Advanced Startup, choose Restart Now. When the blue Choose an Option screen appears, choose Troubleshoot, then Advanced Options, then Windows Startup Settings. Click Restart and you will see the old-fashioned Advanced Boot Options screen. Choose Safe Mode (or Safe Mode with Networking or Safe Mode with Command Prompt) and press Enter. You get logged in to Windows in Safe Mode, using the built-in Administrator account.

Yes, it's that complicated. Microsoft doesn't really want you to use Safe Mode, unless you know what you're doing, and you're willing to bend over backwards to do it.

If you have a local account (not a Microsoft account), and that account has a password (any kind of password), it doesn't matter if you set the password, or somebody else set it up for you. You should take a moment right now to create a Password Reset Disk. If you have multiple Local accounts on one PC (for example, a Regular account and an Administrator account), create a Password Reset Disk for each account. (If you need a refresher on the different types of accounts, flip to Book II, Chapter 4.)

If you have a Microsoft Account, the only way to reset the password is online. Go to `account.live.com/ResetPassword.aspx` and follow the instructions.

I can't emphasize enough how important a Password Reset Disk is, particularly if there's only one Administrator account on your PC, and it's a local account. I get mail practically every day from people who have forgotten their passwords and can't get in. This one simple trick, which takes all of a couple of minutes, will save you untold grief should you forget that lousy password!

"Password Reset Disk" is a misnomer. The part that saves your bacon is a very simple, small file, called `userkey.psw`, which you can copy and move around just like any other file. If you create more than one "Password Reset

Disk," which is to say, you create more than one `userkey.psw` file, make sure you keep track of which file goes with which user ID.

Here's the basic idea: You log on to Windows, using any kind of password — typed, PIN, or picture. Crank up the Forgotten Password Wizard. It will ask you for your typed password, which you must provide. The Wizard then creates this file, `userkey.psw`, on a removable drive. You keep that file someplace handy. If the time ever comes that you forget your password (typed, PIN, or picture), put that file on a removable drive, stick the drive in your computer, say the magic words, and click your heels three times. Bingo, you're in!

It doesn't matter if somebody has changed your password without your knowing. The Password Reset Disk resets your password, *no matter what the password might be.* As long as you have a Local account, you're in like Flynn.

Creating a Password Reset Disk

If you have a password-protected Local account, follow these steps to create a Password Reset Disk (that is, a `userkey.psw` file):

1. **Log on to the account.**

   It doesn't matter what kind of password you use.

2. **Make sure you have a USB flash drive handy, or another type of removable media, such as an SD card, or even an external hard drive.**

   The Wizard won't write anything to a local disk (think about it — D'OH!), and it won't write to a network attached location.

3. **On the desktop, bring up the Control Panel by tapping and holding (or right-clicking) in the lower-left corner and choosing Control Panel. Click the User Accounts and Family Safety link, then the User Accounts link.**

   Windows shows you the User Accounts dialog box, shown in Figure 4-1.

Figure 4-1:
The User Accounts dialog box, with Create a Password Reset Disk on the left.

4. **On the left, click the link that says Create a Password Reset Disk.**

If you can't see a line on the left that says Create a Password Reset Disk, either you don't have a Local account (see the first part of this section), or your account doesn't have a password.

This step launches the Forgotten Password Wizard, which creates a Password Reset Disk. This nifty little program creates a file that you can use to unlock your password and get into your account, even if your precocious seven-year-old daughter changes it to MXYPLFTFFT.

5. **Follow the Wizard and at the final step, click Finish.**

Store that `userkey.psw` file someplace safe. If you ever forget your password, or if someone else changes it for you, follow the steps in the next section to log on to your account.

**Book VI
Chapter 4**

Guard that file! Anybody who has that `userkey.psw` file can log on in your stead, even if he doesn't know your password.

Resetting your password

So you followed the steps in the preceding section and created a Password Reset Disk, which is, in fact, a little file called `userkey.psw`. And the time comes when you forget your password. Here's how to use the file and reset your password:

1. **Copy the file onto some sort of removable drive that your computer can read.**

It'll probably be a USB flash drive, but it could also be an SD card or even a USB-attached hard drive. Make sure it isn't sitting in a folder somewhere; the file has to be in the root directory.

2. **Go through the motions to log on using a typed password.**

If you're accustomed to logging on with a picture password, click the box marked Switch to Password on the logon screen and try there.

I know you don't know the password. Relax. Just type something and press Enter.

3. **When Windows comes back and tells you that The Password is Incorrect. Try Again, click OK.**

That brings up the alternative logon screen shown in Figure 4-2.

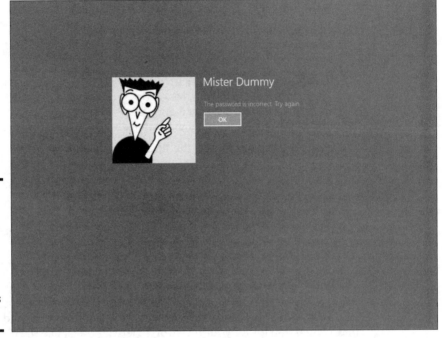

4. **Click Reset Password.**

   Windows brings up the Welcome to the Password Reset Wizard. Glad that you found it, eh?

5. **Make sure your Password Reset Disk — any disk with the `userkey.psw` file on it — is attached to the PC, then tap or click Next.**

6. **Follow the steps in the wizard. The last step in the wizard asks you to type in a new password, as in Figure 4-3.**

   Remember that this is the new password for this account, on this computer. It doesn't affect the Password Reset Disk or the `userkey.psw` file at all.

7. **Type in a new password and hint. Tap or click Next, then Finish. Windows brings you back to the logon screen, where you can log on with the new password.**

   Don't lose that `userkey.psw` file, okay?

To reiterate: As long as you have a Local account, the `userkey.psw` file will log you on to the PC, no matter what password is in effect, no matter who changed the password, when or how.

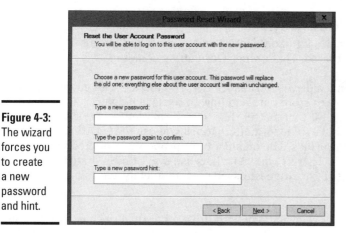

Figure 4-3:
The wizard
forces you
to create
a new
password
and hint.

Maintaining Drives

Drives (hard drives, USB flash drives, CDs, DVDs, even those ancient floppies if you can still find one, and other types of storage media) seem to cause more computer problems than all other infuriating PC parts combined. Why? They move. And, unlike other parts of computers that are designed to move (printer rollers and keyboard springs and mouse balls, for example), they move quickly and with ultrafine precision, day in and day out.

"E pur, si muove"

That's what Galileo said in 1633, after being forced during the Inquisition to recant his beliefs about the earth moving around the sun. "And yet it moves" — and that's the crux of the problem.

As with any other moving mechanical contraption, an ounce of drive prevention is worth ten tons of cure. Unlike other moving mechanical contraptions, a good shot of WD-40 usually doesn't cure the problem.

Solid State Drives are a whole different kettle of fish. SSD manufacturers typically offer diagnostic and health maintenance tools to keep their products in top shape, but they contain no moving parts, and thus aren't subject to the vagaries associated with moving drives. I talk about SSDs later in this chapter.

If you're looking for help installing a new hard drive, you're in the wrong place. I talk about adding new drives and getting Windows 7 to recognize them in Book VIII, Chapter 5.

What is formatting?

Drives try to pack a lot of data into a small space, and because of that, they need to be calibrated. That's where formatting comes in.

When you format a drive, you calibrate it: You mark it with guideposts that tell the PC where to store data and how to retrieve it. Every hard drive (and floppy disk, for that matter) has to be formatted before it can be used. CDs and DVDs have to be formatted, too, if you use the "Live File System" method for storing files. The manufacturer probably formatted your drive before you got it. That's comforting because every time a drive is reformatted, everything on the drive is tossed out, completely and (almost) irretrievably. Everything.

You can format or reformat any hard drive other than the one that contains Windows by starting File Explorer, either from the tile on the Windows Start screen, or from the icon on the desktop taskbar. Then right-click the hard drive, and choose Format. You can also "format" rewritable CDs, DVDs, USB (key) flash drives, and SD or other removable memory cards — delete all the data on them — by following the same approach. To reformat the drive that contains Windows, you have to reinstall Windows. See the instructions for a clean Windows install in Book I, Chapter 4.

Introducing hard-drive-maintenance tools

Hard drives die at the worst possible moments. A hard drive that's starting to act flaky can display all sorts of strange symptoms: everything from long, long pauses when you're trying to open a file to completely inexplicable crashes and other errors in Windows itself.

Windows comes with a grab bag of utilities designed to help you keep your hard drives in top shape.

+ **Storage Spaces:** The best, most comprehensive of the bunch is Storage Spaces (see Book VIII, Chapter 4), which keeps duplicate copies of every file in hot standby, should a hard drive break down. But to use Storage Spaces effectively, you need at least three hard drives and twice as much hard drive space as you have data. Not everyone can afford that. Not everyone wants to dig into the nitty-gritty.

+ **Basic utilities:** Three simple utilities stand out as effective ways to care for your hard drives, and one of them runs automatically once a week. You should get to know Check Disk, Disk Cleanup, and Disk Defragmenter, because they all come in handy at the right times.

You have to be a designated administrator (see the section on using account types in Book II, Chapter 4) to get these utilities to work. I explain how to use Check Disk and Disk Defragmenter in the following two sections.

Running an error check

If a drive starts acting weird (for example, you see error messages when trying to open a file, or Windows crashes in unpredictable ways, or a simple file copy takes hours instead of minutes), run the Windows error-checking routines.

If you're an old hand at Windows (or an even older hand at DOS), you probably recognize the following steps as the venerable CHKDSK routine, in somewhat fancier clothing.

Book VI
Chapter 4

Follow these steps to run Check Disk:

1. **Bring up the drive you want to check in File Explorer. From the tiled Start screen, tap or click the Desktop tile. From the desktop, click the icon that looks like a file folder, down in the taskbar.**

2. **On the left, right-click the drive that's giving you problems and choose Properties.**

You see the Local Disk Properties dialog box.

3. **On the Tools tab, click the Check button, as shown in Figure 4-4.**

Windows may tell you that you don't need to scan the drive, as Windows hasn't found any errors on the drive. If you're skeptical, though, go right ahead.

4. **Tap or click Scan Drive.**

Windows tells you about any problems it encounters and asks for your permission to fix them.

Figure 4-4:
Run a Check
Disk.

Defragmenting a drive

Once upon a time, defragmenting your hard drive — instructing Windows to rearrange files on a hard drive so that the various parts of a file all sit next to one another — rated as a Real Big Deal. Windows didn't help automate running defrags, so few people bothered. As a result, drives started to look like patchwork quilts with pieces of files stored higgledy-piggledy. On the rare occasion that a Windows user ran the defragmenter, bringing all the pieces together could take hours — and the resulting system speed-up rarely raised any eyebrows, much less rocketed Windows fans into hyperthreaded bliss.

Windows 7 changed that by simply and quietly scheduling a disk defragmentation to run every week. Windows 8 continues in that proud tradition. To get defragmented, you don't need to touch a thing.

Windows doesn't run automatic defrags on SSDs, which is to say, flash memory drives that don't have any moving parts. SSDs don't need defragmentation. They also have a finite lifespan, so there's no need to overwork the drives with a senseless exercise in futility.

If you're curious about how your computer's doing in the defrag department, you can see the Defragmenter report this way:

1. **Bring up the Control Panel by tapping and holding (or right-clicking) in the bottom-left corner of the desktop, and choosing Control Panel.**

2. **Tap or click the link to System and Security. Then, under Administrative Tools, tap or click the link to Defragment and Optimize Your Drives.**

Windows shows you the Optimize Drives report, as shown in Figure 4-5.

3. **For a real-time analysis run, showing the fragmentation as of this moment, tap or click Analyze. To move files around into a more optimum ordering, click Optimize.**

4. **If you want to permanently change the schedule for automatic defragging, click Change Settings. When you're done, click Close.**

Defrags run automatically once a week unless you change the settings.

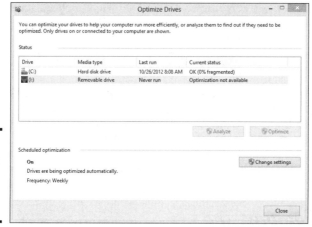

Figure 4-5:
A full report
of defrag-
menting
activities.

Maintaining Solid State Drives

SSDs are a completely different breed of cat. You don't want to run a Checkdisk on them, even if you could, because the results aren't conclusive and you'd end up over-working the SSDs. You certainly don't want to run a defrag because the drives are (depending on how you look at it) already defragmented and/or horrendously fragmented and there's no reason to change.

Most SSDs these days are made from NAND Flash memory, which is memory that doesn't lose its settings when the power's turned off. Although an SSD may fit into a hard drive slot, and behave much like a regular hard drive, the technology's completely different.

While the jury's still out on whether SSDs are *much* more reliable than hard disk drives (HDDs), just about everyone agrees they are more reliable. And there's absolutely no doubt that they're enormously faster. Change your C: drive over from a spinning platter to an SSD, and strap on your seat belt, Nelly.

SSDs have controllers that handle everything. Data isn't stored on SSDs the same way it's stored on HDDs, and many purpose-built hard drive tools don't work at all on SSDs. The controller has to take on all the housekeeping that just comes naturally with HDDs. For example, if you want to erase an HDD, you can format it or just delete all the files on it. If you want to erase an SSD, you should use the manufacturer's utilities, or data can be left behind. See the Computerworld article at `www.computerworld.com/s/article/9211519/Can_data_stored_on_an_SSD_be_secured_` for details.

Windows disables the Windows utilities known as Defrag, Superfetch, and ReadyBoost on SSDs — you should never see Windows offer to run a Defrag on an SSD, for example — and Windows startup works directly with the hardware during boot. That simultaneously makes the boot go faster and reduces unnecessary wear on the SSD.

If you have an SSD or get an SSD, you should drop by the manufacturer's website and pick up any utilities it may have for the care and feeding of the furious little buggers. Windows actually does a very good job of looking after them, but the manufacturer may have a few tricks up its sleeve. Intel's SSD Toolbox at `www.intel.com/support/go/ssdtoolbox/index.htm` is one of the better known utility packs, but you should only use it on Intel SSDs.

Zipping and Compressing

Windows supports two very different kinds of file compression. The distinction is confusing but important, so bear with me.

File compression reduces the size of a file by cleverly taking out parts of the contents of the file that aren't needed, storing only the minimum amount of information necessary to reconstitute the file — extract it — into its full, original form. A certain amount of overhead is involved because the computer has to take the time to squeeze extraneous information out of a file before storing it, and then the computer takes more time to restore the file to its original state when someone needs the file. But compression can reduce file sizes enormously. A compressed file often takes up half its original space — even less, in many cases.

How does compression work? That depends on the compression method you use. In one kind of compression, known as Huffman encoding, letters that occur frequently in a file (say, the letter *e* in a word-processing document) are massaged so that they take up only a little bit of room in the file, whereas letters that occur less frequently (say, *x*) are allowed to occupy lots of space. Rather than allocate eight 1s and 0s for every letter in a document, for example, some letters may take up only two 1s and 0s and others could take up 15. The net result, overall, is a big reduction in file size. It's complicated, and the mathematics involved get quite interesting.

The two Windows file compression techniques are:

✦ Files can be compressed and placed in a *Compressed (zipped) Folder.* The icon for a zipped folder, appropriately, has a zipper on it.

✦ Folders, or even entire drives, can be compressed by using the built-in compression capabilities of the Windows file system (NTFS).

Here's where things get complicated.

NT File System (NTFS) compression is built into the file system: You can use it only on NTFS drives, and the compression doesn't persist when you move (or copy) the file off the drive. Think of NTFS compression as a capability inherent to the hard drive itself. That isn't really the case — Windows does all the sleight-of-hand behind the scenes — but the concept can help you remember the limitations and quirks of NTFS compression.

Although Microsoft would have you believe that Compressed (zipped) Folder compression is based on folders, it isn't. A Compressed (zipped) Folder is really a file — *not* a folder — but it's a special kind of file, called a Zip file. If you ever encountered Zip files on the Internet (they have a .zip filename extension and are frequently manipulated by using programs such as my favorite 7Zip, www.7zip.com), you know exactly what I'm talking about. Zip files contain one or more compressed files, and they use the most common kind of compression found on the Internet. Think of Compressed (zipped) Folders as being Zip files, and if you have even a nodding acquaintance with Zips, you'll immediately understand the limitations and quirks of Compressed (zipped) Folders. Microsoft calls them Folders because that's supposed to be easier for users to understand. You be the judge.

If you have Windows show you filename extensions (see my rant about that topic in the section on showing filename extensions in Book VI, Chapter 1), you see immediately that Compressed (zipped) Folders are, in fact, simple Zip files.

Zipping is very common, particularly because it reduces the amount of data that needs to be transported from here to there. NTFS compression isn't nearly as common. It's more difficult, and hard drives have become so cheap there's rarely any need for most people to use it.

Table 4-1 shows a quick comparison of NTFS compression and Zip compression.

Table 4-1   NTFS Compression versus Compressed (Zipped) Folders Compression

NTFS	*Zip*
Think of NTFS compression as a feature of the hard drive itself.	Zip technology works on any file, regardless of where it is stored.
The minute you move an NTFS-compressed file off an NTFS drive (by, say, sending a file as an e-mail attachment), the file is uncompressed, automatically, and you can't do anything about it: You'll send a big, uncompressed file.	You can move a Compressed (zipped) Folder (it's a Zip file, with a `.zip` filename extension) anywhere, and it stays compressed. If you send a Zip file as an e-mail attachment, it goes over the Internet as a compressed file. The person who receives the file can view it directly in Windows, or use a product such as WinZip to see it.
A lot of overhead is associated with NTFS compression. Windows has to compress and decompress those files on the fly, and that sucks up processing power.	Very little overhead is associated with Zip files. Many programs (for example, antivirus programs) read Zip files directly.
NTFS compression is helpful if you're running out of room on an NTFS-formatted drive.	Compressed (zipped) Folders (that is to say, Zip files) are in a near-universal form that can be used just about anywhere.
You have to be using an Administrator account to use NTFS compression.	You can create, copy, or move Zip files just like any other files, with the same security restrictions.
You can use NTFS compression on entire drives, folders, or single files. They cannot be password protected.	You can zip files, folders, or (rarely) drives, and they can be password protected.

If you try to compress the drive that contains Windows itself (normally your c: drive), you can't compress the files that are in use by Windows.

Compressing with NTFS

To use NTFS compression on an entire drive, follow these steps:

1. **Make sure you're using an Administrator account.**

See Book II, Chapter 4.

2. **Bring up File Explorer. From the tiled Start screen, tap or click the Desktop tile. From the desktop, tap or click the icon on the desktop taskbar.**

3. **On the left, tap and hold (or right-click) the drive you want to compress. Choose Properties, then click the General tab.**

4. **Select the Compress This Drive to Save Disk Space check box. Then click the OK button.**

Windows asks you to confirm that you want to compress the entire drive. Windows takes some time to compress the drive; in some cases, the estimated time is measured in days. Good luck.

Book VI
Chapter 4

Maintaining Your System

To use NTFS compression on a folder, follow these steps:

1. **Make sure you're using an Administrator account.**

See Book II, Chapter 4.

2. **Bring up File Explorer. From the tiled Start screen, tap or click the Desktop tile. From the desktop, tap or click the File Explorer icon on the desktop taskbar.**

3. **On the left, tap and hold (or right-click) the folder you want to compress. Choose Properties, then click the Advanced button.**

4. **Select the Compress Contents to Save Disk Space check box. Then click the OK button.**

Windows asks you to confirm that you want to compress the folder. Unless the folder's enormous, it should compress in a few minutes.

To uncompress a folder, reopen the Advanced Properties dialog box (right-click the file or folder, choose Properties, and then click the Advanced button) and deselect the Compress Contents to Save Disk Space check box.

Zipping the easy way with Compressed (zipped) Folders

The easiest way to create a Zip file, er, a Compressed (zipped) Folder, is with a simple tap and hold (or right-click). Here's how:

1. **Navigate to the files you want to zip.**

If you're on the tiled Start screen, tap or click the Desktop tile. From the desktop, tap or click the File Explorer icon on the taskbar. Then move to wherever the files might be.

2. **Select the file or files that you want to zip together.**

You can tap and hold, or Ctrl+click to select individual files or Shift+click to select a bunch.

3. **Tap and hold (or right-click) any of the selected files and choose Send To⇨Compressed (Zipped) Folder.**

Windows responds by creating a new Zip file, with a `.zip` filename extension, and placing copies of the selected files inside the new Zip folder. File Explorer selects the file, and shows a context tab for Compressed Folder Tools, as shown in Figure 4-6.

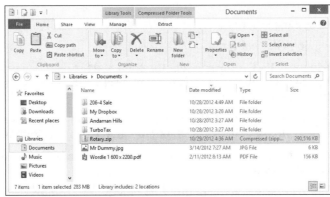

Figure 4-6: Click on a zip, and you get a context tab for Compressed Folder Tools.

The new file is just like any other file: You can rename it, copy it, move it, delete it, send it as an e-mail attachment, save it on the Internet, or do anything else to it that you can do to a file. That's because it *is* a file.

4. **To add another file to your Compressed (zipped) Folder, simply drag it onto the zipped folder icon.**

5. **To copy a file from your Zip file (uh, folder), double-click the zipped folder icon and treat the file the same way you would treat any "regular" file.**

6. **To copy all files out of your Zip file (folder), click the Extract tab on the File Explorer Ribbon.**

   From there you can choose the location, or click the Extract All icon to choose a location other than the ones offered.

By default, the Extract All icon recommends that you extract all the compressed files into a new folder with the same name as the Zip file, which confuses the living bewilickers out of everybody. Unless you give the extracted folder a different name from the original Compressed (zipped) Folder, you end up with two folders with precisely the same name sitting on your desktop. Do yourself a huge favor and feed the wizard a different folder name while you're extracting the files.

Chapter 5: Using Windows (Live) Essentials

In This Chapter

✔ Windows Live is dead, long live Windows Live!

✔ Beating the tiled programs with Windows Essentials

✔ Getting Windows Live

✔ Using Windows Live

I have good news and bad news.

The bad news: Windows Live, the hodge-podge bundle of unrelated programs and services that Microsoft clubbed together in one (actually, many) of its frequent re-branding exercises, is pretty much dead. While Windows Live Essentials were hyped as one of the great reasons to buy Windows 7, in Windows 8 they're going the way of the do-do. *Sic transit gloria computerii.*

The good news: Several of the Windows Live programs are considerably better than their Windows 8 tiled counterparts, in many respects, at least for now. Windows Live programs aren't going away. If you don't mind running orphaned programs on your desktop, a handful of Windows Live programs, in particular, are worth picking up.

Just as this book was going to press, Microsoft released two updated Windows Live programs — Photo Gallery and Movie Maker — and renamed the whole bundle. Where once we had Windows Live Essentials, we now have Windows Essentials, a ragtag collection of free downloadable programs consisting of: Windows Live Family Safety; Windows Live Mail; Windows Live Messenger; SkyDrive for Windows (neither live nor dead, presumably); Windows Movie Maker; Windows Photo Gallery (no Live on either); Windows Live Writer; and Microsoft Outlook Hotmail Connector.

Heaven only knows what Microsoft will rename its Hotmail connector, after the Outlook.com transition has taken over (see Book X, Chapter 4). I'm guessing it won't be called Microsoft Outlook Outlook.com Connector, but in the crazy world of Microsoft branding, it's hard to say.

Windows Essentials and Windows Live applications don't work worth beans on a touch-only tablet. They weren't designed for a touch interface, although they will work, if you have a very high tolerance for pain. Bottom line? Don't even try to install or use the Windows Live/Essentials apps unless you have a functioning keyboard and mouse.

Introducing the Applications and How They've Changed

Windows Live started in 2005 as a re-re-branding of some MSN applications and gradually took on new cloud features. Windows Live Hotmail, Windows Live SkyDrive, Windows Live Calendar, Windows Live Contacts, and Windows Live ID have almost nothing in common, except they all run in the cloud.

"Windows Live" as a brand took on greater prominence when Microsoft decided to pull many applications out of Windows, with the Vista deadlines imminent, and thrust them into a post-Vista-ship-date collection of down-loadable PC programs known as Windows Live Essentials. Such Windows apps as Windows Live Mail, Windows Live Messenger, Windows Live Movie Maker, and Windows Live Photo Gallery also have almost nothing in common, except they run on Windows and they're available for free download to any Windows customer.

Here's what happened to the old Windows Live apps:

✦ **Windows Live ID** (formerly known as Microsoft Wallet, Microsoft Passport, .Net Passport, and Microsoft Passport Network) has been rebranded Microsoft Your Account and referred to informally as your **Microsoft Account.** Your old Microsoft Live ID, typically an e-mail address that ends in @hotmail.com or @live.com, will still work, as will one of the new @outlook.com e-mail addresses. In addition, Microsoft now accepts *any* e-mail address as a Microsoft Account.

✦ **Windows Live Hotmail** (formerly Hotmail, Microsoft Hotmail, and MSN Hotmail) turned into **Hotmail**, once again, and is in the throes of changing to **Outlook.com**, which is very different from Hotmail. Soon, Microsoft assures us, Outlook.com will replace Hotmail entirely. I talk about Hotmail and Outlook.com in Book X, Chapter 4.

✦ **Windows Live SkyDrive** has turned into just plain **SkyDrive for Windows**. There are also SkyDrive variants for Mac, Windows Phone, iPad, and just about any other platform you could mention. Parts of Ray Ozzie's **Windows Live Mesh** (formerly Live Mesh, Windows Live Sync, and Windows Live FolderShare) have been folded into SkyDrive, although Microsoft has squashed PC-to-PC sync. In Windows 8, you can use the tiled SkyDrive app, which I talk about in Book IV, Chapter 4. Or you can access SkyDrive (`www.skydrive.com`) directly through any web browser.

✦ **Windows Live Messenger** sits perched in a particularly precarious position, with Lync on one side and Microsoft Skype on the other. It's been integrated in various degrees into all sorts of sites and apps, including Internet Explorer, Outlook.com and its predecessor Hotmail, SkyDrive, Facebook, MySpace, LinkedIn, the Windows 8 tiled Photos app, Bing, Xbox Live, Windows Phone, and the Zune (which is also biting the dust). Windows Live Messenger is also available for iPhone and iPad from the Apple App Store. While there's a separate tile on the Start screen for Messaging, expect to see Windows Live Messenger show up in all sorts of additional places — without the "Windows Live" part.

✦ **Windows Live Photo Gallery** gained a couple of minor features and is now known as **Windows Photo Gallery**. While Microsoft would love it if everyone would use its Windows 8 tiled Photos app, there's absolutely no question that Windows Photo Gallery runs rings around tiled Photos, if you want to do anything at all with your photos besides just look at them.

✦ **Windows Live Movie Maker**, quite surprisingly, received a major upgrade to become **Windows Movie Maker**. In several *Windows All-In-One For Dummies* books, I've traced the way Movie Maker has gone from pretty good to absolutely awful. Microsoft cut many important features, and just didn't bother to put them back in as it "upgraded" the product. The new, improved, Windows Movie Maker for 2012 has all its old features back, and several impressive new ones to boot. If you ever work with video — even if you only string together clips of your summer vacation — this new Windows Movie Maker is worth a look.

In case you were wondering, the Windows 8 tiled Video app lets you play videos and encourages you to buy more. It doesn't lift a finger to help you make videos.

✦ Then we have all the old Windows Live apps that are slowly (and in some cases, not very successfully) morphing into tiled apps. **Windows Live Mail** gets neglected because its younger cousin the Windows 8 tiled Mail app needs all the attention. **Windows Live Calendar** becomes, more or less, the tiled Calendar; **Windows Live Contacts** turns into the tiled People program.

Windows Essentials apps are still around and available for download from Microsoft, and they're going to be running for many years. That leaves you, the Windows 8 customer, in an enviable position: You can pick and choose which apps you want to use, and which to let stew until Microsoft makes them better.

Microsoft likely will keep improving its tiled apps until they approach, and then supersede, the Windows Essentials apps in terms of functions. But you get to decide if you prefer the Windows Essentials way of doing things, or if you're ready to jump to the tiled side.

People I know who are straddling the tiled and Legacy sides of the fence mention three Windows Essentials apps that are still appealing, in spite of the tiled app candy:

✦ **Windows Live Mail:** The tiled Mail app still won't do much of what advanced Windows Live Mail users want, so they'd rather stick with the devil they know.

✦ **Windows Photo Gallery:** Windows 8's tiled Photos is getting better, but it still doesn't have any of the tools or the user interface that good old Windows Photo Gallery has.

✦ **Windows Movie Maker:** Never one of the most popular Live apps, Windows Movie Maker occupies a unique niche. The tiled Video app is all about selling videos to Windows users. Movie Maker concentrates on letting you build your own.

In the rest of this chapter, I take quick looks at all three of those Essentials apps, starting with an explanation about how to download and install any or all of them with Windows 8.

Getting the Windows Essentials Apps

Want to install a couple of Live-ly ones? Here's how to get the Windows Essentials you want, and let the others sit and stew:

1. **Start your favorite web browser and go to** `download.live.com`**.**

Any browser will do, either on the tiled side, or desktop style.

2. **Click the Download Now button at the lower right.**

Your browser downloads `wlsetup-web.exe`, which is the Windows Live setup program.

3. **Double-click the installer or do whatever you need to do (depending on your browser) to run it.**

4. **When the Windows Essentials 2012 installer asks if you want to install all the Windows Essentials (Recommended), click Choose the Programs You Want to Install.**

You see the program list shown in Figure 5-1.

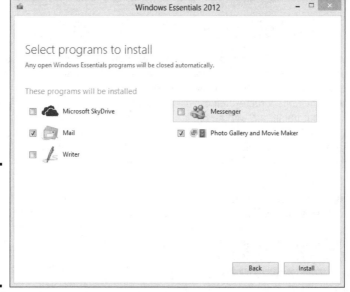

Figure 5-1:
Pick the
Windows
Essentials
programs
you want to
install.

5. **Take a look at the list in the first section of this chapter and choose the Windows Essentials programs that strike your fancy. Click Install.**

   I choose Photo Gallery and Movie Maker (which is one check box because they have to be installed together) and Mail, being very careful to deselect the other boxes.

   The Windows Essentials Installer churns away for a while, and then comes back with a simple message that tells you to click Done, to get going with the programs.

Windows, in its inimitable way, sticks new tiles on your Start screen, one for each of the new applications that you've installed — and the tiles, as usual, go all the way over on the right. It doesn't put anything on your desktop, so in order to start the apps, you have to flip over to the tiled Start screen or modify your taskbar so you can open the programs from the desktop. Book VI, Chapter 2 explains how to beef up your taskbar.

Personally, I use the apps all the time, so I hop over to the Start screen (possibly by pressing the Windows key), drag the tiles over to a more prominent location, then, one by one, right-click each tile and choose Pin to Taskbar.

E-mail client, POP3, and bafflegab

Keeping up with all the e-mail buzzwords is difficult. Here's a quick list that should get you through the major twists and turns of installing and using an *e-mail client* (an e-mail program that runs on your computer) and getting it to retrieve your mail. These terms apply to all e-mail clients, even the tiled Windows 8 Mail app, although tiled Mail tends to hide things.

In a traditional e-mail client, you type a message, list which addresses you want to receive the message, and then send it. When your computer sends the message, it connects to a specific kind of computer attached to the Internet: a *Simple Mail Transfer Protocol (SMTP) server*. The SMTP server is responsible for putting the message onto the Internet, destined for its intended recipient(s).

The Internet routes messages based on the recipients' e-mail addresses. The last part of your e-mail address — the part after the @ sign — is your domain name. In Woody@ AskWoody.com (yes, that's my e-mail address; no, capitalization doesn't matter), AskWoody. com is my domain name. A message sent to me ends up on a particular kind of computer, a *Post Office Protocol 3 (POP3) server* that is tasked with handling messages sent to AskWoody.com.

When you tell your computer that you want to receive messages, it goes out to your POP3 server and downloads all the messages waiting for you in its queue.

Attachments to messages (pictures, files, and so on) travel as text, and your e-mail client (or the web program you use to send and receive mail) takes care of the details using the specific set of rules named *Multipurpose Internet Mail Extensions (MIME)*.

Using Windows Live Mail

Most people know Windows Live Mail as the progeny of the venerable, if quirky Outlook Express.

Choosing an e-mail program

No, you can't use Outlook Express with Windows 8.

Q: What happened to Outlook Express?

A: Oh, it went away a long time ago. Outlook Express was the free e-mail program that shipped in Windows XP. It's kaput. Bygones.

Q: What happened to Windows Mail?

A: It disappeared, too. Windows Mail was a barely warmed-over minor upgrade to Outlook Express. Microsoft shipped Windows Mail as the free e-mail program in Windows Vista. But Microsoft forgot about Windows Mail shortly after it shipped. Orphaned. Abandoned at birth.

Q: So what do we do now, Ollie?

A: If you want to continue to use a desktop e-mail program with quite a few features, Windows Live Mail is a good choice. For Windows 8 users, the tiled Mail app is shaping up to be pretty capable, but the jury's still out on whether the features will match Windows Live Mail, and whether using the tiled Mail with a mouse will ever get to be comparable to Windows Live Mail.

Windows Live Mail pulls mail down and stores it on your computer. Windows Live Mail gobbles up mail sent to your e-mail address, whatever your address may be, using traditional Internet e-mail computers (POP3 servers). It can also grab mail from Hotmail/Outlook.com, Google's Gmail, Yahoo! Mail, and many other online mail services.

Of course, if you want to spend some money, Microsoft has offered Outlook for ages; it's part of Microsoft Office. If you're willing to go online for e-mail, look at Hotmail/Outlook.com (Book X, Chapter 4), Gmail (Book X, Chapter 3), and Yahoo! Mail. And then there's Outlook Web Apps. . . The last time I counted, Microsoft was supporting ten very different e-mail programs.

E-mail alternatives

You have three good reasons to use Windows Live Mail: inertia, inertia, and inertia. All the other reasons aren't convincing. If you have a touch tablet, Windows 8's tiled Mail is a strong contender, and it's getting better. If you're stuck with Windows Live Mail because you have a big collection of old Outlook Express (OE) or Windows Mail (WM) messages, you have my sympathies. If you want to stick with Windows Live Mail because it looks and acts like OE or WM, at least at first glance, I s'pose that's a reasonable fear, er, justification.

But if you're willing to look beyond the tiled Mail, Windows Live Mail, Outlook Express, and Windows Mail, you have all sorts of good options.

Online mail providers (Gmail — see Book VI, Chapter 3; Hotmail/Outlook.com — Book VI, Chapter 4; and Yahoo! Mail) work great if you're usually near a reliable Internet connection.

Mozilla Thunderbird (`Mozilla.org/ thunderbird`) is a free, open-source e-mail

program that particularly appeals to old (and I do mean old) Eudora users.

In my experience, people who rely on e-mail, and want to keep their mail on their own computers, ultimately gravitate to Outlook. I know that's a heretical observation, but it's true. Outlook combines hyperactive spam filtering and so-so antiphishing technology with the kind of industrial strength that many e-mail addicts need. It's also surprisingly easy to use — at least, the common e-mail actions are easy to find and run. The big downside? Outlook is expensive, and many people (present company included) have problems with it hanging from time to time.

I've run Outlook since the dawn of recorded time (or Office 4.1, whichever came first), and I've just recently made the switch to Gmail. It works — and for me, Gmail works better than Outlook 2010.

Running Windows Live Mail

If you've installed Windows Live Mail and want to run it for the first time, take these steps — and precautions:

1. **Start Windows Live Mail by tapping or clicking on the Start menu tile or, if you followed my advice, by clicking on the Windows Live Mail icon on the desktop taskbar.**

   There's a good chance WLM will come back at you with a request to download and install .NET Framework 3.5. If requested, do so. (Windows 8 ships with .NET Framework 4.5, but some Windows Live programs require the earlier version, .NET Framework 3.5.)

   WLM whizzes and gurgles for a bit and then shows you the Add Your Email Accounts dialog box, shown in Figure 5-2.

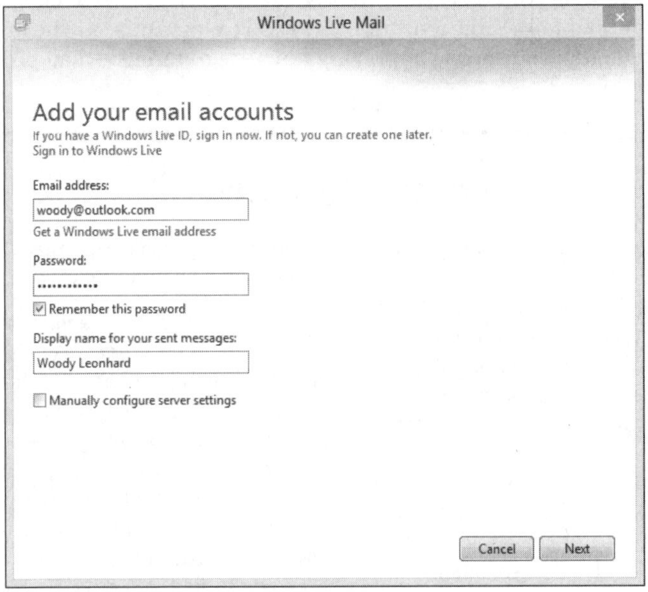

Figure 5-2:
If you have a @hotmail.com or @live.com or @outlook.com ID, type it here to connect.

> ### Windows Live Mail
>
> ### Add your email accounts
> If you have a Windows Live ID, sign in now. If not, you can create one later.
> Sign in to Windows Live
>
> Email address:
> woody@outlook.com
> Get a Windows Live email address
>
> Password:
> ············
> ☑ Remember this password
>
> Display name for your sent messages:
> Woody Leonhard
>
> ☐ Manually configure server settings
>
> [Cancel] [Next]

2. **If you have a Hotmail/Outlook.com account and you want to use Windows Live Mail to access that account, click or tap the line that says Sign in to Windows Live. Fill in the information from your Hotmail account. Click Sign In.**

   Note that you have to fill in your account information, even if you've logged on to Windows with a Microsoft account. Windows isn't smart enough to fill it in for you.

Starting with a Hotmail/Outlook.com account is a quick and easy way to get going with Windows Live Mail: WLM understands Hotmail/Outlook. com, and you don't have to futz with any settings.

On the other hand, you may want to use a conventional e-mail account, in which case you need to fill out the details (see the earlier sidebar, "E-mail client, POP3, and bafflegab"). Your Internet service provider (ISP) should've given you all that information.

If you set up a @hotmail.com or @live.com or @outlook.com account, WLM downloads your messages and shows them to you, as in Figure 5-3.

Book VI Chapter 5

Mail folders   Ribbon changes depending on which tab you click

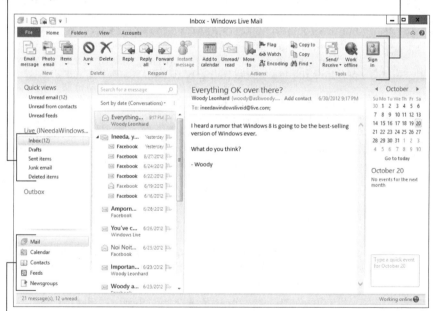

Using Windows (Live) Essentials

Figure 5-3:
Connecting to a Hotmail/ Outlook.com account is two-step easy.

Switch to a different program

You're ready to read, write, send, and receive, so you may as well.

See the next section for details.

You may want to use Windows Live Mail to read your RSS Feeds, but I greatly prefer iGoogle, which is trivially easy to hook up with Chrome or any other web browser (see Book VI, Chapter 6 for details).

Adding e-mail accounts

If you grew up with e-mail, you're lucky. Windows Live Mail should behave more or less the way you expect. If you were born before, oh, 1990, you may not be so adept. This section scratches the surface of what there is to know about e-mail. It should suffice to get you started on the right foot.

The process of setting up mail accounts — and you can set up dozens, if you choose — is a simple one. Get your accounts in order and you're free to create, send, and receive e-mail messages at will. Or to Will.

How many e-mail accounts do you need? Many people have several e-mail addresses — perhaps one for work, one for school, and one for personal use.

I strongly recommend that you not add e-mail accounts for several people in Windows Live Mail. You can add a hundred accounts for yourself, but the minute you add an account for your significant other or your kids or your parents, things get sticky — not just because you all find yourselves reading each other's mail, but because replying, deleting, and forwarding other people's mail gets real hairy, real fast.

If more than one person is using Windows Live Mail, set up a separate Windows account for each person (see Book II, Chapter 4). It doesn't matter if you use Microsoft accounts or Local accounts, just get one account for each person. That way, even if you don't put passwords on the accounts, you can keep the mail sorted out automatically. Little Billy won't accidentally delete Daddy's notification about winning the Irish lottery. Little Melinda won't accidentally leave her love letter in the family Sent Items folder.

To add other e-mail accounts or modify your existing one, follow these steps:

1. **Start Windows Live Mail (probably by clicking the icon on the desktop taskbar, or the tile on the Start screen). When you get there, click the Accounts tab.**

You see the Accounts Ribbon, as shown in Figure 5-4.

Figure 5-4:
The Accounts Ribbon makes adding other e-mail addresses easy.

Click here to add an e-mail account

2. **On the left, click the Email icon.**

   Windows Live Mail shows you the Add Your Email Accounts dialog box, shown in Figure 5-5.

Figure 5-5:
Add just
about any
e-mail
address and
Windows
Live Mail
will handle it.

3. **Fill in the dialog box fields and click Next.**

   Microsoft has a big database of domain names (that's the part of your e-mail address to the right of the @ sign) and if your domain is in that big database, Windows Live Mail can guess at all the settings necessary to set up e-mail service.

4. **If Microsoft can't find the settings for your domain, you see a dialog box that says Configure Server Settings. Using information from your e-mail service provider, fill it out and click Next.**

   Unfortunately, the only place you can find that info is from the people you pay to handle your e-mail.

5. **If you got all the settings right, WLM tells you that it has added your new e-mail account. Click Finish.**

   The mail from your new account appears in a second group of folders on the left.

In case you're wondering, Windows Live Mail doesn't remove any messages from where they're stored "in the cloud." So, for example, if you put your Gmail address in Windows Live Mail, and use WLM to look at your Gmail, you can still log on to Gmail and all your mail will be there.

Someday it'll be easy to set up e-mail accounts. That day hasn't arrived yet.

Creating a message

When you're ready to create a message, follow these steps:

1. **Start Windows Live Mail and click the Home tab. On the left edge of the Home Ribbon, click Email Message.**

   A message window appears, as shown in Figure 5-6, so that you can type your message.

Figure 5-6:
Writing
a new
message.

2. **Choose the recipient for the message.**

   You can enter the person's e-mail address in two different ways:

   • Type the e-mail address on the To line.

   • Click the To... text and select the recipient you want from the Address Book. (To select a recipient, select the contact from the list on the left, click the To button, and then click OK.)

   Note that this is your Hotmail address book, which may or may not be connected to your Windows 8 tiled People app.

3. **Enter a subject for your message. For best results, keep it fairly short and make it descriptive. Then type the body of your message.**

   You have a wide-open space to do just that. You can enter the words the way you want them without any fancy formatting, or you can change the look of the text by choosing a different font and size, changing colors, indenting information, and more.

4. **If you have more than one e-mail account, make sure, on the right, that you have selected the correct account to send the message. Then click Send.**

   You can wait for Windows Live Mail to automatically send the message, a minute or two down the line, or you can click the Send/Receive icon on the Home Ribbon and it is sent immediately.

That should get you started.

Managing Windows Photo Gallery

Remember that photo I took of Dad falling out of the fishing boat? You know, the one from 1998? Or was it 1996? Wait a sec. Gimme a minute. I have it right here. Uh, no, it must be over here. Hmmm, maybe it's in this folder down here. Is it on the network drive? Er, where in the %$#@! did I put that thing?

As this book went to press, the tiled style app called Photos was fancy and glitzy, brought together photos from all over the place, including SkyDrive, and didn't have even rudimentary controls for handling large numbers of pictures. The editing capabilities barely extend beyond the Cro-Magnon level. Compared to the iPad's iPhoto, Microsoft's tiled Photo is just plain embarrassing. You can read about it in Book IV, Chapter 3.

Of course, Microsoft is good at plowing resources into a faltering product if there's a profit to be made, so the Windows 8 tiled Photos app will get better. Until it does, you have a very good alternative, over on the desktop side of the fence.

Windows Photo Gallery brings a handful of sophisticated tools to the thorny problems of gathering, fixing, and, most of all, finding pictures on your computer.

Unfortunately, WPG (as it's known to its friends) can't read your mind. If you want to retrieve that shot of Dad falling out of the fishing boat, you need to tag (mark) the picture with some pertinent keywords that you can later find. I don't know about you, but it'd take me a year or two to go through all my old shots and sort them out. By the time I was done, I'd have to start all over again with new shots. Like the hare versus the tortoise, I'd probably never finish.

That's the fundamental problem with the fancy WPG indexing methods — indeed, with indexing anything. Windows Photo Gallery can't create indexes out of thin air. You have to do the work before you can reap the rewards — and it's debatable whether all the time you might invest in cataloging your pictures will ever pay off.

You have to put the garbage in before you can take it out, eh?

Picasa does many of the same things as WPG: Organizing, viewing, touching up large numbers of photos stored on your PC. When people ask me which is better — Windows Photo Gallery or Picasa — I ask them, "What week is it?" Features in both programs change constantly: When either Photo Gallery or Picasa runs out ahead with a new feature, the other catches up within a month or two. One of these days the tiled Photos app will be in the running, too.

Some people prefer storing their pictures on the Internet, where they're easy to share with other people. Flickr has an enormous array of tools for improving, storing, and retrieving pictures. If that sounds like something you'd like to do, check out Flickr in Book V, Chapter 3.

Leafing through the Gallery

Here's how to get started with Windows Photo Gallery for the first time:

1. **Once you've installed it (see the earlier section, "Getting the Windows Essential Apps"), start Windows Photo Gallery either by tapping or clicking on the Windows Photo Gallery tile on the Start menu or (if you took my advice) by clicking on the Windows Photo Gallery icon on the taskbar.**

   The first time you start WPG, it may ask if you want to use WPG to open files of the following types: JPG, TIF, JXR, PNG, WDP, BMP, and ICO. Those are filename extensions. (In Book VI, Chapter 1, I explain why it's important to be able to see filename extensions. Here's one more example.)

2. **You probably do want WPG to take over those file types, so if you see the notification, click Yes.**

   See Table 5-1 for a comparison of the relative merits of the different file types.

   You may also be asked for your Windows Live ID. If so, sign in, so you can access your SkyDrive photos.

   WPG scans your Pictures and Videos libraries and shows you thumbnails of both in the main window, as shown in Figure 5-7.

Figure 5-7: The main window for WPG.

The WPG development team likes to say that Windows Photo Gallery is designed to store your "digital memories." Gag me with a RAMDAC. What they're really saying is that Windows Photo Gallery works with only the kinds of picture files that are commonly produced by digital cameras — JPG and MPG (and to a lesser extent, TIF) files. You can use RAW format pictures, but only if the camera manufacturer has a program (a *codec*) that can pass them on to WPG. You can't use Photo Gallery to modify GIF, PCX, or WMF files — another reason why it's important to have Windows show your filename extensions (see Book VI, Chapter 1).

3. **You can have WPG show you more or less of the gallery in the ways you would expect, by hopping through the navigation pane on the left: Click, oh, Public Pictures, and WPG shows you only the pictures in the \Public\Pictures folder.**

4. **To edit a still photo, double-click it.**

   WPG shows the photo all by itself, and brings up the Edit Ribbon, as shown in Figure 5-8. See the section "Touching up pictures," later in this chapter.

   If you want to edit a file that's in a format WPG can't edit (for example, GIF or BMP), double-click the file to go into single picture view and tap or click the icon Make a Copy. Windows Photo Gallery lets you save the file in JPG, TIF, or WDP format, all of which are editable in WPG.

   When you're done with the picture, click the big red "X" icon in the upper-right corner that's marked Close File. You go back to the main window (refer to Figure 5-7).

Figure 5-8:
Edit a single picture with WPG's extensive tools.

5. **To view, but not edit, a video, double-click it.**

   WPG shows you the video, with simple tools to start and stop, tag, and delete. If you want to edit your video, you need Windows Movie Maker, which may or may not work — the subject of the next section in this chapter.

6. **When you're done, click the "X" in the upper-right corner to exit WLMP.**

Table 5-1		File Types That WPG Can Handle
Filename Extension	*Relative File Size*	*Description*
JPG	1MB	When you take photos on a camera, they're usually created in JPG format. JPG is *lossy,* which means that this kind of file can be manipulated by the computer (or camera) to make it smaller, even though the quality suffers. If you edit and re-edit a JPG file, the quality of the file may decrease substantially.
TIF	10MB	This *lossless* format is almost universal. Its file sizes are big, but the quality never changes. It's commonly used for scans and archive and fax files.
PNG	6MB	The PNG (pronounced "ping") lossless format is easier to compress than TIF, but it isn't as universally recognized: Many programs can't handle PNG. In fact, WPG can show you PNG files, but it won't help you edit them.
WDP or HDP	Varies	Windows Media Photo, also known as WMPhoto or HD Photo, is a Microsoft proprietary format that can be lossy or lossless. It isn't widely used.
BMP	10MB	The Windows bitmap is lossless and used mostly for screen shots nowadays. WPG can show you BMP files, but it won't help you edit them.
ICO	N/A	Windows icon files typically contain many icons. Windows Live Picture Gallery can "handle" them — in the sense that you can double-click an ICO file and WPG steps you through all the icons in the file. WPG doesn't show the file in the Gallery, though, and it doesn't help you edit the icons.

Adding photos to Photo Gallery

Any pictures or videos that you add to your PC's Pictures or Videos Libraries will get picked up by WPG automatically. So if you want to add photos or videos to WPG, you only need to figure out a way to get them into your Pictures or Videos Libraries.

Although there are sneaky ways to get photos and videos into the Libraries, most people will use one of two methods:

✦ Use File Explorer to copy or move a picture (JPG, TIF, JXR, PNG, WDP, BMP, or ICO file) or video (ASF, AVI, MPEG, MPG, MP4, WMV, MOV) to one of the Libraries.

✦ Use WPG's Picture and Video Import program to pull them off a camera, phone, tablet, or sufficiently advanced toaster oven and add them to the Photo Gallery automatically.

Here's how to import pictures using WPG:

1. **Attach your camera, phone, tablet, camera-equipped toaster oven, or car to your PC, using a USB cable.**

Bluetooth works, too. Sometimes. Alternatively you can take the SD card or other memory card out of your camera and put it in the PC, if you have an SD card reader.

If everything works according to plan, a "toaster" notification appears in the upper-right and invites you to tap (or click) the notification to choose what to do. If you see a notification like that, click or tap it, and choose View Pictures/Photo Gallery.

2. **If you aren't in WPG yet, start it. You end up on the main window (refer to Figure 5-7) with the Home ribbon visible. On the left of the Home ribbon, click Import.**

The Import Photos and Videos app appears, as in Figure 5-9.

Figure 5-9:
WPG will bring in photos and videos, optionally tag them, and put them in your Pictures or Videos Libraries.

3. **Select the Review, Organize, and Group Items to Import option and click Next.**

   The Import app looks at the time and date stamps on the pictures and groups them into suggested folders, based on when you took the pictures. Click and type in names for each of the folders, and optionally add tags by clicking the Add Tags link.

   If you don't like the way the import program breaks up your pictures into groups, you can change the sensitivity of the time grouping by moving the Adjust Groups slider in the lower-right corner.

4. **When your pictures are grouped and tagged appropriately, click Import.**

   The pictures are put in separate folders inside your Pictures folder; similarly, videos go in your Videos folder.

   You can optionally have the Import app delete the pictures and videos as they're being imported.

   Selecting the Delete Files from Device After Importing box requires a small leap of faith, but after you use the Import Pictures and Videos program a couple of times, you'll probably let Windows do the deleting. If something goes bump in the night and you accidentally delete photos on your camera memory card, don't panic. File undelete programs such as Recuva (see Book X, Chapter 5) take advantage of the fact that the data (your picture) isn't deleted until the camera needs to re-use the space on the memory card. With a bit of luck, you can recover pictures that you took a long, long time ago.

5. **Move the pictures around using File Explorer, if you like.**

   They're files. Treat them as such.

Tagging pictures

If you've spent more than ten minutes looking for a photo, you already know that browsing for pictures based on their location on disk can drive you nuts in no time. That's why tags were invented.

When you tag your pictures, the Photo Gallery keeps an index that makes it lightning-quick to find any pic with the specific tag. The problem, of course, is that you have to type a tag or two or three before Photo Gallery has anything to find.

Windows Photo Gallery draws a distinction between *people tags, geo tags,* and *descriptive tags.* It's a useful distinction, as you can see later in this section, but don't let the distinction fool you. Deep down at heart, a people tag or a geo tag is a descriptive tag, where the tag is just the name of the person or the location.

Say you took a picture of your dad falling out of a fishing boat at Lake Isabella. You might want to tag the picture with a people tag of *George* (hey, that's my dad's name), a geo tag of *Kern County,* and, oh, *fishing* and *boat.* After you tag a hundred thousand pictures or so, you can tell Photo Gallery to show all pics that have the name tag *George* or the geo tag *Kern County* or the descriptive tag *boat* and narrow your choices considerably.

To add a tag to a picture or group of pictures, follow these steps:

1. **Start WPG.**

   The Home Ribbon should be showing.

2. **At the top, in the Ribbon, tap or click the Descriptive Tag item. Then select the pictures you want to tag.**

   To give a bunch of pictures the same tag or tags, hold down Ctrl while clicking each picture. Alternatively, if the pictures are contiguous (one after another), you can click the first picture, hold down Shift, and click the last picture, or you can "lasso" them by clicking and dragging a box over the pictures you want to select.

   WPG shows selected pictures with a shaded border around them, as shown in Figure 5-10.

Figure 5-10:
Tagging
pictures of
Yangon's
Shwedagon
Pagoda.

3. **In the pane on the right, click Add Geotag under the Geotag heading (or People Tag or Descriptive Tags), type the tag you want to add, and press Enter.**

   You can separate tags with spaces to give a particular picture or video multiple tags.

Tags that you assign to a picture travel with the picture. Say you tag a photo as George, fishing, and boat, and send a copy of the picture to your brother, and your brother then puts the picture in his Pictures folder. The tags will travel with the photo, and he can use Windows Photo Gallery to find the picture by using any of the tags.

Windows Photo Gallery has several advanced features, one of which — face recognition — can be a huge help in tagging. To use it, click the Find tab, and click the down arrow next to the People icon. Choose All Detected But Not Tagged (see Figure 5-11). Wait a minute or two, and WPG will show you all the pictures that contain faces WPG has detected, but doesn't have People tags associated.

Figure 5-11: WPG can scan for faces that it hasn't yet tagged with a name.

On the right, set up tags for the people (or take them from one of your Windows 8 tiled People app contacts list). After you've done a few, you'll find that WPG can recognize some people, and recommend the correct name to go with the picture.

Scary.

Finding a tagged picture

If your tags are in good shape, Windows Photo Gallery can find the tagged pictures in a split second. Here's how:

1. **Bring up Windows Photo Gallery. Click on the Find tab.**

   You see the Find options shown at the top of Figure 5-12.

Figure 5-12:
WPG's
extensive
Find
capabilities
can search
on all sorts
of criteria —
even, as in
this case, on
a person's
face.

2. **To find a person, select the person's picture in the People box.**

   The "detected" people are ones who match the physical characteristics of the ones you've identified by tagging.

3. **To find any kind of tag (including a People tag), click the Text Search icon on the right, and type the search criteria in the Search box.**

   If you type more than one tag, Photo Gallery retrieves all pictures that match any of the tags — in Boolean terms, the search is an AND search (such as find `George` AND `fishing` AND `boat`).

   WPG looks for the text in any form: People tags, Geo tags, Captions, regular Descriptive tags — even file or folder names.

   Typing on the search bar performs a search only on items that you can see. For example, if you're viewing items tagged `George` and you search for `Rubye`, you see only results tagged with both `George` and `Rubye`.

   If you assign a first and last name to a People tag, you can search on either or both. So if you have a photo tagged `Snidely Whiplash`, and do a text search, that photo will appear in the results for both `Snidely` and `Whiplash`.

Touching up pictures

Windows Photo Gallery offers a small set of the most-used photo touch-up tools, specifically designed to be easy to use and not particularly intimidating — or powerful. You may find them useful, especially if you don't have a more capable program at hand.

There's red in your eye

That devilish glint of red in a photographed eye arises because your camera's flash happened so quickly that the pupil didn't have a chance to contract. Light from the flash gets focused by the eye's lens onto the retina, at the back of the eye. The lens then focuses the light back to the camera. All the blood in the retina results in a vivid red color.

Animals get red-eye, too. Pictures of cats can have red-eye, but it's usually green because of a coating in cats' eyes.

Most modern cameras have red-eye reduction modes that cause the flash to go off multiple times before the real picture is taken. Those preliminary blasts suffice to constrict the pupil.

Red-eye occurs only when the flash goes straight into the eye and straight back. If you have a lot of problems with red-eye, try to bounce your flash. That is, aim the flash at the ceiling or a wall. Another trick: Have the person look away from the camera.

Many picture-editing programs change a picture permanently: Once you change a picture and save it, you can't go back. WPG is smarter than that. It keeps a copy of your original picture in its Original Photos folder, which is located at `C:\Users\<name>\AppData\Local\Microsoft\Windows Photo Gallery\Original Images`. If you ever want to revert to the original picture, on the Edit Ribbon, tap or click Revert to Original.

Here's how to safely and effectively touch up your pictures:

1. **In WPG, double-click the picture you want to edit.**

You see a full-size rendition of the picture, and the Edit Ribbon, as shown in Figure 5-13.

2. **To let WPG try to adjust everything on its own, click the Auto Adjust icon.**

Windows Photo Gallery analyzes the picture and automatically adjusts the brightness, contrast, and color. It also straightens the photo, if it seems a little skewed.

If you don't like what WPG did to your picture, click the tiny Undo icon up at the top.

To undo, click here

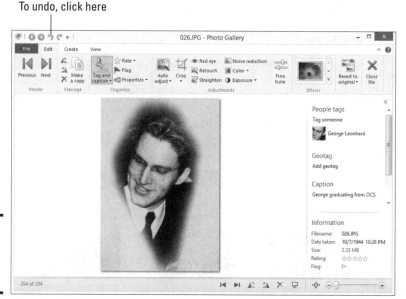

Book VI
Chapter 5

Using Windows
(Live) Essentials

Figure 5-13:
The picture
is ready for
editing.

3. **Choose from the appropriate buttons to crop, adjust red-eye, retouch, straighten, or futz with the color or contrast.**

   To get the most accurate red-eye correction, you usually need to zoom in so that you can pick out the devilish eye. To do so, click and drag the slider in the lower-right corner of the window. Then hold down Alt while you click and drag the picture, moving it around so that you can reach the eye. When you have the eye in, uh, sight, release Alt and click and drag a box around the eye. Make the box as small as you can while still getting all the red. Release the mouse button, and Windows Live does its level best to get the red out. See the sidebar, "There's red in your eye," for more about preventing red-eye.

4. **When you're done, click the "X" Close File icon on the right of the Ribbon.**

   Remember you can always bring back your original picture by opening it, and clicking Revert to Original.

Planning panoramas and fuses

Have you ever taken a series of shots, side by side, trying to convey the vastness of a scene? Have you ever taken a bunch of group photos where Billy's blinking in one shot, Melinda's blinking in another, and little Stevie's sticking out his tongue in the third? Windows Photo Gallery can "stitch" side-by-side shots, tying them together automatically into a panorama, or meld the shots together with Photo Fuse to bring out the best. It's so easy that you won't believe your eyes.

Here's how to stitch together a bunch of photos into a panorama:

1. Get the photos into your Pictures Library, so WPG can get to them.

In Figure 5-14, I import five photos, taken from left to right, from my office balcony.

Figure 5-14:
Five photos, taken from left to right, from my office in Patong.

2. Select the photos that you want WPG to use to create a panorama.

In this case, I press Ctrl+A and select all five shots.

3. On the Create Ribbon, click the icon for Panorama.

WPG stitches the pictures together, then asks you for a filename for the stitched result.

4. WPG creates the new picture and saves it with the filename you specify.

See the result in Figure 5-15.

Mechanically, Photo Fuse works exactly the same way: Choose the photos, go to the Create Ribbon, and choose Photo Fuse. WPG steps you through choosing which of the different pieces look better (so, for example, you can say you don't want Billy's blinking eyes). In the end, give the result a file-name and it's all put together.

Figure 5-15:
The stitched panorama of the five photos in Figure 5-14.

Panning Windows Movie Maker

The Windows 8 tiled Photos app should, some day, be as capable as Windows Photo Gallery. Unfortunately, it isn't at all clear if Microsoft is going to beef up tiled Photos or tiled Video to the point that it can supplant Windows Movie Maker. Right now, tiled Video only looks like an excuse for Microsoft to sell you movies. Although it can play videos in your Videos Library, that only seems to be a come-on to get you to spend money on the Microsoft Video Store.

The latest version of Windows Movie Maker has several worthwhile features. But don't let your Apple-fan friends see WMM. They'll probably want to show you iMovie, and it'll absolutely ruin your day.

If you need a video editor with more oomph, check out Adobe Premiere Elements, which costs around $75 and offers all the capabilities an amateur videographer might need. For help using the program, turn to *Adobe Premiere Elements For Dummies,* by Keith Underdahl.

That said, for a rudimentary video-editing app that connects very easily with YouTube, Facebook, Flickr, and Vimeo, Windows Movie Maker ain't bad. It works in a widely-recognized file format known as H.264. The new Video Stabilization feature works a treat, if your camera doesn't have built-in stabilization. (Most recent cameras do, but phones and small cameras don't.)

Windows Movie Maker also has extensive sound over-dubbing capabilities, with a full, independent narrator track and easy hooks into AudioMicro, Free Music Archive, and Vimeo Music Store to make it easier to find (and perhaps buy) music usage rights — a must if you're going to upload your video to YouTube.

When you install Windows Photo Gallery, Windows Movie Maker comes along for the ride.

Chapter 6: Choosing and Using a Desktop Web Browser

In This Chapter

✔ Evaluating desktop browsers — the good, the bad, and the ugly

✔ Choosing among the browsers on offer

✔ Customizing Internet Explorer, Firefox, and Chrome

✔ Searching on the web and taking control

✔ Getting your news with RSS

✔ Using the reference tools on the web

For hundreds of millions of people, the web and Internet Explorer (IE) are synonyms. It's fair to say that IE has done more to extend the reach of PC users than any other product — enabling people from all walks of life, in all corners of the globe, to see what a fascinating world we live in.

At the same time, IE has become an object of attack by spammers, scammers, thieves, and other lowlifes. As the Internet's lowest (or is it greatest?) common denominator, IE draws a lot of unwanted attention. That's changing, though. Now, all the browsers get some of the flak. It's just that IE continues to get the worst of it.

This chapter looks at desktop browsers: Internet Explorer, sure, but also Firefox and Google Chrome, two viable alternatives, each with its own strengths and weaknesses.

If you're more inclined to use the full-screen touch-friendly browsers on the tiled side of the Windows 8 divide, you're barking up the wrong tree. The tiled version of IE is entirely different from the desktop version. Tiled Chrome carries over many of the features of Desktop Chrome — and it's well worth a look. Take a look at Book IV, Chapter 1.

This chapter takes a look at what's out there, helps you choose one (or two or three) desktop browsers for your everyday use, shows you how to customize your chosen browser, and then offers all sorts of important advice about using the web.

What's an IP address?

When you're connected to the Internet, interacting with a website, the website has to be able to find you. Instead of using names (Billy Bob's broken down ThinkPad), the Internet uses numbers, such as 207.46.232.182, something like a telephone number (that's one of Microsoft's addresses). When you go to a website, you leave behind your IP address. That's the only way the website has to get back to you. Nothing nefarious about it: That's the way the Internet works.

Although your IP address doesn't identify you, uniquely, the IP address for most computers with broadband connections rarely changes. Your IP address changes if you turn off your router and turn it back on again, but for most people, most of the time, the IP address stays constant.

The IP address actually identifies the physical box that's attached to the Internet. For homes and businesses with a network, the address is associated with the router, not individual computers on the Internet. If you're using a mobile (3G or 4G) connection, the IP address is associated with your mobile phone provider's equipment, not yours. In some developing countries, the whole country has a handful of IP addresses, and connections inside the country are handled as if they were on an internal network.

Which Browser's Best?

I must hear that question a dozen times a week.

The short answer: It depends.

The long answer: It depends on a lot of things.

Considering security

Without doubt, the number one consideration for any browser user is security. The last thing you need is to get your PC infected with a drive-by attack, where merely looking at an infected web page takes over your computer.

Fortunately, for the first time in many years, if not forever, I feel confident in telling you that the desktop versions of all three major browsers — Internet Explorer, Firefox, and Chrome — are excellent choices. None has clear superiority over the other. All are (finally!) secure, as long as you follow a few simple rules.

The days of Microsoft taking all the heat for security holes has passed: Although it's true that there are more frontal assaults on Internet Explorer than on the other two, it's also true that Firefox- and Chrome-specific attacks exist.

In fact, browsers aren't the major source of attacks any more. Starting in 2007 or so, the bad guys turned their attention away from browsers and went to work on add-ins, specifically Flash and Acrobat PDF Reader, as well as browser toolbars. According to IBM's X-Force Team, the number of browser-attacking exploits has been declining steadily since 2007, with a concomitant rise in infections based on Flash, Reader, Java, toolbars, and other third-party add-ons.

There are still major security problems with old versions of Internet Explorer. Microsoft's been actively trying to kill IE 6 for years now. But as long as you stick to the latest browser version, keep your browsers reasonably well updated, and don't install any weird toolbars or other add-ons, your only major points of concern for any of the major browsers are Flash, Reader, and Java. I talk about all three in the following sections.

There's a good case to be made for running a browser, not on the old-fashioned desktop, but on the tiled side of the fence.

The tiled Internet Explorer blocks Flash on all sites, except sites that appear on a specific "white list" of allowed sites. Hundreds of sites are on the list. While that adds some control to the wild world of Flash, it comes at a cost: If you use the tiled IE and venture to a site that isn't on the list, and that site has a Flash animation, you may not know why the site doesn't look right.

The tiled version of Chrome, on the other hand, plays all Flash, on all sites, using the built-in (and heavily protected) Flash player that's inside Chrome.

As of this writing, Firefox hasn't weighed in on the Flash debate. Look for details in Book IV, Chapter 1.

IE, Firefox, and Chrome aren't the only games in town. Some people swear by Safari (which is the Apple browser); others go for Opera. Personally, I don't like Safari, but I do like Opera. I have my hands full just juggling the other three.

Looking at privacy

Privacy is one area that differentiates the Big Three. As best I can tell, nobody knows for sure how much data about your browsing proclivities is kept by the browser manufacturers, but this much seems likely:

✦ If you turn on the Suggested Sites feature or SmartScreen Filter in Internet Explorer (see the section on Internet Explorer), IE does send your browsing history to Microsoft, where it is saved and analyzed.

✦ Google keeps information about where you go with Chrome. Get over it.

✦ While Firefox is capable of keeping track of where you're going with your browser, Firefox is the least likely of the Big Three to keep or use the data. Why? Because, in direct contrast to both Microsoft and Google, Firefox doesn't have anything to sell you.

In general, the browser manufacturers can't track you directly, as an individual; they can only track your IP address (see the sidebar, "What's an IP address?"). But both Microsoft and Google mash together information that they get from multiple sources. As Microsoft puts it in the Internet Explorer Privacy Statement:

> "In order to offer you a more consistent and personalized experience in your interactions with Microsoft, information collected through one Microsoft service may be combined with information obtained through other Microsoft services. We may also supplement the information we collect with information obtained from other companies."

Funny the statement doesn't mention targeted advertising.

Google does the same thing: It actively collects information about you from every interaction you have with a Google product or location, including the search site and the browser.

If privacy is very important to you, Firefox is your best choice. No question.

Picking a browser

With all the pros and cons, which browser should you choose?

Although each version of each browser is different, a few generalities about the different browsers seem to hold true:

✦ **Internet Explorer** holds the title for most compatible with ancient websites. Unfortunately, sometimes that compatibility comes at a cost: You may have to install programs (such as ActiveX controls) that can have security holes. IE also has a few features, such as the capability to pin websites to the Windows taskbar, that some people find useful.

✦ **Firefox** has the most extensions, and some of them are quite worthwhile. Ghostery, for example, shows every tracking cookie on every web page; DownThemAll can download every link on a page and manage them all; IE Tab brings IE compatibility to most ancient web pages; NoScript blocks Flash and Java unless you unleash them on a specific site. Firefox is also the least likely to sprout privacy problems (see the preceding section).

What is Do Not Track?

Microsoft has made a huge step in the direction of helping to protect consumer privacy. Yes, *that* Microsoft. They turned on Do Not Track, by default during Windows 8 setup, in both the desktop and tiled versions of Internet Explorer 10. What's DNT? Good question.

Whenever you go to a website, your browser leaves certain fingerprints at each site you visit: the name of your browser, your operating system, your IP address, time zone, screen size, whether cookies are enabled, the address of the last website you visited, that kind of thing. I'm not talking about cookies. I'm talking about data that's inside the "header" at the beginning of the interaction with every web page. Even if you go "incognito" (in Chrome), "private" (in Firefox), or "In Private" (in Internet Explorer), your browser still sends all of that information to every site, every time you visit.

The Do Not Track proposal — and it's only a proposal at this point — would assign one more bit in the header that says, "The person using this browser requests that you not track anything they're doing." DNT was originally developed by Firefox. You can turn on DNT in any recent version of Firefox by clicking the Firefox button, Options, Privacy, and selecting the Tell Web Sites I Do Not Want to Be Tracked check box.

As with everything Internet related, DNT isn't cut-and-dried. There are lots and lots of nuances. First and foremost, it's entirely voluntary: Websites can ignore the DNT bit if the site's programmers want to. Second, the precise definition of "track" can get a little squishy. Third, there's no possible way to enforce the DNT settings — no way to tell which of the dozens of billions of websites now readily accessible even claim to have a DNT policy, much less implement it. Still, it's a start in the right direction.

If you have a browser that supports DNT, you can check to see if it's working at my browser testing site, www.AskWoody.com/testdntflash.

+ **Chrome** usually comes out on top in security tests. With built-in support for both PDF reading and Flash, and the Java programming language, Chrome can handle all three without relying on the Flash, Reader, or Java plug-ins, which are historically riddled with security holes. Chrome's also been a pioneer in new features and standards adoption, and will take your settings along with you as you move from PC to PC.

It isn't an either-or choice, actually. You can easily run Internet Explorer, Firefox, and Chrome side-by-side. Here's what I do:

+ Most of the time, I run Firefox, with NoScript turned on and Ghostery sniffing out the frighteningly large number of cookies watching me. I don't block cookies with Ghostery, although I could. Mostly I want to see how much sites have sold out, reducing my privacy for their profits.

✦ If I want to bookmark something, I usually shift to Chrome, which I keep signed in. I like its bookmarking interface better — and the bookmarks travel with me, wherever I go, because I'm signed in. If I have trouble with a fancy new site in Firefox, Chrome will usually handle it.

✦ And Internet Explorer is always ready, standby, in case I hit an older web page that doesn't work right in Firefox or Chrome. Yes, there are plenty of them (I won't mention my bank by name). Instead of switching Firefox over to the IE Tab add-on, I just jump the monkey and go to IE.

Setting a browser as your default

When you get Windows, Internet Explorer is set up as the default browser: click a web link in a document, say, and Internet Explorer jumps up to load the web page.

Both Firefox and Chrome offer to become your default web browser, as soon as you install them. They also have a check box that basically tells them to quit asking. I always check that box.

It's easy to change your default browser. Here's how:

1. **Tap and hold or right-click the lower-left corner of the desktop, and choose Control Panel.**

2. **Click the Programs link. Then, under Default Programs, click the link that says Set Your Default Programs.**

You see the Set Default Programs dialog shown in Figure 6-1.

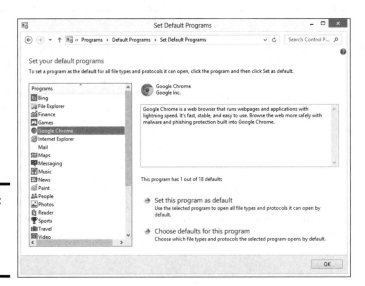

Figure 6-1: Set your default browser here.

The history of Internet Explorer

More than any other product, Internet Explorer reflects the odd and tortured Microsoft approach to the web. After largely ignoring the Internet for many years, Microsoft released the first version of Internet Explorer in 1995, as an add-on to Windows. In 1996, Microsoft built Internet Explorer version 3 into Windows itself, violating antitrust laws and using monopolistic tactics to overwhelm Netscape Navigator.

Having illegally pummeled its competitor in the marketplace, Microsoft made almost no improvements to Internet Explorer between August 2001 and August 2006 — an eternity in Internet time. IE became the single largest conduit for malware in the history of computing, with major security patches (sometimes several) appearing almost every month.

And then there was Firefox. Dave Hyatt, Blake Ross (who was a sophomore at Stanford at the time), and hundreds of volunteers took on the IE behemoth, producing a fast, small, free alternative that quickly grabbed a significant share of the browser market. Microsoft responded by incorporating many Firefox features into Internet Explorer.

Although Google did, and does, provide most of the money that drives Firefox's development — Google pays a pretty penny to be the default search engine in Firefox — the Googlies decided to make their own browser, with a different slant. First released in late 2008, Chrome has grown to the point that Chrome and Firefox often run neck-and-neck in web utilization statistics, with IE on a downward trend around the 50% line.

3. **On the left, select the browser you want to turn into your default, and choose Set This Program as Default.**

If you set any browser other than Internet Explorer as your default, the tiled version of IE won't work. Fortunately, Google Chrome has a tiled version, so setting Chrome as the default browser makes Chrome the default both on the desktop and on the tiled side. If you want to make a lesser-known browser your default, check to make sure it has a tiled version that can fill in when tiled IE gives up.

4. **Click OK.**

Your chosen browser becomes the default.

Using Internet Explorer on the Desktop

I hear the same question over and over: "How can I make Internet Explorer run faster?" The short answer: 99% of the time, you can't. The big problem isn't IE. It's the speed of your Internet connection.

With that question answered, let's see what you *can* do about IE.

Internet Explorer on the desktop is very, very different from the Windows 8 tiled style version of IE. Use them for a few minutes and you'll see:

✦ Tiled IE devotes more of the screen to the website You can bring back the navigation pieces with a swipe — if you can remember how and where. See Book IV, Chapter 1 for details.

Tiled IE handles sites with Flash unevenly — as long as you stick with big-name sites, tiled IE plays Flash animations. But if you venture to lesser-known sites, Flash doesn't play, and tiled IE doesn't warn you at all. Tiled IE also doesn't support ActiveX or Silverlight, two non-standard technologies developed and heavily marketed by Microsoft. Ah, the irony.

✦ The desktop version of IE has the old, familiar interface. It runs all the add-ins you've come to know and love and distrust. With dozens of new features, many of which are actually useful, Internet Explorer 10 on the desktop gives you just about everything a modern browser can give you — except an extensive library of customized add-ons.

Microsoft would have you believe that the tiled and desktop IE are the same browser, with a few minor differences. At some point it turns into an argument over definitions, but to my way of thinking, tiled and desktop IE are two entirely different programs that share one key component — the rendering engine, which draws pictures on the monitor. If you think of tiled IE and desktop IE as two completely different programs, with some components and terminology in common, you'll probably clear up half of the questions that arise at the outset.

Setting a default Internet Explorer

It's like the Abbot and Costello routine, Who's on first? Not all that much has changed since 1937.

Here's how it goes. You either accept the default web browser, or use the steps in the preceding section to set Internet Explorer as your default web browser. That means, among many other things, that when you click a link in, say, a document or e-mail message, Internet Explorer pops up with the linked page on display.

But *which* Internet Explorer? Ay, that's the question.

Does the tiled version of IE appear, over on the full-screen tiled side of Windows 8? Or does the desktop come into view, with the venerable version of IE showing the page? Answer: Unless you change something, the tiled version takes over.

If you want to change things so the desktop version of Internet Explorer runs as the default, you don't go into the Control Panel. The method for changing default programs in general doesn't work. Instead, you go into IE. Here's how:

1. **Start IE on the desktop by touching or clicking the IE icon on the taskbar.**

2. **Touch or click the Settings icon (the one shaped like a gear, at the top right of the IE window). Choose Internet Options.**

The Internet Options dialog box appears.

3. **Click on the Programs tab.**

You see the Opening Internet Explorer options shown in Figure 6-2.

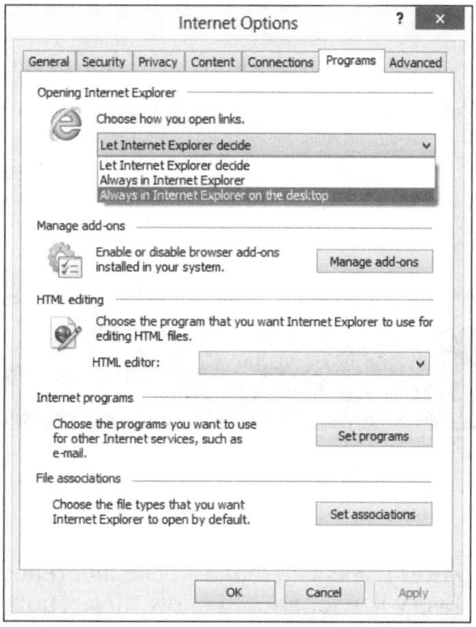

**Book VI
Chapter 6**

**Choosing and Using
a Desktop Web
Browser**

Figure 6-2:
Resolve
the tiled/
desktop
sibling
rivalry here.

4. **In the Choose How You Open Links box, choose Always in Internet Explorer on the Desktop.**

5. **Click OK.**

You've settled the question of which IE is on first.

Navigating in desktop IE

One great thing about the desktop version of Internet Explorer is that you can be an absolute no-clue beginner and, with just a few hints about tools and so on, you can find your way around the web like a pro. Windows 8's tiled IE's a little trickier, in my opinion, because you have to "discover" the navigation methods.

Figure 6-3 gives you a diagram of the basic layout of the Internet Explorer window.

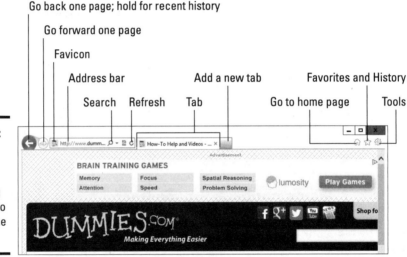

Go back one page; hold for recent history
Go forward one page
Favicon
Address bar · Add a new tab · Favorites and History
Search · Refresh · Tab · Go to home page · Tools

Figure 6-3: The IE window includes everything you need to work on the web.

Don't work too hard

A handful of Internet Explorer tricks can make all the difference in your productivity and sanity. Every IE user should know these shortcuts:

✦ **You rarely need to type www in the address bar at the beginning of an address, and you never need to type http://.** People who build websites these days are almost always savvy enough to let you drop the use of the www at the beginning of the website's name. Unless the site you're headed to was last updated in the late 17th century, you can probably get there by simply typing the name of the site, as long as you include the part at the end. So, you can type **http://www.dummies.com** if you want to, but typing **dummies.com** works just as well.

✦ **IE automatically sticks `http://www.` on the front of an address you type and `.com` on the end if you press Ctrl+Enter.** So, if you want to go to the site `http://www.dummies.com`, you only need to type **dummies** in the address bar and press Ctrl+Enter.

✦ **With a few exceptions, address capitalization doesn't matter.** Typing either **AskWoody.com** or **askwoody.com** gets you to my website — as does **asKwoodY.cOm**. On the other hand, hyphens (-) and underscores (_) aren't interchangeable: `some-site.com` and `some_site.com` would be two completely different sites if they were the real deals. Similarly, the number 0 isn't the same as the letter o, the number 1 isn't a letter l, and radishes aren't the same as turnips. Or so my niece tells me.

The exceptions? Web addresses from one of the thousands of websites that now have shortened URLs. Go to `bit.ly`, for example, or `goo.gl`, feed it a URL that's a gazillion letters long, click a button, and you get back something that looks like this: `goo.gl/XY2Am`. In those kinds of addresses — shortened ones — capitalization *does* matter.

While we're on the topic of working too hard, keeping track of passwords rates as the single biggest pain in the neck in any browser. You have passwords for, what — a hundred different sites? If you haven't yet discovered LastPass (or Roboform), get to Book X, Chapter 5, and check it out.

Moving around the main desktop window

As you can see, IE packs lots of possibilities into that small space. The items you use most often are described in this list:

✦ **Backward** and **forward arrows:** Go to the previously displayed page; hold down to see a list of all previous pages.

✦ **Address bar:** Enables you to type the web address of a page that you want to move to directly. You can also type search terms here; click the spyglass or press Enter, and IE will look them up using your default search engine.

✦ **Refresh:** If you think the page has changed, tap or click this icon to have IE retrieve it for you again.

✦ **Tab:** You can have many pages open at a time, one on each tab. To create a new tab, click the first blank tab on the right.

✦ **Home page:** Replaces the current tab with the tab(s) on your Home page.

✦ **Favorites icon:** Lets you set, go to, and organize favorite websites, as well as look at your browsing history.

✦ **Settings:** Takes you under the covers to change the way IE behaves. Or misbehaves.

If you want to see the old-fashioned toolbar menus (File, Edit, View, and all the others) in Internet Explorer, press Alt. Yep, that's how you get to IE's inner workings.

Tinkering with tabs

Tabs offer you a chance to bring up multiple web pages without opening multiple copies of IE. They're a major navigational aid because it's easy to switch among tabs. If you've never used browser tabs, you might wonder what all the fuss is about. It doesn't seem like there's much difference between opening another window and adding a tab (see Figure 6-4). But after you get the hang of it, tabs can help you organize pages and jump to the one you want.

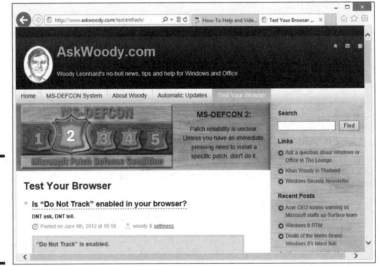

Figure 6-4:
If you've never used tabs, you're in for a treat.

You can add a new tab to IE in any of these four ways:

✦ Click the blank box to the right of the right-most tab. That starts a blank new tab, and away you go.

✦ Ctrl+click a link to open the linked page in a new tab.

✦ Press Ctrl+T to start a new tab. When the tab is open, you get to navigate manually, just as you would in any other browser window.

✦ Right-click a link and choose Open in New Tab.

In addition, the web page you're looking at may specify that any links on the page are to open in a new tab, instead of overwriting the current one.

Why do I like tabs? I can set up a single window with a bunch of related tabs and then bookmark the whole shebang. That makes it one-click easy to open all my favorite news sites, research sites, or financial sites. While my browser's out loading pages, I can go do something else and return to the tabbed window when everything's loaded and ready to go.

If I'm trying to research two different topics at the same time, I frequently start Firefox and create tabs to hunt down the first topic and then start Firefox again — start it in a different window, usually by Shift+clicking a link — or I start Chrome, and traipse through the second topic.

You can reorganize the order of tabs by simply clicking a tab and dragging it to a different location.

Using the address bar

No doubt you're familiar with basic browser functions, or you can guess when you know what the controls mean. But you might not know about some of these finer points:

✦ When you type on the address bar, IE looks at what you're typing and tries to match it with the list of sites it has in your history list and in your favorites. Sometimes, you can get the right address (URL) by typing something related to the site. Watch as you type and see what IE comes up with.

If you turn on Bing Suggestions (sometimes called Suggested Sites), IE sends all your keystrokes to Mother Microsoft, and has Bing try to guess what you're looking for. Depending on how you feel about privacy, that may or may not be a good idea. See the section "Turning on key features," later in this chapter.

✦ Click a link and the web page decides whether you move to the new page in the current browser tab or a new tab appears with the clicked page loaded. Many people don't realize that the web page makes the decision about following the link in the same tab or creating a new one. You can override the web page's setting.

• Shift+click and a new browser window always opens with the clicked page loaded.

• Ctrl+click and the clicked page appears on a new tab in the current browser window. Similarly, if you type in the Search bar and press Ctrl+Enter, the results appear in a new tab.

✦ Even if the web page "hijacks" your Backward and Forward arrows, you can always move backward (or forward) by clicking and holding on the directional arrow, then choosing the page you want.

You can bring up a history of all the pages you visited in the past few weeks by pressing Ctrl+H. To search for a particular word or phrase on a page, press Ctrl+F. Force your browser to refresh a web page (retrieve the latest version, even if a version is stored locally) by pressing F5. If you need to make sure that you have the latest version, even if the timestamps might be screwed up, press Ctrl+F5.

Saving space, losing time

Increasing or decreasing the number of days of browsing history that IE stores doesn't have much effect on the amount of data stored on the hard drive: Even a hyperactive surfer will have a hard time cranking up a History folder that's much larger than 1MB. By contrast, temporary Internet files on your computer can take up 10, 50, or even 100 times that much space.

Those temporary Internet files exist only to speed your Internet access: When IE hits a web page that it has seen before, if a copy of the page's contents appears in the Temporary Internet Files folder, IE grabs the stuff on the hard drive rather than wait for a download. That can make a huge difference in IE's responsiveness, particularly if you have a slow Internet connection, but the speed comes at a price: 250MB, if you haven't changed it.

To clear out the IE temporary Internet files, follow these simple steps:

1. **Start the desktop version of Internet Explorer.**

   The tiled style IE doesn't have access to these settings.

2. **Click the Tools icon, the one shaped like a gear in the upper right, and choose Internet Options.**

   The Internet Options dialog box appears.

3. **On the General tab, under Browsing History, click the Delete button.**

   You see the Delete Browsing History dialog shown in Figure 6-5.

4. **Choose the kinds of data you wish to delete, and click Delete, then OK out of the Internet Options dialog box.**

   You won't hurt anything, but revisited web pages take longer to appear. For advice about cookies, see the next section.

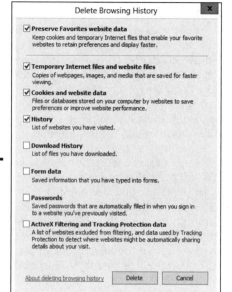

Book VI
Chapter 6

Choosing and Using
a Desktop Web
Browser

Figure 6-5:
You have
full control
over what
kinds of
browsing
history gets
deleted.

Dealing with cookies

A *cookie,* as you probably know, is a text file that a website stores on your computer. The website can put information inside its own cookie (say, the time and date of your last visit or the page you were last viewing or your account number). At least in theory, a website can look at and change only its own cookies: The cookie provides a means for an individual website to store information on your computer and to retrieve it later, using your browser.

In general, that's A Good Thing. Cookies can minimize the amount of futzing around that you need to do on a site. Most shopping cart/checkout sites need cookies.

Of course, nothing ever goes precisely as planned. Bugs have appeared in the way Internet Explorer, in particular, handles cookies and, historically, it's been possible for rogue websites to retrieve information from cookies other than their own.

Because of ongoing problems, sound and fury frequently raised by people who don't understand, and concomitant legislation in many countries, "first-party" cookies these days rarely include any interesting information. Mostly, they store innocuous settings and perhaps a randomly generated number that's used to track a customer in the company's database. To a bad guy, the data stored in most cookies varies between banal and useless.

What's a third-party cookie?

By contrast, *third-party cookies* (or *tracking cookies*) aren't as bland. They have significant commercial value because they can be used to keep track of your web surfing. Here's how: Say ZDNet (`www.zdnet.com`) sells an ad to DoubleClick. When you venture to any ZDNet page (they all have tiny, one-pixel "ads" from DoubleClick), both ZDNet and DoubleClick can stick cookies on your computer. ZDNet can retrieve only its cookie, and DoubleClick can retrieve only its cookie. Cool. DoubleClick might keep information about you visiting a ZDNet site that talks about, oh, an Android phone.

Now say that DealTime (`www.dealtime.com`) sells an ad to DoubleClick. You go to any page on DealTime (they also have tiny one-pixel DoubleClick "ads" on every page) and both DealTime and DoubleClick can look at their own cookies. DealTime might be smart enough to ask DoubleClick whether you've been looking at Android phones and then offer you a bargain tailored to your recent surfing. Or an insurance company may discover that you've been looking at information pages about the heartbreak of psoriasis. Or a car company might find out you're very interested in its latest Stutzmobile.

Multiply that little example by 10, 100, or 100,000, and you begin to see how third-party cookies can be used to collect a whole lot of information about you and your surfing habits. There's nothing illegal or immoral about it. But some people (present company certainly included) find it disconcerting. Oh, you know that Google owns DoubleClick, yes?

I don't get too worked up about cookies these days. If you've ever worked with them programmatically, you're probably at the yawning stage, too. But the potential is there for them to become pernicious.

Deleting cookies

Cookies don't have anything to do with spam — you receive the same junk e-mail even if you tell your computer to reject every cookie that darkens your door. Cookies don't spy on your PC, go sniffing for bank accounts, or keep a log of those . . . ahem . . . artistic websites you visit. They do serve a useful purpose, but like so many other concepts in the computer industry, cookies are exploited by a few companies in questionable ways. I talk about cookies extensively in Book IX, Chapter 1. If you're worried about cookies and want to know what's really happening, that's a great place to start.

In Internet Explorer, to delete all cookies, follow the instructions in the earlier section "Saving space, losing time" to bring up the Delete Browsing History dialog (refer to Figure 6-5). Make sure you select Cookies and Website Data, and click Delete. IE deletes all your cookies.

Internet Explorer has a mechanism for blocking third-party cookies, but I don't think it works very well. It's based on an old "standard" known as P3P, which is actually used by about a dozen websites based in Lower Slobovokia — and that's about it. Even some of Microsoft's own sites don't use P3P. I talk about the problems with IE's third-party cookie blocking in one of my InfoWorld Tech Watch articles, at www.infoworld.com/t/internet-privacy/googles-cookie-runaround-in-ie-not-big-deal-186889.

Changing the home page

Every time you start the desktop version of IE, it whirrs and after a relatively brief moment (how brief depends primarily on the speed of your Internet connection), a web page appears. The information that page contains depends on whether your computer is set up to begin with a specific page known as a *home page*.

Microsoft sets up www.msn.com as the IE home page (see Figure 6-6) by default — a page best known for its, uh, quirky choice of "news" items and phenomenally high density of ads. Many PC manufacturers set the Internet Explorer home page to display something related to their systems.

Figure 6-6: If msn.com is your favorite page on the web, you might want to consider a prefrontal lobotomy.

If the ditzy, ad-laden MSN home page leaves you wondering whether P.T. Barnum still designs web pages (there's one born every minute), or if your PC manufacturer's idea of a good home page doesn't quite jibe with your tastes, you can easily change the home page. Here's how:

1. **Start the desktop version of IE.**

At least in the current version of IE, you can't change the home page by using the tiled version of IE; the settings just aren't available.

2. **Navigate to the page or pages you want to use for a home page.**

You can bring up as many pages as you like on separate tabs. All of the tabs will become your home "page." See the previous section, "Navigating in desktop IE," if you're not sure how to use tabs.

3. **Tap or click the Tools icon (the one in the upper right that looks like a gear), choose Internet Options, then click the General tab.**

You see the Home Page settings shown in Figure 6-7.

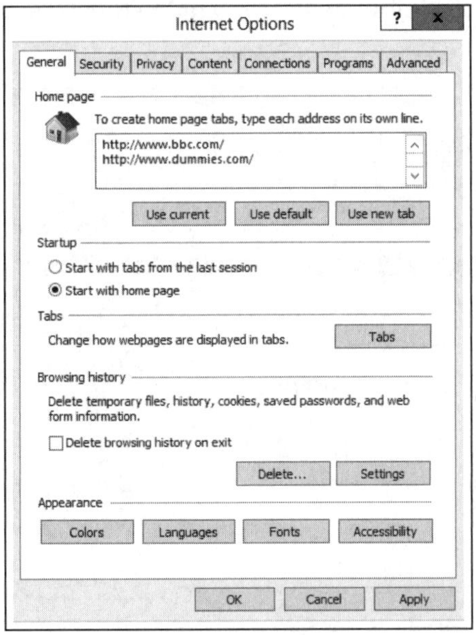

Figure 6-7: Set the home page(s) here.

4. **At the top, make sure you have the list of all the tabs you would like to open as your home page, then tap or click the button marked Use Current.**

If you choose Use New Tab, IE starts with no new page at all. That can be considerably faster than starting with a real home page.

5. Click OK.

Every time the desktop version of IE runs, it will bring up the tabs you selected.

Turning on key features

Microsoft has a long list of improvements to its latest version of Internet Explorer. Most of those improvements operate behind the scenes; you'll only know that they're there when you don't get infected, if you know what I mean.

The last few IE versions have brought along a few worthwhile improvements, which you may not have seen:

✦ **You can pin a specific page to the desktop taskbar.** To pin a site to the taskbar, click the "favicon" next to the page's address, or click the entire tab, and drag it down to the taskbar.

Microsoft says that a website accessed from the taskbar this way "takes on the branding of the site." What Microsoft means is that the background and border colors of the browser take on the main color of the site. Whooo-boy. Some sites, like Facebook, give you notifications about incoming messages.

✦ **IE analyzes add-ons and tells you how much they're dragging your system down,** each time you launch IE. In general, you only see the analysis when your add-ons are causing big problems. There's a detailed explanation on the IE Blog at http://blogs.msdn.com/b/ie/archive/2011/03/23/updates-to-add-on-performance-advisor.aspx.

✦ *Suggested Sites* **(also called Bing Suggestions) is a feature added in IE 8 that keeps track of keys as you type them,** sending your keystrokes to Microsoft (Bing), generating potential matches and suggestions on the fly. Matches are based primarily on your browsing history. To turn on Suggested Sites, click the Star "Favorites" icon, and at the bottom of the box, select Turn on Suggested Sites.

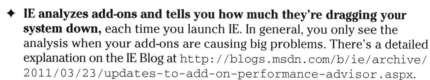

As you might imagine, there's a great deal of controversy about the privacy aspects of Suggested Sites: Microsoft records every keystroke that you type into IE, and it watches your browsing history. Note that Suggested Sites is not turned on by default: You have to enable it. Microsoft has a detailed report on its side of the story on the IE Blog at http://blogs.msdn.com/b/ie/archive/2009/02/05/suggested-sites-privacy.aspx.

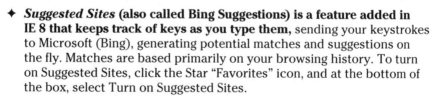

+ *SmartScreen Filter* — **the collaborative Internet Explorer Phishing Filter** — **keeps up-to-the-minute blacklists** of websites that have been identified by other IE users as possible phishing sites. Before you go to a website, SmartScreen Filter compares the site's address to its blacklist, and warns you if the site has been identified as an unsafe site. It also looks on the page for telltale "unsafe behavior" and warns you if the site looks fishy. It also checks files before you download them, to see if they're on Microsoft's whitelist, warning you that the file "is not commonly downloaded" if it's a relative newcomer.

Unlike Suggested Sites, which sends all your information to Microsoft, the SmartScreen Filter maintains a small list of bad sites inside your computer that's updated frequently. That's a very effective trick first employed by Firefox.

To turn on SmartScreen Filter, click the Tools icon (the one that looks like a gear), and choose Safety, then Turn on SmartScreen Filter. If you hit a dicey site — perhaps you were sent there by an apparent phishing e-mail message — you can report the site by clicking on the gear icon and choosing Report Unsafe Website.

+ *InPrivate Browsing* lets you surf anywhere on the web without leaving any records on your PC of where you dallied. It doesn't matter whether it's a racy page, the political headquarters of a candidate you detest, or a squealing fan site for a sappy soap, InPrivate Browsing makes sure that no details are left on your machine.

This kind of cloaking only keeps your PC clean. The sites you travel to can keep track of your Internet address (your IP address; see the earlier section "Looking at privacy," in this chapter, for details). Depending on how you connect to the Internet, your IP address can generally be traced to the router you're using to connect to the Internet. *Caveat surfor.*

Searching with alacrity . . . and Google

It shouldn't surprise you too much to realize that Internet Explorer ships with Microsoft's Bing as its default search engine. If you like Bing, my hat's off to you. But if you want to change to Google (or DuckDuckGo, www.duckduckgo. com, Dogpile, www.dogpile.com, Hotbot, www.hotbot.com, or Wolfram Alpha, www.wolframalpha.com, all of which have their high points), it's remarkably difficult.

Unless Microsoft changes IE 10 (or a judge forces the company to change, to provide better access to alternative search engines), here's the easiest way to move from Bing to Google in IE:

1. **Start the desktop version of IE.**

   Again, it doesn't look like you can do this from the tiled version of IE.

2. **Click the down arrow next to the magnifying glass, up in the address bar, and in the lower-right corner, choose Add.**

   IE takes you to the Internet Explorer Gallery, with Search Providers selected, as in Figure 6-8.

Figure 6-8:
Adding
Google as
a search
provider
ain't easy.

3. **Look. I swear it's there. When you find the Google search logo, click it.**

   When I went looking for Google in all the wrong places, I had to wade through Kenmonjo Search and Mountain Rose Herbs Search and dozens of others (Emglare?) before I found it. Persevere.

   IE brings up the Internet Explorer Gallery highlighting Google Search.

4. **Click Add to Internet Explorer.**

   IE responds with a dialog box called Add Search Provider, shown in Figure 6-9.

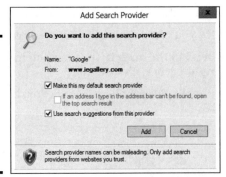

Figure 6-9:
This is the
easy place
to make
Google
your default
search
provider.

5. **Check the box marked Make This My Default Search Provider, and Use Search Suggestions from this Provider. Then click Add.**

IE doesn't say a thing, but it changes your default search provider to Google. How can you tell, without running a search? Click the down arrow next to the magnifying glass icon again, and at the bottom, the tiny Google icon appears to the left of the Bing icon. That's how you know Google's the default search engine.

From that point on, you can type your search terms in the address bar and press Enter, or tap or click the magnifying glass icon, and IE sends the search terms to Google.

I have a section later in this chapter that gives some pointers about searching on the web.

Customizing Firefox

Hey, you can use Internet Explorer if you want to. Without doubt, IE has a few features that other browsers can't match — dragging and dropping websites on the taskbar, Web Slices, InPrivate Filtering, and Accelerators come to mind. It also supports ActiveX controls and fits right in with Silverlight. If those ring your chimes, you need to play the IE game.

I use Firefox. I've used it for years, and I've recommended it in my books for years. Debating the relative merits of web browsers soon degenerates to a fight over the number of angels that can stand on the head of a pin. Suffice it to say that I feel Firefox has more options: more add-ins that make it work better and safer than either IE or Chrome. For me. I also like the fact that Firefox has no vested interest in keeping track of what I'm doing.

I don't mean to imply that Firefox is perfect. It isn't. The Firefox team releases security patches, too, just like IE and Chrome teams, and you need to make sure you keep Firefox updated. But I think you'll enjoy using Firefox more than Internet Explorer. I also would bet that you hit far fewer in-the-wild security problems with the Fox.

Installing Firefox

Installing Firefox couldn't be simpler. You don't need to disable Internet Explorer, pat your head, and rub your belly or jump through any other hoops (although clicking your heels and repeating "There's no place like home" may help). Just follow these steps:

Book VI
Chapter 6

1. **Using any convenient browser (even the tiled version of IE), go to** `www.firefox.com` **and follow the instructions to download and run the installer for the latest version of Firefox.**

Chances are good that you need to click a big, green button and then click Run to get the installer going.

2. **On the installer's splash screen, click Next.**

You see the Setup window.

3. **Click the Standard button and then click Next.**

The Setup wizard finishes and offers to launch Firefox now.

4. **Click Finish.**

Depending on how you install Firefox, the first time you run it, you may be asked whether you want to import bookmarks from Internet Explorer. (I generally choose No because IE has so many useless Microsoft-centric built-in Favorites.) You may also be asked whether you want to make Firefox your default browser. When Firefox gets a tiled version that works, I'll check the box Yes; for now, I clear the box to signify No. (Keep up with the latest on `www.askwoody.com`.) You end up with a screen that looks like Figure 6-10.

Firefox is a little different from IE in that it has a search bar in addition to the address bar. In fact, you can type search terms into the address bar or the search bar, and Firefox brings up your preferred search engine to look for them.

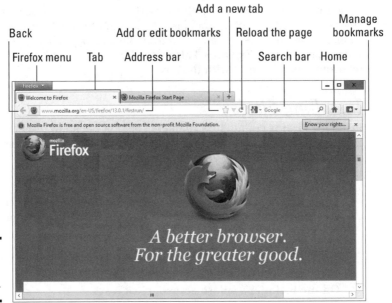

Back | Firefox menu | Tab | Add or edit bookmarks | Address bar | Add a new tab | Reload the page | Search bar | Home | Manage bookmarks

Figure 6-10:
Firefox up
and running.

All the tricks I mention in the earlier IE section called "Don't work too hard," also perform in Firefox. You never need to type **http://**, almost never need to type **www**, and typing something like **dummies** followed by a Ctrl+Enter puts you spot-on for http://www.dummies.com.

Setting a home page in Firefox is similar to setting one in IE. To get to the right place, click the Firefox menu, choose Options, then Options again. Home page settings are on the General tab.

Browsing privately in Firefox

Firefox has a private browsing feature similar to IE's InPrivate browsing, which I describe in the section "Turning on key features" in the IE part of this chapter. Firefox's version is called, er, Private Browsing. (Hey, Firefox invented it!)

To start a Private Browsing session, click the Firefox menu and choose Start Private Browsing.

Some people prefer to always work in Private Browsing mode. There's a lot to be said for that approach, although you won't get the advantages of having cookies hanging around. Staying in Private Browsing mode is easy to do in Firefox. Here's how:

1. **Start Firefox on the desktop. Click the Firefox menu button and choose Options, then Options again. At the top, click the Privacy icon.**

You see the Options dialog box shown in Figure 6-11.

Figure 6-11:
It's easy to have Firefox always start in Private Browsing mode.

2. **In the Firefox Will box, choose Use Custom Settings For History.**

3. **Then select the box marked Always Use Private Browsing Mode.**

4. **If you want to turn on Do Not Track (see the sidebar, "What is Do Not Track?" earlier in this chapter), select the Tell Websites I Do Not Want to Be Tracked check box.**

Admittedly, DNT doesn't do much right now, but it doesn't hurt, and might actually block a few sites.

5. **Click OK.**

The next time you start Firefox, it'll be in Private Browsing mode. If you ever want to drop back into regular mode, click the Firefox menu and choose Stop Private Browsing.

Bookmarking with the Fox

Firefox handles bookmarks differently from Internet Explorer. (In IE, they're called Favorites. Same thing.)

The easiest way to understand Firefox bookmarks? Start with the Unsorted Bookmarks folder.

If you hit a website that you want to bookmark, follow these steps:

1. **In Firefox, go to the site you want to bookmark, and tap or click the Bookmark icon (the big star) on the right edge of the address bar.**

   This step bookmarks the page and puts the bookmark in a kind of All Other folder named Unsorted Bookmarks.

2. **If you'd rather stick your bookmark in a place where you can find it later or assign a tag to it, click the bookmark star once again.**

   Firefox opens its Edit This Bookmark dialog box, shown in Figure 6-12.

Figure 6-12:
Pull your bookmark out of the Unsorted Bookmarks morass in this dialog box.

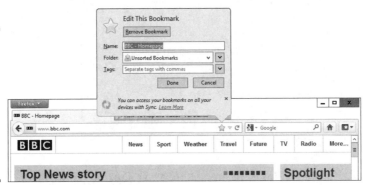

3. **Type any tags you want to associate with the bookmark in the Tags box, at the bottom.**

   Tags help you find things on the address bar. For example, if you assign a `Stuxnet` tag to the bookmark, typing **stux** in the address bar brings up this particular bookmark.

4. **To organize your bookmarks into folders, or to place this bookmark on the Bookmark bar, click the down arrow to the right of the Folder box.**

   Firefox lets you choose the bookmark folder that should contain your new bookmark or create a new folder to hold the bookmark (see Figure 6-13).

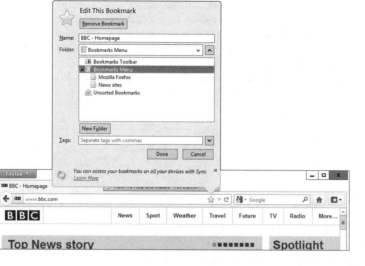

Figure 6-13:
Add new
folders here.

5. **If you create a new folder, you can leave it in the Unsorted Bookmarks folder, but if you want to make it more readily accessible from the Bookmarks menu, click and drag the new folder in the Edit This Bookmark dialog box so that the folder appears under the Bookmarks Menu folder.**

In Figure 6-13, I put the News sites folder under the Bookmarks Menu folder.

6. **If you want to put the new folder on the Bookmarks toolbar, to the right of the Latest Headlines button, click and drag it to the Bookmarks Toolbar folder.**

The Bookmarks toolbar is convenient, but it takes up precious space on the screen. Many people prefer to work with the Bookmarks icon, on the far right.

After the folder has been created (and, optionally, located on the Bookmarks menu or the Bookmarks toolbar), you can place any bookmark in the folder by double-clicking the bookmark star.

Adding Firefox's best add-ons

One of the best reasons for choosing Firefox over IE and Chrome is the incredible abundance of add-ons. If you can think of something to do with a browser, chances are good there's already an add-on that'll do it.

An enormous cottage industry has grown up around Firefox. The Firefox people made it relatively easy to extend the browser itself. As a result, tens of thousands of add-ons cover an enormous range of capabilities.

To search for add-ons, mosey over to `addons.mozilla.org` (see Figure 6-14). You can search for the add-ons recommended by Firefox itself or look for the most frequently downloaded add-ons.

Figure 6-14: Firefox makes it easy to extend the browser with add-ons made by other groups.

Here are some of my favorites. I always install the first four on any Firefox system I come into contact with:

+ **NoScript** lets you shut down all active content — Java, JavaScript, Flash, and more — either individually or for a site as a whole. Many sites don't work with JavaScript turned off, but NoScript gives you a fighting chance to pick and choose the scripts you want. Between JavaScript and Flash blocking, NoScript significantly reduces your exposure to online malware.

+ **Ghostery** keeps an eye on sites that are watching you. It tells you when sites contain "web beacons" or third-party cookies that can be used to track your surfing habits. I don't use Ghostery to stop cookies, but I do use it to watch who's watching me.

+ **Adblock Plus** blocks ads. (What did you expect?) It blocks a lot of ads — so much so that you may want to pull it back a bit. That's easy, too. See a demo at `adblockplus.org/en`.

✦ **DownThemAll** "scrapes" all downloadable files on a web page and presents them to you so that you can choose which files you want to download. Click Start and they all come loading down.

✦ **Greasemonkey** adds a customizable scripting language to Firefox. After you install Greasemonkey, you can download scripts from `userscript.org` that perform an enormous variety of tasks, from tweet assistance to downloading Flickr files.

✦ **IETab** embeds Internet Explorer inside Firefox. If you hit a site that absolutely won't work with Firefox, right-click the link, choose Tools⇨Open This Link in IETab, and Internet Explorer takes over a tab inside Firefox.

✦ **eBay Sidebar** watches your trades while you're doing something else.

✦ **Video Download Helper** makes it easy to download videos from the web. **Easy YouTube Video Downloader** does the same thing, but it's specialized for YouTube.

✦ **Linky** lets you open all links or images on a page, all at once, either on separate tabs or in separate windows. It's a helpful adjunct to Google image search.

To install the latest edition of any of these add-ons, go to `http://addons.mozilla.org` and search for the add-on's name. Each add-on's page has download and installation instructions — usually just a click or two, and a possible re-start of Firefox.

Optimizing Google Chrome

Google Chrome on the desktop has several advantages over IE and Firefox. Foremost among them: built-in Flash, Java, and PDF support, which greatly reduces the chances of getting stung by the largest source of infections these days.

The tiled version of Chrome is one of the shining examples (in my opinion anyway) of how the Windows 8 tiled side could work, if developers aren't saddled with Microsoft's design restrictions. You can find more details in Book IV, Chapter 1.

Installing Chrome

Installing Google Chrome is like falling off a log:

1. **With any browser (even a tiled style browser), go to** `http://chrome.google.com`.

You probably see a big blue button that says Download Google Chrome.

2. **Click the button to download.**

   You see a user agreement. Read all 214,197 pages of it, deselect the check box marked Set Google Chrome as My Default Browser, and click Accept and Install.

3. **Click run, or save and then run, depending on what browser you're using to download Chrome.**

   The installer takes a minute or two, then comes up with a Welcome to Chrome page, as shown in Figure 6-15.

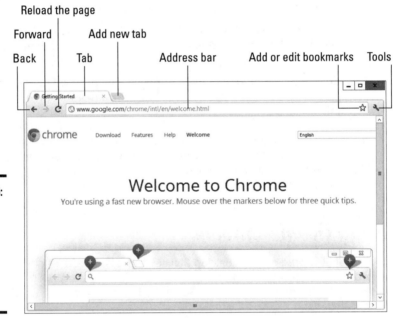

Reload the page

Forward   Add new tab

Back   Tab   Address bar   Add or edit bookmarks   Tools

Figure 6-15: Google Chrome has all of the usual controls, easily available.

4. **The first time you use Chrome, it will ask if you want to Sign In to Chrome. If you want your Chrome settings to follow you, onto any computer, tablet, or phone, sign in with a Google ID, such as a Gmail address.**

   I do. Syncing across many kinds of devices is one of the best parts about Chrome.

Navigating in Chrome

Navigation in Chrome is very similar to that in Firefox, except there's no search bar. Chrome doesn't need one: You just type into the address bar.

All the tricks I mention in the earlier IE section called "Don't work too hard" also perform in Chrome. You never need to type **http://**, almost never need to type **www**, and typing something like **dummies** followed by a Ctrl+Enter puts you directly into http://www.dummies.com.

The home page in Chrome is a little different from both IE and Firefox. The default in Chrome is to show what Chrome calls the New Tab page, which has icons to link you to the Chrome Web Store, Tweetdeck (for Twitter), YouTube (which is owned by Google, eh?), Gmail, and Google Search. The New Tab page adds more entries as you use the browser.

If you want to change the home page in Chrome, navigate to the page(s) you want to use. Click the wrench on the far-right side and choose Settings. A new tab opens with various Chrome settings. Under the heading On Startup, select the option Open a Specific Page or Set of Pages, then tap or click the link to Set Pages. In the lower left, tap or click Use Current Pages. You see a list like the one in Figure 6-16. Verify that you have the right pages, and then tap or click OK.

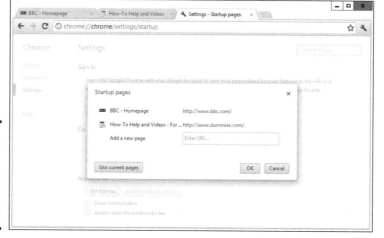

Figure 6-16:
Settings for
the home
page(s)
are on the
Settings tab.

Here's part of the magic of Chrome: If you signed in to Chrome using a Google ID (such as a Gmail e-mail address), changing the home page(s) here will change your Chrome home pages on all the computers — whether they're on PCs, tablets, phones — anywhere you go.

The following Chrome features are helpful as you move around the web using Chrome:

✦ **The default search engine:** The default search engine setting is on the same settings tab shown in Figure 6-16. Bing is one of the listed options, but you can add just about any search engine. Compare and contrast that with IE's default search engine hunting game.

✦ **Private browsing:** Chrome's version of InPrivate Browsing is called Incognito. To start a new Incognito window, click the wrench and choose New Incognito Window.

✦ **Bookmarks:** I find Chrome's Bookmarks capability much easier to use than Firefox's. To see why, go to a web page that you'd like to bookmark, then click the Bookmark star icon, on the right. If you want to rearrange your bookmark folders, click the Edit button and you can work with a full, hierarchical organization of folders, as in Figure 6-17.

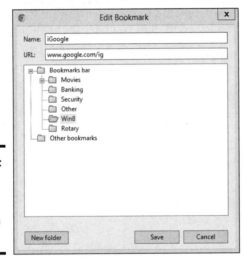

Figure 6-17:
Chrome
bookmarks
are simple
and easy to
organize.

While the Chrome Web Store won't make you shun the iTunes Store, it comes with a few cool items, including a free version of Angry Birds. Just start a new tab, and click the icon for the Chrome Web Store.

Chrome does have many add-ons (there's an Adblock for Chrome, for example), but it has never reached the depth or breadth of the Firefox add-on menagerie.

Ever since Google released its tiled version of Chrome, I find myself using Chrome more and more. No-hassle Flash inside the tiled part of Windows makes a difference to me. The ability to sync my browser settings — bookmarks, home pages, history — among many machines really helps, although IE has a similar feature, as long as I'm on Windows. It's easy to see why Chrome is slowly overtaking Internet Explorer in market share. Build a better browser, and the world will come.

Searching on the Web

Internet searching can be a lonely business. You're out there, on the Internet range, with nothing but gleaming banner ads and text links to guide you. What happens when you want to find information on a specific subject but you're not sure where to start? What if Google leads you on a wild goose chase? What if the Microsoft Bing "decision engine" takes the wrong turn?

Book VI
Chapter 6

Google's good. It's the search engine I use every day. But there are some good alternatives, several of which can help in specific situations. For example:

✦ Microsoft's **Bing** (www.bing.com) isn't all that bad, and it's getting better. Remains to be seen if Bing can come up with any really compelling reasons to switch from Google. Microsoft's dumping a ton of money into search — more than a billion dollars a year, at last count — and I'm not sure they've come up with anything that puts Bing clearly in the lead.

✦ **DuckDuckGo** (www.duckduckgo.com) is an up-and-comer that I find fascinating. It relies heavily on information from crowd-sourced sources, including Wikipedia. At this point, the results DuckDuckGo delivers aren't as close to what I want as Google's, but they're getting better. One big point in this search engine's favor: Like Firefox, DuckDuckGo doesn't track what you do.

✦ **Dogpile** (www.dogpile.com), an old favorite, aggregates search results from Google, Bing, Yahoo!, and other engines, and smashes them all together, in a remarkably quick way. If I can't find what I need on Google, I frequently turn to Dogpile.

✦ **Wolfram Alpha** (www.wolframalpha.com) isn't exactly a search engine. It's a mathematical deduction engine that works with text input. So, for example, it can compare methanol, ethanol, and isopropanol. Or it can describe to you details of all the hurricanes in 1991. Or it can analyze the motion of a double pendulum.

But I find myself going back to Google.

Google has gone from one of the most admired companies on the web to one of the most criticized — on topics ranging from copyright infringement to pornography to privacy and censorship — and the PageRank system has been demonized in terms rarely heard since the Spanish Inquisition. Few people now believe that PageRank objectively rates the "importance" of a web page; millions of dollars and thousands of months have been spent trying to jigger the results. Like it or not, Google just works. The Google spiders (the programs that search for information), which crawl all over the web, night and day, looking for pages, have indexed billions of pages, feeding hundreds of millions of searches a day. Other search engines have spiders, too, but Google's outspider them all.

As this book went to press, Google was worth about $190 billion, the verb *google* had been embraced by prestigious dictionaries, the company was taking on Microsoft *mano a mano* in many different areas, and many other search engines offered decent alternatives to the once almighty Google. Everything's changing rapidly, and that's good news for us consumers.

In this section, I show you several kinds of searches you can perform with Google (and the other search engines). No matter what you're looking for, a search engine can find it!

Finding what you're looking for

Google has turned into the 800-pound gorilla of the searching world. I know people who can't even find AOL unless they go through Google. True fact.

The more you know about Google, the better it can serve you. Getting to know Google inside and out has the potential to save you more time than just about anything in Windows proper. If you can learn to search for answers quickly and thoroughly — and cut through the garbage on the web just as quickly and thoroughly — you can't help but save time in everything you do.

You can save yourself a lot of time and frustration if you plot out your search before your fingers hit the keyboard.

Obviously, you should choose your search terms precisely. Pick words that will appear on any page that matches what you're looking for: Don't use *Compaq* when you want *Compaq S710*.

Beyond the obvious, the Google search engine has certain peculiarities you can exploit. These peculiarities hold true whether you're using Google in your browser's search bar or you venture directly to www.google.com:

✦ **Capitalization doesn't matter.** Search for *diving phuket* or *diving Phuket* — either search returns the same results.

✦ **The first words you use have more weight than the latter words.** If you look for *phuket diving*, you see a different list than the one for *diving phuket*. The former list emphasizes websites about Phuket that include a mention of diving; the latter includes diving pages that mention Phuket.

✦ **Google shows you only those pages that include all the search terms.** The simplest way to narrow a search that returns too many results is to add more specific words to the end of your search term. For example, if *phuket diving* returns too many pages, try *phuket diving beginners*. In programmer's parlance, the terms are banded together.

✦ **If you type more than ten words, Google ignores the ones after the tenth.**

✦ **You can use OR** to tell Google that you want the search to include two or more terms — but you have to capitalize OR. For example, *phuket OR samui OR similans diving* returns diving pages that focus on Phuket, Samui, or the Similans.

✦ **If you want to limit the search to a specific phrase, use quotes.** For example, *diving phuket "day trip"* is more limiting than *diving phuket day trip* because in the former, the precise phrase *day trip* has to appear on the page.

✦ **Exclude pages from the results by putting a hyphen in front of the words you don't want.** For example, if you want to find pages about diving in Phuket but you don't want to associate with lowly snorkelers, try *diving phuket-snorkeling*.

✦ **You can combine search tricks.** If you're looking for overnight diving, try *diving phuket-"day trip"* to find the best results.

✦ **Google supports wildcard searches** in quite a limited way: The asterisk (*) stands for a single word. If you're accustomed to searches in, say, Word or Windows, the * generally indicates a sequence of characters, but in Google it only stands for an entire word. You might search for *div** and expect to find both diver and diving, but Google won't match on either. Conversely, if you search for, oh, *email * * wellsfargo.com*, you find a lot of e-mail addresses. (The second * matches the at sign [@] in an address. Try it.)

If you use Google to search for answers to computer questions, take advantage of any precise numbers or messages you can find. For example, googling *computer won't start* doesn't get you anywhere; but *two beeps on startup* may. If you're trying to track down a Windows error message, use Google to look for the precise message. Write it down, if you have to.

Using Advanced Search

Didn't find the results you need? Use Google Advanced Search. There's a trick.

If you need to narrow your searches — in other words, if you want Google to do the sifting rather than do it yourself — you should get acquainted with Google's Advanced Search capabilities. Here's a whirlwind tour:

1. **Run your search and, if it doesn't have what you want, click the gear icon and choose Advanced Search.**

The Google gear icon is located in the upper-right corner *of the search results page* — it's not part of your browser, it's actually on the search results page.

Google brings up its Advanced Search page (see Figure 6-18).

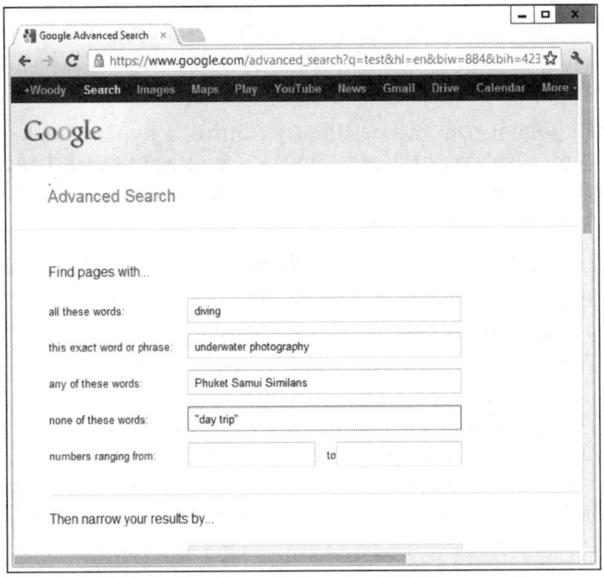

Figure 6-18: Advanced Search lets you narrow your Google search quickly and easily.

> **Google Advanced Search** ×
>
> https://www.google.com/advanced_search?q=test&hl=en&biw=884&bih=423
>
> +Woody Search Images Maps Play YouTube News Gmail Drive Calendar More ▾
>
> **Google**
>
> Advanced Search
>
> Find pages with...
>
> | | |
> |---|---|
> | all these words: | diving |
> | this exact word or phrase: | underwater photography |
> | any of these words: | Phuket Samui Similans |
> | none of these words: | "day trip" |
> | numbers ranging from: | to |
>
> Then narrow your results by...

2. **Fill in the top part of the page with your search terms.**

In Figure 6-18, I ask for sites that include the word *diving* and the exact phrase *underwater photography*. I also want to exclude the phrase *day trip* and return only pages pertaining to Phuket, Samui, or the Similans.

Anything you can do in the top part of this page can also be done by using the shorthand tricks mentioned in the preceding section. If you find yourself using the top part of the page frequently, save yourself some time and brush up on the tricks (such as typing **OR**, -, "") that I mention in the earlier section, "Finding what you're looking for."

3. **In the bottom part of the Advanced Search page, further refine your search by matching on the identified source language of the page (not always accurate); a specific filename extension (such as** `.pdf` **or** `.doc`**); or the domain name, such as** `www.dummies.com`**.**

   You can also click the link at the bottom to limit the search to pages stamped with specific dates (notoriously unreliable), pages with specific licensing allowances (not widely implemented), and ranges of numbers.

4. **Press Enter.**

   The results of your advanced search appear in a standard Google search results window (see Figure 6-19).

Figure 6-19: Running the stringent search specified in Figure 6-18 turns up 40,600 hits.

You can find more details about Google Advanced Search on the Google Advanced Search page, `www.google.com/help/refinesearch.html`.

Pulling out Google parlor tricks

Google has many tricks up its sleeve, some of which you may find useful — even if it's just to win a bet at a party. For example:

✦ To find the status of your UPS, FedEx, or USPS delivery, just type the package number (digits only) in the Google search box.

✦ The search box is a stock ticker. Type a symbol such as MSFT, GOOG, or AAPL.

✦ To use Google as a calculator, just type the equation in the Google search box. For example, to find the answer to $1,234 \times 5,678$, type **1234*5678** in the search box. Or, to find the answer to $3 \div \pi$, type **3/pi**. No, Google doesn't solve partial differentials or simultaneous equations — yet. For that, check out Wolfram Alpha.

✦ Google has a built-in units converter. The word in triggers the converter. Try **10 meters in feet** or **350 degrees F in centigrade** (or **350 f in c**) or **20 dollars in baht** or (believe me, this is impressive) **1.29 euros per liter in dollars per gallon**.

✦ To find a list of alternative (and frequently interesting) definitions for a word, type **define**, as in **define booty**.

✦ You can see movie reviews and local showtimes by typing **movie** and then the name of the movie, such as **movie hunger games**.

✦ Try quick questions for quick facts. For example, try **height of mt everest** or **length of mississippi river** or **currency in singapore**.

Working with RSS Feeds

If you haven't yet pulled together a few RSS Feeds, you're in for a treat.

Though IE can handle RSS Feeds all by itself, there's a much better way, using the website www.igoogle.com. If you use www.igoogle.com, you can put together RSS Feeds in IE, Firefox, or Chrome, no problem at all.

Here's how RSS, or Really Simple Syndication, works — really:

1. **A website (usually with "newsy" topics, but sometimes just a site that wants to get noticed) creates a specific kind of file, an RSS Feed.**

2. **When the website has, uh, new news, it adds a short new item to the beginning of the RSS Feed file and drops the last item off the end.**

   Typically, the new item is just a few sentences long. That keeps the RSS Feed short and simple and reasonably up to date.

3. **If you go to a website that maintains an RSS Feed, the site usually advertises that fact by placing a little orange box with "radio waves" somewhere near the top of the page.**

4. **When you find a site with an RSS Feed you want to follow, you *subscribe* to the feed.**

   It's kind of like subscribing to a newspaper or magazine, or a little bit like following someone on Twitter.

5. **A program on your computer, an *RSS reader,* periodically looks at the RSS Feeds for all web pages on your subscription list, and keeps track of the latest items.**

Many different RSS readers are running around. If you like, you can use the RSS readers built into Internet Explorer, Firefox, or Chrome, or one of several e-mail programs, or one of many for the tiled side of Windows. Personally, I find all of them intrusive and hard to work with. My personal choice for an RSS reader is the iGoogle customized page from Google.

Here's how to set up a custom iGoogle page, with your own RSS reader:

1. **If you don't already have one, go to** `www.gmail.com` **and create a Gmail account.**

   You don't have to use your real name. Larry Page doesn't.

2. **Fire up your favorite browser (tiled or desktop version) and go to** `www.igoogle.com`.

   You see a getting started page like the one shown in Figure 6-20.

Book VI Chapter 6

Choosing and Using a Desktop Web Browser

Figure 6-20: Get your own RSS reader going through iGoogle.

3. **Choose things that interest you, give your location if you like, then tap or click See Your Page.**

   iGoogle shows you your initial iGoogle home page.

4. **Click on the link to sign in with your Google id.**

   That automatically saves all of your changes. Your new iGoogle RSS page will be waiting for you any time you sign in to Google — anywhere.

   After you have the page set up, you can add more RSS Feed content by using the steps coming up next.

Feel free to use iGoogle as your browser's home page. I do.

With an iGoogle account set up, you have everything you need to keep on top of every site on earth. Here's how to start feeding your iGoogle page:

1. **Go to the desktop. (This doesn't work on the tiled side of Windows.) In any convenient browser, navigate to the site that you want to add to your RSS reader.**

   You should see the orange Radio Waves button featured prominently on the page. That tells you the site has an RSS feed.

2. **Go to** www.igoogle.com.

   Your browser shows you the iGoogle page which, depending on how many site Gadgets you've added, will look more or less like Figure 6-21. (Note that the term "Gadgets" in iGoogle is very different from the term "Gadgets" inside Windows itself.)

3. **Click on the tile marked Add Gadgets (see Figure 6-21).**

   Google shows you a page with many suggested sites.

Figure 6-21:
Go to the iGoogle page to set up an RSS feed "gadget" for your new site.

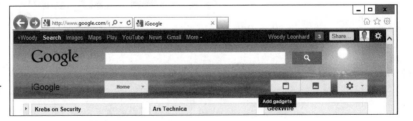

4. **You can use the search function, but in my experience it doesn't work very well. Far better is to click the link at the lower left that says Add Feed or Gadget.**

Google gives you a place to type in the address of the site that provides the feed, as shown in Figure 6-22.

Book VI
Chapter 6

Choosing and Using a Desktop Web Browser

Figure 6-22:
Type the site that offers an RSS Feed on the lower left.

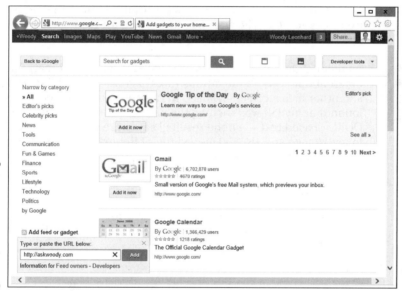

5. **Type the address of the site that you want to add to iGoogle, and then tap or click Add.**

If you got the address right, iGoogle shows a small notification that says it's added the site.

6. **In the upper-left corner, tap or click Back to iGoogle.**

You go back to the main iGoogle page. The new Gadget RSS feed appears as a box in the upper-left corner.

7. **You can click and drag the new RSS Feed Gadget anywhere on the page.**

Every few minutes, iGoogle reaches out to all sites on your iGoogle home page and retrieves the latest news from the sites' RSS Feeds.

You can customize the iGoogle home page till the cows come home. A series of tutorials is at www.google.com/support/websearch/?ctx=web.

Referring to Internet Reference Tools

I get questions all the time from people who want to know about specific tools for the Internet. Here are my choices for the tools that everyone needs.

Internet speed test

Everybody, but everybody, needs (or wants) to measure her Internet speed from time to time. The site I use these days for testing is `www.dslreports.com/speedtest`.

A million different speed tests are available on the Internet, and two million different opinions about various tools' accuracy, reliability, replicability, and other measurements. I used to run speed tests at Speakeasy, but then found that my ISP was caching the data — in fact, caching all the data from OOKLA-based test — so the results I saw were just local; they didn't reflect long-distance speeds. So I moved to DSLReports, with its tests that can't be cached, and haven't looked back.

DNSStuff

Ever wonder whether the website `BillyJoeBobsPhishery.com` belongs to BillyJoeBob? Head over to `www.dnsstuff.com` (see Figure 6-23) and find out.

Figure 6-23: DNSStuff offers a wide array of web- and Net-related tools.

You give DNSStuff a domain name and the site divulges all the public records about the site, commonly known as a whois: who owns the site (or at least who registered it), where the rascals are located, and whom to contact.

DNSStuff also tells you the official "abuse" contact for a particular site (useful if you want to lodge a complaint about junk mail or scams), whether a specific site is listed on one of the major spam databases, and much more.

3d Traceroute

So where's the hang-up? When the Internet slows down, you probably want to know where it's getting bogged down. Not that it will do you much good, but you might be able to complain to your ISP.

Book VI
Chapter 6

My favorite tool for tracing Internet packets is the free product 3d Traceroute, from German Holger Lembke in Braunschweig. You can download it at this website: `http://d3tr.de`. 3d Traceroute has no installer — it just runs. I like that.

Choosing and Using a Desktop Web Browser

When you run 3d Traceroute, you feed it a target location — a web address to use as a destination for your packets. As soon as you enter a target, 3d Traceroute runs out to the target and keeps track of all the hops — the discrete jumps from location to location — along the way. It measures the speed of each hop (see Figure 6-24).

Figure 6-24:
Why is the
Internet so
slow? 3d
Traceroute
pinpoints
pileups.

If you look at the ASN column, on the far-right end in Figure 6-24, you can see a list of AS numbers. Each number uniquely identifies a network operator.

You can search for the AS number at `www.google.com` and see where your packets hit a roadblock.

Down for everyone or just me?

So you try and try and can't get through to Wikipedia, or Hotmail has the hiccups: The browser keeps coming back and says it's timed out, or it just sits there and does nothing.

It's time to haul out the big guns. Hop over to `www.downforeveryoneor justme.com` (no, I don't make this stuff up) and type the address of the site that isn't responding. The computer on the other end checks to see whether the site you requested is still alive. Cool.

The Wayback Machine

He said, she said. We said, they said. Web pages come and go, but sometimes you just have to see what a page looked like last week, or last year. No problem, Sherman: Just set the Wayback Machine for November 29, 1975. (That's the day Bill Gates first used the name Micro Soft.)

If you're a Mr. Peabody look-alike and you want to know what a specific web page really said in the foggy past, head to the Internet Archive at `www.archive.org`, where the Wayback (or is it WABACK?) Machine has more than 85 billion web pages archived and indexed for your entertainment (see Figure 6-25).

Figure 6-25: Everything old is new again with the Archive.org Wayback Machine. This is what windows.com looked like 15 years ago, on October 11, 1997.

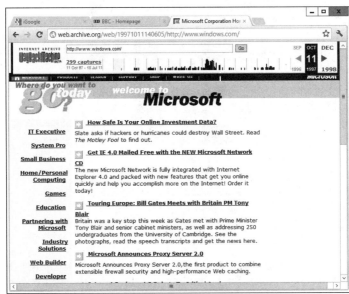

Chapter 7: Music on the Desktop

In This Chapter

✓ **Getting started with Windows Media Player**

✓ **Making the most out of your music**

✓ **Ripping and burning**

✓ **Creating and using playlists**

✓ **Using alternatives to WMP**

✓ **Finding more music**

Music on the Windows desktop rates as hard to find, a little bit boring, and certainly less enticing than the tiled version, over on the Start screen. But if you're listening to music because you like to listen to music (as opposed to buying more music from the Windows Store), the experience isn't bad at all.

Windows 8 comes with Windows Media Player (WMP), which is a decent application, and the subject of most of this chapter. Better players are out there, and I talk about a couple of them in this chapter, too.

If you're looking for tips about iTunes, I have a bunch (see Book X, Chapter 1). I don't like running iTunes on Windows; it works much better on a Mac. If you've installed and use iTunes as an alternative to Windows Media Player, I direct you to Book X, Chapter 1.

Windows Media Player has one additional good point: With WMP, you have a lot of control over your privacy — what data's sent to Mother Microsoft, and what stays private. If you don't like the idea of Microsoft collecting your playing history, you'll appreciate the control WMP offers over the tiled Music app.

Getting Started with Windows Media Player

The first problem you're likely to have with Windows Media Player? Finding it! This section helps you track down WMP and, if you're starting it for the first time, walks you through the setup screens that appear. If you've already found and fired up WMP a time or ten, this section explains how to adjust your privacy settings, if you so choose.

Pinning WMP to the Start menu or taskbar

In Book VI, Chapter 3, I go through a long list of applications that are built into Windows, but are hard to find. Windows Media Player is probably the most often used program on the list.

Here's the quick way to bring it back:

1. **Flip over to the Start screen.**

   If you're looking at the desktop, press the Windows key on your keyboard or push the Windows button on your tablet. Say hello to the tiled interface.

2. **Immediately type** windows media.

   As shown in Figure 7-1, Windows Media Player appears on the left side of the screen, under Apps.

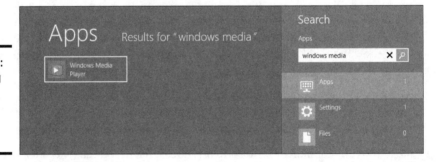

Figure 7-1:
Searching
for the
Windows
Media
Player.

3. **Tap and hold or right-click the Windows Media Player link in the upper-left corner.**

   Windows shows you the notification bar at the bottom of the screen.

4. **Tap or click Pin to Start if you want a tile for WMP to appear on the Start screen. Tap or click Pin to Taskbar if you want to put a WMP icon on your desktop taskbar.**

   I put WMP on my Start screen, but not on my taskbar. Why? I generally use VLC to play media — a subject I discuss several times later in this chapter. But sometimes I really do want to use WMP, so I look (and look and look) for it in the Start screen.

The competition

Windows Media Player isn't the only game in town. Although WMP excels in some respects, several competitors deserve your attention — if not your ears.

Lots of folks swear by Winamp, a mercifully compact, surprisingly capable player from Nullsoft (www.winamp.com). The basic player is free. If you want to add MP3 ripping and fast CD burning, it costs all of $19.95 — and you aren't pestered until the day you die to buy and download songs from a proprietary library. I use the free version of Winamp to sync songs with my Android phone. It'll also import my entire iTunes Library.

My favorite media program? A free, open-source, low-overhead player named VLC, created and maintained by the VideoLAN Project (www.videolan.org/vlc/ download-windows.html). Don't let its name fool you: VLC isn't just for LANs anymore, although it works great over home networks. Mostly, I use VLC when I don't want to stare at the gussy Windows Media Player interface, or when WMP just doesn't work. You'd be amazed at how many different video files, in particular, are a hassle to play in WMP but play immediately with VLC.

If you're looking for something a bit more glitzy — with a whole lot of capabilities, including the capability to handle enormous music collections — check out Media Monkey (www.mediamonkey.com). It's more than a player, something closer to a full-fledged movie and music library. The free version handles almost everything; the $24.95 version adds faster burning and unlimited MP3 ripping.

Setting WMP right the first time

The first time you fire up WMP, you're presented with a bunch of inscrutable choices.

If you haven't run WMP yet, here's how to get off on the right foot:

1. **Get WMP running. If you have a tile on the Start screen, click it. If you have an icon on the taskbar, click it.**

Either way, you're propelled to the desktop, and presented with the Welcome screen shown in Figure 7-2.

2. **Click the Custom Settings button, and then click the Next button.**

WMP shows you the Select Privacy Options dialog box, shown in Figure 7-3, which enables you to limit Windows Media Player's snooping. I think that's a good idea. You may feel that I'm being too harsh, and that Microsoft should be able to keep records of everything you're playing. Fair enough.

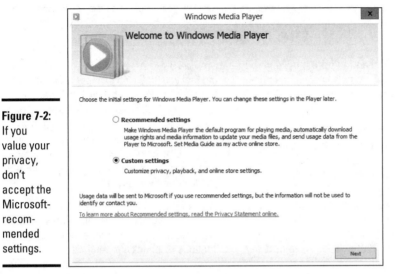

Figure 7-2:
If you
value your
privacy,
don't
accept the
Microsoft-
recom-
mended
settings.

Windows Media Player

Welcome to Windows Media Player

Choose the initial settings for Windows Media Player. You can change these settings in the Player later.

○ **Recommended settings**
Make Windows Media Player the default program for playing media, automatically download usage rights and media information to update your media files, and send usage data from the Player to Microsoft. Set Media Guide as my active online store.

◉ **Custom settings**
Customize privacy, playback, and online store settings.

Usage data will be sent to Microsoft if you use recommended settings, but the information will not be used to identify or contact you.

To learn more about Recommended settings, read the Privacy Statement online.

[Next]

Windows Media Player

Select Privacy Options

| Privacy Options | Privacy Statement |

Enhanced Playback Experience
☑ Display media information from the Internet
☑ Update music files by retrieving media information from the Internet
☐ Download usage rights automatically when I play or sync a file
Note: Media information that is retrieved may not be in your language.

Enhanced Content Provider Services
☐ Send unique Player ID to content providers
Click Cookies to view or change privacy settings that affect cookies   [Cookies]

Windows Media Player Customer Experience Improvement Program
☐ I want to help make Microsoft software and services even better by sending Player usage data to Microsoft

History
Store and display a list of recently/frequently played:
☐ Music   ☐ Pictures   ☐ Video   ☐ Playlists

[Back]   [Next]

Figure 7-3:
Big Brother
wants your
permission.

---

3. **Select or deselect the various check boxes, depending on your preferences.**

Microsoft has a long, tumultuous history of using Windows Media Player to gather all sorts of personal information about you and your media-playing habits. (Of course, the tiled Music app collects everything with wild abandon anyway.) Approach this dialog box with skepticism. I select only the Display Media Information from the Internet and the Update Music Files by Retrieving Media Information from the Internet check boxes. You may want to send Microsoft more, but unless you have an overwhelming reason to do so, I suggest that you limit your exposure. Of course, if you choose the option Display Media Information from the Internet, Microsoft keeps tabs on you, too. I guess it all boils down to a question of how much privacy you're willing to give up to get cool features such as automatically downloaded album covers and correct song titles.

The check box marked Download Usage Rights Automatically when I Play or Sync a File only applies to DRM-protected files that you bought long ago from Microsoft, which is why I never let WMP check for Usage Rights. Anything Microsoft sold you in the recent past doesn't have DRM protection. Anything that still has DRM protection deserves to be deleted.

4. **When you're comfortable with your privacy choices, click the Next button.**

WMP then asks whether you want it to be used as the default music and video player. If you haven't yet installed a competing product, such as VLC, go ahead and make WMP your default music and video player.

5. **Choose whether you want WMP to be your default player, and click the Next button.**

Finally, WMP asks if you want to set up an online store. In this case, the option is called Media Guide, and it's an option because Microsoft owns the Media Guide. You can buy music in much better ways, as I explain in the last section in this chapter.

6. **Choose Don't Set Up a Store Now, and click Finish.**

WMP springs to life, scans your Music library, and displays the available songs, as shown in Figure 7-4.

Book VI
Chapter 7

Music on the Desktop

Figure 7-4: Windows Music Player opens, shouting "Put me in, Coach! I'm ready to play, today."

WMP may take a while to scan your Music library and add songs as it bumps into them. (I talk about libraries in general, and the Music library in particular, in Book VII, Chapter 3.) Initially, your Music library includes your own Music folder, plus the Music folder in your computer's Public folder. WMP also reaches out across your network and HomeGroup, to see whether any media collections have been made available. Later in this chapter, I show you how to expand the library's reach.

Tweaking privacy options after installation

If you already installed WMP, or the latest version came preinstalled on your PC, take a moment now to turn off the $#@! Usage Rights setting. Follow these steps to do so:

1. **Start WMP.**

If you put a tile on your Start screen, tap or click it. If you put an icon on your desktop taskbar, click it. If you haven't done either, go to the Start screen, type **windows media**, and click Windows Media Player.

2. **Press Alt to open the main menu. (If you used an older version of WMP, I bet you wondered where it was hidden.) Then choose Tools⇨Options and click the Privacy tab (see Figure 7-5).**

3. **In particular, make sure the Download Usage Rights Automatically When I Play or Sync a File check box isn't selected. Personally, I deselect all check boxes except for the first two (refer to Figure 7-5).**

You might be wondering about the Automatically Check If Protected Files Need to Be Refreshed and the Set Clock on Devices Automatically check boxes. Both of those are related to subscription services — where you pay by the month for the capability to play music (or video) files. Both of those are obsolete, with Xbox Music now in the subscription driver's seat.

4. **Click the OK button.**

Your changes take affect immediately — although, if you didn't make these changes soon enough, Microsoft may already have your unique player ID on file. That isn't a horrible lapse of personal security, but it does add to the stockpile of personal information Microsoft has on file.

If you have questions about the other tabs in the Options dialog box, see the section "Customizing WMP," later in this chapter.

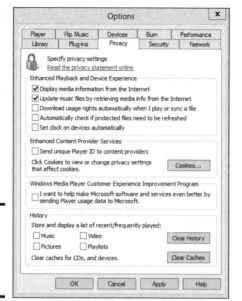

Figure 7-5:
Control
WMP
privacy
settings.

Playing with Now Playing

So much for the preliminaries. Let's get to the music, shall we?

After WMP scans your music — assuming you have any! — the screen
appears in Library view, which looks like Figure 7-6.

Library view, shown in Figure 7-6, enables you to leaf through the music
that WMP has identified. (See the earlier section "Setting WMP right the first
time" for details about what's imported.) From Library view, you see the
identified albums and songs in the middle, and get a plethora of tools for
finding and playing music and videos arrayed all around the window.

You control Windows Media Player by using the three tabs in the upper-right
corner of the window, and you control the music/videos by using the bar at
the bottom.

+ **Play tab:** Click or tap the tab to see the current *playlist* — the songs or
  videos that are going to be played. See the section, "Managing Playlists,"
  later in this chapter.

+ **Burn tab:** Sets up WMP to burn a CD or DVD — transfer music from your
  computer to a CD or DVD. See the section, "Burning CDs and DVDs,"
  later in this chapter.

✦ **Sync tab:** Synchronizes chosen songs with a supported plugged-in device. There aren't many devices that sync with Windows Media Player. No, it won't work with an iPad.

✦ **Controls:** The controls to play, pause, stop, and so on are labeled with their universal icons. See the next section, "Controlling the playback buttons," for details.

Navigation pane

Address bar   Albums and songs   Control WMP with these tabs

Figure 7-6:
Library view, where you can leaf through your music.

Controls for playing media   Switch to Now Playing mode

Library view, shown in Figure 7-6, enables you to leaf through the music that WMP imported when you first launched the program. (See the earlier section, "Setting WMP right the first time," for details about what's imported.) To get there, double-click an album, and then click the Play tab on the right. From Library view, you see the album and songs in the middle, and the following navigation tools are at your disposal:

✦ **Navigation pane:** Lets you choose the type of media you want to see or hear, look at it by album or artist, pick a playlist, or open up folders that aren't in your Music library.

Windows Media Player mashes together all the music in your Music library, but it doesn't include the albums (or video tracks or recorded

TV shows) outside your Music library (or Video Library or Recorded TV Library). To see music from a CD, USB flash drive, MP3 player, or any of the exposed music libraries on your network, you must pick that specific library in the navigation pane on the left or click the wedge to the left of the word Library and choose a different source.

✦ **Address bar:** In WMP, the address bar lets you choose a type of media and, in the case of music, navigate to specific albums.

The location of the music on your hard drive doesn't matter; as long as an album is in your Music library, WMP picks it up. That said, if you can't find an album you're looking for, flip to the section, "Leafing through the library," later in this chapter.

✦ **Playlist:** When the Play tab is selected, you see a playlist on the right side of the Now Playing window. A playlist is a sequence of tracks. You can create your own playlists or rely on the ones built into WMP. The Now Playing playlist, for example, is the list of tracks that are queued up to play, one after the other. To play a different track from the current playlist, double-click the track in the list of playlist contents. See the section, "Managing Playlists," later in this chapter, for details.

If you click the small bunch of squares in the lower-right corner of WMP (refer to Figure 7-6), the program shrinks to an appearance that Microsoft calls **Now Playing mode**, as shown in Figure 7-7.

Book VI
Chapter 7

Music on the
Desktop

Figure 7-7:
WMP in
Now Playing
mode.

Controlling the playback buttons

The buttons along the bottom of the library window (refer to Figure 7-6) are similar to the buttons on a conventional CD player. From left to right:

✦ **Shuffle** jumps quasi-randomly among all the songs in the current playlist.

✦ **Repeat** plays all the items in the current playlist and then goes back to the top and plays them again.

You can turn on both Shuffle and Repeat, in which case WMP picks tracks randomly from the playlist and doesn't stop until you turn it off.

✦ The **Stop** button stops the playing. Click the Play button to start playing again. Unlike Pause/Resume, the Stop/Start button returns to the start of the track. To start a different track, double-click that track in the playlist.

✦ **Play/Pause** work just the way you expect. When playing is paused, the Pause button toggles to a Play button. Click it again to make playing resume.

✦ The **Previous Track** button skips to the start of the preceding track. From the first track in the playlist, it skips to the beginning of the last track on the playlist.

✦ The **Next Track** button skips to the start of the next track. From the last track in the playlist, it skips to the first.

✦ The **Mute** button silences the sound. Click the button again to restore the sound. Unlike the Pause button, the Mute button does not halt playing. If you mute the sound for ten seconds, you miss hearing ten seconds of the track. If you mute Snoop Dogg for ten seconds, you get un-rapped (heh-heh-heh).

That's about all you need to know to play music from a playlist.

Playing a CD

Want to play a CD? Here's how:

1. **Take the CD out of its plastic case, if it's in one.**

2. **Wipe the pizza stains off the shiny side. (Don't worry about the other side.)**

The correct method: Hold the CD with one finger in the hole in the middle, the other on the edge, and wipe gently from the middle to the outside. Start with a clean soft cloth, and if that doesn't work, try rubbing alcohol or plain ol' soap and water.

3. **Stick the CD in the PC's drive and close it.**

Windows shows you a toaster notification, sliding in from the right, that asks you to tap to choose what happens with Audio CDs. If you tap or click the toaster notification, Windows then gives you the option to Play the Audio CD with Windows Media Player, or to take no action. (See Figure 7-8.)

Figure 7-8:
The toaster notification on top appears when you insert an audio CD. If you tap or click it, the choices appear below.

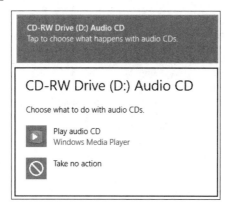

4. **Tap or click the No, I'd Rather Clip My Toenails — What Did You Think I Wanted to Do? or the Play Audio CD Windows Media Player button, whichever suits your fancy.**

If WMP isn't running already, it starts all by itself. Then you wait a few seconds and WMP starts playing the first track, using the Now Playing visage (refer to Figure 7-7).

Be aware of the fact that if you do tap or click to play the CD in Windows Media Player, you've set a precedent: In the future, every time you insert an audio CD, it'll start playing unless you change the AutoPlay settings (as I explain in the sidebar, "How to change AutoPlay settings").

How does WMP know what's on an audio CD? After it identifies the CD from information encoded along with the recorded tracks, it gets the CD's description and track titles over the web, from a database maintained for that purpose.

If a CD is quite obscure — or really good — it may not be in the Microsoft database. Then WMP can display only the information it finds on the CD itself: the number of tracks and the playtime of each track. If a CD isn't in the Microsoft database, you can enter the names of the songs manually. (To do so, right-click any song and choose Edit, and then type a new name.)

How to change AutoPlay settings

Whenever you insert a new CD into a PC, Windows 8 analyzes the CD and takes an action based on what you've told it to do. If you don't change anything, Windows pops up the query in Figure 7-8 and does whatever you say.

That's true not only for CDs, but also true for memory cards, DVDs, blank CDs or DVDs, or removable drives such as USB flash drives.

If you want Windows 8 to start automatically playing, say, audio CDs, bring up Control Panel (right-click in the lower-left corner), and in the Search box, type **autoplay**. Click AutoPlay and you have options for every conceivable combination of inserted media and file types: audio CDs, Blue-ray movies, blank DVDs, you name it.

Copying from a CD (Also Known As Ripping)

When you *rip* a CD, your computer converts the audio tracks on the CD into files that your computer can understand. Most people rip to MP3 files, because they're universal — they'll play on anything. But if you're an audiophile, you may want to rip to FLAC files, which carry all of the original music information. If you're happy with the CD ripping settings in Windows Media Player, all you need to do is put the CD in your drive, wait for WMP to start, and then click the Rip CD icon at the top. Ripping a CD onto your computer is that easy.

If you haven't ripped a CD yet, it helps to understand and adjust the settings before you rip that first CD. In WMP, the settings are sticky, so they remain the same until you adjust them again. In the following sections, I explain a little about music file formats and then walk you through the settings that you can adjust in WMP.

Understanding music file formats

Microsoft wants you to store music in its format. The *Windows Media Audio* format, created and owned by Microsoft, is the default format in which Windows Media Player rips files from a CD onto your computer. The WMA format has advantages: It creates files that are higher in quality and/or smaller in size than the MP3 format that I suggest you use. However, WMA has major disadvantages:

✦ First, at least in theory, WMA files can be locked down with Digital Rights Management (DRM) restrictions. It appears as if Microsoft (following Apple's lead) has finally gotten over its DRM dreams, but WMA still leaves your files potentially vulnerable. Why fill your libraries with files that could, at some point, be protected.

✦ Second, not every player can play WMA files. Apple and Microsoft are duking it out in the marketplace, and they aren't always interested in interoperability. Furthermore, the next awesome music widget may come from who-knows-where. Copying your music in a proprietary format means you may have trouble playing it wherever you want down the road.

By contrast, the MP3 format is inherently more flexible. MP3 rates as a more-or-less standard format, free to everyone. (That is, no one has to pay to license MP3, unlike with WMA; the cost can be a deterrent to supporting a format.) MP3 is also an open format, which is to say that no one can apply Digital Rights Management restrictions to MP3 files, making them infinitely more portable than files in a proprietary format.

So, when you copy new music files to your computer, you want those files to be MP3.

Adjusting the WMP ripping settings

If you want to rip CD files into the MP3 format, you have to change the settings inside Windows Media Player. Don't worry; it's easy if you know how.

Here's how to rip a CD that any computer can work with:

1. **Put the audio CD that you want to copy into the CD drive.**

Windows responds with notifications like the ones in Figure 7-8. Sooner or later you end up in the Library view of Windows Media Player, similar to Figure 7-6.

2. **When your CD starts playing, press the Alt key, then choose Tools⇨Options. Then click the Rip Music tab.**

You see the Rip Music Options dialog box, shown in Figure 7-9.

3. **(Optional) In the Rip Music to This Location box (refer to Figure 7-9), tap or click the Change button. Navigate to your Public Music folder and click OK.**

Easiest way to find your Public Music folder is by starting with your Libraries, then choosing Music⇨Public.

This step ensures that the audio files you rip end up in your computer's Public Music folder, where other people using your computer, and other people on your network, can find them. See Book VI, Chapter 1 for an introduction to Public folders.

Of course, if you're the only one who listens to the music on your computer, you can skip this step.

Figure 7-9:
Set rip
parameters
before you
start ripping.

4. **In the Rip Settings Format drop-down box, choose MP3.**

5. **Slide the Audio Quality slider over to 192 Kbps or 256 Kbps.**

   At 192 Kbps, the quality of the songs you rip is close to the original quality of the CD recording. If you don't mind making your files bigger for
   higher-quality songs, choose 256 Kbps or even 320 Kbps (which is, in my
   opinion, indistinguishable from the original).

   See Table 7-1 for a thumbnail comparison of sound quality and file size.

6. **(Optional) If you're trying to rip a really scratchy CD, and don't mind
   allowing WMP extra time to try to recover all the music it can possibly
   ferret out, on the Devices tab, click your CD drive, then click Properties.
   Select the box marked Use Error Correction, and click OK.**

   For details, see the section "Customizing WMP," near the end of this
   chapter.

7. **Click OK.**

8. **Back in Windows Media Player (see Figure 7-10), make sure that
   Windows Media Player has correctly identified the name of the album
   and all the tracks, er, songs.**

Click here to rip

Figure 7-10:
Windows
Media
Player is
ready to let
'er rip.

If any information is missing — rare, in my experience, even with obscure CDs — right-click the incorrect entry and choose Find Album Info. WMP phones home and retrieves as many matches for the album as it can find. You can then choose the correct album or right-click the track, choose Edit, and type your own information.

9. **(Optional) If you want to choose specific songs to copy, select the check boxes to the left of each track that you want to copy and deselect the check boxes next to the ones you want to leave behind.**

To rip all tracks (copy all songs) on the CD, you don't need to do anything.

10. **Click the Rip CD link.**

The Rip settings are "sticky," so after you set them correctly, there's no need to reset them. Thus, the second time you rip a CD (and all subsequent times), you can click Rip Music and rip away.

Windows Media Player dutifully copies the tracks you selected, placing the "ripped" files in the default folder, which (if you followed Step 5) is your Public Music folder.

Table 7-1	Number of CDs That Fit on a 32GB iPad	
MP3 Quality	*Sound Quality*	*Number of CDs*
128 Kbps	Excellent on a portable player and so-so on good sound equipment	More than 500
192 Kbps	Very good on normal consumer audio systems	More than 350
256 Kbps	Indistinguishable from the original CD	More than 280
320 Kbps	As good as it gets	More than 200

Why can't I rip a video DVD?

I once had dinner with a senior Microsoft exec who told me, point blank, "As far as Bill's concerned, ripping any DVD is illegal." Full stop. Bill isn't around anymore, but his sentiment still permeates the Redmond offices.

That's why Microsoft doesn't make tools that allow you to rip DVDs. Microsoft doesn't want the legal hassles. It doesn't want to alienate movie companies. It doesn't want to be viewed as soft on copyright violation. There's a whole lotta upside to being friendly with movie companies, and exactly zero potential profit in providing DVD-ripping software.

The legalities of the situation vary depending on where you live, but in my opinion, everyone should be able to create digital backups of DVDs they own. DVDs die. Bits don't. Or, at least they don't die as frequently as DVDs. My observation may be against the law in your neck of the woods — or it may be legal today and illegal tomorrow. To be sure, ask your lawyer how she rips *her* DVDs. If ripping DVDs is illegal where you live this week, please take a thick black pen and mark out the rest of this sidebar.

There's nothing particularly unique about a DVD movie disc. The movie consists of a handful of files. A typical DVD movie disc contains two folders: AUDIO_TS and VIDEO_TS, and the AUDIO_TS folder is usually empty. The VIDEO_TS folder contains files with names ending in BUP, IFO, and VOB. All the video tracks, including the sound tracks and subtitles, are in the VOB files. Each VOB file runs about 15 minutes.

If you run VLC (see the sidebar "The competition," earlier in this chapter), you have everything you need to watch VOB files: Simply start VLC, choose Media⇨Open File, and open the VOB. You can choose the language track and subtitles by using the VLC menu. Fifteen minutes later, when the first VOB is finished, open the next one. It's that simple.

For those with VLC who don't mind interruptions every 15 minutes, you can copy an entire DVD by just clicking the VOB filenames and dragging them to your computer.

You can use VLC to rip your DVDs, but I've started using a program that's easier. WinX DVD Ripper, from a company known as Digiarty, works like a champ, and it's free. See www.winxdvd.com.

To a first approximation, WMP makes a folder for each artist, and inside the artist's folder, it makes a subfolder for each album. The music tracks go into the album's folder. (Things get a little hairy when two artists collaborate on a song. In that case, WMP puts all the songs in one folder, and that folder usually goes under the name of the artist who performed most of the album. If WMP can't decide, you may find a folder named Various Artists or Unknown Artist. Frequently, classical music is filed under the name of the composer, not the artist performing the piece.)

If you're connected to the Internet, WMP grabs all associated album information — track titles, album cover art, and artist — and sticks it in the folder along with the music. Sweet.

Because you ripped the album into your Public Music folder, your newly ripped album appears in the Music library list, and in the Windows Media Player Library list, for you, for other people who use your computer, and for anyone who can connect to your Public Music folder. Even Macs on your home network can get to it. Smart, eh

Organizing Your Media Library

Windows Media Player picks up all the songs in your Windows 8 Music library, which you can sort through to find and select songs to play, but that isn't always the best way to find the music you want. This section introduces to you the library-based organization and explains ways to further organize and find your files using built-in WMP tools for rating, sorting, and searching.

Leafing through the library

When you start WMP, it's in Library mode, which displays a window split into three panes, with the library's structure on the left, the contents of the selected item on the right, and the current playlist also on the right, as shown in Figure 7-11.

WMP uses the Windows 8 libraries — Music, Video, Pictures — to organize soundtracks, videos, TV shows, and so on. When you understand how Windows libraries work, you can organize your music just the way you want. I talk about Windows 8 libraries in Book VII, Chapter 3.

Figure 7-11:
My Music
library, or
at least a
small part
of it, seen
through
the eyes of
Windows
Media
Player.

You can see the media-related Windows 8 libraries along the left side: Music, Videos, and Pictures. Also along the left are additional categories that are specific to (and handled by) Windows Media Player. You can choose from among the categories by clicking the category. Here's the rundown of categories you find:

✦ **Playlist:** Every playlist you've created appears here. See "Managing Playlists," later in this chapter, for details about creating a playlist.

✦ **Music:** Contains all the audio tracks in your Windows Music library, such as those you ripped from CDs, copied from other computers, or bought via the tiled Music app. You can have WMP sort and gather audio tracks by artist, album, or genre (rock, classical, comedy, folk, jazz, dance, or Cajun, for example).

The Music library contains only items in your Windows Music library. If you haven't changed anything, that includes your \Music folder and your computer's \Public\Music folder. If you want to look in other libraries in your HomeGroup or network, you have to click the specific library, as listed under Other Libraries, at the bottom of the list.

✦ **Videos:** Contains the contents of your Windows Video Library. WMP can play video files in many formats, including ASF, AVI, MPG, WMV, and many others — but not the Apple-protected M4V format, or the Apple MOV format, and not in the native DVD movie VOB format. (See the earlier sidebar "Why can't I rip a DVD?").

✦ **Pictures:** Contains various kinds of image files that happen to be located in your Windows Pictures Library. WMP may be the worst place to work with pictures. See the discussion of Windows Photo Gallery in Book VI, Chapter 5.

✦ **Other Libraries:** Most of the time this includes links to shared media on PCs attached to your HomeGroup.

Changing album and song data

The Windows Media Player library folders are powerful tools for keeping your recordings organized because they offer so many different ways of looking at the same information.

It behooves you to keep your data clean. Misfiled and misidentified songs lead to endless frustration when you can't find a song that you know should be in the library. If you want to change the data associated with a bunch of songs (for example, if the songs are all by the same artist or on the same album), follow these steps:

1. **Find them in the library, and get the library to list the individual songs.**

   If you can only see an album cover, double-click the cover and WMP shows you a list of songs.

2. **Select the songs.**

   Ctrl+click to select individual songs or Shift+click to select a group of songs.

3. **Right-click one of the fields (for example, Album or Artist) and choose Edit. Click the Content tab.**

   You'll find that the descriptions on the Content tab don't match WMP's column headings (for example, Artist on the tab, Contributing Artist in WMP), but the correlation isn't hard to divine.

4. **Choose the tag you want to change. Type the new value and press Enter.**

   All selected songs are changed at the same time.

If you want to get serious about manipulating tags like these, get Media Monkey (www.mediamonkey.com). Media Monkey handles tags like a, well, like a monkey. You can use Media Monkey and WMP on the same Library, no problem.

Rating songs

One of the most powerful WMP capabilities, creating and manipulating playlists based on your own ratings of individual songs or videos, works only if you take the time to rate your songs. To rate any track or album at any time, right-click it, choose Rate, and give it a rating from 1 to 5 stars. You can even select multiple tracks or albums and rate them all in one fell swoop. In the WMP list shown in Figure 7-11, you can just click the stars next to a track.

If you have WMP show you albums rather than individual songs, the really cool rating system doesn't work as well. When WMP rates an album, it uses the average rating of all the songs in the album. So, if you have an absolutely great song inside an otherwise rather dull album and then you sort the albums by rating, you might not even get around to that truly great song. The only solution? Lie. Rate all songs in the album with five stars. That way, the album floats to the top of the charts.

Sorting songs

You have a great deal of flexibility in the ways you can sort. If you want to look at all your rap and hip-hop albums, for example, make sure that you're looking at the Music category (in the upper-left area) and then double-click Album to list all albums by album name. Now click the top of the Genre column to sort the list of tracks by genre, from A to Z. Click Genre again to sort the list backward.

If your collection of recordings is large, sorting the list in different ways can help you find items you want. Microsoft claims that Windows Media Player can handle tens of thousands — even hundreds of thousands — of tracks. Go ahead. Put it to the test.

Searching

You can search the Music library (or any of the other libraries, for that matter) for items that have certain words in their titles or for artist names, album names, composer names, conductor, date, or genres. When your collection of recordings becomes too large to inspect easily, searching is a convenient way to find things in it.

To find what you want, simply start typing in the Search box, in the upper-right part of the screen. WMP responds immediately, narrowing its list of found items as you type. The following tips can help you with searching and discerning WMP's search results:

✦ **You can use the Windows search tricks,** which I describe in Book VI, Chapter 8. For example, AND, OR, and NOT work in the Search box: A search on Willie Nelson AND minuet brings up Willie's "Bach Minuet in G" from his album The Promiseland. No, I'm not kidding.

✦ **Results include titles and genre.** In Figure 7-12, my search for *blue* brought up Eric Clapton's song "Blues Power," as I would expect, but also Eric Bibb's Get Onboard album. Why? The album is filed under the genre Blues.

Figure 7-12:
Searches
look for
titles, artist
names,
album
names,
genres,
composers,
and other
ancillary
meta
information.

✦ **You might have to navigate through a link to see search results.**
Depending on where you perform the search, WMP may display a list
of how many artists, albums, or songs match the search criteria. In that
case, simply click the underlined link to view the results.

Strangely, Windows Media Player doesn't participate in the Charms bar
based Search that's touted on the tiled side of the Windows 8 fence. If you
try to use the Search charm in WMP, you won't find anything.

Searching the Music library is much like searching in File Explorer on the
desktop — no doubt because they use the same search engine.

Managing Playlists

Er, maybe that should be mangling playlists.

WMP gives you all sorts of control over which songs you hear, and it does so
through playlists. Did you ever want to rearrange the order of the songs on
The Beatles' White Album? My son just about croaked when he found out he
could burn a CD that plays Britney Spears's "Oops! . . . I Did It Again" immediately after Eminem's homage "Oops! . . . The Real Slim Shady Did It Again."
You've got the power. Hmmm. That's a catchy tag line, isn't it?

Windows Media Player helps you create your own playlists, and you can
modify them to your heart's content.

Creating a new playlist

If you have a favorite set of tracks that you like to hear in a particular order and the tracks are in the Music library (or Video Library), you can build a playlist that gives you precisely what you want. It's like being able to create your own, custom CD.

In fact, you can use a playlist to make your own custom CD if you have a CD burner. (er, recorder). Nothing to it. The section "Burning CDs and DVDs," later in this chapter, explains how.

To make your own playlist, follow these steps:

1. **In Windows Media Player, make sure that the Music library is showing (on the left edge). On the right, click the tab marked Play.**

2. **If the Playlist area on the right has a bunch of music in it, click the Clear List link at the top of the Playlist area.**

   Windows Media Player invites you to drag items to create a new playlist, as shown in Figure 7-13.

3. **On the left, navigate to each song that you want to have on the playlist, and then drag it to your preferred location on the right.**

   You can use any of the navigation tools: Choose an artist, album, or genre, or use the Search box. Everything's fair game.

   WMP adds the track to the playlist. In Figure 7-14, I build a playlist of rock songs by the Thai-American artist Tata Young.

Figure 7-13: Build a new playlist by dragging tracks to the area on the right.

Figure 7-14:
Various
tracks from
my favorite
Thai rock
singer.

4. **If you decide that you don't want a specific song on the playlist, right-click it and choose Remove from List.**

5. **Click and drag a song to move it up or down in the playlist.**

6. **When you're happy with your playlist, click the Save List button at the top of the Playlist area.**

   WMP highlights the Untitled Playlist text box, inviting you to type a name for the new playlist.

7. **Type a name for your new playlist in the Untitled Playlist text box and press Enter.**

   WMP saves your new playlist. It appears anywhere playlists appear, anywhere in Windows Media Player.

That's how easy it is to create a new playlist.

Note how Windows Media Player shows you the common decency of not arbitrarily rearranging the order of the songs.

Renaming and deleting playlists

To change a playlist's name, you can right-click the playlist name on the left, in the Playlists list, and choose Rename. Or, you can simply click the playlist name near the top of the Playlist area on the right, and type the new name.

To delete a playlist, follow these steps:

1. **Tap and hold or right-click the playlist in the Playlists list (say that ten times really fast) and choose Delete. Or, just click the playlist and press Delete.**

   WMP responds with a confusing dialog box, as shown in Figure 7-15.

Figure 7-15:
Select an option to delete a playlist.

Don't worry. Removing a playlist does *not* remove the songs from your computer. Where the dialog box says Delete from Library and My Computer, it isn't referring to the songs. The songs stay on your computer no matter which choice you make. The dialog box is referring to the *playlist* — and you can delete a playlist from your computer with no ill effect.

2. **Choose either the Delete from Library Only or the Delete from Library and My Computer check box, and then click OK.**

   There's essentially no difference between the two choices, unless you want to copy playlists from computer to computer.

Burning CDs and DVDs

If your computer has a CD or DVD writer, you can create an audio CD by using tracks in the Music library. Windows Media Player makes it easy.

Most audio players these days will play MP3 files: You don't need to create an audio CD, if it's going to be used in any reasonably modern CD or DVD player. I mention this because you can fit a bunch more songs on a CD if you just burn the MP3 files without formatting it as an audio CD. A standard audio CD can hold one album (or maybe half of a very long album — you get the idea), whereas a CD packed with MP3s can hold 100 to 200 songs.

From a bit's point of view, a CD holds about 650MB (megabytes = millions of bytes). That's enough for eight or ten typical songs, if they're in normal audio format. But a typical song that's been ripped and converted to a normal MP3 runs 3MB to 5MB. It isn't at all unusual for a CD filled with MP3 files to hold 10 or 12 or more albums.

Which leads to the big question: If you need to make a CD to play in a CD player, should you use File Explorer or Windows Media Player? The short answer:

✦ **If you need to play the CD in an old CD player that doesn't understand MP3 files,** then you have to burn in Windows Media Player — and you'll only get a dozen typical songs or so on a CD. See the next section, "Burning an audio CD."

✦ **If you're going to play the CD in a CD player that understands MP3s,** my preference is to burn it in Windows Media Player, too. It's a little harder to set up than in File Explorer, where you just click and drag and you're done. But WMP has a bunch of support that just doesn't exist in File Explorer. See "Burning data CDs and DVDs with Media Player," a little later in this chapter, for details.

Burning an audio CD

In this section, I only deal with *audio CDs,* the old-fashioned CDs that only hold one album per CD, give or take a bit.

The process of writing data to a CD is called *burning.* Rip and burn. Rip and burn. WMP enables you to burn a plain, old-fashioned, everyday audio CD very, very easily. Here's the quickest way I know to put together a dynamite audio CD:

1. **Stick a blank CD-R disc in your CD drive.**

Assuming that you have a CD drive that's capable of burning CDs, and that this is the first time you've put a blank CD in your PC, Windows responds with a notification that says "CD-RW Drive: Tap to Choose What Happens with Blank CDs." If you then tap or click the notification, you get a second notification, shown in Figure 7-16.

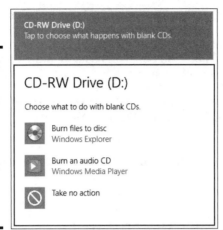

Figure 7-16:
The toaster notification on top appears first. Click or tap on it, and you get the choices shown below.

2. **Tap or click the Burn an Audio CD Using Windows Media Player icon.**

Keep in mind that this is a "sticky" choice: The next time you insert a blank CD, Windows will assume that you want to burn an audio (not a data) CD, and take you to the appropriate place in Windows Media Player. If you want to reset or change the Windows default action, follow the instructions in the sidebar, "How to change AutoPlay settings," earlier in this chapter.

Windows opens WMP and starts a burn list for you on the right (see Figure 7-17).

Figure 7-17:
Ready to create a burn list.

3. **Using any tricks you can muster (listing by artist or album, sorting, searching, pulling up an existing playlist — whatever), click and drag the tracks you want to burn, and arrange them on the right, in the burn list.**

Keep an eye on the "Remaining" number at the top of the list. WMP has been known to overestimate the available room on a CD, so it's a good idea to leave a minute or two or three, unused, on the CD.

If you try to put too much music on a CD, WMP breaks out the burn list, with horizontal lines marking the current disc, the next disc, the next disc, and so on. When you burn a multidisc list, you just have to keep feeding CDs into the drive. Easy.

4. **As a precaution, if you just created a unique playlist, save it by clicking the name Burn List at the top of the playlist on the right (see Figure 7-18) and typing a new name.**

The saved playlist can come in handy if a problem crops up with the burn that you don't find out about for a day or two or three. You can select your saved playlist rather than redo the working of choosing and arranging the tracks just the way you want them.

Figure 7-18:
Save your
Burn List in
case you
need it later.

5. **Before you burn, double-check the burn options so that you don't, uh, get burned. Press the Alt key, and then choose Organize⇨Options and then click the Burn tab. See Figure 7-19.**

Figure 7-19:
Set the
basic burn
character-
istics.

6. **Follow the advice in Table 7-2 to set up the burn the way you want it.**

7. **When you're happy with your choices, click the OK button.**

   WMP goes back to the main Burn window (refer to Figure 7-18).

8. **Click the Start Burn button, at the top of the burn list.**

   WMP processes each track in turn, converting it from a music file into data that's required on an audio CD and, when it's done converting, writing each one to the CD.

   It's truly that simple. When WMP is done, pull the CD out of the CD burner and plop the CD into any CD player. The magic's the music.

Table 7-2	**Recommended Burn Options**	
Setting	*Recommendation*	*Reason*
Burn Speed	Slow	Greatly reduces the chances of turning out a coaster. If it takes longer, it takes longer, okay?
Apply Volume Leveling Across Tracks	Select	It takes more time but ensures that a rogue song doesn't blast your ears.

Burn CD without Gaps	Select	If you deselect this check box, WMP inserts an additional 2-second gap between each track.
Add a List of All Burned Files	M3U	Use M3U, the universal playlist format. WPL is the Microsoft format.
Use Media Information to Arrange Files	Deselect	Keep this option deselected so that WMP leaves the sequence of your tracks the way you set them when you burn a "data disc" — a disc full of MP3 files. (Note that WMP always honors your sequencing when you burn an old-fashioned audio CD.) If you select the box, WMP groups data disc songs by album, no matter how you laid out the tracks in the burn list. The files appear in \Music\Artist\Album folders, where the artist and album information is pulled from each individual track.

The copying process takes, oh, a third to a fifth of the time it would take to play the copied tracks, the exact time depending on the speed of your CD writer.

If you interrupt the writing process by clicking the Stop Burn button or by removing the CD from the writer before the burn is complete, WMP goes bananas and the whole process stops. A fried CD-R ain't good for anything but a coaster.

Burning data CDs and DVDs with Media Player

The procedure for burning data CD-Rs, CD-RWs, DVD-Rs, and DVD-RWs with Windows Media Player is essentially the same as that described in the preceding section, except that . . .

. . . you can fit a whole lot more music on a data CD than on an audio CD. In spite of that fact, the burning process for a data CD can go faster than that for an audio CD. Why? WMP doesn't have to preprocess data files — it doesn't need to convert them into a form that works with audio CD players.

If you already set the data disc's options in the preceding section's Step 6 (refer to Table 7-2), you've done everything you need to do to produce top-notch MP3 CDs and DVDs. Just remember to click the check box icon above the burn list and choose Data CD or DVD, as shown in Figure 7-20.

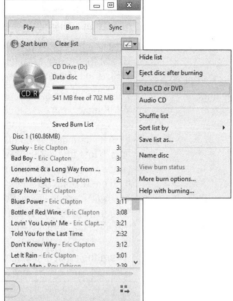

Figure 7-20: To burn a data disc (full of MP3s), be sure to choose Data CD or DVD before you start the burn.

Sharing Your Windows Media Player Media

Windows Media Player can make media in its libraries available to other computers on your network by using the streaming technique. To a first approximation, streaming involves using your Windows PC to send signals to a digital media player, which can then play the music or show a movie on a television. That can be mighty handy if you want to hook up an Xbox, or some other network digital media player, to play songs or movies.

The mechanics for setting up a network in your house or small office are straightforward. The mechanics for sharing things over the network aren't quite so easy.

If your Windows computer is part of a HomeGroup (see Book VII, Chapter 5) and you haven't changed any settings, your computer automatically shares everything in its media libraries (Music library, Video Library, Picture Library) with all other computers in the HomeGroup and with every user on every computer in the HomeGroup.

If you have an Xbox or some other kind of networked digital media player that doesn't understand HomeGroups, you should hop into Windows Media Player and give Windows permission to share your media — assuming that you want to share your media.

Here's how to share all your media:

1. **Start Windows Media Player and click the Play tab.**

2. **In the upper-left corner, choose Stream⇨More Streaming Options.**

   You see the Media Streaming Options dialog box. Depending on how many computers you have connected to your network, it looks more or less like Figure 7-21.

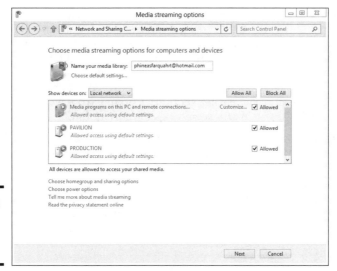

Figure 7-21:
Media
sharing
options.

3. **In the Show Devices On drop-down box, choose All Networks.**

4. **Click the button marked Allow All.**

   This step sets up streaming for any device now connected to your network. It also opens your media libraries to other computers on your network. Windows Media Player on those other computers shows your media libraries under the Other Libraries entry on the left side of the main Windows Media Player window.

If you get stuck with a copy-protected file that plays only on your computer, or an odd file format that works only on your computer, streaming in this way may be a viable option — if your network is fast enough to handle the load.

Customizing WMP

You can customize WMP in several ways. You get to most of the settings by pushing the Alt key on your keyboard (or the onscreen keyboard), then choosing Organize⇨Options. This command displays a dialog box with a bunch of tabs for customizing many aspects of WMP behavior:

✦ **Player:** Controls general aspects of WMP behavior, such as checking for automatic updates.

✦ **Rip Music:** Controls aspects of the copying process, including, most importantly, the format of ripped CDs (which you set to MP3 already, right?). You can also control the amount of data compression to apply when copying a CD. (More compression makes the copied tracks occupy less space, but reduces sound quality.) It also controls the folder to which music is copied. (You changed it to your computer's Public Music folder, right?) The earlier section, "Copying from a CD (Also Known As Ripping)," explains these settings in more detail.

✦ **Devices:** Lists available devices that WMP can use (such as CD drives and portable players) and enables you to control certain aspects of their behavior. If you tend to rip CDs with lots of scratches, click the Devices tab, click your DVD drive, and then choose Properties. In the Rip section at the bottom (see Figure 7-22), select the Use Error Correction check box and click OK. That makes ripping go slower, in some circumstances, but increases the chances that you perform a clean rip, even from an iffy CD.

Figure 7-22: Tell Windows to keep trying, over and over, to produce a high-quality rip.

✦ **Burn:** A subject I talk about extensively in the section "Burning CDs and DVDs," earlier in this chapter.

✦ **Performance:** Lets you control how WMP handles streaming media.

✦ **Library:** Controls whether WMP looks for video files in the Pictures Library, whether volume-leveling information should be calculated for new files, and how WMP retrieves information from the Internet.

Although there's a setting here for overwriting media information with the information taken from the Internet, in my experience, you have to manually apply that information. WMP doesn't go behind your back to update your album covers or track descriptions, willy-nilly, with anything it finds in the Microsoft music data website.

✦ **Plugins:** Lets you decide what happens with your WMP plugins (which are few and far between) and visualizations (which abound on the web).

✦ **Privacy and Security:** Primarily controls how much information you send to Microsoft every time you use WMP. See the section "Tweaking privacy options after installation," earlier in this chapter.

My privacy settings are shown at the beginning of this chapter (refer to Figure 7-3). If you decide to give Microsoft more information than the amount shown in that figure, I strongly recommend that you click the Read the Privacy Statement Online link and read the information with a thoroughly jaundiced eye.

✦ **Network:** Lets you select the network protocols that WMP may use to receive streaming media. It also lets you control proxy settings, which you may have to change if your computer is on a local-area network protected by a separate firewall.

It would take an advanced degree in computer science to even begin to understand many of these settings. Come to think of it, I have an advanced degree in computer science and *I* don't understand some of those settings. It's a good policy to change one of the options only if you understand it well and keep careful notes so that you can restore the original setting if anything goes wrong.

There's no harm in looking at the options, though. You can discover a lot by rummaging through each tab of the Options dialog box.

Where to Find and Buy Good Music

Saving the hardest part for last . . . .

Finding music that you're going to like has gotten considerably simpler because of some very fancy mathematical matching algorithms. But even after you've found the good stuff, it can be hard to buy. Let me start with the easier of the two.

Buying music and videos online

Once upon a time, buying music online was easy. Now you're faced with myriad choices, all fiercely competitive, and the details about each of the offerings change just about once a week.

The big three music stores — Amazon, Google, and Apple — have been around for years. Microsoft's also trying to enter the fray, although as of this writing it's too early to tell if it will be able to compete with the entrenched three. Aside from easy access to the tiled Music app, it isn't at all clear what Microsoft can or will bring to the party.

Here's the current skinny on each of the main services:

✦ Although it wasn't the first online store to go with cheap MP3 files, **Amazon** brought unfettered music to the masses. Amazon usually has the best prices, and loads of discounted music — with an ever-changing array of free downloads (go to www.amazon.com and search for *free MP3*). With 16 million different tracks at last count, you'll be hard pressed to find more music, and everything's in blissfully unencumbered 256 Kbps MP3 format.

Amazon will store your music, if you like, and let you get to it with the Amazon Cloud Player application, which runs on PCs, Macs, iPads, and all kinds of phones. It's free for the first 5GB of storage, including unlimited storage of any songs you buy at Amazon, and $20 per year for 20GB plus unlimited amounts of music from any source. Visit www.amazon.com/clouddrive/learnmore for details.

What's not to like? If you're buying music to play on an iPhone or iPad, you have to go through the additional step of copying the music from the download location to iTunes, or into the iCloud. The iTunes Store also has a separate downloader (see the next section) that complicates things, the first time you download.

✦ **iTunes** converted to the copy-protection-free religion shortly after Amazon made big cuts into Apple's market share: Apple was selling copy-protected music, and everybody in the know went with Amazon's unencumbered MP3s. It didn't take long at all for iTunes to get rid of copy protection.

The result was historic. With 20 million titles or so and enormous volume, iTunes is, by far, the largest online music and video store — although Amazon and Microsoft are trying hard to catch up, and Google may not be far behind. iTunes frequently gets new albums out before the others, because of sweetheart deals with the major labels. Although iTunes isn't the cheapest, it's cheap enough for most Mac, iPad, and iPhone owners, and it's integrated with those devices to be tap-tap-tap easy. If you buy an album or video once, you get it on all your devices, no questions asked, and if you ever lose your copy, getting a replacement is like falling off a log.

One relatively new feature, called iTunes Match, lets you keep all your music, no matter where you bought it, on the Internet, for $25 per year. Details are in Book X, Chapter 1.

Downsides? iTunes (the program) doesn't download nice, neat MP3 files. You can get iTunes to convert the files you've bought to MP3, but it takes several steps. As long as you live in an Apple world, it's all neat and easy — but it's hard to break out of the walled garden.

✦ **Google's Music Store,** the latecomer to the list, has lots of hooks into Android devices. In addition to offering plain, unfettered MP3s at 320 Kbps, Google also has a web player, Google Play, that works very well as long as you're in the U.S. Amazon and Apple don't have web players. Google prides itself on nurturing indie bands, so if you're looking for something slightly out of the mainstream (or way out, for that matter), Google may have what you're looking for. You can store up to 20,000 songs on Google's website, free, and any songs that you buy from Google get stored free without denting your 20,000 allowance. When you buy a song from Google, it's immediately available inside your Android phone or tablet, or on the web player. You can also download the MP3 any time you like.

Where should you buy your music? Tough choice. At this moment (and I'm sure the offerings will change by the time you read this), I tend to buy everything from Amazon, just because I'm old-fashioned and like to have real MP3s on my PC. But I'm sorely tempted with Google's offer to keep copies of my music for me, where I don't have to worry about backing it up. And, yes, sometimes I'm lazy and buy an album from iTunes for my iPad.

Using the Amazon music store

Last night I went to the Phuket Blues and Rock Festival (www.phuketblues festival.com) and saw an absolutely riveting performance by Eric Bibb, a tremendous blues guitarist and singer. Today I dropped by my friendly local music shop and couldn't find a single CD by Eric Bibb.

Many people think they have to use the music ordering mechanism that's attached to their player to get new music simply. Not true. Yes, I could've used the Metro Music buying mechanism to get Eric's latest. Ordering it from the iTunes Store for my iPad or iPhone would've been a cinch. But it's also easy to buy from alternate sources — a Good Thing if you don't particularly want to enrich Microsoft or Apple.

So I hopped on Amazon and was listening to Eric's latest album in a few minutes. Here's how:

1. **Point your web browser to** www.amazon.com.

2. **At the top of the Amazon page, in the Search box, choose MP3 Downloads, and on the right, type the name of the artist or album you're looking for. Click Go.**

   I searched for Eric Bibb, and Amazon responded with 297 songs and albums from Eric Bibb (see Figure 7-23). I peeled myself off the floor.

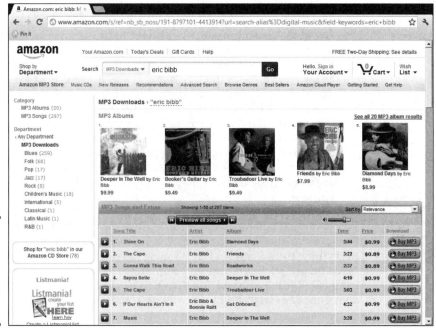

Figure 7-23:
Amazon boasts an extensive collection of MP3s.

3. **You can click the album cover to get more information, but if you know what you want, click the Download MP3Album link.**

   I decided to download Eric's latest, "Deeper in the Well."

4. **Amazon takes me to the ordering page for the album. I have 1-Click set up with Amazon, so I click the 1-Click link.**

   If I was new to Amazon, it'd take a couple of extra steps to sign up.

   Amazon says I must install the Amazon MP3 Downloader.

5. **Follow the instructions and install the downloader.**

   It takes about 30 seconds.

6. **After the downloader is installed, Amazon prompts you to click the Download Album button. Do so.**

   It may take a few minutes, but ultimately the Amazon downloader downloads all the tracks and puts them in your `\Music` folder, in a newly created folder named `\Amazon MP3`. In this case, I found a new folder named `\Music\Amazon MP3\Eric Bibb\Deeper in the Well` that contains MP3s for all songs in the album.

Thank heaven for MP3 files: No restrictions on where they can go. No restrictions on who can play them.

Finding new music you'll like

My first piece of advice: Start with Norah Jones, and move from there.

Okay, okay. Start with Metallica . . . er, Nickelback . . . uh, Linkin Park . . . all right, I give up, what *do* you like?

If you have an iPad or iPhone or some sort of iMusic player, you probably already know about Genius, the Apple program that tries to guess what you're going to like based on what you've been listening to. Genius works well, as long as most of your music listening goes through Apple one way or another.

I've been impressed with a blog called Google Play Magnifier, `www.magnifier.blogspot.com`, that keeps on top of the music industry and tells me about music that I find interesting. An interview with Mick Jagger, reminiscing about the Stones' American invasion? New stuff from Corinne Bailey Rae? Hey, they've got me hooked.

The easiest way to find new music, though, is to listen to one of the sites that specializes in helping you discover music that's similar to what you're listening to now. Both Pandora (`www.pandora.com`) and Last.fm (`www.last.fm`) build custom channels — actually playlists — based on the music that you choose, and then let you vote thumbs-up or thumbs-down on songs they dig out of their archives. Each refines the offerings based on the songs you choose, and they're quite remarkable. Both have free versions, with extra perks for those who pay.

Pandora chooses music based on The Music Genome Project (`www.pandora.com/mgp.shtml`), which tries to identify parts of songs that people like: "Since we started back in 2000, we've carefully listened to the songs of tens of thousands of different artists — ranging from popular to obscure — and analyzed the musical qualities of each song one attribute at a time. This work continues each and every day as we endeavor to include all the great new stuff coming out of studios, clubs, and garages around the world."

Last.fm, on the other hand, relies on a crowdsourcing technique it calls *scrobbling* to have many, many people make recommendations based on what they like. "Millions of songs are scrobbled every day. This data helps Last.fm to organize and recommend music to people; we use it to create personalized radio stations, and a lot more besides."

One last tip: If you remember a song's melody, or a few words, but can't figure out what song it is, try Midomi (www.midomi.com). You can hum or sing a few bars, or type in some lyrics, and Midomi will run out and find songs that match your criteria. Amazing what it can find.

Chapter 8: Searching on the Desktop

*I*n Book III, Chapter 2, I talk about using search on the tiled side of the Windows 8 fence. That chapter covers a simple introduction to the kind of Windows searches most people use. Unfortunately, if you're accustomed to real searching — where you can look for characters that don't appear at the beginning of words, for example — Search with training wheels can feel stifling. In fact, as I describe in that chapter, the simplistic Windows approach can lead to all sorts of unexpected errors — where a search for *Shell*, for example, won't find the program called *PowerShell*.

In this chapter, I talk about the real search engine inside Windows — the one that isn't documented anywhere, except in a few musty corners of the Microsoft websites and here. While you can use the techniques mentioned in this chapter over on the tiled side, it's usually easier to construct an advanced search on the desktop. File Explorer helps.

File Explorer comes packed with all sorts of search options that you can use in a variety of situations. You can even save a desktop search and pin it on your desktop, the Start screen, or the taskbar. You can't do that in the tiled part of Windows 8.

Desktop search has two different personas. There's a Ribbon-based plethora of tools for expanding or limiting searches — setting the location to be searched, or looking based on date or file type or size. But to really narrow down a search, you have to use an ancient specification language known as *Advanced Query Syntax*. AQS looks weird, but it brings back many of the search capabilities you may have found in other operating systems (such as, oh, DOS) or applications, including Microsoft Office. I take you through AQS in this chapter, too.

Surprisingly, you can use AQS queries in the Start screen's type-and-Search box. It's a bit like taking off the search training wheels and strapping on a pair of rocket engines. Don't fret: You can do it.

Indexing to Speed Up Searches

There are two different ways to look for things on a computer.

First, you can *scan* — the brute-force approach — looking at every file, one at a time, searching for whatever you seek. Think of going through the *Encyclopedia Britannica,* one sentence at a time. It's a tough way to look.

If you're smarter, you'll *index* first. Windows creates an index of all the designated files in the most commonly searched locations, and then keeps the index updated on the fly. That way, when you're looking for a specific term, Windows only needs to look in the index. Bang.

Indexing has long been the Achilles heel of the search industry. Earlier add-ons took forever to compile and then update the indices. The indexer took over the machine from time to time, and slowed everything to a painful crawl. With the latest versions of Windows, though, the indexing takes place reasonably effectively while the machine's idle. Although you may have to wait for initial indices to be built, once they're in place, the updates go through with a minimum of fuss and bother.

I talk about extending the Windows indexing — making Windows create indices any place you like — in the last section of this chapter.

Using Search Wisely and Sparingly

File Explorer has a search box in the upper-right corner of every File Explorer window, as shown in Figure 8-1.

There are also search boxes in many major applications' File Open dialog boxes. The Office applications use the Windows search engine.

Search ribbon

Type search terms here

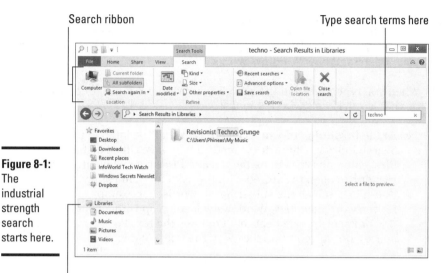

Figure 8-1:
The
industrial
strength
search
starts here.

Search covers this folder and all subfolders

If you type a word or phrase in a search box, Windows checks against the index, looking for matches in the current folder and all the folders underneath the current folder. Windows searches for all kinds of files — documents and text files, naturally, but also the tags ("metadata") in pictures and music, e-mail messages (if you use one of the Microsoft mail programs), even the contents of web pages. So the trick is to go to the right folder — one likely to contain the information you want — and start your search from that folder.

In particular, if you're looking for an e-mail message, fire up your e-mail program and search from there. If you're looking for a song, use Windows Media Player. (Some other media players have search capabilities, but many of them, including iTunes, don't use the Windows search routines.) Looking for a tag on a picture? Try going into the Pictures Library and search from there.

Knowing Search's Idiosyncrasies

Most people who can't find what they want get tripped up by a Windows idiosyncrasy. It's important that you understand exactly what Search looks for, and what it skips. Windows Search is nothing like searching the web.

If you're used to the old DOS-style search, Windows Search is nothing like that, either. In particular, the "*.*" style searches you may be accustomed to from the Days of the DOS Dinosaur don't work the same way, so make sure you understand how Windows works.

When you type a word in the search box, Windows looks for an **exact match** on that word. Here's where it looks:

✦ **At the beginning of words inside files** that the indexer understands. Search looks in Office documents, if you have Office installed, text files, common types of metadata, and PDFs if a sufficiently capable PDF reader has been registered with the system. Confusingly, Windows doesn't search all the substrings in words. For example, if you search for the word *dummies*, Windows will come up with a match on a Word doc or Excel spreadsheet that contains the text `For dummies` (note the space), but it won't find files with the text `Fordummies`.

A lot of people get tripped up by that little gem.

✦ **At the beginning of filenames.** Except in unusual circumstances, Windows does NOT search substrings of the filename. The unusual circumstances: Windows will match a search string if it appears in a file-name after a space or a period. So, for example, searching on *Dummies* won't match `ForDummies.docx`, but it will match `For Dummies.xlsx` and `For.Dummies`.

Betcha didn't know that, either. Don't believe me? Try it.

Those two gotchas, which are more or less undocumented, account for about 90 percent of the confusion I see concerning Windows Search. There are ways to compensate for Windows's searching indiscretions. I talk about them in the section "Introducing AQS" later in this chapter.

Limiting and Expanding Searches through the Ribbon

If you type something in the File Explorer Search box, a Search Tools tab appears at the top of Explorer. Click on it and you see the Search Ribbon (refer to Figure 8-1).

The Ribbon gives you a lot of control over the search. Here are some of the options:

✦ **Search Again In** lets you switch the location that will be searched. Options include your entire Homegroup (which could take a little while), Libraries, inside you e-mail program (for some e-mail programs), Sticky Notes (!), and Internet (which brings up Internet Explorer). It may also include SkyDrive, if you're signed in with your Microsoft account.

+ **Date Modified** includes a very handy list (see Figure 8-2) of days based on the current date.

+ **Kind** lets you choose from many different kinds of files, as in Figure 8-3.

As you make choices from the drop-down lists, File Explorer modifies the search query, as shown in Figure 8-3. Those funny "kind:document" modifiers in the search box are simple forms of the Windows Advanced Search Query language, which I discuss in the next section.

Date modified list

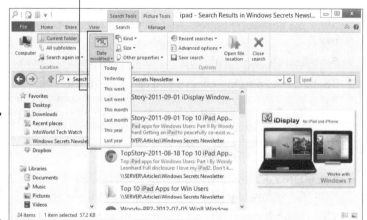

Figure 8-2:
Remember
when
you last
changed the
file?

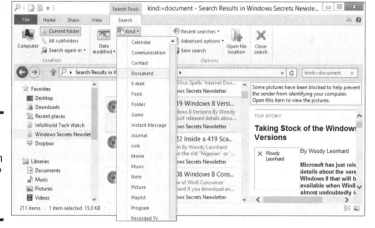

Figure 8-3:
Only
interested in
documents?
Choose it
here.

If you only use the tiled Mail app for your e-mail, a search here on E-mail won't bring up anything.

+ **Size** allows you to limit the search based on file sizes: Empty, Tiny (0–10KB), Small (10–100KB), Medium (100KB–1MB), Large (1MB–16MB), Huge (16MB–128MB), and Gigantic (> 128MB).

+ **Recent searches** contains a list of your recent searches.

+ **Advanced options** lets you search in locations that haven't been indexed. It also has a line for partial matches. If that line isn't selected, in theory, File Explorer only matches full filenames or full words inside files. If it is selected, the search proceeds as described earlier, where the match is only on the beginning of filenames, or the beginning of text inside the file. It's a confusing option — and I've encountered many bugs trying to use it.

+ **Save Search** saves a file that, when clicked, runs the search again.

That's a cool option because you can save the search file anywhere you like. Once saved, go back to it in File Explorer, and you can tap and hold (or right-click) on the file and choose Pin to Start, which pins the search on your Start screen. You can also click and drag the file onto your desktop. Or you can drag it to the taskbar, in which case, it's added to the File Explorer Jump List (see Book VI, Chapter 1).

+ **Open File Location** if you tap once on a file, or click on it. Choosing this icon moves File Explorer over to the folder that contains the file.

+ **Close Search** closes the results list, the same as tapping or clicking the "X" at the end of the Search box.

While the Ribbon's mighty powerful, it doesn't give you any reliable way to search for text inside of filenames, or text inside a document, if it isn't at the beginning of a word. (Sorry, but in my experience the Advanced Options selection doesn't work.) That's a real shortcoming — one that's overcome by Windows Search's antique Advanced Query Syntax language.

Introducing AQS

Here's how most experienced Windows users get turned off by Windows Search: They type something in the File Explorer Search box, and wait while Windows comes back, first with bushels, then with reams, and finally an avalanche of results. "Whooooa!" they say (or something slightly less printable), "I only wanted to find files with that text in the filename. Obviously, Windows is useless; it shows me all of this garbage but didn't even find the file that I wanted."

Yes, I still hear from old-timers who cluck-cluck-cluck that DOS did it better.

Typing text in the File Explorer Search box is a bit like sticking a straw in a fire hydrant. As I recommend earlier, if you have any idea where the text you seek may be located, you're far better off going to that location (with File Explorer, say, or Outlook), and starting the search from that folder or one above it.

Searching for a filename

What if you're just looking for a filename? Not so long ago (Windows XP, for example), that's all you *could* look for. Ends up that looking for filenames is pretty easy with Windows Search (if you use AQS), although the rules and syntax are a bit strange.

If you want to find text inside a filename, anywhere in the filename, not just at the beginning or before a space, use * as I show in this example:

```
file:*dummies
```

That will match a file with the name `Dummies.docx`, just like a regular search for `dummies`, but it will also find `ForDummies.jpg` (without a space).

If you need an exact match, try =

```
file:"ForDummies.txt"
```

It matches `ForDummies.txt` and `fordummies.txt` (capitalization doesn't matter in a filename), but it doesn't match `For Dummies.txt` (with a space).

It's important to realize that the file: trick works all over the place — inside File Explorer, of course, but also in Start screen searches, and in the File Open dialog boxes in various Windows and Office applications. I have a yellow sticky note on my monitor that says file:

Using wildcards in ways that make sense

If you've used DOS, or the Windows command line, or written a BAT file, or gone searching for text using older versions of Word or Excel, you may be familiar with wildcards: characters that serve as placeholders. For example, in DOS, searching for a string like `Invoice*.xls` will turn up all the `.xls` files that start out with `Invoice`: say, `Invoice1.xls`, `Invoice420.xls`, and so on. On the Windows command line, or in a BAT file, searching for `win32.*` gives you all the files with `win32.` at the beginning and any filename extension. The asterisk (*) is a wildcard, and in the Land of DOS, it matches anything.

If you think you know how to use a wildcard in a search, think again: Windows Search doesn't work that way. That's another major reason why Windows veterans think the latest versions of Windows don't work.

When you type an asterisk in a Windows search box, Windows takes the characters following the asterisk and uses them to match any part of a filename. It's another idiosyncrasy that leads some old-timers to drink. Or at least, to cluck.

Say you're in File Explorer, or running a Search from the Start screen, or you click File, Open in Word, and you type ***doc** in the search box. Here's what happens:

Windows starts scanning filenames, matching any files with the characters doc in the filename. So you get a hit on `For Dummies.doc`, but you also get a hit on `DryDock.jpg`. You also get a hit on any file that's in a folder with doc in the name of the folder.

If you type ***doc** and expect to get a list of all `.doc` files, you'll get those — but you'll also get the odd file with the text doc inside the name.

Windows ace Rob Oppenheim ran down the details on searching with and without wildcards in Windows 8. He started with the official Windows documentation on AQS, and then subjected the assertions in the documentation to a little bit of real-world hard work. You can see his conclusions in Table 8-1.

Table 8-1	Using Wildcards in Windows 8 Searches	
Search For	*Finds This in Filenames*	*Finds This in File Contents*
Dummies	Finds "dummies" if it begins a word in a filename, or follows a period in a filename	Finds "dummies" if it begins a word in a file's contents
*dummies	Finds "dummies" anywhere in a filename	Finds "dummies" if it begins a word in a file's contents (same as searching for "dummies")
file:dummies	Finds "dummies" if it begins a word in a filename, same as searching for "dummies"	Doesn't match any text inside any files
file:*dummies	Finds "dummies" anywhere in a filename	Doesn't match any text inside any files
content:dummies	Doesn't match any filenames	Finds "dummies" if it begins a word in a file's contents
content:*dummies	Doesn't match any filenames	Finds "dummies" if it begins a word in a file's contents, same as searching for content:dummies

That's just the beginning. Windows Search has a host of keywords, Boolean operators such as OR and AND, NOT, and some odd variations. See the official syntax document at `http://msdn.microsoft.com/en-us/library/aa965711(VS.85).aspx`.

Making Windows Index Where You Search

Indexing is a speed thing.

Out of the box, Windows indexes files in all of your libraries. (See Book VII, Chapter 3 for details about libraries.) If you have a PDF Viewer, such as Adobe Reader, or Foxit, the PDF files inside those libraries get indexed. If you use Outlook or Windows Live Mail, your mail gets indexed (other mail clients may or may not index your mail — the tiled Mail app being a case in point, at least as of this writing).

But what if you frequently search for files in folders that aren't being indexed? Unless you can add those folders to your libraries (which is a good idea, in general), you need to tell Windows where to build its indices. You can only add a folder to your PC's index if the folder is located on the PC. You can't manually add a networked folder.

Here's how to add a folder to your index:

1. **Wait until you can leave your computer alone for a few hours, or overnight.**

   Indexing can take forever. The initial indexing only has to be done once, but that once may take eons.

2. **Go to the Start screen, and type** index. **On the right, tap or click Settings. On the left, tap or select Indexing Options.**

   You see the Indexing Options dialog box, as shown in Figure 8-4.

3. **Tap or click Modify.**

   The Indexed Locations dialog box appears, as shown in Figure 8-5.

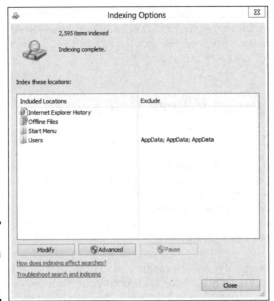

Figure 8-4:
Add location
for indexing
here.

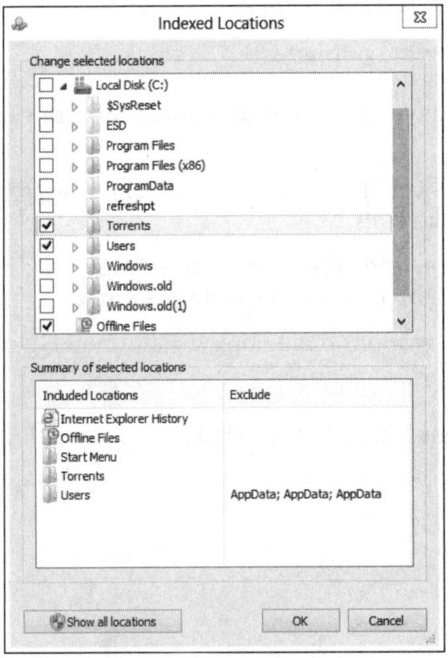

Figure 8-5:
You can tell
Windows
exactly
which
folders you
want to
include in
your search
index.

4. **In the upper panel, click on the wedges(s) next to the drive(s) that contain the folder(s) you want to add. Select the check box(es) next to the folder(s). When you've added all the folders you want to index, click OK.**

It'll take a while, but by the time Windows is done, you'll have all those new locations indexed, and searching there will go faster than ever.

Book VII

Controlling Your System

Now maybe these folks got a decent disaster recovery plan and maybe they don't...

DANGER
WILD RHINOCEROS

Contents at a Glance

Chapter 1: Controlling Control Panel

In This Chapter

✔ **Rooting around in the Control Panel**

✔ **Updating device drivers**

✔ **Taking control of AutoPlay**

✔ **Working with programs and features**

✔ **Rewinding the clocks**

✔ **Switching languages**

✔ **Accessing easily**

The inner workings of Windows reveal themselves inside the mysterious (and somewhat haughtily named) Control Panel.

The Control Panel itself isn't a program or an app; it's kind of a gathering of dozens of programs — a fairly easy way to get to a plethora of programs that watch and adjust Windows settings. Those individual programs, the ones that do the work, are Control Panel *applets*. The applets are grouped together and categorized, and the main categories are what you see as the eight categories in the Control Panel.

Most of this book is peppered with descriptions of Control Panel applets: After all, they're the key to controlling much of Windows behavior, both good and bad.

In this chapter, I give you an overview of what's available in the Control Panel, point you to detailed explanations elsewhere in this book, and explain some of the key settings that don't fit into other chapters.

Exploring the Real Control Panel

Over on the tiled side of the Windows 8 fence, people seem to get to either the Settings panel or the Change Settings (sometimes called PC Settings) screen and figure they're in the Control Panel.

That's a bit like getting off a plane in a Rome airport and thinking you're in the Sistine Chapel. The Control Panel, which lives on the desktop side of Windows 8, isn't nearly as pretty as its stunted tiled-side wannabes — and it has many, many more nooks and crannies.

Bringing up the Control Panel

Among the dozens of ways to bring up the Control Panel in its understated glory, use one of two methods:

✦ **With your fingers,** switch to the desktop by tapping the Desktop tile on the Start screen. Then swipe from the right to bring up the Charms bar. Tap the Settings charm and then at the top, tap the Control Panel entry.

✦ **With a mouse,** right-click in the lower-left corner of the screen (you know, where the Start button used to be — okay, I'm being catty) and choose Control Panel. Yep, that works on both the new tiled Start screen, and on the old-fashioned desktop.

The real Control Panel looks like Figure 1-1. If you don't see a window sitting on the desktop, filled with icons and a decidedly touch-unfriendly network of tiny hot links, you haven't found the Holy Grail. Try again, pilgrim.

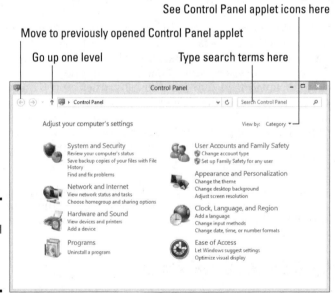

Figure 1-1: Navigational aids in the Control Panel.

Scouting out the Control Panel

The main categories of the Control Panel span the breadth (and plumb the depth) of Windows. Here's how the Control Panel breaks them out:

✦ **System and Security:** Use an enormous array of tools for troubleshooting and adjusting your PC, backing up your data, controlling how Windows conducts searches, checking your performance rating, and generally making your PC work when it doesn't want to. Unfortunately, this category also includes all the tools you need to shoot yourself in the foot, consistently and reliably, day in and day out. Use this part of the Control Panel with discretion and respect. I talk about Device Manager and checking drivers later in this chapter. I cover the following components elsewhere in this minibook:

  • *Action Center and the Troubleshooter:* Book VII, Chapter 2

  • *Windows Firewall, Defender, and other components of the mighty security arsenal:* Book IX, Chapter 3

  • *The Windows Experience Index:* Book VIII, Chapter 4

  • *Remote Assistance:* Book VII, Chapter 2

    If you're here because someone you don't know has asked you whether it's okay to connect to your computer, STOP and think about it! The Remote Assistance scam ranks very high on many a creep's social engineering list. Yes, even if they say they're from Microsoft.

  • *Windows Update:* Book VIII, Chapter 4

  • *Power Options:* Book VI, Chapter 1

  • *File History:* Book VIII, Chapter 1

  • *BitLocker:* Book IX, Chapter 4

  • *Storage Spaces:* Book VII, Chapter 4

  • *Admin Tools, including Disks and Event Logs:* Book VIII, Chapter 4

✦ **Network and Internet:** Covers just about everything you need to hassle with networking. Many security settings in this category duplicate those in the Security category. I cover three topics in this category elsewhere in this book:

  • *Network Status and troubleshooting:* Book VIII, Chapter 4

    This includes the frequently asked question regarding the Windows notification that makes your computer accessible to the rest of your network and a brief discussion of virtual private networks (VPNs).

  • *HomeGroups:* Book VII, Chapter 5

  • *The Internet Options applet:* Book VI, Chapter 6

The applet in this category pertains only to Internet Explorer. (Isn't it just like Microsoft to list Internet Options in the Control Panel, when they aren't Internet options at all — just IE options?) I also cover Firefox and Chrome.

✦ **Hardware and Sound:** The "all other" category. I talk about AutoPlay settings later in this chapter. Other topics include

- *Devices and Printers:* Book VII, Chapter 7

- *Display Resolution:* Book VI, Chapter 2

- *Power Options:* Book VI, Chapter 1

✦ **Programs:** Covers many actions you want to perform on Windows and other programs, short of stomping on them and yanking out their still-beating hearts, offering them to the merciless demons who dwell within (and you thought I didn't have any issues with Windows). In this chapter, I talk about uninstalling/changing programs, turning Windows features on and off, and changing default filename associations and default programs. I cover View Windows Updates in Book VIII, Chapter 3.

✦ **User Accounts and Family Safety:** Family Safety built into the Control Panel is laughable and easily defeated; I don't talk about them in this book at all. But I do cover two other topics in this category:

- *User Accounts:* Book II, Chapter 4

  The tiled PC Settings method for creating and handling User Accounts runs rings around the method here in the Control Panel.

- *Windows Credentials:* Book VII, Chapter 5

✦ **Appearance and Personalization:** In this chapter, I talk about the Ease of Access Center, which has some cool tricks for everybody, whether you need to ease your access or not; see the upcoming Ease of Access bullet. These other topics appear in other chapters in this book:

- *Desktop, themes, colors, and the like:* Book VI, Chapter 2

- *Display:* Book VI, Chapter 2 (desktop)

✦ **Clock, Language, and Region:** I cover all these topics in this chapter. Set the time and date — although double-clicking the clock on the Windows taskbar is much simpler — or tell Windows to synchronize the clock automatically. You can also add support for complex languages (such as Thai) and right-to-left languages (such as Arabic), and change how dates, times, currency, and numbers appear. And what the heck is an input method? All is revealed later in this chapter.

✦ **Ease of Access:** Change settings to help you see the screen, use the keyboard or mouse, or ask Windows to flash part of your screen when the speaker would play a sound. Also set up speech recognition for the built-in Windows speech recognition routines. I have more details about the options — and a recommendation — at the end of this chapter.

Many Control Panel settings duplicate options you see elsewhere in Windows, but some capabilities that seem like they should be Control Panel mainstays remain mysteriously absent. You have at least 157 different ways in the Control Panel to turn on Windows automatic updating, for example (okay, so I exaggerate a little), but you don't find the controls for choosing whether you want the tiled, "immersive" IE or desktop IE to be your default browser. Just sayin'.

If you want to change a Windows setting, by all means, try the Control Panel but don't be discouraged if you can't find what you're looking for. Instead, look in this book's Table of Contents or index.

Relying on Device Manager

Device Manager is your point of first resort when something goes wrong with the hardware — the *devices* — on your system. It's a Control Panel applet that gives you limited access to information about every piece of hardware Windows identifies on your system.

Unless your network card implodes or the cat takes a leak on one of your PC's exhaust vents, the most common source of hardware problems lies in the *device driver* — the program (sometimes a huge program) that handles the interaction between Windows and your device.

When you install a new piece of hardware, chances are very good that it'll install all by itself, without any intervention from you. Simply plug most USB devices into a Windows machine, Windows installs all the drivers it needs, and you're off and running in no time.

However, once in a blue moon, Windows either can't find or has trouble installing the device driver. When that happens, I never — absolutely *never* — use the device driver software that came in the box with the new hardware (by the time the manufacturer ships the box, and you buy it, the driver may have gone through ten revisions!). Instead, I go to the manufacturer's website and download the latest version of the driver. Here are a few tips on downloading the right driver:

+ **If you can't find a Windows 8 version,** use a Windows 7 (or even a Vista) version.

+ **If you're running a 32-bit version of Windows (see Book I, Chapter 3),** be careful to get the 32-bit version of the driver. Similarly, the 64-bit version of Windows takes only a 64-bit driver. Drivers don't mix and match bittedness.

Don't update a driver just because it's newer than the one you have. That way lies madness. You should update a driver only if the old one isn't working right, or if you know for a fact that the new driver has some specific capability you really need. Fixing what isn't broken can often break what didn't need to be fixed, and life's too short to fix a problem caused by what you didn't need to fix in the first place.

With a good driver in hand, use Device Manager to install the new driver. Follow these steps:

1. Bring up the Control Panel by swiping on the desktop or right-clicking in the lower-left corner, and then choosing Settings.

Details at the beginning of this chapter in the section "Bringing up the Control Panel."

2. Choose System and Security, and in the System section, choose Device Manager.

Windows opens the Device Manager applet, as shown in Figure 1-2.

Figure 1-2:
The Device Manager applet.

3. Tap or click the wedge sign next to the heading that contains the device you want to update.

In Figure 1-2, I selected the wedge sign next to Display Adapters (also known as a video card). Windows shows which display adapters are installed and recognized.

You may have to try several headings to find the right one. If you guess wrong, just tap or click again to collapse the heading you expanded. Don't worry. You aren't breaking anything. Yet.

4. **Tap and hold or double-click the device to open the Device Properties dialog box (see Figure 1-3), and then tap or click the Driver tab to display details about the driver.**

**Book VII
Chapter 1**

Controlling Control
Panel

You can identify the latest driver by its date, version number, or both.

5. **If your new driver is on a USB drive, put it in the PC; if it's sitting on the hard drive, make sure you know where it is.**

6. **Tap or click the Update Driver button.**

   Windows asks whether it should search automatically for updated driver software, or browse your computer for driver software.

If you tell Windows to search automatically, it goes out to Microsoft's big driver database in the sky and retrieves whatever Microsoft thinks is the best driver. Unfortunately, Microsoft has a bad track record for storing and proffering old, sluggish (but usually stable) drivers. That's why you went out and retrieved the manufacturer's recommended driver in the first place.

Note that Windows does *not* automatically check the manufacturer's site for the latest drivers. Instead, it relies on the drivers that have been checked in to its driver database — and many of those drivers are weeks, months, or years out of date.

7. **Tap or click Browse My Computer for Driver Software; then point Windows to the location of your updated driver and tap or click Next.**

Windows may step you through installing the new driver. Or it may tell you that the driver you have is the best one for your device. In either case, I suggest you take Microsoft's suggestion and leave it at that.

I always, always reboot my PC after installing a new driver, even if it isn't required. That gives Windows a chance to trip and fall while the event's still clearly in my mind. It also gives me a chance to reboot to the Last Known Good Configuration if I want to roll back the driver. See Book VIII, Chapter 2 for a discussion of Last Known Good Configuration.

Stuffing AutoPlay

I talk about AutoPlay settings briefly in Book VI, Chapter 7, when I discuss how to handle audio CDs and video DVDs when you insert them into your PC. Here's the rest of the story.

When you put a CD, DVD, or USB drive into a PC, Windows pops up with a notification that asks you what it should do with the new data. This AutoPlay capability has been around since the times of Windows XP. AutoPlay was invented to make it easier for people to play CDs, transfer photos from SD cards, or move data around on a USB.

A typical AutoPlay interaction goes in two steps. First you see a blue toaster notification rolling out of the right side of the screen that asks whether you want to choose what happens when that particular event (such as inserting an audio CD) happens. If you tap or click that toaster notification, you get a second notification that asks what you want to do. See Figure 1-4.

Figure 1-4: Windows asks whether you want to set an AutoPlay option. If so, you get to choose how to handle the situation.

Unfortunately, AutoPlay can be used for insidious purposes. All hell broke loose in January, 2009, when somebody figured out how to jigger AutoPlay so it gave Windows users a bogus option to Open Folder to View Files. The option appears in the Install or Run Program section, but many people didn't notice the subtlety. If you clicked the Open Folder . . . option, Windows didn't open a folder at all. It ran a program that infected the PC with the Conficker worm.

There was quite an uproar at the time as Microsoft had trouble plugging the hole. And a whole lot of people got infected with Conficker, in many cases from dodgy USB drives.

Windows finally has some robust tools for handling inserted media. For example, you're asked how you want to handle a newly inserted CD with music on it. If you choose to play the music, your choice is remembered, and from that point on, any new music CD you insert in your PC gets played — Windows doesn't ask, it just does. Similarly for SD cards and pictures, or USB drives and files — if you tell Windows to open the folder to view files once, in the future, Windows always opens similar USB drives so you can view the files.

Windows performs this magic by analyzing the kinds of files on the inserted media and then consulting a list to see what it should do with a specific kind of file on a specific kind of media: Music on CDs, for example, may be treated differently than music on USB drives; an inserted blank CD will trigger yet another action.

You may have set Windows to perform some AutoPlay function that you really don't want. Or you might want to go back to the blissful state where Windows doesn't assume anything, and asks you every time how to handle inserted media. Here's how to set things right:

1. **Bring up Control Panel by swiping on the desktop or right-clicking in the lower-left corner, and then choosing Settings.**

    Details at the beginning of this chapter in the section "Bringing up the Control Panel."

2. **Select the Hardware and Sound category, and then tap or click the AutoPlay link.**

    The AutoPlay dialog box, as shown in Figure 1-5, appears.

**Book VII
Chapter 1**

Controlling Control Panel

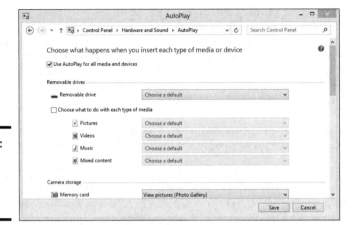

Figure 1-5:
Set
AutoPlay
defaults
here.

3. **To turn off AutoPlay, deselect the Use AutoPlay for All Media and Devices check box.**

   It's a good choice if you're concerned about getting infected.

4. **If you aren't quite so paranoid, choose default actions associated with each of the indicated kinds of media.**

   For example, with Memory Card, you can choose to import pictures and videos with the tiled Windows 8 Photos app. Under CDs, you can have audio CDs play with Windows Media Player.

5. **Tap or click Save.**

   Your changes take effect immediately. If you ever find yourself doubting your choices, come back to the dialog box and, at the bottom, tap or click the Reset All Defaults button. That starts you out again with a clean slate.

If you're curious about the gory details, I have an analysis on how Conficker jimmies Windows into showing bogus AutoPlay entries in my Windows Secrets Newsletter article at `http://tinyurl.com/dbgndc` with further details at `http://tinyurl.com/mck9ys`.

Uninstalling/Changing Programs

Windows lives only to serve — or so I'm told — and, more than anything, Windows serves programs. Most people spend time working inside programs, such as Outlook, Word, Adobe Photoshop, or QuickBooks. Windows acts as traffic cop and nanny, but doesn't do the heavy lifting. Programs rule. Users rely on Windows to keep the programs in line.

Installing programs on the desktop side of Windows is easy. When you want to install a program, you typically download the program and double-click the downloaded file, or insert a CD into your CD drive and follow the instructions. You've done that a hundred times.

Installing tiled Windows 8 apps is simpler still: Windows does it for you, when you get the app from the Windows Store (see Book III, Chapter 5). In fact, that's the only way to install tiled apps — Microsoft doesn't let you do it any other way.

Removing well-behaved programs on the desktop side is just as easy, if you follow the instructions in this section. Changing programs, on the other hand, is a different kettle of fish, as you soon discover.

Windows includes a one-stop shopping point for removing and making massive changes to desktop programs. To get to it, bring up the Control Panel (find out how at the beginning of this chapter), and then under the Programs heading, tap or click the Uninstall a Program link. You see the dialog box shown in Figure 1-6.

**Book VII
Chapter 1**

Controlling Control Panel

Figure 1-6:
Remove a program the proper way.

When Windows talks about changing programs, it isn't talking about making minor twiddles — this isn't the place to go if you want Microsoft Word to stop showing you rulers, for example. The Uninstall or Change a Program dialog box is designed to activate or deactivate big chunks of a program — graft on a new arm or lop off an unused head (of which there are many, particularly in Office). In the Uninstall or Change a Program dialog box for Office 2010, for example, you may tell PowerPoint that you want to use its Organization Chart add-in. Similarly, you may use the Uninstall or Change a Program dialog box to obliterate Publisher, if you don't want it darkening your drives. That's the kind of large-scale capability I'm talking about.

Yes, it's true. If you want to install a big chunk of a program, you have to tap or click the Uninstall a Program link in the Control Panel. The terminology stinks. Windows really should say something like "Bring up a program's installer or uninstaller." But I guess speaking the truth plainly would be too confusing.

Windows itself doesn't do much in the Uninstall or Change a Program dialog box. Windows primarily acts as a gathering point: Well-behaved programs, when they're installed, are supposed to stick their uninstallers where the Uninstall or Change a Program dialog box can find them. That way, you have one centralized place to look in when you want to get rid of a program. Microsoft doesn't write the uninstallers that the Uninstall or Change a Program dialog box runs; if you have a gripe about a program's uninstaller, you need to talk to the company that made the program.

A few school-of-hard-knocks comments pertain:

✦ If you have any problems at all uninstalling a program using the Windows uninstaller, get a free copy of Revo Uninstaller and give it a shot. I talk about Revo Uninstaller in Book X, Chapter 5.

✦ If you want to remove a program and it isn't listed here, there's a 99 percent chance that the program you want to remove is a piece of scumware. Hop onto Google and search for the name of the program — make sure you copy it precisely — and add the term *uninstall*. You may be in for some interesting times.

✦ You rarely use the Uninstall or Change a Program dialog box to remove parts of a program. Either you try to add features in a program that you forgot to include when you originally installed the program — most commonly with Office — or you want to delete a program entirely, to wipe its sorry tail off your hard drive.

Why sweat the small stuff? When you install a program, install it all. With large hard drives so cheap that they're likely candidates for a landfill, it never pays to cut back on installed features to save a few megabytes. In for a penny, in for a pound.

✦ Some uninstallers, for reasons known only to their company's programmers, require you to insert the program's CD into your CD drive before you uninstall the program. That's like requiring you to show your dog's vaccination records before you kick it out of the house.

When you start a program's uninstaller, you're at the mercy of the uninstaller and the programmers who wrote it. Windows doesn't even enter into the picture.

Turning Windows Features On and Off

The ability to turn certain parts of Windows on or off goes back to the days of Windows 3.1. Once upon a time, the feature was useful to reduce the bloat — the footprint — of Windows. Now, that isn't such a compelling reason. But it's become an interesting location for adding gonzo programs like Hyper-V, which piggyback on the Add a Feature approach to run heavy-duty installers.

Most frequently, parts of Windows get blocked off in order to minimize the chances of you shooting yourself in the foot. The theory goes that if you're smart enough to turn on a feature, you're smart enough to use it.

So much for theories.

On rare occasions, you might want to intentionally disable a part of Windows because you don't want to deal with the consequences of having it available. People used to disable Internet Explorer to minimize their chances of getting infected with IE-borne viruses — although it's highly debatable whether they actually accomplished anything by doing so.

If you find instructions to enable or disable certain pieces of Windows — turn Windows features on or off, in the parlance — here's how to do it:

Book VII
Chapter 1

Controlling Control Panel

1. **Bring up the Control Panel by swiping on the desktop or right-clicking the lower-left corner, and choosing Settings.**

Details at the beginning of this chapter in the section "Bringing up the Control Panel."

2. **In the lower left, select the Programs category; then in the Programs and Features section, tap or click the Turn Windows Features On or Off link.**

The Windows Features dialog box appears, as shown in Figure 1-7.

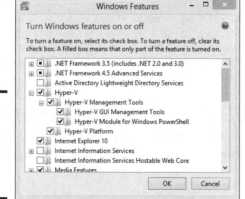

Figure 1-7:
Enable or disable big swathes of Windows here.

3. **Enable or disable Windows features by selecting or deselecting, respectively, the appropriate boxes.**

   Note that you can tap or click the + sign next to some features, to allow you to enable or disable specific pieces of the programs.

   In Figure 1-7, I selected the Hyper-V check box to enable Microsoft's Virtual Machine hypervisor. Details in Book VIII, Chapter 5.

4. **Click OK.**

   The pieces of Windows get added or blocked immediately.

Setting Default Programs

The term *default program* gets confusing because the phrase has four completely different meanings in The Land of Windows. To-wit:

✦ **You can set up default programs to handle newly inserted media.** I talk about AutoPlay earlier in this chapter. For example, you can tell Windows to run Windows Media Player when you put a music CD in your CD drive.

✦ **You can tell Windows to associate a default program with a specific filename extension.** (See Book VI, Chapter 1.) The chosen program is the one that gets run when you double-click a file in File Explorer or an attachment to an e-mail. For example, if you associate the filename extension .docx with Microsoft Word, when you double-click a DOCX file inside File Explorer or attached to an e-mail message, Word appears with the DOCX file loaded and ready for bear.

✦ **Similarly, you can associate a default program with a specific Internet (or Windows) protocol.** For example, you can tell Windows that you want it to have Firefox handle http:// addresses. That way, if you click a hot link http:// address in, say, your word processor or e-mail program, Windows hauls out Firefox and has it bring up the indicated address.

✦ **You can choose a specific program as your default web browser or e-mail program.** You can also tell Windows that you want a specific program to handle picture or music files. This capability is related to the filename extension association, but there are differences, explained in a moment.

Changing the default for a filename extension

Here's how to set the default program for a specific filename extension or Internet protocol:

1. **Bring up Control Panel by swiping on the desktop or right-clicking the lower-left corner, and choosing Settings.**

   Details at the beginning of this chapter, in the section "Bringing up the Control Panel."

2. **In the lower-left, select the Programs category; then in the Default Programs section, tap or click the Make a File Type Always Open in a Specific Program link.**

   Microsoft doesn't call the letters at the end of a filename (such as .doc or .jpg) a "filename extension" here because the phrase is verboten — "file type" is much more politically correct, but less descriptive. Windows doesn't show filename extensions by default, but you've followed the instructions in Book VI, Chapter 1 and turned them on, right?

   When you tap or click the link, the Associate a File Type or Protocol with a Specific Program dialog box appears, as shown in Figure 1-8. The list shows more than 650 filename extensions that are already recognized by Windows, in addition to several dozen Internet and Windows protocols.

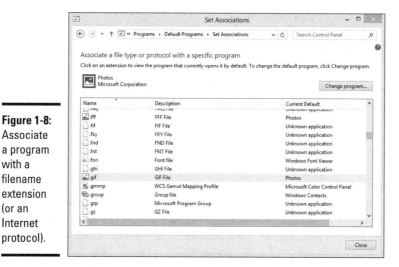

Figure 1-8: Associate a program with a filename extension (or an Internet protocol).

Book VII Chapter 1

Controlling Control Panel

3. **To change the default program associated with a filename extension, tap or click the extension, tap or click Change Program, and choose the program that you want to handle it.**

   For example, you could click the gif extension, which may or may not have an association on your machine, and assign it to Microsoft Paint.

4. **Tap or click Close, and your change takes place immediately.**

   You might want to run out to File Explorer and open a file with the extension to ensure that your change works right.

Changing the default browser or e-mail program

Changing the default program assigned to a filename extension is pretty straightforward. But setting your default browser, e-mail program, music player, picture editor, and the like, is considerably more complicated.

The mechanics of making the change aren't hard at all. The complicated part is what Windows does behind the scenes to make your changes work. Many programs inside Windows, and many programs you install, can handle a wide variety of filename extensions and Internet protocols. For example, Firefox can handle HTM, HTML, SHTM, XHT, and XHTML files, as well as the protocols `fpt://`, `http://`, and `https://`.

When you install Firefox, the installer tells Windows which kinds of files and protocols Firefox can handle. If you set Firefox as your default browser, it takes control over all those filename extensions and protocols. But if you choose another browser as your default browser, it takes all (or almost all) those filename extensions and protocols.

That's a brief explanation of what can happen — and a warning about what can go wrong. If you go messing with individual filename extension defaults, you may put Windows in a difficult position, with some kinds of browser functions being handled by one program, and other functions handled by a different program.

So with that bit of warning — *don't mess with individual associations* — here's how to set a default web browser, e-mail program, music or video player, picture editor, maps handler, Contacts program, and so on:

1. **Bring up Control Panel by swiping on the desktop or right-clicking the lower-left corner, and choosing Settings.**

   Details at the beginning of this chapter in the section "Bringing up the Control Panel."

2. **In the lower left, select the Programs category; then in the Default Programs section, tap or click the Set Your Default Programs link.**

   Windows opens the Set Default Programs dialog box, as shown in Figure 1-9.

Number of possible associated programs

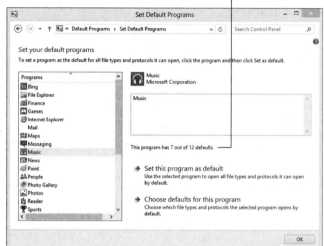

Figure 1-9:
Set a default
browser,
e-mail
program,
and many
others here.

3. **Pick the program, such as a browser, e-mail program, and so on, that you want to make your default, and then tap or click Set This Program as Default.**

   Behind the scenes, Windows pulls up all the possible filename extensions and protocols that could be assigned to that program, and switches them all over to the program.

4. **(Optional) To see what's actually happening, tap or click Choose the Defaults for This Program. Then look at — *but don't touch* — the filename extensions and protocols up for offer.**

   Be very aware that changing the default browser will prevent Internet Explorer from running on the tiled side of Windows. If you set Chrome as your default browser, Chrome takes over on the tiled side of the fence (and does a fine job, it must be said). If IE isn't the default browser, Windows won't run IE on the tiled part of Windows. Windows will, however, run any browser you like on the desktop side.

   If you change your default browser to, say, Chrome, and later decide that you really prefer to use the tiled version of Internet Explorer, you can always come back here and set IE as your default web browser.

5. **Tap or click OK.**

   Your changes take place immediately.

If you changed a default program with many filename extensions, it'd be a good idea to run out to File Explorer and make sure that it behaves the way you think it should.

Adding and Switching Clocks

If you want to change the clock in the lower-right corner of the desktop — perhaps add a clock, change the time, or change the format of the date or time — it's easy. Here's how:

1. **In the lower-right corner of the desktop, tap or click and hold on the clock. Choose Adjust Date and Time.**

   The Date and Time dialog box appears, as shown in Figure 1-10.

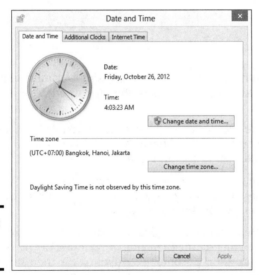

Figure 1-10:
Change the
time.

2. **To change the current date and time, or set up a new time zone, tap or click the appropriate buttons.**

   Be aware that some calendar programs don't take kindly to having their time zones changed. Some of them get confused, and can't decide whether to adjust the time of your appointments or leave them as is. (If you were in Los Angeles when you set an appointment for 9:00 Monday morning, and you fly to New York, what should happen to your appointment? It's not a simple question!)

3. **To change the date format (to show day-month-year, for example), tap or click the Change Date and Time button, and then tap or click the Change Calendar Settings link.**

   I'm partial to displaying dates in the dd-mmm-yy format, such as 25-Sep-12, so I set my Short Date format to dd-MMM-yy, and then clicked OK three times.

4. **(Optional) To put a second digital clock in the system notification area — the bottom-right corner of the desktop — tap or click the Additional Clocks tab and follow the instructions.**

5. **When you're happy with the changes, tap or click OK.**

   Your clocks change at once.

Changing Languages

Windows language support has improved enormously in the past few versions. One very common request is to change the keyboard: You may have a German, British, or Thai keyboard, which is completely different from anything you've ever seen. Although you can fake an umlaut, for example, using the Character Map program (see Book VI, Chapter 3), if you use a lot of umlauts, it makes sense to get a keyboard that has umlauts built in.

When you change the keyboard language — Windows calls the program behind it the *Input Method Editor* — Windows doesn't really change the keyboard at all. It just re-assigns things, so what you see on the keycaps corresponds to what appears onscreen. It's a mapping function, even with enormously complex languages.

Here's how to change the mapping that Windows uses, to accommodate different languages and their keyboards:

1. **Bring up Control Panel by swiping on the desktop or right-clicking the lower-left corner, and choosing Settings.**

   Details at the beginning of this chapter in the section "Bringing up the Control Panel."

2. **On the right side, in the Clock, Language and Region section, tap or click the Add a Language link.**

   The Change Your Language Preferences dialog box appears, as shown in Figure 1-11.

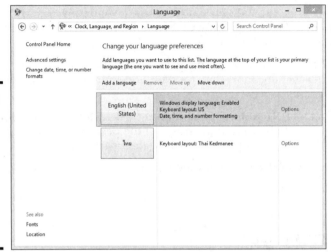

Figure 1-11:
To make
a specific
language's
keyboard
available to
Windows,
install the
language
first.

3. **If you don't see the language that you want to use, tap or click the Add a Language link.**

If you *do* see the language you want — say, you want to add a Dvorak keyboard layout as an option for U.S. English — tap or click the Options link on the right, and then tap or click Add an Input Method. Windows shows you dozens of different U.S. keyboards, and you can take your pick.

After you tap or click Add a Language, you're presented with a list of more than a hundred languages.

4. **Pick the language(s) you want and then tap or click Add.**

Tamazight Tifinagh, anyone? You return to the Change Your Language Preferences dialog box in Figure 1-11.

5. **If you have more than one language or keyboard layout installed, make sure your preferred language is on top by tapping or clicking the Move Up/Move Down links, and then close the dialog box.**

Windows puts a small icon on the taskbar, immediately to the left of the clock. If you started in the English language, the ENG icon appears.

6. **To change languages — that is, to change the mapping Windows uses from your keyboard to the characters displayed onscreen — tap or click the icon, and choose your language or keyboard.**

Enabling Ease of Access Features

Windows has a large number of Assistive Technology options that make it easier for people who need help to interact with the beast. For example, Ease of Access settings can make it easier to see what's on the screen, interact with the computer, hear the audio output, and much more.

The easiest way to set up Ease of Access options is to run through the five-question wizard Microsoft puts under the Let Windows Suggest Settings link. To get there, bring up the Control Panel using the method described at the beginning of this chapter under "Bringing up the Control Panel." Then, on the lower right, under Ease of Access, tap or click Let Windows Suggest Settings.

The questions cover problems you may have with vision, manual dexterity, hearing, speech, and reasoning/dyslexia. Answer the questions, and Windows comes up with a custom-tailored set of recommended settings, which you can accept or reject, one by one.

**Book VII
Chapter 1**

Controlling Control Panel

Chapter 2: Troubleshooting and Getting Help

In This Chapter

✔ Using the Windows troubleshooting tools

✔ Checking your system's stability

✔ Working with Windows Help and Support

✔ Snapping your problems

✔ Getting help from other folks without losing the farm

✔ Getting help on the web — effectively

Your PC ran into a problem that it couldn't handle, and now it needs to restart. You can search for the error online: *There's an error message that goes by so fast, you can't possibly read it.*

Wish I had a nickel for every time I've seen that "blue screen" message. People write to me all the time and ask what caused the message, or one like it, to appear on their computers. My answer? Could be anything. Hey, don't feel too bad: Windows couldn't figure it out, either, and Microsoft spent hundreds of millions of dollars trying to avoid it.

Think of this chapter as help on Help. When you need help, start here.

Windows arrives festooned with automated tools to help you pull yourself out of the sticky parts. The troubleshooters really do shoot trouble, frequently, if you find the right one. The error logs, event trackers, and stability graphs can keep you going for years — even the experts scratch their heads. Windows abounds with acres and acres — and layers and layers — of Help. Some of it works well. Some of it would work well, if you could figure out how to get to the right help at the right time.

This chapter tells you when and where to look for help. It also tells you when to give up and what to do after you give up. Yes, destroying your PC is an option. But you may have alternatives. No guarantees, of course.

This chapter also includes detailed, simple, step-by-step instructions for inviting a friend to take over your computer, via the Internet, to see what is going on and lend you a hand while you watch. I believe that this Remote Assistance capability is the most powerful and useful feature ever built into any version of Windows.

Troubleshooting in the Action Center

If something goes bump in the night and you can't find a discussion of the problem and its solution in this book, your first stop should be the Action Center. They don't call it Action fer nuthin'.

Windows ships with a handful of troubleshooters. *Troubleshooters,* as the name implies, take you by the hand and help you figure out what's causing problems — and, just maybe, solve them.

If you run into a problem and you're stumped, see whether Microsoft has released a pertinent troubleshooter by following these easy steps:

1. **Go to the tiled Start screen and type** trouble. **On the right, tap or click Settings, and then on the left, tap or click Troubleshooting.**

   The Troubleshooting dialog box appears, as shown in Figure 2-1.

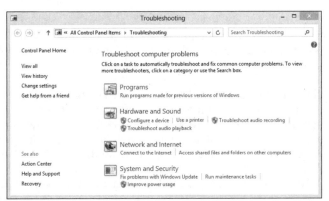

Figure 2-1: Trouble-shooting wizards can cut to the heart of a problem, if you can find one.

You can also get to the Troubleshooting dialog box the old-fashioned way by bringing up the Control Panel (right-click the lower-left corner of the screen and choose Control Panel) and choosing Find and Fix Problems under System and Security.

2a. *If you see a troubleshooter that seems to address your problem,* **tap or click it.**

   The selection is limited, but if you're lucky, the Troubleshooting Wizard steps you through the entire process of fixing the problem.

26. *If you don't see a troubleshooter that seems to address your problem,* **type a key word or two in the Search box and see whether Windows can find one for you.**

Microsoft has dozens of troubleshooters online. You can search for them by using the Search box in the upper-right corner of the Troubleshooting dialog box. For example, there are troubleshooters for power settings, searching and indexing, system maintenance, Windows Update, Internet Explorer, and many others.

Frequently, troubleshooters just can't shoot the trouble, and they end up with an error message dialog box that says something like, This error cannot be automatically repaired. You can tap or click Next and end up with informative messages such as The Error '5' was encountered. (I don't make this stuff up — that's exactly the error message I once received while running the connection troubleshooter.)

If you can't find a worthy troubleshooter, you may be able to unearth worthwhile content from your systems log using the Event Viewer, a topic that I tackle in Book VIII, Chapter 4.

System Stability and the Reliability Monitor

The Reliability Monitor's a useful tool that can help pinpoint problems that you can only vaguely identify. Say your computer suddenly starts getting those blue screen messages saying, Your PC ran into a problem that it couldn't handle, and now it needs to restart. You know for sure that your PC didn't have those problems last week. But something happened in the past few days, and now, suddenly, Windows encounters more problems than Kiefer Sutherland in a season of *24*.

Windows watches all, knows all, sees all — and keeps notes. Windows *events,* as they're called, get stored in a giant database, and you can look into that database with the Event Viewer, which I describe in Book VIII, Chapter 4.

One specific subset of the events get collected into a report — a Reliability Monitor report — that you can see in a nonce.

If you're looking at the Reliability Monitor because somebody on the phone told you that he's trying to help you fix your computer, be very, very suspicious. The Reliability Monitor will show that your computer has problems. Everybody's Reliability Monitor, sooner or later, shows problems. Scammers often use that fact to talk people into paying for services they don't need, or allowing them to connect to your computer for nefarious reasons. Don't be conned! It's not unusual to have a string of problems showing in the Reliability Monitor.

Here's the easy way to bring up the Reliability Monitor:

1. **On the Start screen, type** reliability. **On the right, tap or click Settings, and then on the left, tap or click View Reliability History.**

The Reliability Monitor report appears, as shown in Figure 2-2.

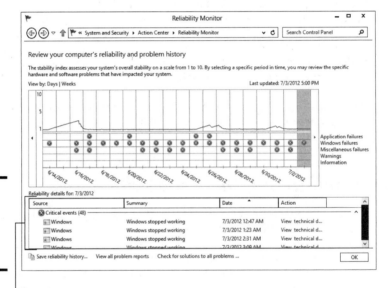

Figure 2-2:
The
Reliability
Monitor
report.

Double-click or tap to see details

2. **Tap or click any item in the list at the bottom of the report to bring up details.**

You can also tap or click an event, and coalesce reports by days or weeks, by choosing the appropriate option at the top.

The Reliability Monitor calculates an aggregate score, based on how many problems appear in this graph, taken as a rolling (or in some cases, *roiling*) average.

If you take the Stability score with a small grain of salt, you may be able to glean some useful information from the graph. For example, if you install a new driver and your system goes from ten to five that day, you can bet that the driver had something to do with the decline. The Reliability Monitor shows you significant events for each day and leaves it to you to draw inferences.

Tricks to Using Windows Help

The kind of Windows help you're offered depends on where you start:

✦ **If you start at the tiled Start screen,** swipe from the right (or hover your mouse in the upper-right corner), choose the Settings charm, and then choose Help, you get the very abbreviated list shown in Figure 2-3.

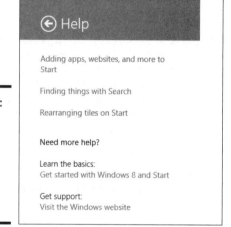

Figure 2-3: The very reduced Help Lite available from the tiled Start screen.

Book VII Chapter 2

Troubleshooting and Getting Help

✦ **If you start on the desktop** and perform the same actions, you're dropped into the Microsoft Internet-based Windows Help and Support, as shown in Figure 2-4.

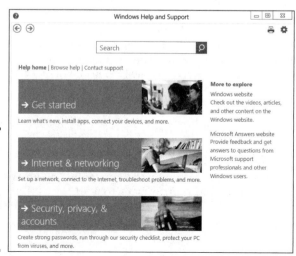

Figure 2-4: Go at it from the desktop, and you get access to all the support options.

Microsoft hopes to make finding what you need easier for you, even if you don't know the answer to your question in advance — a common problem in all versions of Windows Help.

The problem (s) with Windows Help

Windows Help offers only the Microsoft party line. If a big problem crops up with Windows, you find only a milquetoast report here. If a product from a different manufacturer offers a better way to solve a problem, you won't find that information here. Want searing insight or unbiased evaluations? That's why you have this book, eh?

Windows Help exists primarily to reduce Microsoft support costs, which is both good and bad. Microsoft has tried hard to enable you to solve your own problems, and to help you connect with other people who may be willing to volunteer. That's good. At the same time, Microsoft has made it difficult to figure out how to pick up the phone and chat with somebody in Product Support Services. That's bad. I spill the beans — and give you some much better alternatives — in a later section of this chapter, "How to Really Get Help."

Windows Help puts a happy face on an otherwise sobering (and bewildering!) topic. After you click past the sugarcoating, you find the following gotchas that you should know about:

✦ **You can't configure the Help search engine.** The Windows Help engine already looks in all the places it can. Your only option is to cut off online searches — which makes about as much sense as cutting off your clicking finger. You don't have anywhere near as many choices as with, say, a standard Google search (see "Getting Help Online," later in this chapter).

✦ **Live, one-on-one support from Microsoft is notoriously uneven.** One day you reach a support rep (who probably doesn't actually work for Microsoft) who can solve your problem in the blink of an eye. The next day, you spend hours on hold, only to be told that you need to reformat your hard drive and reinstall Windows. If you get bumped up to Level 2 live support, you're more likely to find someone who knows what she's doing, but you have to persist to Level 3 before you get to talk to a real, live, breathing guru. Few customers have the patience or the savvy to convince Microsoft product support droids to escalate their problem to Level 3.

Using different kinds of help

Windows Help has been set up for you to jump in, find an answer to your problem, resolve the problem, and get back to work.

Unfortunately, life is rarely so simple. So too, with Help. You probably won't dive into Help until you're feeling lost. And when you're there, well, it's like the old saying, "When you're up to your *<insert favorite expletive here>* in alligators, it's hard to remember that you need to drain the swamp."

Windows Help morsels fall into the following categories:

✦ **Overviews, articles, and tutorials:** Explanatory pieces aimed at giving you an idea of what's going on, as opposed to solving a specific problem.

✦ **Tasks:** Step-by-step procedures for solving a single problem or changing a single setting.

✦ **Walk-throughs and guided tours:** Marketing demos . . . uh, multimedia demonstrations of capabilities that tend to be, uh, light on details and heavy on splash.

✦ **Troubleshooters:** Walks you through a series of (frequently complex) steps to help you identify and resolve problems. I talk about troubleshooters earlier in this chapter.

Staying online

If you aren't connected to the Internet when you open Windows Help and Support, Windows falls back to a stunted version of the Help system. If you really need help with almost anything that's fairly complex, you have to be online.

The Windows Help system has few options that you can set, but you should check the one key setting that keeps Help talking to the mother ship. Follow these steps:

1. **On the Start screen, type** help, **and then on the left, choose Help and Support.**

You can bring up Help and Support in other ways, but that's the easiest. The Windows Help and Support main page appears (refer to Figure 2-4).

2. **In the upper-right corner, tap or click the gear icon.**

Windows Help has just two settings, but one of them is vital.

3. **Ensure that the Get Online Help (Recommended) check box is selected. Tap or click OK, and then tap or click the X button to close Windows Help.**

When Help is connected to the Internet, you see the Online Help icon in the lower-left corner of every Help screen.

Choosing the index versus search

Just as this book has an index, so too does Windows Help. To find the index, tap or click the Browse Help link.

The Windows Help index is quite thorough but, like any index, it relies heavily on the terminology being used in the Help articles themselves. That leads to frequent chicken-and-egg situations: You can find the answer to your question quite readily if you, uh, know the answer to the question — or if you know the terminology involved (which is nearly the same thing, eh?).

Generally, typing keywords in the Search text box is the best way to approach a problem, but the index comes in handy from time to time. Don't hesitate to use it.

How to Really Get Help

You use Windows Help when you need help, right? Well, yes. Sorta.

In my experience, Help works best in the following situations:

✦ When you want to understand what functions the big pieces of Windows perform, and you aren't overly concerned about solving a specific problem (for example, *Windows Media Player*)

✦ When you have a problem that's easy to define (for example, *my printer doesn't print*)

✦ When you have a good idea of what you want to do but you need a little prodding on the mechanics to get the job done (for example, *touch gestures*)

Help doesn't do much for you if you have only a vague idea of what's ailing your machine, if you want to understand enough details to think your way through a problem, if you're trying to decide which hardware or software to buy for your computer, or if you want to know where the Windows bodies are buried.

For example, if you type **how much memory do I need?**, the 60 answers you see talk about all sorts of things, but they don't tell you how much memory you need.

For all that, and much more, you need an independent source of information — this book, for example.

Beware of "Microsoft" tech support scams!

Somebody calls you, claims to be from Microsoft, and points you to a fancy website that says the caller's a Microsoft Registered Partner. The caller may even know your name, or your phone number, or he may act like he knows what version of Windows, or what computer, you're using. The scammer offers to check whether your system is still under warranty. Invariably, it just went out of warranty, and oh golly, you have to pay $35 or $75 or $150 to get all your problems solved.

These folks are very clever. Many don't live in your home country, although they may sound like it. They may scrape your name from a tech support site and look up your phone number, or they may just make cold calls and figure there's likely to be a warm reception for anyone who says they're from Microsoft, and they want to help.

The websites with Microsoft Registered Partner qualifications might look impressive, but anybody — even you — can become a Microsoft Partner; it takes maybe two minutes, and all you need is a Hotmail or Oulook.com account or other Microsoft account (formerly Windows Live ID). Drop by `http://partner.microsoft.com/40032508` and sign up!

I have a general explanation of the scam in Book IX, Chapter 1, and a detailed report at `http://windowssecrets.com/top-story/watch-out-for-microsoft-tech-support-scams`.

**Book VII
Chapter 2**

**Troubleshooting
and Getting Help**

My website, AskWoody.com (`www.askwoody.com`), can come in handy, especially if you're trying to decide whether you should install the latest Microsoft security patch of a patch of a patch. AskWoody.com links to the (absolutely free) Windows Secrets Newsletter Lounge, where hundreds of volunteers help thousands of bewildered Windows victims! You find more than 850,000 searchable posts, absolutely free. Drop by from time to time to see what's happening.

If you can't find the help you need in Windows Help and Support or at AskWoody.com, expand your search for enlightenment in this order:

1. Use simple bribery, which is far and away the best way to get help.

Buttonhole a friend who knows about this stuff, and get her to lend you a virtual hand. Promise her a beer, a pizza, a night on the town — whatever it takes. If your friend knows her stuff, it's cheaper and faster than the alternatives.

If you can cajole your machine into connecting to the Internet — and get your friend to also connect to the Internet — Windows makes it easy for a friend to take over your computer while you watch with the Remote Assistance feature, which I discuss a little later in this chapter.

2. If your friend is off getting a tan at Patong Beach, you may be able to find help elsewhere on the Internet.

   See the section "Getting Help Online," later in this chapter.

3. If you have a problem with a security patch — and can prove it — you may qualify for free support.

   Microsoft used to have a website where you could request a free support ticket, but it has withdrawn the old site. Now, apparently you have to call (see the next step) and convince the person on the other end of the phone that you're having a problem with a security patch, and that your tech support call should be free.

   For the life of me, I can't find *any* e-mail address — or pointer to an e-mail address — for tech support at Microsoft. Even the chat lines appear to be blocked off.

4. As a last resort, you can try to contact Microsoft by telephone.

   Heaven help ya.

Microsoft offers support by phone — you know, an old-fashioned voice call — but some pundits (including yours truly) have observed that you'll probably have more luck with a psychic hotline. Be that as it may, the telephone number for tech support in the United States is (800) 642-7676, and you may have to press 0 three or more times to get a live person, or (425) 635-3311. In Canada, it's (905) 568-4494. Have your computer handy. Be prepared to pay.

Snapping and Recording Your Problems

Raise your hand if you've heard the following conversation:

Overworked Geek (answering the phone): "Hi, honey. How's it going?"

Geek's Clueless Husband: "Sorry to call you at work, but I'm having trouble with my computer."

OG: "What kind of trouble?"

GCH: "I clicked the picture, and it went into Microsoft, you know, and I tried to look at this report my boss sent me, but the computer said it couldn't."

OG: "Huh?"

GCH: "I'm sure you've seen this a hundred times. I clicked the picture, but the computer said it couldn't. How do I look at the report?"

OG: "Spfffft!"

GCH: "What's wrong? Why don't you say anything? You have time to help the other people in your office. Why can't you make time for me?"

OG wonders, for the tenth time that day, how she ever got into this bloody business.

At one time or another, you may have been on the sending or receiving end of a similar conversation — probably both, come to think of it. In the final analysis, one thing's clear: When you're trying to solve a computer problem, being able to look at the screen is worth ten thousand words. Or more.

Taking snaps that snap

Since the dawn of WinTime, you could take a snapshot of your desktop and put it on the Windows Clipboard by simply pressing the PrtScr or Print Screen key on your keyboard. Similarly, hold down the Alt key and press PrtScr, and Windows puts a screen shot of the currently active window on the Windows Clipboard. From there, you can open Paint (or any of a hundred other picture-savvy programs, including Word), paste, and do what you will with the shot. That approach still works in Windows — even on the Start screen, and in the tiled apps — and in some circumstances, it's exactly the right tool for the job.

Windows Vista introduced the Snipping Tool, which is a more advanced tune on the same theme. With the Snipping Tool (see Figure 2-5), you tap or click New, then drag and draw a rectangle around the area you wish to capture. You can also capture a free-form area anywhere on the screen, or automatically capture the current window, or the full screen.

Figure 2-5: The Snipping Tool can take screen shots in a couple of steps.

The Snipping Tool has rudimentary tools for drawing on the captured screen, and the result can be copied to the Clipboard and/or saved as a PNG, GIF, JPG, or HTML file, or automatically attached to a newly generated e-mail message.

To bring up the Snipping Tool, go to the Start screen, type **snip**, and choose Snipping Tool. The Snipping Tool runs immediately, but it will capture only desktop screens.

Now Windows has a third screen capture option, and in many circumstances, it's much handier than its two older brethren. If you hold down the Windows key and press PrtScr or Print Screen on your keyboard, Windows takes a screen shot of the entire screen, converts it to a PNG file, and stores it in your Pictures library. The file is given the name `Screenshot (x).png`, where the number *x* is increased by one with each shot.

Unlike the Snipping Tool, the new screen capture tool does work on the Start screen, or in any tiled app. Unlike the Snipping Tool, you can't select a part of the screen — you get the whole thing. Also unlike the Snipping Tool, you can't pick a format for the shot, or a destination location. Still, for quick screens, it works well.

Recording live

If a screen shot's worth a thousand words, a video of the screen in action must be worth a thousand and one at least, right?

Windows includes the magical *Problem Steps Recorder (PSR),* recently renamed the Steps Recorder, which lets you take a movie of your screen. To a first approximation, anyway, it's actually a series of snapshots, more like an annotated slide show. You end up with a file that you can e-mail to a friend, a beleaguered spouse, or an innocent bystander, who can then see which steps you've taken and try to sort things out. To read the file, your guru has to run Internet Explorer.

Steps Recorder creates a slide show of your screen, with automatically generated detailed annotations, good, bad, ugly, problem-infested or rosy-cheeked. If you have a rosy-cheeked background, anyway.

Steps Recorder's fast and easy, and it works like a champ.

Here's how to record your problems, er, screen:

1. **Make sure you remember which steps you have to take to make the problem (or rosy cheeks) appear.**

   Practice, if need be, until you figure out just how to move the whatsis to the flooberjoober and click the thingy to get to the sorry state that you want to show to your guru friend.

Realize that anything appearing on the screen, even fleetingly, may be recorded, and your friend may be able to see it. So don't send your salary information, okay?

2. Go to the Start screen, type steps, **and on the left, tap or click Steps Recorder.**

You can start the Steps Recorder from the Control Panel, but this method is a whole lot easier.

The Steps Recorder, which resembles a full-screen camcorder, springs to life (see Figure 2-6). It isn't recording yet.

Figure 2-6:
The unassuming Steps Recorder.

Steps Recorder
Start Record   Stop Record   Add Comment

3. Tap or click Start Record.

The recorder starts. You know it's going because the title flashes Steps Recorder — Recording Now.

Note that the recorded slide show will include the Steps Recorder window, so you may have to move it out of the way in order to show what you want to show.

4. (Optional) If you want to type a description of what you're doing or why or anything else you want your guru friend to see while she's looking at your home movie:

a. Tap or click the Add Comment button.

The recording pauses, and the screen grays out a bit. A Highlight Problem and Comment box appears at the bottom of the screen.

b. Tap or click the screen wherever your problem may be occurring, and drag the mouse to highlight the problematic location.

c. Type your edifying text in the box, and tap or click OK.

Recording continues.

5. When you're done with the demo, tap or click Stop Record.

Steps Recorder responds with the Recorded Steps dialog box, as shown in Figure 2-7.

Take a good look at the file because what you see in the Save As box is precisely what gets saved — each of the screen shots, in a slide show, precisely as presented. Remember, this isn't a video. It's an annotated slide show.

Book VII
Chapter 2

Troubleshooting and Getting Help

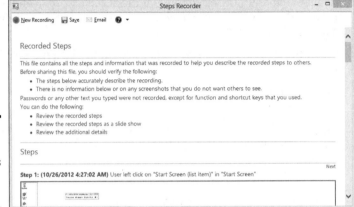

Figure 2-7:
Save the
recording as
soon as you
finish it.

6. **Type a name for the file (it's a regular Zip file), and tap or click Save.**

   The Zip file contains an MHT file, which can be reliably read only by
   Internet Explorer — although you may have some luck reading the file in
   Firefox, if it's running the MAFF or UnMHT add-ons.

7. **Send the file to your guru friend.**

   Sneakernet — the old-fashioned way of sticking the file on a USB drive
   and hand delivering it — works.

8. **Tell your friend to double-click the Zip file when she receives it and
   then double-click the MHT file inside.**

   Internet Explorer appears and shows the MHT file. You have several
   options; my favorite is to show the file as a slide show (see Figure 2-8).

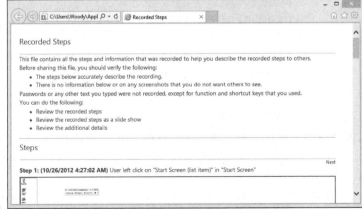

Figure 2-8:
The
recording
appears as
a series of
snapshots,
with detailed
accounts
of what has
been clicked
and where.

9. **When you're done, click the red X button to close the Steps Recorder.**

Magical. Okay, Snagit (see Book X, Chapter 5) does the screen recording shtick better, but still.

Connecting to Remote Assistance

Windows has long boasted the Remote Assistance feature, which lets a person on one computer control a second computer, long distance, while both watch what's on the screen. It's a great puppet/puppet master capability that allows someone to solve your problems remotely, while you watch. (Or, if you're the guru, Remote Assistance allows you to solve others' problems while they watch.)

If you're looking at these instructions because someone you don't know wants to get into your computer, stop. Right now. **Seriously. Stop.** Ask yourself how much you know about the person who's trying to look at your PC. Do you trust her to take control of your PC — is it possible she'll pull a fast one on you, even drop an infected file? If you have any qualms at all, DON'T DO IT. Scammers love to talk people into using Remote Assistance because they get full control over the PC, and if they work fast enough (or talk fast enough to convince you that what they're doing is legitimate), they can easily plant anything they want on your computer.

Understanding the interaction

Windows includes the Remote Assistance feature, which lets you call on a friend (or friendly guru) to take over your PC.

The basic interaction goes something like this:

1. You create an invitation file for your guru friend, asking him to look at your computer. Windows creates a password for the invitation, and shows it on your screen.

2. You send or give the file to the guru. Separately, you send your guru the password.

The file can go any way you can imagine: Attach it to an e-mail message, send it via an instant messaging program that allows you to transfer files, put it on a network shared drive, post it on your company's intranet, copy it to a shared folder on SkyDrive, stick it on a USB key drive, burn it on a CD, or strap it to a carrier pigeon. It's just a text file. Nothing fancy.

Similarly you can send the password if you like, but it's smarter to call your guru and repeat it over the phone, just in case somebody's scraping your e-mail.

3. Your guru friend receives the message or file and responds by clicking it and then typing the password.

4. Your PC displays a message saying that your guru friend wants to look at your computer.

5. If you give the go-ahead, your guru friend can see what you're doing — look, but not touch.

6. Your guru friend may ask whether he can take over your computer. If you give your permission, he takes complete control of your machine.

   He can switch between the Start screen and the desktop, bring up the charms, go into Control Panel, run programs . . . the whole nine yards. You watch as your friend types and clicks, just as *you* would if you knew what the heck you were doing. Your friend solves the problem as you watch.

7. Either of you can break the connection at any time.

The thought of handing your machine over to somebody on an Internet connection probably gives you the willies. I'm not real keen on it either, but Microsoft has built some industrial-strength controls into Remote Assistance. Your guru friend must supply the password that you specify before he can connect to your computer. He can take control of your computer only if he requests it and you specifically allow it. And you can put a time limit on the invitation: If your friend doesn't respond within an hour, say, the invitation is canceled.

Making the connection

When you're ready to set up the connection for Remote Assistance, the following is what you need to do. (I'm writing this from the point of view of the Dummy requesting assistance from a guru. If you're the guru in the interaction, you have to kind of stand on your head and read backward, but, hey, you're the guru and no doubt you knew that already, huh?)

1. **Make sure that your guru friend is ready.**

   Call him or shoot him an e-mail and make sure that he will have his PC on, connected to the Internet, and running Windows 8, 7, Vista, XP, Windows Server 2003, Windows Server 2008, or Windows Server 2012. Also, make sure that he has his instant messenger program cranked up, will check e-mail frequently, or will wait for you to hand him a file or make one available on your network.

Make sure that you can contact your guru friend using your selected method: If you're using e-mail, make sure that he's in your address book and send him a test message to make sure that you have his e-mail address down pat; if you're going to send a floppy disk by carrier pigeon, make sure that the pigeon knows the route and has had plenty of sleep.

2. **Start your machine (the PC that your Remote Assistance friend, the guru, will take over), and make sure that it's connected to the Internet.**

   Make sure you aren't running any programs that you don't want the guru to see. Yes, that includes the Sudoku with the lousy score.

3. **Flip over to the Start screen and type** invite. **On the right, choose Settings, and on the left, choose Invite Someone to Connect to Your PC and Help You, or Offer to Help Someone Else.**

   The Windows Remote Assistance dialog box appears, as shown in Figure 2-9.

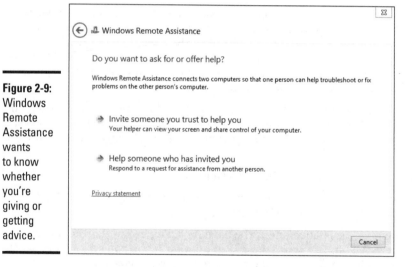

Figure 2-9:
Windows
Remote
Assistance
wants
to know
whether
you're
giving or
getting
advice.

4. **Tap or click Invite Someone You Trust to Help You.**

   You don't actually have to trust him but, well, you get the idea.

   Remote Assistance responds with the dialog box shown in Figure 2-10.

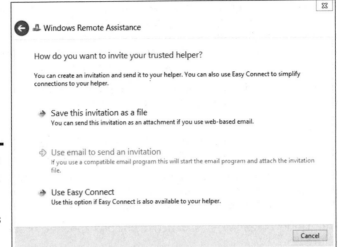

How do you want to invite your trusted helper?

You can create an invitation and send it to your helper. You can also use Easy Connect to simplify connections to your helper.

→ Save this invitation as a file
You can send this invitation as an attachment if you use web-based email.

→ Use email to send an invitation
If you use a compatible email program this will start the email program and attach the invitation file.

→ Use Easy Connect
Use this option if Easy Connect is also available to your helper.

Cancel

Figure 2-10:
The surest way is to save the invitation as a file.

Easy Connect is an advanced version of Remote Assistance. It works for some people, if they're connecting with another person who's running Windows 7 or Windows 8. Unfortunately, sometimes network routers get in the way. The big gain with Easy Connect is that you set it up once, and then you can reuse the same connection any time you like, without going through the invitation/password routine.

The method I describe in the following steps works whether your router likes it or not. If you want to try Easy Connect, by all means, choose that option in Figure 2-10 and see whether your guru can connect. If it works, it's, uh, easy.

5. **Choose Save This Invitation as a File.**

   Even if you're going to e-mail the file, it's easier to save the file first and then attach it to an e-mail message.

   Remote Assistance opens the Save As dialog box and prompts you to save the file Invitation.msrcIncident. You can change the name, if you like, but it's easier for your guru friend if you keep the filename extension msrcIncident.

6. **Save the file in a convenient place.**

   Remote Assistance responds with an odd-looking dialog box, the Windows Remote Assistance control bar, as shown in Figure 2-11. It advises you to provide your helper (that's your guru friend) with the invitation file and the automatically generated 12-character password.

Windows waits for your guru friend to contact you. You can continue to work, swear, play Minesweeper, or do whatever it takes to keep you sane until your friend can connect.

Figure 2-11:
The Windows Remote Assistance control bar.

7. **Send the invitation file to your guru friend via e-mail, in a shared SkyDrive folder, or a USB slipped into his hamburger at lunch.**

8. **Tell your friend to double-click the invitation file to initiate the Remote Assistance session.**

   Your friend's computer asks for the password that's in your Windows Remote Assistance control bar. He types it in the indicated box on his computer and clicks OK.

   Windows Remote Assistance then asks whether it's okay to allow your guru friend to connect to your computer (see Figure 2-12).

Figure 2-12:
Remote Assistance requires your explicit permission.

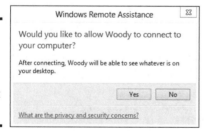

9. **Tap or click the Yes button.**

   Two things happen simultaneously:

   • Your computer's Remote Assistance bar shows that you're connected, as shown in Figure 2-13.

   • Your guru friend's computer sets up a window that shows him everything on your computer, as shown in Figure 2-14.

Figure 2-13:
Your computer gets this Remote Assistance bar.

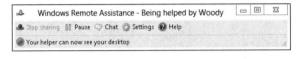

Figure 2-14:
Your guru friend sees your entire desktop, in a special Remote Assistance window.

If your guru friend wants to take control of your PC, he needs to click the Request Control icon on his Remote Assistance bar.

If he does that, your machine warns you that your guru friend is trying to take control, as shown in Figure 2-15.

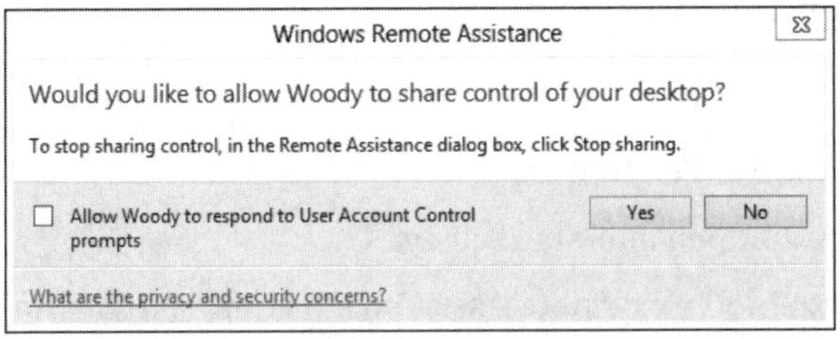

Figure 2-15:
Allow your guru friend to take over.

Windows Remote Assistance

Would you like to allow Woody to share control of your desktop?

To stop sharing control, in the Remote Assistance dialog box, click Stop sharing.

☐ Allow Woody to respond to User Account Control prompts   Yes   No

What are the privacy and security concerns?

10. **On your machine, tap or click Yes to allow your guru friend to take control of your PC.**

Your guru friend can now control your computer, move the mouse, and type on the keyboard while you watch.

11. **Anytime either of you wants to sever the connection, tap or click the Disconnect icon on the Remote Assistance bar.**

In addition, you — the person who requested the session — can cancel the session at any time by pressing Esc.

After a Remote Assistance session is underway and you release control to your friend, your friend can do anything to your computer that you can do — anything at all, except change users. (If either logs off, the Remote Assistance connection is canceled.) Both of you have simultaneous control over the mouse pointer. If either or both of you type on the keyboard, the letters appear onscreen. You can stop your friend's control of your computer by pressing Esc.

Your friend can rest assured that this is a one-way connection. He can take control of your computer, but you can't do anything on his computer. He can see everything that you can see on your desktop, but you aren't allowed to look at his desktop. Whoever said life was fair?

Limiting an invitation

Unless you change things, an invitation that you send requesting Remote Assistance expires after six hours. To change the expiration time, follow these steps:

1. **Bring up the Control Panel (right-click the lower-left corner of the screen and choose Control Panel) and on the left, tap or click the System and Security link.**

2. **Under the System link, tap or click the Allow Remote Access link.**

3. **Make sure that the Remote tab displays, and in the Remote Assistance box, tap or click the Advanced button.**

4. **In the Invitations box, choose the amount of time you want invitations to remain open.**

5. **Tap or click OK twice, and then tap or click the X to close the Control Panel.**

Troubleshooting Remote Assistance

Plenty of pitfalls lurk around the edges of Remote Assistance, but it mostly rates as an amazingly useful, powerful tool. The following are among the potential problems:

+ You and your guru friend have to be connected to the Internet or to the same local network. If you can't connect to the Internet — especially if that's the problem you're trying to solve — you're outta luck.

+ Both of you have to be running Windows 8, 7, Vista, XP, Windows Server 2003, Windows Server 2008, Windows Server 2012, or another operating system that supports Remote Assistance. Sorry, your iPad doesn't qualify.

+ You have to be able to give (or send) your guru friend a file so that he can use the invitation to connect to your PC.

+ If a firewall sits between either of you and the Internet, it may interfere with Remote Assistance. Windows Firewall (the firewall that's included in Windows 8, 7 and Windows Vista, as well as Windows XP Service Pack 2 and later) doesn't intentionally block Remote Assistance, but other firewalls may. If you can't get through, contact your system administrator, or dig into the firewall's documentation and unblock *Port 3389* — the communication channel that Remote Assistance uses.

You — the person with the PC that will be taken over — must initiate the Remote Assistance session. Your guru friend can't tap you on the shoulder, electronically, and say something like this (with apologies to Dire Straits): "You an' me, babe, how 'bout it?"

Getting Help Online

Once upon a time, Microsoft made it fairly easy to call for tech support, or send e-mail to the tech support staff. Now, it's almost impossible to find a living human being who will respond to your requests for help.

It just isn't efficient. You may have the same question that a hundred other people have, and it doesn't make sense to answer your one question, without making that answer available to anybody else who takes the time to look.

That's one of the reasons why Microsoft encourages you to use the support forums. The other big reason? Lots of people join in on the forums to help. Many of them are *MVPs — Microsoft Most Valued Professionals —* who work without pay, just for the joy of knowing that they're helping people. Microsoft gives the MVPs recognition and thanks, and some occasional benefits such as being able to talk with some people on the development teams. In exchange, the MVPs give generally good — sometimes excellent — support to anyone who asks.

My personal bias, of course, is to direct you to the free online help forum that a bunch of friends, and I started 15 years ago. It's at `http://windows secrets.com/forums`. I mention it earlier in this chapter.

Microsoft has a massive support complex known as the Microsoft Answers forum. If you specifically want help with Windows 8 questions, go to the Win8 section: `http://answers.microsoft.com/en-us/windows/forum/windows_8`.

Search for an answer before you post a question. Chances are very good that somebody else has already hit the same problem.

Chapter 3: Working with Libraries

*W*hen you start File Explorer, icons for four libraries appear. That should give you a hint about the central role libraries play in the way Microsoft wants you to think about your data.

A lot of experienced Windows users get confused when they start thinking about libraries. That's because they have a long-imprinted misconception that data has to be located in one place. Your files are on your C: drive or on a DVD, or you download them from the Internet. You open a file, and if you don't find what you want, you look in another file in the same folder. If the folder doesn't have what you want, you go up one level and look again.

All those concepts are locked into the idea that your data has to be located in just one place.

Although your files have to sit somewhere, Windows has introduced a concept that makes it easier to handle collections of files and folders.

Understanding Libraries

You know what a file is, right? (If not, I talk about it in Book I, Chapter 1.) Files hold data. Typically, you have one photo or video in one file. You have one song in one file. You have one document, spreadsheet, or PowerPoint presentation in one file. Of course, there are lots of nuances, but at its heart, a *file* is just a collection of data that you stick in one place. Files can be empty. They can be huge.

And you know about folders, yes? *Folders* are collections of files and other folders. Folders can also be empty. They can be huge. They can have lots of little files or many big files, or any combination of little and big files and folders. You put a bunch of files and folders together in one place, and that place is a folder.

Note how I said "in one place." The physical details may get a little hairy, but at least conceptually, all the data in the file is in one place. All the files in a folder are in one place. That's how libraries are different.

Libraries aren't all in one place. Libraries bring together folders that can be sitting just about anywhere: on your C: drive, on your D: drive, on a USB stick, on an external drive, even someplace else on your network, if you have one. A *library* is a collection of folders that's broken free of the "in one place" restriction. But libraries use pointers to make it *seem* like these files are all in one place.

Working with Your Default Libraries

When you start File Explorer, icons for the four libraries that Windows itself builds appear (see Figure 3-1).

Four default libraries

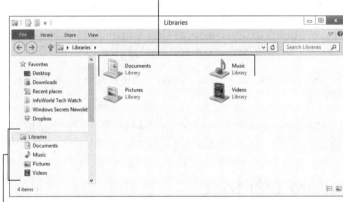

Figure 3-1:
The four horses of the library apocalypse.

Navigate to a library

You might be tempted to think that Windows magically identifies the kinds of files you're working with and shows them in the appropriate library — all your pictures appear in the Pictures library, for example. That isn't how libraries work.

Windows builds the four libraries you see by slamming together the contents of your My folder of the appropriate type, and your Public folder of the same type. Thus

✦ Everything that appears in the Documents library comes from the \My Documents folder, mashed together with the \Public\Documents folder.

+ Same for the Music library.

+ Everything in the Pictures library comes from either the \My Pictures or \Public Pictures folder.

+ Same for the Videos library.

The converse is also true. Every file in the \My Music folder appears in the Music library, as does every file in the \Public\Music folder. Windows doesn't dig into the file and see whether it's a music file. The Music library doesn't consist of music files, necessarily. It's just a mash-up of all the files in those two folders.

Why would you want to bother with libraries? Ends up that they're pretty powerful, after you get used to them. Probably the most valuable timesaver for most people is in the search that spans across multiple folders. Here are two examples:

+ If you want to search all your music for an album by Nickelback, go to the Music library and in the upper-right corner, search for *Nickelback.*

+ If you want to search for documents and spreadsheets that contain the word *defenestrate,* bring up the Documents library, type **defenestrate** in the search box, and Windows returns all the documents in both \My Documents and \Public\Documents that contains the word.

Imagine how that searching can make your life easier if you keep, say, all of your music in a folder on one computer that's attached to your network. Set up your Music library to include that folder, and your searching just got a whole lot easier.

Libraries for old Windows hands

If you've used any modern version of Windows Media Player, you already know about libraries. WMP starts with your Music folder and your PC's Public Music folder, and allows you to add other folders to its library. So, for example, you can add a folder full of music on an external hard drive to the WMP library, or link to Music folders on other networked computers, or even a Music folder on a Windows Home Server server.

When you add a folder to the WMP library, it doesn't copy the music anywhere. WMP merely provides easy access to all the files (the songs) in the library, keeps track of them, and lets you search and work with them as a group.

There are no limitations to the folders you can add to a WMP library: As long as your computer can get at the folders — the external drive is plugged into the computer, say, or there are no security rules blocking access to another computer — WMP treats the music in those folders more-or-less the same way they'd be treated if they were sitting on your own PC.

When an application running under Windows looks for the Documents folder, Windows hands it the entire Documents library. If you start a graphics program and choose File⇨Open, you don't go to your Pictures folder any more. Instead, you open the Pictures library. Imagine. If you have a folder on another computer that contains documents you commonly use, and you add that folder to your Documents library, every time you crank up Word and choose File⇨Open, that folder's staring right at you. Unlike earlier versions, Windows Media Player doesn't need separate settings to handle libraries because Windows takes care of everything.

Think of libraries as Folders: The Next Generation.

Customizing Libraries

You can add folders to a library above and beyond the default folders. ("Working with Your Default Libraries" earlier in this chapter explains what the default folders are.) You can also change where a library saves data when you add items to it. Read on for the details.

Adding a folder to a library

The most common change I see people make to their libraries is to add a new folder to the Pictures or Music library. Typically, you have pictures or maybe music strewn in several locations, either on your computer or on your network. Here's how easy it is to add a folder from far away into your library:

1. **Using File Explorer, navigate to the folder you want to add.**

It can be located just about anywhere.

2. **Tap and hold or right-click the folder, select Include in Library, and choose the library.**

In Figure 3-2, I add the Family Pics folder to my Pictures library.

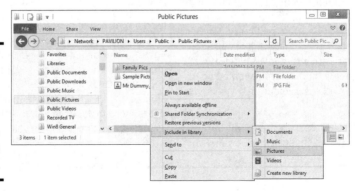

Figure 3-2:
Adding a folder to a library is easy, if you start by going to the folder.

3. **Go back to the library and make sure that the folder was added properly.**

   In Figure 3-3, you can see that the Family Pics folder, which sits on a different computer, is now in my Pictures library.

Figure 3-3:
Even though
the folder
hasn't
moved,
it's now
included in
the library.

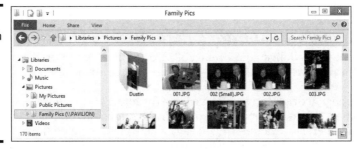

Family Pics

It's important to realize that Windows *doesn't move anything.* The pictures are still in their old location. But the library has been expanded to include the folder in the remote location. If you search your Pictures library, Windows will not only look at the contents of the \My Pictures and \Public\Pictures folders, it will also look inside the Family Pics folder.

Libraries go better with tags

Whereas most music files have (at least rudimentary) tags associated with them, photos usually don't come with tags, other than the ones your camera may put on them — *EXIF data*, such as the time and date the picture was taken. Nor do videos. To keep massive amounts of media organized, you have to come to grips with tags, the index data (or *metadata*) that you can stick on every file you own.

Although you can't create a library based on tags, you can search on tags, and that makes it infinitely easier to keep large libraries organized.

Windows Media Player and Live Photo Gallery have good tools for handling tags. In general, you can assign your own tags to just about any file (except GIFs) as follows:

1. **Locate the file in File Explorer and make sure it's selected.**

2. **Open the Details pane (the link is under the Preview pane) and edit the tags in the pane at the right.**

   Alternatively, you can right-click the file, choose Properties, and click the Details tab. Many free programs are available for editing tags on MP3 files, too.

At the risk of paraphrasing Beyoncé (and the Chipettes), if you like it then you shouldda put a tag on it. Whoa whoa whoa. If you want to find a file, put a tag on it!

Libraries aren't exclusive. You can put one folder in multiple libraries. You can put a folder in one library, and a subfolder of that folder in a different library.

If you ever want to remove a folder from a library, tap and hold or right-click the folder's name on the left in the Navigation pane. Choose Remove Location from Library.

Changing a library's default save location

Want to challenge your brain a bit? Don't short-circuit on this one, but "libraries" *itself* is a library — a library that contains libraries.

When you drag, copy, or move a file (or folder) into a library, the file (or folder) has to physically go somewhere — it has to be placed in a real, physical folder. For example, if you save a new picture called Dummy.pic to the Pictures library, Windows has to put the file Dummy.pic someplace; it has to stick it in a real folder. Because the Pictures library isn't a real folder, Windows needs to figure out which folder inside the Pictures library should get the copy of Dummy.pic.

The folder is the *default save location* for the library. The save location for the Documents library is the My Documents folder. The save location for the Music library is the My Music folder, and so on.

It's easy to change the default save location for any of the libraries.

I, personally, change the save location of the Music library to the \Public\ Music folder, so any time I drag or save music into the Music library, it automatically ends up in a place where other people who use my PC, and other people on my network, can access that music easily.

Here's how to change the default save location:

1. Start File Explorer.

The libraries appear, as shown in Figure 3-1.

2. On the left, tap or click a library. Then at the top, tap or click the Library Tools tab.

The Library Tools Manage tab opens and exposes the Manage Library Ribbon, which looks like Figure 3-4.

3. On the left, in the Navigation pane, tap or click whichever library you wish to change.

4. **At the top, tap or click Set Save Location and choose the folder that you wish to set as the default save location.**

Your change takes place immediately.

Set the default save location

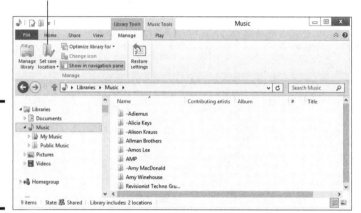

Figure 3-4:
Manage
your
libraries
from this
Ribbon.

Creating Your Own Library

Windows ships with four libraries, but you can add as many as you like.

You might want to create your own library if, for example, you have a bunch of information about a house you want to sell. The info might include Word documents, an Excel spreadsheet, multiple photos and maybe a video or two. You have the documents in a folder in My Documents, the photos are in a separate folder in My Pictures, and the video is in a separate folder in My Videos. Here's how to make a library that ties them all together:

1. **Start File Explorer and make sure your libraries show (refer to Figure 3-1).**

2. **Tap and hold or right-click any blank location on the right, and choose New⇨Library.**

Windows creates a new library, giving it the name New Library.

3. **Immediately type a name for the library and hit Enter (or tap the new icon).**

   In Figure 3-5, I typed the name *House for Sale* and pressed Enter, and File Explorer showed me my new, empty library.

   Windows lets you out to pick and choose your first folder.

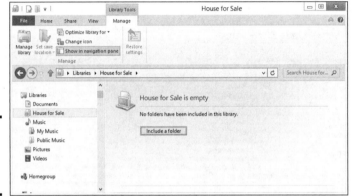

Figure 3-5:
Start your own custom library.

4. **Tap or click the Include a Folder button.**

5. **Navigate to the first folder you want to include, and tap or click Include Folder.**

   The first folder becomes the default save folder.

6. **To add additional folders to the library, navigate to the folder, tap or right-click and hold, choose Include in Library, and choose the name of the new library.**

   The new library appears everywhere that the four default libraries appear, including the Navigation pane on the left of File Explorer and in the right-click menu for folders.

Chapter 4: Storing in Storage Spaces

In This Chapter

✔ Virtualizing Storage Spaces

✔ Setting up Storage Spaces

✔ Care and feeding of Storage Spaces

*F*or people who want to make sure that they never suffer a data loss — in spite of dying hard drives or backup routines that don't run properly — the Windows Storage Spaces feature may, in and of itself, justify buying, installing, and using Windows 8.

If you're using Drobo, ReadyNAS, or some other expensive network attached storage device for file mirroring, you can toss your old hardware. Windows 8 handles it all as part of the operating system itself.

In this chapter, I introduce you to the Windows 8 approach to drive virtualization and how it enables Storage Space to work. Then you walk through setting up Storage Spaces, and the tips and tricks you need to know to make Storages Spaces work for you. Using Storage Spaces for backup is quick and easy, and it works.

Understanding the "Virtualization" of Storage

You're going to get sick of the term *virtualization* sooner or later. People who want to sell you stuff use the term all the time. But if you'll pinch your nose and wade through the offal, there's a solid core of real-world good stuff in this particular kind of virtualization technology.

Windows Storage Spaces takes care of disk management behind the scenes so you don't have to. You'll never even know (or care) which hard drive on your computer holds what folders, or which files go where. Volumes and folders get extended as needed, and you don't have to lift a finger.

Storage Spaces' roots in Windows Home Server

The crazy thing about Storage Spaces? Microsoft's already shipped a fully functional version, long before Windows 8. The original Windows Home Server, released in July 2007, had a Drive Extender feature that's very, very similar to what Microsoft now offers in Windows 8.

I know. Drive Extender is featured prominently in my book, *Windows Home Server For Dummies*; it's one of the greatest features Microsoft has ever offered to home and small business users.

The really crazy part: Microsoft yanked Drive Extender from the second version of Windows Home Server, which was released in April 2011. The claim, at the time, was that the technology had bugs deep inside that couldn't be exorcised

in the normal course of upgrading from version 1 to version 2. I hollered and moaned at the time, to no avail. Drive Extender was one of two really cool features (the other was Automatic Backup) in Windows Home Server that I relied on all the time, and Microsoft threw it away.

I felt so strongly about Microsoft's defenestration of Drive Extender that I refused to upgrade to version 2 of Windows Home Server — to this day, I run the original version of WHS. Drive Extender really is that cool.

Now I know why MS took Drive Extender out of Windows Home Server 2. It built the same technology, re-worked from the ground up, in Windows 8 and in Windows 2012 Server. You gotta see it to believe it.

You don't have to worry about your `D:` drive running out of space because you don't *have* a `D:` drive. Or an `E:` drive. Windows just grabs all the hard drive real estate you give it and hands out pieces of the hard drive as they're required.

As long as you have two or more physical hard drives of sufficient capacity, any data you store in a Storage Space pool is automatically mirrored between two or more independent hard drives. If one of the hard drives dies, you can still work with the one(s) that are alive, and you never miss a beat — not one bit is out of place. Run out and buy a new drive, stick it in the computer, tell Windows that it can accept the new drive into the Drive Spaces borg, wait an hour or two while Windows performs its magic, and all your data is back to normal. You never miss a beat. It's really that simple.

When your computer starts running out of disk space, Windows tells you. Install another drive — internal, external, USB, SATA, whatever — and, with your permission, it's absorbed into the pool. More space becomes available, and you don't need to care about any of the details — no new drive letters, no partitions, no massive copying or moving files from one drive to another, no homebrew backup hacks. For those accustomed to Windows' whining and whining, the Storage Spaces approach to disk management feels like a breath of fresh air.

When you add a new hard drive to the Storage Spaces pool, everything that was on that new hard drive gets obliterated. You don't have any choice. No data on the drive survives — it's all wiped out. That's the price the drive pays for being absorbed into the Storage Spaces borg.

Here's a high-level overview of how you set up Storage Spaces with data mirroring:

1. Tell Windows that it can use two or more drives as a storage pool.

   Your C: drive — the drive that contains Windows — cannot be part of the pool.

   The best configuration for Storage Spaces: Get a fast solid state drive for your system files and make that the C: drive. Then get two or more big, hunking drives for storing all your data. The big drives can be slow, and you'll hardly notice.

2. After you set up a pool of physical hard drives, you can create one or more Spaces.

   In practice, most home and small business users will want only one Space. But you can create more, if you like.

3. Establish a maximum size for each Space and choose a mirroring technology, if you want the data mirrored.

   The maximum size can be much bigger than the total amount of space available on all your hard drives. That's one of the advantages of virtualization: If you run out of physical hard drive space, instead of turning belly up and croaking, Windows just asks you to feed it another drive.

   For a discussion of the available mirroring technologies, see the sidebar "Mirroring technologies in Storage Spaces."

4. If a drive dies, you keep going and put in a new drive when you can. If you want to replace a drive with a bigger (or more reliable) one, you tell Windows to get rid of (or *dismount*) the old drive, wait an hour or so, turn off the PC, yank the drive, stick in a new one, and away you go.

   It's that simple.

**Book VII
Chapter 4**

**Storing in Storage
Spaces**

Mirroring technologies in Storage Spaces

When it comes to mirroring — Microsoft calls it *resiliency* — you have four choices:

✔ You can choose to *not mirror* at all. That way you lose the automatic real-time backup, but you still get the benefits of pooled storage.

✔ You can designate a space as a *two-way mirrored* space, thus telling Windows that it should automatically keep backup copies of everything in the space on at least two separate hard drives, and recover from dead hard drives automatically as well. It's important to realize that your programs don't even realize the data's being mirrored. Storage Spaces takes care of all the details behind the scenes.

✔ You can use *three-way mirroring*, which is only for the most fanatical people with acres of hard drive space to spare.

✔ There's another form of redundancy called *parity* that calculates check sums on your data and stores the sums in such a way that the data can be reconstructed from dead disks without having two full copies of the original file sitting around. This approach takes up less room than full mirroring, but there's higher overhead in processing input/output. MS recommends that you use parity mirroring only on big files that are accessed sequentially — videos, for example — or on files that you don't update very often.

If you've ever heard of RAID (Redundant Array of Inexpensive Discs) technology, you might think that Storage Spaces sounds familiar. The concepts are similar in some respects, but Storage Spaces doesn't use RAID at all. Instead of relying on specialized hardware and fancy controllers — both hallmarks of a RAID installation — all of Storage Spaces is built into Windows itself, and Storage Spaces can use any kind of hard drive — internal, external, IDE, SATA, USB, eSATA, you name it — in any size, mix or match. No need for any special hardware or software.

Setting Up Storage Spaces

Even though you can set up Storage Spaces with just two hard drives — your c: system drive, plus one data drive — you don't get much benefit out of it until you move up to three drives. So in this section, I assume that you have your c: drive, plus two more hard drives — internal, external, eternal, infernal, whatever — hooked up to your PC. I further assume that those two hard drives have absolutely nothing on them that you want to keep. Because they will get blasted. Guaranteed.

Ready to set up a Space? Here's how:

1. **Hook up your drives; then go into File Explorer and verify that Windows has identified three drives.**

   In Figure 4-1, I have three drives. The C: drive has my Windows system on it; C:'s the boot drive. The other two have miscellaneous junk that I don't want to keep.

Figure 4-1: Start with three drives, two for your storage pool.

Book VII
Chapter 4

Storing in Storage Spaces

2. **Bring up the Control Panel (right-click the lower-left corner of the screen and choose Control Panel); tap or click System and Security, and then tap or click Storage Spaces.**

   Equivalently, you can go to the Metro Start screen, type **storage spaces**, and look under Settings.

   If you choose either Storage Spaces or Manage Storage Spaces, you see the Storage Spaces dialog box, as shown in Figure 4-2.

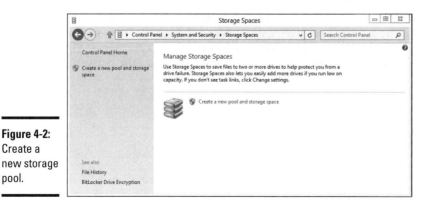

Figure 4-2: Create a new storage pool.

3. **Tap or click the Create a New Pool and Storage Space link.**

   You have to create a storage pool first — that is, assign physical hard drives to Windows available pool of hard drives. Windows offers to create a storage pool, as shown in Figure 4-3.

Figure 4-3: Windows allows you to pool any drives other than those that contain the boot and system partitions.

4. **Select the check boxes next to the drives that you want to include in the storage pool. Note that if you accidentally select a drive that contains useful data, your data's going to disappear. Irretrievably.**

   And I do mean *irretrievably*. You can't use Recuva or some other disk scanning tool to bring back your data. After the drive's absorbed into the storage pool borg, it's gone.

5. **Tap or click Create Pool.**

   Windows whizzes and wheezes and whirs for a while, and then comes up with the Create a Storage Space dialog box, as shown in Figure 4-4.

6. **Give your Storage Space a name and a drive letter.**

   You use the name and the letter in the same way that you now use a drive letter and drive name — even though the Storage Space spans two or more hard drives. You can format the Storage Space "drive," copy data to or from the "drive," and even partition the "drive," even though there's no real, physical drive involved.

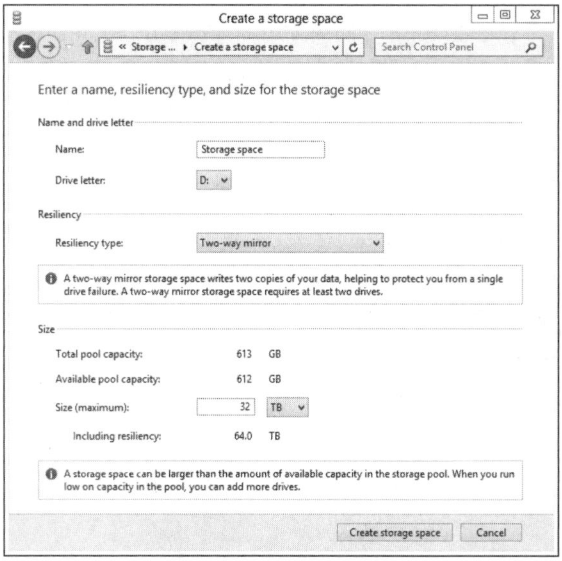

Figure 4-4:
Windows
wants you
to give
the new
Storage
Space
a name
and drive
letter, and
choose the
mirroring
and the
maximum
size.

7. **Choose a resiliency.**

   For a discussion of your four choices — no mirroring, two-way, three-way, and parity — see the nearby sidebar "Mirroring technologies in Storage Spaces" earlier in this chapter.

8. **Set a logical size for the Storage Space.**

   As mentioned, the logical size of the Storage Space can greatly exceed the available hard drive space. There's no downside to having a very large logical size, other than a bit of overhead in some internal tables. Shoot for the moon. In this case, I turned less than 1 terabyte of actual, physical storage into a 32TB virtual monstrosity.

9. **Tap or click Create Storage Space.**

   Once again, Windows whirs and sets up a freshly formatted Storage Space.

10. **Go back out to File Explorer and verify that you have a new "drive" which is, in fact, an enormously humongous Storage Space.**

    You see something like Figure 4-5.

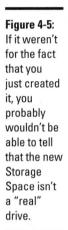

Figure 4-5:
If it weren't
for the fact
that you
just created
it, you
probably
wouldn't be
able to tell
that the new
Storage
Space isn't
a "real"
drive.

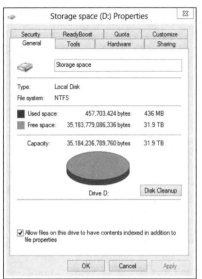

Working with Storage Spaces

Have a new Storage Space? Good. Go kick some tires.

First, realize that to the outside world, your Storage Spaces looks just like any other hard drive. You can use the drive letter the same way you'd use any drive letter. The folders inside work like any other folders; you can add them to libraries or share them on your network. You can back it up. If you have a cranky old program that requires a simple drive letter, the Storage Spaces won't do anything to spoil the illusion.

That said, Storage Space "drives" can't be defragmented or run through Checkdisk.

Here's the grand tour of the inner workings of your Storage Spaces:

1. **Bring up the Control Panel (right-click the lower-left corner of the desktop screen and choose Control Panel); tap or click System and Security, and then tap or click Storage Spaces.**

    Equivalently, you can go to the Metro Start screen, type **storage spaces**, and look under Settings.

    If you choose either Storage Spaces or Manage Storage Spaces, the Storage Spaces dialog box appears, this time with a Storage Space.

2. **At the bottom, tap or click the down arrow next to Physical Drives.**

   The full Storage Spaces status report appears, as shown in Figure 4-6.

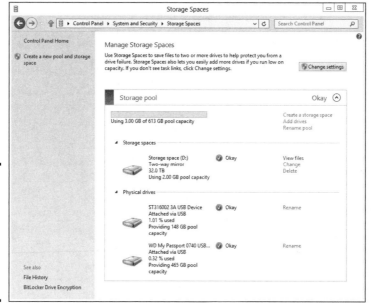

Figure 4-6:
Full details
of your
Storage
Space, and
the storage
pool it
sits on.

The Storage Spaces report tells you how much real, physical hard drive space you're using; what the Storage Space looks like to your Windows programs; and how your physical hard drives have been carved up to support all that glorious, unfettered space.

It's quite a testament to the Storage Space designers that all this works so well — and invisibly to the rest of Windows. This is the way storage should've been implemented years ago!

Chapter 5: Getting the Most from HomeGroups

In This Chapter

↳ **Setting up the prerequisites for HomeGroups**

↳ **Joining, sharing, and navigating a HomeGroup**

↳ **Making changes to your HomeGroup**

↳ **Sharing with XP and Vista and with a Mac**

*I*f you've ever used a house key, you know how to use HomeGroups. Okay, that's Microsoft's analogy, and the process isn't quite that easy, but it's close.

The *HomeGroup* bundles a bunch of settings in quite a handy — I'm tempted to use the word *brilliant* — way. When your PC joins a HomeGroup, Windows strips away a lot of the hassle and mind-numbing details generally associated with sharing folders and printers and replaces the mumbo jumbo with a cookie-cutter method of sharing that works quite well, in almost all home and many small-business networks.

All the computers in a HomeGroup share their Pictures, Music, and Videos libraries, and with an extra click, you can share your Documents library as well. The computers also share printers and some other peripherals. All it takes is a couple of taps. Or clicks.

Don't be put off by the term *HomeGroup*. If you have a business and need to share information, a HomeGroup may provide exactly what you want.

Preparing a PC for a HomeGroup

When you first establish a network connection, Windows asks whether you want to turn on sharing and connect to devices, per Figure 5-1.

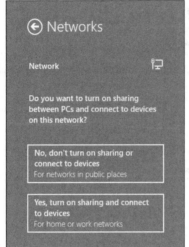

Figure 5-1:
Tell
Windows
if you're
connected
to a friendly
network,
or one
that might
include a lot
of bad PCs.

If you turn on sharing and connect to devices, your Windows 8 PC can participate in a HomeGroup. All you need is the password of an existing HomeGroup. Microsoft likens it to having a key to a house. At the risk of stretching a metaphor, if you have the key to the house (the HomeGroup password), you can get into anything in the house (printers, folders, and files inside those folders, in particular). If you don't have the password, or if there's no HomeGroup on your network, you can create a new HomeGroup and set a new password. Find out how in the upcoming section, "Setting up a new HomeGroup."

A few points to remember as you're getting a PC ready for the HomeGroup:

✦ **HomeGroups work only with Windows 7 and Windows 8 computers.** You can have a zillion computers on your home or office network, running Windows, OS X, Linux, iOS, and Android, laughing and printing and crashing together, but only the ones running Windows 8 with sharing turned on and Windows 7 PCs with a designated Home network type can participate in a HomeGroup. (See the sidebar "What happened to home, work, and public networks?")

✦ **HomeGroups can exist within a bigger network of HomeGroup-incompatible computers.** If you have computers that run something other than Windows 7 or 8, you have Windows 7 computers that are set up with work or public networks, or you have Windows 8 computers without sharing turned on, you can think of a HomeGroup as a clique inside your network. See "Venturing beyond HomeGroups" for details.

What happened to home, work, and public networks?

Windows 7 had three specific network "types" that you had to assign to every network connection. As soon as the connection was made, you were required to classify the connection as home, work, or public. Presumably, *home* networks are attached computers that could be trusted; they were allowed to join a HomeGroup. *Work* networks were also trusted, but not as much — they couldn't participate in HomeGroups. *Public* networks were completely locked down — Windows wouldn't broadcast its presence on the networks, and it blocked any unexpected incoming traffic.

When I wrote *Windows 7 All-In-One For Dummies,* I had a very hard time explaining in layman's terms what the big difference was between home and work types. There's a good reason why it was hard to explain: There *isn't* any difference at all between home and Work, with the exception that home networks can participate in HomeGroups, whereas work networks cannot.

The sins of 7 are visited upon everyone today. The current version of Windows supports HomeGroups for systems that have sharing and connect to devices enabled (see Figure 5-1). But if you want to put a Windows 7 PC in your HomeGroup and let it play with the big boys . . . er, the newer versions of Windows, you must first make sure that the Win7 PC identifies its network connection as a Home connection.

If your Windows 7 PC doesn't identify its network connection as a Home connection, it's easy to change:

1. **Choose Start➪Control Panel and under the Network and Internet heading, click the View Network Status and Tasks link.**

2. **In the View Your Active Networks box, click the link that mentions the network type you now have.**

3. **Click Home and then OK.**

   Your network is now a home network.

Connecting to a HomeGroup

Every time you attach a Windows 8 PC to a network and you tell Windows Yes, Turn On Sharing and Connect to Devices (refer to 5-1), Windows starts sniffing around the network to see whether any Windows 7 or 8 PCs are attached to the network and, if so, whether any of them belong to a HomeGroup.

When Windows is done sniffing around, here's what you may see and a tip or two about your next best step toward a HomeGroup connection:

✦ **You see a message that says the HomeGroup isn't available because you're not connected to your Home network.** Realize that Windows is just guessing. It doesn't *really* know whether you're connected to your Home network: There's no Orwellian camera looking to see where you're sitting. What it's really saying is, "You didn't turn on sharing and connecting to devices, so you can't participate in a HomeGroup." In order to right the wrong, tap or click the Change Network Location link. That brings up the friendly network notification, as shown in Figure 5-1. Select Yes, Turn On Sharing and Connect to Devices, and you should be on your way.

Several of you have written to me and complained that PCs newly attached to a network don't discover an existing HomeGroup. The most common reason? All the PCs in the HomeGroup are sleeping. To solve the problem, make sure at least one of the PCs that belongs to the HomeGroup wakes up. It only takes one.

✦ **Windows doesn't detect any kindred spirits on the network connected to a HomeGroup, and it offers to set up a HomeGroup for you, as shown in Figure 5-2.** If no existing HomeGroup is detected and you know a HomeGroup is on your network, make sure that at least one of the PCs in the HomeGroup is up, awake, and alive.

✦ **Windows detects a HomeGroup.** In this case, you see the notification shown in Figure 5-3. Jump to the section "Joining an existing HomeGroup."

Figure 5-2: Windows offers to set up a HomeGroup.

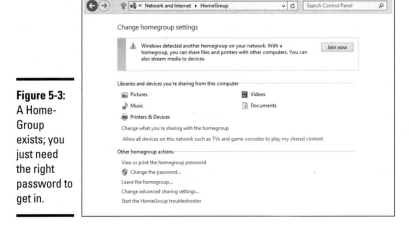

Figure 5-3: A Home-Group exists; you just need the right password to get in.

Setting up a new HomeGroup

So you have the first PC in your network that's going to have a HomeGroup. Here's how to set it up if Windows hasn't found a HomeGroup:

1. **Tap or click Create a HomeGroup in the dialog box (see Figure 5-2).**

   Windows tells you a little bit about HomeGroups and tells you that it's protected with a password.

2. **Tap or click Next.**

   The Create a HomeGroup dialog box appears, as shown in Figure 5-4.

3. **Select which libraries to offer to other PCs.**

   For most people, the big question about HomeGroups is whether you want to share your Documents library with other PCs attached to the HomeGroup. By default, Windows doesn't put your Documents library out for sharing. You can, if you want. I do.

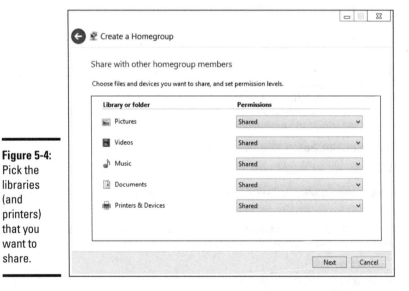

Figure 5-4:
Pick the libraries (and printers) that you want to share.

Book VII
Chapter 5

Getting the Most from HomeGroups

4. **Tap or click Next.**

   Windows sets up the HomeGroup and generates a random password. The password appears in the Use This Password dialog box. You can safely ignore it — no need to write down the password because you're going to change it.

5. **Tap or click Finish.**

   The Change HomeGroup Settings dialog box appears, as shown in Figure 5-5.

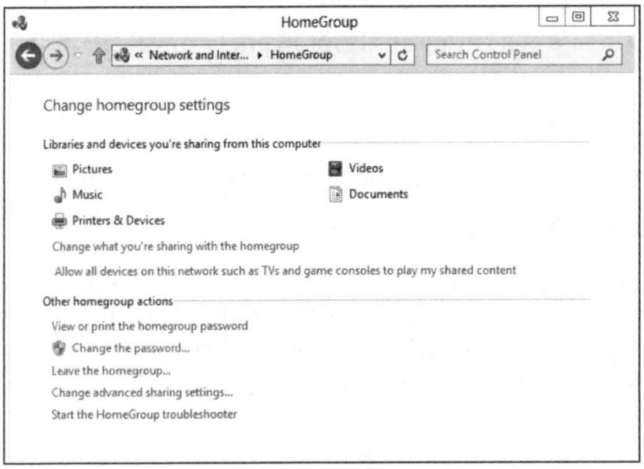

Figure 5-5:
Before
you go,
change the
password to
something
you'll
remember.

6. **Tap or click the Change the Password link.**

   Windows warns you that changing the HomeGroup password will disconnect everyone. Of course, there isn't an "everyone" — you just set up the HomeGroup. Now you're going to change the password from the monstrosity that Windows pulled out of thin air, and turn it into a password that you can remember.

7. **Tap or click Change the Password (again).**

   Windows offers you a box in which you can type your own password.

8. **Type a new password — one that you can remember — and tap or click Next.**

   No need to be Sherlock Holmes about it. Remember this password applies only to people who are *already connected* to your home (or office) network.

   Windows treats you to another shhhhh-super-secret password box like the one in Step 4. You know the password now. And you can always retrieve it. So fuhgeddaboutit.

More than one HomeGroup can exist on a single network, but things get complicated quickly. A particular computer can only be part of one HomeGroup at a time: You can leave one HomeGroup and join another one, but you can't do two at once. By the by, HomeGroups work great with Windows Home Server.

Joining an existing HomeGroup

If Windows found an existing HomeGroup, here's how to get in:

1. **At the bottom of the Share with Other Home Computers or the top of the Change Homegroup Settings dialog box, as shown in Figure 5-3, tap or click the Join Now button.**

   Windows tells you that you can join, but you need a password.

2. **Tap or click Next.**

   You see a Share with Other HomeGroup Members dialog box, similar to the one in Figure 5-4.

3. **Choose which libraries you want to share and whether you want to share printers; then tap or click Next.**

   I always share everything, including the Documents library. Isn't that what sharing's all about?

   Windows asks you for the HomeGroup's password. Note that HomeGroups don't have names — they only have passwords.

4. **Type the password for the HomeGroup, and tap or click Next.**

   Windows advises that you have joined the HomeGroup.

5. **Tap or click Finish, and then close the HomeGroup Settings dialog box, if you see one.**

If you have the password, joining the HomeGroup's very easy. If you don't have the password, go to one of the other PCs in the HomeGroup, bring up Control Panel, and tap or click Change HomeGroup Settings on the left under Network and Internet. Then tap or click or the View or Print the HomeGroup Password link. The instructions are the same for both Windows 7 and 8.

Sharing Files and Printers in a HomeGroup

HomeGroups are great, and there's more to them than meets the eye. When you dig a little deeper, here's what you find:

✦ **A HomeGroup connects computers and printers, but users have to give their permission to share libraries.** If you attach a Windows PC to a HomeGroup, all the people using that PC — all its user accounts — gain access to the data that's available to the HomeGroup. They also get access to any printers in the HomeGroup. But it doesn't work the other way. Each user, individually, has to give permission for their libraries to appear in the HomeGroup.

✦ **Although you can override the default choices (see Figure 5-4), when you join your PC to a HomeGroup, you make all Pictures, Music, and Videos libraries and printers on your PC available to other PCs in the HomeGroup.**

I said *libraries*, not folders. (I talk about libraries in Book VII, Chapter 3.) If you share the Pictures libraries on your PC with the HomeGroup, for example, all folders in your Pictures library are shared. If you add a folder from a Windows XP computer to your Pictures library and your PC is in a HomeGroup, that folder on the Windows XP computer becomes accessible to every user on every computer in the HomeGroup. That's a very powerful capability, almost as good as connecting an XP computer to the HomeGroup (even though XP computers can't participate in HomeGroups).

More than that, you can put folders from other HomeGroup computers' libraries into your libraries. So if a computer in your HomeGroup has a Pictures library that includes a folder from a Windows XP PC, you can simply copy that folder into your Pictures library and, it works like any other folder in your Pictures library. Combining HomeGroups and libraries leads to enormously powerful capabilities.

When you share a file, it's important to understand whether other people in your HomeGroup can open the file, modify its contents, or delete it. The default permissions level for HomeGroup-shared folders is a bit convoluted, but it makes sense. Unless you specifically modify the permissions (more about that in the "Caring for Your HomeGroup" section, later in this chapter), here's what you get:

✦ **Other users in your HomeGroup can open all files in your libraries (Pictures, Music, Videos, and optionally, Documents).**

✦ **Other users in your HomeGroup can't change files in your personal folders (your \Pictures, \Music, \Videos, and, optionally, \Documents folders).** But they can change or delete files in your computer's Public folders (\Public\Pictures, \Public\Music, \Public\Videos, and optionally, \Public\Documents). They can also add new files to the public folders. Book VI, Chapter 1 introduces you to personal versus public folders.

✦ **If you have other folders in your libraries, the folders inherit the restrictions that are set on the computer containing the folders.**

You can change the permissions level at any time — restrict access to folders or add new folders on your PC to the HomeGroup, for example. I show you how, in the section "Caring for Your HomeGroup," later in this chapter.

You can hook up to printers on HomeGroup computers just as easily as you set up a printer on your own computer. Printers on a HomeGroup-connected computer are shared automatically with all other Windows computers on the HomeGroup. You may be asked for permission to copy drivers from a different PC in your HomeGroup, but it's very easy.

Navigating to a HomeGroup Folder

Navigating to a folder or file in a shared library in a HomeGroup, is as easy as navigating to a folder or file on your computer. When your computer is attached to a HomeGroup, you see a direct link to the HomeGroup on the left side of the File Explorer window (see Figure 5-6). From that jumping-off point, you can easily look at all shared folders on all computers in your HomeGroup.

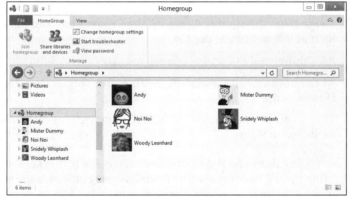

Figure 5-6:
Your
HomeGroup
appears
on the left
side of the
Explorer
window.

HomeGroups are also baked into every nook and cranny of Windows:

+ **Windows Media Player:** HomeGroup links appear in the Navigation pane on the left. Media streaming from HomeGroup computers works in a flash.

+ **Windows Media Center:** Look for a HomeGroup link in the shared section of the browser.

+ **Office applications:** If you fire up Word and choose File⇨Open, for example, the HomeGroups are right there.

After the hassles people have had sharing files and printers over the years, I bet you'll find HomeGroups like a breath of fresh air. Finally.

Caring for Your HomeGroup

So you have a HomeGroup, with one or more PCs connected to it. This section explains how to change your HomeGroup so it suits you to a *T*.

Using the tiled HomeGroup interface

Microsoft built a very serviceable interface for HomeGroups for the tiled side of the Windows 8 fence. You can use the full-screen HomeGroup Settings screen to join a HomeGroup, change which folders you're sharing, and leave the HomeGroup.

The tiled side's HomeGroup settings can be very handy if you don't want to use a mouse and keyboard. Here's how to get it working:

1. **Bring up the Start screen.**

   If you're looking at the desktop, press the Windows key.

2. **Swipe from the right to bring up the Charms bar and tap the Settings icon at the bottom of the list.**

   An abbreviated PC Settings panel appears on the right.

3. **At the bottom, tap Change PC Setting; then on the left, tap HomeGroup.**

   The full-screen version of the HomeGroup Settings dialog box appears, as shown in Figure 5-7.

As with many things on the tiled side of Windows 8, this screen hits almost everything you'll ever need with HomeGroups. You can bring up the desktop version of Windows to access all the options.

Operationally, there's only one big difference: When you join a HomeGroup using the desktop interface, by default, you elect to share your Music, Pictures, and Videos libraries and share your printers. The full-screen version doesn't share anything by default: You have to choose each item, one at a time.

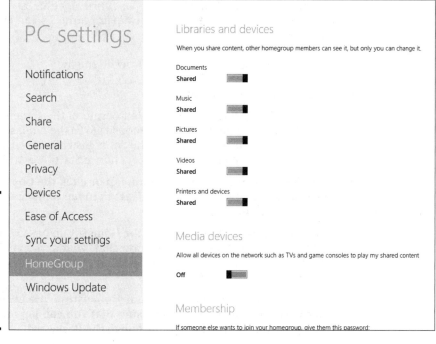

Figure 5-7: Most HomeGroup settings can be handled with the full-screen interface.

Changing the HomeGroup password

Want to know why Windows automatically generates that gargantuan password every time you start a new HomeGroup? Because early testers needed it. When the folks at Microsoft watched people trying to use HomeGroups for the first time, they discovered that many people would stop, worry, and fret about typing a password. In many cases, that's because the person setting up the HomeGroup uses only a small set of passwords, and they didn't want to hand out those passwords to everyone in the house or company. So the testers spent quite a bit of time trying to figure out whether they should create a completely new password and, if so, which one to use. Brain overload.

To make your life easier, Windows assigns a somewhat arbitrary password when you create a HomeGroup. If you're smart, you'll change it before you add any more PCs to the HomeGroup. That's precisely the procedure I describe in the "Setting up a new HomeGroup" section earlier in this chapter.

In fact, you can change a HomeGroup's password any time, and it's easy as long as all the computers in the HomeGroup are turned on and you can log on to them all.

To change the HomeGroup password, proceed thusly:

1. **Bring up the Control Panel.**

In Windows 8, right-click the lower-left corner of the screen and choose Control Panel. (If you don't have a mouse, go to the old-fashioned desktop, swipe from the right, choose the Settings charm, then at the top, choose Control Panel.) In Windows 7, choose Start⇨Control Panel.

2. **In the Network and Internet section, tap or click the Choose HomeGroup and Sharing Options link; then tap or click the Change the Password link.**

Windows warns you that changing the HomeGroup password will disconnect everyone. Well, yes, you know that. That's why you've made sure that all the PCs in your HomeGroup are awake, and that you can log on to them all. If not, well. . . .

3. **Make sure that all computers in your HomeGroup are awake (not hibernating or asleep), and make sure that you can log on to them all. When you're ready, tap or click Change the Password.**

Windows offers a new password for you to use, or you can type one of your own.

4. **Tap or click Next.**

Your HomeGroup password changes dutifully.

5. **One by one, go to each of the other computers in your HomeGroup and follow Steps 1 and 2 to Choose HomeGroup and Sharing Options.**

The warning shown in Figure 5-8 appears. Some scurvy brigand has changed the password on your HomeGroup! Avast and alack, and buckle my swash . . . .

6. **Tap or click the Type New Password button and do precisely that.**

You reconnect to the HomeGroup. By supplying the correct password — the new one — your PC hooks up with the new HomeGroup, and all your settings carry across.

If you have problems reconnecting to the HomeGroup, tap or click the link (refer to Figure 5-8) to leave the HomeGroup, and then tap or click the Join Now button. Continue with Step 2 in the instructions in the "Joining an existing HomeGroup" section, earlier in this chapter.

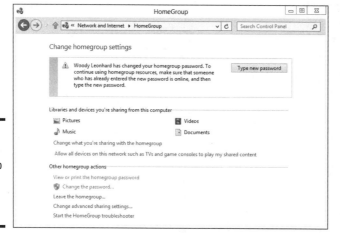

Figure 5-8:
Change the
HomeGroup
password
for each
computer.

To change the password using the full-screen interface (which I describe in the section "Using the tiled HomeGroup interface" earlier in this chapter), you have to go through two steps. To do so, at the bottom, tap or click the Leave button for the HomeGroup; then type the HomeGroup password, and tap or click Join.

Adding or blocking folders in the HomeGroup

If you want to make a folder available to everyone in your HomeGroup, the simplest approach is to add it to one of your shared libraries. See Book VII, Chapter 3 for details.

If you share your Documents library, for example, adding a folder to your personal Documents folder makes the folder available so that anybody attached to the HomeGroup can open and read the items in it. Adding the folder to your Public Documents folder allows everyone in the HomeGroup to read, modify, or delete the items in the folder.

Sometimes, though, you just want to make a folder available to the HomeGroup, and you don't want to go through the steps to add it to a shared library. For example, I like to share my Downloads folder so that other people in my HomeGroup can easily copy or run the files I download.

Here's how to add the Downloads folder to your HomeGroup, without adding the Downloads folder to any of your shared libraries:

1. **Navigate to the folder you want to put in the HomeGroup.**

In Figure 5-9, I started File Explorer and clicked the Downloads link on the left.

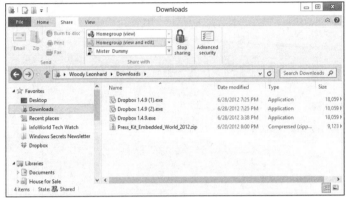

Figure 5-9:
Adding
a folder
to your
HomeGroup
is easy, if
you know
the trick.

2. **At the top, tap or click the Share tab.**

3. **On the Share Ribbon, choose HomeGroup (View) if you want to give everyone in your HomeGroup read access to the files, or choose HomeGroup (View and Edit) if you trust them not to delete or otherwise clobber the files.**

    It can take a few minutes, but eventually the shared folder becomes available across the HomeGroup, as shown in Figure 5-10.

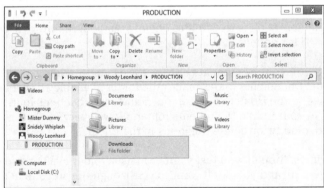

Figure 5-10:
The
Downloads
folder
becomes
available
on all
computers
that belong
to the
HomeGroup.

Venturing beyond HomeGroups

If you have computers on your network that don't work with HomeGroups, this section is for you. You find out how to set up fine-grained permissions for folders and documents, whether or not they're in a HomeGroup (a task not for the faint of heart). This chapter wraps up with a section about sharing across a mixed network that has computers in and out of a HomeGroup clique.

Password-protecting the Public folder

You have fairly complex ways to force people accessing the \Public folder from the network to provide a password before opening the folder. If you set a password, anybody on your computer can get at the \Public folder without hindrance, but someone coming from the outside has to provide the password. You can also establish read/write permissions for people accessing the \Public folder from the network. See *Networking All-In-One For Dummies* by Doug Lowe for details.

Sharing and granting permissions

Using the \Public folder to share files, as described in Book VI, Chapter 1, constitutes a quick 'n' dirty approach to sharing: Everybody using your computer gets full access to all the \Public files, and people coming from the network either get in or they don't. You have a little bit of fine control over who gets in and what they can do, but by and large, \Public is a blunt object.

The Windows ability to establish sharing permissions for individual files and folders on your PC gives you much finer control than the plain ol' Public folder method. You can assign fine-grained permissions for your HomeGroup or for individual users with Windows built-in permission levels.

The permission levels come in two flavors:

+ **View** allows the chosen individuals or groups to open or copy the file, but not change or delete them.

+ **Edit** lets the designated user or group do anything such as open, change, delete, or move the files.

This kind of fine-grained sharing is a minefield that you should not undertake unless you're willing to keep permissions updated. You should also be tolerant of many potential problems because I guarantee you'll bump into them. Rather than assign detailed sharing permissions to a folder, you might find it smarter (and much easier) to put the files you want to share in \Public and use the application that created the files to assign read-only or read/write passwords, controlling access to the data in those files. All Office applications, and many others, have heavy-duty password protection available.

If you're convinced that using file/folder sharing permissions is the way to go, here's how to set up fine-grained sharing for a file or folder that's not in the \Public folder:

1. **Navigate to the file or folder you want to share. Tap or click the Share tab to bring up the Share Ribbon.**

   In Figure 5-11, I went to the Software folder within the Downloads folder.

Choose the type of sharing here

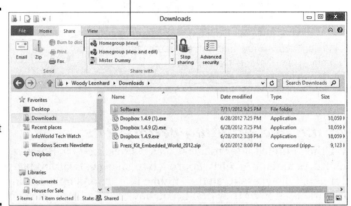

Figure 5-11: You can easily assign sharing restrictions for any file or folder, but it's a bear keeping them up to date.

2. **Choose one of these options:**

   • *HomeGroup (View)* so that anyone in the HomeGroup can open or copy the file.

   • *HomeGroup (View and Edit)* so that anyone in the HomeGroup can open, copy, change, or delete the file.

   • *One of the listed users,* who is then granted the View (not edit) permission.

3. **Click the Specific People link at the bottom of the list to bring up the File Sharing dialog box, as shown in Figure 5-12.**

   Anyone accessing your computer from the network who isn't in the HomeGroup has to know a username and password that works on your computer. That's the username that Windows uses to assign permissions in the File Sharing dialog box.

4. **To stop sharing the file or folder, select it (see Figure 5-11) and tap or click the Stop Sharing icon at the top.**

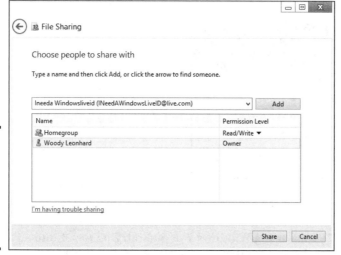

Figure 5-12:
You can
set sharing
permissions
for each
individual, if
you like.

Sharing on mixed HomeGroup, workgroup, and Apple networks

Sharing with the \Public folder is quick and dirty. As long as the person trying to get into your \Public folder is connected to your network and he can supply a valid username and password — one that will log on to your computer — he can get at the contents of \Public. (Find out about the Public folder in Book VI, Chapter 1.)

As I mention earlier in this chapter, HomeGroups work only with Windows 7 and Windows 8 computers. That's it. If you have a Vista or (shudder!) XP PC on your network, it can't join the HomeGroup, so it has to access the shared data directly. Toss a Mac into the mix and, *oy vez!*

Sharing with XP and Vista computers

Windows XP and Vista support *workgroups,* which aren't nearly as fancy as HomeGroups. Workgroups and HomeGroups co-exist peacefully, but you have to jump through some extra hoops to cross from one to another. Here's how:

✦ **If you try to connect a Windows XP or Vista PC to a Windows 7 or 8 PC,** you get a challenge like the one in Figure 5-13. The person using the Windows XP PC has to provide a valid username and password for the machine that she's trying to get into.

**Book VII
Chapter 5**

Getting the Most
from HomeGroups

Figure 5-13:
Windows XP
PCs can't
get into your
HomeGroup-
protected
PC, unless
they can
provide a
username
and
password.

+ **If you're using Windows 7 or 8 and trying to get into a PC that isn't in your HomeGroup,** you see a challenge like the one in Figure 5-14. Again, the person using the PC has to provide a username and password that's valid on the PC that he's trying to access.

Figure 5-14:
Windows 7
and 8 PCs
also get
challenged
if they
aren't part
of the same
HomeGroup.

Sharing with a Mac

Surprisingly, connecting a Mac to a Windows 7 or 8 PC is quite similar. The Mac can't join your HomeGroup, no way no how, but it can get into the \Public folder of a specific PC. Here's how:

1. **In the Mac OS X Finder, choose Go⇨Connect to Server.**

The Mac responds with the dialog box shown in Figure 5-15.

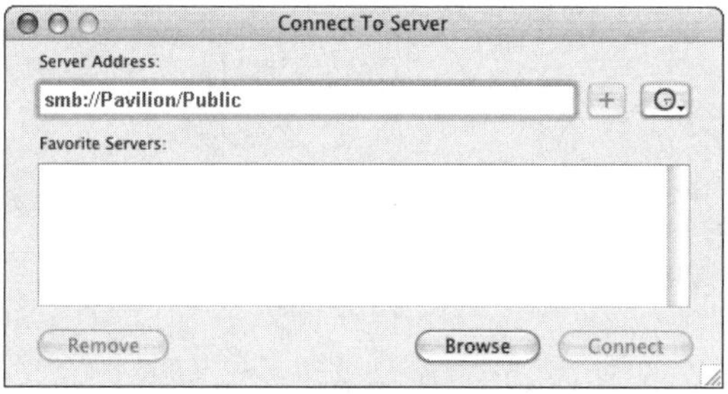

Figure 5-15:
Connecting
from a
Mac to a
Windows
PC is fairly
straight-
forward.

```
● ○ ○                Connect To Server
Server Address:
┌─────────────────────────────────────┐ ┌─┐ ┌──┐
│ smb://Pavilion/Public                │ │+│ │ ⊙ │
└─────────────────────────────────────┘ └─┘ └──┘
Favorite Servers:
┌───────────────────────────────────────────┐
│                                             │
│                                             │
│                                             │
│                                             │
└───────────────────────────────────────────┘
( Remove )            ( Browse )  ( Connect )
```

2. **In the Server Address box, type** smb:// **followed by the name of the PC you're trying to connect to, then** /Public. **Click Connect.**

    In Figure 5-15, I connected from OS X Lion to a Windows 8 PC called Pavilion.

3. **When you see the challenge, enter a username and password that's valid on the computer you're trying to get into. If you're asked for a workgroup name, type** workgroup.

    You end up in the \Public folder.

You can also enable Windows-style file sharing on your Mac, so you can pull files from the Mac into your PC. At least, theoretically. See `http://mac-connect.com/win_mac_samba.php` for details.

Chapter 6: Running the Built-In Desktop Applications

In This Chapter

✔ **Writing with Notepad and WordPad for free**

✔ **Mapping characters**

✔ **Calculating and painting**

✔ **Creating sticky notes**

The tiled "Windows 8" apps are coming, but it isn't yet clear if any of them can top what you already have, for free, on the desktop.

In this chapter, I introduce you to a handful of useful programs that you've already paid for. They aren't the greatest, but they're more than adequate in many situations — and when better, free alternatives exist, I tell you about them, too.

Even if they do come from a Microsoft competitor.

Keep your eyes open for new Windows Store tiled applications that can match some of the functions in these free built-in Windows programs. As time goes by, the tiled apps will get better — although it's going to be a little difficult to beat the price on these guys.

Getting Free Word Processing

If you commonly work with complicated documents, I hate to tell you, but you don't have much choice besides dishing out the money to buy Microsoft Office. If you edit other people's Word documents, you need Word, too.

Sorry.

But if you don't need the absolutely best (and most temperamental and confusing) word processor — if fairly straightforward formatting is good enough — you have a host of choices, including:

✦ **Notepad:** For just plain text, use Notepad, or its beefed-up (free) brother, Notepad++. I talk about Notepad in this chapter and Notepad++ in Book X, Chapter 5.

✦ **WordPad:** If you need just a little bit of formatting, use WordPad. I talk about WordPad in this chapter.

✦ **LibreOffice:** If you need moderate-to-heavy duty editing and formatting, check out LibreOffice — formerly known as OpenOffice at `www.libre office.org/download`. Some Word documents don't survive the trip to LibreOffice Writer and back: LibreOffice can lop off massive amounts of formatting sometimes. But for basic documents (and spreadsheets, presentations, and a draw program), LibreOffice works great. And it's free. 100 percent free. All the time.

✦ **Google Docs:** If you're connected to the Internet all the time, look at Google Docs, `http://docs.google.com`. Google Docs delivers a word processor over the Internet, so you can use it where you can connect online and store your documents online, too. Google Docs won't replace Word for fancy documents or editing existing Word documents, but Google's Write app works well in any browser, on any platform. Yes, that includes the Mac and iPad. An offline option gives you rudimentary document viewing capabilities even when you aren't connected to the Internet. Docs includes a word processing, spreadsheet, and presentation program. I talk about getting started with Google Docs and its overarching brother Google Drive in Book X, Chapter 3.

That said, I admit that I use Word almost all the time. Word is a great program — and one that can serve you well, along with the other useful programs in the Office suite. Personally, I've been swearing at Office for almost a decade — my first four books were about it. But even I would admit that it's overkill for a lot of people, in a lot of situations. The newer, smaller writing apps — Pages on the iPad, for example — don't have the depth of Word (not by a long shot!), but they're phenomenally easy to use and much less intimidating.

Microsoft offers a free online version of Word as part of its Office Web Apps package. I hesitate to call it a "version of Word" because it doesn't really have even a small fraction of Word features, but it is free. Its one saving grace is that it doesn't seem to mangle existing Word documents as badly as Google Docs. Docs is notorious for opening an Office doc and turning it into a wobbling mass of undifferentiated jelly.

If you're interested in either Google Docs or Office Web Apps, consider investing in the paid version of Google Apps or Microsoft Office 365. Both offer a lot of additional features, and the price isn't bad at all — $5 or so per person, per month. You can find a detailed analysis of the first versions of both at `www.infoworld.com/d/cloud-computing/office-365-vs-google-apps-the-infoworld-review-447`.

Running Notepad

Reaching back into the primordial WinOoze, Notepad was conceived, designed, and developed by programmers, for programmers — and it shows. Although Notepad has been vastly improved over the years, many of the old limitations pertain. Still, if you want a fast, no-nonsense text editor (certainly nobody would have the temerity to call Notepad a word processor), Notepad's a decent choice.

Notepad understands only plain, simple, unformatted text — basically the stuff you see on your keyboard. It wouldn't understand formatting, such as bold, or an embedded picture if you shook it by the shoulders, and heaven help ya if you want it to come up with links to web pages.

On the other hand, Notepad's shortcomings are, in many ways, its saving graces. You can trust Notepad to show you exactly what's in a file — characters are characters, old chap, and there's none of this froufrou formatting stuff to mess up things. Notepad saves only plain, simple, unformatted text; if you need a plain, simple, unformatted text document, Notepad's your tool of choice. To top it off, Notepad is fast and reliable. Of all the Windows programs I ever met, Notepad is the only one I can think of that has never crashed on me.

The following tidbits of advice are all you'll likely ever need to successfully get in and around Notepad:

✦ **To start Notepad,** flip over to the Start screen, type **Notepad**, and choose Notepad. You can also double-click any text (`.txt`) file in File Explorer. You see something like the file shown in Figure 6-1.

✦ **Notepad can handle files up to about 48MB in size.** (That's not quite the size of the *Encyclopedia Britannica,* but it's close.) If you try to open a file that's larger, a dialog box suggests that you open the file with a different editor.

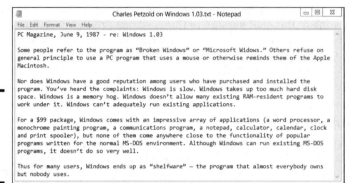

Figure 6-1:
Notepad
rocks in a
geriatric
sort of way.

✦ **You can change the font, sorta.** When you first start Notepad, it displays a file's contents in the 10-point Lucida Console font. That font was chosen by Notepad's designers because it's relatively easy to see on most computer monitors.

Just because the text you see in Notepad is in a specific font, don't assume for a moment that the characters in the file itself are formatted. They aren't. The font you see on the screen is just the one Notepad uses to show the data. The stuff inside the file is plain-Jane, unformatted, everyday text.

To change the font that's displayed onscreen, choose Format⇨Font and pick from the offered list. You don't need to select any text before you choose the font because the font you choose is applied to all text onscreen, and it doesn't affect the contents of the file. The default Notepad font is *monospaced* — all the characters are the same width. If you change the font, text files that are designed for a fixed-width world can look very odd.

✦ **You can wrap text, too.** Usually text extends way off the right side of the screen. That's intentional. Notepad, ever true to the file it's attached to, skips to a new line only when it encounters a line break — usually that means a *carriage return* (or when someone presses Enter), which typically occurs at the end of every paragraph.

Notepad allows you to wrap text onscreen, if you insist, so that you don't have to scroll all the way to the right to read every single paragraph. To have Notepad automatically break lines so that they appear onscreen, choose Format⇨Word Wrap.

✦ **Notepad has one little geeky timestamp trick** that you may find amusing — and possibly worthwhile. If you type **.LOG** as the first line in a file, Notepad sticks a time and date stamp at the end of the file each time it's opened.

Many, many alternatives to Notepad exist: Programmers need text editors, and many of them take up the mantle to build their own. Over the years, I've used a lot of them. Right now, I use Notepad++ — and, yes, I do type text quite a bit. Native HTML. But that's another story.

I walk you through Notepad++ in Book X, Chapter 5. It's free and works very well.

Writing with WordPad

If you really want and need formatting — and you're too cheap to buy Microsoft Word or too lazy to download LibreOffice, or you don't trust working online — Windows WordPad will do. If you've been locked out of Word by the nefarious Microsoft Office (De)Activation Wizard, you'll no doubt rely on WordPad to keep limping along until Microsoft can reactivate you.

If you find yourself reading these words because Office has slipped into Reduced Functionality mode (gawd, I love that phrase!), take heart, but be forewarned: If you aren't careful, you can clobber your Word files by saving them with WordPad.

WordPad plays nice (at least, reasonably so), with DOCX format documents — the kind that are generated automatically in Word version 2007 and later. But if you have to edit a Word DOC or DOCX file with WordPad, whether it's from Word 97, 2000, 2002, 2003, 2007, or 2010, follow these steps:

1. **Make a copy of the Word document and open the copy in WordPad.**

Do not edit original Word doc files with WordPad. You'll break them as soon as you save them. Do not open Word docs in WordPad, thinking that you'll use the Save As command and save with a different name. You'll forget.

2. **When you get Word back, open the original document, choose Tools➪Compare and Merge Documents (in Word 2007 and later, on the Review Ribbon, choose Compare➪Combine), pick the WordPad version of the document, and click the Merge button.**

The resulting merged document probably looks like a mess, but it's a start.

3. **Use the Revisions toolbar (which is available in Word 2003 and earlier) or the Review tab (in Word 2007 and later) to march through your original document and apply the changes you made with WordPad.**

This is the only reliable way to ensure that WordPad doesn't accidentally swallow any of your formatting.

**Book VII
Chapter 6**

**Running the
Built-In Desktop
Applications**

WordPad works much the same as any other word processor, only less so. Its feature set reflects its price: You can't expect much from a free word processor — at least not from Microsoft. That said, WordPad isn't encumbered with many of the confusing doodads that make Word so difficult for the first-time e-typist, and it may be a decent way to start figuring out how simple word processors work.

To get WordPad going, go to the Start screen, type **wordpad** and choose WordPad (see Figure 6-2).

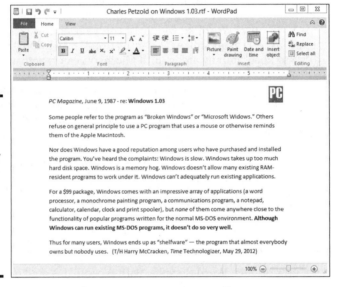

Figure 6-2: WordPad includes rudimentary formatting capabilities and the ability to embed images for free.

Some people like the Ribbon interface across the top of the WordPad window. I find it familiar (like Word 2007) but annoying (like, uh, Word 2007).

WordPad lets you save documents in any of the following formats:

✦ **Rich Text Format (RTF)** is an ancient, circa-1987 format developed by Microsoft and the legendary Charles Simonyi (yes, the space tourist) to make it easier to preserve some formatting when you change word processors. RTF documents can have some simple formatting, but nothing nearly as complex as Word 97, for example. Many word processing programs from many manufacturers can read and write RTF files, so RTF is a good choice if you need to create a file that can be moved to a lot of places.

✦ **OOXML Text Document (DOCX)** is the new Microsoft document standard file format, introduced in Word 2007. If you're going to use the document in Word, this is the format to choose.

Note that WordPad can read and write DOCX files. Unfortunately, WordPad takes some, uh, liberties with the finer formatting features in Word: If you open a Word-generated DOCX file in WordPad, don't expect to see all the formatting. If you subsequently save that DOCX file from WordPad, expect it to clobber much of the original Word formatting.

✦ **ODF Text Document (ODT),** the OpenDocument format, is the native format for LibreOffice and OpenOffice.

✦ **Text Document (TXT)** strips out all pictures and formatting and saves the document in a Notepad-style regular old text format. The two alternatives — MS-DOS format and Unicode — control the way WordPad handles non-Roman characters in the document.

If you're just starting out with word processing, keep these facts in mind:

✦ **To format text,** select the text you want to format; then choose the formatting you want from the Font part of the Home Ribbon. For example, to change the font, click the down arrow next to the font name (it's Calibri in Figure 6-2) and choose the font you like.

✦ **To format a paragraph,** simply click once inside the paragraph and choose the formatting from the Paragraph group in the Ribbon.

✦ **General page layout is controlled by settings in the Page Setup dialog box.** General page layout includes things like margins and whether the page is printed vertically or horizontally, for example. To open the dialog box, choose File⇨Page Setup.

✦ **Tabs are complicated.** Every paragraph starts with tab stops set every half inch. You set additional tab stops by clicking in the middle of the ruler. (You can also set them by clicking the tiny side arrow to the right of the word Paragraph and then clicking the Tabs button.) The tab stops that you set up work only in individual paragraphs: Select one paragraph and set a tab stop, and it works only in the selected paragraph; select three paragraphs and set the stop, and it works in all three.

**Book VII
Chapter 6**

Running the
Built-In Desktop
Applications

WordPad treats tabs like any other character: A tab can be copied, moved, and deleted, sometimes with unexpected results. Keep your eyes peeled when using tabs and tab stops. If something goes wrong, click the Undo icon (to the right of the diskette-like Save icon) or press Ctrl+Z immediately and try again.

WordPad has a few features worthy of the term *feature*: bullets and numbered lists; paragraph justification; line spacing; super and subscript; and indent. WordPad lacks many of the features that you may have come to expect from other word processors: You can't even insert a page break, much less a table. If you spend any time at all writing anything but the most straightforward documents, you'll outgrow WordPad quickly.

Might be time to start typing with your iPad.

Taming the Character Map

Windows includes the Character Map utility, which may prove a lifesaver if you need to find characters that go beyond the standard keyboard. Using the Character Map, you can ferret odd characters out of any font, copy them, and then paste them into whatever word processor you may be using (including WordPad).

Windows ships with many *fonts* — collections of characters — and several of those fonts include many interesting characters that you may want to use. To open the Character Map, on the Start screen, type **cha** and choose Character Map. You see the screen shown in Figure 6-3.

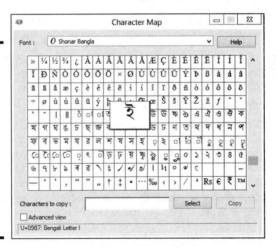

Figure 6-3:
Need a character from a different language? Use the desktop Character Map. Klingon, anyone?

You can use many characters as pictures — arrows, check marks, boxes, and so on — in the various Wingdings and Webding fonts. Copy them into your documents, and increase the font size as you like.

Calculating — Free

Windows includes a capable calculator. Actually, Windows contains four capable calculators, with several options in each one. Before you run out and spend 20 bucks on a scientific calculator, check out the two you already own!

To run the Calculator, go to the Start screen, type **calc** and choose Calculator. You probably see the standard Calculator, or one of its gussied-up forms, as shown in Figure 6-4.

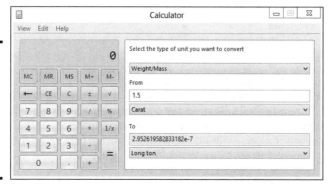

Figure 6-4: The standard Calculator, showing its Unit Conversion option.

To use the Calculator, just type whatever you like on your keyboard or tap the keys, and then press Enter when you want to carry out the calculation. For example, to calculate 123 times 456, you type or tap **123 * 456** and then press Enter.

The Calculator comes in four modes: Standard, Scientific (which adds *sin* and *tan*, and *x to the y*, and the like), Programmer (hex, octal, Mod, Xor), and Statistics (averages and summations). You can also choose three options, which appear as a separate slide-out Calculator to the right of the "real" Calculator. The Unit Conversion option appears in Figure 6-4. Date Calculation makes you choose dates from built-in calendars. The Templates option gives you a quick way to calculate gas mileage, lease payments, and simple mortgage amortization.

Personally, I use Google for all the options. You can type **32 C in F** in Google and get the answer back immediately. (Google can calculate *1.2 euro per liter in dollars per gallon*, in one step — way beyond Windows Calculator.) Do a Google search for *mileage, lease payment,* or *amortization* and you can find hundreds of sites with far more capable calculators.

A few Calculator tricks:

✦ Nope, an X on the keyboard doesn't translate into the times sign. I don't know why, but computer people have had a hang-up about this for decades. If you want to say "times," you have to tap the asterisk on the Calculator, or press the asterisk key (*) or Shift+8.

✦ You can use the number pad, if your keyboard has one, but to make it work, you have to get Num Lock going. Try typing a few numbers on your number pad. If the Calculator sits there and doesn't realize that you're trying to type into it, press the Num Lock key. The Calculator should take the hint.

Painting

The Windows Paint program has taken a lot of hard knocks for a lot of years, but it can actually do a few things that you might need. It's a just-barely-good-enough application for manipulating existing pictures, and it helps you convert among the various picture file formats (JPEG or GIF, for example). But it's certainly no competition for a real drawing tool like Adobe Photoshop or Illustrator, or even a free graphics editor like IrfanView (www. irfanview.com) or www.paint.net (see Book X, Chapter 5). And, if you want to correct red-eye or adjust for a bad exposure, Windows Live Photo Gallery or Picasa (or iPhoto on the iPad) have the tools that you need (see Book VI, Chapter 5).

That said, you can have a lot of fun with Windows Paint. To bring it to life, bring up the Start screen, type **paint**, and choose Paint. You see a screen like the one shown in Figure 6-5.

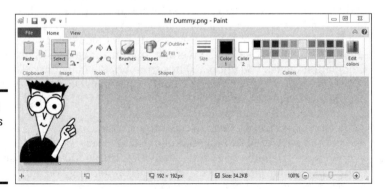

Figure 6-5: Paint offers a handful of useful features.

Opening, saving, and closing pictures in Paint is a snap; it works just like any other Windows program, once you figure out that you have to tap or click the File tab.

Scanning pictures into Paint goes like a breeze: Choose File⇨From Scanner or Camera. To draw one of the prebuilt shapes, just tap or click the shape, and then tap/click and drag on the drawing paper to adjust the size. Crop, resize, or rotate by choosing the corresponding icon in the Image group of the Ribbon. Easy.

Where you're bound to get in the most trouble is in free-form drawing, which can be mighty inscrutable until you understand the following points:

✦ You select a line color (used by all the painting tools as their primary color) by tapping or clicking the Color 1 icon, and then choosing the color in the Colors group on the Ribbon.

✦ You select a fill color (used to fill the inside of the solid shapes, such as the rectangle and oval) by tapping or clicking the Color 2 icon, and then choosing a color in the Colors group on the Ribbon.

✦ Many painting tools let you choose the thickness of the lines they use — in the case of the spray can, you can choose the heaviness of the spray — in the Size drop-down list on the Ribbon.

General rules for editing are a lot like what you see in the rest of Windows — select, copy, paste, delete, and so on. The only odd editing procedure I've found is for the Free-form Selection tool, which hides behind the Select icon on the Image group on the Ribbon. If you tap or click this tool and draw an area on the picture, Paint responds by selecting the smallest rectangle that encloses the entire line you drew. It's . . . different.

Sticking Sticky Notes

Do you really like little yellow sticky notes on your screen? Really? I guess the electronic ones are better than the meatspace version — at least they won't get your screen gummy.

Anyway, if you really want one, here's how to make a yellow sticky note to yourself:

1. **On the Start screen, type** stick **and choose Sticky Notes.**

2. **Start typing.**

Really. That's all there is to it.

Your new sticky note appears, as shown in Figure 6-6.

Figure 6-6:
Sticky notes
are cool, but
the margin
is too small
for the
proof.

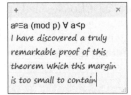

After you have a sticky note, you can create a new one by tapping or clicking the + sign in the upper-left corner.

You can change the color to something other than that eyestrain-inducing cadmium yellow by right-clicking the note (or tap and hold) and choosing a new color.

Sticky notes live on your desktop. You can drag and move them like any other denizen of the desktop. They're easy to resize. You can alternately show or hide all sticky notes on your desktop by tapping or clicking the Sticky Notes icon on the toolbar.

Hate the sticky note font? I don't blame you. If you open any program that'll format text — Word, or even WordPad, for example — type the text you want, format it the way you like it, then copy and paste the text into a sticky note, the formatting stays. That's how I created Fermat's Last Theorem in Figure 6-6.

And you thought sticky notes didn't have any hidden secrets . . .

Chapter 7: Working with Printers

In This Chapter

✔ **Attaching a new printer to your PC or network**

✔ **Solving print queue problems**

✔ **Troubleshooting other problems with printers**

✔ **Stopping a runaway printer**

A h, the paperless office. What a wonderful concept! No more file cabinets bulging with misfiled flotsam. No more hernias from hauling cartons of copy paper, dumping the sheets 500 at a time into a thankless plastic maw. No more trees dying in agony, relinquishing their last gasps to provide pulp as a substrate for heat-fused carbon toner. No more coffee-stained reports. No more paper cuts.

No more . . . oh, who the heck am I trying to kid? No way.

Industry prognosticators have been telling people for more than two decades that the paperless office is right around the corner. Yeah, sure. Maybe around *your* corner. Around *my* corner, I predict that PC printers will disappear about the same time as the last *Star Trek* sequel. We're talking geologic time here, folks.

The biggest problem? Finding a printer that doesn't cost two arms and three legs to, uh, print. Toner cartridges cost a fortune. Ink costs two fortunes. That bargain-basement printer you can get for $65 will probably print, oh, about ten pages before it starts begging for a refill. And four or five refills can easily cost as much as the printer.

Gillette may have originated the razor-and-blades business model, but it took the likes of HP, Brother, Canon, and Samsung to perfect it. Thank heavens Gillette hasn't figured out a way to put a microchip in the blades, to guarantee their obsolescence.

There has been one important — even exciting — development in the printer arena, over the past 6 years. Network connected printers — ones that attach to a network router, either through a wire or a WiFi connection, bypassing PCs entirely — are finally affordable. Relatively. In my experience anyway, network attached printers have fewer problems than the ones that are tethered to a specific machine.

Windows has excellent printer support. It's easy after you grasp a few basic skills.

Installing a Printer

You have three ways to make a printer available to your computer:

+ Attach it directly to the computer.

+ Connect your computer to a network and attach the printer to another computer on the same network.

+ If the printer can attach directly to a network, connect your computer to a network and attach the printer directly to the network's hub, either with a network cable or via a wireless connection.

Connecting a computer directly to a network hub isn't difficult, if you have the right hardware. Each printer controller is different, though, so you have to follow the manufacturer's instructions.

Although choosing a new printer is beyond the scope of this book, you can find free tips — inkjet or laser, basic or multifunction? — at `www.dummies.com`.

Attaching a local printer

So you have a new printer and you want to use it. Attaching it *locally* — which is to say, plugging it directly into your PC — is the simplest way to install a printer, and it's the only option if you don't have a network.

All modern printers have a USB connector that plugs into your computer. In theory, you plug the connector into your PC's USB port and turn on the printer, and then Windows recognizes it and installs the appropriate drivers. You're done.

If you're watching the desktop while Windows is doing its thing, you see an icon flashing. If you're curious, click the flashing icon and you see something like Figure 7-1.

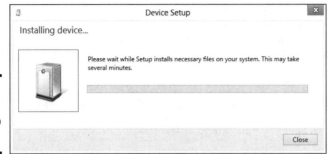

Figure 7-1:
Letting
Windows do
all the work.

I *don't* recommend that you install the manufacturer's software, no matter what the instructions in the box with the printer may say. Most printers come with a CD loaded with . . . junk.

When the printer is installed properly, you can see the printer in your Devices list. (See Book III, Chapter 4 for details on the Devices list.) To see your devices, swipe on the right or hover your mouse in the upper-right corner, and choose the Settings charm. Choose Change PC Settings; then on the left, choose Devices. You see a list similar to the one in Figure 7-2.

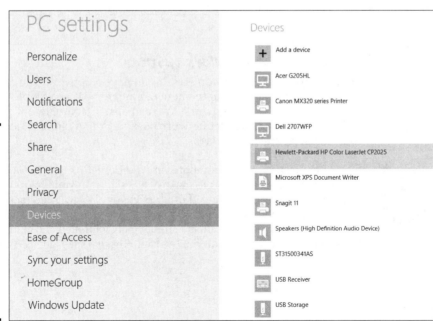

Figure 7-2:
After my
LaserJet
printer is
automat-
ically
recognized
and
installed, it
appears in
the Devices
list.

Once in a very blue moon, and sometimes with very new models of printers, Windows may have trouble locating a driver. If that happens, you can use the CD that came with your printer or, better, go to the manufacturer's website and download the latest driver. See Table 7-1 for a list of websites.

Table 7-1	Driver Sites for Major Printer Manufacturers
Manufacturer	*Find Drivers at This URL*
Brother	`http://brother-usa.com/downloads/default.aspx?ProductGroupID=1`
Canon	`http://usa.canon.com/cusa/consumer/standard_display/support`
Dell	`http://support.dell.com/filelib/criteria.aspx?c=us`
Epson	`http://epson.com/cgi-bin/Store/support/SupportIndex.jsp`
HP	`http://www8.hp.com/us/en/support-drivers.html`
Samsung	`http://www.samsung.com/us/support/downloads`

Connecting a network printer

Windows networks work wonders. If you have a network, you can attach a printer to any computer on the network and have it accessible to all users on all computers in the network. You can also attach different printers to different computers and let network users pick and choose the printer they want to use as the need arises.

If you attach a printer to a computer in your HomeGroup, Windows automatically recognizes it and offers to make it accessible on your computer. You can turn off the automatic sharing of printers in your HomeGroup (see Book VII, Chapter 5), but unless you changed something, every printer attached to every computer in your HomeGroup is automatically identified and added to the Devices list on every computer in the HomeGroup (see Figure 7-3). Very slick.

Figure 7-3:
This printer
was
automat-
ically
identified
on my
HomeGroup
and made
available
to all the
computers
in it.

If you have printers attached to your network but not in your HomeGroup —
for example, you may have a printer on a Windows Vista or Windows XP
machine, or on a Windows 7 or 8 machine, that isn't set up to share devices —
you can still add it to your collection of shared printers. Here's how:

1. **Swipe from the right or hover your mouse over the upper-right corner
   to bring up the Charms bar.**

2. **At the bottom, choose the Settings charm, choose Change PC Settings,
   and then on the left, choose Devices.**

   The Devices list appears (refer to Figure 7-2).

3. **At the top, tap or click the Add a Device button.**

   Windows looks all through your network — not just your HomeGroup —
   to see whether any printers are available. If any printers are available,
   you get a notification like the one in Figure 7-4.

Figure 7-4:
You have
to manually
hook up any
printer not
attached to
computers
in your
HomeGroup.

4. **Tap or click the printer to add it.**

   In Figure 7-4, scanning for a printer identified a laser printer that's attached to my network's router. Because it isn't attached to a PC, it isn't part of the HomeGroup; so I have to add it manually to at least one PC in the HomeGroup.

   Windows looks to see whether it has a driver handy for that particular printer. If there's no driver immediately available, it asks *Do You Trust This Printer?*

5. **Check to see whether a button says, "Golly, it's always been a good printer to me, but you never really know if it suddenly acquired subversive tendencies — right? — so how can I tell for sure?" If you don't find that button, tap or click Install Driver.**

   Windows whirs and clanks for a while and then tells you that you've successfully added the printer.

6. **Tap or click Next.**

   You're asked whether you want to make the new printer your *default* printer (the one that an application uses unless you explicitly tell it otherwise).

7. **If you want to make the printer your default, tap or click Yes.**

8. **Tap or click Finish.**

   Your new printer appears in the Devices list, as shown in Figure 7-5.

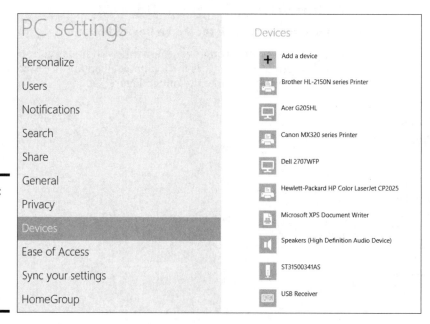

Figure 7-5:
Windows adds the network attached HL-2150N printer to the list.

Using the Print Queue

You may have noticed that when you print a document from an application, the application reports that it's done before the printer finishes printing. If the document is long enough, you can print several more documents from one or more applications while the printer works on the first one. This is possible because Windows saves printed documents in a *print queue* until it can print them.

If more than one printer is installed on your computer or network, each one has its own print queue. The queue is maintained on the *host PC* — that is, the PC to which the printer is attached.

If you have a network attached printer, the printer itself maintains a print queue.

Windows uses print queues automatically, so you don't even have to know that they exist. If you know the tricks, though, you can control them in several useful ways.

Displaying a print queue

You can display information about any documents that you currently have in a printer's queue by following these steps:

1. **Bring up the Control Panel by right-clicking in the lower-left corner of the screen and choosing Control Panel.**

    If you don't have a mouse, go to the old-fashioned desktop, swipe from the right, choose Settings. At the top, tap Control Panel.

2. **Under the Hardware and Sound category, choose View Devices and Printers. Double-click (or tap and hold) the printer you're interested in. Then tap or click See What's Printing.**

    The print queue appears, as shown in the lower right of Figure 7-6. If you have documents waiting for more than one printer, you get more than one print queue report.

    In many cases, Windows has to notify the printer that it's canceling the document, so you may have to wait awhile for a response.

    The Owner column tells you which user put the document in the print queue. The jobs in the print queue are listed from the oldest at the top to the newest at the bottom. The Status column shows which job is printing.

Figure 7-6:
All the
documents
you have
waiting to
print display
in the
queue.

3. **To cancel a document, tap and hold, or right-click the document you wish to cancel; choose Cancel.**

4. **Keep the print queue window open for later use, or minimize the print queue window and keep it in the taskbar.**

   That can be quite handy if you're running a particularly long or complex print job — Word mail merges are particularly notorious for requiring close supervision.

Pausing and resuming a print queue

When you *pause* a print queue, Windows stops printing documents from it. If a document is printing when you pause the queue, Windows tries to finish printing the document and then stops. When you *resume* a print queue, Windows starts printing documents from the queue again. Follow these guidelines to pause and resume a print queue:

✦ **To pause a print queue,** when you're looking at the print queue window (refer to the lower-right corner of Figure 7-6), choose Printer➪Pause Printing.

✦ **To resume the print queue,** choose the same command again. The check mark in front of the Pause Printing line disappears, and the printer resumes.

Why would you want to pause the print queue? Say you want to print a page for later reference, but you don't want to bother turning on your printer to print just one page. Pause the printer's queue, and then print the page. The next time you turn on the printer, resume the queue, and the page prints.

Sometimes, Windows has a hard time finishing the document — for example, you may be dealing with print buffer overruns (see the "Troubleshooting Printing" section, later in this chapter) — and every time you clear the printer, it may try to reprint the overrun pages. If that happens to you, pause the print queue and then turn off the printer. As soon as the printer comes back online, Windows is smart enough to pick up where it left off.

Also, depending on how your network is set up, you may or may not be able to pause and resume a print queue on a printer attached to another user's computer or a network attached printer.

Pausing, restarting, and resuming a document

If you've followed along so far, here are some other reasons you might want to pause a document. Consider the following:

✦ Say you're printing a web page that documents an online order you just placed, and the printer jams. You already finished entering the order, and you have no way to display the page again to reprint it. Pause the document, clear the printer, and restart the document.

✦ Here's another common situation where pausing comes in handy. You're printing a long document, and the phone rings. To make the printer be quiet while you talk, pause the document. When you're done talking, resume printing the document.

Here's how pausing, restarting, and resuming work:

✦ **Pause a document:** When you pause a document, Windows is prevented from printing that document. Windows skips the document and prints later documents in the queue. If you pause a document while Windows is printing it, Windows halts in the middle of the document and prints nothing on that printer until you take further action.

✦ **Restart a document:** When you restart a document, Windows is again allowed to print it. If the document is at the top of the queue, Windows prints it as soon as it finishes the document that it's now printing. If the document was being printed when it was paused, Windows stops printing it and starts again at the beginning.

✦ **Resume a document:** Resuming a document is meaningful only if you paused it while Windows was printing it. When you resume a document, Windows resumes printing it where it paused.

To pause a document, right-click the document in the print queue or tap and hold, and choose Pause. The window shows the document's status as Paused. To resume or restart the paused document, right-click or tap and hold that document, and choose Resume.

Canceling a document

When you *cancel* a document, Windows 7 removes it from the print queue without printing it. You may have heard computer jocks use the term *purged* or *zapped* or something totally unprintable.

Here's a common situation when document canceling comes in handy. You start printing a long document, and as soon as the first page comes out, you realize that you forgot to set the heading. Cancel the document and change the heading, and print the document again.

To cancel a document, select that document. In the print queue window, choose Document⇨Cancel. Or, tap and hold, or right-click the document in the print queue window and choose Cancel. You can also select the document and press Delete.

When a document is gone, it's gone. No Recycle Bin exists for the print queue.

Conversely, most printers have built-in memory that stores pages while they're being printed. Network attached printers can have sizable buffers. You may go to the print queue to look for a document, only to discover that it isn't there. If the document has already been shuffled off to the printer's internal memory, the only way to cancel it is to turn off the printer.

Troubleshooting Printing

The following list describes some typical problems with printers and the solutions to those sticky spots:

✦ **I'm trying to install a printer. I connected it to my computer, and Windows doesn't detect its presence.** Be sure that the printer is turned on and that the cable from the printer to your computer is properly connected at both ends. Check the printer's manual; you may have to follow a procedure (such as push a button) to make the printer ready for use.

✦ **I'm trying to install a printer that's connected to another computer on my network, and Windows doesn't detect its presence. I know that the printer is okay; it's already installed and working as a local printer on that system!** If the printer is attached to a Windows XP or Vista PC, the printer may not be shared. If it's attached to a Windows 7 PC, the PC may be set to treat the network as a public network — in which case, it doesn't share anything. To rectify the problem, right-click the printer and choose Sharing. (For details, see *Windows XP All-in-One Desk Reference For Dummies* or *Windows Vista All-in-One Desk Reference For Dummies* or *Windows 7 All-In-One For Dummies*, all by yours truly.)

If the printer is attached to a Windows 7 or Windows 8 PC and it's part of your HomeGroup, make sure that the HomeGroup is working. If it isn't part of your HomeGroup, read Book VII, Chapter 5 and get with the system!

✦ **I can't use a shared printer that I've used successfully in the past. Windows says that it isn't available when I try to use it, or Windows doesn't even show it as an installed printer any more.** This situation can happen if something interferes with your connection to the network or the connection to the printer's host computer. It can also happen if something interferes with the availability of the printer, for example, if the host computer's user has turned off sharing.

If you can't find a problem, or if you find and correct a problem (such as file and printer sharing being turned off) but you still can't use the printer, try restarting Windows on your own system. If that doesn't help, remove the printer from your system and then reinstall it.

To remove the printer from your system, swipe from the right and choose Settings on the Charms bar. At the bottom, choose PC Settings, and then on the left, choose Devices. Tap and hold or right-click the printer and choose Remove Device. Windows asks whether you're sure you want to remove this printer. Tap or click the Yes button.

To reinstall the printer on your system, use the same procedure you used to install it originally. (See the "Connecting a network printer" section, earlier in this chapter.)

✦ **I printed a document, but it never came out of the printer.** Check the printer's print queue on the host PC (the one directly attached to the printer). Is the document there? If not, investigate several possible reasons:

- *The printer isn't turned on.* Hey, don't laugh. I've done it. In some cases, Windows can't distinguish a printer that's connected but not turned on from a printer that's ready, and it sends documents to a printer that isn't operating.

- *You accidentally sent the document to some other printer.* Hey, don't laugh — you've heard that one.

- *Someone else unintentionally picked up your document and walked off with it.*

- *The printer is turned on but not ready to print, and the printer (as opposed to the host PC) is holding your whole document in its internal memory until it can start printing.* A printer can hold as much as several dozen pages of output internally, depending on the size of its internal memory and the complexity of the pages. Network attached printers frequently have 16MB or more of dedicated buffer memory, which is enough for a hundred or more pages of lightly formatted text.

If your document is in the print queue but isn't printing, check for these problems:

- *The printer may not be ready to print.* See whether it's plugged in, turned on, and properly connected to your computer or its host computer.

- *Your document may be paused.*

- *The print queue itself may be paused.*

- *The printer may be printing another document that's paused.*

- *The printer may be "thinking."* If it's a laser printer or another type of printer that composes an entire page in internal memory *before* it starts to print, it appears to do nothing while it processes photographs or other complex graphics. Processing may take as long as several minutes.

  Look at the printer and study its manual. The printer may have a blinking light or a status display that tells you it's doing something. As you become familiar with the printer, you develop a feel for how long various types of jobs should take.

- *The printer is offline, out of paper, jammed, or unready to print for some other reason.*

Catching a Runaway Printer

This topic has to be the most common, most frustrating problem in printer-dumb.

You print a document and, as it starts to come out the printer, you realize that you're printing a zillion pages you don't want. How do you stop the printer and then reset it so that it doesn't try to print the same bad stuff, all over again?

Here's what you do:

1. **Pull the paper out of the printer's paper feeder.**

   This step stops the immediate problem, uh, immediately.

2. **On the desktop, in the lower-right corner, look among the notification icons for one that looks like a printer; tap and hold it, or double-click it.**

   The print queue appears (refer to Figure 7-6).

3. **Right-click (or tap and hold) the runaway print job and choose Cancel.**

   If this step deletes the bad print job, good for you.

4. **If it doesn't delete the bad print job, wait a minute and then turn off the printer and unplug it from the wall. (Really.) Reboot Windows. When Windows comes back, wait another minute, plug the printer back in and turn the printer back on.**

   Your bad job is banished forever.

Book VIII

Maintaining Windows 8

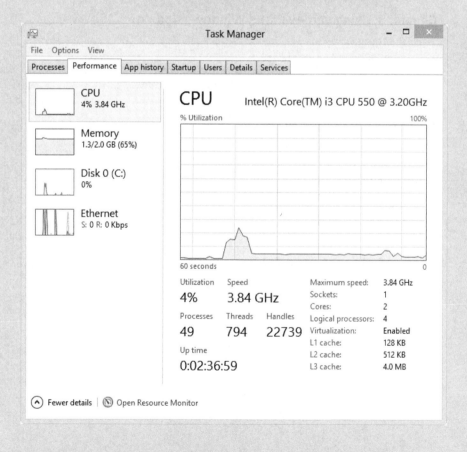

Contents at a Glance

Chapter 1: File History, Backup, Data Restore, and Sync

In This Chapter

✓ **Discovering what happened to the Windows 7 backup**

✓ **Backing and restoring your data**

✓ **Storing via the cloud**

*I*f you're accustomed to using earlier versions of Windows to back up or restore data, to "ghost" a whole drive, or to set restore points, you're probably in this chapter looking for something that no longer exists.

Although you can set manual restore points — much the same process as it was in Windows ME, many moons ago — the way to do so is buried deep inside the new Windows, and frankly, your need for them is highly debatable.

Microsoft has, in one stroke, made backup and restore much simpler and much less controllable. Or perhaps I should say *micro-manageable*.

In this chapter, I talk about how to back up your data: running backups, restoring them, being smart about where to store them, and accessing them if something goes wrong. (In Chapter 2 of this minibook, I talk about Refresh and Reset, two ways of bringing Windows back to life. Refresh keeps all your data. Reset wipes out everything and returns your PC to its out-of-the-box state.)

In this chapter and Chapter 2 of this minibook, I don't talk about a whole lot of old Windows topics that just don't apply any more. These include system repair discs, restore points, image backups, recovery mode, and safe mode. You can find vestiges of those features in Windows 8 if you look hard enough. But they aren't recommended any more — and they're rarely supported.

What Happened to the Windows 7 Backup?

If you're an experienced Windows 7 user, you may be looking for specific features that have been renamed, morphed, or axed in the current version of Windows. Here's a little pocket dictionary to help you figure out the landmarks:

✦ **Shadow Copies (or Previous Versions) of files are now called File History.** It's functionally very similar to the Apple Time Machine — just not as cool, visually.

✦ **Image Backup (or System Image or Ghosting) is still available, but well hidden.** In the not-so-good old days, you could make a very precise copy of your C: drive if you felt so consumed. Nowadays, you need to know the trick — or just use a third-party utility, such as Acronis True Image.

If you're absolutely convinced that you really, really want to create a system image with Windows, you can do it. On the Start screen, type **file recovery**, choose Settings, and look for Windows 7 File Recovery. Happy hunting.

✦ **Windows Backup and the Backup and Restore Center are also available using the same Windows 7 File Recovery option.** But it's much smarter to use File History.

✦ **You can boot into safe mode if you really want to, but Microsoft makes it very difficult to get there.** Follow the instructions in Book VIII, Chapter 2 to get into the Windows Recovery Environment.

Replicating Windows Home Server backup

Many people use Windows Home Server. I love it. Even wrote a book about it, *Windows Home Server For Dummies.* But Microsoft's giving up on WHS, and it isn't coming back.

With the new version of Windows, though, I'm not going to miss WHS. The absolutely best feature in WHS was its ability to back up data on connected PCs and keep redundant copies of the data. That way, any drive on the server or on my PC could fail, and all it takes is a new drive and an hour or two, to restore all my data as if nothing had happened.

And you can do all that and more by combining Storage Spaces (see Book VII, Chapter 4) with File History (see the nearby section "Backing Up and Restoring Files with File History").

WHS has one more significant feature that isn't replicable in Windows 8: It not only backs up your data, it backs up the entire contents of all your drives. When I was using WHS, if my C: drive decided to crack into a million pieces, restoring it was quite simple. Without WHS, but using Windows 8 and File History, I can restore everything except my desktop applications.

Microsoft is *deprecating* (killing, zapping) all the old backup, restore, system restore, and safe mode options — slowly getting rid of them, but leaving vestiges around — in favor of completely new (and much easier-to-use) backup and restore options.

Backing Up and Restoring Files with File History

Windows File History not only backs up your data files, it also backs up many versions of your data files, and makes it very easy to retrieve the latest version and multiple earlier versions.

By default, File History takes snapshots of all the files in your libraries (see Book VII, Chapter 3), your desktop, your Contacts data, and your Internet Explorer favorites. The snapshots get taken once an hour and are kept until your backup drive runs out of space.

You can change those defaults. I explain how later in this section.

Setting up File History

To use File History, Windows demands that you have an external hard drive, a second hard drive, or a network connection that leads to a hard drive. In this example, I use a simple, cheap 500GB external hard drive. You can pick up one at any computer store.

If you have a lot of photos in your Photos library, or a zillion songs in the Music library, the first File History backup takes hours and hours (and longer!). If you have a lot of data and this is your first time, don't even try to set up things until you're ready to leave the machine for a long, long time.

To get File History going:

1. **On the Start screen, type** file history; **on the right choose Settings, and then on the left, choose File History.**

If you don't remember how to get to the tiled Start screen, press the Windows key on your keyboard or the Windows button on your tablet.

The File History applet appears in the desktop Control Panel, as shown in Figure 1-1.

If you don't have a drive set up for File History, you see the banner that starts, We recommend that you use an external drive for File History...

Figure 1-1:
Set up File
History
here.

2. **Attach your external drive, or tap or click the User Network Location link and navigate to a networked drive.**

   If you're using a clean hard drive, the banner disappears. If data's on your drive, or your drive installs a driver of some sort, you may need to tap or click Use Network Location, and point to the drive.

   After your drive is connected, File History presents you with the dialog box shown in Figure 1-2.

Figure 1-2:
With an
external
drive
connected,
time to
turn on File
History.

3. **Tap or click the Turn On button.**

   If you have a HomeGroup, File History asks whether you want to recommend the drive to other members of your HomeGroup.

4. **If you have a HomeGroup and want to recommend the drive to other members, so they can also use it for File History, tap or click Yes; if you don't want to recommend the drive, tap or click No.**

File History goes out to lunch for a long time. Possibly a very long time. It gathers everything in your libraries (see Book VII, Chapter 3), everything on your desktop, all your Contacts, and your Internet Explorer favorites.

You can go back to work, or grab a latte or three. Go home. Take a nap. If you have a lot of pictures in your library, you might want to consider re-reading *War and Peace*. When File History is good and ready, a Run Now link appears in the File History dialog box, per Figure 1-3 appears.

Figure 1-3:
File History
is on the
job.

5. **Don't tap or click Run Now, just yet. Before you leave the topic entirely, make sure that the backup actually happened by following the next steps.**

Instead of relying on the File History program to tell you that the backup occurred, take matters into your own hands and look for the backup with File Explorer. To find the backup files with File Explorer:

1. **On the desktop, tap or click the File Explorer icon on the taskbar.**

   File Explorer opens and shows you your libraries.

2. **Navigate to the drive that you just used in the preceding steps for a backup.**

   This may be an external or a networked drive; it might even be a second drive on your PC, although I don't recommend that.

3. **Tap or double-click your way through the folder hierarchy:**

   - *FileHistory*
   - *Your username*
   - *Your PC name*

- *Data*
- *The main drive you backed up* (probably C:)
- *Users*
- *Your username* (again)
- *Desktop* (assuming you had any files on your desktop that you backed up)

A File Explorer screen like the one in Figure 1-4 appears.

Figure 1-4:
Your backup data appears waaaay down in a chain of files; they're stored on the hard drive.

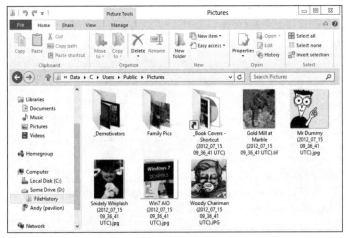

4. **Check whether the filenames match the files that are on your desktop, with dates and times attached.**

5a. **If the files match,** you can close File Explorer and close the File History dialog box.

Although you can restore data from this location via File Explorer, it's easier to use the File History retrieval tools. (See the next section for details.)

5b. *If you don't see a list of filenames that mimics the files on your desktop,* **go back to Step 1 of the preceding steps list and make sure you get it right!**

File History doesn't run if the backup drive gets disconnected, or the network connection to the backup drive drops — but Windows produces File History files anyway. As soon as the drive's reconnected, or the network starts behaving, File History dumps all its data to the correct location.

Restoring data from File History

File History stores snapshots of your files, taken every hour, unless you change the frequency. If you've been working on a spreadsheet for the past six hours and discovered that you blew it, you can retrieve a copy of the spreadsheet that's less than an hour old. If you've been working on your résumé over the past three months and decide that you really don't like the way your design changed five weeks ago, File History can help you there, too.

If you're accustomed to the Windows 7 way of bringing back Shadow Copies, you need to unlearn everything you think you know about bringing back old files. Windows 8 works differently.

Here's how to bring back your files from cold storage:

1. **On the Start screen, type** file history; **on the right choose Settings, and then on the left, choose Restore Your Files with File History.**

The File History Restore Home page, as shown in Figure 1-5, appears.

Figure 1-5:
You need to find the file you want to restore, starting at the top.

2. **Navigate to the location of the file you want to restore.**

In Figure 1-5, I went to my desktop, where the file I want to resuscitate is stored.

You can use several familiar File Explorer navigation methods inside the File History program, including the up arrow to move "up one level," the forward and back arrows, and the search box in the upper-right corner. See Figure 1-6.

Figure 1-6:
First, find
the location.
Then, find
the correct
version.

3. Check the time and date in the upper-left corner.

4a. *If that's the time and date of the file you want to bring back,* tap and hold or right-click the file, then choose Restore, or (usually easier, if you have a mouse) simply click and drag the file to whatever location you like.

   You can even preview the file by double-clicking it.

4b. *If this isn't the right time and date,* at the bottom, tap or click the left arrow to take you back to the previous snapshot.

   Tap or click left and right arrows to move to earlier and later versions of the files, respectively.

5. If you want to restore all the files you can see, at any given moment, tap or click the arrow-in-a-circle at the bottom of the screen.

   You're given options to replace the files (which deletes the latest version of each file) or to choose which files you want to replace.

Personally, I always restore by clicking and dragging. It's much easier to see exactly what's happening, and avoid mistakes before they happen.

If you accidentally replace a good file, be of good cheer. There was a snapshot of that file taken less than an hour ago. You just have to find it. Kinda cool how that works, eh?

Changing File History settings

File History has several settings you may find valuable.

File History backs up *every file in every library* on your computer. If you have a folder that you want to have backed up, just put it in a library. Any library. Invent a new library if you want. You don't have to *use* the library; just put the folder in a library. File History takes care of all the details.

I have an extensive discussion of libraries in Book VII, Chapter 3, but if you only want to stick an existing folder in a newly minted library, it's easy: Tap and hold or right-click the folder, choose Include in Library➪Create New Library, and give your new library a name. You're done.

Here's how to change some other key settings:

1. **On the Start screen, type** file history; **on the right, choose Settings, and then on the left, choose File History.**

   The File History main page appears (refer to Figure 1-3).

2. **If you want to exclude some folders in your libraries so they don't get backed up, on the left, choose Exclude Folders.**

   File History opens a simple dialog box with an Add button that lets you put folders on the exclude list.

3. **Tap or click the back arrow to get back to the File History applet.**

4. **To change how backups are made, on the left, tap or click the Advanced Settings link.**

   The Advanced Settings dialog box in Figure 1-7 appears.

   In this dialog box, you can change the frequency of backups; the size of the cache where File History stores your temporary backups when you aren't connected to your regular backup drive; and how long versions should be kept.

Figure 1-7:
Take control of your backups here.

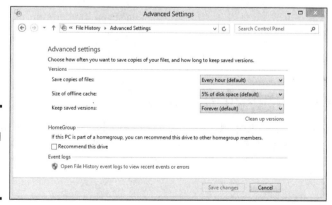

5. **See my recommendations for these settings in Table 1-1, and choose accordingly.**

6. **Tap or click Save Changes.**

   Your next File History backup follows the new rules.

Table 1-1	File History Advanced Settings	
Setting	*Recommendation*	*Why*
Save Copies of Files	Every 30 Minutes	This is mostly a tradeoff between space (more frequent backups take a tiny bit of extra space) and time — your time. If you have a lot of backups, you increase the likelihood of getting back a usable version of a file, but on the other hand, you have to wade through many more versions. I find 30 minutes strikes the right balance, but you may want to back up more frequently.
Size of Offline Cache	10% of Disk Space	Controls how much space File History will take up on your main hard drive if your backup drive is offline (or the network connection to your backup drive goes dead). I figure 10 percent is an easy price to pay for extra insurance, and I'm tempted to run it up to 20 percent.
Keep Saved Versions	Forever (default)	If you choose Until Space Is Needed, File History won't raise a holy stink if you run out of room on your backup drive. By leaving it at Forever, File History sends notifications when the hard drive gets close to full capacity, so you can run out and buy another backup drive.
If This PC Is Part of HomeGroup	Checked	Other people who use your PC, and other people in your HomeGroup, probably need backups, too.

Storing To and Through the Cloud

File History's a great product. I use it religiously. But it isn't the be-all and end-all of backup storage. What happens if my office burns down?

The best solution I've found is to have File History do its thing, but I also back up data, from time to time, to the Internet. Doing so is fast, cheap, and easy — but it does have problems. I talk about the mechanics of using SkyDrive in Book IV, Chapter 4, and SkyDrive's certainly a good choice. But other choices are available, and I want you to know about them.

Backing up to the Internet has one additional, big plus: Depending on which package you use and how you use it, the data can be accessible to you, no matter where you need it — on the road, on your iPad, even on your phone. You can set up folders to share with friends or co-workers, and in some cases, have them help you work on a file while you're working on it, too.

Two years ago, only one big player — Dropbox — was in the online storage and sharing business. Now there's Dropbox, Microsoft SkyDrive, Google Drive, the Apple iCloud (which is a bit different), Amazon Cloud Drive, and Facebook's storage — all from huge companies — and SugarSync, Box (formerly Box.net), SpiderOak, and many smaller companies.

What happened? People have discovered just how handy cloud storage can be.

I'm not talking about the mega-file uploading companies. Megaupload (which as of this writing has been taken down, rightly or wrongly), RapidShare, Hotfile.com, SoundCloud, and many others specialize in offering parking places for large files, and making it easy to download single files. They're in a slightly different business.

The cloud storage I'm talking about is specifically designed to allow you to store data on the Internet, and retrieve it from just about anywhere, on just about any kind of device — including a phone or tablet. They also have varying degrees of interoperability and sharing so, for example, you can upload a file and have a dozen people look at it simultaneously. Some cloud storage services (notably Google Drive) have associated programs (such as Google Apps) that let two or more people edit the same file simultaneously.

Considering cloud storage privacy concerns

I don't know how many times I've heard people tell me that they just don't trust putting their data on some company's website. But although many people are rightfully concerned about privacy issues and the specter of Big Brother, the fact is that the demand for storage *in the cloud* is growing by leaps and bounds.

**Book VIII
Chapter 1**

**File History,
Backup, Data
Restore, and Sync**

The concerns I hear go something like this:

✦ **I have to have a working Internet connection in order to get data to or from the online storage.** Absolutely true, and there's no way around it. If you use cloud storage only for offsite backup, it's sufficient to be connected whenever you want to back up your data or restore it. Some of the cloud storage services have ways to cache data on your computer when, say, you're going to be on an airplane. But in general, yep, you have to be online.

✦ **The data can be taken or copied by law enforcement and local governments.** True. The big cloud storage companies get several court orders a day. The storage company's legal staff takes a look, and if it's a valid order, your data gets sent to the cops. Or the feds. Or the tax people.

Moral of the story: If you're going to store data that you don't want to appear in the next issue of a certain British tabloid, it would be smart to encrypt the file before you store it. Word and Excel 2007 and later use very effective encryption techniques. Couple that with a strong password, and your data isn't going anywhere soon. Unless, of course, you're required by the court to give up the password.

✦ **Programs at the cloud storage firm can scan my data.** True, once again. Cloud storage company programs can see your data. There's been a big push in the past few months to hold cloud storage companies responsible for storing copyrighted material: If you upload a pirate copy of *Men in Black 3*, the people who hold the copyright are going to get very upset.

Different cloud storage companies handle the task differently, but with the takedown of Megaupload in January 2012, everybody's concerned about incurring the wrath of the *MPAA* and *RIAA,* the companies that defend movie and music copyrights, respectively. The net result is that most cloud storage companies will be performing routine scans — either now or in the not-too-distant future — to see whether you're trying to upload something that's copyright-protected.

✦ **Employees at the cloud storage firm can look at my data.** True again. Certain cloud storage company employees *can* see your data. They have to be able to see your data, in order to comply with court orders.

Does that mean Billy the intern can look at your financial data, or your family photos? Well, no. It's more complicated than that. Every cloud storage company has very strict, logged and monitored rules for who can authorize, and who can view, customer data. Am I, personally, absolutely sure that every company obeys all its rules? No, not at all. But I don't think my information is interesting enough to draw much attention from Billy, unless he's trying to swipe the manuscript of my next book.

✦ **Somebody could break into the cloud storage site and steal my data.** Well, yes, that's true, but it probably isn't much of a concern. Each of the cloud storage services scrambles its data, and it'd be very, very difficult for anyone to break in, steal, and then decrypt the stolen data. Could it happen? Sure. Will I lose sleep over it? Nah.

Reaping the benefits of backup and storage in the cloud

So much for the negatives. Time to look at the positives. On the plus side, a good cloud storage setup gives you:

✦ **Offsite backups** that won't get destroyed if your house or business burns down.

✦ **Access to your data from anywhere,** using just about any imaginable kind of computer, including phones and tablets.

✦ **Controlled sharing** so you can password-protect specific files or folders. Hand the password to a friend, and he can look at the file or folder.

✦ **Broadcast sharing** from a Public folder that anyone can see.

✦ **Direct access from application programs that run in the cloud**. Google Apps is a good example.

✦ **Free packages, up to a certain size limit,** offered by almost all the cloud storage services.

Choosing an online backup and sharing service

So which cloud storage service is best? Tough question. Personally, I use four of them — three for PCs and Android, and iCloud for my Mac, iPad, and iPhone stuff — different services for different purposes.

Dropbox, Microsoft SkyDrive, and Google Drive have programs that you run on your PC or Mac to set up folders that are shared. Drag a file into the shared folder, and it appears on all the computers you have connected (with a password) to the shared folder. Go on the web and log on to the site, and your data's available there, too. Install an app on your iPhone, Android, or Blackberry phone or tablet, and the data's there as well. Here's a rundown of what each cloud storage service offers:

✦ **Dropbox,** as shown in Figure 1-8, offers 2GB of free storage, with 100GB for $99/year. It's very easy to use, reliable, and fast. I use it for synchronizing project files — including the files for this book. Dropbox also connects to Facebook to retrieve or post pictures. (www.dropbox.com)

✦ **SkyDrive** has 7GB of free storage, with 50GB for $25/year. I talk about SkyDrive in Book IV, Chapter 4. (`www.skydrive.com`)

✦ **Google Drive,** as shown Figure 1-9, has 5GB of free storage, with 100GB for $60/year. Google Drive isn't as slick as the other two, and there's no Facebook connection, but it works well enough. There's an optical character recognition facility, and the ability to launch web apps directly. Most of all, it's fall-down simple to use Google Drive with Google Apps, which includes Gmail, and several not-very-compatible writing and spreadsheet apps. See Book X, Chapter 3. (`http://drive.google.com`)

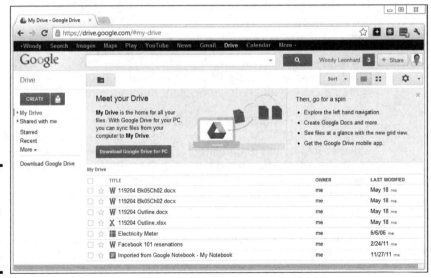

Figure 1-9:
Google
Drive works
very well
with Google
Apps.

✦ **Apple iCloud,** as shown in Figure 1-10, is really intended to be an Apple-centric service. The first 2GB is free, then $20 per year for an additional 10GB. It works great with iPads and iPhones and even my new Mac, with extraordinarily simple backup of photos. In fact, photo and video backup and sharing takes place automatically, and I don't have to do a thing. But it's not really set up for open data sharing. (`http://icloud.com`)

Figure 1-10: iCloud works with Apple products, but makes it difficult to share files among PCs.

The other services have specific strong points:

✦ **Amazon Cloud Drive** ties in with Amazon purchases and the Kindle, but not much else. (`www.amazon.com/clouddrive`)

✦ **SugarSync** lets you synchronize arbitrary folders on your PC. That's a big deal if you don't want to drag your sync folders into one location. (`www.sugarsync.com`)

✦ **Box** is designed for large companies. It gives companies tools to control employee sharing. (`www.box.com`)

✦ **SpiderOak** is the most secure of the bunch: It doesn't keep the keys to your files, and unlike the other services in this chapter, it's impossible for SpiderOak to see your files. (`www.spideroak.com`)

Like so many other things in the PC business, cloud storage is changing very, very rapidly. If you're interested in backing up to the cloud — and sharing files on the Internet, too, by the way — stay on top of the latest at my site, AskWoody.com (`www.askwoody.com`).

Book VIII
Chapter 1

File History, Backup, Data Restore, and Sync

Chapter 2: A Fresh Start: Restore and Reset

In This Chapter

✓ Refreshing, resetting, and restoring your PC

✓ Introducing the Windows Recovery Environment

*I*n this chapter, I look at how you can bring back to life a computer that's been possessed. (This chapter doesn't talk about bringing files back from the dead. That's the purview of Book VIII, Chapter 1.)

If you've worked with Windows for any length of time at all, you know that from time to time Windows PCs simply go out to lunch . . . and stay there. The problem could stem from a bad drive, or a scrambled Registry entry, or a driver that's suddenly taken on a mind of its own, a revolutionary new program that's throwing its own revolution, or that dicey tuna sandwich you had for lunch.

Windows is a computer program, not a Cracker Jack toy, and it will have problems. The trick lies in making sure that *you* don't have problems, too. This chapter walks you through the important tools you have at hand to make Windows do what you need to do, to solve problems as they (inevitably!) occur.

If you're the family's resident voodoo doctor — or the Windows go-to-gal in the office — this chapter can save your hide.

Microsoft has gone through a great deal of effort to make restoring a recalcitrant PC much simpler than ever before. The goal is to keep *you* out of the details and let Windows handle it: Computer, heal thyself, as it were. To a large degree, Microsoft has succeeded.

The Three R's — and a Fourth RE

When resuscitating a machine with Windows gone bad, consider the three R's — Reset, Refresh, and Restore. Two of them are readily available, but they make major changes to your machine. One's not nearly so destructive, but it's harder to understand and use.

Here are the three R's that every Windows medic needs to know, starting with the most destructive:

✦ **Reset** removes everything on your PC, and re-installs Windows. Your programs, data, and settings all get wiped out — they're irretrievably lost. This is the most drastic thing you can do with your computer, short of shooting it. (Did you see that viral video of the guy shooting his daughter's laptop? I digress.) If you like, you can tell Reset to do a *thorough* reformatting of the hard drive, in which case, random patterns of data are written to the hard drive, to make it almost impossible to retrieve anything you used to store on the disk.

✦ **Refresh** keeps some Windows settings (accounts, passwords, the desktop, Internet Explorer favorites, wireless network settings, drive letter assignments, and BitLocker settings), and all personal data (in the \User folder). It wipes out all programs and then restores the apps available in the Windows Store (primarily the tiled apps). This one's pretty drastic, too, but at least it keeps the data stored in the most common locations — Documents folder, the desktop, Downloads, and the like. And as an added bonus, the Refresh routine keeps a list of the apps it zapped and puts that list on your desktop, so you can look at it when your machine's back to its chirpy self.

If you've tried to bring back an older Windows machine from purgatory, in previous years, you may have encountered System Restore. In fact, System Restore still exists, but Microsoft really doesn't want you to use it. Refresh is a combination of System Restore, safe mode, Recovery Console, and all sorts of minor earlier system recovery techniques, wrapped into one neat one-click bundle — with none of the hassles, but none of the old controls.

✦ **Restore** is very hard to find — Microsoft doesn't want everyday users to find it — but it rolls Windows back to an earlier *restore point*, which I describe in the section "Restoring to an Earlier Point" later in this chapter. Restore doesn't touch your data or programs; it simply resets the Registry to an earlier point in time. If your problems stem from a bad driver or a problematic program change you made recently, Restore may do all you need. If you're familiar with earlier versions of Windows, the Windows 8 Restore is almost identical to Restore in the earlier version; you just access it a little differently.

Why does Microsoft make it hard to find Restore? As far as I know, the logic goes something like this: If you don't use Restore right, you can shoot your machine; in which case, you'll bother the folks at Microsoft mercilessly and accuse them of all sorts of mean things. Even if you *do* use Restore right, it fixes only a small percentage of all Windows-breaking problems, so if you try Restore and it doesn't work, you'll also bother the folks at Microsoft mercilessly — a classic lose-lose situation for the company. Importantly, there's nothing analogous to Restore with any competing operating system, tablet, or phone. The iPad doesn't have anything that resembles Restore; Android tablets and phones aren't in any shape to Restore; OS X wouldn't know a Restore from a hole in the ground; and my Linux friends start tittering obnoxiously anytime I say "Restore." In short, only Windows has a Registry, and Restore works almost exclusively on the Registry, so only Windows needs a Restore. There's not much competitive benefit to offering Restore to the average Windows consumer — and a lot of downside.

All three of these resuscitation methods play out in the *Windows Recovery Environment (WRE),* a special proto-Windows system. If you run Reset or Refresh, you won't even know that WRE is at work behind the scenes, but it's there.

When there's trouble and Windows can't boot normally, Windows instead boots into WRE, not into Windows itself. WRE has the special task of giving you advanced tools and options for fixing things that have gone bump in the night.

Reset, Refresh, and Restore — and several more (Recycle, Re-Use, Reduce?) are available in WRE.

I talk about WRE — and your advanced boot options — toward the end of this chapter.

A note about terminology

I *hate* the terminology Microsoft uses for its Windows-resuscitation technology.

If you and I get confused about Reset, Refresh, Restore, Recovery Environment, and Recombobulate (okay, I made up that last one), just imagine how confused normal, everyday users are going to get when they're confronted with choices that could, quite literally, obliterate all their data.

Further confusing the issue: Restore also applies to bringing back files. Reset applies to network settings. Refresh applies to screen scanning. Recovery is something you do with the aid of Jack Daniel's after Windows dies again.

It's very important that you watch carefully when you apply any of these "R"s. The implications of your actions are spelled out reasonably well on all the screens that Windows uses. But you can still very easily get confused.

And for heaven's sake, don't tell your mom to reset her PC when you meant to tell her to refresh it. You might not get invited over for dinner next Thanksgiving.

Refreshing Your PC

You don't really know or care about restore points, and you don't want to dig into Windows to make it work right. Mostly, you just want a one-tap (or click) solution that reams out the old, replaces it with known good stuff, and doesn't destroy your files in the process. That's what Microsoft has tried to offer with Refresh.

Have I got a Refresh for you. Here are the ground rules. Don't say I didn't warn you.

Running Refresh *keeps* all these:

+ **Many of your Windows settings:** These include accounts and passwords, backgrounds, wireless network connections and their settings, BitLocker settings and passwords, drive letter assignments, and your Windows installation key.

+ **Files in the \User folder:** That includes files in every user's Documents folder, the desktop, Downloads, and so on. Refresh also keeps folders manually added to the root of the C: drive, such as C:\MyData. Refresh keeps File History versions, and it keeps folders stored on drives and in partitions that don't contain Windows (typically, that means Refresh doesn't touch anything outside of the C: drive).

Files that *aren't* kept can be retrieved for several weeks from the C:\Windows.old folder. Yes, Microsoft keeps a secret stash of the files that it really wants to delete — and it's up to you to find them, if something disappears unexpectedly.

+ **Apps from the Windows Store:** Their settings are saved, too. So if you're up to the 927th level of Cut the Rope before you run a Refresh, afterward, you're still at the 927th level.

Running Refresh *destroys* all these:

+ **Many of your Windows settings:** Display settings, firewall customizations, and file type associations are wiped out. Windows has to zap most of your Windows settings because they could be causing problems.

+ **Files — including data files — not in the \User folder:** If you have files tucked away in some unusual location, don't expect them to survive the Refresh.

+ **Desktop apps — basically anything that you didn't install from the Windows Store:** Their settings disappear, too, including the keys you need to install them, passwords in such programs as Outlook — everything. You need to re-install them all.

The Refresh routine, helpfully, makes a list of the programs that it identifies on the kill list, and puts it on your desktop.

Here's how to run Refresh:

1. **Make very, very sure you understand what will come through, and what won't.**

   See the preceding bullet lists.

2. **From the Start screen, swipe from the right or hover your mouse in the upper-right corner.**

3. **Choose the Settings charm; at the bottom, tap or click Change PC Settings; and on the left, tap or click General.**

   Toward the bottom of the General list is the Refresh setting, as shown in Figure 2-1.

4. **Under the heading Refresh Your PC Without Affecting Your Files (which is only a slight exaggeration), tap or click Get Started.**

   The message in Figure 2-2 appears; take it to heart.

Click here to refresh

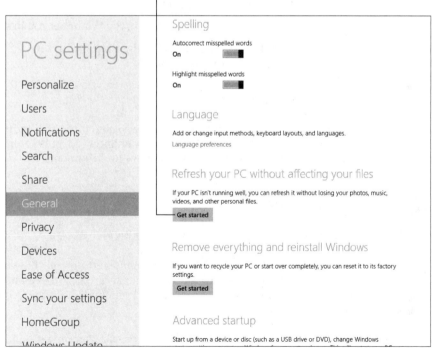

Figure 2-1:
Run Refresh
from the
tiled side of
the fence.

Book VIII
Chapter 2

A Fresh Start:
Restore and Reset

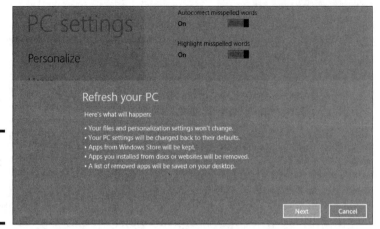

Figure 2-2:
What won't
make it
through
Refresh.

5. **Tap or click Next, and then tap or click Refresh**.

   The whole process takes about ten minutes on a reasonably well-seasoned PC, but it can take longer, particularly on a slow tablet.

   When Refresh is done, you end up on the Windows Log in screen.

6. **Tap or click the Desktop tile, and then tap or double-click the new Removed Apps file on the desktop.**

   Your default browser appears and shows you a list of all the programs it identified that didn't make it through the Refresh.

If Windows 8 can't boot normally, you're tossed into the Windows Recovery Environment. See the last section in this chapter for a description of how to start Refresh from the Windows Recovery Environment.

Resetting Your PC

Running Reset is very similar to running Refresh except . . .

Warning! Warning! Danger, Will Robinson! Resetting your PC wipes out everything and forces you to start all over from scratch. You even have to enter new account names and passwords, and re-install everything, including Windows Store apps.

If you're selling your PC, giving it away, or even sending it off to a recycling service, Reset is a good idea. If you're keeping your PC, only attempt Reset when you've run two or more refreshes, and they haven't solved the problem. Reset is very much like a clean install (which I discuss in Book I, Chapter 4). You're nuking everything on your PC.

With that as preamble, here's how to nuke, er, reset your PC:

1. **Make very, very sure you understand that your PC will turn out like a brand-new PC, fresh off the store shelves. Also make sure that you have your 25-character Windows installation key.**

   Absolutely nothing survives the wipeout.

2. **From the Start screen, swipe from the right or hover your mouse in the upper-right corner.**

3. **Choose the Settings charm; at the bottom, tap or click Change PC Settings; and on the left, tap or click General.**

   Near the bottom of the General list is the Reset setting, under the heading Remove Everything and Reinstall Windows, as shown in Figure 2-1.

4. **Under the heading Remove Everything and Reinstall Windows, tap or click Get Started.**

   The Reset routine shows a warning message, per Figure 2-3. Heed it well.

Figure 2-3:
Nothing
makes it
through
Reset.

5. **Tap or click Next.**

   Refresh asks whether you want to merely delete your old files, or whether you want to positively nuke them, as shown in Figure 2-4.

   - The *Just Remove My Files* option reformats the hard drive, but as you no doubt know, data can be recovered from a reformatted hard drive.

   - The *Fully Clean the Drive* option writes random data on every sector of the hard drive. Although, in theory, the NSA may be able to reconstruct what's on the hard drive, in practice, it'll be very difficult to retrieve anything.

   PCs with solid state drives will be handled correctly, in accordance with your instructions.

Figure 2-4:
How
thoroughly
do you want
to wipe out
your old
hard drive?

6. **Tap or click the Just Remove My Files option or the Fully Clean the Drive option, depending on your intended disposition of the PC; then tap or click Reset.**

The **Just Remove My Files** option takes about five minutes on a PC with a small hard drive. **The Fully Clean the Drive option** can take hours. Many hours.

Regardless of which option you choose, when Reset is done, you end up staring at a screen that asks for your product key. Now *that's* a complete, scorched-earth install.

Restoring to an Earlier Point

If you've used an earlier version of Windows, you may have stumbled upon the System Restore feature. Windows 8 has full support for System Restore and restore points; it just hides all the pieces from you.

Why? Because Microsoft spends a fortune every year answering phone calls and e-mail messages from people who bork System Restore. Instead of trying to handle all the picayune questions — and there are hundreds of thousands of them — Microsoft said, "That's enough!" and invented Refresh.

With a few exceptions, Refresh takes you all the way back in time to when you first set up your PC; it adds the Windows 8 tiled apps that ship with Windows, and it's careful not to step on your data. Aside from a few Windows settings, that's about it. Refresh is a sledgehammer, when sometimes the tap of a fingernail might be all that you need.

Smashing with a sledgehammer is easy. Tapping your fingernail requires a great deal more finesse. And that brings me to System Restore in Windows 8.

Windows takes snapshots of its settings, or *restore points,* before you make any major changes to your computer — install a new hardware driver, perhaps, or a new program. You can roll back your system settings to any of the restore points.

Windows automatically takes System Restore *restore points* once a day. It also automatically saves a restore point every time you successfully start Windows. A restore point contains Registry entries and copies of certain critical programs including, notably, drivers and key system files — a *snapshot* of crucial system settings and programs. When you roll back (or, simply *restore*) to a restore point, you replace the current settings and programs with the older versions.

When Windows can tell that you're going to try to do something complicated, such as install a new network card, it sets a restore point. Unfortunately, Windows can't always tell when you're going to do something drastic — perhaps you have a new CD player and the instructions tell you to turn off your PC and install the player before you run the setup program. So it doesn't hurt one little bit to run System Restore from time to time, and set a restore point, all by yourself.

Creating a restore point

Here's how to create a restore point:

1. **Wait until your PC is running smoothly.**

    No sense in having a restore point that propels you out of the frying pan and into the fire, eh?

2. **On the Start screen (yes, the Start screen, not the desktop), type** restore point **and on the right, tap or click Settings.**

    The first result in Windows Search is Create a Restore Point.

3. **Tap or click the Create a Restore Point tile.**

    Windows flips you over to the desktop, brings up the System Properties Control Panel dialog box, and opens it to the System Protection tab. (Cool, huh? Sometimes it's much easier to use the tiled side of Windows 8.) See Figure 2-5.

4. **At the bottom, next to Create a Restore Point Right Now, tap or click the Create button.**

    The Create a Restore Point dialog box appears (see Figure 2-6).

Figure 2-5:
The hard-to-find System Restore command point.

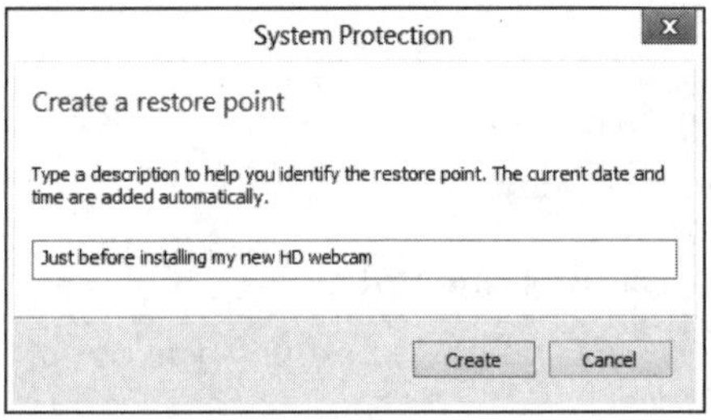

Figure 2-6:
Give your restore point a name.

5. **Type a good description, and then tap or click Create.**

   Windows advises that it's creating a restore point. When it's done, it shows a message that says, `The restore point was created successfully.`

6. **Tap or click Close on the message, and then tap or click the X button to close the System Properties dialog box.**

   Your new restore point is ready for action.

Rolling back to a restore point

If you don't mind getting your hands a little dirty, the next time you think about running Refresh, see whether you can roll your PC back to a previous restore point, manually, and get things working right. Here's how:

1. **Save your work and then close all running programs.**

System Restore doesn't muck with any data files, documents, pictures, or anything like that. It works only on system files, such as drivers, and the Registry. Your data is safe. But System Restore can mess up settings, so if you recently installed a new program, for example, you may have to install it again after System Restore is done.

2. **On the Start screen, type** restore point **and on the right, tap or click Settings.**

The first result in Windows Search is Create a Restore Point.

3. **Tap or click the Create a Restore Point tile.**

Windows flips you over to the desktop, brings up the System Properties Control Panel dialog box, and opens it to the System Protection tab (refer to Figure 2-5).

4. **Near the top, tap or click the System Restore button.**

The System Restore Wizard appears, as shown in Figure 2-7.

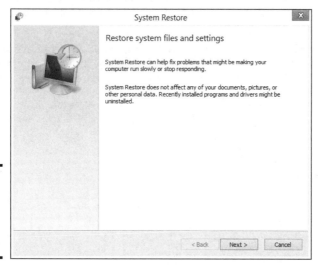

Figure 2-7: See, wizards are in Windows 8.

5. **Tap or click Next.**

A list of recent restore points appears, as shown in Figure 2-8.

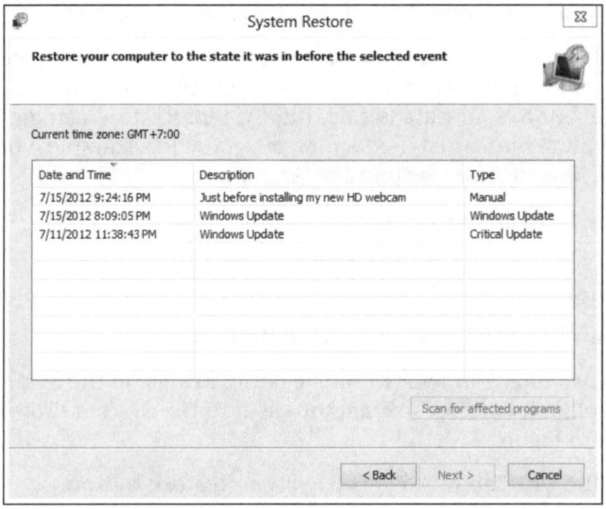

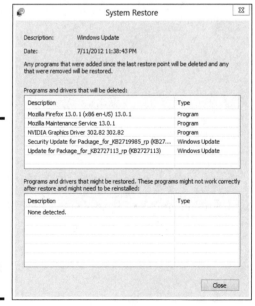

Figure 2-8:
The latest
restore
point isn't
always the
best restore
point.

6. **Before you roll your PC back to a restore point, tap or click to select the restore point you're considering and then tap or click the Scan for Affected Programs button.**

   System Restore tells you which programs and drivers have system entries (typically in the Registry) that will be altered and which programs will be deleted if you select that specific restore point. See Figure 2-9.

Figure 2-9:
Windows
can scan
the restore
point to
see what
programs
will be
affected by
rolling back
to it.

7. **If you don't see any major problems with the restore point — it doesn't wipe out something you need — tap or click Close, and then tap or click Next.**

    (If you do see a potential problem, go back and choose a different restore point, or consider using Refresh, as I describe earlier in this chapter.)

    System Restore asks you to confirm your restore point. You're also warned that rolling back to a restore point requires a restart of the computer, and that you should close all open programs before continuing.

8. **Follow the instructions to save any open files, close all programs, and then tap or click Finish.**

    True to its word, System Restore reverts to the selected restore point and restarts your computer.

System Restore is a nifty feature that works very well. The folks at Microsoft figure it's too complicated for the general computer- and tablet-buying consumer public. They may be right but, hey, all it takes is a little help and a touch of moxie, and you can save yourself a Refresh.

Entering the Windows Recovery Environment

In Windows 8, the Windows Recovery Environment has become a very sophisticated, almost eerily intelligent fix-everything program that works very well.

Except, of course, when it doesn't.

You know you're in the Windows Recovery Environment if you see a blue Choose an Option screen, or a blue Troubleshoot screen like the one in Figure 2-10. (If you find yourself facing a blue Choose an Options screen, choose Troubleshoot!)

From the Troubleshoot screen, you can run Refresh or Reset directly: They behave precisely as I describe earlier in this chapter. You can also choose Advanced Options, which brings you to several interesting — if little-used — options, as shown in Figure 2-11.

**Book VIII
Chapter 2**

**A Fresh Start:
Restore and Reset**

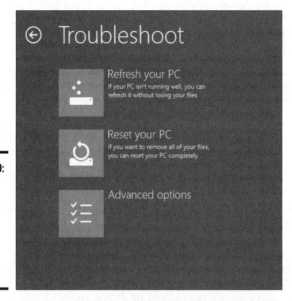

Figure 2-10:
The
hallmark
of the
Windows
Recovery
Environ-
ment.

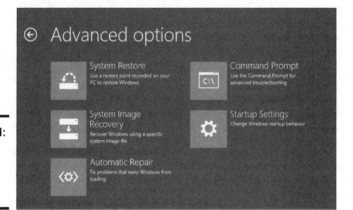

Figure 2-11:
The
advanced
boot
options.

You can also get to this screen by choosing Advanced Startup from the General list (refer to Figure 2-1). After you choose Advanced Startup, choose Troubleshoot, and then choose Advanced Options.

Here's what the Advanced Options can do:

✦ **System Restore** puts your system back to a chosen restore point, following the same steps in the section "Rolling back to a restore point" earlier in this chapter.

✦ **System Image Recovery** requires a system image that you can make only by using the DOS command line in a very geeky way. Details at `http://blogs.msdn.com/b/b8/archive/2012/01/04/refresh-and-reset-your-pc.aspx`.

✦ **Automatic Repair** reboots into a specific Windows Recovery Environment program known as Start Repair, and runs a diagnosis and repair routine that seeks to make your PC bootable again. I've seen this program run spontaneously when I'm having hardware problems. A Start Repair log file is generated at `\Windows\System32\Logfiles\Srt\SrtTrail.txt`. If you find yourself running Start Repair, you can't do anything: Just hold on and see whether it works.

✦ **Command Prompt** brings up an old-fashioned DOS command prompt, just like you get if you go into safe mode. Only for the geek at heart. You can hurt yourself in there.

✦ **Startup Settings** reboots Windows and lets you change video resolution, start debugging mode or boot logging, run in safe mode, disable driver signature checks, disable early launch anti-malware scans, and disable automatic restart on system failure. Definitely not for the faint of heart.

Chapter 3: Using and Avoiding Windows Update

In This Chapter

✔ **Finding out the trouble with patches**

✔ **Choosing your update level**

✔ **Patching selectively**

✔ **Looking at a security bulletin**

✔ **Removing Windows patches**

*W*indows Automatic Update is for *chumps*.

I've taken a lot of flak over the years for advising people to turn off automatic updating. If you're sophisticated enough to be reading this book, you're sophisticated enough to keep Windows from clobbering your system.

I think you should tell Windows to advise you when patches are available and then wait and see whether the patches do more harm than good before applying them to your PC.

Face it: You have to patch, sooner or later. Patching isn't like brushing your teeth, where you can ignore it for a year or two and things turn smelly and then gradually rot and fall out. If you don't patch today, by next month, your computer can look and act and feel like toast. The bad guys know what's been patched, and they prey on people who don't get their updates.

On the other hand, you don't need to follow Microsoft's dictates and apply patches the moment they're available. More than a few Dummies have seen their computers melt down because of a bad patch that has been force-fed to them by the Automatic Update mechanism.

Almost everyone — certainly, anyone reading this book — needs to check out the latest Microsoft missives before applying updates. Blindly updating Windows can lead to all sorts of problems.

Windows Update stinks. Massively. Permit me to elaborate: Both the security patches that Microsoft dribbles out to users and the method by which Microsoft delivers those patches to users stink. Massively. But you can still keep your system patched while working around the worst that these patches and Windows Update have to offer.

TIP

If you're setting up a Windows computer for someone else to use and she shows no interest at all in keeping her system safe, by all means, set her up with Automatic Updates. Sooner or later, everybody should patch. But if you're savvy enough to be reading this book, and concerned enough to check the Internet from time to time, you can save yourself a whole lotta headache by waiting for other people to shake out the problems with new patches. Let them get the arrows in their backs. Patch in haste; repent in leisure. Wait until Microsoft has had a chance to test its monthly patches on a hundred million PCs — and zapped a few hundred or tens of thousands along the way. It's easy. I explain it all in this chapter.

Patching Woes

Any large computer program has bugs. Heck, any *small* computer program has bugs. When a program grows as large as Windows — tens of millions of lines of code — the bugs start stacking up like planes at O'Hare in a snowstorm.

Patching non-Microsoft products

To keep your computer secure, you need to stay up to date on patches for all your programs. Microsoft takes the lion's share of the blame for messed-up PCs, but in fact, more PCs fall to unpatched Java, Flash, and Adobe Reader security holes.

The bad guys frequently target these other programs because they're ubiquitous: The folks at Adobe claim that there are more computers that have Flash Player, for example, than there are computers running Windows — and they're probably right. Oracle (the company that owns Java) says that Java runs on three billion computers.

The best way I've found to stay on top of non-Microsoft patches is by using the free-for-personal-use, fast, and quite talented program Secunia Personal Software Inspector (PSI) at `http://secunia.com/vulnerability_scanning/personal`. The security intelligence company Secunia makes PSI available for free to advertise its other services. Secunia PSI knows about thousands of programs. It scans your computer and advises you on which ones need security patches, and then it takes you by the hand and helps you install updates. Details in Book X, Chapter 5.

Microsoft issues hundreds of updates each year. Some updates fix bugs that make Windows crash. Many updates plug security holes. Most updates come in the form of *patches,* or fixes to an individual Windows program that isn't working right. Some patches are small. Most are big. Many Microsoft security bulletins, which appear to handle a single bug and its patch, in fact cover many big, frequently unrelated, patches.

Microsoft periodically releases security and "high priority" patches for Windows, generally on the second Tuesday of every month. Anyone with a recent copy of Windows (including Windows 7, Windows Vista, and Windows XP) who has taken the defaults when first running Windows, or chosen the Install Updates Automatically (Recommended) option gets those patches pushed, automatically, to their machines, as soon as the PC is connected to the Internet. You don't need to lift a finger: When automatic updating is turned on, you come in one morning, and your PC has been patched and you never hear a word about it.

Or, you come in one morning and your machine sits there with a blue screen and you can't get it to start, or you can't print your tax forms, or the patch installer runs and runs but Windows says it still needs to be patched, or running a program you've always run suddenly locks up your machine, or your machine has re-booted itself and all the work you left open is gone . . . and you have no idea why.

Most of the time, on most machines, the patches perform as advertised — they fix a defect in the product. Fair enough. Beats a product recall, I guess. Sometimes, though, the patches don't work right or they offer bonus, uh, features that users neither asked for nor want. A few of my favorites:

✦ **The tax printing predicament:** On April 10, 2012, a Tuesday, Microsoft released an update to the Windows programming package .NET Framework, known cryptically as MS12-025. (For a description of the "MS12-XXX" patch numbers, see the "Decoding a security bulletin" section, later in this chapter.) Most Windows users in the United States didn't get the patch until Thursday or Friday. On the weekend before tax returns were due, thousands (possibly tens of thousands) of Windows consumers found themselves unable to print their TurboTax forms because of Microsoft's botched patch. On Saturday, Microsoft pulled the patch from Automatic Update.

✦ **The installer won't stop:** On February 14, 2012, Patch Tuesday, Microsoft released another .NET Framework update, this one called MS12-016. Many Windows users with ATI video cards reported the control program locked up their machines because of the patch. An unknown number of users reported that Windows tried installing the patch over and over again.

✦ **Everything crashes:** On January 10, 2012, Patch Tuesday, Microsoft
released a patch, MS12-006, that was supposed to solve a problem with
Secure Sockets Layer, the "s" in `https://`. Except it broke dozens of
programs. Microsoft pulled the patch, then reinstated it, then pulled it
again, and issued a warning on the MS Developer Network blog about
ongoing problems.

That's just the first four months of 2012. Going back to 2011, a big bunch
of bad patches occurred in August (MS11-066, MS11-069, and others), and
another run of really bad patches in June, several of which (MS11-039, MS11-
044) couldn't be fixed: You had to remove Windows programs and re-install
them to get them to work. In January, 2011 was a Windows 7 "reliability
update" delivered by Automatic Update — KB 2454826 — that started crashing Windows 7 machines. That same month, Automatic Updates inexplicably
started installing the MS10-090 October 2010 Internet Explorer patch all over
again. December 2010 saw a big problem with MS10-092, which crashed or
froze many machines.

Get the picture here? I didn't even mention the time a Windows patch on tax
weekend made it impossible to see your \Documents folder (MS06-015), or
the one that broke Outlook Express (MS06-016), or the way Microsoft used
the Automatic Update mechanism to surreptitiously install new registration
validation software, declaring many perfectly valid systems "not genuine" —
the "Windows Genuine Spyware" incident.

Almost every batch of patches that Microsoft releases these days contains
at least one stinker — a patch that, on a certain percentage of PCs, makes
things much worse. It's like the cure is worse than the disease.

I've been at this business for a long time — I've used Windows since the
days of Windows 286, which shipped on a single floppy disk, and I wrangled
with DOS long before that. Of all the Microsoft features that I don't trust —
and there are many — Windows Automatic Update rates as the single
Microsoft feature that I trust the least. Microsoft has gone to extraordinary
lengths over the past decade to reinforce my distrust and to demonstrate
plainly and unambiguously that when it comes to updating Windows,
Microsoft doesn't have a clue.

Don't get me wrong. You need to apply Windows patches at some point —
Windows Update itself is a hugely complex program that works reasonably
well most of the time. The problem is with *Automatic* Updates. Month after
month, Microsoft pushes out updates, automatically, that break things. By far
the best approach is to let Microsoft push whatever it wants to push, while
you sit back and watch how its updates fare with those who uninstall them
automatically — the cannon fodder. After a week or two or three, when the

dust has settled and Microsoft has had a chance to fix its fixes, *that's* when you should apply the patches. I have a (free!) website that will help you judge when patching time is right for you at AskWoody.com (`www.askwoody.com`).

Choosing an Update Level

When you install Windows, or when you first start a new Windows PC, if you don't take the default Installation settings, Windows asks you to `Help protect and update your PC`, allowing you three choices (see Figure 3-1):

✦ **Automatically Install Important and Recommended Updates:** You allow Microsoft to turn on Automatic Updates (more about that in this section), and generally let Microsoft have its way with your computer.

  Those may be the recommended Microsoft settings. They certainly aren't mine.

✦ **Automatically Install Important Updates:** You allow Microsoft to turn on Automatic Updates. See the theme here?

✦ **Don't Set Up Windows Update (Not Recommended):** This option is — you guessed it — my recommendation.

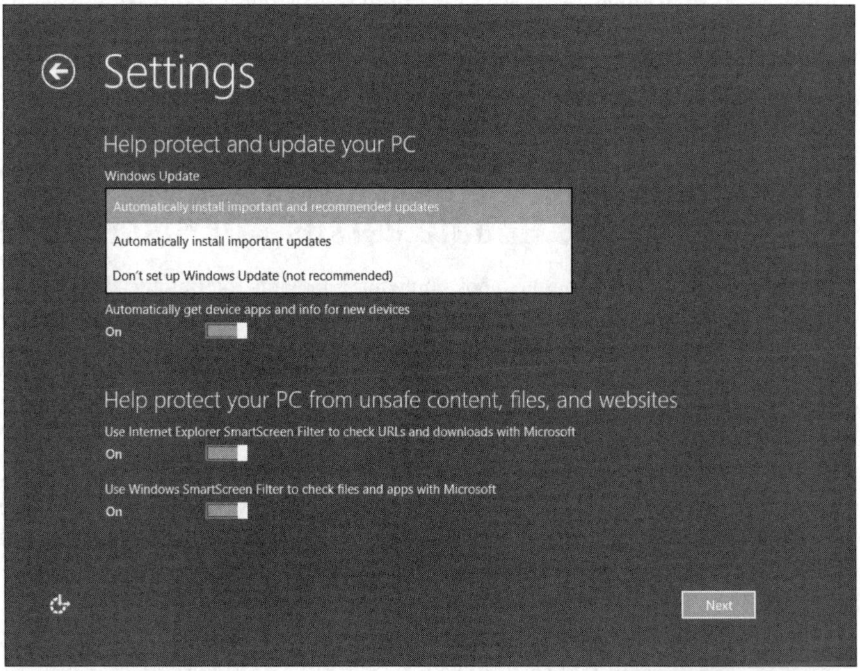

Figure 3-1:
A loaded
question.

No matter which option you choose, Windows Defender updates itself automatically. That's as it should be: Bad Windows Defender updates aren't unheard of, but they're usually fixed in short order, and I've never heard of one that froze a thousand machines. I also have no problem with updates to the junk mail filters in various Microsoft packages, which also update automatically, regardless of your choice here.

Microsoft wants you to turn on Automatic Updates. Heck, most Windows gurus suggest that you turn on Automatic Updates. One of those gurus says that it's better for Microsoft to automatically install its software on your PC than to leave your system wide open for some malicious kid to install his software on your PC.

He has a good point.

Still, I disagree. I believe that Microsoft has proven conclusively that it can't be trusted to produce reliable security fixes. If Microsoft distributes an automatic patch that's so badly flawed that thousands or tens of thousands of PCs suddenly stop working, the people with those PCs won't have the slightest idea that the culprit was a bad patch from Redmond. In my opinion, savvy Windows users should let the Automatic Update service advise them when new patches are available — but they should wait to apply those patches until there's enough real-world experience with the patches to ensure that they solve more problems than they create. I cover the latest problems and recommend when to patch and when to hold off on AskWoody.com (`www.askwoody.com`). You can also get important, up-to-date analyses by subscribing to Windows Secrets Newsletter, (`www.windowssecrets.com`).

Windows Update versus Microsoft Update

Windows, right out of the box, looks only for updates to Windows — makes sense.

If you have Microsoft Office (or any of a small handful of additional Microsoft products) installed on your computer, the dialog box shown in Figure 3-2 takes on an additional Give Me Updates for Microsoft Products and Check for New Optional Microsoft Software When I Update Windows option.

If you select that check box — and I recommend that you do — Windows Update starts looking for patches that apply to not only Windows but also Office (and, potentially, other modern Microsoft products). It also, annoyingly, may start offering you such stellar updates as Microsoft Silverlight, which you most assuredly don't want.

This supercharged pan-Microsoft version, dubbed Microsoft Update, works the same way as Windows Update: You can choose to notify but not download patches; uninstall patches; and in general, do everything else mentioned in this chapter — applied to Microsoft Office.

No matter what you chose when you first started Windows, it's never too late to take back control of your computer. Here's how:

1. **From the desktop, swipe from the right, choose the Settings charm, and then choose Control Panel; or right-click the lower-left corner of the desktop and choose Control Panel.**

The full-fledged Control Panel appears, not the tiled side Wimpy version.

2. **Tap or click System and Security; under Windows Update, tap or click the Turn Automatic Updating On or Off link; and then choose how you want to work with Important Updates.**

Windows Update lets you choose from four different levels of control so that you have some choice over what it does — or doesn't do — to your system. It's worth taking a few minutes to peruse Table 3-1, think through what Windows has to offer, and decide which approach works best for you.

I recommend the third option, Check for Updates but Let Me Choose Whether to Download and Install Them, as shown in Figure 3-2.

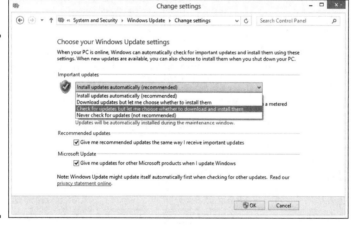

Figure 3-2: You can keep Microsoft's mitts off your machine, until you're ready to install patches.

Although the gestation period for new worms is shrinking — the bad guys are picking up on the Microsoft security patches and figuring out how to exploit the holes shortly after the patches are announced — it's quite rare that a freshly patched security hole turns into an active exploit in a few days. And generally, word of botched security patches surfaces within a few days.

On the other hand, if Great-Aunt Mildred frets about breaking her computer if she plays a round of Solitaire, she's a good candidate for automatic updating. Go ahead and set it up for her — but as you do so, recognize your technological co-dependence: You may be bailing her out of patch problems for as long as she has your telephone number.

3. **Select the Give Me Recommended Updates the Same Way I Receive Important Updates check box.**

   There's a very thin line between Important and Recommended in Microsoft parlance. (See the nearby "What's a critical update?" sidebar.) As long as you have a chance to review the updates before they're installed, you might as well look at recommended updates, too.

4. **Take note of the, uh, note.**

   The note warns you that Windows Update might update itself automatically first when checking for other updates. It's the Microsoft response to widespread criticism in August 2007, when it started changing the Windows Update program even if automatic updates were turned off.

   Microsoft feels that Windows Update has to be able to update itself, even without your permission: "Windows Update automatically updates itself from time to time to ensure that it is running the most current technology, so that it can check for updates and notify customers that new updates are available."

   Windows Update updated itself, without permission, in July 2012, to revoke certain, scandalously ancient, Microsoft security certificates that had been used in widely publicized attacks in the Flame virus.

5. **When you're happy with your settings, tap or click OK.**

   Your changes take effect immediately.

Table 3-1	Choosing a Windows Update Option	
Option	*What It Does*	*Recommended For*
Install Updates Automatically (Recommended)	Windows checks with the Microsoft update site daily to determine when new updates are available, downloads them when you're not on a metered Internet connection, and installs them automatically for you — typically, in the middle of the night.	People who are easily confused by the process of telling Windows that it's okay to install new updates. It's also a good option if you don't have the time or inclination to look online to see whether a specific update has major problems, or if you have a PC located in a public place.

Option	What It Does	Recommended For
Download Updates but Let Me Choose Whether to Install Them	Windows checks with the Microsoft update site daily to determine when new updates are available. If updates are available, WU downloads them when you're not on a metered Internet connection and then asks your permission to install them.	Not recommended. Unfortunately, because of the way Windows shuts down, you may be forced to install updates before you're ready.
Check for Updates but Let Me Choose Whether to Download and Install Them	Windows checks with the Microsoft update site daily to determine when new updates are available. If they are, Windows notifies you and asks for your permission to download and install them.	Folks who are willing to wait a week or two to install a new patch and who check online to see whether a patch is causing more harm than good.
Never Check for Updates (Not Recommended)	Automatic Update is turned off for Windows (although Windows Defender and spam filter updates still go through).	Not recommended. (See, I can sound like Microsoft when I have to.) It's hard to imagine any situation where this option makes sense.

When Windows Update reaches into your computer to see what you have installed, which patches have been applied, and so on, it doesn't retrieve any personally identifiable information. It doesn't even retrieve your activation key. As far as I've been able to tell, Microsoft doesn't attempt to spy on your machine via the Automatic Update program. So don't turn it off entirely unless you're really, really paranoid.

Selectively Patching: A Panacea for Those Woes

Microsoft really, really wants you to allow Windows to automatically update itself. Unless you have much more faith in Microsoft than I do, seriously consider defying the Party Line and decide for yourself when (and whether!) patches should be applied. The Windows Genuine Spyware debacle alone (see the "Patching Woes" section, earlier in this chapter) amply demonstrates that Microsoft automatic updating can't be trusted.

What's a critical update?

Microsoft has extremely strict definitions for its various levels of security patches. The official Severity Rating System defines these levels of security holes:

- **Critical:** "A vulnerability whose exploitation could allow the propagation of an Internet worm without user action."

- **Important:** "A vulnerability whose exploitation could result in compromise of the confidentiality, integrity, or availability of users' data, or of the integrity or availability of processing resources."

- **Moderate:** "Exploitability is mitigated to a significant degree by factors such as default configuration, auditing, or difficulty of exploitation."

- **Low:** "A vulnerability whose exploitation is extremely difficult, or whose impact is minimal."

In addition, Microsoft publishes an Exploitability Index that reflects the company's anticipation that some cretin will produce a piece of malware that can take advantage of the security hole in relatively short order. Here are the ratings:

- **Consistent Exploit Code Likely:** The Microsoft security team figures that somebody can come up with a piece of malware that uses the security hole to zap systems left and right.

- **Inconsistent Exploit Code Likely:** This rating also anticipates that somebody will be able to come up with a working program that takes advantage of the security hole, but the program probably won't work reliably.

- **Functioning Exploit Code Unlikely:** For any number of reasons, the security hole is well protected by other security settings, or it's so obscure that a big attack probably isn't in the cards.

Lest you truly believe that you should install *critical* updates before you install *important* updates — or that you can, say, ignore *moderate* updates — you need to realize that Microsoft's use of the terms is, in fact, quite arbitrary and at times, highly debatable. Many "critical" patches don't address unassisted worm propagation. In at least one instance, the severity level of a security hole was changed after enough people complained. One "critical" update removed a symbol from one font in Office 2003. The assignment of a security level seems to reflect internal Microsoft politics more than anything else. So take the severity level and Exploitability Index ratings with a grain of salt, okay?

Let Microsoft notify you when it wants to install something on your computer, but don't blindly allow the 'Softies to install whatever they want. Wait until millions and millions of hapless Windows customers unknowingly run the Microsoft patch beta tests and then install the patch after the cannon fodder has raised the alarm.

Microsoft officially releases new security patches on the second Tuesday of every month (except when it doesn't). If you hear of a security patch coming out on any date other than the second Tuesday of the month — an *out-of-band patch* — chances are good that a major security breach needs to get fixed fast. Microsoft also tends to release non-security patches on the fourth Tuesday of the month. These patches generally aren't as interesting as the security patches, but they can still hose your system.

Patching Windows manually

In the best of all possible worlds, patching Windows manually isn't a difficult process. It takes a little bit of time, but in the end, your computer's worth it, yes?

Here's how I patch. You can do it, too, with a little help from your friends. Follow these steps:

1. **Make sure you've followed the steps in the "Choosing an Update Level" section, earlier in this chapter, so that the Windows updater notifies you when a patch is available, but doesn't download or install it.**

    That's easy.

    Whenever a patch (or, more likely, a slew of patches) becomes available, you see a balloon in the notification area, near the clock, that says something like `Updates are available for your computer. Click here to download updates.`

2. **When you have a few spare minutes, tap or click the balloon.**

    The exact terminology may change, but you see a notification that updates are ready. Don't worry if you can't get to the updates right away. If the balloon disappears, you can bring it back by tapping or clicking the flag in the notification area (down near the clock) and choosing to read the message.

    When you click the balloon or the flag, Windows Update shows you a notification box like the one shown in Figure 3-3.

3. **Don't click the Install Updates button. Instead, tap or click the *X* Important Updates Are Available link.**

    The updates offered appear, as shown in Figure 3-4. The term Important is meant to reflect a level in Microsoft's rating system for patches. See the earlier sidebar, "What's a critical update," for details.

Figure 3-3:
Updates
are ready to
download.

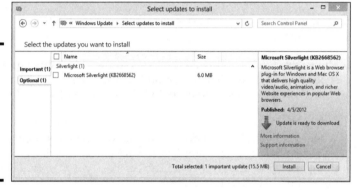

Figure 3-4:
Windows
Update
offers
details
about each
available
patch.

4. **Select the box next to each patch you want to install.**

On the left, you can alternate between important and optional patches. Important patches are usually selected automatically (although there can be exceptions — when Microsoft pulls a flakey patch, it will show the patch in the "important" list, but deselect the box). Optional patches may or may not be selected — you have to select the check boxes next to the ones you want.

You can tap or click any links in the update list, refer to the appropriate security bulletin or Knowledge Base article (see the "Getting What You Need from a Security Bulletin" section, later in this chapter), check my MS-DEFCON status (see the "MS-DEFCON: Your guide to patch safety" sidebar, later in this chapter), look at your favorite security website, or consult that really wired astrologer who hangs out in the park. Bring your own tea leaves.

MS-DEFCON: Your guide to patch safety

Big companies hire people — sometimes groups of people — to check the latest Microsoft patches, verify that they don't break anything, and then deploy the patches, slowly, throughout the corporate network.

If you can afford to hire a patch-busting team, my hat's off to you. But what are you, a typical Windows user, to do? Where can you turn for understandable, unbiased reporting on Windows flaws and fixes — and flaws in the fixes?

I have a rating system on my website, AskWoody.com (www.askwoody.com), that lets individual Microsoft consumers know when it's safe to install patches. I call it the *Microsoft Patch Defense Condition Level — MS-DEFCON*, for short. It's modeled after the U.S. Armed Forces DEFCON system, with the following levels:

The MS-DEFCON level advises you when it's safe to install patches.

✔ **MS-DEFCON 1:** Current Microsoft patches are causing havoc. Don't patch.

✔ **MS-DEFCON 2:** Patch reliability is unclear. Unless you have an immediate, pressing need to install a specific patch, don't do it.

✔ **MS-DEFCON 3:** Patch reliability is unclear, but widespread attacks make patching prudent. Go ahead and patch, but watch out for potential problems.

✔ **MS-DEFCON 4:** Isolated problems exist with current patches, but they are well known and documented on www.askwoody.com. Check the site's latest entries to see whether you're affected, and if things look okay, go ahead and patch.

✔ **MS-DEFCON 5:** All's clear. Patch while it's safe.

Watch the MS-DEFCON level for an independent, somewhat jaundiced analysis of threats, from hackers and from Microsoft.

---

5. **Don't be afraid to wait; tap or click the X to get out of the list and come back at any time.**

The world may be jumping up and down. Heck, the U.S. Department of Homeland Security once issued an emergency bulletin recommending the immediate installation of a Microsoft security patch — a patch that turned into a dud. Keep your head while those about you are losing theirs.

Within a few days, problems with new patches appear — sometimes with disastrous vigor. The mainstream press frequently carries distorted, sensationalized reports either (a) warning you to patch immediately because the sky is falling (I call them Chicken Littles), or (b) describing disasters that didn't really occur (I call them he-said-she-said rumors — or something distinctly less printable).

Windows continues to pester you, mercilessly, with the same balloon warning, `Updates are ready for your computer`. That's good. You need to hear the geese cackling.

6. **When you're convinced that patching will cause more good than harm, click that infernal balloon (or click the flag), open the update details (refer to Figure 3-4), make sure that you want to take the plunge, and tap or click Install.**

   The Windows update routine retrieves the updates and asks you for permission to install them.

7. **Follow the prompts from Windows.**

   Downloading and installing updates can take anywhere from a few minutes to a few hours.

Windows reboot improvements

Some patches require a reboot. There's nothing you can do about it. Like changing a wheel while your Maserati's in motion, you just have to shut off the dern thing to get the innards fixed.

Historically, Microsoft's combination of automatic updating and forced, unattended rebooting led to an interesting phenomenon: You sat down at your PC in the morning, and it suddenly didn't work. Blue screens, black screens, no screen at all. The patch that was automatically installed clobbered the machine when it rebooted. If you have Automatic Updates installed, that's always going to be a problem.

There's a different problem with rebooting. Windows 7 had a nasty habit of installing updates when you turned off or manually rebooted the computer. There was no way to avoid the (sometimes very lengthy) installation sequence when you wanted to shut down the PC. Sometimes the Do Not Shut Off Your PC message sat on the screen for an hour or two while you waited for the updater to do its thing. I winged and whined about the problem during

the Windows 7 testing phases, but Microsoft didn't listen to me. Again.

Windows 8 has a little more class. Two disturbing behaviors have been improved, if not fixed:

- First, Microsoft promises that it will consolidate patches that require a reboot, regardless of when they come out during the month, and synchronize the rebooting step to coincide with the once-a-month Patch Tuesday releases (see the nearby "Selectively Patching: A Panacea for Those Woes" section for an explanation of Black Tuesday).

- Second, Microsoft promises you that it will warn you at least three days before a reboot takes place. You see notifications in the lock screen, when you log in, warning that a system reboot is imminent.

Will Microsoft live up to those promises? I doubt that it can all the time, but it can probably do it most of the time. The changes are certainly a step in the right direction.

8. **When Windows finishes installing the updates, restart your computer.**

Even if Windows doesn't require a reboot, it's an excellent idea. Keep your eyes open for any problems and if you encounter one, check AskWoody.com (www.askwoody.com) or use your favorite search engine to get to the bottom of it.

Once more, for emphasis: *You have to keep Windows patched.* But you don't have to do it on Microsoft's terms. Take the bull by the horns, be mindful about the potential problems, and go out and do it your way.

Checking for updates manually

You can also check for patches manually, any time they become available, by running Windows Update. Here's the easy way:

1. **From the Start screen, swipe from the right or hover your mouse in the upper-right corner to bring up the Charms bar. At the bottom, choose Settings.**

2. **At the bottom of the Settings pane, choose Change PC Settings; on the left, choose Windows Update.**

The Windows Update settings pane appears. If you've told Windows to Check for Updates but Let Me Choose Whether to Download and Install Them, as I recommend earlier, or Download Updates but Let Me Choose Whether to Install Them, a screen similar to the one in Figure 3-5 appears.

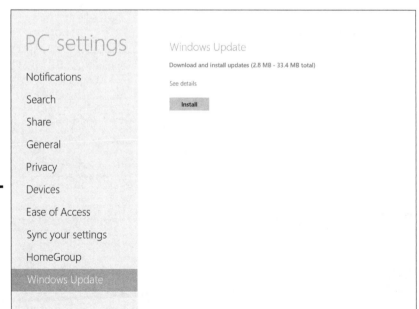

Figure 3-5:
The simple Windows Update settings, on the tiled side of Windows.

3. **If there are any updates on offer, tap or click the See Details link.**

   Windows Update runs out to the Microsoft mother ship and sees which updates are available. If it finds updates, it presents you with a list (see Figure 3-6) and, in some cases, offers an option to Choose Important Updates (tap or click this link to flip over to the Control Panel).

4. **If you want to pick and choose updates, tap or click the Choose Important Updates to Install, or Install Optional Updates link.**

   That flips you over to the old-fashioned desktop, and puts you in the Select Updates to Install Control Panel dialog box (refer to Figure 3-4). If you go over to the old-fashioned desktop side, you can complete the update over there, if you feel so inclined (you aren't returned to the tiled side automatically).

5. **If you're absolutely convinced that you want to install the updates Microsoft has chosen, tap or click outside of the *X* Important Updates box, to return to Figure 3-5, and then tap or click Install.**

   The installation proceeds exactly the same way as it would if you installed updates from the old-fashioned desktop side of Windows.

You may need to restart your computer for all the changes to take effect. In general, it's a good idea to restart after applying any major update.

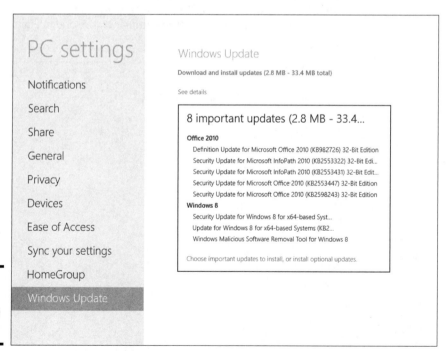

Figure 3-6:
Windows patches are available.

Getting What You Need from a Security Bulletin

When Microsoft patches a security hole in Windows, it issues a security bulletin (like the one shown in Figure 3-7). A *security bulletin* gives you some brief information about a particular patch (or patches) and offers a way to download patches without Windows Update. Security bulletins contain official notice from Microsoft about things that go bump in the night. They're frequently laden with so much jargon that the interpreters need interpreters to translate them into plain English.

To find the latest security bulletins, check the Microsoft Security Response Center blog, `http://blogs.technet.com/msrc`. Notices of new or revised security bulletins frequently appear on the MSRC blog long before any of the other Microsoft delivery mechanisms get the word out.

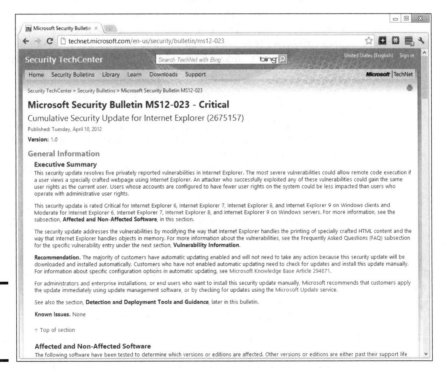

Figure 3-7: Security bulletin MS12-023.

Decoding a security bulletin

When you open a security bulletin, you need a few helpful pointers on interpreting what Microsoft has to say:

+ **Security bulletins are assigned sequential numbers, such as MS12-002, denoting the second security bulletin issued in 2012.**

    You might think that bulletin MS12-002 would talk about the second security *patch* in 2012, but you'd be wrong. Microsoft bunches up security patches, sometimes releasing several completely unrelated patches in one security bulletin. Why? Because it knows that the world at large correlates the number of security bulletins with the relative "holiness" of its software. If Windows releases only 30 patches in a year and Linux releases 48, which operating system sounds more secure?

    This particular security bulletin, MS12-023 (refer to Figure 3-7), is an Internet Explorer rollup patch. Microsoft releases similar patches every couple of months. This one includes fixes for five separately identified security holes that affect 42 different versions of Internet Explorer. In total, *more than a thousand files* are patched by this one security bulletin.

+ **Security bulletins are dated.** Usually they get revision numbers, too, but revision numbering seems to be, uh, subject to revision, if you know what I mean — the numbering can be a bit subjective. If you see a security bulletin that has been updated recently, there's a reason — usually something has gone wrong. If you see a security bulletin with a revision number such as 2.3 or 4.2, you know that problems bedevil the patches and that Microsoft has had to revise and re-revise (and re-re-revise) its explanations.

+ **Each security bulletin refers to one or more Knowledge Base (KB) articles, which give further details about the patch.** The six-digit KB article number appears at the end of the description of the patch.

The Knowledge Base article number is important if you need to remove a patch. Frequently, this number is the only way you have to identify the patch. If you need to remove the patch because, say, it clobbers an important part of Windows, you need the KB article number. (See the "Checking and Uninstalling Updates" section, later in this chapter.)

+ **Many patches have a second Knowledge Base article, referenced in the Caveats section, which exists solely to track the (acknowledged) bugs in the patch.** These KB articles contain a list of the bugs, updated as they're identified.

Getting patches through a security bulletin

Although you can use Windows Update to identify the patches your computer requires, download the patches, and even install them, you can download a patch manually and run it without Windows Update's interference, er, assistance. That can come in handy if you need to apply the same patch to numerous PCs or if you want to download the patch when your Internet connection isn't busy but wait to install the patch later.

To download and install a security bulletin patch manually, tap or click the Download the Update link for Windows 8 in the security bulletin and then follow the instructions to download the patch.

 Generally, it's much simpler to have Windows keep track of which patches are required and to download them automatically by using Windows Update, but if you need to apply the same patch to multiple machines, a manual download can save hours of trouble.

Checking and Uninstalling Updates

Want to know which patches have been installed? Do you suspect that a wayward patch has clobbered your machine, so you want to uninstall it?

As long as you don't mind wading through a bunch of Knowledge Base article numbers, getting to the list is easy. Here's how:

1. **On the desktop, to bring up the Control Panel, swipe from the right, choose Settings, and then tap or click Control Panel; or right-click the lower-left corner of the desktop and choose Control Panel.**

2. **Tap or click the System and Security link; then in the Windows Update section, tap or click the View Update History link.**

Windows Update presents you with a list of installed updates, as shown in Figure 3-8.

3. **(Optional) If you want to see details about a particular update, tap and hold or double-click the update and then, at the bottom, tap or click the More Information link.**

The Knowledge Base article for that particular patch appears.

4. **To remove a patch, at the top, tap or click the Installed Updates link.**

You see a list like the one in Figure 3-9.

Some Windows patches cannot be uninstalled — after you got 'em, you got 'em, and no amount of wailing or gnashing of teeth will tear them out of Windows.

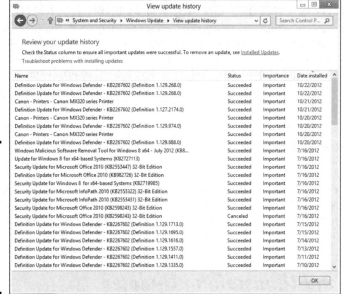

Figure 3-8:
Installed
updates
appear
with cryptic
names and
Knowledge
Base article
numbers.

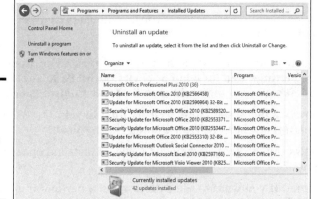

Figure 3-9:
Only
updates
that can be
uninstalled
make it on
this list.

5. **To uninstall a patch, tap or click it and choose Uninstall. When you're done, tap or click the X (Close) button to close the Installed Updates window.**

   Although you don't have to, you should restart your computer to ensure that the uninstalled patch is truly uninstalled.

Chapter 4: Monitoring Windows

In This Chapter

✔ **Watching Windows with the built-in tools**

✔ **Finding and fixing problems**

✔ **Judging your system's performance**

✔ **Viewing connections**

✔ **Working with the Event Viewer**

✔ **Tracking reliability over time**

*W*indows 8 ships with a tremendous array of tools designed to help you look at your system, and warn you if something's wrong. It also has a simple scoring mechanism that gives you a fairly good idea of where your PC excels, and where it's falling down on the job.

In Microsoft's zeal to make Windows less intimidating to new users, some of those tools are tucked away in rather obscure corners. But if you know what you're doing, you cannot only find them, but you can also use them to help make your machine hum.

Or at least burble.

One of the tools, the *Event Viewer,* is a favorite foil of scammers and charlatans, who use it to convince you that your PC needs fixing (for a fee, of course) when it's just fine. I talk about that in this chapter, too.

Obeying the Action Center

The Windows *Action Center* may sound like the title of a Grade B movie or the locus of a local television news program, but it serves a simple and worthwhile purpose: Whenever Windows wants to get your attention, it nags you through the Action Center.

What's a notification?

Notifications on the tiled side of the Windows fence are quite different from notifications on the desktop.

On the desktop, the notification area is in the lower-right corner of the screen, next to the system clock. That's where you find the Action Center flag icon. Programs can put their own icons in the notification area, and they can raise bubble messages alerting you to important events. The Action Center raises bubbles from time to time. You have complete control over the icons in the notification area, although you can't delete the Action Center flag, the Internet Access icon, or the Volume control.

Compare and contrast that, class, with the tiled notification — which can take any of several forms. I talk about them in Book II, Chapter 3. Most commonly a notification on the tiled side of Windows appears as a *toast* notification — yes, that's the technical term. *Toast* is a message that pops out from the upper-right edge of your screen. Just like, well, toast from a toaster.

In this chapter when I talk about notifications, I'm talking about the icons and bubbles in the lower-right corner of the desktop screen.

The Action Center consolidates security warnings with status notifications about updates, backups, and various troubleshooting tips. The Center's most important work revolves around security.

In theory, the Windows Action Center offers one-stop shopping for all your security needs. In practice, it's a short stop indeed — and taking control of security settings that aren't accessible through the Action Center can be quite a headache.

But, hey, at least you don't see the notice "There are unused icons on your desktop" every time you boot Windows. See, there have been some real improvements since Windows XP.

Entering the Action Center

If you go looking for it, the Windows Action Center sits buried in an obscure corner of the desktop infrastructure. But the Security flag sits up front and, uh, center. The easiest way to get to it: on the desktop, tap or click the flag near the system clock and choose Open Action Center from the pop-up menu. The Action Center appears in all its glory, which, if you've been a moderately good Windows custodian, looks like Figure 4-1.

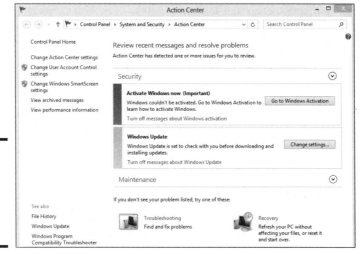

Figure 4-1:
The Action
Center,
ready for,
oh, you
know.

The little flag on the desktop can take on three personas:

✦ **A plain, unfettered flag means that you conform to Microsoft expectations.** You may have security messages waiting or troubleshooting tips available in the Action Center but, on the whole, you're doing fine and needn't upset the applecart.

Surprisingly, refreshingly, Windows shows you a flag without an overlay if you tell it to check for Windows Updates but don't download them. That's a big improvement over earlier versions of Windows, which would go into conniption fits if you prevented Microsoft from reaching into your machine and applying any change it deemed appropriate. (See Book VIII, Chapter 3 for details.)

✦ **A yellow exclamation point means that a portion of Windows wants your attention, and you should attend to it rather quickly.** Important security releases that haven't been applied fall into this category — at least, updates that Microsoft feels are important — as do hardware problems that leave a piece of your computer out of order.

✦ **A red circle with an X through it (see Figure 4-2) means that something is wrong and you need to check it quickly.**

**Book VIII
Chapter 4**

**Monitoring
Windows**

Figure 4-2:
The dreaded
red X
appears.

In some respects, the Action Center works as a central clearinghouse for Windows problems: In many cases, if a Windows program hits a problem, the program notifies the Action Center and the Action Center talks to you. In other respects, the Action Center takes on a proactive stance: It actively goes out and checks to see whether something is wrong and reports on its findings.

Unfortunately, these notifications don't work in lockstep with tiled notifications, which are far more dramatic: You can get a tiled notification without a concomitant desktop notification, and vice versa.

Working with the Action Center

The Action Center itself consolidates a wide range of settings from many different parts of Windows — indeed, from places outside of Windows — all in one place.

Watching Security settings

To see the monitored Security items, click the down arrow to the right of the Security heading as shown in Figure 4-3. The Action Center monitors the status of the following elements:

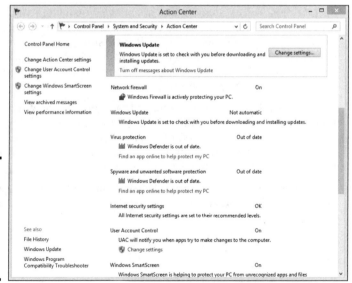

Figure 4-3:
The security components of Action Center status reporting.

♦ **Network Firewall:** Blocks access to your computer from the Internet. Although there are many firewalls available, the vast majority of Windows users employ the one built into Windows, which is Windows Firewall. (I talk about Windows Firewall in Book IX, Chapter 3.)

A *firewall* program insulates your PC (or network) from the Internet. At its heart, the Windows inbound firewall keeps track of requests that originate on your PC. When data from the Internet tries to make its way into your PC, the firewall checks to make sure that one of your programs requested the data. Unsolicited data gets dropped; requested data comes through. That way, rogues on the Internet can't break in.

Windows also has an outbound firewall, which is basically unusable. In my experience, an outbound firewall is more hassle than it's worth; see Book IX, Chapter 3 for details. The Network Firewall line in the Action Center says On even if you don't have outbound firewall protection.

You may be using the Windows Firewall, or you may have a third-party firewall installed. It's possible (but maddening) to run more than one firewall at the same time.

♦ **Windows Update:** Allows Windows to phone home and check for patches and patches to patches of patches. If you trust Microsoft, you can even allow Windows to patch itself, kinda like getting a license for self-administered lobotomies. I don't recommend this, however, and explain why in Book VIII, Chapter 3.

♦ **Virus Protection:** Tells you whether you have a functional antivirus (AV) program. Windows Defender comes built-in (see Book IX, Chapter 3), but if you got suckered into buying an AV product, it'll appear here.

♦ **Spyware and Other Unwanted Software Protection:** Looks at your computer and tries to determine whether you have spyware/scumware detection and blocking in force. Of course, Microsoft Windows Defender appears here — it's built into Windows itself. But if you have a different antispyware package, it'll appear here, too.

♦ **Internet Security Settings:** Refers only to your security settings in Internet Explorer.

♦ **User Account Control:** Refers to Windows' effort to put dialog boxes like the one shown in Figure 4-4 on the screen. I explain how to control UAC in Book IX, Chapter 3.

Figure 4-4:
User
Account
Control
settings
trigger
messages
like this one.

✦ **Windows SmartScreen**: Tries to keep you from installing potentially malicious software. There are pros and cons to its use, but as long as you understand what's going on, it's relatively innocuous. I talk about it in Book IX, Chapter 3.

✦ **Network Access Protection:** Covers a feature that works only in large, client-server domain networks. If you have a problem with your NAP settings, you need to contact your network administrator.

✦ **Microsoft Account:** If you use a Microsoft account to sign in (typically an @hotmail.com or @live.com or @outlook.com ID, but it can be any e-mail address), this item tells you of any problems with the account. Foremost among them is the possibility that you don't know the current password to the account. See Book II, Chapter 4.

All these settings focus on preventing bad stuff outside your PC from getting inside — a noble goal, to be sure, but the baddies that lurk outside your box are only part of the problem. The other part? You. To get — and keep — your security and sanity in Windows, you must understand how your PC can be attacked and what you can do to forestall those attacks, both from a computer point of view and by thinking "outside the box." (That's the theme of Book IX, Chapter 1.)

Checking Maintenance settings

To see the general Windows programs that the Action Center monitors, tap or click the down arrow to the right of the Maintenance heading. You see the following options (see Figure 4-5):

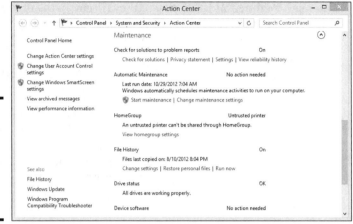

Figure 4-5:
The mainte-
nance
compo-
nents of
the Action
Center.

✦ **Check for Solutions to Problem Reports:** This is one of the passive settings. Windows Action Center monitors problem events as they occur
and keeps tabs on your computer's reliability history.

You can go back and see whether Microsoft has posted any solutions
to problems that your computer has reported in the past. It's rare, but
it does happen. If you want to see which problems your computer has
reported, tap or click the View Archived Messages link.

If you tap or click the View Reliability History link, you see the Reliability
Monitor, as shown in Figure 4-6. (I talk about the Reliability Monitor later
in this chapter, in the "Gauging system reliability" section.)

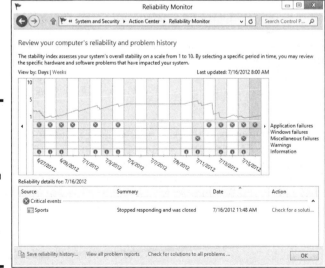

Figure 4-6:
The
Windows
Reliability
Monitor can
help you
pinpoint
faulty
software or
hardware.

✦ **Automatic Maintenance:** Gives you the current status of the programs Windows automatically schedules to keep your system running, from mundane tasks like defragmenting drives, to system updates, and reboots as needed.

✦ **HomeGroup**: Tells you whether you're connected to a HomeGroup. (I talk about HomeGroups in Book VII, Chapter 5.)

✦ **File History**: Lets you know whether your backups are working properly. (I talk about File History in Book VIII, Chapter 1.)

✦ **Drive Status:** Warns you whether you should expect giant flames and acrid smoke. If your status turns red, increase your house insurance, like, right away, okay? Actually, this monitors the automatic reporting of problems by your hard drive and raises a flag if your drive says it's having problems. In my experience, it isn't very reliable.

Running Your Windows Experience Index

Hardware benchmarks have suffered a long, checkered history. Once the mainstay of the computer magazine industry ("Buy a GefilteFlop because it rates 7.9 on the FlippIndex and its competitor rates only a 7.7"), hardware manufacturers since the dawn of the Bronze Age have tweaked and mangled and goosed their designs to boost meaningless benchmark numbers. Scandals erupted when manufacturers cooked their products to increase ratings at the big-name computer magazines, frequently sacrificing overall performance to gain a slight advantage with a specific test. Once the quantification of the PC Holy Grail, over time benchmarking became enormously complex and arcane and gradually fell out of favor with the general computer-buying public.

Microsoft turned that all around with the advent of Vista and its simple numerical ratings for processor speed, memory, video, and storage. In the Brave New Windows World, every computer completes a battery of tests, and ultimately receives a number between 1.0 and 9.9 that represents the PC's Windows Experience Index. (That's like calling the U.S. 1040 Tax Form a Wealth Assistant.) Microsoft says the Windows Experience Index isn't a benchmark. Yeah, sure.

When you look at your computer's Windows Experience Index (WEI), and when you comparison-shop for products based on their WEIs, remember that benchmarks always lie, but the best ones don't lie as much. A 20 percent difference in any single WEI score isn't perceptible to any normal human. Moreover, the WEI scores are calculated in a way that, in some cases, defies any sort of logic I can discern. But there's learning to be had from WEI, if you know when to pay attention to it and when to tune it out. In the following sections, I offer up the details of my, uh, experience.

Getting a faster Internet connection trumps anything and everything Windows has to offer.

Checking your Windows Experience score

Before you waste time and money chasing an elusive performance boost, make sure you understand the numbers and their limitations.

To see how your system stacks up, follow these steps:

1. **On the Start screen, type** system, **choose Settings on the right, and choose System on the left. Or, on the desktop, right-click the lower-right corner and choose System.**

2. **Under the System heading, tap or click the Windows Experience Index link.**

   The Performance Information and Tools dialog box appears, with a big number for the overall rating and with five smaller numbers delineating Microsoft's take on your computer's performance in five key areas (see Figure 4-7). The big number — your *base score* — is simply the lowest of the five component scores.

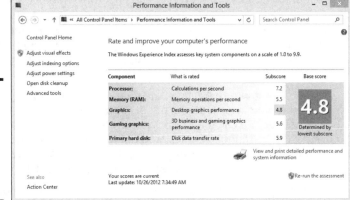

Figure 4-7: An overall performance rating, er, Experience Index of 4.8.

3. **If you think that your system hasn't been given a fair shake, tap or click the Re-Run the Assessment link.**

Windows runs through all its performance benchmarks, recalculates the component ratings, and comes up with a new number. Unless you changed hardware lately, or somebody jimmied the system, the new number is precisely the same as the old number.

Interpreting the numbers

At this moment, every component on every computer receives a rating between 1.0 and 9.9, except for hard drives, which all run from 2.0 to 9.9. You could install the fastest overclocked gigacore pipelined processor on the planet with ten terabytes of L2 cache, and your CPU score wouldn't hit 10.0. You could have two chipmunks spinning hard drive platters for peanuts, and your disk wouldn't fall below 2.0.

Microsoft has scaled the scores. Over time, the maximum values increase, but for now 9.9 is as good as it gets. Think of the open-ended Richter scale, where you haven't seen a big enough quake yet.

A higher number is better. That part's easy. Understanding the rest of the numbers isn't nearly as straightforward. Here's what the performance scores *really* measure:

✦ The **processor score** measures how quickly your processor runs a battery of CPU-intensive tests, such as compressing and decompressing data, encryption and decryption, and encoding video. It doesn't attempt to measure many compute-intensive activities that you see in other processor benchmarks, such as recalculating huge spreadsheets or repaginating *War and Peace* or morphing George W's old publicity stills. Depending on the kind of work you do, the benchmark may or may not reflect your kind of work.

✦ In spite of what Figure 4-7 says, the **memory component** doesn't rely solely on "memory operations per second." Instead, Windows looks at how much memory you have on your system, subtracts the amount of memory dedicated to graphics, and determines a maximum score based on Table 4-1. If you're running the 64-bit version of Windows and you have 4GB of memory, the highest score you can hit is 5.9.

✦ The **graphics component score** emphasizes two-dimensional performance, with specific tests geared to the *Desktop Windows Manager*, video memory bandwidth, and video decoder capability. As this book went to press, the exact tests and their meaning weren't clear.

◆ The **gaming graphics component,** confusingly, deals with 3D graphics. Internally, it's the *D3D* score, short for Direct3D, Microsoft's proprietary set of commands for high-performance 3D picture rendering. The benchmark measures blending and shading performance. If your graphics card doesn't support the Pixel Shader 3.0 spec, the score is clipped at 4.9, no matter how fast your card.

◆ The **primary hard disk component** tests your hard drive by measuring read speeds while overflowing the hard drive with changed data that needs to be written to disk. If you have a Solid State Drive (SSD), this score's going to be higher than with a standard hard disk drive.

Table 4-1	Maximum Memory Component Scores
Amount of Memory	*Maximum Memory Component Scores*
Less than 256MB	1.0
Less than 500MB	2.0
Less than 512MB	2.9
Less than 704MB	3.5
Less than 960MB	3.9
Less than 1.5GB	4.5
Less than 3GB	5.5

The *Windows System Assessment Tool* is a program (it's actually a big bunch of programs) that runs all the benchmarks and boils down the results to the WEI numbers you see on the screen. The raw scores are stored in XML files in the folder `c:\Windows\Performance\WinSAT\DataStore`.

Turning the numbers into real improvement

Used properly, the WEI scores can help you assemble a kick-butt Windows system for a very low price. As with any good benchmark, the Windows Experience Index tells you how well a piece of hardware works. Forget the salesdroid's palaver. Toss the glossy brochure in the trash. The WEI can tell you whether a piece of hardware delivers the goods — or whether it's all hat and no cattle, if yaknowhatimean.

You really need to focus on improving the lowest-scoring parts of your setup. That's where the greatest bang for your buck can be had.

While I was writing *Windows 7 All-In-One For Dummies*, I hopped down to my friendly local PC dealer, looking for a dirt-cheap PC to run Windows 7. I found a discontinued HP Pavilion — dozens of them — that the retailer had marked down to $225. Very basic stuff: dual core Pentium, 1GB of memory, 160GB hard drive, integrated Intel GMA 3100 video driver, PCI Express slots, running Vista Home Basic. The bone-stock Vista WEI came in at a toe-curling 1.0 (see Figure 4-8). The WEI told me at a glance that my graphics and gaming graphics scores were the trouble spots: Both scores were several points below the others.

Figure 4-8: My wimpy new Pavilion, with a Vista WEI of 1.0.

Bravely pursuing Windows enlightenment, I tore open the case and installed a used video card that I had lying around the office. It sports an NVIDIA GeForce 8600 GT chip with 256MB of memory. These days, you can buy a considerably more powerful card at many discount shops for $50 or less. I also added one 2GB stick of memory, worth about $20, to bring the total memory to 3GB.

That's the main machine I run today: a $225 Pavilion with a $50 video card and $20 in memory. It worked well with Windows 7, and it works even better with Windows 8. The WEI? I didn't hit 9.9 on any scores, but it scoots along pretty well, for an old geezer. See for yourself, in Figure 4-7.

Moral of the story: Even a cheap PC can make a great Windows 8 computer, providing you use a decent video card and get the memory up to 3 or 4GB.

Reviewing Your Network Status

Windows keeps you well informed about the status of your Internet connection, with a badge icon on the lock screen, an icon in the desktop's notification area, and easy access to the latest info through the Settings charm: right-swipe (or hover your mouse in the upper-right corner), and then choose Settings, and the Internet Access icon is in the upper-left corner, per Figure 4-9.

Figure 4-9: Quick network status is only a right-swipe and tap away.

If you want to see more about your network status, you have to flip over to the desktop. In the notification area, next to the time, tap and hold or right-click the Internet Access icon, and then choose Open Network and Sharing Center. An overview of your network appears (see Figure 4-10).

Figure 4-10: For more details on network status, you have to venture over to the desktop side.

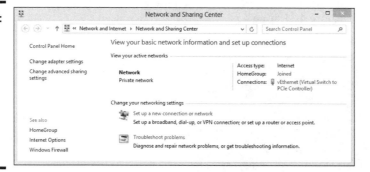

Book VIII
Chapter 4

Monitoring
Windows

From the Network and Sharing Center, you can troubleshoot all sorts of networking problems. For a host of details, see Doug Lowe's *Networking All-In-One for Dummies.*

Turning sharing on or off

If you have a network and other computers on the network can't "see" your PC, the most likely cause is that you've turned off sharing. Conversely, if you can't see other computers on your network, you probably turned off sharing. Finally, if you can't get a HomeGroup working (see Book VII, Chapter 5), chances are good you turned off sharing.

See a pattern here?

If you're sitting in a coffee shop using the WiFi, you don't want sharing. If you're in an office where people don't share much — not even their printers — go ahead and turn off sharing. But for most situations, most of the time, sharing's a very smart thing to do.

Everything you know about network admin you learned in kindergarten, right?

Fortunately, turning on sharing is very easy. Here's how:

1. **Swipe from the right, or hover your mouse in the upper-right corner. When the Charms bar appears, choose Settings.**

   The status pane appears. Depending on where you were when you swiped from the right, the status pane may look a little different, but there's always a network icon.

2. **Tap or click the network icon.**

   It's the top one on the left. A network connections pane like the one in Figure 4-11 appears.

Figure 4-11: Network connections appear here.

3. **Tap and hold or right-click Connected.**

   A Turn Sharing On or Off box appears.

4. **Tap or click the box.**

You're given the choices shown in Figure 4-12.

Figure 4-12:
Open your
network
connection.

5. **To turn off sharing, tap or click the top box; and to turn on sharing, tap or click the bottom box.**

It may take a few minutes for Windows to change the sharing setting to open itself to the network and, if necessary, run out to the network and shout, "I'm here! I'm here!"

Sharing and discovery is, in fact, a very complex topic, with all sorts of gotchas. Anyone who's ever tried to get a Windows XP computer to talk to a Mac knows just what I mean. If you find yourself trying to plumb the depths of networking hell, get a copy of *Networking All-In-One For Dummies*, by Doug Lowe.

Troubleshooting network adapters

When I have trouble with a network, and the standard Windows Troubleshooter doesn't work (it appears at the bottom of Figure 4-10, if your network isn't working), I always start pushing and prodding my network adapters.

There are several ways to see your network adapters. This is the method I like best because of the detour through the Network and Sharing Center. Try this:

1. **Bring up Control Panel:**

   - *Without a mouse,* flip over to the desktop, swipe from the right, choose Settings, and then, at the top, choose Control Panel.

   - *With a mouse,* right-click the lower-left corner of the screen and choose Control Panel.

2. **Under the Network and Internet heading, tap or click the View Network Status and Tasks link.**

   The Network and Sharing Center appears, (refer to Figure 4-10).

   The Network and Sharing Center gives you a solid overview of what's connected, and to where.

3. **On the left, tap or click the Change Adapter Settings link.**

   Windows shows you a list of all your adapters, as shown in Figure 4-13.

Figure 4-13:
Network adapters — the pieces of hardware that connect your PC with the outside world — appear here.

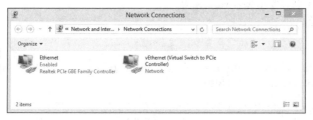

4. **Tap or click an adapter that may be causing problems, and then tap or click Diagnose This Connection.**

   Windows performs a full diagnostic on the adapter. You also have the options to disable and then re-enable the adapter (which often works wonders), or to view the status of the connection (where you can change some heavy duty settings, such as a manual override of the adapter's IP address, or locking in a DNS Server — see *Networking All-In-One For Dummies*, by Doug Lowe for details).

5. **When you've solved the problem (or you're ready to give up), tap or click the X's to get out of Control Panel.**

   That should fix it.

Setting up a virtual private network

I use virtual private networks all the time. Sometimes I need to look like I'm accessing the Internet from someplace I'm not — I'm sitting on the beach in Phuket, say, but I have to look to a client like I'm getting on the Internet from Los Angeles. Sometimes I want to bypass throttling by my Internet service provider (ISP), when I'm doing something they may not like, such as accessing a streaming movie. Other times I'll try to trick a scammer into believing that I'm just down the street from where they're located. Lots of good reasons.

I always, always use a virtual private network when I hook up my laptop to a public WiFi signal. *Firesheep,* a very simple Firefox add-on, lets anybody in the vicinity snoop on WiFi traffic, if the snooper knows the WiFi password. Without a VPN, somebody using a laptop near you can intercept everything you do, unless you happen to be dealing only with secured HTTPS sites. Scary stuff.

Here's how a VPN works:

1. **You set up an account with a VPN provider.**

   Typically the VPN provider has locations — or servers — located in several places around the world.

2. **You connect to the Internet using the VPN's server.**

   After you're connected to the VPN server, all your interactions with the Internet go through the server, and communication between your computer and the server is quite secure.

   So, for example, if I have a VPN account on a server in Los Angeles, I log on to that server using my account. From the moment that I establish the connection, all my interactions with the Internet look like they're coming from Los Angeles. The only people who know that I'm using the connection are the ones who sell me the VPN service. To everyone else, I'm coming from an anonymous location in LA.

   As long as you don't break the connection — disconnect or intentionally log off the VPN server — all your interactions with the server are encrypted, and all your interactions with the outside world can be traced only to the server.

   Even your ISP is in the dark. To your ISP, it just looks like you're pushing a lot of data through a server in Los Angeles.

VPNs originated as a way for traveling corporate types — bankers, stockbrokers, spies — to dial in to their company (or The Company) computers, and have a secured connection all the way. These days, VPNs are for just about everybody — especially anybody who's connected to a public WiFi hotspot.

There are hundreds of free VPNs but, as you might guess, they're wholly dependent on the ability of their server(s) to keep up with the load. Google can help you find many of them. My experience with free VPNs has been spotty at best.

Years ago, I switched to a paid VPN service, VyprVPN. It works on Windows, but it's also great for my iPad, iPhone, and Android phone. (Don't tell anybody, but I use it on my Mac, too.) If you've read some of my earlier books, you probably recognize the name: VyprVPN (www.vyprvpn.com) comes from the same people who run the Giganews Usenet service (www.giganews.com) and is a good option if you get tired of the free VPNs.

Viewing Events

Every Windows user needs to know about Event Viewer, if only to protect themselves from scammers and con artists who make big bucks preying on peoples' fears.

As I explain in Book X, Chapter 1, scammers are calling people in North America, Europe, Australia, and other locations all around the world, trying to talk Windows users into allowing these con artists to take over victims' systems via Remote Assistance. The scammers typically claim to be from Microsoft, or associated with Microsoft. They may get your phone number by looking up names of people posting to help forums.

Some of them just cold call: Any random phone call to a household in North America or Europe stands a very good chance of striking a resonating chord when the topic turns to Windows problems. If you randomly called ten people in your town, and said you were calling on behalf of Microsoft to help with a Windows problem, and you sounded as if you knew what you were talking about, I bet at least one or two of your neighbors would take you up on the offer. In my neighborhood, it'd probably be closer to nine.

The scam hinges around the Windows Event Viewer feature. It's an interesting, useful tool — but only if *you* take the initiative to use it, and don't let some fast talker use it to bilk you out of hundreds of bucks.

Using Event Viewer

Windows has had an Event Viewer for almost a decade. Few people know about it. At its heart, the Event Viewer looks at a small handful of logs that Windows maintains on your PC. The logs are simple text files, written in XML format. Although you may think of Windows as having one Event Log file, in fact, there are many — Administrative, Operational, Analytic and Debug, plus application log files.

Every program that starts on your PC posts a notification in an Event Log, and every well-behaved program posts a notification before it stops. Every system access, security change, operating system twitch, hardware failure, and driver hiccup all end up in one or another Event Log. The Event Viewer scans those text log files, aggregates them, and puts a pretty interface on a deathly dull, voluminous set of machine-generated data. Think of Event Viewer as a database reporting program, where the underlying database is just a handful of simple flat text files.

In theory, the Event Logs track "significant events" on your PC. In practice, the term "significant" is in the eyes of the beholder. Or programmer. In the normal course of, uh, events, few people ever need to look at any of the Event Logs. But if your PC starts to turn sour, the Event Viewer may give you important insight to the source of the problem.

Here's how to use the Event Viewer:

1. **On the Start screen, type** event. **On the right, choose Settings; then on the left, choose View Event Logs.**

   The Event Viewer appears.

2. **On the left, choose Event Viewer↪Custom Views↪Administrative Events.**

   It may take a while, but eventually you see a list of notable events like the one in Figure 4-14.

3. **Don't freak out.**

   Even the best-kept system (well, my production system anyway) boasts reams of scary-looking error messages — hundreds, if not thousands of them. That's normal.

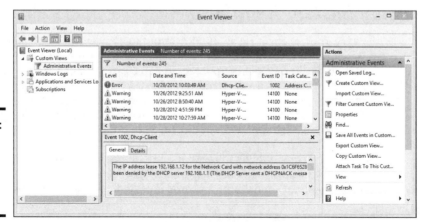

Figure 4-14: Events logged by various parts of Windows.

Events worthy — and not worthy — of viewing

Before you get all hot and bothered about the thousands of errors on your PC, look closely at the date and time field. There may be thousands of events listed, but those probably date back to the day you first installed the PC. Chances are good that you can see a handful of items every day — and most of the events are just repeats of the same error or warning. Most likely, they have little or no effect on the way you use Windows. An *error* to Windows should usually trigger a yawn and "Who cares?" from you.

For example, looking through my most recent Event Log, I see a bunch of errors generated by a source called DistributedCOM, telling me that the server Microsoft.WindowsLive.Mail.App didn't register with DCOM within the required timeout. Really and truly, no biggie. Fugeddaboutit.

That's exactly my advice. If you aren't experiencing problems, don't sweat what's in the Event Viewer. Even if you are experiencing problems, the Event Viewer may or may not be able to help you.

How can Event Viewer help? See the Event ID column? Make note of the ID number, and look it up at www.eventid.net. They may be able to point you in the right direction, or at least translate the event ID into something resembling plain English. If you're trying to track down a specific problem, and you see an event that may relate to the problem, use Google to see whether you can find somebody else who's had the same problem. Event Viewer can also help you nail down network access problems because the Windows programs that control network communication spill a large amount of details into the Event Logs. Unfortunately, translating the logs into English can be a daunting task, but at least you may be able to tell where the problem occurs — even if you haven't a clue how to solve it.

Gauging System Reliability

Every Tom, Dick, 'n Hairy Windows routine leaves traces of itself in the Windows Event Log. Start a program, and the ignoble event gets logged. Stop it, and the Log gets updated. Install a program or a patch, and the Log knows all, sees all. Every security-related event you can imagine goes in the Log. Windows Services leave their traces, as do errors of many stripes. Things that should've happened but didn't get logged, as well as things that shouldn't have happened but did. Soup to nuts.

The Event Log contains items that mere humans can understand. Sometimes. It also logs things that only a propeller head could love. The Event Log actually consists of a mash-up of several files that are maintained by different

Windows system programs in different ways. The Event Viewer, discussed in the preceding section, looks at the trees. The Reliability Monitor tries to put the forest in perspective.

The Windows Reliability Monitor slices and dices the Event Log, pulling out much information that relates to your PC's stability. It doesn't catch everything — more about that in a moment. But the stuff that it does find can give you instant insight into what ails your machine.

Here's how to bring up the Reliability Monitor:

1. **On the Start screen, type** reli. **On the right, choose Settings; then on the left, choose View Reliability History.**

The Reliability Monitor springs to life, as shown in Figure 4-15.

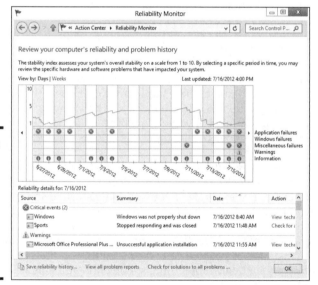

Figure 4-15: When something goes out to lunch, it leaves a trace in the Reliability Monitor.

2. **In the View By line, flip between Days and Weeks.**

Reliability Monitor goes back and forth between a detailed view and an overview.

Once again, please, don't freak out. There's a reason why Microsoft makes it hard to get to this report. It figures if you're sophisticated enough to find it, you can bear to see the cold, hard facts.

The top line in the monitor is supposed to give you a rating, from one to ten, of your system's stability. In fact, it doesn't do anything of the sort, but if you see the line drop like a wood barrel over Victoria Falls, something undoubtedly has gone bump in the night.

Your rating more-or-less reflects the number and severity of problematic Event Log events in four categories: Application, Windows failures, Miscellaneous failures, and Warnings. The Information icons (circled i's) generally represent updates to programs and drivers; if you installed a new printer driver, for example, there should be an Information icon on the day it was installed. Microsoft has a detailed list of the types of data being reported in its TechNet documentation, at `http://bit.ly/HW3rSF`.

If you tap or click a day (or a week), the box at the bottom shows you the corresponding entries in your Windows Event Log. Many events at the bottom have a more detailed explanation, which you can see by tapping/clicking the View Technical Details link.

The Reliability Monitor isn't meant to provide a comprehensive list of all the bad things that have happened to your PC, and in that respect, it certainly meets its design goals. It isn't much of a stability tracker, either. The one-to-ten rating uses a trailing average of daily scores where more recent scores have greater weight than old ones, but in my experience, the line doesn't track reality: My system can bounce like a Willy's in four wheel drive, and it doesn't affect the rating; conversely my system can be purring like a cat while my rating score goes to the dogs.

The real value of the Reliability Monitor lies in showing you a time sequence of key events — connecting the temporal dots so you may be able to discern a cause and effect. For example, if you suddenly start seeing blue screens repeatedly, check the Reliability Monitor to see whether something untoward has happened to your system. Installing a new driver, say, can make your system unstable, and the Reliability Monitor can readily show you when it was installed. If you see your rating tumble on the same day that a driver update got installed, something's fishy, and you may be able to readily identify the scaly culprit.

Proverbial bottom line: The Reliability Monitor doesn't keep track of everything, and some of it is a bit deceptive, but it can provide some worthwhile information when Windows starts kicking. The Reliability Monitor is well worth adding to your Win bag of tricks.

TECHNICAL STUFF

Other performance monitors

Windows has two other monitors — *perfmon,* the Performance Monitor, and *resmon,* the Resources Monitor — that have been largely rendered obsolete because of the new (and very cool!) Task Manager. I talk about Task Manager in Chapter 5 of this minibook. If you really want to see either perfmon or resmon in action, type the appropriate name on the Start screen and then tap or click the only app that appears.

But I think you're going to like the new Task Manager a whole lot better.

Chapter 5: Using System Tools

*W*indows abounds with tools that can help you do everything from taking out the dog to making the perfect espresso — at least, if your computer runs hot. In this chapter, I step you through three specific tools that can come in very handy:

✦ The new, greatly improved and expanded *Task Manager* has turned into the Swiss Army knife of Windows applications. In Windows 7, you had to bring up, navigate to, download and/or install a half dozen different tools to even come close to what Task Manager does right out of the box. In earlier versions of Windows, many of the tools existed only in vestigial form.

✦ Windows includes all the tools you need to install a new hard drive, and the steps are easier than you think. All it takes is a trip to the Disk Management application. In this chapter, I show you how.

✦ Finally, I have a bonus section on the virtual machine generator that ships with Windows 8 Pro only. (Sorry, if you have standard Windows 8, you don't get it.) A *virtual machine* is a make-believe fully contained PC that runs inside your regular PC. You can use it to run Windows XP programs, for example, without setting up a dual boot on your Windows 8 system. You can also use a VM to check out new tricks, or try some different Windows settings, without gumming up your working machine. Hyper-V works a treat, if you know how to treat it.

Tasking Task Manager

Windows has a secret command post that you can get to if you know the right handshake, uh, key combination. Whatever. The key combination (or tap sequence) works all the time, unless Windows is seriously out to lunch.

Task Manager can handle any of these jobs:

+ **Kill a program.** That comes in very handy if, say, Internet Explorer freezes and you can't get it to do anything. Doesn't matter if the tiled full-screen version of IE freezes, or the desktop version. Either way, one trip to Task Manager and *zap!*

   Windows tries to shut down the application without destroying any data. If it's successful, the application disappears from the list. If it isn't successful, it presents you with the option of summarily zapping the application (called End Now to the less imaginative) or simply ignoring it and allowing it to go its merry way.

+ **Switch to any program.** This is convenient if you find yourself stuck somewhere — in a game, say, that doesn't "let go" — and you want to jump over to a different application. You can easily go to a tiled- or desktop-style program.

+ **See which processes are hogging your CPU.** There's a bouncing list of program pieces — called *processes* — and an up-to-the-second ranking of how much computer time each one's taking. That list is invaluable if your PC is working like a slug, and you can't figure out which program(s) are hogging the processor.

+ **See which processes take up most of your memory, use your disk, or gab over the network.** Sometimes it's hard to figure out which program's at fault. Task Manager knows all, sees all, and tells all.

+ **Get running graphs of CPU, memory, disk, or network usage.** They're cool and informative, and may even help you decide whether you need to buy more memory.

+ **See which tiled Windows Store apps use the most resources over a specified period of time.** Did the Camera take up the most time on your PC in the past month? Pinball?

+ **Turn off auto-starting programs.** This used to be a huge headache, but now it's surprisingly easy. The simple fact is that almost everybody has automatically starting programs that take up boot time, add to your system overhead, cause aggravation, and may even be dangerous. Task Manager shows you major programs that start automatically, and gives you the option to disable the program.

+ **Send a message to the other users on your PC.** The message shows up on the lock screen when you log off.

+ **Force Task Manager to stay on top of all other windows.** This includes "immersive" full-screen windows.

Who da man?

Here's how to bring out the full glory of the Swiss Army knife version of Windows Task Manager:

1a. ***If you have a keyboard,*** **press Ctrl+Alt+Delete; tap or click the Task Manager link in the screen that appears.**

1b. ***If you don't have a keyboard,*** **go to the Start screen, type** Task, **and on the left, tap or click Task Manager.**

In either case, the Task Manager appears with a list of all running applications (see Figure 5-1). Notably, the list includes all the running tiled apps, as well as all the running desktop programs.

Figure 5-1:
Windows
Task
Manager
lets you
control
running
programs.

2. **To kill one of your running programs, tap or click it and then tap or click End Task.**

The program may continue for a minute or two — some programs hold on tenaciously — but in the end, almost every program succumbs to the preemptive force.

3. **To see the other options, tap or click More Details.**

The Processes tab of the full-fledged Task Manager appears. See Figure 5-2.

**Book VIII
Chapter 5**

Using System Tools

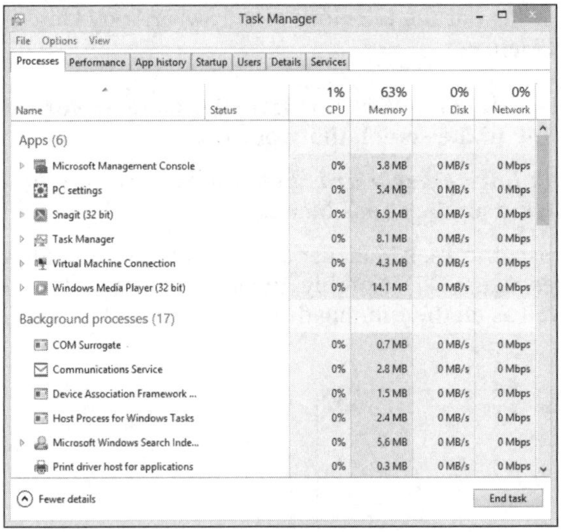

		1% CPU	63% Memory	0% Disk	0% Network

Task Manager

File Options View

Processes | Performance | App history | Startup | Users | Details | Services

Name | Status | CPU | Memory | Disk | Network

Apps (6)

▷ 🖳 Microsoft Management Console		0%	5.8 MB	0 MB/s	0 Mbps
🔧 PC settings		0%	5.4 MB	0 MB/s	0 Mbps
▷ 🖼 Snagit (32 bit)		0%	6.9 MB	0 MB/s	0 Mbps
▷ 🖥 Task Manager		0%	8.1 MB	0 MB/s	0 Mbps
▷ 🖥 Virtual Machine Connection		0%	4.3 MB	0 MB/s	0 Mbps
▷ 🖥 Windows Media Player (32 bit)		0%	14.1 MB	0 MB/s	0 Mbps

Background processes (17)

🖥 COM Surrogate		0%	0.7 MB	0 MB/s	0 Mbps
✉ Communications Service		0%	2.8 MB	0 MB/s	0 Mbps
🖥 Device Association Framework ...		0%	1.5 MB	0 MB/s	0 Mbps
🖥 Host Process for Windows Tasks		0%	2.4 MB	0 MB/s	0 Mbps
▷ 🖥 Microsoft Windows Search Inde...		0%	5.6 MB	0 MB/s	0 Mbps
🖨 Print driver host for applications		0%	0.3 MB	0 MB/s	0 Mbps

⌃ Fewer details   End task

Figure 5-2:
Task
Manager
ranks
processes
in real time.

Task Manager Processes

On the Processes tab, Task Manager groups running programs depending on the type of program:

✦ **Apps** are just regular, everyday programs. They're ones you started, or ones that are set up to start automatically.

✦ **Background processes** keep the pieces of your programs and drivers working.

✦ **Windows processes** are similar to background processes, except they're parts of Windows itself.

TIP

You can tap or click a column heading (such as CPU, Memory, Disk, or Network), and Task Manager sorts on that particular value. To update the report, choose View⟹Refresh Now.

As you start new programs, they appear on the Apps list, and any background programs that they bring along appear on the Background processes list. Tiled, full-screen apps, in particular, go to sleep when they aren't being used, so they drop off the Task Manager list. One glance at the Processes tab should give you a good idea if any programs are hogging your machine — for CPU processor cycles, memory, disk access, or tying up the network.

Task Manager Performance

The Performance tab (see Figure 5-3) gives you running graphs of CPU usage, allocated memory, disk activity, and the volume of data running into and out of your machine.

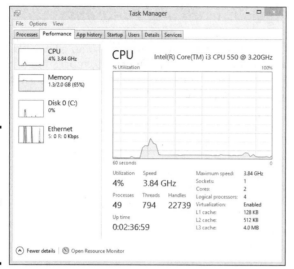

Figure 5-3:
Keep tabs on the four key components of your PC's perfor- mance.

If you want to see much more detailed information — including utilization of each of the cores of a multi-core CPU — tap or click the Open Resource Monitor link at the bottom.

Task Manager App History

The App History tab (see Figure 5-4) keeps a cumulative count of all the time you've spent on each of the various tiled apps from the Windows Store. Tap or click a column header to sort.

Figure 5-4:
A compre- hensive list of all the time you've spent playing, er, using each of the tiled Windows Store apps.

Book VIII
Chapter 5

Using System Tools

Task Manager Startup and Autoruns

No doubt you know that Windows automatically runs certain programs every time you start it, and that those programs can prove, uh, cantankerous at times. The Startup tab, as shown in Figure 5-5, represents a giant step forward for Windows usability. It shows you all the programs that are started automatically each time you log on to Windows.

Figure 5-5:
A subset of those cycle-stealing auto-startup programs.

If you want to disable an autorunning program, tap or click the program, choose Disable, and then reboot Windows.

The Task Manager Startup tab shows you the application programs, their helper programs, and sometimes problematic programs that use well-known tricks to run every time Windows starts. Unfortunately, really bad programs frequently find ways to squirrel themselves away, so they don't appear on this list.

Microsoft distributes an Autoruns program that digs into every nook and cranny of Windows, ferreting out autorunning programs — even Windows programs.

Autoruns started as a free product from the small Sysinternals company, and owes its existence to Mark Russinovich (now a celebrated novelist) and Bryce Cogswell, two of the most knowledgeable Windows folks on the planet. In July 2006, Microsoft bought Sysinternals. Mark became a Microsoft Demigod, er, Fellow. (He's since become a phenomenal fiction writer, as well.) Microsoft promised that all the free Sysinternals products would remain free. And wonder of wonders, that's exactly what happened.

To get Autoruns working, download it as a Zip file from `http://technet.microsoft.com/en-us/sysinternals/bb963902.aspx` and extract the Zip. `Autoruns.exe` is the program you want. Tap or double-click to run it; no installation required.

After Autoruns is working on your computer, the following tips can help you start using the program:

✦ **Autoruns lists an enormous number of auto-starting programs,** some of which appear in the most obscure corners of Windows. The Everything list shown in Figure 5-6 lists every auto-starting program, in the order they're run.

Figure 5-6: Autoruns shows you every program that starts automatically.

✦ **Autoruns has many options** — you can get a good overview on the Microsoft Ask the Performance Team blog, `http://bit.ly/I2VUxa`. The one I use most is the ability to hide all the auto-starting Microsoft programs. It's easy. Choose Options⇨Filter Options and then select the Hide Microsoft Entries box. The result is a clean list of all the foreign stuff being launched automatically by Windows.

✦ **Autoruns can suspend an auto-starting program.** To do so, deselect the box to the left of the program and reboot Windows. If you zap an auto-starting program and your computer doesn't work right, run Autoruns again and select the box. Easy.

Of course, you shouldn't disable an auto-starting program just because it looks superfluous, or even because you figure it contributes to global warming or slow startups, whichever comes first. As a general rule, if you don't know *exactly* what an auto-starting program does, don't touch it. It's not nice to fool with the support for those tiled apps, in particular..

On the other hand, if you concentrate on auto-starting programs that don't come from Microsoft, you may find a few things that you don't want or need — items that deserve to get consigned to the bit bucket.

Task Manager Users

If you're using an administrator account, the Users tab lets you look at what's happening with every person who's currently logged on to your computer, as shown in Figure 5-7.

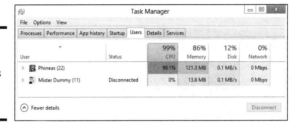

Figure 5-7:
See what
other users
are doing
right now.

The number that appears to the right of the User's name is the number of processes the user has going at that point. Tap or click the wedge to the left of the user's name and you see a full list of processes.

It's pretty creepy in a voyeur kind of way, but one interesting capability is available — and mislabeled — on this tab. You can write a message that will appear on the Windows lock screen. To do so, tap and hold or right-click a username, and then choose Send Message. Task Manager shows you the dialog box in Figure 5-8.

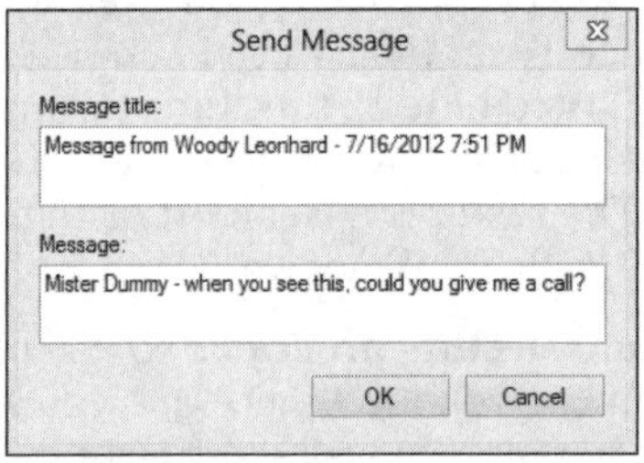

Figure 5-8:
Create a
message
for the
Windows
lock screen.

You'd think that the message would be sent to the person you "send" it to, but it isn't. Instead, it appears on the computer's lock screen, the next time the lock screen appears. Before anyone can sign in to the computer, they have to click OK to get rid of the message.

Task Manager Details and Services

If you used Task Manager in Windows 7 or earlier, you've seen this version, shown in Figure 5-9. The Details tab shows all the running processes, regardless of which user is attached to the process.

Figure 5-9:
All the details about every process appear here.

Name	PID	Status	User name	CPU	Memory (p...	Description
dwm.exe	4568	Running	DWM-2	00	208 K	Desktop Window M...
dwm.exe	1228	Running	DWM-3	98	22,596 K	Desktop Window M...
dasHost.exe	1324	Running	LOCAL SE...	00	724 K	Device Association F...
svchost.exe	760	Running	LOCAL SE...	00	13,016 K	Host Process for Wi...
svchost.exe	980	Running	LOCAL SE...	00	4,076 K	Host Process for Wi...
svchost.exe	1144	Running	LOCAL SE...	00	7,596 K	Host Process for Wi...
svchost.exe	1864	Running	LOCAL SE...	00	2,980 K	Host Process for Wi...
svchost.exe	2284	Running	LOCAL SE...	00	3,020 K	Host Process for Wi...
taskhost.exe	2168	Running	LOCAL SE...	00	2,024 K	Host Process for Wi...
explorer.exe	4136	Running	Mister Du...	00	5,720 K	Windows Explorer
GoogleUpdate.exe	3364	Running	Mister Du...	00	1,108 K	Google Installer
GoogleUpdate.exe	3820	Running	Mister Du...	00	692 K	Google Installer
LiveComm.exe	4468	Running	Mister Du...	00	4,200 K	Live Communicatio...
rundll32.exe	4588	Running	Mister Du...	00	936 K	Windows host proce...
RuntimeBroker.exe	2952	Running	Mister Du...	00	1,384 K	Runtime Broker
taskhost.exe	4300	Running	Mister Du...	00	1,396 K	Host Process for Wi...
taskhost.exe	4308	Running	Mister Du...	00	1,316 K	Host Process for Wi...

The Services tab, similarly, shows all the Windows services that have been started. Once in a very blue moon, you may find a Windows error message that some Windows service or another (say, the printer service, or some sort of networking service) isn't running. This tab is where you can tell whether the service is really running.

Installing a Second Hard Drive

You probably know how hard it is to install an external hard drive in a Windows 8 PC. Basically, you turn off the computer, plug the USB or eSATA cable into your computer, turn it on . . . and you're done.

Yes, external hard drive manufacturers have fancy software. No, you don't want it. Windows knows all the tricks. If you install one additional hard drive, internal or external, you can set up File History (see Book VIII, Chapter 1). Install two additional drives, internal or external, and you can turn on Storage Spaces (see Book VII, Chapter 4). None of the Windows programs need or want whatever programs the hard drive manufacturer offers.

Book VIII
Chapter 5

Using System Tools

Installing a second internal hard drive into a PC that's made to take two or more hard drives is only a little bit more complex than plugging an external drive into your USB port. Almost all desktop PCs can handle more than one internal hard drive. Some laptops can, too.

Here's how to do it:

1. **Turn off your PC. Crack open the case, put in the new hard drive, attach the cables and secure the drive, probably with screws. Close the case. Turn on the power and log in to Windows.**

If you need help, the manufacturer's website has instructions. Adding the physical drive inside the computer case is really very simple — even if you've never seen the inside of your computer.

2. **On the Start screen, type** disk man, **choose Settings on the right, and choose Create and Format Hard Disk Partitions on the right. Or right-click the lower-left corner of the screen and choose Disk Management.**

The Disk Management dialog box appears, as shown in Figure 5-10.

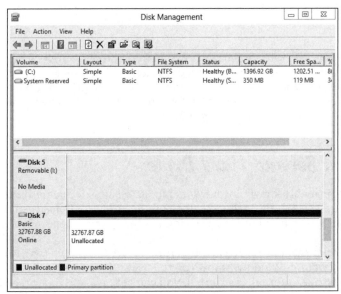

Figure 5-10:
Add the new
drive here.

3. **Scroll down the list at the bottom and find your new drive, probably marked Unallocated.**

In Figure 5-10, the new drive is identified as Disk 7.

4. **On the right, in the Unallocated area, tap and hold or right-click, and then choose New Simple Volume.**

   The New Simple Volume Wizard appears, as shown in Figure 5-11.

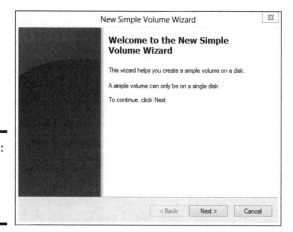

Figure 5-11:
The wizard takes you through all the steps.

5. **Tap or click Next.**

   You're asked to specify a volume size.

6. **Leave the numbers just as they are — you want to use the whole drive — and tap or click Next.**

   The wizard asks you to specify a drive letter. `D:` is most common.

7. **If you really, really want to give the drive a different letter, go ahead and do so (most people should leave it at `D:`). Tap or click Next.**

   The wizard wants to know whether you want to use something other than the NTFS file system, or to set a different allocation unit. You don't.

8. **Tap or click Next; then tap or click Finish.**

   Windows whirs and chunks, and when it's done, you have a spanking new drive, ready to be used.

If you have three or more drives in, or attached to, your PC, consider setting up Storage Spaces. It's a remarkable piece of technology that'll keep redundant copies of all your data and protect you from catastrophic failure of any of your data drives. See Book VII, Chapter 4 for details.

**Book VIII
Chapter 5**

Using System Tools

Changing your C: drive

Whoa nelly! If you've never seen a Windows 8 PC running an SSD (Solid State Drive) as the system drive, you better nail down the door and shore up the, uh, windows. Changing your C: drive from a run of the mill rotating platter to a fast, shiny new Solid State Drive can make everything work so much faster. Really.

Unfortunately, getting from an HDD (hard disk drive) C: to an SSD C: ain't exactly 1-2-3.

Part of the problem is the mechanics of transferring your Windows 8 system from an HDD to an SSD: You need to create a copy (not exactly a clone) that'll boot Windows. Part of the problem is moving all the extra junk off the C: drive, so the SSD isn't swamped with all the flotsam and jetsam you've come to know and love in Windows.

Most of the drive cloning/backup/restore techniques developed over the past decade work when you want to move from a smaller drive to a bigger one. However, replacing your HDD C: drive with an SSD C: drive almost always involves going from a larger drive to a smaller one.

As this book went to press, there weren't any clearly superior methods for swapping your main hard drive (or C: drive). Opinions vary on using third-party software (such as Acronis True Image or Macrium Reflect Free), with some people encountering problems and others saying it worked fine. Windows 7 had a Create System Image function that could be coerced into performing the kind of backup and restore that are required (see http://ssdfreaks.com/content/664/how-to-clone-hdd-to-ssd-with-windows-7s-own-software). But Windows 8 hides those functions (see Book VIII, Chapter 1), and Microsoft doesn't recommend using them.

My best advice at this point? Bite the bullet and re-install Windows 8. You can do it. Your SSD will thank you for the fresh, new copy of Windows.

Running a Virtual Machine

At its heart, a virtual machine (or VM) is a sleight of hand. A parlor trick. You set up a "machine" inside Windows that isn't really a machine; it's a program. Then you stick other programs inside the virtual machine. The programs think they're working inside a real machine, when they aren't — they're working inside another program.

Windows 8 Pro (and Enterprise) includes Hyper-V and all the ancillary software (drivers and such) you need to run a virtual machine inside of Windows. If you only have the "regular" version of Windows 8, you need to look elsewhere. (Hint: Use Google and find a copy of VirtualBox.)

In addition, to get the Hyper-V program going, you must be running the 64-bit version of Windows 8 Pro, with at least 2GB of memory. The hardware itself has to be fairly up to date because it has to support the *Second Level Address Translation (SLAT)* capability. You can find a good overview of testing for SLAT on the How-To Geek site, `www.howtogeek.com/73318/how-to-check-if-your-cpu-supports-second-level-address-translation-slat`.

Why would you want to use a VM? Many reasons:

+ Say you have an old program that runs only under Windows XP or Windows 95 (or even DOS, for that matter). You set up a VM, install XP or 95 (or DOS), and then stick the old program inside the VM. The old program doesn't know any better — it's fat, dumb, and happy working inside of XP. But you're watching from the outside. You can interact with the old program, type inside it, click inside it, give it disk space to play with, or attach it to a network interface card. A fake ("virtual") one, of course, that works just like the real thing.

+ You want to try a different operating system. Maybe you want to play with Linux for a while, or take Windows Server 2012 for a ride. Or you get nostalgic for the days of Windows Me. Or Microsoft Bob. Set up a virtual machine for each of the operating systems and install the operating system in the VM. Then close each VM and save it. When you want to play with one of the OSs, just crank up the right VM, and you're on your way.

+ You need to isolate your "real" system while you try something that's tricky or experimental or potentially dangerous. If you have a VM that gets infected with a virus, the virus doesn't necessarily spread to your main machine. If you try a weird program inside a VM and it crashes, restarting the VM is much easier than restarting your PC, and if there are any bizarre side effects — say, weird Registry changes — they won't affect your main machine.

+ I use VMs when I'm experimenting with hooking computers together. It's pretty easy to set up several VMs, one running XP, say, another with Win7, and one more with Win8. Each of them thinks that it's connected to the other two. That way, I can test settings and figure out how to get them to communicate with each other.

Hyper-V is a big, complex product, worthy of a book unto itself. In this chapter, I just get you started and then point you to some sources of information that'll help you take full advantage of the product.

Here's how to turn on Hyper-V:

1. **On the Start screen, type** features.

2. **On the right, tap or click Settings; on the left, tap or click the Turn Windows Features On or Off link.**

The Windows Features dialog box appears, as shown in Figure 5-12.

Figure 5-12: Hyper-V has to be turned on before you can use it.

3. **Select the Hyper-V box, and then tap or click OK.**

Windows installs two programs, the Hyper-V Manager and the Hyper-V Virtual Machine Connection. Both appear as tiles on the far right side of the Start screen.

4. **Reboot after the installation finishes.**

When Windows comes back, you're ready to set up your first virtual machine. Here's how:

1. **On the Start screen, tap or click the Hyper-V Manager tile.**

Hyper-V brings up the rather intimidating screen shown in Figure 5-13.

2. **On the right, tap or click Virtual Switch Manager.**

The Virtual Switch Manager for your PC appears, as shown in Figure 5-14.

I assume you want your new VM to be able to communicate with the outside world — for an Internet connection, if nothing else — and it's easiest to set up that connection before you create the VM. The connection is done through a *virtual switch,* which ties a connection inside the virtual machine to a physical device on the outside, in the real world.

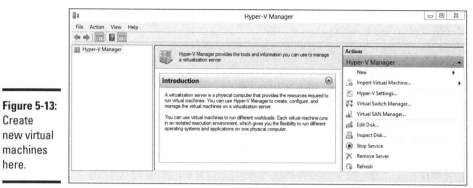

Figure 5-13:
Create
new virtual
machines
here.

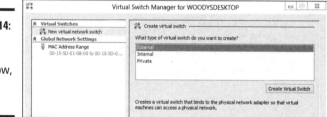

Figure 5-14:
Set up
a virtual
switch now,
while it's
easy.

3. **On the left, tap or click New Virtual Switch.**

You're asked to set up properties for the new virtual switch, as shown in Figure 5-15.

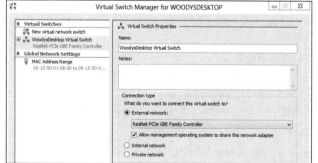

Figure 5-15:
Flesh out
the virtual
switch here.

4. **Give the new virtual switch a name and tap or click OK.**

Chances are good you want your VM to connect to a physical network adapter in the outside world, so leave the default selections the way they are.

**Book VIII
Chapter 5**

Using System Tools

Hyper-V goes back to the Hyper-V Manager dialog box (refer to Figure 5-13).

5. **On the right, choose New⇨Virtual Machine.**

The New Virtual Machine Wizard starts.

6. **Tap or click Next.**

You're asked to specify a name and location for the VM, as shown in Figure 5-16.

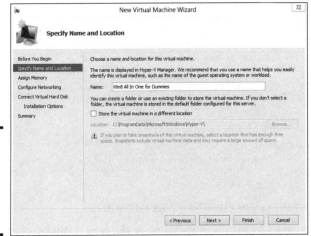

Figure 5-16:
Start by giving the VM a name you will recognize.

7. **Type a name that will immediately tell you what you're running on this VM; and if you need to move the location of the VM (remember the VM is a program, and needs to store its files somewhere), change the location.**

8. **Tap or click Next.**

VMs take up a lot of room, and each time you take a "snapshot," you store away the entire status of the VM — including any data on the disks, copies of installed programs, and all settings.

The wizard asks how much memory you want to assign for startup.

9. **If you're going to run Windows 7 or Windows 8, set startup memory at 1024MB and select the Use Dynamic Memory for this Virtual Machine box.**

Linux fans can get by with 512MB and no Dynamic Memory.

10. **Tap or click Next.**

You want enough memory so the VM doesn't start thrashing, but you don't want to specify too much in case you try to start many VMs at the same time.

Hyper-V wants to know whether you want to connect the VM to a network adapter. You set up the virtual connection already, so it's easy.

11. **In the Connection box, choose the name of the connection that you created in Steps 3 and 4. Tap or click Next.**

Hyper-V wants you to set up the virtual hard disk.

In case you're wondering, the virtual hard disks inside Hyper-V are quite different from the disk virtualization done in Windows Storage Spaces. Don't be confused. They work in completely different worlds.

12. **Type a new name if you like, and then tap or click Next.**

The defaults here are fine.

You see the final key step in the wizard, which asks you how you want to install the operating system on the VM, as shown in Figure 5-17.

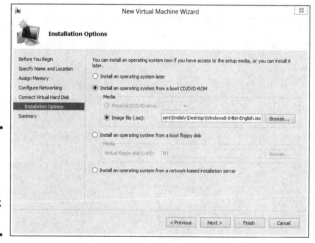

Figure 5-17:
Every VM needs an operating system. Pick yours here.

13. **If you have a Windows installation disk or file, select Install an Operating System from a Boot CD/DVD-ROM and tell Hyper-V where to find the Boot CD/DVD (or ISO file, if you have one).**

14. **Tap or click Next.**

   Hyper-V gives you a last look at your settings.

15. **Tap or click Finish.**

   Your new VM appears in the list of virtual machines.

To start the VM, tap or double-click it, and then if necessary choose Action⇨Start. You see something like the VM in Figure 5-18, which runs Windows 8 in a VM inside Windows 8.

The first thing you want to do with your new VM is add an Integration Services Setup Disk, so you can control the VM more readily. To do so, choose Action⇨Insert Integration Services Setup Disk.

That just barely scratches the surface of Hyper-V. For more info, start at Microsoft's Hyper-V support center at `http://technet.microsoft.com/en-us/windowsserver/dd448604`.

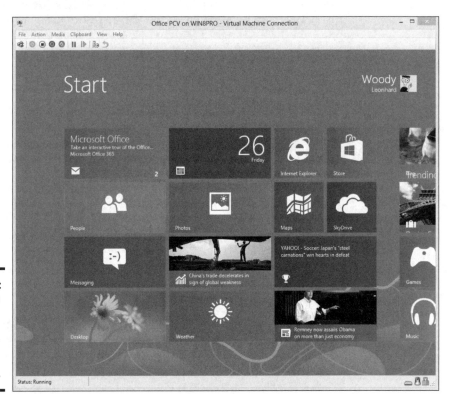

Figure 5-18: A Windows 8 virtual machine running inside Windows 8.

Book IX

Securing Windows 8

The 5th Wave   By Rich Tennant

"Well, the first level of Windows 8 security seems good – I can't get the shrink-wrapping off."

Contents at a Glance

Chapter 1: Spies, Spams, Scams — They're Out to Get You

*W*indows XP had more holes than a prairie-dog field. Vista was built on top of Windows XP, and the holes were hidden better. Windows 7 included truly innovative security capabilities; it represented the first really significant break from XP's lethargic approach to security.

Windows 8 includes marginal security improvements to Windows itself, but better safety nets to keep you from shooting yourself in the foot. Also a fully functional, very capable antivirus program is built in. That's important.

When you hear about a mass infection, it's invariably on XP computers. There's a reason why. It's getting harder and harder to take out Windows. Of course, the bad guys are getting smarter and smarter — and they have more money these days.

In this chapter, I explain the source of real threats. (More details follow in the upcoming chapters in this minibook.) I bet it'll surprise you to find out that Adobe and Oracle let more bad guys into Windows boxes than Microsoft. I also take you outside the box, to show you the kinds of problems people face with their computer systems and to look at a few key solutions.

Most of all, I want you to understand that (1) you shouldn't take a loaded gun, point it at your foot, aim carefully, and pull the trigger, and (2) if you're smart and can control your clicking finger, you don't need to spend a penny on malware protection.

Understanding the Hazards — and the Hoaxes

Many of the best-known Internet-borne scares in the past decade — the Rustocks, Waledacs, Esthosts, Confickers, Mebroots, Bagles, Netskys, Melissas, ILOVEYOUs, Blasters and Slammers, and their ilk — work by using the programmability built into the computer application itself or by taking advantage of Windows holes to inject themselves into unprotected machines (see Figure 1-1).

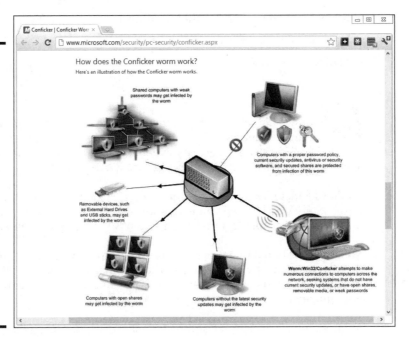

Figure 1-1: The ways the Conficker worm can enter a computer, employing program-mability built into Windows or security holes that had been patched months earlier.

Fast-forward a dozen years and the concepts have changed. The old threats are still there, but they've taken on a new twist: The scent of money, and sometimes political motivation, has made *cracking* (or breaking into PCs for nefarious ends) far more sophisticated. What started as a bunch of miscreants playing programmer one-upmanship at your expense has turned into a profitable — sometimes highly profitable — business enterprise.

Where's the money? At least at this moment — and for the foreseeable future — the greatest profits are made by using botnets and phishing attacks. That's where you should expect the most sophisticated, most damnably difficult attacks. Unless you're running a nuclear reactor.

The primary infection vectors

How do people *really* get infected?

According to Microsoft's Security Intelligence Report 11, the single greatest security gap is the one between your ears. See Figure 1-2.

Many years ago, the biggest PC threat came from newly discovered security holes: The bad guys use the holes before you get your machine patched, and you're toast. They traded 'em like baseball cards. Those holes still get a lot of attention, especially in the press, but they aren't the leading cause of infection. Not even close. A very large majority of infections happen when people get tricked into clicking something they shouldn't.

In the last couple of years, security holes in Windows have fallen by the wayside, when it comes to infecting Windows machines. Depending on whose statistics you read, something like 70 to 90 percent of all Windows infections in recent years came through Java, Flash, and Adobe Reader. You go to a malicious website; click something you shouldn't click; and Java, Flash, or a bad PDF file processed by Adobe Acrobat Reader jumps out and takes over your machine. Sometimes you don't need to click, especially if you're using older versions of Internet Explorer.

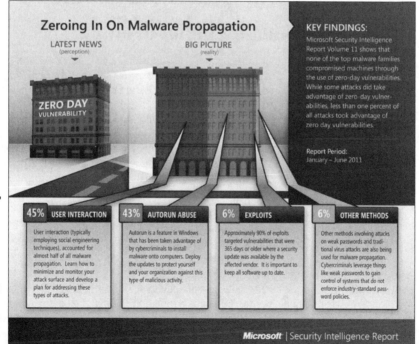

Figure 1-2: Most infections happen when people don't think about what they're doing.

Zombies and botnets

Every month, Microsoft posts a new Malicious Software Removal Tool that scans PCs for malware and, in many cases, removes it. In a recent study, Microsoft reported that 62 percent of all PC systems that were found to have malicious software also had backdoors. That's a sobering figure.

A *backdoor* program breaks through the usual Windows security measures and allows a cretin to take control of your computer over the Internet, effectively turning your machine into a zombie. The most sophisticated backdoors allow creeps to adapt (upgrade, if you will) the malicious software running on a subverted machine. And they do it by remote control.

Backdoors frequently arrive on your PC when you install a program you want, not realizing that the backdoor came along for the ride.

Less commonly, PCs acquire backdoors when they come down with some sort of infection: The ZeuS, Rustock, Waledac, TDL4/Alureon, Conficker, Mebroot, Mydoom, and Sobig worms installed backdoors. Many of the infections occur on PCs that haven't kept Java, Flash, or the Adobe Acrobat Reader up to date. The most common mechanism for infection is a *buffer overflow* (see the nearby "What's a buffer overflow" sidebar).

What's a buffer overflow?

If you've been following the progress of malware in general, and the beatings delivered to Windows in particular, you've no doubt run across the term buffer overflow or buffer overrun — a favorite tool in the arsenal of many virus writers. A buffer overflow may sound mysterious, but it is, at its heart, quite simple.

Programmers set aside small areas in their programs to transfer data from one program to another. Those places are buffers. A problem arises when too much data is put in a buffer (or if you look at it from the other direction, when the buffer is too small to hold all the data that's being put in it). You might think that having ten pounds of offal in a five-pound bag would make the program scream bloody murder, but many programs aren't smart enough to look, much less cry uncle and give up.

When too much data exists in the buffer, some of it can spill into the program itself. If the cretin who's stuffing too much data into the buffer is very clever, he/she/it may be able to convince the program that the extra data isn't data, but is instead another part of the program, waiting to be run. The worm sticks a lot of data in a small space and ensures that the piece that flops out will perform whatever malicious deed the worm's creator wants. When the offal hits the fan, the program finds itself executing data that was stuffed into the buffer — running a program that was written by the worm's creator. That's how a buffer overrun can take control of your computer.

Every worm that uses a buffer-overrun security hole in Windows takes advantage of a stupid programming error inside Windows, but nowadays it's more common for the buffer overflows to happen in Flash or Java.

A cretin who controls one machine by way of a backdoor can't claim much street "cred." But someone who puts together a *botnet* — a collection of hundreds or thousands of PCs — can take his zombies to the bank:

✦ A botnet running a *keylogger* (a program that watches what you type and sporadically sends the data to the botnet's controller) can gather all sorts of valuable information. The single biggest problem facing those who gather and disseminate keylogger information? Bulk — the sheer volume of stolen information. How do you scan millions of characters of logged data and retrieve a bank account number or a password?

✦ Unscrupulous businesses hire botnet controllers to disseminate spam, "harvest" e-mail addresses, and even direct coordinated distributed denial-of-service (DDoS) attacks against rivals' websites. (A *DDoS attack* guides thousands of PCs to go to a particular website simultaneously, blocking legitimate use.)

There's a fortune to be made in botnets. The Rustock botnet alone was responsible for somewhere between 10 and 30 *billion* pieces of spam per day. Spammers paid the Rustock handlers, either directly or on commission, based on the number of referrals.

The most successful botnets run as *rootkits,* programs (or collections of programs) that operate deep inside Windows, concealing files and making it extremely difficult to detect their presence.

You probably first heard about rootkits in late 2005, when a couple of security researchers discovered that certain CDs from Sony BMG surreptitiously installed rootkits on computers: If you merely played the CD on your computer, the rootkit took hold. Several lawsuits later, Sony finally saw the error of its ways and vowed to stop distributing rootkits with its CDs. Nice guys. (The researchers, Mark Russinovich and Bryce Cogswell, were later hired by Microsoft.)

Microsoft deserves a lot of credit for taking down botnets in innovative, lawyer-laden ways. In October 2010, 116 people were arrested worldwide for running fraudulent banking transactions, thanks to Microsoft's tracking abilities. When the folks of Microsoft went after the ZeuS botnet, they convinced a handful of companies whose logos were being used to propagate the botnet to go to court. The assembled group used the RICO laws — the racketeering laws in the U.S. — to get a takedown order. On March 23, 2012, U.S. Marshals took out two command centers — one in Illinois, the other in Pennsylvania — and effectively shut down ZeuS. Microsoft also led the efforts to take down the Waledac, Rustock, and Kelihos botnets.

What about Stuxnet?

Few computer topics have sucked in the mainstream press as thoroughly as the Stuxnet worm — the Windows-borne piece of malware that apparently took out several centrifuges in Iran's uranium enrichment facility.

Here's what I know for sure about Stuxnet: It's carried by Windows, but doesn't do anything dastardly until it finds that it's connected to a specific kind of Siemens computer that's used for industrial automation. When it finds that it's connected to that specific kind of Siemens computer, it plants a rootkit on the computer that disrupts operation of whatever the computer's controlling. And that specific Siemens computer controlled the centrifuges at Iran's enrichment plant.

Anything beyond that is speculation. The people who wrote Stuxnet are very, very adept at both Windows infection methods and Siemens computer programming. David Sanger, Chief Washington Correspondent for The New York Times, claims convincingly in his book Confront and Conceal (published by Crown) that Stuxnet originated as a collaboration between the U.S. National Security Agency and a secret Israeli military unit. But there's no definitive confirmation about the source of Stuxnet — nor about the damage it caused.

That said, Microsoft has been roundly criticized by members of the security community for "hampering and even compromising a number of large international investigations in the U.S., Europe, and Asia" while trying to dispense swift justice (www.krebsonsecurity.com/2012/04/microsoft-responds-to-critics-over-botnet-bruhaha).

Phishing

Do you think that message from Wells Fargo (or eBay, the IRS, PayPal, Citibank, a smaller regional bank, Visa, MasterCard, or whatever) asking to verify your account password (Social Security number, account number, address, telephone number, mother's maiden name, or whatever) looks official? Think again.

Did you get a message from someone on eBay saying that you had better pay for the computer you bought or else he'll report you? Gotcha. Perhaps a notification that you have received an online greeting card from a family member — and when you try to retrieve it, you have to join the greeting card site and enter a credit card number? Gotcha again.

Phishing — sending e-mail that attempts to extract personal information from you, usually by using a bogus website — has in many cases reached levels of sophistication that exceed the standards of the financial institutions themselves. Some phishing messages, such as the bogus message in Figure 1-3, warn you about the evils of phishing, in an attempt to persuade you to send your account number and password to a scammer in Kazbukistan (or New York).

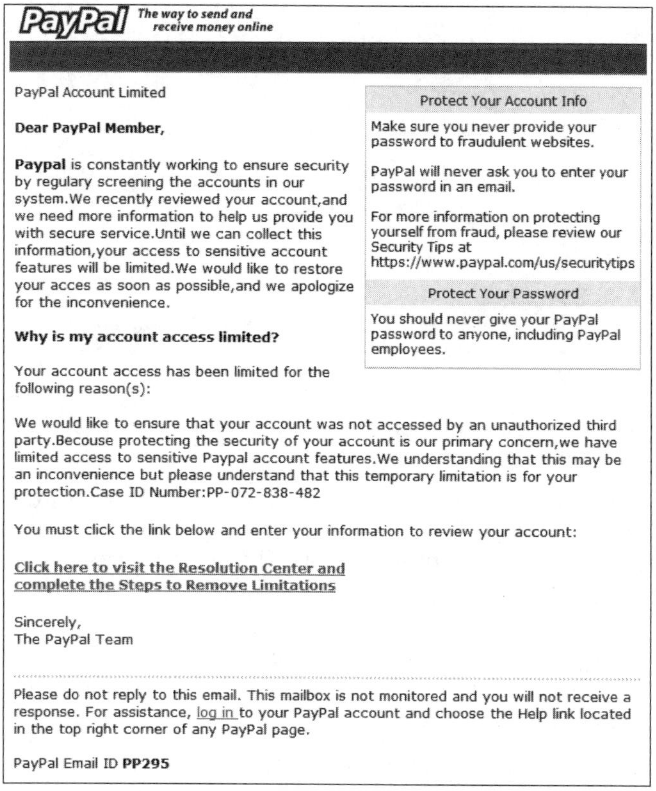

Figure 1-3:
If you click
the link, you
open a page
that looks
much like
the PayPal
page,
and any
information
you enter
is sent to a
scammer.

> **PayPal** The way to send and receive money online
>
> PayPal Account Limited
>
> **Dear PayPal Member,**
>
> **Paypal** is constantly working to ensure security by regulary screening the accounts in our system.We recently reviewed your account,and we need more information to help us provide you with secure service.Until we can collect this information,your access to sensitive account features will be limited.We would like to restore your acces as soon as possible,and we apologize for the inconvenience.
>
> **Why is my account access limited?**
>
> Your account access has been limited for the following reason(s):
>
> We would like to ensure that your account was not accessed by an unauthorized third party.Becouse protecting the security of your account is our primary concern,we have limited access to sensitive Paypal account features.We understanding that this may be an inconvenience but please understand that this temporary limitation is for your protection.Case ID Number:PP-072-838-482
>
> You must click the link below and enter your information to review your account:
>
> **Click here to visit the Resolution Center and complete the Steps to Remove Limitations**
>
> Sincerely,
> The PayPal Team
>
> ----
>
> Please do not reply to this email. This mailbox is not monitored and you will not receive a response. For assistance, log in to your PayPal account and choose the Help link located in the top right corner of any PayPal page.
>
> PayPal Email ID **PP295**
>
> **Protect Your Account Info**
> Make sure you never provide your password to fraudulent websites.
>
> PayPal will never ask you to enter your password in an email.
>
> For more information on protecting yourself from fraud, please review our Security Tips at https://www.paypal.com/us/securitytips
>
> **Protect Your Password**
> You should never give your PayPal password to anyone, including PayPal employees.

Here's how phishing works:

1. A scammer, often using a fake name and a stolen credit card, sets up a website.

   Usually it's quite a professional-looking site — in some cases, indistinguishable from the authentic site.

2. The website asks for personal information — most commonly, your account number and password or the PIN for your ATM card. See Figure 1-4 for an example.

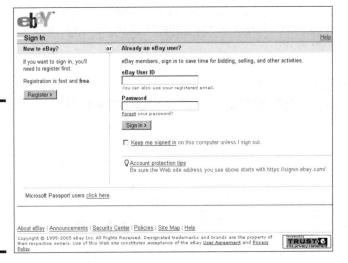

3. The scammer turns spammer and sends hundreds of thousands of bogus messages.

   The messages include a clickable link to the fake website and a plausible story about how you must go to the website, log on, and do something to avoid dire consequences. The From address on the messages is spoofed so that the message appears to come from the company in question.

   The message usually includes official logos — many even include links to the real website, even though they encourage you to click through to the fake site.

4. A small percentage of the recipients of the spam e-mail open it and click through to the fake site.

5. If they enter their information, it's sent directly to the scammer.

6. The scammer watches incoming traffic from the fake website, gathers the information typed by gullible people, and uses it quickly — typically, by logging on to the bank's website and attempting a transfer or by burning a fake ATM card and using the PIN.

7. Within a day or two — or sometimes just hours — the website is shut down and everything disappears into thin ether.

Phishing has become hugely popular because of the sheer numbers involved. Say a scammer sends 1 million e-mail messages advising Wells Fargo customers to log on to their accounts. Only a small fraction of all the people who receive the phishing message will be Wells Fargo customers, but if the hit rate is just 1 percent, that's 10,000 customers.

Most of the Wells Fargo customers who receive the message are smart enough to ignore it. But a sizable percentage — maybe 10 percent, maybe just 1 percent — will click through. That's somewhere between 100 and 1,000 suckers, er, customers.

If half the people who click through provide their account details, the scammer gets 50 to 500 account numbers and passwords. If most of those arrive within a day of sending the phishing message, the scammer stands to make a pretty penny indeed — and she can disappear with hardly a trace.

I'm not talking about using your credit card online. Online credit card transactions are as safe as they are face to face — more so, actually, because if you use a U.S.-based credit card, you aren't liable for any loss caused by somebody snatching your card information or any other form of fraud. I use my credit cards online all the time. You should, too. (See "Using your credit cards safely online," later in this chapter, for more information.)

Here's how to fight against phishing:

✦ **Use the latest versions of Internet Explorer, Firefox, or Chrome.** All three contain sophisticated — although not perfect — antiphishing features that warn you before you venture to a phishy site. See the warning in Figure 1-5.

Figure 1-5:
If enough people report a site as being dangerous, you see a warning like this one from Firefox.

Reported Web Forgery!

This web page at new11010scb.com has been reported as a web forgery and has been blocked based on your security preferences.

Web forgeries are designed to trick you into revealing personal or financial information by imitating sources you may trust.

Entering any information on this web page may result in identity theft or other fraud.

[Get me out of here!] [Why was this page blocked?]

Ignore this warning

✦ **If you encounter a website that looks like it may be a phishing site, report it.** Use the tools in IE, Firefox, or Chrome. Use all three, if you have a chance! Here's how:

- *In the desktop version of Internet Explorer,* tap or click the Tools icon (the one that looks like a gear) and choose Safety, Report Unsafe Website. In the tiled full-screen version of IE, swipe from the top or bottom, or right-click, choose the Page Tools icon (which looks like a wrench), and choose View on the Desktop. That takes you to the desktop version of IE, where you can report the page.

- *Chrome and Firefox* use the same malicious site database. To report a site, go to `www.google.com/safebrowsing/report_badware`.

✦ **If you receive an e-mail message that contains any links to the web, don't click them.** Nowadays, almost all messages with links to commercial sites are phishing come-ons. Financial institutions, in particular, don't send messages with links any more — and few other companies would dare. If you feel motivated to check out a dire message — for example, if it looks like somebody on eBay is planning to sue you for something you didn't do — open the tiled full-screen version of your favorite browser (which is inherently less exposed) and type the address of the company by hand.

You can see which site a link *really* points to by hovering your mouse over the link. There's no tap equivalent just yet.

✦ **Never include personal information in an e-mail message and send it.** Don't give out any of your personal information unless you manually log on to the company's website. Remember that unless you encrypt your e-mail messages, they travel over the Internet in plain text form. Anybody who's "sniffing" the mail can see everything you've written. It's roughly analogous to sending a postcard.

✦ **If you receive a phishing message that may be new or different, check** `www.millersmiles.co.uk` **to see whether it's a well-known, uh, phish.** If you don't see your phish listed, submit a copy using the instructions at `www.millersmiles.co.uk/submit.php`. Hold on to the message for a while to see whether the authorities need a copy of the message header: If so, it'll send you instructions.

MillerSmiles (see Figure 1-6) has a wealth of information on phishing — more than 2 million samples of phishing messages, at last count — including an invaluable description of the steps you should take if you accidentally give your personal information to a phisher. See `www.millersmiles.co.uk/identitytheft/oah-6.htm`.

Figure 1-6:
MillerSmiles
maintains
a huge
database
of phishing
messages
and offers
sage advice
about
identifying,
reporting,
and
recovering
from
phishing
attacks.

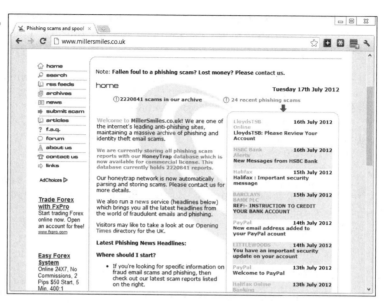

419 scams

> *Greetings,*
>
> *I am writing this letter to you in good faith and I hope my contact with you will transpire into a mutual relationship now and forever. I am Mrs. Omigod Mugambi, wife of the late General Rufus Mugambi, former Director of Mines for the Dufus Diamond Dust Co Ltd of Central Eastern Lower Leone . . .*

I'm sure you're smart enough to pass over e-mail like that. At least, I hope so. It's an obvious setup for the classic 419 ("four one nine") scam — a scam so common that it has a widely accepted name, which derives from Nigerian Criminal Code Chapter 38, Article 419.

Much more sophisticated versions of the 419 scam are making the rounds today. The basic approach is to convince you to send money to someone, usually via Western Union. If you send the money, you'll never see it again, no matter how hard the sell or dire the threatened consequences.

There's a reason why everybody gets so much 419 scam e-mail. It's a huge business. Some people reckon it's the third to fifth largest revenue-generating business in Nigeria. I have no way of verifying independently whether that's true, but certainly these folks are raking in an enormous amount of money. And they don't all work out of Nigeria: 419 scams are a significant source of foreign exchange in Benin, Sierra Leone, Ghana, Togo, Senegal, and Burkina

Faso, plus just about anywhere else you can mention. Some even originate in the U.S. although, as you see shortly, there are big advantages to working out of small countries.

Here's one of the new variations of the old 419. It all starts when you place an ad that appears online. It doesn't really matter what you're selling, as long as it's physically large and valuable. It doesn't matter where you advertise — I've seen reports of this scam being played on Craigslist advertisers and major online sites, tiny nickel ad publishers, local newspapers, and anywhere else ads are placed.

The scammer sends you an e-mail from a Gmail address. I got one recently that said, "I will like to know if this item is still available for sale?" I wrote back and said, yes, it is, and he'd be most welcome to come and take a look at it. He wrote back:

> "Let me know the price in USD? I am OK with the item it looks like new in the photos I am from Liverpool U.K., i am sorry i will not be able to come for the viewing, i will arrange for the pickup after payment has been made, all documentation will be done by the shipper, so you don't have to worry about that. Thanks"

Three key points:

+ The scammer is using a Gmail address, which can't be traced with anything short of a court order.

+ He claims to be out of the country, which makes pursuing him very difficult.

+ He claims that he has a shipper who will pick up the item. The plot thickens.

Also, his grammar falls somewhere between atrocious and unintelligible. Unfortunately, that isn't a sure sign, but it's not bound to inspire confidence.

I wrote back and gave him a price, but I expressed concern about the shipper. He wrote that he would send the shipper from the U.K. for pickup and said, "I will be paying the PayPal charges from my account and i will be paying directly into your PayPal account without any delay, and i hope you have a PayPal account."

I gave him a dormant PayPal account, listing my address as that of the local police station. He wrote back quite quickly:

> "I have just completed the Payment and i am sure you have received the confirmation from PayPal regarding the Payment. You can check your paypal e-mail for confirmation of payment.a total of 25,982usd was sent,

24,728usd for the item and the extra 1,200usd for my shipper's charges, which you will be sending to the address below via western union" and then he gave me the name of someone in Devon, U.K. "You should send the money soon so that the Pick Up would be scheduled and you would know when the Pick Up would commence, make sure you're home. I advice you to check both your inbox or junk/spam folder for the payment confirmation message."

I then received a message that claimed to be from Service-Intl.PayPal.Com:

"The Transaction will appear as soon as the western union information is received from you,we have to follow this procedure due to some security reason... the Money was sent through the Service Option Secure Payment so that the transaction can be protected with adequate security measures for you to be able to receive your money. The Shipping Company only accept payment through Western Union You have nothing to doubt about, You are safe and secured doing this transaction and your account will be credited immediately the western union receipt of *1,200USD* is received from you."

There's the hook. Of course, the message didn't come from PayPal, much less from `www.paypal.com`. I strung the scammer along for several days. Ultimately he threatened me with legal action, invoking PayPal and the FBI as antagonists, see Figure 1-7.

Figure 1-7: Oh me, oh my, he's going to send the FBI.

In the end, the scammer and his cohorts were quite sloppy. Most of the time when scammers send e-mail from "PayPal," they use a virtual private network (VPN; see Book VIII, Chapter 4) to make it look like the mail came from the U.S. But on three separate occasions, the scammer I was conversing with forgot to turn on the VPN. Using a very simple technique, I traced all three messages back to one specific Internet service provider in Lagos, Nigeria.

So I had three scamming messages with identified IP addresses, the name of a large Internet service provider in Nigeria, and a compelling case for PayPal (to defend its name) and Western Union (which was being used as a drop) to follow up.

I sent copies of the messages to Western Union and PayPal. I got back form letters — it's unlikely that a human even read them. I wrote to the ISP, MTN Nigeria. They responded, but the upshot is disheartening:

> "All our 3G network subscribers now sit behind a small number of IP addresses. This is done via a technology called network address translation (NAT). In essence, it means that one million subscribers may appear to the outside world as one subscriber because they are all using the same IP address."

So now you know why Nigerians love to conduct their scams over the Nigerian 3G network. No doubt MTN Nigeria could sift through their NAT logs and find out who was connected at precisely the right time, but tracing a specific e-mail back to an individual would be difficult, if not impossible — and it would certainly require a court order.

If you know anybody who posts ads online, you might want to warn them.

I'm from Microsoft and I'm here to help

This kind of scam really hurts me, personally, because I've made a career out of helping people with Microsoft problems.

Someone calls and says she's been referred by Microsoft to help with your Windows problem. She's very convincing. She says that she heard about your problem from a post you made online, or from your Internet service provider, or from a computer user group. She even gives a website as reference, a very convincing site that has the Microsoft Registered Partner logo.

You explain the problem to her. Then one of two things happens. Either she requests your 25-character Windows activation key, or she asks for permission to connect to your computer, typically using Remote Assistance (see Book VII, Chapter 2).

If you let her onto your machine, heaven knows what she'll do. (Believe me, these guys are fast and convincing: It's like playing three card monte with a tech support guru.)

If you give her your activation key — or she looks up your validation key while she's controlling your PC — she'll pretend to refer to the "Microsoft registration database" (or something similar), and give you the bad news that your machine is all screwed up, and it's out of warranty, but she can fix it for a mere $189.

As proof positive that your machine's on its last legs, she'll probably show you the Event Viewer. As I mention in Book VIII, Chapter 4, the Event Viewer on a *normal* machine shows all sorts of scary warnings. And that Microsoft Registered Partner stuff? Anybody can become a Microsoft Registered Partner — it takes maybe two minutes, and all you need is a Microsoft account — a Hotmail, Live, or Outlook.com ID. Don't believe it? Go to `http://partner.microsoft.com/40032508` and fill out the forms.

The overwhelming con give-away — the big red flag — in all of this: *Microsoft doesn't work that way.* Think about it. Microsoft isn't going to call you to solve your problems, unless you've received a very specific commitment from a very specific individual in the organization — a commitment that invariably comes only after repeated phone calls on your part, generally accompanied by elevation to lofty levels of the support organization on multiple continents, frequently in conjunction with high-decibel histrionics. Microsoft doesn't respond to random online requests for help by calling a customer. Sorry. Doesn't happen.

If you aren't sure whether you're being conned, ask the person on the other end of the line for your Microsoft Support Case *tracking number* — every MS tech support interaction has a tracking number or Support ID. Then ask for a phone number, and offer to call them back. Con artists won't leave trails.

If the con is being run from overseas — much more common in these days of nearly-free VoIP cold calling — your chances of nailing the perpetrator runs from extremely slim to none. So be overly suspicious of any "Microsoft Expert" who doesn't seem to be calling from your country.

If you've already been conned — given out personal information, or a credit card number — start by contacting your bank or the credit card issuing company, and follow their procedures for reporting identity theft.

0day exploits

What do you do when you discover a brand-new security hole in Windows or Office or another Microsoft product? Why, you sell it, of course.

When a person writes a malicious program that takes advantage of a newly discovered security hole — a hole that even the manufacturer doesn't know about — that malicious program is a *0day exploit*. (Fuddy-duddies call it "zero-day exploit." The hopelessly hip say "sploit.")

0days are valuable. In some cases, very valuable. HP has a subsidiary — *TippingPoint* — that buys 0day exploits. TippingPoint works with the software manufacturer to come up with a fix for the exploit, but at the same time, it sells corporate customers immediate protection against the exploit. "TippingPoint's goal for the Zero Day Initiative is to provide our customers with the world's best intrusion prevention systems and secure converged networking infrastructure." TippingPoint offers up to $10,000 for a solid security hole.

Rumor has it that several less-than-scrupulous sites arrange for the buying and selling of new security holes. Apparently, the Russian hacker group that discovered a vulnerability in the way Windows handles WMF graphics files sold its new hole for $4,000, not realizing that it could've made much more. In 2012, *Forbes Magazine* estimated the value of 0days as ranging from $5,000 to $250,000. You can check it out at the following URL:

```
www.forbes.com/sites/andygreenberg/2012/03/23/shopping-
for-zero-days-an-price-list-for-hackers-secret-
software-exploits/
```

According to Forbes, some government agencies are in the market. Governments certainly buy 0day exploits from Vupen, a notorious 0day brokering firm.

How do you protect yourself from 0day exploits? In some ways, you can't: By definition, nobody sees a 0day coming, although most antivirus products employ some sort of heuristic detection that tries to clamp down on exploits based solely on the behavior of the offensive program. Mostly, you have to rely on the common sense protection that I describe in the section "Getting Protected," later in this chapter. You must also stay informed, which I talk about in the next section.

Staying Informed

When you rely on the evening news to keep yourself informed about the latest threats to your computer's well-being, you quickly discover that the mainstream press frequently doesn't get the details right. Hey, if you were a newswriter with a deadline ten minutes away and you had to figure out how the new Bandersnatch 0day exploit shreds through a Windows TCP/IP stack buffer — and you had to explain your discoveries to a TV audience, at a presumed sixth grade intelligence level — what would you do?

The following sections offer tips on getting the facts.

Relying on reliable sources

Fortunately, some reliable sources of information exist on the Internet. It would behoove you to check them out from time to time, particularly when you hear about a new computer security hole, real or imagined:

✦ **The Microsoft Security Response Center (MSRC) blog** presents thoroughly researched analyses of outstanding threats, from a Microsoft perspective. (`http://blogs.technet.com/msrc`)

The information you see on the MSRC blog is 100 percent Microsoft Party Line — so there's a tendency to add more than a little "spin control" to the announcements. Nevertheless, Microsoft has the most extensive and best resources to analyze and solve Windows problems, and the MSRC blog frequently has inside information that you can't find anywhere else.

✦ **SANS Internet Storm Center (ISC)** pools observations and analysis from thousands of active security researchers. You can generally get the news first — and accurately — from the ISC. (`http://isc.sans.org`)

✦ **Windows Secrets newsletter,** the most-read Windows weekly ever, contains excellent recaps of all the latest problems. Also, my site, AskWoody.com (`www.askwoody.com`), strives to present the latest security information in a way that doesn't require a Ph.D. in computer science. (`www.windowssecrets.com`)

Take a moment right now to look up those sites and add them to your Firefox or Chrome Bookmarks or Internet Explorer Favorites. Unlike the anti-malware software manufacturers' websites, these sites have no particular ax to grind or product to sell. (Well, okay, Microsoft wants to sell you something, but you already bought it, yes?)

Microsoft releases security patches, usually on the second Tuesday of every month. You can get advance notice about upcoming patches on the MSRC blog. When the patches become available, they're described and presented in security bulletins bearing sequential numbers, such as MS13-001, MS13-002, and so on. The patches themselves are attached to Microsoft Knowledge Base (KB) articles with numbers resembling KB 912345. Microsoft keeps the bulletins separate from the patching programs because a single security bulletin may have many associated patches. I talk about the bulletins in Book VIII, Chapter 3.

From time to time, Microsoft also releases security advisories, which generally warn about newly discovered 0day threats in Microsoft products. You can find those, too, at the MSRC blog.

It's hard to keep all the patches straight without a scorecard. I maintain an exhaustive list of patches and their known problems and also the Microsoft patches of the patches (of the patches) on AskWoody.com.

Ditching the hoaxes

Tell me whether you've heard any of these:

✦ "Amazing Speech by Obama!" "CNN News Alert!" "UPS Delivery Failure," "Hundreds killed in *[insert a disaster of your choice],*" "Budweiser Frogs Screensaver!" "Microsoft Security Patch Attached."

✦ A virus will hit your computer if you read any message that includes the phrase "Good Times" in the subject line. (That one was a biggie in late 1994.) Ditto for any of the following messages: "It Takes Guts to Say 'Jesus'," "Win a Holiday," "Help a poor dog win a holiday," "Join the Crew," "pool party," "A Moment of Silence," "an Internet flower for you," "a virtual card for you," or "Valentine's Greetings."

✦ A deadly virus is on the Microsoft *[or insert your favorite company name here]* home page. Don't go there or else your system will die.

✦ If you have a file named *[insert filename here]* on your PC, it contains a virus. Delete it immediately!

They're all hoaxes — not a breath of truth in any of them.

Some hoaxes serve as fronts for real viruses: The message itself is a hoax, a red herring, designed to convince you to do something stupid and infect your system. The message asks (or commands!) you to download a file or run a video that acts suspiciously like an .exe file.

Other hoaxes are just rumors that circulate among well-intentioned people who haven't a clue. Those hoaxes hurt, too. Sometimes, when real worms hit, so much e-mail traffic is generated from warning people to avoid the worm that the well-intentioned watchdogs do more damage than the worm itself! Strange but true.

Do yourself (and me) a favor: If somebody sends you a message that sounds like the following examples, just delete it, eh?

✦ A horrible virus is on the loose that's going to bring down the Internet. (Sheesh. I get enough of that garbage on the nightly news.)

✦ Send a copy of this message to ten of your best friends, and for every copy that's forwarded, Bill Gates will give *[pick your favorite charity]* $10.

✦ Forward a copy of this message to ten of your friends, and put your name at the bottom of the list. In *[pick a random amount of time],* you will receive $10,000 in the mail, or your luck will change for the better. Your eyelids will fall off if you don't forward this message.

✦ Microsoft (Intel, McAfee, Norton, Compaq — whatever) says that you need to double-click the attached file, download something, not download something, go to a specific place, avoid a specific place, and on and on.

If you think you've stumbled on the world's most important virus alert, by way of your uncle's sister-in-law's roommate's hairdresser's soon-to-be-ex-boyfriend (remember that he's the one who's a really smart computer guy, but kind of smelly?), count to ten twice and keep these four important points in mind:

✦ No reputable software company (including Microsoft) distributes patches by e-mail. You should never, ever, open or run an attachment to an e-mail message until you contact the person who sent it to you and confirm that she intended to send it to you.

✦ Chances are very good (I'd say, oh, 99.9999 percent or more) that you're looking at a half-baked hoax that's documented on the web, most likely on the Snopes urban myths site (www.snopes.com).

✦ If the virus or worm is real, Brian Krebs has already written about it. Go to www.krebsonsecurity.com.

✦ If the Internet world is about to collapse, clogged with gazillions of e-mail worms, the worst possible way to notify friends and family is by e-mail. D'oh! Pick up the phone, walk over to the water cooler or send a carrier pigeon, and give your intended recipients a reliable web address to check for updates. Betcha they've already heard about it anyway.

Try hard to be part of the solution, not part of the problem, okay? And if a friend forwards you a virus warning in an e-mail, do everyone a big favor: Shoot him a copy of the preceding bullet points, ask him to tape it to the side of his computer, and beg him to refer to it the next time he gets the forwarding urge.

Am I Infected?

So how do you know whether you're infected?

The short answer is this: Many times, you don't. If you think that your PC is infected, chances are very good that it isn't. Why? Because malware these days doesn't usually cause the kinds of problems people normally associate with infections.

Whatever you do, don't fall for the scamware that tells you it removed 39 infections from your computer but you need to pay in order to remove the other 179 (see "Shunning scareware," a little later in this chapter).

Evaluating telltale signs

Here are a few telltale signs that might — *might* — mean that your PC is infected:

✦ **Someone tells you that you sent him an e-mail message with an attachment — and you didn't send it.** In fact, most e-mail malware these days is smart enough to spoof the From address, so any infected message that appears to come from you probably didn't. Still, some dumb old viruses that aren't capable of hiding your e-mail address are still around. And, if you receive an infected attachment from a friend, chances are good that both your e-mail address and his e-mail address are on an infected computer somewhere. Six degrees of separation and all that.

✦ **You suddenly see files with two filename extensions scattered around your computer.** Filenames such as kournikova.jpg.vbs (a VBScript file masquerading as a JPG image file) or somedoc.txt.exe (a Windows program that wants to appear to be a text file) should send you running for your antivirus software.

Always, always, always have Windows show you filename extensions (see Book VI, Chapter 1).

✦ **Your antivirus software suddenly stops working.** If the icon for your antivirus product disappears from the notification area (near the clock), something killed it — and chances are very good that the culprit was a virus.

✦ **You can't reach websites that are associated with anti-malware manufacturers.** For example, Firefox or Internet Explorer or Chrome works fine with most websites, but you can't get through to www.microsoft.com, www.symantec.com, or www.mcafee.com. This problem is a key giveaway for several infections.

Where did that message come from?

In my discussion of 419 scams, I mentioned that I could trace several scammer messages back to Nigeria. If you've never traced a message before, you'll probably find it intriguing — and frustrating.

You know that return addresses lie. Just like an antagonist in the TV series, *House*. You can't trust a return address because "spoofing" one is absolutely trivial. So what can you do?

If you receive a message and want to know where it came from, the first step is to find the header. In the normal course of events, you never see message headers. They look like the gibberish in Figure 1-8.

Figure 1-8: The header for the 419 message in Figure 1-7.

Here's how to find a message's header:

✦ **If you're using Outlook 2003 and earlier,** open the message and then choose View⇨Options.

✦ **In Outlook 2007,** you have to open the message and then click the tiny square with a downward, right-facing arrow in the lower-right corner of the Options group.

✦ **Outlook 2010** hides the header entirely. To get it, you need a program like the free PocketKnife Peek, www.xintercept.com/peek/pkpeek. htm. Download and install it, per the site's instructions, and you can right-click a Message in Outlook 2010, choose Peek, and then click the Header tab to see the full header.

✦ **In Gmail,** click the down arrow next to the message subject and choose Show Original. That shows you the entire message, including the header.

✦ **In Hotmail or Outlook.com,** click the down arrow next to Reply, which is near the sender and subject.

Other e-mail programs work differently. You may have to jump on to Google to figure out how to see a message's header.

After you have the header, copy it, and head over to the ipTracker site, www. iptrackeronline.com/header.php. Paste the message's header into the top box, and then tap or click Submit Header for Analysis. A report like the one in Figure 1-9 appears.

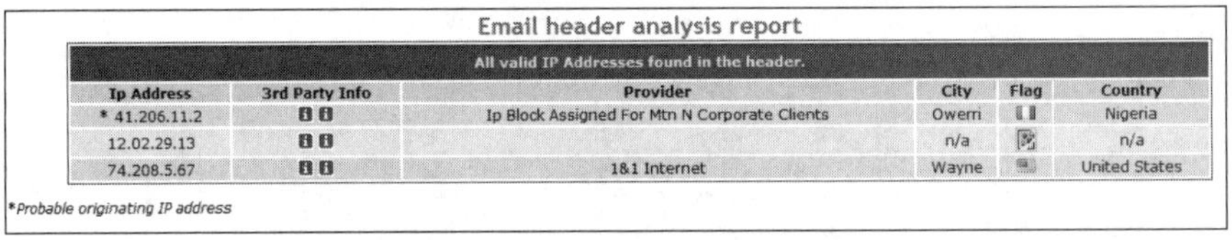

Figure 1-9:
Confirmation that a message came from Nigeria.

Email header analysis report					
All valid IP Addresses found in the header.					
Ip Address	**3rd Party Info**	**Provider**	**City**	**Flag**	**Country**
* 41.206.11.2	🔲 🔲	Ip Block Assigned For Mtn N Corporate Clients	Owerri	▮▮	Nigeria
12.02.29.13	🔲 🔲		n/a	▨	n/a
74.208.5.67	🔲 🔲	1&1 Internet	Wayne	▥	United States

*Probable originating IP address

Realize that the header can be faked, too. Really clever scammers can disguise the origin of a message by faking the header. It's difficult, though, and scammers tend not to be, uh, the brightest bulbs on the tree.

What to do next

If you think that your computer is infected, follow these steps:

1. Don't panic.

Chances are very good that you're not infected.

2. DO NOT REBOOT YOUR COMPUTER.

You may trigger a virus update when you reboot. Stay cool.

3. Run a full scan of your system. If you're using Windows Defender, go to the Start screen, type def, and choose Windows Defender.

If you aren't using Windows Defender, get your antivirus package to run a full scan.

The Windows Defender main interface appears (see Figure 1-10). See Book IX, Chapter 3 for details about Windows Defender.

4. On the right, tap or click Full, and then tap or click Scan Now.

A full scan can take a long time. Go have a latte or two.

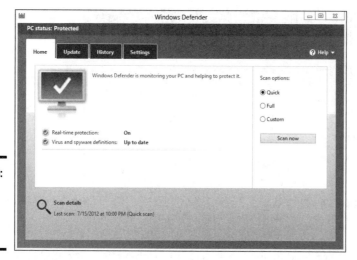

Figure 1-10:
Windows
Defender
ready for
action.

5. **If Step 4 still doesn't solve the problem, go to Jim Eshelman's AumHa site (**www.aumha.net/viewtopic.php?t=4075**) and post your problem on the Malware Removal forum.**

   Make sure that you follow the instructions precisely. The good folks at AumHa are all volunteers. You can save them — and yourself — lots of headaches by following their instructions to the letter.

6. **Do not — I repeat — do not send messages to all your friends advising them of the new virus.**

   Messages about a new virus can outnumber infected messages generated by the virus itself — in some cases, causing more havoc than the virus itself. Try not to become part of the problem. Besides, you may be wrong.

In recent years, I've come to view the mainstream press accounts of virus and malware outbreaks with increasing skepticism. The antivirus companies are usually slower to post news than the mainstream press, but the information they post tends to be much more reliable. Not infallible, mind you, but better. I also cover security problems at AskWoody.com.

Shunning scareware

A friend of mine brought me her computer the other day and showed me a giant warning about all the viruses residing on it (see Figure 1-11). She knew that she needed XP Antivirus, but she didn't know how to install it. Thank heaven.

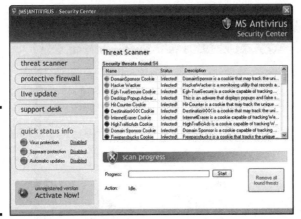

Figure 1-11:
Rogue anti-
malware
gives you
reason to
pay.

Another friend brought me a computer that always booted to a Blue Screen of Death that said

```
Error 0x00000050 PAGE_FAULT_IN_NON_PAGED_AREA
```

It took a whole day to unwind all the junkware on that computer, but when I got to the bottom dreck, I found Vista Antivirus 2009.

I've received messages from all over the world from people who want to know about this fabulous new program, Security Essentials 2010 or Antivirus 2012 (or XP Antivirus or MS Antivirus Security Center or Total Win7 Security or similar wording). Here's what you need to know: It's malware, plain and simple, and if you install it, you're handing over your computer to some very sophisticated folks who will install keyloggers, bot software, and the scum-miest, dirtiest stuff you've ever seen on any PC.

Here's the crazy part: Most people install this kind of scareware voluntarily. One particular family of rogue antivirus products, named Win32/FakeSecSen, has infected more than a million computers; see Figure 1-12.

The exact method of infection can vary, as will the payloads. Almost always, people install rogue antivirus programs when they think they're installing the latest, greatest virus chaser — and they're hastened to get it working because they just *know* there are 179 more viruses on their computers that have to be cleaned.

Figure 1-12:
Win32/
FakeSecSen
scares you
into thinking
you have
to pay to
clean your
computer.

If you have it, how do you remove it? For starters, don't even bother with
Windows Add or Remove Programs. Any company clever enough to call a
piece of scum Antivirus 2012 won't make it easy for you to zap it. Personally,
I rely on `www.malwarebytes.com` — but removing some of these critters is
very difficult (see Book IX, Chapter 4).

One of my favorite anti-malware industry pundits, Rob Rosenberger, has
an insightful analysis of this type of scareware in the article "Two decades
of virus hysteria contributes to the success of fake-AV scams," at `www.`
`vmyths.com/2009/03/22/rogue-av`.

Microsoft has an excellent review of rogue antivirus products in its Security
Intelligence Report Volume 6, available at `www.microsoft.com/sir`.

Getting Protected

The Internet is wild and woolly and wonderful — and, by and large, it's
unregulated, in a Wild West sort of way. Some would say it cannot be regu-
lated, and I agree. Although some central bodies control basic Internet
coordination questions — how the computers talk to each other, who doles

out domain names such as Dummies.com, and what a web browser should do when it encounters a particular piece of HyperText Markup Language (HTML) — no central authority or Web Fashion Police exists.

In spite of its Wild West lineage and complete lack of couth, the Internet doesn't need to be a scary place. If you follow a handful of simple, common sense rules, you'll go a long way toward making your Internet travels more like Happy Trails and less like *Doom III*.

Protecting against malware

"Everybody" knows that the Internet breeds viruses. "Everybody" knows that really bad viruses can drain your bank account, break your hard drive, and give you terminal halitosis — just by looking at an e-mail message with *Good Times* in the Subject line. Right.

In fact, botnets and keyloggers can hurt you, but hoaxes and lousy advice abound. Every Windows user should follow these tips:

✦ **Don't install weird programs, cute icons, automatic e-mail signers, or products that promise to keep your computer oh-so-wonderfully safe.** Unless the software comes from a reputable manufacturer whom you trust and you know precisely *why* you need it, you don't want it. Don't be fooled by products that claim to clean your Registry or clobber imaginary infections.

You may think that you absolutely must synchronize the Windows clock (which Windows does amazingly well, no extra program needed), tune up your computer (gimme a break), use those cute little smiley icons (gimme a bigger break), install a pop-up blocker (IE, Firefox, and Chrome do that well), or install an automatic e-mail signer (your e-mail program already can sign your messages — read the manual, pilgrim!). What you end up with is an unending barrage of hassles and hustles.

✦ **Never, ever, open a file attached to an e-mail message until you contact the person who sent you the file and verify that she did, in fact, send you the file intentionally.** You should also apply a bit of discretion and ask yourself whether the sender is smart enough to avoid sending you an infected file. After you contact the person who sent you the file, don't open the file directly. Save it to your hard drive and run Windows Defender on it before you open it.

✦ **Follow the instructions in Book VI, Chapter 1 to force Windows to show you the full name of all the files on your computer.** That way, if you see a file named `something.cpl` or `iloveyou.vbs`, you stand a fighting chance of understanding that it might be an infectious program waiting for your itchy finger.

✦ **Don't trust e-mail.** Every single part of an e-mail message can be faked, easily. The return address can be spoofed. Even the header information, which you don't normally see, can be pure fiction. Links inside e-mail messages may not point where you think they point. Anything you put in a message can be viewed by anybody with even a nodding interest — to use the old analogy, sending unencrypted e-mail is a lot like sending a postcard.

✦ **Check your accounts.** Look at your credit card and bank statements, and if you see a charge you don't understand, question it. Log on to all your financial websites frequently, and if somebody changed your password, scream bloody murder.

Disabling Java and Flash

As I'm fond of saying, "It's time to run Java out of town." More precisely, I think developers should stop developing programs that require the Java Runtime Environment, or JRE.

I also salute the rapid change from Flash, for automating websites, to HTML5, which does a better job in a faster and more secure way.

Neither Java nor Flash will run unfettered on the tiled side of the Windows 8 fence — the implementations I've seen so far are surrounded by impressive malware-containing barriers — which leads me to my main browser safety recommendation: *Use the tiled, full-screen version of your favorite browser whenever you can.*

If you can't use the tiled version, or if you can but you just hate dealing with the tiled interface, get the free NoScript Firefox extension (`www.noscript.net`), which automatically blocks both Java and Flash in Firefox. You can allow Java and Flash to run, on a case-by-case basis, but for general surfing, NoScript and Firefox is the safest way to go.

If you really have to use Internet Explorer or Chrome, it's relatively easy to turn off Java and Flash in both browsers. Google shows you how.

Using your credit card safely online

Many people who use the web refuse to order anything online because they're afraid that their credit card numbers will be stolen and they'll be liable for enormous bills. Or they think the products will never arrive and they won't get their money back.

If your credit card was issued in the United States and you're ordering from a U.S. company, that's simply not the case. Here's why:

✦ **The Fair Credit Billing Act protects you from being charged by a company for an item you don't receive.** It's the same law that governs orders placed over the telephone or by mail. A vendor generally has 30 days to send the merchandise, or it has to give you a formal, written chance to cancel your order. For details, go to the Federal Trade Commission (FTC) website (www.ftc.gov/bcp/edu/pubs/consumer/credit/cre28.shtm).

✦ **Your maximum liability for charges fraudulently made on the card is $50 per card.** The minute you notify the credit card company that somebody else is using your card, you have no further liability. If you have any questions, the Federal Trade Commission can help (www.ftc.gov/bcp/edu/pubs/consumer/tech/tec01.shtm).

The rules are different if you're not dealing with a U.S. company and using a U.S. credit card. For example, if you buy something in an online auction from an individual, you don't have the same level of protection. Make sure that you understand the rules before you hand out credit card information. Unfortunately, there's no central repository (at least none I could find) of information about overseas purchase protection for U.S. credit card holders: Each credit card seems to handle cases individually. If you buy things overseas using a U.S. credit card, your relationship with your credit card company generally provides your only protection.

Some online vendors, such as Amazon, absolutely guarantee that your shopping will be safe. The Fair Credit Billing Act protects any charges fraudulently made in excess of $50, but Amazon says that it reimburses any fraudulent charges under $50 that occurred as a result of using its website. Many credit card companies now offer similar assurances.

Regardless, take a few simple precautions to make sure that you aren't giving away your credit card information:

✦ **When you place an order online, make sure that you're dealing with a company you know.** In particular, don't click a link in an e-mail message and expect to go to the company's website. Type the company's address into Internet Explorer or Firefox, or use a link that you stored in your Internet Explorer Favorites or the Firefox Bookmarks list.

✦ **Type your credit card number only when you're sure that you've arrived at the company's site and when the site is using a secure web page.** The easy way to tell whether a web page is secure is to look in the lower-right corner of the screen for a picture of a lock (see Figure 1-13). Secure websites scramble data so that anything you type on the web page is encrypted before it's sent to the vendor's computer. In addition, Firefox tells you a site's registration and pedigree by clicking the icon to the left of the web address. In Internet Explorer, the icon appears to the right of the address.

Figure 1-13:
Major
browsers
show a lock
to indicate a
secure site.

🔒 https://plus.google.com/u/0/

Be aware that crafty web programmers can fake the lock icon and show an `https://` (secure) address to try to lull you into thinking that you're on a secure web page. To be safe, confirm the site's address and click the icon to the left of the address at the top to show the full security certificate.

✦ **Don't send your credit card number in an ordinary e-mail message.** E-mail is just too easy to intercept. And for heaven's sake, don't give out any personal information when you're chatting online.

✦ **If you receive an e-mail message requesting credit card information that seems to be from your bank, credit card company, Internet service provider, or even your sainted Aunt Martha, don't send sensitive information back by way of e-mail.** Insist on using a secure website and type the company's address into your browser.

Identity theft continues to be a problem all over the world. Widespread availability of personal information online only adds fuel to the flame. If you think someone may be posing as you — to run up debts in your name, for example — see the U.S. government's main website on the topic at `www.ftc.gov/bcp/edu/microsites/idtheft`.

Defending your privacy
"You have zero privacy anyway. Get over it."

That's what Scott McNealy, CEO of Sun Microsystems, said to a group of reporters on January 25, 1999. He was exaggerating — Scott has been known to make provocative statements for dramatic effect — but the exaggeration comes awfully close to reality. (Actually, if Scott told me the sky was blue, I'd run outside and check. But I digress.)

I continue to be amazed at Windows users' odd attitudes toward privacy. People who wouldn't dream of giving a stranger their telephone numbers fill out their mailing addresses for online service profiles. People who are scared to death at the thought of using their credit cards online to place an order with a major retailer (a very safe procedure, by the way) dutifully type their Social Security numbers on web-based forms.

I suggest that you follow these few important privacy points:

✦ **Use work systems only for work.** Why use your company e-mail ID for personal messages? C'mon. Sign up for a free web-based e-mail account, such as Gmail (www.gmail.com), Yahoo! Mail (www.mail.yahoo.com), or Hotmail/Outlook.com (www.hotmail.com and www.outlook.com).

In the United States, with few exceptions, anything you do on a company PC at work can be monitored and examined by your employer. E-mail, website history files, and even stored documents and settings are all fair game. At work, you have zero privacy anyway. Get over it.

✦ **Don't give it away.** Why use your real name when you sign up for a free e-mail account? Why tell a random survey that your annual income is between $20,000 and $30,000? (Or is it between $150,000 and $200,000?)

All sorts of websites — particularly Microsoft — ask questions about topics that, simply put, are none of their dern business. Don't put your personal details out where they can be harvested.

✦ **Know your rights.** Although cyberspace doesn't provide the same level of personal protection you have come to expect in *meatspace* (real life), you still have rights and recourses. Check out www.privacyrights.org for some thought-provoking notices.

Keep your head low and your powder dry!

Reducing spam

Everybody hates spam, but nobody has any idea how to stop it. Not the government. Not Bill Gates. Not your sainted aunt's podiatrist's second cousin.

You think legislation can reduce the amount of spam? Since the U.S. CAN–SPAM Act (www.fcc.gov/cgb/consumerfacts/canspam.html) became law on January 7, 2003, has the volume of spam you've received increased or decreased? Heck, I've had more spam from politicians lately than from almost any other group. The very people who are supposed to be enforcing the antispam laws seem to be spewing out spam overtime.

The Doubleclick shtick

A website plants a cookie on your computer. Only that website can retrieve the cookie. The information is shielded from other websites. ZDNet.com (the PCMag website) can figure out that I have been reading reviews of digital cameras. Dealtime.com knows that I buy shoes. But a cookie from ZDNet can't be read by Dealtime, and vice versa. So what's the big deal?

Enter Doubleclick.net, which is now a division of Google. For the better part of a decade, both ZDNet.com and Dealtime.com have included ads from a company named Doubleclick.net. Don't believe it? Use Internet Explorer to go to each of the sites, press the Alt key, and choose View⇨Web Page Privacy Policy. (In Firefox, you can do the same thing by choosing Tools⇨Options⇨Privacy⇨Show Cookies and then watching the bottom of the list.) Unless ZDNet or Dealtime has changed advertisers, you see Doubleclick.net featured prominently in each site's privacy report.

Here's the trick: You surf to a ZDNet web page that contains a Doubleclick.net ad. Doubleclick kicks in and plants a cookie on your PC that says you were looking at a specific page on ZDNet. Two hours (or days or weeks) later, you surf to a Dealtime page that also contains a Doubleclick.net ad — a different ad, no doubt — but one distributed by Doubleclick. Doubleclick kicks in again and discovers that you were looking at that specific ZDNet page two hours (or days or weeks) earlier.

Now consider the consequences if a hundred sites that you visit in an average week all have Doubleclick ads. They can be tiny ads — 1 pixel high, or so small that you can't see them. All the information about all your surfing to those sites can be accumulated by Doubleclick and used to "target" you for advertising, recommendations, or whatever. It's scary.

Want to look at who's watching you? Install the Ghostery browser (www.ghostery.com/download). It shows you exactly which cookies are tracking you on every page you visit.

By and large, Windows is only tangentially involved in the spam game — it's the messenger, as it were. But every Windows user I know receives e-mail. And every e-mail user I know gets spam. Lots of it.

Why is it so hard to identify spam? Consider. There are 600,426,974,379,824,381,952 different ways to spell *Viagra*. No, really. If you use all the tricks that spammers use — from simple swaps such as using the letter *l* rather than *i* or inserting e x t r a s p a c e s in the word, to tricky ones like substituting accented characters — you have more than 600 quintillion different ways to spell Viagra. It makes the national debt look positively tiny.

Hard to believe? See www.cockeyed.com/lessons/viagra/viagra.html for an eye-opening analysis.

Spam scanners look at e-mail messages and try to determine whether the contents of the potentially offensive message match certain criteria. Details vary depending on the type of spam scanner you use (or your Internet service provider uses), but in general, the scanner has to match the contents of the message with certain words and phrases stored in its database. If you've seen a lot of messages with odd spellings come through your spam scanner, you know how hard it is to see through all those sextillion, er, septillion variations.

Spam is an intractable problem, but you can do certain things to minimize your exposure:

✦ **Don't encourage 'em.** Don't buy anything that's offered by way of spam (or any other e-mail that you didn't specifically request). Don't click through to the website. Simply delete the message. If you see something that might be interesting, use Google or another web browser to look for other companies that sell the same item.

✦ **Opt out of mailings only if you know and trust the company that's sending you messages.** If you're on the Costco mailing list and you're not interested in its e-mail any more, click the Opt Out button at the bottom of the page. But don't opt out with a company you don't trust: It may just be trying to verify your e-mail address.

✦ **Never post your e-mail address on a website or in a newsgroup.** Spammers have spiders that devour web pages by the gazillion, crawling around the web, gathering e-mail addresses and other information automatically. If you post something in a newsgroup and want to let people respond, use a name that's hard for spiders to swallow: woody (at) ask woody (dot) com, for example.

✦ **Never open an attachment to an e-mail message or view pictures in a message.** Spammers use both methods to verify that they've reached a real, live address. And, you wouldn't open an attachment anyway — unless you know the person who sent it to you, you verified with her that she intended to send you the attachment, and you trust the sender to be savvy enough to avoid sending infected attachments.

✦ **Never trust a website that you arrive at by "clicking through" a hot link in an e-mail message.** Be cautious about websites you reach from other websites. If you don't personally type the address in the Internet Explorer address bar, you might not be in Kansas any more.

Ultimately, the only long-lasting solution to spam is to change your e-mail address and give out your address only to close friends and business associates. Even that strategy doesn't solve the problem, but it should reduce the level of spam significantly. Heckuva note, ain't it?

Chapter 2: Fighting Viri and Scum

In This Chapter

✔ **Quick security checklist — do's and don'ts**

✔ **Getting the lowdown on malware**

✔ **Understanding how Windows Defender works**

✔ **Scanning for rootkits via Windows Defender Offline**

✔ **Deciphering your browser's cryptic security signs**

*W*indows 8 is the first version of Windows to ship with a complete anti-virus/anti-spy/anti-malware package baked right into the product.

You don't need to buy an antivirus, firewall, or anti-everything product. Windows 8 has all you need. It's already installed and working, and it doesn't cost a penny.

On the other hand, you need to hold up your end of the bargain by not doing anything, uh, questionable. I wanted to say "stupid" but some of the tricks the scummeisters use these days can get you even if you *aren't* stupid. Book IX, Chapter 1 helps you understand the tactics online creeps use and keep your guard up.

I start this chapter with a very simple list of do's and don'ts for protecting your computer, and your identity. They're important. Even if you don't read the rest of this chapter, make sure you read — and understand, and follow — the rules in each list.

Basic Windows Security Do's and Don'ts

Here are the ten most important things you need to do, to keep your computer secure:

✦ **Check daily to make sure Windows Defender is running.** If something's amiss, a red "X" appears on the Action Center flag, down in the desktop's notification area, near the time. To check Defender's status, on the Start screen, type **def** and choose Windows Defender. If Defender's running, a green check mark appears, as shown in Figure 2-1.

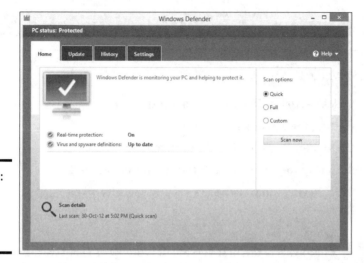

Figure 2-1:
Windows
Defender
is up and
running.

Actually, Windows should tell you if Defender stops, either via a toaster notification from the right side or a red X on the flag in the lower-right corner of the desktop. But if you want to be absolutely sure, there's no better way than to check it yourself. Only takes a second.

✦ **Run the tiled, "immersive" full-screen version of your Internet browser, if you can stand it.** If you absolutely have to run your browser on the desktop, use Firefox or Chrome with NoScript or a similar Java and Flash blocker installed and working. (You can use Internet Explorer, but if you do, disable Java and Flash.) Chrome has been working on a *sandbox* — a fortified running cocoon — for Flash. The sandbox is still experimental but may become the safest way to run a browser on the desktop.

Most Windows infections come in the door through Java, Flash, or Adobe Reader (see Book IX, Chapter 1). The tiled browsers won't run Java or Flash, except inside a fortified "sandbox."

✦ **Use the Microsoft Reader app to look at PDF files.**

It's free, from the Windows Store. Go to the Store and search for *Reader*. Although Microsoft Reader can have as many security holes as Adobe Reader, the fact that Adobe Reader is used by so many people makes it a much larger target for people who want to crack your system.

✦ **Every month or so, run Windows Defender Offline.** WDO scans for rootkits. I talk about WDO later in this chapter.

✦ **Every month or so, run Malwarebytes.** The Malwarebytes program gives you a second opinion, possibly pointing out questionable programs that

Windows Defender doesn't flag. I talk about Malwarebytes in Book IX, Chapter 4.

✦ **Delete chain mail.**

I'm sure that you'll be bringing down the wrath of several lesser deities for the rest of your days, but do everyone a favor and don't forward junk. Please.

If something you receive in an e-mail sounds really, really cool, it's probably fake — an urban legend, or a come-on of some sort. Look it up at www.snopes.com.

✦ **Keep up to date with Windows patches and (especially) patches to other programs running on your computer.** See my diatribe about Windows Automatic Update in Book VIII, Chapter 3. For help keeping your other programs updated, use Secunia Personal Software Inspector, which I describe in Book IX, Chapter 4.

✦ **Check your credit cards and bank balances regularly.**

I check my charges and balances every couple of days, and suggest you do the same.

✦ **If you don't need a program any more, get rid of it.** Use the Windows Uninstaller that I describe in Book VII, Chapter 1. If it doesn't blast away easily, use Revo Uninstaller in Book X, Chapter 5.

✦ **Change your passwords regularly.** Yeah, another one of those things everybody recommends, but nobody does. Except you really should. See the admonitions in Book II, Chapter 4 about choosing good passwords, but especially take a look at LastPass and RoboForm, which I describe in Book IX, Chapter 4.

Here are the ten most important things you *shouldn't* do, to keep your computer secure:

✦ **Don't trust any PC unless you, personally, have been taking close care of it.** Even then, be skeptical. Treat every PC you might encounter as if it's infected. Don't stick a USB drive into a public computer, for example, unless you're prepared to disinfect the USB drive immediately when you get back to a safe computer. Assume that everything you type into a public PC is being logged and sent to a pimply-face genius who wants to be a millionaire.

✦ **Don't install a new program unless you know precisely what it does, and you've checked to make sure you have a legitimate copy.**

Yes, even if an online scanner told you that you have 139 viruses on your computer, and you need to pay just $49.99 to get rid of them.

If you install apps from the Windows Store, you're safe. But any programs you install on your desktop should be vetted ten ways from Tuesday, downloaded from a reputable source (such as www.cnet.com, www.sourceforge.net, www.softpedia.com, www.majorgeeks.com, www.tucows.com, www.snapfiles.com), and *even then* you need to ask yourself whether you really need the program.

✦ **Don't use the same password for two or more sites.** Okay, if you reuse your passwords, make sure you don't reuse the passwords on any of your e-mail or financial accounts.

True confession time. Yes, I reuse passwords. Everybody does. LastPass (see Book IX, Chapter 4) makes it easier to create a different password for every website, but I'm lazy sometimes.

E-mail accounts are different. If you reuse the passwords on any of your e-mail accounts and somebody gets the password, he may be able to break into everything, steal your money, and besmirch your reputation. See the nearby "Don't reuse your e-mail password" sidebar.

✦ **Don't use WiFi in a public place unless you're running exclusively on HTTPS encrypted sites, or through a virtual private network (VPN).**

If you don't know what HTTPS is and have never set up a VPN, that's okay. Just realize that anybody else who can connect to the same WiFi station you're using can see *every single thing* that goes into or comes out of your computer. See Book VIII, Chapter 4.

✦ **Don't fall for Nigerian 419 scams, "I've been mugged and I need $500 scams," or anything else where you have to send money.** There are lots of scams — and if you hear the words "Western Union," or "Postal Money Order," run for the exit. See Book IX, Chapter 1.

✦ **Don't tap or click a link in an e-mail message or document, and expect it to take you to a financial site.** Take the time to type the address into your browser. You've heard it a thousand times, but it's true.

✦ **Don't open an attachment to any e-mail message until you've contacted the person who sent it to you and verified that she intentionally sent you the file.** Even if she did send it, you need to use your judgment as to whether the sender is savvy enough to refrain from sending you something infectious.

No, UPS didn't send you a non-delivery notice in a Zip file, Microsoft didn't send you an update to Windows attached to a message, and your winning lottery notification won't come as an attachment.

✦ **Don't forget to change your passwords.** Yeah, another one of those things everybody recommends, but nobody does. Except you really should.

Don't reuse your e-mail password

Say you have a Gmail account. You run over to an online classified advertising site and sign up for an account there. You're lazy, so you use the same password for both accounts.

A day, month, or year later, you place an ad on the classified advertising site. You have to provide your e-mail address. Hey, no problem.

The next week, somebody breaks into the classified advertising site and steals the information from 10,000 accounts. Unbeknownst to you, the people who created and maintain the classified advertising site stored the passwords and e-mail addresses in a way that can be cracked.

The person who broke into the site posts his booty on some underground file-sharing site, and within minutes of the break-in, two dozen people are trying every combination of your Gmail address and password, trying to break into banking sites, brokerage sites, PayPal, whatever.

If they hit on a financial site that requires only an e-mail address in order to retrieve the account information, bingo, they use your Gmail address and ask for a new password. They log on to Gmail with your password and wait for the password reset instructions. Thirty seconds later, they're logged into the financial site.

Happens every day.

+ **Don't trust anybody who calls you and offers to fix your computer.** The "I'm from Microsoft and I'm here to help" scam has gone too far. Stay skeptical, and don't let anybody else into your computer, unless you know who they are. See Book IX, Chapter 1.

+ **Don't forget that the biggest security gap is between your ears**. Use your head, not your tapping or clicking finger.

Making Sense of Malware

Although most people are more familiar with the term *virus,* viruses are only part of the problem — a problem known as malware. *Malware* is made up of the elements described in this list:

+ **Viruses:** A computer virus is a program that replicates. That's all. Viruses generally replicate by attaching themselves to files — programs, documents, or spreadsheets — or replacing "genuine" operating system files with bogus ones. They usually make copies of themselves whenever they're run.

You probably think that viruses delete files or make programs go belly-up or wreak havoc in other nefarious ways. Some of them do. Many of them don't. Viruses sound scary, but most of them aren't. Most viruses have such ridiculous bugs in them that they don't get far "in the wild."

Lies, damn lies, and malware statistics

Computer crime has evolved into a money-making operation, with some espionage tacked on for good measure, but when you hear statistics about how many viruses are out and about and how much they cost everyone, take those statistics with a grain of salt.

As *The New York Times* puts it so accurately, "A few criminals do well, but cybercrime is a relentless, low-profit struggle for the majority..." (www.nytimes.com/2012/04/15/opinion/sunday/the-cyber-crime-wave-that-wasnt.html)

Here's what you need to know about those cost estimates:

✔ There's no way to tell how much a virus outbreak "costs." You should expect that any dollar estimates you see are designed to raise your eyebrows, nothing more.

✔ Although corporate cyberespionage certainly takes place all the time, it's very hard to identify — much less quantify. For that matter, how can you quantify the effects of plain old everyday industrial espionage?

✔ Instead of flinging meaningless numbers around, it's more important to consider the amount of hassle people and companies encounter when they have to clean up after a group of cybercretins. One hundred thousand filched credit card credentials may not lead to a lot of lost money, but it'll certainly cause no end of mayhem for a lot of people.

Although the major antivirus companies release virus-catching files that identify tens of millions of signatures, almost all the infections in any given year come from a handful of viruses. The threat is real, but it's way overblown.

✦ **Trojans:** Trojans (occasionally called Trojan horses) may or may not be able to reproduce, but they always require that the user do something to get them started. The most common Trojans these days appear as programs downloaded from the Internet, or e-mail attachments, or programs that helpfully offer to install themselves from the Internet: You tap or double-click an attachment, expecting to open a picture or a document, and you get bit when a program comes in and clobbers your computer, frequently sending out a gazillion messages, all with infected attachments, without your knowledge or consent.

✦ **Worms:** Worms move from one computer to another over a network. The worst ones replicate very quickly by shooting copies of themselves over the Internet, taking advantage of holes in the operating systems (all too frequently, Windows).

Some malware can carry bad *payloads* (programs that wreak destruction on your system), but many of the worst offenders cause the most harm by clogging networks (nearly bringing down the Internet itself, at times) and by turning PCs into zombies, frequently called *bots,* which can be operated by remote control. (I talk about bots and botnets in Book IX, Chapter 1.)

The most successful pieces of malware these days run as *rootkits,* programs that evade detection by stealthily hooking into Windows in tricky ways. Some nominally respectable companies (notably, Sony) have employed root-kit technology to hide programs for their own profit. Rootkits are extremely difficult to detect, and even harder to clean. Windows Defender Offline, discussed later in this chapter, is your best bet to clobber the beasts.

All these definitions are becoming more academic and less relevant, as the trend shifts to *blended-threat* malware. Blended threats incorporate elements of all three traditional kinds of malware — and more. Most of the most successful "viruses" you read about in the press these days — Rustock, Aleuron, and the like — are, in fact, blended-threat malware. They've come a long way from old-fashioned viruses.

Scanning for Rootkits with Windows Defender Offline

Windows Defender Offline (WDO) sniffs out and removes rootkits. WDO should occupy a key spot in your bag of tricks. It works like a champ on Windows XP, Vista, Windows 7, and Windows 8 systems and should be able to catch a wide variety of nasties that evade detection by more traditional methods.

Windows Defender Offline can help in two very different situations:

✦ When Windows won't boot, you can boot your machine with a WDO CD or USB drive, and have WDO perform a malware scan.

✦ If you think you might have a rootkit — or even if you're just curious — WDO can scan your system and remove many different kinds of rootkits.

It's important to understand that, even though Microsoft makes and distributes WDO, it is *not* a Windows application; it doesn't use the copy of Windows installed on your PC. Rather, it's completely self-contained — you boot with the WDO CD or USB drive, and WDO looks at your system without any interference from the installed copy of Windows.

To find rootkits, a rootkit detector has to do its job when Windows isn't running. If the rootkit detector was running on Windows, it would never be able to see underneath Windows, to catch the rootkits.

To get WDO up and running, make sure you have a blank CD, DVD, or USB flash drive with at least 250MB of free space. Then follow these steps:

1. **Figure out the "bittedness" of the computer that's going to get scanned.**

If you don't already know whether your PC is running 32-bit or 64-bit Windows, right-click the lower-left corner of the screen and choose System. (If you don't have a mouse, flip to the desktop, swipe from the right, choose the Settings charm, and at the top, tap Control Panel. Tap the System and Security link, and then tap the System link. And consider buying a mouse.) Windows responds with the System window, as shown in Figure 2-2, and near the middle, it tells you whether you have a 32-bit or 64-bit system.

The number of bits is here

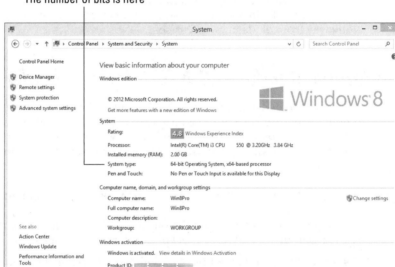

Figure 2-2:
The System window tells you the bittedness of your PC.

You can use any Windows computer for the following steps — you don't have to use the PC that's going to get scanned.

If you're going to create a CD or DVD to boot WDO, you do have to use a PC with a CD or DVD writer. To create a bootable USB drive, the down-loading computer has to have a USB port.

2. **Go to the Windows Defender Offline site, click and download either the 32-bit or 64-bit version, depending on the bittedness of the system you're going to scan. Tap or double-click to run the downloaded file.**

The WDO site can be found at `www.windows.microsoft.com/en-US/ windows/what-is-windows-defender-offline`.

The welcome pane appears, as shown in Figure 2-3.

Figure 2-3:
You need
to sacrifice
a CD, DVD,
or USB
drive to hold
the WDO
booter.

3. **Tap or click Next, accept all the defaults, choose whether you want to use a CD, DVD, or USB drive, and then tap or click Finish.**

   The ISO file option is primarily for people who are going to run WDO on systems that can boot from an ISO file, which usually means a virtual machine.

   If you're going to create a bootable USB drive, be aware that this installer wipes out everything on the drive.

   The installer downloads the latest version of the software and signature files (about 210MB for the 32-bit version or 230MB for the 64-bit version), then creates the boot drive, or the ISO file.

4. **With a bootable CD, DVD, or USB drive properly inserted, boot the PC you want to examine from the device.**

   If you've never booted the machine from CD or USB before, and can't figure out how to jimmy the BIOS to make it work, Microsoft has some suggestions for getting it to work at www.windows.microsoft.com/en-US/windows/windows-defender-offline-faq.

5. **If you have a multiboot system, choose which OS you wish to scan.**

   WDO will scan only one system at a time.

   With the OS chosen, you see a Windows 7-like startup screen which dissolves into the Windows Defender Offline screen, as shown in Figure 2-4.

Figure 2-4:
Windows
Defender
Offline may
need to be
updated
before it will
scan your
system.

6. **Update the definitions if need be, by tapping or clicking the Update button. Choose a Quick, Full, or Custom scan, and then tap or click the Scan Now button.**

   The Full scan option is very thorough — it looks inside all the files on the system, including ancient backed-up e-mails — and can run for six or eight hours. The Custom option lets you select drives and folders for scanning. In my tests on a fresh Windows 8 machine, the Full scan took only 30 minutes.

   If WDO finds potential threat(s), it displays warning(s) identical to the warning dialog box in Windows Defender.

7. **Choose to Remove, Quarantine, or Ignore the threat.**

   See Book IX, Chapter 3 for a discussion of the options and what they mean. *Hint:* Unless you have an overwhelming need to do otherwise, choose Remove.

Deciphering Browsers' Inscrutable Warnings

One last trick that may help you head off an unfortunate online incident: Each browser has subtle ways of telling you that you might be in trouble. I'm not talking about the giant Warning: Suspected Phishing Site or Reported Web Forgery signs. Those are supposed to hit you upside the head, and they do.

Understanding how Windows Defender works

Windows Defender in Windows 8 is a fully functional, very capable, fast, small anti-malware program that works admirably well. There's absolutely no reason to spend any money on any other anti-malware/anti-whatever program. You have the best, inside Windows 8, already working, and you don't have to lift a finger.

Windows Defender in Windows 8 is built on the Microsoft Security Essentials foundation,

which I've raved about for years. It incorporates all of the MSE pieces (so there's no reason to install Microsoft Security Essentials on a Win8 machine), while adding new features, including the ability to work with the new UEFI boot system to validate secure boot operating systems.

I talk about Windows Defender, UEFI, and secure boot in Book IX, Chapter 3.

I'm talking about the gentle indications each browser has that tell you whether there's something strange about the site you're looking at. Historically, if you're on a secured page — where encryption is in force between you and the website — you see a padlock. That simple padlock indicator has grown up a bit, so you can understand more about your secure (or not-so-secure) connection with a glance.

Chrome

Chrome browsers have four different icons that can appear to the left of a site's URL, as shown in Figure 2-5.

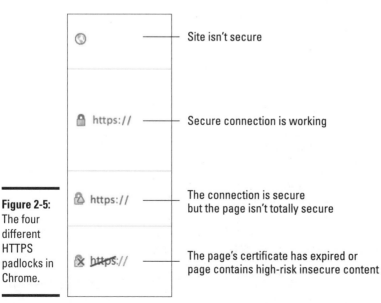

Figure 2-5:
The four
different
HTTPS
padlocks in
Chrome.

Site isn't secure

Secure connection is working

The connection is secure
but the page isn't totally secure

The page's certificate has expired or
page contains high-risk insecure content

Here's what they mean:

✦ The world icon doesn't look like a padlock because it indicates that the site isn't secure. As long as you don't have to type anything into a site, there's no great reason to require a secure site. If you're asked to provide information on an unsecure site, be intensely aware that it can be seen by anybody who's snooping on your connection.

✦ The green padlock says that there's a secure connection in place, and it's working. As long as you're looking at the correct domain — you didn't mistype the domain name, for example — you're safe.

 If the site has an Extended Validation certificate (see the nearby "What is Extended Validation?" sidebar), you will also see green highlighting in the address bar.

✦ The yellow warning on a padlock says that Chrome has set up a secure connection, but there are parts of the page that could, conceivably, snoop on what you're typing. That's what the "insecure content" warning means.

✦ The red X on a padlock tells you that there are problems with the site's certificate, or that "insecure content" on the page is known to be high risk. When you hit a red X, you have to ask yourself whether the site's handlers just let the certificate lapse (I've seen that on banking sites, and other sites that shouldn't go bad), or if there's something genuinely wrong with the site.

Firefox

Firefox handles things a little differently. Firefox puts a box to the left of the URL — called a Site Identity Button (see Figure 2-6) — that's color-coded to give you an idea of what's in store. If you tap or click the button, you see detailed information about the security status of the site.

Figure 2-6: Firefox gives detailed site security information, like the fact that Wells Fargo doesn't identify its site.

The three colors indicate:

✦ **Gray:** Not a secure site

✦ **Blue:** Basic security information

✦ **Green:** Complete security information, including an Extended Validation certificate (see the "What is Extended Validation?" sidebar)

Internet Explorer 10

Internet Explorer 10 has yet another way to tell you about potential problems. It has a padlock icon that works much like the analogous icons in Chrome and Firefox, as shown in Figure 2-7.

Security info padlock

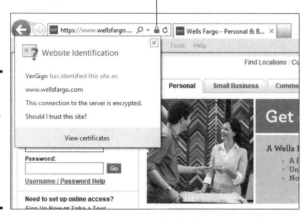

Figure 2-7:
IE shows
site security
information
if you tap
or click the
padlock
icon.

The padlock icons in the desktop version of Internet Explorer look like this:

✦ No padlock means the connection isn't secure.

✦ A gray padlock is for standard security.

✦ A gray padlock plus green highlights in the address bar is for Extended Validation sites (see the "What is Extended Validation?" sidebar).

In addition, IE has a huge variety of nuanced messages, such as the one in Figure 2-8. This Microsoft-constructed demo page shows how an HTTPS site may not trigger a padlock icon in Internet Explorer 10. (Note: There's no padlock indication next to the web address.)

What is Extended Validation?

Companies have to pay to get a secure certificate, and use it correctly on their site before the major browsers will display a padlock for the site.

Unfortunately, in recent years, there have been many problems with faked, stolen, or otherwise dubious certificates. Part of the difficulty lies in the fact that just about anybody can get a website security certificate. Several years ago, a couple of people applied for a security certificate for Microsoft.com. They sweet-talked their way into having a certificate issued.

Starting in April 2008, a second level of certification, an *Extended Validation certificate,* was put into effect. In order to buy an EV certificate, the organization or individual applying for the certificate has to jump through many hoops to establish their legal identity, physical location, and prove that the people applying for the certificate do, in fact, own the domain name that they're trying to certify.

EV certificates aren't infallible, but they're much more trustworthy than regular certificates.

More than a dozen messages can appear at the top or bottom of the screen. For details, see `blogs.msdn.com/b/ie/archive/2011/06/23/internet-explorer-9-security-part-4-protecting-consumers-from-malicious-mixed-content.aspx`.

Site should be secure...

...but there's no padlock

Figure 2-8: A supposedly secure HTTPS site contains parts that aren't secure.

Chapter 3: Running Built-In Security Programs

In This Chapter

✔ **Making Windows Defender work your way**

✔ **Coping with SmartScreen**

✔ **Working with UEFI and Secure Boot**

✔ **Controlling User Account Control**

✔ **Understanding Windows Firewall**

Windows 8, right out of the box, ships with a myriad of security programs, including a handful that you can control.

This chapter looks at the things you can do with the programs on offer: Windows Defender, SmartScreen, UEFI (don't judge it by its name alone), User Account Control, and Windows Firewall. What you find in this chapter is like a survey of the tip of an iceberg. Even if you don't change anything, you'll come away with a better understanding of what's available, and how the pieces fit together. With a little luck, you'll also have a better idea of what can go wrong, and how you can fix it.

Working with Windows Defender

Fast, full-featured and free, Microsoft Windows Defender draws accolades from experts, and catcalls from competitors.

If you've ever put up with a bloated and expensive security suite exhorting/ extorting you for more money, or you've struggled with free AV packages that want to install a little toolbar here and a funny monitoring program there — and *then* ask you for money — you're in for a refreshing change . . . from an unexpected source.

Windows Defender takes over antivirus and antispyware duties, and tosses in bot detection and anti-rootkit features for good measure. In independent tests, Microsoft has consistently received high detection and removal scores for Windows Defender (and Microsoft Security Essentials, Windows Defender's kissin' cousin) for years.

Windows Defender conducts periodic scans and watches out for malware in real time. It vets e-mail attachments, catches downloads, deletes or quarantines at your command, and in general, does everything you'd expect an antivirus, anti-malware, and/or anti-rootkit product to do.

The beauty of Windows Defender is that it just works. You don't have to do anything — although you should check from time to time to make sure it hasn't been accidentally (or maliciously) turned off. To check whether Windows Defender is running, go to the Start screen, type **def**, and on the left, choose Windows Defender. If you see the green check mark, you're doing fine. (You can see the check mark in the upcoming Figure 3-1.)

Microsoft maintains a very active online support forum for Windows Defender at Microsoft Answers, www.answers.microsoft.com/en-us/windows/forum/windows_8-security.

When you use Windows Defender, here are a few caveats you need to be aware of:

✦ It's *never* a good idea to run two antivirus products simultaneously, and Windows Defender is no exception: If you have a second antivirus product running on your machine, Windows Defender has been disabled, and you shouldn't try to bring it back.

  If you don't like your AV product, and don't particularly want to keep paying and paying and paying for it, use Windows Remove Programs to get rid of it. Reboot your machine, and Windows Defender returns.

  In summary, Windows Defender works great, but if you get a second antivirus program, do *not* run Windows Defender and the usurper at the same time.

✦ Windows Defender updates itself, no matter what setting you may have for Windows Automatic Update or Microsoft Automatic Update.

  You may see updates listed for Windows Defender, if you go into Windows Update and look. Just leave them alone. They'll install all by themselves. See Book VIII, Chapter 3 for details about Automatic Update.

✦ No matter how you slice it, real-time protection eats into your privacy. How? Say Windows Defender (or any other antivirus product) encounters a suspicious looking file that isn't on its zap list. In order to get the latest information about that suspicious looking file, Windows Defender has to phone back to Mother Microsoft, drop off telltale pieces of the file, and ask whether there's anything new. You can opt out of real-time protection, but if you do, you won't have the latest virus information — and some viruses travel very fast.

Adjusting Windows Defender

Unlike many other antivirus products, Windows Defender has a blissfully small number of things that you can or should tweak. Here's how to get to the settings:

1. **On the Start screen, type** def **and then on the left, tap or click Windows Defender.**

   The main Windows Defender screen appears, as shown in Figure 3-1.

Green checkmark means everything is OK

For a manual scan, choose level of scanning

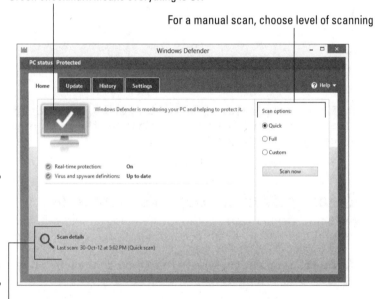

Figure 3-1:
The
Windows
Defender
main
screen.

Results of most recent scan

2. **Tap or click the Settings tab.**

   Here you can make minor changes in Windows Defender's behavior.

   It's rare that you would want to change any of these settings, except the Microsoft Access Protection Services (MAPS), as shown in Figure 3-2.

3. **Adjust the MAPS setting if you wish by tapping or clicking the MAPS entry on the left.**

   Generally, I don't like it when Microsoft gathers information about my system, but in this case I make an exception, and set MAPS at Basic Membership, which is the default. That's the only way to get the full benefit of real-time checking for updated definitions. As I explain earlier in this chapter, you're caught between a rock and a hard place.

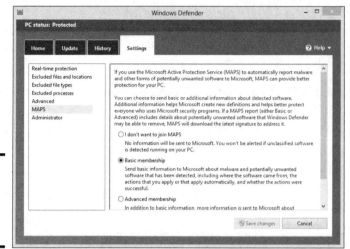

Figure 3-2:
The MAPS
settings for
Windows
Defender.

4. **If you change anything on the Settings tab, tap or click Save Changes, and then tap or click X to close Windows Defender. (If you didn't change anything, just tap or click X.)**

Your changes take effect immediately.

Running Windows Defender manually

Windows Defender works without your doing a thing, but you can tell it run a scan if something on your computer is giving you the willies. Here's how:

1. **On the Start screen, type** def **and then on the left, tap or click Windows Defender.**

The main Windows Defender screen appears (refer to Figure 3-1).

2. **On the Update tab (see Figure 3-3), to get the latest anti-malware definitions, tap or click Update.**

When you tap or click Update, Windows Defender retrieves the latest signature files from the Microsoft site, but it doesn't run a scan. If you want to run a scan, you need to go back to the Home tab and run it.

3. **To perform a manual scan, tap or click one of the three buttons on the left, and then tap or click Scan Now.**

Here's what the Scan options mean:

- *Quick* looks in locations where viruses and other kinds of malware are likely to hide.

- *Full* runs a bit-by-bit scan of every file and folder on the PC.

- *Custom* is like Full, but you get to choose which drives and folders get scanned.

4. To see what Windows Defender has caught and zapped, historically, tap or click the History tab (see Figure 3-4).

Once upon a time, Windows Defender would flag infected files and offer them up for you to decide what to do with the offensive file. It appears as if that behavior has been scaled back radically. As best I can tell, in almost all circumstances, when Windows Defender hits a dicey file, it *quarantines* the file — sticks it in a place you won't accidentally find — and just keeps going. You're rarely notified, (although a toaster notification may slide out from the right side of the screen), but the file just disappears from where it should've been.

If you just downloaded a file, and it disappeared, there's a very good chance that it's infected, Windows Defender has whisked it away to a well-guarded location, and the only way you'll ever find it is in the History tab of the Windows Defender program.

Should you decide to bring the file back, for whatever reason, select the check box next to the file and then tap or click Restore. Rub your lucky rabbit's foot a couple of times while you're at it.

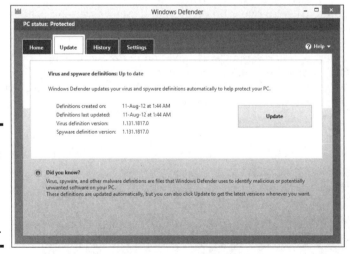

Figure 3-3:
The current status of Windows Defender signature file updates.

Figure 3-4:
A full
history of
the actions
Defender's
taken
appear
here.

Judging SmartScreen

Have you ever downloaded a program from the Internet, then clicked to install it — and then, a second later, think, "Why did I do that?"

Microsoft came up with an interesting technique it calls SmartScreen that gives you an extra chance to change your mind, if the software you're trying to install has drawn criticism from other Windows customers. It was built into the older version of Internet Explorer, version 9. It's now part of Windows 8.

One part of SmartScreen works in conjunction with Windows Defender. In fact, sometimes I've seen an infected file trigger a toaster notification from Windows Defender, and later had the same infected file prompt the SmartScreen warning shown in Figure 3-5.

Figure 3-5:
Smart-
Screen may
take the
credit for
the bust, but
Windows
Defender
did the
work.

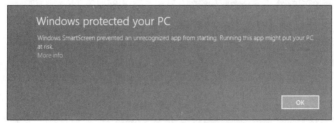

If you tap or click the More Info link in Figure 3-5, Windows shows you the filename and the publisher (if one can be identified), and gives you the option to run the program anyway. If you don't run the program, it gets stuffed into the same location that Windows Defender puts its quarantined programs — out of the way where you can't find it, unless you go in through Windows Defender's History tab (refer to Figure 3-4).

There's a second part of SmartScreen that works completely differently. Something like this:

1. You download something — anything — from the Internet.

   Most browsers and many e-mail programs and other online services (including instant messengers) put a "brand" on the file that indicates where the file came from.

2. When you try to launch the file, Windows checks the name of the file and the URL of origin to see whether they're on a "trusted" white list.

3. If the file doesn't pass muster, you see the notification in Figure 3-5.

4. The more people who install the program from that site, the more "trusted" the program becomes.

   Again, Microsoft is collecting information about your system — in this case, about your downloads — but it's for a good cause.

Microsoft claims that SmartScreen helped protect IE9 users from more than 1.5 billion attempted malware attacks and 150 million phishing attacks. MS also claims that, when a Windows user is confronted with a confirmation message, the risk of getting infected is 25–70 percent. Of course it's impossible to independently verify those figures — and the gap from 25–70 percent gapes — but SmartScreen does seem to help in the fight against scumware.

So what can go wrong? Not a lot. If SmartScreen can't make a connection to its main database when it hits something phishy, er, fishy, you see a blue screen like the one in Figure 3-6 telling you that SmartScreen can't be reached right now. The connection can be broken for many reasons, such as the Microsoft servers go down or maybe you downloaded a program and decided to run it later. When that happens, if you can't get your machine connected, you're on your own.

Figure 3-6:
If Smart-
Screen
can't phone
home, it
leaves
you on
your own.

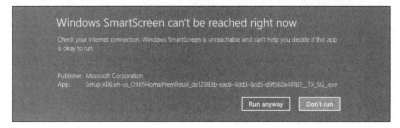

Turning off SmartScreen is an option when you install Windows 8. You can also turn it off manually. Normally, overriding a SmartScreen warning requires the okay of someone with an administrator account. You can change that, too. Here's how:

1. **On the Start screen, type act; on the right, choose Settings and on the left, choose Action Center.**

   The Windows Action Center appears.

2. **Tap or click the down arrow to the right of Security.**

   A lengthy list of security options appears.

3. **Under Windows SmartScreen, tap or click the Change Settings link.**

   The Windows SmartScreen dialog box appears, as shown in Figure 3-7.

Figure 3-7:
Think twice
before
turning
off Smart-
Screen.

4. **Tap or click the appropriate button to drop the requirement for an administrative account in order to okay a SmartScreen warning override, or to turn off SmartScreen entirely.**

5. **Tap or click OK.**

   If you disabled SmartScreen, you see a near-immediate reaction in the desktop's notification area, warning you that SmartScreen has been turned off.

Booting Securely with UEFI

If you've ever struggled with your PC's BIOS — or been knee-capped by a capable rootkit — you know that BIOS should've been sent to the dugout a decade ago.

Windows 8 will pull the industry kicking and screaming out of the BIOS generation and into a far more capable — and controversial — alternative, *Unified Extensible Firmware Interface* (UEFI). Although UEFI machines in the time of Windows 7 were unusual, starting with Windows 8, every new machine with a Runs Windows 8 sticker is required to run UEFI; it's part of the licensing requirement. Tis a brave new world.

A brief history of BIOS

To understand where Windows is headed, it's best to look at where it's been. And where it's been with BIOS inside PCs spans the entire history of the Personal Computer. That makes PC-resident BIOS more than 30 years old. The very first IBM PC had a BIOS, and it didn't look all that different from the inscrutable one you swear at now.

The Basic Input/Output System, or *BIOS*, is a program responsible for getting all your PC's hardware in order and then firing up the operating system — in this case, Windows — and finally handing control of the computer over to the OS. BIOS runs automatically when the PC is turned on.

Older operating systems, such as DOS, relied on BIOS to perform input and output functions. More modern OSs, including Windows, have their own device drivers that make BIOS control obsolete, once the OS is running.

Every BIOS has a user interface, which looks a lot like the one in Figure 3-8. You press a key while the BIOS is starting and, using obscure keyboard incantations, take some control over your PC's hardware, select boot devices (in other words, tell BIOS where the operating system is located), overclock the processor, disable or rearrange hard drives, and the like.

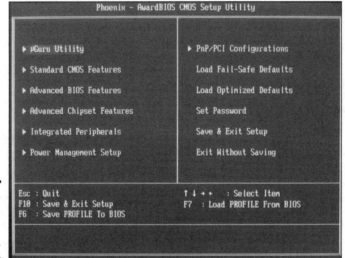

```
              Phoenix - AwardBIOS CMOS Setup Utility

    ▶ µGuru Utility                    ▶ PnP/PCI Configurations

    ▶ Standard CMOS Features           Load Fail-Safe Defaults

    ▶ Advanced BIOS Features           Load Optimized Defaults

    ▶ Advanced Chipset Features        Set Password

    ▶ Integrated Peripherals           Save & Exit Setup

    ▶ Power Management Setup           Exit Without Saving


    Esc  : Quit                    ↑ ↓ → ←    : Select Item
    F10  : Save & Exit Setup       F7   : Load PROFILE From BIOS
    F6   : Save PROFILE To BIOS
```

Figure 3-8:
The
AwardBIOS
Setup Utility.

The PC you're using right now may or may not have UEFI, and even if it does have UEFI, you may not be able to get to it. Windows 8 runs just fine on BIOS systems, but it can protect you even better — especially from rootkits — if your PC supports UEFI.

How UEFI is different from/better than BIOS

BIOS has all sorts of problems, not the least of which is its susceptibility to malware. Rootkits like to hook themselves into the earliest part of the booting process — permitting them to run underneath Windows — and BIOS has a big Kick Me sign on its tail.

UEFI and BIOS can coexist: UEFI can run on top of BIOS, hooking itself into the program locations where the operating system might call BIOS, basically usurping all the BIOS functions after UEFI gets going. UEFI can also run without BIOS, taking care of all the run-time functions. The only thing UEFI can't do is perform the *POST* power-on self test, or run the initial setup. PCs that have UEFI without BIOS need separate programs, for POST and setup, that run automatically when the PC is started.

Unlike BIOS, which sits inside a chip on your PC's motherboard, UEFI can exist on a disk, just like any other program, or in non-volatile memory on the motherboard, or even on a network share.

UEFI is very much like an operating system that runs before your final operating system kicks in. UEFI has access to all the PC's hardware, including the mouse and network connections. It can take advantage of your fancy video card and monitor, as shown in Figure 3-9. It can even access the Internet. If you've ever played with BIOS, you know that this is in a whole new dimension.

Compare Figure 3-8 with 3-9, and you'll have some idea where technology's been and where it's heading.

BIOS — the whole process surrounding BIOS, including POST — takes a long, long time. UEFI, by contrast, can go by quite quickly. The BIOS program itself is easy to reverse-engineer, and has no internal security protection. In the malware maelstrom, it's a sitting duck. UEFI can run in any irascible, malware-dodging way its inventors contrive.

Dual boot in the old world involves a handoff to a clunky text program; in the new world, it can be much simpler, more visual, and controlled by mouse or touch.

Figure 3-9:
The UEFI
interface
on an
ASUS PC.

More to the point, UEFI can police operating systems prior to loading them. That could make rootkit writers' lives considerably more difficult by, for example, refusing to run an OS unless it has a proper digital security signature. Windows Defender can work with UEFI to validate OS's before they're loaded. And that's where the controversy begins.

How Windows 8 uses UEFI

A UEFI *Secure Boot* option validates programs before allowing them to run. If Secure Boot is turned on, Operating System loaders have to be "signed" using a digital certificate. If you want to dual boot between Windows 8 and Linux, the Linux program has to have a digital certificate — something Linux programs have never required before.

After UEFI validates the digital key, UEFI calls on Windows Defender to verify the certificate for the OS loader. Windows Defender (or another security program) can go out to the Internet and check to see whether UEFI is about to run an OS that has had its certificate yanked.

So, in essence, in a dual boot system, Windows Defender decides whether an operating system gets loaded on your Secure Boot-enabled machine.

That curls the toes of many Linux fans. Why should their operating system be subject to Microsoft's rules, if you want to dual boot between Windows 8 and Linux?

If you have a PC with UEFI and Secure Boot, and you want to boot an operating system that doesn't have a Microsoft-approved digital signature, you have two options:

✦ **You can turn off Secure Boot**.

✦ **You can manually add a key to the UEFI validation routine,** specifically allowing that unsigned operating system to load.

Some PCs won't let you turn off Secure Boot. So if you want to dual boot Windows 8 and some other operating system on a Windows 8 certified computer, you may have a lot of hoops to jump through. Check with your hardware manufacturer.

Controlling User Account Control

User Account Control *(UAC)* is a pain in the neck, but then again, it's supposed to be a pain in the neck. If you try to install a program that's going to make system-level changes, you see the obnoxious prompt in Figure 3-10.

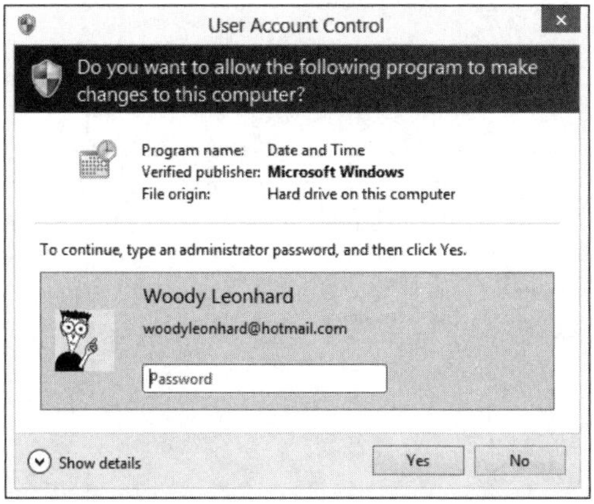

Figure 3-10:
User
Account
Control tries
to keep
you from
clobbering
your system.

UAC's a drama queen, too. The approval dialog box in Figure 3-10 appears front and center, but at the same time, your entire desktop dims, and you're forced to deal with the UAC prompt.

UAC grabs you by the eyeballs and shakes once or twice for a good reason: It's telling you that a program wants to make changes to your system — not piddling things like changing a document or opening a picture, but earthshaking things like modifying the Registry or poking around inside system folders.

If you go into your system folders manually, or if you fire up the Registry Editor and start making loose and fancy with Registry keys, UAC figures you know what you're doing and leaves you alone. But the minute a program tries to do those kinds of things, Windows whups you upside the head, warns you that a potentially dangerous program is on the prowl, and gives you a chance to kill the program in its tracks.

Windows lets you adjust User Account Control so it isn't quite as dramatic — or you can get rid of it entirely.

To bring up the slider and adjust your computer's UAC level, follow these steps:

1. **Using an administrator account, on the Start screen, type** user; **on the right, choose Settings, and on the left, choose Change User Account Control Settings.**

The slider shown in Figure 3-11 appears.

Figure 3-11: Windows allows you to change the level of UAC intrusiveness.

2. **Adjust the slider according to Table 2-1, and then tap or click OK.**

Perhaps surprisingly, as soon as you try to change your UAC level, Windows hits you with a User Account Control prompt (refer to Figure 3-10). If you're using a standard account, you have to provide an administrator username and password to make the change. If you're using an administrator account, you have to confirm the change.

3. **Tap or click Yes.**

Your changes take effect immediately.

Table 2-1	User Account Control Levels	
Slider	*What It Means*	*Recommendations*
Level 1	Always brings up the full UAC notification whenever a program tries to install software or make changes to the computer that require an administrator account, or when you try to make changes to Windows settings that require an administrator account. You see these notifications even if you're using an administrator account. The screen blacks out, and you can't do anything until the UAC screen is answered. The default setting.	This level offers the highest security but also the highest hassle factor.
Level 2	Brings up the UAC notification whenever a program tries to make changes to your computer, but generally doesn't bring up a UAC notification when you make changes directly.	The default — and probably the best choice.
Level 3	This level is the same as Level 2 except that the UAC notification doesn't lock and dim your desktop.	Potentially problematic. Dimming and locking the screen presents a high hurdle for malware.
Level 4	UAC is disabled — programs can install other programs or make changes to Windows settings, and you can change anything you like, without triggering any UAC prompts. Note that this doesn't override other security settings. For example, if you're using a standard account, you still need to provide an administrator's ID and password before you can install a program that runs for all users.	Choosing Level 4 automatically turns off all UAC warnings — not recommended.

This description sounds simple, but the details are quite complex. Consider. Microsoft's Help system says that if your computer is at Level 2, the default setting in Windows, "You will be notified if a program outside of Windows tries to make changes to a Windows setting." So how does Windows tell when a program is "outside of Windows" — and thus whether actions taken by the program are worthy of a UAC prompt at Levels 2 or 3?

UAC-level rules are interpreted according to a special Windows security certificate. Programs signed with that certificate are deemed to be part of Windows. Programs that aren't signed with that specific certificate are "outside of Windows" and thus trigger UAC prompts if your computer is at Level 1, 2, or 3.

Poking at Windows Firewall

A *firewall* is a program that sits between your computer and the Internet, protecting you from the big, mean, nasty gorillas riding around on the information superhighway. An *inbound firewall* acts like a traffic cop that, in the best of all possible worlds, allows only "good" stuff into your computer and keeps all the "bad" stuff out on the Internet, where it belongs. An *outbound firewall* prevents your computer from sending bad stuff to the Internet, such as when your computer becomes infected with a virus or has another security problem.

Windows includes a usable (if not fancy) inbound firewall. It also includes a snarly, hard-to-configure, rudimentary outbound firewall, which has all the social graces of a junkyard dog. Unless you know the magic incantations, you never even see the outbound firewall — it's completely muzzled unless you dig into the Windows doghouse and teach it some tricks.

Everybody needs an inbound firewall, without a doubt. You already have one, in Windows 8, and you don't need to do anything to it.

Outbound firewalls tend to bother you mercilessly with inscrutable warnings saying that obscure processes are trying to send data. If you simply click through and let the program phone home, you're defeating the purpose of the outbound firewall. On the other hand, if you take the time to track down every single outbound event warning, you might spend half your life chasing firewall snipes.

I have a few friends who insist on running an outbound firewall. They uniformly recommend Comodo Firewall, which is available in a free-for-personal-use version at `http://personalfirewall.comodo.com`.

I think outbound firewalls are a complete waste of time. Although I'm sure some people have been alerted to Windows infections when their outbound firewall goes bananas, 99.99 percent of the time the outbound warnings are just noise. Outbound firewalls don't catch the cleverest malware, anyway.

Hardware firewalls

Most modern routers and wireless access points include significant firewalling capability. It's part and parcel of the way they work, when they share an Internet connection among many computers.

Routers and wireless access points add an extra step between your computer and the Internet. That extra jump — named network address translation — combined with innate intelligence on the router's part can provide an extra layer of protection that works independently from, but in conjunction with, the firewall running on your PC.

Understanding Firewall basic features

All versions of Windows 8 ship with a decent and capable, but not foolproof, *stateful* firewall named Windows Firewall (WF). (See the nearby sidebar, "What's a stateful firewall?")

The WF inbound firewall is on by default. Unless you change something, Windows Firewall is turned on for all connections on your PC. For example, if you have a LAN cable, a wireless networking card, and a 3G USB card on a specific PC, WF is turned on for them all. The only way Windows Firewall gets turned off is if you deliberately turn it off or if the network administrator on your Big Corporate Network decides to disable it by remote control or install Windows service packs with Windows Firewall turned off.

In extremely unusual circumstances, malware (viruses, Trojans, whatever) have been known to turn off Windows Firewall. If your firewall kicks out, Windows lets you know loud and clear with balloon notifications near the system clock on the desktop, toaster notifications from the right on the Start screen, and a crescendo from Ride of the Valkyries blaring on your speakers.

You can change WF settings for inbound protection relatively easily. When you make changes, they apply to all connections on your PC. On the other hand, WF settings for outbound protection make the rules of cricket look like child's play.

WF kicks in before the computer is connected to the network. Back in the not-so-good old days, many PCs got infected between the time they were connected and when the firewall came up.

What's a stateful firewall?

At the risk of oversimplifying a bit, a *stateful* firewall is an inbound firewall that remembers. A stateful firewall keeps track of packets of information going out of your computer and where they're headed. When a packet arrives and tries to get in, the inbound firewall matches the originating address of the incoming packet against the log of addresses of the outgoing packets to make sure that any packet allowed through the firewall comes from an expected location.

Stateful packet filtering isn't 100 percent foolproof. And, you must have some exceptions so that unexpected packets can come through for reasons discussed elsewhere in this chapter. But a stateful firewall is a fast, reliable way to minimize your exposure to potentially destructive probes from out on the big, bad Internet.

Speaking your firewall's lingo

At this point, I need to inundate you with a bunch of jargon so that you can take control of Windows Firewall. Hold your nose and dive in. The concepts aren't that difficult, although the lousy terminology sounds like it was invented by a first-year advertising student. Refer to this section if you become bewildered when wading through the WF dialog boxes.

As you no doubt realize, the amount of data that can be sent from one computer to another over a network can be tiny or huge. Computers communicate with each other by breaking the data into *packets* (or small chunks of data with a wrapper that identifies where the data came from and where it's going).

On the Internet, packets can be sent in two ways:

+ **User Datagram Protocol (UDP):** UDP is fast and sloppy. The computer sending the packets doesn't keep track of which packets were sent, and the computer receiving the packets doesn't make any attempt to get the sender to resend packets that vanish mysteriously into the bowels of the Internet. UDP is the kind of *protocol* (transmission method) that can work with live broadcasts, where short gaps wouldn't be nearly as disruptive as long pauses, while the computers wait to resend a dropped packet.

+ **Transmission Control Protocol (TCP):** TCP is methodical and complete. The sending computer keeps track of which packets it's sent. If the receiving computer doesn't get a packet, it notifies the sending computer, which resends the packet. Almost all communication over the Internet these days goes by way of TCP.

Every computer on a network has an *IP address,* which is a collection of four sets of numbers, each between 0 and 255. For example, 192.168.1.2 is a common IP address for computers connected to a local network; the computer that handles the Dummies.com website is at 208.215.179.139. You can think of the IP address as analogous to a telephone number. See Book VI, Chapter 6 for details.

Peeking into your firewall

When you use a firewall — and you should — you change the way your computer communicates with other computers on the Internet. This section explains what Windows Firewall does behind the scenes so that when it gets in the way, you understand how to tweak it. (You find the ins and outs of working around the firewall in the "Making inbound exceptions" section, later in this chapter.)

When two computers communicate, they need not only each other's IP address but also a specific entry point called a *port* — think of it as a telephone extension — to talk to each other. For example, most websites respond to requests sent to port 80. There's nothing magical about the number 80; it's just the port number that people have agreed to use when trying to get to a website's computer. If your web browser wants to look at the Dummies.com website, it sends a packet to 208.215.179.139, port 80.

Windows Firewall works by handling all these duties simultaneously:

✦ **It keeps track of outgoing packets and allows incoming packets to go through the firewall if they can be matched with an outgoing packet.** In other words, WF works as a stateful inbound firewall.

✦ **If your computer is attached to a private network, Windows Firewall allows packets to come and go on ports 139 and 445, but only if they came from another computer on your local network and only if they're using TCP.** Windows Firewall needs to open those ports for file and printer sharing. WF also opens several ports for Windows Media Player if you've chosen to share your media files, as you might within a HomeGroup (see Book VII, Chapter 5), for example.

✦ **Similarly, if your computer is attached to a private network, Windows Firewall automatically opens ports 137, 138, and 5355 for UDP, but only for packets that originate on your local network.**

✦ **If you specifically told Windows Firewall that you want it to allow packets to come in on a specific port and the Block All Incoming Connections check box isn't selected, WF follows your orders.** You might need to open a port in this way for online gaming, for example.

✦ **Windows Firewall allows packets to come into your computer if they're sent to the Remote Assistance program, as long as you created a Remote Assistance request on this PC and told Windows to open your firewall (see Book VII, Chapter 2).** Remote Assistance allows other users to take control of your PC, but it has its own security settings and strong password protection. Still, it's a known security hole that's enabled when you create a request.

✦ **You can tell Windows Firewall to accept packets that are directed at specific programs.** Usually, any company that makes a program designed to listen for incoming Internet traffic (Skype is a prime example, as are any instant messaging programs) adds its program to the list of designated exceptions when the program is installed.

✦ **Unless an inbound packet meets one of the preceding criteria, it's simply ignored.** Windows Firewall swallows it without a peep. Conversely, unless you've changed something, any and all outbound traffic goes through unobstructed.

Making inbound exceptions

Firewalls can be absolutely infuriating. You may have a program that has worked for a hundred years on all sorts of computers, but the minute you install it on a Windows 8 machine with Windows Firewall in action, it just stops working, for absolutely no apparent reason.

You can get mad at Microsoft and scream at Windows Firewall, but when you do, realize that at least part of the problem lies in the way the firewall has to work. (See the "Peeking into your firewall" section, earlier in this chapter, for an explanation of what your firewall does behind the scenes.) It has to block packets that are trying to get in, unless you explicitly tell the firewall to allow them to get in.

Perhaps most infuriatingly, WF has to block those packets by simply swallowing them, not by notifying the computer that sent the packet. Windows Firewall has to remain "stealthy" because if it sends back a packet that says, "Hey, I got your packet but I can't let it through," the bad guys get an acknowledgment that your computer exists, they can probably figure out which firewall you're using, and they may be able to combine those two pieces of information to give you a headache. It's far better for Windows Firewall to act like a black hole.

Some programs need to "listen" to incoming traffic from the Internet; they wait until they're contacted and then respond. Usually, you know whether you have this type of program because the installer tells you that you need to tell your firewall to back off.

If you have a program that doesn't (or can't) poke its own hole through the Windows Firewall, you can tell WF to allow packets destined for that specific program — and *only* that program — in through the firewall. You might want to do that with a game that needs to accept incoming traffic, for example, or for an Outlook extender program that interacts with mobile phones.

To poke a hole in the inbound Windows Firewall for a specific program:

1. **Make sure that the program you want to allow through the Firewall is installed.**

2. **On the Start screen, type** firewall**; on the right, choose Settings, and then on the left, choose Allow an App Through Windows Firewall.**

Windows Firewall presents you with a lengthy list of programs that you might want to allow (see Figure 3-12): If a box is selected, Windows Firewall allows unsolicited incoming packets of data directed to that program and that program alone, and the column tells you whether the connection is allowed for private or public connections.

These settings don't apply to incoming packets of data that are received in response to a request from your computer; they apply only when a packet of data appears on your firewall's doorstep without an invitation.

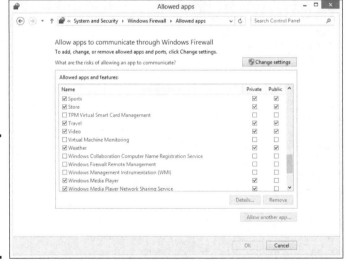

Figure 3-12:
Allow installed programs to poke through the firewall.

In Figure 3-12, the tiled Weather app is allowed to receive inbound packets whether you're connected to a private or public network. Windows Media Player, on the other hand, may accept unsolicited inbound data from other computers only if you're connected to a private network: If you're attached to a public network, inbound packets headed for Windows Media Player are swallowed by the WF Black Hole (patent pending).

3a. ***If you can find the program that you want to poke through the firewall listed in the Allow Programs list,*** **select the check boxes that correspond to whether you want to allow the unsolicited incoming data when connected to a home or work network and whether you want to allow the incoming packets when connected to a public network.**

It's rare indeed that you'd allow access when connected to a public network but not to a home or work network.

3b. ***If you can't find the program that you want to poke through the firewall,*** **you need to go out and look for it. Tap or click the Change Settings button at the top and then tap or click the Allow another App button at the bottom.**

You have to tap or click the Change Settings button first and then tap or click Allow another Program. It's kind of a double-down protection feature that ensures you don't accidentally change things.

Windows Firewall goes out to all common program locations and finally presents you with the Whack a Mol . . . er, Add an App list like the one shown in Figure 3-13. It can take a while.

Figure 3-13:
Windows Firewall suggestions for programs you might want to poke through it.

4. **Choose the program you want to add, and then tap or click the Add button.**

Realize that you're opening a potential, albeit small, security hole. The program you choose had better be quite capable of handling packets from unknown sources. If you authorize a renegade program to accept incoming packets, the bad program could let the fox into the chicken coop. If you know what I mean.

You return to the Windows Firewall Allowed Apps list (refer to Figure 3-12), and your newly selected program is now available.

5. **Select the check boxes to allow your poked-through program to accept incoming data while you're connected to a private or a public network. Then tap or click OK.**

Your poked-through program can immediately start handling inbound data.

In many cases, poking through the Windows Firewall doesn't solve the whole problem. You may have to poke through your modem or router as well — unsolicited packets that arrive at the router may get kicked back according to the router's rules, even if Windows would allow them in. Unfortunately, each router and the method for poking holes in the router's inbound firewall differs. Check the site `www.portforward.com/routers.htm` for an enormous amount of information about poking through routers.

Chapter 4: Top Security Helpers

In This Chapter

✓ **Deciding whether to pay for BitLocker**

✓ **Keeping on top of all those passwords**

✓ **Watching your programs for updates**

✓ **Blocking Java and Flash in your browser**

✓ **The ultimate antiscumware scan**

*1*n Chapter 3 of this minibook, I talk about built-in Windows programs that are available to every Windows 8 owner. In this chapter, I cast the web out a bit further, to include one Microsoft encryption program you have to pay for — *BitLocker* for Windows 8 Pro — and a handful of free-for-personal use programs that belong on every Windows 8 user's desktop.

Windows covers a lot of security bases, but it doesn't touch them all.

Two very good programs will store all your passwords, and automatically fill in the username/password prompts at the websites you visit. One of them, *LastPass,* is based in the *cloud,* which means you can get at it even when you're on a dive boat in the Similans. The other, *RoboForm,* stores its data on your computer, or on a USB drive. I take you through the pros and cons of both approaches in this chapter.

Sometimes you — or one of your friends — will get an infection that even Windows Defender (and Windows Defender Offline) can't handle. Usually it's because you (or, say, "they") installed a program they didn't research. If you (er, they) get hit bad, there's one place to turn. *Malwarebytes,* a combination of software and a very competent website, can crack just about any infection.

Secunia Personal Software Inspector is free and does an amazing job of helping you keep all your software up to date.

Finally, I know of one specific Java and Flash blocker that works very well in the Firefox browser. *NoScript* can be customized in many ways. Although there are more-or-less similar choices for Chrome and Internet Explorer, NoScript works the best of them all. It's the primary reason why I use Firefox as my main browser.

The Encrypting File System (EFS)

The Microsoft *Encrypting File System* works with or without BitLocker. EFS is a method for encrypting individual files or groups of files on a hard drive. EFS starts after Windows boots: It runs as a program under Windows, which means it can leave traces of itself and the data that's being encrypted in temporary Windows places that may be sniffed by exploit programs. The Windows directory isn't encrypted by EFS, so bad guys (and girls!) who can get access to the directory can hammer it with brute-force password attacks. Widely available tools can crack EFS if the cracker can reboot the, uh, crackee's computer. Thus, for example, EFS can't protect the hard drive on a stolen laptop/notebook. Windows has supported the Encrypting File System since the halcyon days of Windows 2000.

BitLocker and EFS protect against two completely different kinds of attacks. Given a choice, you probably want BitLocker.

All these programs are free, well known, tested — and they need to be part of your Windows system.

Deciding about BitLocker

BitLocker encrypts an entire drive. (Actually, it encrypts a volume, not a drive, but you get the idea.) Unlike the Encrypting File System (see the nearby "The Encrypting File System [EFS]" sidebar), you have to encrypt full drives, or nothing at all. BitLocker runs *underneath* Windows: It starts before Windows starts. The Windows partition on a BitLocker protected drive is completely encrypted. Even if a thief gets his hands on your laptop or hard drive, he can't view anything on it — not even your settings or system files.

BitLocker To Go is quite similar to BitLocker, except it works on USB drives.

BitLocker is part of Windows 8 Pro. It is not part of the regular version of Windows 8. If you have Windows 8 and you want to get BitLocker, you have to upgrade to Windows 8 Pro. There's no other way to get it.

I talk about the various versions of Windows 8 in Book I, Chapter 3. Suffice it to say that some people feel their information is sufficiently valuable that BitLocker, all by itself, justifies paying the extra bucks for Windows 8 Pro.

Here's how to encrypt your hard drive with BitLocker:

1. **Wait until you have several hours free.**

Encrypting a drive can take a long, long, long, time.

2. **On the Start screen, type** bit; **on the right, choose Settings, and on the left, tap or click BitLocker Drive Encryption.**

The BitLocker Drive Encryption dialog box appears, as shown in Figure 4-1.

Figure 4-1:
Encrypt
full drives
(actually,
volumes)
using a key
you specify.

3. **Next to the drive (volume) you want to encrypt, tap or click Turn On BitLocker.**

4. **If you get a message asking you to verify, choose Yes.**

If your PC doesn't have a built-in Trusted Platform Module system, you see a message that says, Your administrator must set the 'Allow BitLocker without a compatible TPM' option. The only easy way to solve that problem is to run the Local Group Policy Editor program, gpedit.msc. If you need advice, check out the TechNet article at http://technet.microsoft.com/en-us/library/cc732725(v=ws.10).aspx#BKMK_S5.

The BitLocker Drive Encryption setup dialog box appears.

5. **Tap or click Next.**

On Operating System drives (such as your drive C:), the Preparing Your Drive dialog box appears.

6. **Tap or click Next.**

On removable drives, BitLocker asks how you want to unlock the drive, as shown in Figure 4-2.

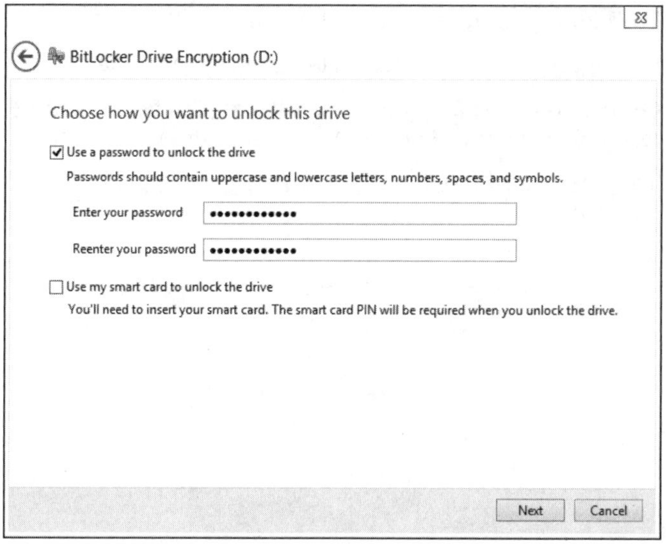

[BitLocker Drive Encryption (D:)]

Choose how you want to unlock this drive

☑ Use a password to unlock the drive

Passwords should contain uppercase and lowercase letters, numbers, spaces, and symbols.

Enter your password   ••••••••••••

Reenter your password   ••••••••••••

☐ Use my smart card to unlock the drive

You'll need to insert your smart card. The smart card PIN will be required when you unlock the drive.

[Next] [Cancel]

Figure 4-2:
Enter your
password.

7. **Enter your password twice and tap or click Next.**

   On an operating system drive, BitLocker asks how you want to unlock the drive.

8. **Tap or click Require a Startup Key at Every Startup.**

   That ensures data on a stolen laptop can't be purloined.

   On an operating system drive, BitLocker asks how you want to store your recovery key.

9. **Choose Save the Recovery Key to a USB Flash Drive.**

   The wizard takes you through the steps.

10. **Select the Run BitLocker System Check check box and then choose Continue.**

    BitLocker asks for your permission and then reboots your system. After rebooting, it starts encrypting — a process that can take a few minutes on a USB drive, or many hours on a full C: drive.

If you encrypted your operating system drive — typically your C: drive — keep that USB drive in a safe place. You need it every time you want to boot your computer.

Oh. In case you were wondering. Yes, you can use BitLocker on Storage Spaces. BitLocker encrypts the whole Storage Space.

Managing Your Passwords

You can find no end of advice on creating strong passwords, using clever tricks, stats, mnemonics, and such. But all too frequently people (myself included in this rebuke) tend to reuse little passwords at what people think are inconsequential sites. It's a big mistake. If somebody hacks into that small-time site and steals your password — a process that's frighteningly common these days — any other place where you've used that same password is immediately vulnerable.

There have been some spectacular examples of ultra-secure sites getting hacked in the past few years, where the hacker stole a username and password off a little, inconsequential site, and then discovered that the same username and password opened the doors to a trove of top secret — even politically sensitive — corporate e-mail or customer bank account information. The usernames and passwords were stolen from seasoned security professionals and admins at sensitive sites. You'd think they'd know better.

Using password managers

I don't know about you, but I have more than a hundred usernames and passwords that I use fairly regularly. There's just no way I could remember them all. And my monitor isn't big enough to handle all the yellow sticky notes they'd demand.

That's where a password manager comes in. A *password manager* keeps track of all your online passwords. It can generate truly random passwords with the click of a button. Most of all, it remembers the username and password necessary to log on to a specific website.

Every time I go to `www.ebay.com`, for example, my password manager fills in my username and password. Amazon, too. Facebook. Twitter. My bank. Stock brokerage house. I have to remember the one password for the password manager, but after that, everything else gets filled in automatically. It's a huge timesaver.

A password manager won't log on to Windows for you, and it won't remember the passwords on documents or spreadsheets. But it does keep track of every online password, and regurgitates the passwords you need with absolutely no hassle.

Which is better: Online or inhand?

I have used two password-remembering programs for many years. I like — and trust — them both. The big difference between them? One is on a USB drive; the other is on the Internet:

✦ **RoboForm,** which can store passwords on your hard drive or on a USB drive, works with all the major web browsers, and has simple tools for synchronizing passwords between your hard drive and a USB drive.

✦ **LastPass,** which stores passwords on its website, uses an encryption technique that guarantees your passwords won't get stolen or cracked. I talk about the encryption method in the section "Liking LastPass," later in this chapter.

Which one is better? It depends on how you use your computer.

If you always use the same computer, or you can always remember to sync and take your RoboForm2Go USB drive with you, RoboForm works great.

Unfortunately, I don't meet either of those two criteria, so in recent years, I've been using LastPass. Of course, there's an additional security concern because your data's stored on LastPass's servers and not on the USB drive in your pocket. Of course, you need an Internet connection to get to LastPass — but then if you don't have an Internet connection, you probably don't need RoboForm, either.

Rockin' RoboForm

RoboForm (www.roboform.com) has all the features you need in a password manager. It manages your passwords, of course, with excellent recognition of websites, automatically filling in your login details, but it'll also generate random passwords for you, if you like, fill in forms on the web, and create backups either on a USB drive or on another computer on your network.

RoboForm stores all its data on a disk in AES-256 encrypted format. If somebody steals your RoboForm database, you needn't worry. Without the master key — which only you have — the whole database is gibberish.

RoboForm has versions for Windows, Mac, Linux, iPhone, iPad, Android phones and tablets, and BlackBerry. You need to buy a separate license for each computer, device, or USB drive.

The evaluation version of RoboForm (which can store up to ten passwords) is free. The Pro version, with unlimited storage and several additional features, runs $29.95.

There's a new RoboForm Everywhere offering that I haven't tried. It will store all your information on RoboForm's servers, so you can download it and use it anywhere — even on an unlimited number of computers. The trick is the price: Unlike the other versions, where you pay once and have a license for that specific version forever, RoboForm Everywhere costs $19.95 per year. The first year's discounted to $9.95.

What is AES-256?

The most effective encryption method that's commonly used on PCs conforms to the U.S. National Institute of Standards and Technology's Advanced Encryption Standard 256-bit specification.

AES is the first widely available, open encryption technique (yes, you can look at the program) that's been approved by the U.S. National Security Agency for Top Secret information. Of course, that fact has led to speculation that the

NSA has cracked the algorithm, so they can decrypt AES-256 data, but there doesn't seem to be any corroboration. I guess the conspiracy theory makes for good beer drinking banter, but not much more.

It's been estimated that if you took all the computer horsepower currently on the face of the earth, and set it to work on a single AES-256 encrypted file, cracking the encryption would take far longer than the age of the universe.

Liking LastPass

LastPass (www.lastpass.com) stores everything "in the cloud" on LastPass's servers. Like RoboForm, LastPass keeps track of your user IDs, passwords, and other settings and offers them to you with a click.

Using LastPass couldn't be simpler. Download and install it, and it'll appear with a red asterisk in the upper-right corner of your browser (see Figure 4-3).

LastPass

Figure 4-3:
LastPass is on the job if you can see a red asterisk in the upper-right corner.

You don't really need to do anything. LastPass will prompt you for the master password when you start using your browser. If LastPass is turned off, the star icon turns gray. Tap or click it, provide the master password, and the LastPass icon turns red again, ready to roll.

When you go to a site that requires a username and password, if LastPass recognizes the site, it fills them both in for you. If LastPass doesn't recognize the site, you fill in the blanks and click, and LastPass will remember the credentials for the next time you surf this way.

Form filling works similarly.

You can maintain two (or more) separate usernames and passwords for any specific site — say, you log on to a banking site with two different accounts. If LastPass has more than one set of credentials stored for a specific site, it'll take its best guess as to which one you want, but then give you the option of using one of the others.

Any time you want to look at the usernames and passwords that LastPass has squirreled away, tap or click the red LastPass icon. You have a chance to look at your *Vault* — which is your password database — or look up recently used passwords, and much more.

The way LastPass handles your data is quite clever. All your passwords are encrypted using AES-256. They're encrypted and decrypted *on your PC.* Only you have the master password. So if the data is pilfered off LastPass's servers, or somebody is sniffing your online communication, all the interlopers get is a bunch of useless bits.

LastPass is free for individual use. If you want versions for iPhone, iPad, Android, Windows Phone, or to run LastPass without installing a plugin (important for the tiled "immersive" version of Windows 8 web browsers), you need the Premium edition, which costs $12 a year.

Keeping Your Other Programs Up to Date

You have Windows Update to keep Windows working and patched.

But what about all the other programs on your PC? Considering that something like 80 percent of all new infections come from *third-party* programs (read: software written by some company other than Microsoft), keeping those other programs updated is a crucial task.

That's where Secunia Personal Software Inspector — Secunia PSI to its friends — comes into play. Secunia PSI keeps tabs on every program in your computer. (Well, some really weird programs may not make the cut.) Secunia PSI keeps on top of the latest patches for every single program, and it warns you if the software you have is out of date.

If you use the Automatic Update features — which I recommend — Secunia PSI will even install updates for you, as they become available.

Ironic that I don't recommend Automatic Update for Windows, but I do for all the non-Microsoft programs, eh? That's because massive mess-ups with the other programs usually won't bring your PC to its knees. A bad update in, say, Java, or Flash, will make some websites crash, but you can probably work around that. A bad update in Windows can bring your whole computer down. Big difference.

Here's how to install Secunia Personal Software Inspector:

1. **Go to the Secunia main site (www.secunia.com) and tap or click the Download the Free Secunia PSI link.**

2. **Tap or click the Download button, and depending on your browser, either save or run the file.**

   The Setup Wizard starts.

3. **Accept all the defaults, including when the wizard asks whether you want to Install Updates Automatically, make sure you select the box before choosing Install.**

   Automatic updates are an important feature of Secunia PSI.

   After the wizard ends, it asks whether you want to Launch Secunia PSI now.

4. **Choose Yes.**

   The first run can take a long, long time, so be patient.

5. **If PSI prompts you to run a scan, do so.**

   When the scan finishes, you see a screen like Figure 4-4.

Figure 4-4:
Secunia
PSI's first
scan usually
brings
surprises.

6. **If any programs in the upper part of the screen need attention — for example, if you need to select the language for a particular program — tap or click the program and follow the instructions.**

   Secunia PSI may take a few minutes, it may take a few hours, but when it's done, all your applications are updated.

PSI offers only two options, under the Settings wheel:

✦ **Start on Boot:** You may or may not want to because it does tie up your machine for a while.

✦ **Install Updates Automatically:** Almost everybody needs this.

Blocking Java and Flash in Your Browser

Giorgio Maone has done the world a favor by bringing the NoScript add-on to the Firefox browser. NoScript selectively blocks Java, JavaScript, Flash, and other plugins — you control when and how. NoScript doesn't work in Chrome or Internet Explorer.

NoScript is so good that I use Firefox as my main browser on the desktop, simply because it's the only browser that supports NoScript.

As this book went to press, Google announced that they have a new, improved "sandbox" in Chrome that effectively keeps Flash safely tied up in a separate cocoon, where Flash can't crash or control the PC. If the sandbox lives up to its advance billing, I may end up using Chrome as my number-one browser. Follow the latest on www.AskWoody.com.

Although Java and Flash may or may not be able to poke through their sandboxes in tiled "immersive" full-screen browsers, there's no question you have to worry about Java and Flash — the two leading sources of Windows infections, by far — if you use a browser on the desktop.

Installing and using NoScript is easy. Here's how:

1. **Start Firefox, and in the upper-left corner, tap or click Firefox and then choose Add-Ons.**

   The standard Firefox add-ons page appears.

2. **In the search box, in the upper right, type** noscript **and then press Enter or tap the magnifying glass icon.**

   Firefox comes up with a list of about a zillion add-ons, and the first is NoScript.

3. **To the right of NoScript, tap or click Install.**

   Firefox downloads and installs NoScript. You have to restart Firefox.

   The NoScript S appears in the lower-left or lower-right corner of Firefox (depending on the version).

4. **Tap or click the NoScript S icon and choose Options, or tap or click the Options button and choose Options. Then tap or click the Embeddings tab.**

   The NoScript Options dialog box appears, as shown in Figure 4-5.

5. **Consult Table 4-1 and see whether you want to change any of the settings. If you do, select or deselect the appropriate box(es) and tap or click OK.**

   The NoScript Release Notes page may appear. If it does, ignore everything about running Registry cleaners.

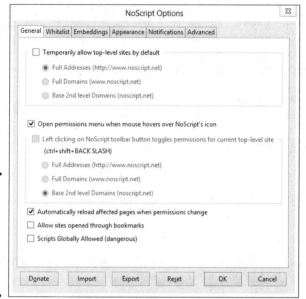

Figure 4-5:
NoScript's
default
configura-
tion really
locks things
down.

6. **Review the annotated directions at** `www.noscript.net/screenshots`.

You may have to click the S icon and select Temporarily Allow All on This Page for the video to run.

By the time you've gone through the video and the tutorial, you're in very good shape.

Getting used to NoScript may take a while. You're going to find that some of the sites you visit all the time — including financial sites and most sites with ordering baskets — won't work unless you allow scripts on the site. You may even hate me for recommending it to you. Fair enough.

At the same time, you should feel much more secure, knowing that the largest source of Windows infections are being blocked before they even have a chance to get into your PC.

NoScript is absolutely free. The effort's supported a little bit by those cloying Clean Your Registry and other ads, when they appear, but primarily by donations from people like you and me. If you use NoScript, take a minute to make a donation via the Donate button in the upper-right corner. You'll be helping to make the web a safer place for everybody. And, yes, PayPal is already on NoScript's "allowed" white list.

Table 4-1	NoScript Restrictions
Forbid	*And You Block*
Java	Both JavaScript and Java. In spite of the names, Java (which is a complex programming language that interacts with the Java Runtime Environment on your PC) and JavaScript (which is a much simpler language that runs on your PC all by itself) are very different. Historically, JavaScript was used by malicious websites to wreak havoc. More recently, Java — particularly aided by bugs in the Java Runtime Environment — has become a very fertile ground for attacks. Shopping sites, such as Amazon and eBay, use Java programs to keep track of your shopping cart and purchases. E-mail sites, such as Hotmail/Outlook.com and Gmail, also need Java, as do forums. You have to tell NoScript to back off on those sites.
Flash	Any Flash videos on a site won't play. If you think that means you can't watch videos on YouTube, you're wrong: YouTube has spent years converting the vast majority of its videos to other formats, including formats that work with NoScript. If you have NoScript set to block Flash, and you go to a YouTube site, YouTube is smart enough to understand that it can't play Flash, and will switch to a different format if it's available. The web is finally getting rid of Flash. Slowly.
Silverlight	Microsoft's answer to Flash is so bad that Microsoft *itself* isn't allowing Silverlight into the tiled full-screen part of Windows 8. That should tell you something. Don't need it. Don't want it.
Other Plugins	A motley assortment of plugins get stopped in their tracks including, notably, any PDF rendering plugins. Select this box and you can't read PDF files directly in your browser; you have to go through the extra step of downloading the PDF file and opening it in a viewer, preferably one other than Adobe Acrobat Reader, which has been plagued with security holes for years. Choosing this box also blocks QuickTime files.

Fighting Back at Tough Scumware

Windows Defender works great. But sometimes you need a second opinion. Sometimes you get hit with an infection that's so nasty, absolutely nothing will clean it up.

That's when you want to check out Malwarebytes (`www.malwarebytes.org`).

Malwarebytes is a last resort. If your system is running normally, there's no reason to bother with it. In fact, if your system is really messed up, you can probably fix things with a full scan in Windows Defender (see Book IX, Chapter 3) or Windows Defender Offline — or even a System Refresh (see Book VIII, Chapter 2). If you've tried all that and still can't get your furshlinger machine to work properly, time to haul out the big guns.

Malwarebytes has long been my software (and site) of choice for going after absolutely intractable infections — viruses, Trojans, scumware, spyware, retroware, introware, sticky gooey messyware, you name it, Malwarebytes can probably get rid of it.

When you're ready to tear out your hair, you've run Windows Defender and Windows Defender Offline, and performed Refresh, and you *still* can't get rid of the beast that's plaguing your system, here's what to do:

1. **Go to the Malwarebytes support forum,** `http://forums.malware bytes.org`, **see whether anyone has the same problem, and if so, log on and talk to them.**

2. **If that doesn't work, go to the Malwarebytes Anti-Malware Free site,** `http://malwarebytes.org/products/malwarebytes_free`, **and install the free version of its anti-malware package.**

During the installation phase, Malwarebytes disables parts of Windows Defender. Not to worry. You don't want to run two antivirus packages at the same time.

3. **Run Malwarebytes and, if it doesn't get rid of your problem, post your results on the support forum.**

Start at `http://forums.malwarebytes.org/index.php?show topic=9573` and follow the instructions precisely.

4. **If Malwarebytes fixes your problem, pay for its Pro package.**

Even if you only use it occasionally. It's only $24.95, and you're helping to keep the Malwarebytes effort solvent.

You should only run Malwarebytes manually: Don't let it run all the time because you'll hit inevitable conflicts with Windows Defender. When Malwarebytes is done with a manual scan, it returns Windows Defender to its full and upright position.

Book X

Enhancing Windows 8

Contents at a Glance

Chapter 1: Using Your iPad and iPhone with Windows

In This Chapter

✔ Discovering the best peripheral your PC ever had

✔ Running iTunes on Windows

✔ Breaking the iTunes link with iCloud

✔ Recommending great iPad apps to use with Windows

✔ Letting your kids use iPads and iPhones

*L*ike it or not — and I know that many don't — tablets are changing the way the world works and plays. Whether it's an iPad, a Kindle, a Nook, or an Android, mobile devices are rolling over the computing landscape like rainclouds over Redmond. Big rainclouds.

Some people moan about the way "toy computers" are taking over. I, for one, relish it. A tablet is vastly superior to a notebook — even an ultrabook, or any other kind of book — in performing very specific tasks. And they're tasks I do all the time: surfing the web, watching videos, keeping up on Facebook and Twitter, even light e-mail.

Sure, I would never use a tablet or a phone to write a book, or build a complex investment-tracking spreadsheet. But (appearances to the contrary) I don't write books all day, every day. And online investment-tracking software is so good now, there's very little reason for me to futz with obtuse Excel formulas.

Although Microsoft certainly disagrees with me, I see the iPad as the best peripheral a Windows PC ever had. And, yes, I include Windows 8 in that assessment, too. Although I can flip back and forth from the desktop to the Start screen when necessary in Windows 8, I find it much simpler to just walk away from Windows 8 and pick up the iPad when I need to do something the iPad's good at.

As this book went to press, Windows RT remains the big unknown. I, personally, have doubts that Microsoft will be able to make Windows RT tablets (especially the Windows RT Surface) better than the iPad, but I suppose it's possible. Certainly, Windows desktop and laptop users have millions of reasons to bring a tablet into the mix of computers they use every day. Perhaps Microsoft can come up with a compelling reason to choose Windows RT over iOS, the operating system in the iPad. We'll see.

In this chapter, I'm not going to try to turn you to the iPad Side of the Force. But I do want to point out places where real, live everyday Windows users such as yourself should seriously consider using an iPad if you have one. I explain how to wrangle with iTunes, but only when you have to, and point you to apps and techniques for combining Windows and the iPad.

I also won't try to introduce you to the iPad, or take you through an iPad tutorial. *iPad For Dummies* by Edward Baig and Bob LeVitus does a great job with the basics, and *Exploring iPad For Dummies* by Galen Gruman and *iPad All-in-One For Dummies* by Nancy Muir tackle deeper subjects. Instead, I'm going to concentrate on how you can use your iPad with Windows 8, and vice versa.

Running iTunes on Windows, Or Maybe Not

iTunes is Apple's program originally designed to sync your Windows PC or Mac with iPods and later other mobile devices. Apple's iDevices used to be kind of like dumb boxes without iTunes on a computer to sync and organize contacts, playlists, and the like. You don't really *need* iTunes for your iPad or iPhone any more. Apple has made the iPad and the iPhone free-standing devices, ready to connect directly to the iCloud. But if you overlook the fact that iTunes is simply one of the worst Windows applications ever created, it has some good points, too.

Never mind me. I've been complaining about the iTunes program running on Windows for more than a decade now. (iTunes on the Mac is a completely different kettle of fish.) And iTunes on Windows does have a sharing capability that makes it possible for one PC on your home network to play music that's available to iTunes on another. Still, as a Windows program, iTunes leaves much to be desired.

I'm most assuredly not dissing the iTunes Store, the online shop where you can buy music, video, apps, and more from Apple, all of which are formatted to work on Apple's devices. The iTunes Store has its own problems, but it's revolutionized the way I buy music. In 2009, in response to Amazon's launching a DRM-free MP3 store, iTunes put one of the final nails in the coffin of music *Digital Rights Management* — where the people who sell music control how it's played, even after you buy it. Apple made an incredible array of music relatively affordable and easy to access, to a whole lotta people, and it's made a bundle of money out of the effort.

Music on iCloud — iTunes Match

If you're willing to pay $24.99 per year, and you have a lot of (upload) time on your hands, iTunes Match lets you upload *all* your music — it doesn't matter where it came from. That music will become available on all your iPhones and iPads, and it'll be available through iTunes for Windows on all your PCs. (Not to mention iTunes on the Mac as well.)

Yes, that's a good reason to install iTunes on your Windows PC. But it's also a good reason to hook your iPad directly into iCloud, so you can retrieve all your music, all the time.

Apple doesn't copy your music, *per se.* It uses sophisticated matching software to identify the music you have on your PC and match it with the music Apple already has on file — millions of exceedingly high quality recordings. If Apple can't match your music (live recordings of Juice Newton, anyone?), it stores the unidentified tracks on Apple's servers and makes them

available to you directly. Those unidentified tracks are counted against your free allowance of 5GB of iCloud storage. Ship too many oddball songs to iCloud, and you end up paying for storage. But the songs that iTunes Match identifies get stored without eating into your free 5GB.

After you sign up for the service and let iTunes scan your music, you can download up to 25,000 matching tracks — all in 256 KB (high quality) MP3 files. When you download those matching tracks, you can either replace your current tracks or keep the old ones — up to you. If you stop paying $25 per year, the music's all yours; you just can't pull it down from the iCloud any more — so you can't stream to your iPhone, iPad, or iTunes.

iTunes Match is one of the great bargains on the Internet. And one of the few good reasons for installing iTunes for Windows.

Why you may need or want iTunes for Windows

As long as all your iPhone/iPad music, videos, or books reside in (or can be retrieved from) the iTunes Store, you're better off starting and staying with the iCloud. (iCloud is Apple's service that stores and syncs your iPhone or iPad data over the Internet.) Don't install the Windows iTunes app, and don't even try to understand it. Just follow the instructions to set up iCloud at www.apple.com/icloud/setup.

Switching your iPad or iPhone over to using iCloud is simple: In the iPad or iPhone Settings app, on the left, tap iCloud. Make sure you have the right account set up (believe me, you don't want to hassle with mismatched accounts), on the right at the bottom, tap Storage and Backup. Slide the iCloud Backup setting to On. Then wait — it took two hours for my initial backup.

If you have some music, videos, or books on your computer that aren't in iCloud, or if you want to be able to pull your iCloud stuff (especially music) into your PC, the iTunes app is something you have to bear with. Two reasons why you might want iTunes:

✦ **iTunes is the only way to sideload non-iTunes stuff from your PC onto your iPad.** For example, if you've acquired books, movies, TV shows from someplace other than the iTunes Store, it's easier to use the iTunes Windows app to put them on an iPad.

✦ **If you've paid for iTunes Match, running iTunes on your PC is the only way to pull music from iCloud and use it on your PC.** If you have a sizable collection of music, see the nearby "Music on iCloud — iTunes Match" sidebar.

Installing iTunes

Fair warning. iTunes is one of the snarliest Windows programs I've ever used: It takes over the computer and doesn't let go until it's good and ready. It's slow to switch services (links on the left side). Double-clicking anything can result in really odd behavior. All in all, it doesn't look or work like a Windows app. And it's been like that for ten years.

iTunes uses another Apple program, QuickTime — a video-playing program that I've sworn at for many years. When you install iTunes, you install QuickTime, whether you want to or not.

From time to time, Apple also tries to get you to install other pieces of software, such as Safari, Bonjour Services, the Apple Updater, and MobileMe, and it's been known to use sneaky techniques to convince you to install other software. So keep your guard up, and keep your clicking finger at bay. The idea is to install iTunes because you have to — and nothing extra. If that friendly Apple update reminder appears miraculously on your screen three months from now and says you need to install another wonderful Apple product, you have my permission to guffaw and obliterate the reminder.

Here's how to get your Windows PC iTuned:

1. **Crank up your favorite browser and head to** www.itunes.com.

   Apple redirects your browser to a different page, but that's okay. You end up in the right place, which looks like Figure 1-1.

Figure 1-1:
The landing
page for
installing
iTunes.

2. **Tap or click the Free Download button.**

    Apple kindly offers you an opportunity to sign up for its spam, er, mailing
    lists, and requests your e-mail address. Don't give it to them.

3. **Deselect any boxes, don't type your e-mail address, but do tap or click
    the Download Now button.**

    Your browser downloads the correct version — 32-bit or 64-bit. Depending
    on which browser you're using, you may have to tap or click something
    to save and run the downloaded file.

4. **In the standard splash screen that appears, tap or click Next.**

    The options in Figure 1-2 appear.

5. **Deselect the Use iTunes as the Default Player for Audio Files and the
    Automatically Update iTunes and Other Apple Software check boxes.**

    In the past, Apple has used the update "permission" to bother iTunes
    users into installing Safari and putting ten new icons on the desktop.

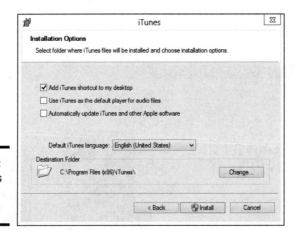

Figure 1-2:
The iTunes installer options.

If you let iTunes take over all your audio files, it appears in all sorts of weird places and does things that aren't at all intuitive — to me, anyway. Most importantly, if iTunes is your default audio player, every time you click an audio file, you have to wait and wait and wait and wait for iTunes to get itself put together and start playing the tune.

6. **Tap or click Install.**

The installer splashes an ad on your screen, does its thing, and ends several minutes later with a Congratulations! message.

7. **Tap or click Finish.**

You can quit at this point, or you can continue on to start iTunes for the first time. See the next section.

Setting up iTunes

Before you use iTunes for the first time, you run through the iTunes Setup Assistant program. Here's how to minimize your ongoing headaches:

1. **If you quit immediately after iTunes is installed (see the preceding section) or if iTunes was preinstalled on your PC, tap the iTunes tile on the Start screen or double-click the iTunes icon on the desktop to run iTunes for the first time.**

If you didn't quit iTunes, you automatically come to this step after iTunes has been successfully installed.

2. **Tap or click through another license agreement, which is considerably longer than the U.S. Constitution. Choose "I Agree, yer honor."**

Then head over to YouTube and look up the *South Park* episode where Butters reads the iTunes agreement. You don't want to mess with these people.

The iTunes Tutorials home page appears, as shown in Figure 1-3.

Figure 1-3: Take the tutorials. They're worth the effort.

3. **When the tutorials are done, close the Tutorials home page.**

The initial iTunes Music page appears, as shown in Figure 1-4.

Figure 1-4: Time to get your music files set up, the iTunes way.

4. **At the bottom of the screen, tap or click the Find MP3 and AAC Files in My Home Folder link.**

   Pardon Apple's weird terminology. It doesn't actually look for music in a Home folder; it looks in your Music library.

   Depending on how much music you have stored in your Music library, the scan can take minutes or hours.

   If you're curious about what iTunes actually does with your music, don't be overly concerned. Unlike earlier versions, the latest version of iTunes doesn't move any files. Instead, it builds a database that points to your music, and stores it in the new \Music\iTunes folder. Still worried? Crank up File Explorer and go look. And breathe a sigh of relief.

   You may or may not want to use iTunes to import *(rip)* music CDs — I explain how to do that using Windows Media Player in Book VI, Chapter 7. But even if you don't want to use iTunes to rip CDs, it's a good idea to make one simple change, right now.

5. **Choose Edit⇨Preferences. Tap or click the Import Settings icon near When You Insert a CD.**

   The Import Settings dialog box appears, as shown in Figure 1-5.

Figure 1-5:
Make sure
iTunes rips
to MP3
format.

6. **Choose MP3 Encoder in the Import Using drop-down list.**

   That ensures the ripped music files appear as MP3 files. You may prefer AAC format, (or WMA format, for that matter), but there's nothing as clean — or as ubiquitous — as MP3.

7. **Unless you rip many CDs every day, select the Use Error Correction When Reading Audio CDs check box.**

Although using error correction may make the ripping process run a little slower, it'll guarantee that you get the best recordings possible from those old, dirty scratched CDs. You know you have them.

8. **Tap or click OK, and then tap or click OK again.**

   You end up back in iTunes.

If you ever discover that iTunes failed to pick up a new song — one that you ripped from a CD, downloaded from the Internet, or bought from an online service — simply locate the song file or album folder in File Explorer and drag it into iTunes.

Pulling Internet videos onto your iPad

Most (but not all) of the videos that you can see on the Internet can be *scraped* and stored permanently on your iPad or iPhone. That can be very useful if you're going to be someplace that doesn't have an Internet connection for your iPad, or if you're going to watch the same video over and over (hey, you have kids, yes?) and you don't want to pay for repeatedly downloading the same clip.

Many products will scrape videos off the Internet. KeepVid (`www.keepvid.com`) was one of the first, and it works well for most videos on YouTube, DailyMotion, Megavideo, Metacafe, and Vimeo. To use the free version of KeepVid, go to the KeepVid website and paste in the URL of the video you want to save.

My personal preference is the Firefox Video DownloadHelper add-in (`http://addons.mozilla.org/en-US/firefox/addon/video-download-helper`). When you install Video DownloadHelper in Firefox, it watches to see whether scrapable videos are on the page you're viewing. If there are, a little icon starts rotating. Tap or click the icon, and download the video. Easy.

The trick with KeepVid, Video DownloadHelper, or any other video scraper you find is that you need to have it produce videos in MP4 format. Although MP4 isn't a format as much as it's a group of formats (details too boring to recount here), almost all the time, MP4 files play just fine on an iPad.

Of course, you don't do this for copyrighted material or on sites that otherwise expressly forbid it.

Here's how to get videos off the Internet and into your iPad. Follow these steps:

1. **Use Video DownloadHelper, or a similar scraper, to produce MP4 files.**

2. **Start iTunes. On the left, under Library, tap or click the Movies line.**

   iTunes doesn't have any way to make a playlist of movies just yet, but you can still play individual movies with your iPad's built-in Video app.

3. **Locate the MP4 files in File Explorer. Then drag and drop them into the iTunes Movies folder.**

   A thumbnail of the movie appears, as shown in Figure 1-6.

Figure 1-6:
Drag MP4 movies into iTunes and then sync to get them on your iPad.

4. **When you're done dragging all your MP4 files into the Movies folder, connect your iPad or iPhone, and sync.**

   If the movie will play on your iPad or iPhone, it gets copied over to the device.

Once in a while, the movie won't sync properly. I have no idea why, but I've found that if you drag the movie from the iTunes \Library\Movies folder to the iPad \Movies folder, it gets copied onto the iPad.

Creating a movie playlist

For reasons known only to The Most Valuable Company on Earth, it's impossible to string iPad movies together in a playlist. You're forced to play them one at a time; playlists don't exist in the Video app. If you want to play one MP4 file followed by another followed by another, with no human intervention required, you have to get tricky.

It's trivial to put music in a playlist: On the iPad, go into the iPod app. Tap or click the Plus (+) icon at the bottom left, type a playlist name, and tap or click the blue (+) icon to the left of any songs you want to add to the list. Tap or click the blue Done button and you're, uh, done. The iPod app on the iPad has all sorts of capabilities to help you build playlists — you can sort your songs by genre or bring up album covers, or add podcasts or audiobooks. You can even make new playlists by stringing together old playlists. But you can't make a playlist in the iPad's Video app. And you can't make a playlist of videos inside iTunes and get it to work on the iPad.

There's a trick, though — one that I've never seen documented anywhere. By using iTunes on your PC, you can trick your iPad into thinking that it has a Movie playlist, and play all the movies you want with just one click. How? Use iTunes to make the iPad think that the video playlists are, in fact, TV shows. I know it doesn't make any sense. But it works. Here's how:

1. **Plug the iPad into your PC and fire up iTunes. Inside the iTunes Movies list, Ctrl-click or Shift-click to select the videos that you want to put in your playlist. Right-click and choose Get Info.**

Maybe someday iTunes for Windows will get a touch interface. For now, no such luck.

The Multiple Item Information dialog box appears.

2. **Tap or click the Options tab. In the Media Kind drop-down list, choose TV Show.**

That turns all your videos into TV Shows. Yeah, it doesn't really change anything. But it works.

3. **Tap or click the Video tab. Type a name for your new video playlist, in the Show box.**

That gives your video playlist — er, your TV shows — a name. See Figure 1-7.

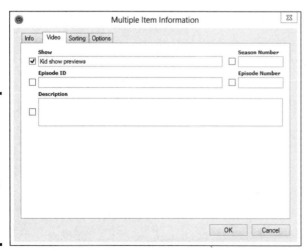

Figure 1-7:
Create a video playlist by making iTunes think your videos are "TV shows."

4. **Tap or click OK.**

   The next time you sync your iPad (or iPhone), the playlist appears in the iPad's Video app, but you have to tap or click (the grayed-out and hard to see) TV Shows link at the top of the app to bring them up.

Perhaps not surprisingly, this method comes with limitations. After you put a video in a "TV Show" playlist, it disappears from the Movie folder, and it won't appear inside the Movies part of the Video app. So if you put *The Muppets: Bohemian Rhapsody* in a TV Show playlist, it won't appear with the other videos. You can get around that shortcoming as follows:

✦ Stick another copy of *The Muppets: Bohemian Rhapsody,* if you have one, in the Movie folder.

✦ When you're done with your playlist, return the video to the Movie folder: Go to the TV Shows list, right-click the video, choose Get Info, click Options, and change the Media Kind back to Movie.

By default, your iPad plays the videos in a TV Show playlist in alphabetical order. If you want to choose the sequence in which videos appear on the playlist, the easiest approach I've found is to modify the Sort Show. In the TV Shows section, right-click a video and choose Get Info. Click the Sorting tab and type in the Sort Show box (see Figure 1-8).

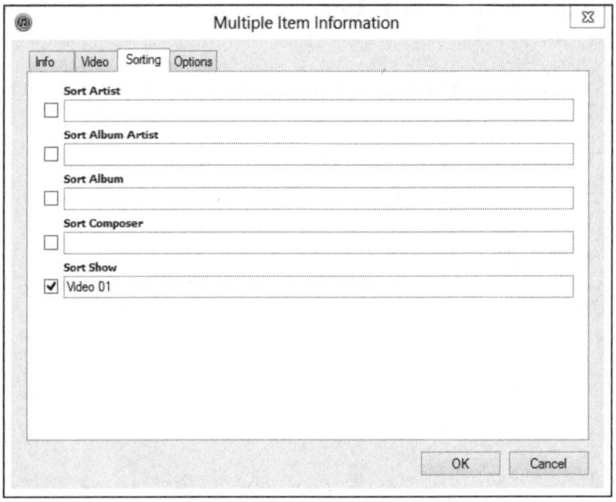

Figure 1-8: Change the names of the "TV Shows" so they sort alphabetically in the order you want.

Great iPad Apps to Use with Windows

Full disclosure: I love my new iPad. Don't know how I ever lived without it.

On the other hand, as you have probably surmised by a quick perusal of the thousand or so pages in this book, I have a complex love-hate relationship with Windows. The PC runs rings around the iPad in a dozen different areas. The converse is just as true. How to get the best out of both? It ain't easy.

If you're like me, you've been using Windows for a long time, but got an iPad on something of a lark — it's cute, does a few things very well, and it's very good with kids and not-so-computer-savvy members of the family. I talk about that at length in the next section.

**Book X
Chapter 1**

The iPad is also hell for a touch typist, incompatible with many Windows-friendly programs like Office and Flash, and too expensive to just sit in a closet most of the time. Unlike a smartphone with a camera, an iPad doesn't have any compelling, redeeming social graces.

So now that you have it, what do you do with it — how can you make your iPad work within your Windows-centric life?

I don't claim to have The Answer. In fact, everything's changing so quickly, I doubt that anybody caught straddling both the Win and iPad worlds has more than a tiny piece of the equation figured out. But I've found a handful of apps, and a couple of tricks, that you may find useful.

Controlling Windows from your iPad

More than a dozen PC remote control apps are available in the Apple App Store. Some of them work surprisingly well:

✦ **LogMeIn Ignition:** A favorite among reviewers, although at $29.95 for the iPad application, it's pricey. You have to run LogMeIn on both the iPad and the Windows machine. If you go with LogMeIn Free on the Windows PC, you can't transfer files, print remotely, hear sounds from the PC, or share desktops. To do any of that, you have to spend an additional $69.95 per year for the Windows PC's software.

✦ **GoToMyPC**: Another name that should sound familiar to Windows aficionados, it also draws good reviews, but it turns even pricier quickly. Figure on spending $9.99 per month per computer, after the initial 30-day free trial period.

✦ **Desktop Connect:** A lesser-known product that demands you run a Virtual Network Computing (VNC) program on your Windows PC. You also have to connect with a hard-coded IP address.

✦ **Splashtop:** Another lesser-known product works well on a WiFi system, connecting to PCs on the same network, but going outside the local network can get more difficult. I use Splashtop to play videos that aren't in MP4 format on my iPad.

✦ **TeamViewer:** My favorite remote control program (free for non-commercial use) can run in one of two ways. You either install the TeamViewer program on your Windows PC and let it control the interaction, or you simply run the program on your PC, manually, any time you want to be able to access the Windows PC from your iPad (see Figure 1-9). When you run the program manually on your Windows PC, it generates a random user ID and password, which you use on the iPad to initiate the session.

After TeamViewer's connected, it lets you use the iPad keyboard, pinch to expand or reduce the size of the screen, tap with two fingers to emulate a right-click, use the buttons on the top of the screen for Alt and Ctrl and Esc, and much more. Even Flash animations come through remarkably quickly.

Figure 1-9: TeamViewer lets you control your PC from an iPad — and it's free. This shot of Win8 was taken from an iPad.

Delivering PowerPoint presentations with your iPad

I'll never forget the first time I saw a PowerPoint presentation delivered from an iPad. Actually, it combined a laptop, a projector, and an iPad. The presenter had a reasonably good PowerPoint presentation, running on a plain-vanilla Win7 laptop connected to a projector. Instead of hiding behind his laptop and mousing his way through the slides, or staring at the projector screen and using a clicker, he was actually looking at the audience, glancing at the slides and notes on the iPad in front of him, swiping his way through the presentation. The presentation went extraordinarily well because the presenter interacted with the audience, not with his PC, not with the projector screen. He had the right tools for the job.

If you have a Windows 8 tablet that weighs less than a Volkswagen and doesn't overheat, you can use the tablet to make the presentation from the desktop. But if you're running Win8 on a laptop, holding the computer while delivering the presentation just isn't in the cards. I know. I've tried.

If you haven't yet seen, or delivered, a PowerPoint presentation with an iPad, you're in for a treat. The liberating little tablet changes the entire dynamic of making PowerPoint presentations.

The presenter was using Slideshow Remote, from LogicInMind. It's $4.99, from the App Store. Slideshow Remote shows you the slides on your iPad, of course, but it also shows notes and it previews the next slide. You can even bring up a full slide thumbnail list, just like in PowerPoint itself, and jump to specific slides with a swipe and a tap.

Extending your Windows display with iDisplay

What? You didn't know that you can use your iPad to extend your Windows PC's display?

iDisplay — $4.99 in the App Store — works using WiFi, not a cable, and you don't have to invest in a fancy video card with two outputs. Instead, you download and run the iDisplay app on both your iPad and your Windows PC. Go into the Windows app, find the iPad, and then start the iDisplay app on it. Stick the monitors side by side (see Figure 1-10), and you can click and drag from one screen to the other.

**Book X
Chapter 1**

**Using Your iPad
and iPhone with
Windows**

Figure 1-10:
iDisplay
extends your
Windows
PC's desktop
without a
fancy video
card.

iDisplay is best suited for shuffling relatively static information off to the side of your screen — all the bits have to travel by WiFi, and they don't move quickly. I use iDisplay to run TweetDeck on the side of my screen.

Move files between your PC and the iPad

The iPad's file system can best be described as, uh, rudimentary. Actually, *nonexistent* comes to mind. Be that as it may, from time to time, you may want to transfer a file other than a typical iTunes file — music, video, podcast, photo, or book — to or from your iPad.

My personal favorite? Dropbox. I talk about Dropbox in Book VIII, Chapter 1, in the context of cloud backup. But for normal, everyday files, the Dropbox iPad app (free, from the App Store), works fine. Download and install the app, give it your username and password, and you're done. Dropbox handles syncing across multiple platforms, invisibly and reliably. Even if your Internet connection goes down, the files are still in the box.

You can use iCloud to transfer files, but it's considerably more complicated than Dropbox.

Working with Windows documents on the iPad

If you're looking for a Microsoft Office replacement for the iPad, you're out of luck.

The iPad doesn't do Office, and none of the alternatives come close to "genuine" Office. Sorry, but it's trivially easy to construct documents in Word, Excel, or PowerPoint that get plastered when edited in any of the Microsoft Office alternatives. Of course, the same can be said for Microsoft's own online version of Office, the Office Web Apps.

My best advice is to avoid editing existing Word, Excel, or PowerPoint files on your iPad. If you want to create new files, simple files, that stand some chance of being properly interpreted in the original Office programs, consider using Apple's own iWork for iPad.

iWork consists of three applications, each of which can be purchased separately for $9.99:

+ **Pages** handles word processing.

+ **Numbers** is for spreadsheets.

+ **Keynote** produces presentations.

Parts of iWork will drive any Office aficionado mad — documents are selected from a gallery, and you don't save them because they're saved automatically. Techniques for selecting and modifying text are quite different, but if you follow the onscreen tutorial, you'll get the hang of it quickly. If you plan on using any of the iWork apps for more than 30 seconds, invest in the iPad Keyboard Dock ($69) or any of the zillions of external keyboards now available for the iPad.

Moving iWork files in and out of the iCloud is easy, but that doesn't help much if your main machine's running Windows.

Getting Dropbox files into the iWork apps is easy — you just open them. But getting modified files back into Dropbox is a monumental pain in the neck. You can e-mail the files, or sync them with iTunes, but if you want to make modified files available in Dropbox, follow these instructions on the Techinch site: `www.techinch.com/2011/02/02/integrate-dropbox-with-pages-keynote-and-numbers-on-ipad`.

If you want to work with PDF files on the iPad, get GoodReader, $4.99 in the App Store. GoodReader lets you read PDFs, but it also allows you to mark up and annotate PDF and TXT files, and sync with Dropbox or remote servers. It's an amazing, legendary program.

Playing with Kids on Your iPad or iPhones

Permit me to end this chapter with a bit of personal advice, aimed at the parents (and grandparents!) in the crowd.

In 2010 and 2011, there was a rash of articles in the popular press saying that iPads and iPhones would rot your kids' brains. I mean, it's hard to wade through a bunch of headlines like these from *The New York Times* and not feel like an iPad's the root of all kiddy evil: "Growing Up Digital, Wired for Distraction" and "The Risks of Parenting While Plugged In" and "An Ugly Toll of Technology: Impatience and Forgetfulness." I forgot what the other headlines said, but you get my drift. Typical admonishment: People are raising a generation of kids in front of screens whose brains are going to be wired differently.

Well, yes. That's exactly the point.

When I was a kid, the child development experts said that any more than 45 minutes of television per day would make a kid irresponsible, incapable of concentrating, unable to interact with people, and a developmental basket case. Look what happened to me. Oh, wait. That isn't a good comparison. Look at what happened to the entire generation. Perhaps everyone suffered from short attention spans and terminal halitosis. But somehow I think we all pulled through it, give or take a few politicians.

I don't claim to be a child development expert. But I do know this. Putting an iPad (or Android, Kindle, whatever) into your child's hands isn't a brain cell death sentence. It's opening an important new world.

Yes, I've read about the studies that show toddlers who grow up on tablets don't develop vocabularies until a later age. I know about the teen tech idiot savants, who can't write a sentence, but spin out programs to solve algebra problems. The high schoolers who send 20,000 SMSs a month, but can't find time to finish a homework assignment. The kids who play so many games they forget to sleep at night.

On the other hand, I've seen the toddlers who spend hours and hours practicing their letters and numbers, shapes and words, colors and coordination, exploring with their parents' help, and going right back to the iPad at every opportunity — because it's fun. And I know a whole lot of people in Silicon Valley who make a living, not by writing book reports, but by churning out miles of incredible code. The best of the bunch started as teenagers. Young teenagers.

The trick, in my opinion, is to use the technology to interact with your kids. Sure, my toddler and I still read books — real, dead tree books — every day. But most of the day when we're playing indoors, the topics are generally educational, and they're invariably on the iPad, or the PC.

Am I setting up my toddler for having his brain wired the wrong way? Pshaw. Will his interpersonal skills suffer? Not if he gets some time playing with other kids. Will he be able to use all the tools he'll need as he gets older? Yeah, I think so. Most of all, he won't be intimidated by these talking pieces of glass. It'll be second nature, and when the time comes, he'll be able to start standing on the shoulders of giants. It's just that, in the meantime, he has to learn that he can't tap or swipe a TV screen and get it to change channels, or slide his finger on a magazine and expect it to move forward a page.

So I say take your kids to the library. Watch TV with them. Make sure they have time with other kids their own age. And get a tablet into their hands at an early age, so you can play with them.

A friend of mine asked me to come up with a list of iPad apps that my wife and I like to play with our toddler. Here's the list:

+ The Cat in the Hat
+ Dr. Seuss Band
+ Anything by the GiggleBellies
+ Any Sandra Boynton books
+ Pat the Bunny
+ Twinkle Twinkle (Super Simple Learning)
+ My First Words Baby Picture dictionary
+ Starfall ABCs
+ Elmo Loves ABCs
+ Any Duck Duck Moose stories
+ Nighty Night!
+ Pepi Bath
+ The Little Critter books

You can also scrape videos off YouTube. I leave it to your search skills to find videos on YouTube for your kids. And, of course, you can watch YouTube directly, if you hook the iPad up to your WiFi.

All the apps I listed are in the Apple App Store — immediately accessible from the iPad, or if you want to surf, go to `www.apple.com/itunes`. The YouTube app comes preloaded on your iPad or iPhone.

Computers are going to give your kids (and grandkids, and their grandkids) abilities I can hardly dream about today. Don't be afraid to teach them well. In spite of what the experts say.

Chapter 2: Kindle, Nook, Android, and Windows 8

In This Chapter

✓ Demystifying book file formats

✓ Using calibre

✓ Getting media from your PC to your Kindle

✓ Syncing your calendars and contacts

*I*f you think that the iPhone rules the smartphone roost, you're wrong. Android phones (that is, smart phones that run the Android operating system) outsell iPhones by a very wide margin.

On the other hand, the iPad holds the top spot among tablets, but Android tablets (the Google Nexus, Galaxy Tabs, ASUS Transformers, and Motorola XOOMs of the world) and even Windows 8 tablets get some traction. The e-reader market helps: Few people realize it, but the Amazon Kindle is an Android tablet. So is the Barnes & Noble/Microsoft Nook. Inside the understated exteriors and behind the gorgeous eye-friendly displays beat hearts of pure Android. Android's market share is increasing, too. As I write this chapter, more than 300 million Android devices are in use, and more than 1,000,000 are being activated every day. That's a whole lotta Android.

In this chapter, I talk a little bit about the interaction among Windows 8 and Android devices, primarily the Amazon Kindle, but also Android phones and other tablets. Because books remain the forte of the Kindle, I dig into electronic books and their foibles extensively.

There's a lot of activity in this area right now — in fact, with so many people doing so many things, Android may be the target of more change than any other platform, including the iPad and (emphatically) Windows. So my emphasis in this chapter is on showing you Android techniques that are likely to survive as long as Windows 8 remains on the market.

By the time Windows 9 hits the stands, the world will be a different place, especially on the Android end.

Apple's walled garden versus Android's open source

When you deal with iPhones and iPads (and the iCloud, iMacs, iTVs, iPods, and all those other iThingies), you're living in a walled garden. Apple controls it from beginning to end. That's one of the reasons why all the different iDevices work together so well — the hardware and software come from the same company, they're designed to fit together, and Apple's designers are absolutely first-class. But you pay for the privilege.

On the other hand, Android devices come from a huge array of manufacturers, many with very different ideas of what's right and what's almost

right. Although Google's in the driver's seat — Google bought Android, give or take a patent claim or two or ten, and has released Android to the world — hardware manufacturers, to a first approximation, are free to take Android in any direction they like.

Android is *open source* under the Apache License, which means that not only is the program free, the source code for the program is free and readily available as well. (It's a little more complicated than that; for details see www.apache.org.)

Android isn't Android isn't Android. The Android device you buy today may not be capable of running the new Android of tomorrow. Actually, that's true of Windows Phone, iPad, and iPhone, too, and it will probably prove true for Windows 8 and Windows RT tablets. But Android seems to be less upgradable than its competitors. Be careful.

Wrangling E-Book Files

Someday a single format will exist for all electronic books. In my utopian future, you will buy a book in one format, and that format will just work, no matter what device you want to use to read it.

Unfortunately, the world isn't at that point yet. In fact, it isn't even close. The single biggest headache you're likely to have with electronic books revolves around book formats, and how to get one device to show you books that were made for a competing device.

If you can afford to stick with just one device and bookstore — only buy books from Amazon and read them on the Kindle, for example, or only buy books from the iTunes Store and read them on the iPad, or the Barnes & Noble and the Nook — I salute you. Your life will be considerably less complicated. Most people aren't so lucky.

If you're one of them, you can simplify e-book management by buying your books online through your PC's web browser, using calibre to convert files into whatever format your reader requires, and then syncing your e-books with your e-reader on your PC. (You can also read any e-book on your Windows computer, but that may be beside the point, huh?)

Introducing popular e-book formats

Here are the most popular book file formats:

✦ **EPUB** comes closest to being a universal format. The iPhone and iPad handle EPUB natively; there are many third-party Windows EPUB readers (more about which after this list); Nook reads EPUB natively; and many Android apps read EPUB. The only major holdout for the EPUB format, as this book went to press, was Kindle — and it's entirely possible that Kindle will be able to accept EPUB format books by the time you read this.

Given a choice, unless you live in a Kindle-only world, get your books in EPUB format.

✦ **MOBI** and **PRC** formats are the Kindle's bread and butter. Amazon has a format converter — *KindleGen* — that changes EPUB files into MOBI. It works surprisingly well.

✦ **PDF** is the original format for publications that have to survive a transition from one kind of computer to another. Although every common device can read PDF, most of the readers just display the original document without trying to reflow pages or add any features, such as note-taking. Reading a PDF file in most readers is a frustrating and headache-inducing experience.

Reading e-book files on your PC

Whether or not you have e-books you bought with an e-reader, you can read anything on a Windows 8 PC. Sometimes, though, you have to get a little creative, and bring in apps that can do the heavy lifting.

Windows EPUB readers are a dime a dozen. Actually, they're free. Before you try to download and install one on the desktop, run through the Windows Store (just tap or click the Store tile on the Start screen) and see whether any highly rated EPUB readers are available. Just use the Search charm to look for the text *EPUB*. Details in Book III, Chapter 2.

If you can't find a tiled EPUB reader that you like, you have several choices for desktop apps that can read EPUB files. Arguably the best of the bunch is Adobe Digital Editions (ADE), which is free, from `www.adobe.com/products/digitaleditions`. ADE does yeoman's work of rendering EPUB and PDF/A files accurately, and it includes note-taking features.

ADE also allows you to read files that have been copy-protected with the ADEPT (Adobe Digital Experience Protection Technology) technique. Barnes & Noble uses a form of ADEPT copy-protection on its books. ADEPT was reverse-engineered years ago, and several programs (including programs called *inept* and *ignoble*) can crack the encryption.

PDF viewers are also a dime a dozen. If you don't already have the Microsoft Reader installed (you can get it in the Windows Store) and aren't running the latest version of Word (which finally has a built-in PDF viewer), you can always use the old desktop standby Foxit Reader (`www.foxitsoftware.com`). Just be careful when you install it that you don't let it install any crapware that you don't want.

Organizing your e-book files with calibre

Before you lose any sleep over different book file formats, realize that one desktop app has been translating among the formats for years. In fact, calibre's more than a Babel fish; it's also a book manager; for free. See Figure 2-1.

Much like Windows Media Player or iTunes, calibre keeps track of all your books, translates them into the correct format if need be, and offers the files up for easy transfer to the reader of your choice.

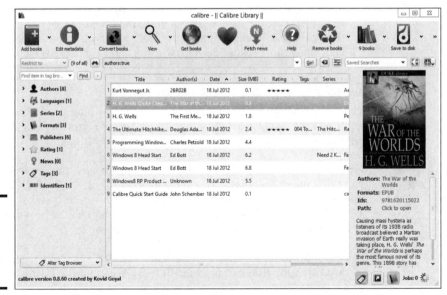

Figure 2-1:
calibre
translates
and
organizes.

Here's a quick look at calibre's capabilities:

1. **Bring up your favorite browser, go to** `http://calibre-ebook.com`, **and then download and install calibre.**

   The installer doesn't have any options.

2. **Tap or click Finish, and then run calibre for the first time.**

   When calibre asks for your e-book device (see Figure 2-2), don't panic — it converts any format to any other. This just sets up things so calibre knows which format you favor and makes it easier to choose your most common format.

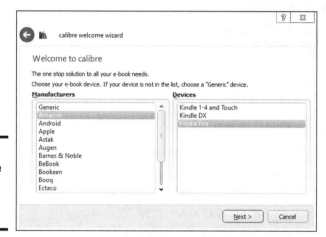

Figure 2-2:
Choose the device you use most commonly.

calibre scans your Documents library for books — just about any format you can imagine — and lists each book (see Figure 2-1).

It's important to realize that calibre lists books, not files. If you have a book that's in two different formats — say, a MOBI file and an EPUB file — it appears only as one book on this main screen.

3. **To see the details about an individual book, right-click it and choose Edit Metadata⇨Edit Metadata Individually.**

   (Someday calibre will have a touch option; for now, it's mouse only.)

   calibre shows you an enormous amount of information about the book, including the formats that are available. See Figure 2-3.

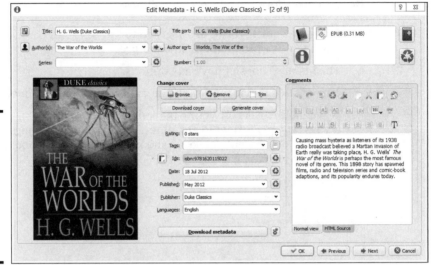

Figure 2-3: calibre shows, and allows you to edit, an enormous amount of data about each book.

4. **When you're done looking at, or modifying, the data, close the book's dialog box.**

   You return to calibre library, as shown in Figure 2-1.

5. **To convert a book to a different format, right-click the book and choose Convert Books⇨Convert Individually.**

   A Convert dialog box appears, similar to Figure 2-4.

6. **In the upper right, choose the format you want to convert the book to; and then in the lower right, tap or click OK.**

   calibre converts the book to the format you choose and places the new file next to the old ones.

This just touches on calibre's capabilities; it's an amazingly versatile program. For a more detailed rundown of what calibre can do, start at `http://manual.calibre-ebook.com/gui.html`.

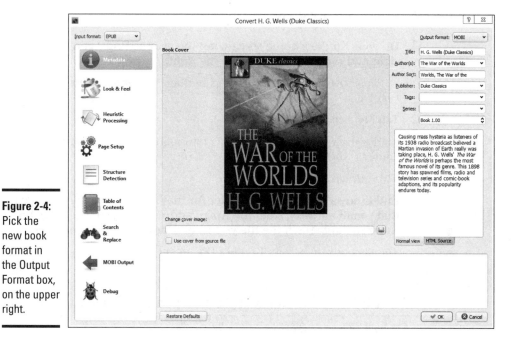

Figure 2-4:
Pick the
new book
format in
the Output
Format box,
on the upper
right.

Getting Media from Your PC to Your Kindle

If you use your PC to manage your books and music, you need a way to get those files onto your e-reader or tablet. This section is here to help. Unfortunately, the methods for each device are specific to that device. So, I focus on the Kindle e-reader in this section because the Kindle is the most popular e-reader out there.

If you use a Nook or other Android tablet and you need help syncing files, check out the articles and tutorials available at www.dummies.com.

E-mailing books from your PC to your Kindle

The easiest way to transfer books to your Kindle? E-mail them via the Kindle Personal Documents Service. As long as you need to transfer a file type listed in Table 2-1, e-mailing is the best, quickest way.

Here's how to transfer a file:

1. **On your Kindle's home screen, tap the gear settings icon in the upper right and then choose More on the right.**

   Kindle shows you several settings options, starting with Help & Feedback.

2. **Tap My Account.**

   Kindle shows you the registration information, including an e-mail address, such as woody_217b64@kindle.com.

3. **Write down the e-mail address.**

4. **In Windows (or on any computer for that matter), send a message to that e-mail address, from the e-mail address that you use to log into Amazon, and attach the file you want to transfer to the message.**

   The file ends up in your Kindle's Documents folder.

Table 2-1   Document Types That Can Be E-Mailed to a Kindle

File Type (Filename Extension)	Description
MOBI	Kindle native MOBI format
TXT	Plain text files (looks surprisingly good on the Kindle)
DOC, DOCX	Doesn't handle complex Word documents very well, but simple ones are fine
RTF	Rich Text Format
HTML	Web pages
ZIP, X-ZIP	Kindle unpacks the files
PDF	Amazon converts them to MOBI and then passes them along to your Kindle; "experimental" but works well
JPG, GIF, BMP, PNG	Images show up fine

Amazon has a Send to Kindle application that lets you right-click a file in the desktop File Explorer and choose Send To⇨Kindle. That sends the file to your Kindle, using the e-mail method described earlier. You can also print from any desktop application and choose Send to Kindle. I don't use either because e-mailing is very simple and clean, and I don't have to worry about the Amazon application gumming up things.

Receiving e-mailed books from a friend

If you want a friend to send books or documents to your Kindle, you have to give her permission by adding her e-mail address to your allowed list. Here's how to let others e-mail books and documents directly to your Kindle:

1. **Sign on to** www.amazon.com **with the same ID that you use on your Kindle.**

Your personalized Amazon screen appears, as shown in Figure 2-5.

2. **Tap and hold or hover your mouse over Your Account, and then choose Manage Your Kindle.**

Amazon shows you a list of all the titles you've bought and placed on your Kindle.

3. **On the left, under Your Kindle Account, tap or click the Personal Document Settings link.**

You see the options shown in Figure 2-6.

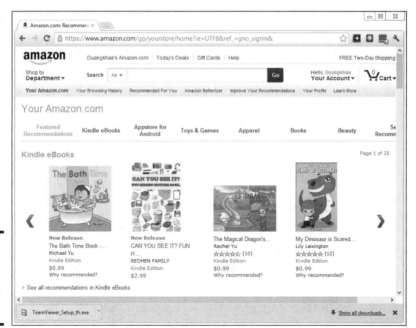

Figure 2-5:
Your
Account
settings are
here.

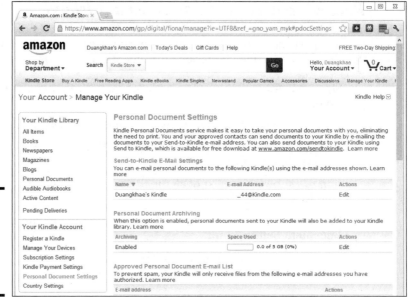

Figure 2-6:
Add your
send-
enabled
friends to
this list.

4. **At the bottom, tap or click the Add a New Approved E-Mail Address link.**

   A box that lets you add e-mail addresses appears.

5. **Type the address of anyone you want to allow to send stuff directly to your Kindle, and then tap or click Add Address.**

   To add multiple addresses, simply repeat the preceding steps.

   The changes take effect immediately.

Adding music to your Kindle

To get music into the Kindle, you need to connect it to your PC and drag the files across. Follow these simple steps:

1. **Plug a standard Mini-USB cable into your Kindle (one may have come with the device) and stick the other end in your PC.**

2. **Slide the Start Screen slider on your Kindle.**

   The You Can Now Transfer Files from Your Computer to Kindle screen appears.

Windows hums and haws for a while, and then may ask (in a toaster notification on the right side) what you want to do with newly inserted hard drives.

3. **If a Windows notification appears, ignore it.**

4. **Bring up File Explorer by tapping or clicking the Explorer icon on the taskbar.**

   It may take a minute, or two, or even three, but sooner or later, your Kindle appears on the left side of File Explorer, somewhere on the list of other hard drives on your computer.

5. **Find a favorite MP3 file, or folder full of MP3 files, and drag it from your PC into the Kindle \Music folder.**

   All the music in the \Music and \Audible folders is available to the Kindle music player.

6. **When you've transferred all the music that's fit to play, tap Disconnect on the Kindle and then unplug the USB cable.**

   Your music is loaded and ready to rock.

7. **On the Kindle's home page, tap Music.**

   A list of all the MP3 files appears in either the \Music or \Audible folders.

8. **(Optional) To create a playlist, tap the Playlists link and follow the instructions to build a playlist.**

9. **To simply play your music, tap the Shuffle and Play button, or simply tap a song.**

   The song starts playing. There are individual controls for volume, pause, fast-forward, rewind, shuffle, and cycle. After the music starts, you can go back to the Kindle's home page and read books. The music keeps going even after the screen has gone dark.

10. **To turn off the music, tap Music and, at the bottom of the screen, tap the Pause button.**

You can also copy your music to the Amazon Cloud Drive and play it on your Kindle from there. Amazon has even made it easy to copy your iTunes songs over to the Amazon Cloud Drive. For details, go to `www.amazon.com/mp3` and tap or click the Amazon Cloud Player link. Follow the instructions and tap or click Upload to Your Cloud Drive. Go through the steps to install the Amazon MP3 Uploader. The Amazon MP3 Uploader scans your computer for music files and automatically uploads them to your Amazon Cloud Drive.

If you own a Kindle, Amazon gives you free Amazon Cloud Drive storage for everything you've bought from Amazon, plus 5GB of free storage for things you've acquired elsewhere — even songs from iTunes. Very slick.

Using the Tiled Kindle App

Amazon may improve its tiled Kindle app by the time you read this, but if not, the app's a disappointment. The Kindle app is available from the Windows Store, just like all tiled Windows 8 apps, but don't expect too much from it. See Figure 2-7.

Basically, the app has you sign in to Amazon with your Amazon ID. It then lets you read any of the books you've bought from Amazon. After you tap a book to open it, you can use the navigator (tap and hold or right-click the book, and then choose Go To) to go to locations inside the book. You can set bookmarks or annotate the book. Or you can pin a tile for the book on the Start screen.

There's no way to *sideload* books or music (copy them on your computer so the tiled Kindle app can see them). Until somebody cracks it anyway.

Figure 2-7:
An early
incarnation
of the tiled
Kindle app.

Syncing Contacts and Calendars

The iPhone and iPad sync with a Mac like two lovebirds in a tree. Three.

Android phones and Windows? Not even close.

The trick with syncing Android phones with your Windows data is to go through Google. And syncing your Outlook contacts or Windows People with Google's contacts list is a Herculean task. I introduce the tools I think work best so far in this section.

Syncing Outlook contacts with Android devices

The best Outlook Contacts-to-Android phone contacts sync intermediary I've found is Soocial (www.soocial.com). Soocial is free for the first 250 contacts, and then increases to $5 per month.

The general approach works like this:

1. Use Soocial to pull your Outlook contacts into the Soocial database.

2. Then use Soocial to sync with your Gmail contacts. You end up with all your Outlook contacts in Gmail and all your Gmail contacts in Outlook.

3. At this point, you can either

• Use your phone's sync with Gmail to pull in the combined list of contacts

• Use Soocial's Android app to work directly with your Soocial database

Presumably at some point in time, Soocial will have a sync capability working with the Windows tiled People app. That may be your best bet for syncing Outlook, tiled People, Gmail, and your phone.

Syncing calendars

For syncing Outlook Calendar items with Google, I use Google Calendar Sync (http://dl.google.com/googlecalendarsync/GoogleCalendar Sync_Installer.exe). It's easy to install and works well. As this book went to press, there was no way to sync Windows tiled Calendar entries with Google Calendars.

Chapter 3: Getting Started with Gmail, Google Apps, and Drive

In This Chapter

✔ Using Google alternatives to Windows

✔ Setting up your Gmail account

✔ Using Google Docs (Drive)

✔ Moving your domain to Google

*I*n spite of the rivalry between Microsoft and Google, Google's so important to today's computer users that Microsoft builds hooks into Windows 8 that try to get you to add your Gmail account to the tiled, "immersive" Mail app, and add your Gmail contacts to the tiled People app. Of course, Google is happy to return the favor, with easy ways to put your Hotmail/Outlook.com mail inside Gmail, and to import your Hotmail/Outlook.com contacts into Gmail.

There's a reason why Microsoft wants you to put your Google eggs in its basket. Google has very good competitors to the Microsoft online stable, er, stables, including the following:

✦ *Microsoft Hotmail/Outlook.com,* the *Windows 8's tiled Mail app,* the mail part of Microsoft's Outlook, and the *desktop Windows Live Mail* all compete with *Google Gmail,* in different ways.

✦ The *Windows 8 tiled Messaging app,* the *desktop Windows Live Messenger,* and the messaging component of *Microsoft Skype* compete with *Google Talk.* Few people use Google Talk as a standalone app, but they use it from inside Gmail and *Google+,* the Google social networking site at `http://plus.google.com`.

✦ The *Microsoft Windows 8 tiled Calendar app* and the *Office Outlook calendar* compete with *Google Calendar.*

✦ The *Microsoft Windows 8 tiled People app* and *Hotmail/Outlook.com contacts* compete with *Google Gmail contacts.*

Worth noting: Every app in *italics* in the preceding list is *free* if you're running Windows 8. Absolutely free. Microsoft and Google give away the apps to draw you in to their corner, with the hope of selling you something in the future.

You can use Gmail to send and receive mail using your own, private domain, and it's free for up to ten mailboxes. So, for example, I can use Gmail to handle all the mail coming into and going out of AskWoody.com, without changing my e-mail address, and without anyone knowing that I'm using Gmail: All the mail going out says it's from Woody@AskWoody.com, and all the mail sent to Woody@AskWoody.com ends up in my Gmail Inbox. It's a feature in Google Apps, and except for one step, it's pretty easy. See the last section in this chapter, "Moving Your Domain to Google," for details.

All this wrangling takes place against a backdrop of increased competition from Apple and new assaults from Facebook. All the companies really want to get you hooked on their way of working.

Don't forget that "free" services aren't free, in the sense of being zero-sum. The companies offering the "free" service gather information about you, unabashedly, and show you targeted ads, in the hope of selling you something. As a poster named *blue_beetle* on the site MetaFilter (www.metafilter. com/95152/Userdriven-discontent#3256046) put it so succinctly, "If you're not paying for it, you're not the customer; you're the product being sold."

In the following section, I take a very brief look at Google alternatives to Microsoft products, from the perspective of a Windows user.

Finding Alternatives to Windows with Google

Google has a handful of free online products and offerings that warrant your attention. Microsoft has two or three handfuls, but that's the subject of the rest of this book.

Here are the four Google products that serve as alternatives to Microsoft offerings:

✦ **Gmail:** A free online mail program, similar to Microsoft's Hotmail/ Outlook.com. Features change constantly, but it's fair to say that if you find a feature you like in Hotmail/Outlook.com, it'll be in Gmail soon — and vice versa. Some people prefer one interface over the other; I'm ambivalent, but for now I've settled on Gmail, primarily because I prefer the interface. If you use Google's Chrome web browser, you can even use Gmail when you aren't connected to the Internet.

✦ **Google Drive:** A new service from Google that gives you up to 5GB of free online storage, similar to Microsoft SkyDrive. I talk about the different online storage services in Book VIII, Chapter 1. Google Drive's main advantage is its ability to work easily with Google Apps.

✦ **Google Docs:** Contains online programs for creating and editing word processing documents, spreadsheets, fill-in-the-blank forms, presentations, and drawings. Although the programs are rudimentary, they can work collaboratively — two or more people can edit the same document at the same time, with no ill effect and no weird restrictions.

Google is gradually phasing out the use of the term *Google Docs* and rolling all the programs into the umbrella *Google Drive.* In this chapter, I talk about Google Docs occasionally to give you a reference point for when you see instructions (even from Google!) that refer to Google Docs. But the distinction between Google Docs and Google Drive is fading fast. You can use the two terms interchangeably.

✦ **Google Apps:** A combination of several web apps — Gmail, Docs, Calendar, Groups (see the next bullet), and Sites (team collaboration) — and Google Drive storage with a framework that lets you run your own domain name through Google's programs.

Think of Google Apps as a way to leverage Google's software and servers for your organization. It's free for ten or fewer business users, free for non-profits up to 3,000 users, free for schools up to 30,000 users. Beyond that, every seat costs you or your organization $5 a month or $50 a year.

Google Apps competes more-or-less with Microsoft Office 365 (which isn't Office at all, but that's a different story; see the nearby "Office 365 isn't Office" sidebar).

✦ **Google Groups:** If you belong to an organization, Google Groups offers an alternative to a Facebook page for keeping the members of the organization updated on what's happening, and to give members of the organization a chance to talk to each other.

One person, the *manager,* sets up a group at `http://groups.google.com`. The manager then sends invitations to people, who can respond by joining the group. The invitations can go to any e-mail address — they don't have to go to `@gmail.com` addresses. Members can post messages to the group, which are then e-mailed to every member of the group.

The manager can set herself up as *moderator* for the group — in which case, she must approve each message before it's relayed to the members — or whether the group should be allowed to receive messages un-moderated. She also has control over each individual, such as who can post messages and who will receive them, and she can remove an individual from the group.

Technologically, Google Groups has been more-or-less upstaged by Facebook private pages, and by Google+ Hangouts (a real-time video meeting place). But for people who feel more comfortable dealing with e-mail than with Facebook — or cameras — it's a good option.

Office 365 isn't Office

Microsoft's entry in the holistic online service wars is *Office 365*. I have no idea why. Office 365 isn't anything at all like Office, but I guess Office 365 has a good marketing ring to it. Office 365 and Google Apps are vastly different.

I have a lengthy analysis of the differences between Google Apps and Office 365 in the InfoWorld review, www.infoworld. com/d/cloud-computing/office-365-vs-google-apps-the-info world-review-447. The short version goes like this.

Office 365 incorporates all the backend server features that people expect from Exchange Server, SharePoint Server, and Lync Server — locked-down security, direct feed into the Windows 8 tiled Mail app, coordination between phone calls, SMSs and e-mail, videoconferencing, and much more. The beauty of Office 365 is that you get all those services without having to install and manage your own Exchange Server farm. Microsoft does all the heavy lifting.

Office 365 is meant to be used with a locally installed version of Office, whereas Google Apps lives 100 percent in the browser. You can get a version of Office 365 that uses only the (free) Office Web Apps — stunted versions of the desktop apps you've known for years — but most people and companies stick with the desktop versions they've grown accustomed to.

By contrast, Google Apps is small, light, and easy to set up and maintain — but it doesn't have anywhere near the bells and whistles of Office 365. Of course, it doesn't cost as much, either. Google Apps is free for up to ten people. Office 365 has a bunch of different price points, but a typical small organization pays about $ 4 per user per month for just Exchange Server e-mail support, up to $20 per user per month for the full-blown package, including Office.

With Office 2013, Microsoft is changing the nature of Office 365 — taking out the server functions, pushing you to use SkyDrive, and charging by the month. I cover Office 365 and Office 2013 extensively at www.askwoody.com.

Setting Up Gmail

If you don't yet have a Gmail account, get one. Doing so is free and easy. Besides, every new Gmail account gets 50 free SMSs. Here's how to set up an account:

1. **With your favorite browser, go to** www.gmail.com.

In the upper-right corner is the Create an Account button.

2. **Tap or click the Create an Account button.**

The sign-up form in Figure 3-1 appears.

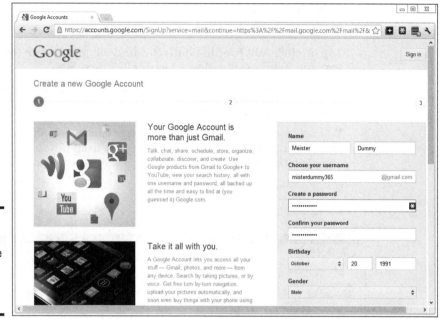

Figure 3-1:
Signing up
for a Google
account is
free and
easy.

3. Fill in the form as creatively as you wish.

If you type a real phone number, Google can use it to help you get into
your account if you're locked out. Similarly, your current e-mail address
may help you get back into your account if somebody hijacks it. Don't
let Google change your home page.

In some countries, you're required to give a valid mobile number, and
Google sends you an SMS to verify that phone number before you can
sign in. Currently, the U.S., most of the countries in Europe, and India
require valid mobile numbers, but the requirement could change from
day to day. If you're reticent to give Google your phone number, ask a
friend whether it's okay to use his number, just to get this one SMS from
Google. Google says it "won't use this number for anything else besides
account verification."

It might be worth a beer, or a pizza, if your friend prefers. What are
friends for . . .

4. (Optional) Turn off the +1 tracker.

I deselect the box that allows Google to use my account information to
personalize +1's on content and ads on non-Google websites. You may
feel differently about your privacy, but think about turning it off.

5. **At the bottom, tap or click Next Step.**

   Google offers you a chance to add a public profile photo.

6. **Tap or click Add Profile Photo and find an appropriate (or inappropriate) one. When you're done, tap or click Next Step.**

   Google thanks you on a job well done. Don't let it go to your head.

7. **Tap or click Continue to Gmail.**

   You now have an official Google account and a new Gmail address. Google dangles the default Gmail screen in front of you (see Figure 3-2), and it's already populated with three e-mail messages.

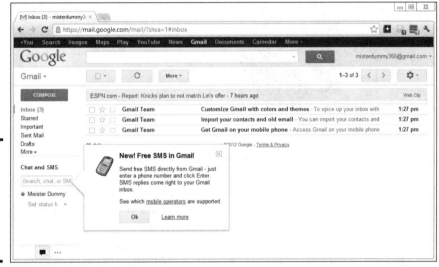

Figure 3-2: Your brand-new Gmail account comes with four e-mail messages.

A good way to get started is to simply send an e-mail to yourself. Follow these simple steps for an orientation:

1. **In the upper-left corner, tap or click Compose.**

   The mail composition page shown in Figure 3-3 appears.

2. **In the To: field, type your new Gmail address; add a subject; write a message; and try formatting parts of the message using the string of formatting icons at the top of the typing box.**

When you're done typing a message, click Send

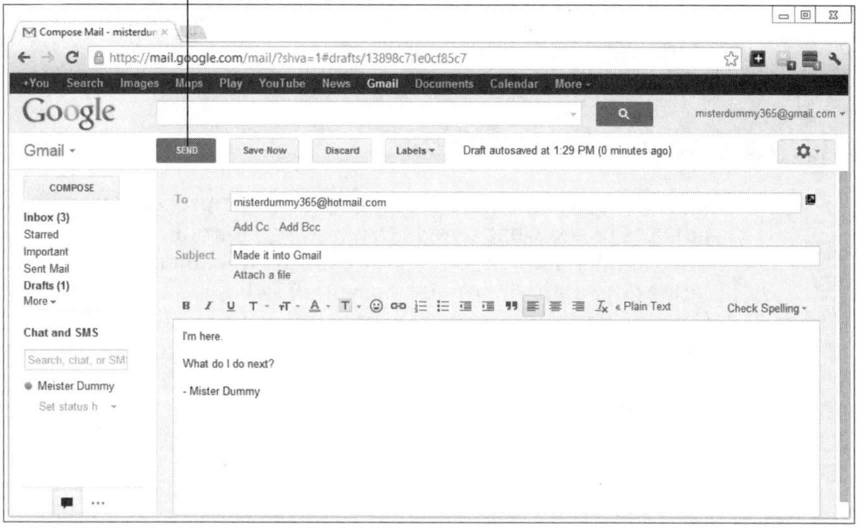

Figure 3-3:
Create a
new e-mail
message
here.

3. **When you tire of talking to yourself, in the upper-left corner, tap or
click Send.**

   Wait a minute or two. If you get bored, click the round arrow at the top,
   to force your browser to look again.

4. **When the message arrives, play with it a bit.**

   Gmail is different from other mail programs. For starters, it groups messages by the subject. With one click, change to a conversation view that
   looks a lot like the list seen in forum messaging. Its folders — called
   labels — work differently from other mail programs. Some people like
   the organization, some people hate it, but it's well worth taking some
   time to see whether this method feels better to you than the method
   you're using now.

   After you have a few messages under your belt, hop over to the Gmail learning
   center at `http://support.google.com/mail` and figure out the options
   Gmail has to offer. They're extensive, and impressive. It probably won't
   surprise you to know that Gmail has search down cold — you can find any
   message in seconds, if you know the tricks. But you might be surprised to
   see how Gmail can work offline — when you aren't connected to the Internet
   (but you have to use the Chrome browser) — and its support for huge
   (25MB!) messages.

Now that you have a Google account, take a few minutes to set up iGoogle as one of your browser's home pages, so you can see updated news via RSS feeds. See Book VI, Chapter 6 for details on using iGoogle as your default start page.

Using Google Docs/Drive

After you get a free Google account (see the preceding section), take a few minutes to see what Google Drive can do for you. Remember that Google Docs and its applications — for creating documents, spreadsheets, presentations, fill-in-the-blanks forms, and drawings — are being absorbed into Google Drive. If you see the name *Google Docs* while working with *Google Drive,* it's only because Google is slow in getting its names sorted out.

Everything's free, of course.

Here's how to start with Google Docs, er, Drive:

1. **With your favorite browser, go to** `www.drive.google.com`.

2. **If you aren't logged in to Google, provide your Google account and password. Tap or click Get Started.**

   The Google Drive signup page appears, as shown in Figure 3-4.

Figure 3-4:
Sign up
for Google
Drive.

3. **Play the video, scroll down the page to see what's in store, and then in the upper-right corner, tap or click the Get Started with X GB Free button.**

Google Drive appears, with an interface that's uncannily similar to Gmail. See Figure 3-5.

Figure 3-5:
Google Drive is familiar to anyone who's seen Gmail.

4. **Tap or click the Install Google Drive for PC link.**

Google Drive requires a very simple installation. When it's done, the Google Drive sign-in screen appears.

5. **Type your Google account and password, and then follow the steps in the Getting Started sequence to install Google Drive on your PC.**

Google Drive installs a new folder on your computer called, uh, Google Drive (see Figure 3-6). If you drag files into that folder, those files become available in Google Drive on the Internet and on any other PC where you've installed Google Drive using the same Google account.

6. **Drag an assortment of files into the Google Drive folder.**

Try grabbing a simple Word document, a spreadsheet, some graphic files, some PowerPoint slides, and maybe a PDF. Get a handful of them so you can experiment with the Google Drive apps.

7. **Go back to your browser and, once again, go to** `www.drive.google.com`.

All the files that you put in the Google Drive folder appear, as shown in Figure 3-6.

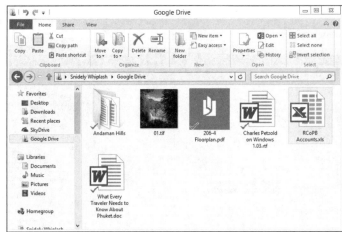

Figure 3-6: Files you drag or copy into the Google Drive folder on your desktop appear inside Google Drive on the Internet.

8. **Open one of the documents (a Word document, Excel spreadsheet, or PowerPoint slide, if you have one) that you copied into the Google Drive folder.**

If you have the corresponding Office program installed and working on your computer, Google Drive opens the document inside the correct program.

If you didn't spend the exorbitant amount of money for Office — there's no Office or Office-wannabe on your computer — and the document's fairly simple, as you can see in Figure 3-7, Google Drive does a reasonably good job of *rendering* it — showing it on the screen.

More complex documents, though, can have all sorts of problems, from missing pieces to jumbled text. Although Google Drive does yeoman work trying to display Office documents, it's far from 100-percent accurate.

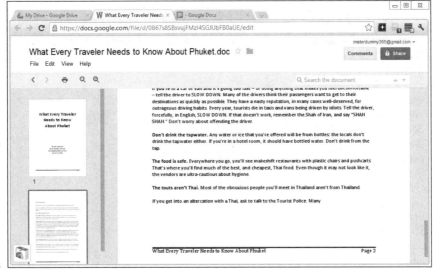

Figure 3-7:
Simple Microsoft Office documents render quite well.

9. **To edit the document, choose File⇨Export to Google Document.**

A copy of the document is saved in Google format (Word documents become `.gdoc`; Excel files become `.gsheet`; and PowerPoint slides become `.gslides`, for example), which you can then edit.

At this point, converting from the Office format to the Google format is a one-way trip. At least as of this writing, you can't change a Google document back to an Office document, although Google has at times offered a File⇨Export as Word option. Although you can treat Google documents just like any other file — copy or e-mail them, for example — they can be edited only by Google Drive applications.

Don't be surprised if the Google applications fall over when converting documents from Microsoft format (or even PDF) to Google format. `An error has occurred and we cannot save your changes.` The conversion feature is very much a work in progress.

10. **To create a new document, on the Google Drive home page, tap or click the Create button and choose what kind of document you want.**

You can create a new document, presentation, spreadsheet, fill-in-the-blanks form (which is stored as a spreadsheet), or drawing (which is stored as a `.gdraw` file). See Figure 3-8.

Figure 3-8:
It's safer to create new documents from inside Google Drive, rather than importing and switching from Microsoft Office format.

11. **Edit the file using the Google Drive apps' comparatively limited tools (although the spreadsheet app does support Pivot Tables).**

    In fact, more than one person can edit the file simultaneously.

12. **When you're done, close the browser tab.**

    Your files are saved automatically, and the latest versions appear almost immediately in the Google Drive folder on your desktop.

After you play with Google Drive a bit, take a few minutes to read the manual. You can find the Google Docs (ooops — there's that word again) help system at `http://support.google.com/docs`.

Moving Your Domain to Google

The terminology's confusing. Permit me to review quickly.

Google Docs, now Google Drive, has a bunch of apps — word processing, spreadsheet, presentation, drawing, and fill-in-the-blanks forms. The apps are tied together with a Dropbox-like online file storage and synchronization app.

Google Calendar, which I didn't cover in this chapter, is a standalone calendar with lots of advanced features, including the ability to sync with many other calendars. To read more about Google Calendar, go to `www.google.com/calendar`.

All those apps — word processing, spreadsheet, presentation, forms, drawing, and calendar — together with Google Groups (which is being edged out by other technologies), and 5GB or more of online synced storage, are available free for anybody, any time. I talk about most of the apps in this chapter.

Google Apps is a horse of a slightly different color; it's ad-supported, so you see ads everywhere you turn. Fair enough.

Although Google Apps includes all the apps and services I just mentioned, that's kind of a side issue: Those apps are all free, all the time, anyway. More than the, uh, apps, Google Apps ties together organizations (companies, yes, but charities and clubs and all sorts of other kinds of organizations) that operate with a single domain, such as AskWoody.com or Dummies.com. When your organization (and your domain) hooks up with Google Apps, you get to use Gmail for handling all your mail, and you aren't tied to `@gmail.com` e-mail addresses.

Here are several Google Apps packages that you're most likely to be interested in:

+ **Google Apps:** This is the free edition, for up to ten e-mail addresses.

+ **Google Apps for Business:** This costs $50 per e-mail address, per year. It includes all the free stuff, such as running your domain through Gmail and shared calendars. The $50 also buys your organization 25GB of storage in each account and 24/7 phone support. You aren't limited to just ten e-mail addresses — you can have tens of thousands.

+ **Google Apps for Education:** This is free for schools, colleges, and universities with up to 30,000 users.

+ **Google Apps for Non-Profits:** This is free for up to 30,000 users in a 501(c)3 organization; same service as Google Apps for Business. Larger organizations qualify for a 40 percent discount on the Google Apps for Business price.

Why would an individual or small group want Google Apps? Good question. The most persuasive arguments I know are these:

+ It's simple, effective, cheap (or free) and easy, especially if you know and like Gmail.

✦ If the Google Drive apps do everything you need — straightforward documents, spreadsheets, presentations — you can save yourself and your organization a ton of money by not buying Microsoft Office.

This, to me, is the crucial question: Do you need to spend the money to get all the frills in the Office apps, or do the Google Drive apps give you enough of what you need? Tough question, and one only you can answer after you try it for a while.

✦ If you set things up properly, you can share documents with everyone in your group, and it doesn't take any extra work. In fact, you can all collaborate on a document at the same time with basically zero effort.

✦ Everyone can work on the device they prefer; whether the device is a PC, a Mac, an iPad, a Nexus, or an abacus (okay, I exaggerated a little bit), Google Apps has you covered. And you can switch from machine to machine, location to location, without any concerns about syncing or dropping files.

✦ Google's reliability is second to none. It isn't up 100 percent of the time, but it's mighty close.

Before you go screeching to your terminal to sign up for Google Apps, understand that, although the day-to-day use of Google Apps is as simple as using Gmail, setting it up has a couple of gotchas. Converting to the free version of Google Apps isn't too difficult, but it'd be wise to make sure you understand the steps before you commit yourself.

Also ensure that you understand what will and won't happen with your e-mail after you switch. For example, Google Apps doesn't move your old messages over to Gmail: If you want your old messages to come across, you have to run its migration program. You can find a comprehensive discussion about moving to Google Apps Gmail at `http://learn.googleapps.com/gmail`.

I assume that you already have a domain name for yourself or your organization. If not, you can register a domain name with thousands of different web hosting companies. I use `www.greengeeks.com`, but your friends may have better recommendations.

In general terms, here's how to get your domain grafted onto the free version of Google Apps (read all the steps before you get started):

1. **Go to** `www.google.com/enterprise/apps/business/pricing.html` **and, in the Google Apps column, tap or click the Start Now button.**

Google hides the free version, but it's there if you know where to look.

The sign-up sheet appears, as shown in Figure 3-9.

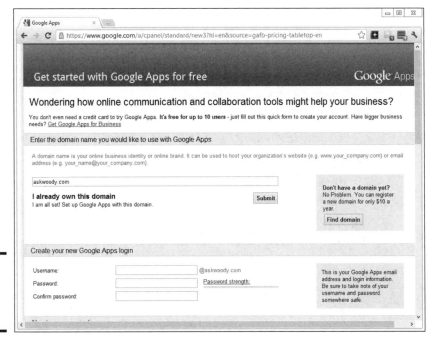

Book X Chapter 3

Getting Started with Gmail, Google Apps, and Drive

Figure 3-9: Sign up for the free service.

2. **Tap or click Start Free Trial. A form appears. Fill out the form and at the bottom, tap or click I Accept! Create My Account.**

   Now comes the hard part.

3. **Verify that you do, in fact, own the domain that you're moving over to Google Apps.**

   Google gives you three weeks to modify your website by putting a unique identifier on it that confirms it is, indeed, your domain.

   Look at the video at `http://support.google.com/a/bin/answer.py?hl=en&answer=60216` for details.

   Although you may be uncomfortable performing the upload yourself, if you have a person who helps you with your website, he may well find it to be a piece of cake. Google has detailed instructions for more than 50 different web hosts. Yes, it has step-by-step instructions for Go Daddy, in case you were wondering.

4. **After you verify that you own the domain and Google confirms that it's received the verification, change your site so it starts routing e-mail to the Google Apps servers.**

You do that by changing the so-called MX Records that are associated with the domain.

This part's easier than Step 3, but it takes some concentration, especially if you're not accustomed to bumping around inside your domain's records. Details at `http://support.google.com/a/bin/answer.py?hl=en&answer=140034`.

5. **Wait for the changes to take effect.**

   Usually that's less than an hour. In my case, it took only a few minutes.

   Mail starts flowing to your Gmail account, and you can use it immediately.

6. **If you want to move any mail over from your current program to Gmail, follow the instructions at** `http://learn.googleapps.com/gmail.`

All in all, setting up Google Apps is a bit of a pain, but after you're over the hump, using Gmail for all your mail can be a liberating experience.

Chapter 4: Using Hotmail and Outlook.com

In This Chapter

↙ **Getting the scoop on Hotmail's long and tortured history**

↙ **Starting out with Outlook.com**

↙ **Organizing Outlook.com**

↙ **Finding out if Outlook.com went down**

↙ **Getting some advanced Outlook.com tips**

T wo months before Microsoft shipped Windows 8, the folks in Redmond dropped a bomb on the online e-mail world. Hotmail — one of the best-recognized brands on the planet — would be put out to pasture, replaced by something completely different.

Welcome to Outlook.com, the website and service that's slated to completely replace Hotmail. Chances are good that, by the time you read this, there won't be any Hotmail any more: point your web browser to `www.hotmail.com`, and you're likely to end up in the Outlook.com service. Or you may end up on the Hotmail.com website, but it'll look like the new Outlook.com. Or you could end up in live.com. The Microsoft web developers can't keep up with all the changes. Sooner or later, though, you won't be able to get into the old Hotmail, and you'll have to adjust to Outlook.com.

In this chapter, I step you through Outlook.com, with a nod and a wink to Hotmail. If your old Hotmail account hasn't been switched over to Outlook.com, many of the tricks in this chapter will work in the old Hotmail, too. You just have to poke around a bit to find out where.

Getting Started with Outlook.com

If you don't yet have an `@hotmail.com` or `@live.com` or `@outlook.com` e-mail address, getting one is easy. Follow these steps:

1. **With your favorite web browser, go to** `www.outlook.com`.

 The main screen asks whether you have a Microsoft account.

2. To get a new Microsoft account, tap or click Sign Up.

The sign-up form appears, as shown in Figure 4-1.

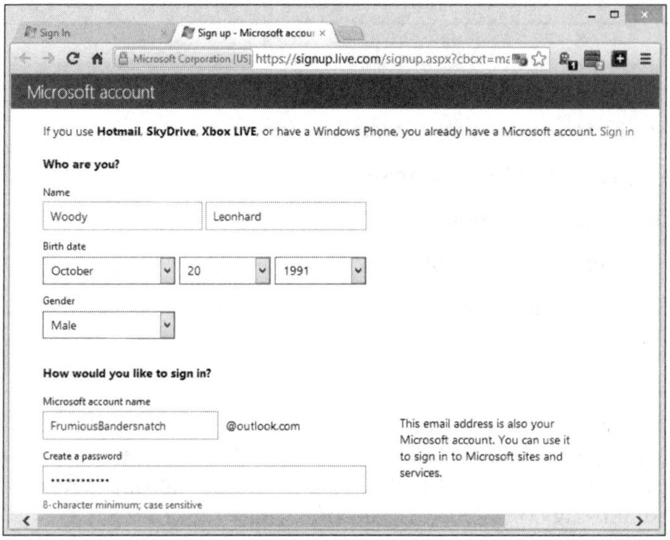

Figure 4-1: Sign up for an @hotmail.com or @live.com e-mail address.

3. Fill out the form creatively; type the CAPTCHA codes, if you can figure them out; deselect the Send Me Mail check box; and then tap or click I Accept.

The sign-up form asks for your telephone number. If you really don't want to give Microsoft your phone number — I can think of about a hundred million reasons why — click or tap on the link that says Or Choose a Security Question. While it isn't at all obvious from the way the form is filled out, if you select a security question (Mother's birthplace, Name of first pet, or something else) and type in an answer, you don't have to give a phone number.

Having a phone number on file with Microsoft makes it easier to reset your password if you lose it — Microsoft sends an SMS to your phone with a reset key. Only you can decide if the additional convenience (and greater security) of having a working SMS phone number on file is worth the dent in your privacy.

Outlook.com whirrs for a minute or so, and then shows you the Outlook.com welcome screen (see Figure 4-2).

That's it.

Axing the advertising

Yes, the entire third column of your Outlook.com home page is taken up by advertising. Want to get rid of the ads? That's gonna cost you, bucko.

If you upgrade to Outlook.com Plus for the princely sum of $20 a year, Microsoft will give you the right column back. Sorta. If you pay to get rid of the ads, the rightmost column will contain either a search link or, if the mail came from someone on your Windows 8 People contact list, you will see a picture of the sender along

with his or her latest Twitter tweets and Facebook posts. Saints preserve.

If you really want to spend the money, go to the Hotmail Plus site, `www.windows.microsoft.com/en-US/Hotmail/Hotmail-plus`. At some point, Microsoft's webmeisters will catch up with the rebranding and make that an Outlook.com Plus site, but the old link should continue to work. At $20 per year, it better.

Book X Chapter 4

Using Hotmail and Outlook.com

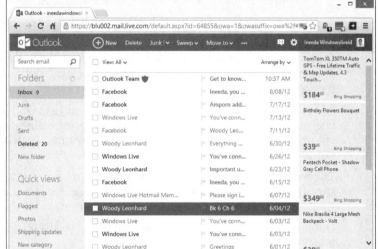

Figure 4-2:
Your new Outlook.com e-mail address is alive and working.

You can now use your new Outlook.com account as a Windows logon ID. You can use it for e-mail, Messenger, just about anything.

Take a quick spin around Outlook.com, starting from the welcome screen, which you see when you log on to Outlook.com (`www.outlook.com`) using your favorite `@hotmail.com` or `@live.com` or `@outlook.com` e-mail address (refer to Figure 4-2):

✦ **The default folders on the left are Junk, Drafts, Sent, and Deleted.** You click each folder to open it. Make sure you understand what each one is supposed to contain:

  • *Junk* holds mail that was sent to you but that Outlook.com has identified as being junk. Outlook.com and Gmail have very effective junk identifiers, but occasionally a message will get tossed in here that really isn't junk. If that happens, tap or click the box next to the "good" junk message, and at the top, choose Move To⇨Inbox.

    You can also drag and drop the message into whatever folder you like.

    If you get a piece of junk mail in your Inbox, don't delete it. You can help the Hotmail filters, and other Hotmail users, by marking the message as Junk. Just check the box next to the message, and at the top, tap or click Junk.

  • *Drafts* holds mail that you were working on, but didn't send.

  • *Sent* contains copies of everything that's gone out.

  • *Deleted* is the place where messages go when you "delete" them.

    You can create new folders. Just tap or click the New Folder link.

✦ **The search box in the upper-left is the most important location on the Outlook.com main page.** People go nuts trying to organize their mail. The Search function finds things amazingly quickly. But that's the topic for the next section.

If you use the Windows Search charm while you're in Outlook.com, the charm doesn't search your mail: Search performs a Bing search on the entire Internet, not inside your mail. To look for mail, you have to use the Search box in the upper-left corner.

✦ **The Sweep feature enables you to move all the messages sent from a specific address into a folder.** Select one message from the sender you want to move and choose Sweep⇨Move All From.

Outlook.com offers to move all the mail from the given address into a folder that you choose.

Similarly, you can delete all the messages from a specific sender.

✦ **Quick Views in the lower left enable you see only messages that meet specific criteria.**

The Quick Views options are a little unusual. Here's how they work:

  • *Documents:* If you receive a message with a "document" attachment that Outlook.com recognizes — primarily Word, Excel, or PowerPoint documents — the message appears in the Documents Quick Views list until you delete it. Strangely, PDF files don't qualify.

  • *Flagged:* If you flag a message by clicking the flag icon (it shows up faintly in Figure 4-2, next to the subject), the message gets elevated to the top of your Inbox list, and it also appears in the Flagged quick view. There doesn't appear to be any difference between looking at the list of flagged messages at the top of the Inbox, and the list of flagged messages in the Flagged Quick Views category, and apparently you can't assign different kinds of flags.

- *Photos:* If you receive a message with an attachment that Outlook.com recognizes as a photo, the message appears in the Photos Quick Views until you delete it.

- *Shipping Updates:* Arguably most bizarre of all, if an inbound message contains text that Outlook.com recognizes as a tracking number (UPS, FedEx, and so on), the message appears in the Shipping Updates Quick Views until you delete it.

With the addition of a few obvious features that you see when you poke around — tapping or clicking a column heading, for example, sorts that column — that's the extent of navigating in Outlook.com.

In the next section, I talk about organizing mail so you can use it effectively.

A brief history of Hotmail

Hotmail blazed new ground as the first major free web-based e-mail service when Sabeer Bhatia (a native of Bangalore and a graduate of Caltech and Stanford) spent $300,000 to launch it in 1996.

On December 31, 1997, Microsoft bought Hotmail for $400 million, and the service has never been the same. Microsoft struggled with Hotmail for many years, adding new users like flies, but always suffering from severe performance problems and crashes heard round the world. Ultimately, Hotmail was shuffled under the Microsoft Network (MSN) wing of the corporate umbrella, its free services were clipped, and its user interface was subjected to more facelifts than an aging Hollywood actor, which is saying something.

As MSN lost its luster and competitors, such as Gmail and Yahoo! Mail, battered at the, uh, Gates, the Hotmail subscription-based income model died almost overnight and the company's market share fell precipitously. Why pay for 20MB of Hotmail message storage when Google gave away 1GB for free? Hotmail became the number-one candidate for a "Live" makeover and the poster child for Microsoft's entire Live effort.

Microsoft has gone through a series of well-intentioned but horrendously implemented rebrandings and a few minor upgrades, passing through (get out your scorecard) MSN Hotmail, Windows Hotmail, Windows Live Hotmail, Microsoft Hotmail, and now Outlook.com. Hotmail's final facelift, pre-Outlook.com came in early 2012. Few people cared, and among the ones who did, the reaction was not universally positive.

Although e-mail as a whole isn't an endangered species, it isn't growing very quickly. Social networking sites are starting to pick up a substantial portion of traditional one-to-one email traffic, and IMs, SMSs and VoIP/Skype calls eat away at the numbers.

Bringing Some Sanity to Outlook.com Organization

Here's my number-one tip for Outlook.com users:

Create a new folder and call it Save.

When you hit a message in your Inbox that's worth saving, drag it to the Save folder.

Here's my number-two tip for Outlook.com users:

Don't create any other folders.

That way lies madness.

Yes, you can create a folder hierarchy that mimics the filing cabinets in the Pentagon. You can fret for an hour over whether an e-mail about your trip to the beach should go in the Trips folder or the Beaches folder — or both. You can slice and dice and organize 'til you're blue in the face, and all you'll have in the end is a jumbled mess.

If you want to save that message about your trip to the beach, just drag it into the Save folder.

If you want to find all the messages about Trips, use the Search box. If you want to find all the messages about Beaches, use the Search box. And if you want to find all the messages about Trips *and* Beaches . . . wait for it . . . use the Search box!

By the way, I don't mention this tip in the Gmail discussion for a reason. Gmail already has a Save folder. It's called Archive, and Archive has its own little button at the top of the page.

People get caught up in flags (you can tap or click the silhouette of a flag next to a message to set it) as a way to organize and sort mail. If you work well that way, hey, knock yourself out. But note that there's only one kind of flag; you can't set up different flag colors, as you can in many other e-mail programs. My general approach is to blast through e-mail as quickly as I can, responding to what needs responding and filing the rest immediately. *De gustibus non est disputandum.*

Handling Outlook.com Failures

Although any computer system in general — and any online system in particular — has failures, Outlook.com, and Hotmail before it, seems (at least to me) to be more susceptible than Gmail.

I recall one particular incident in January 2011, when Hotmail went down and took all the mail from 17,000 users with it. In the grand Hotmail scheme of things, 17,000 users is a very tiny drop in the 300-million-plus subscribers bucket. But if you're one of the 17,000, your opinion may well vary. Ultimately, all those customers got their mail back, but it took up to three days to restore from tape backups (yes, tape!).

If Outlook.com starts acting up on you, here are two websites you should consult:

Book X
Chapter 4

✦ **The Microsoft Hotmail Service Status site** (see Figure 4-3) gives you the latest information about Outlook.com's current health — from Microsoft's point of view. (Yes, the site is still called the "Hotmail" Status site.) Unfortunately, in the past, the site has been criticized for being very slow to recognize reality. In the past few years, Microsoft's network going down has, at times, also taken the status reporting sites down, too. (`http://status.live.com/detail/hotmail`)

Using Hotmail and Outlook.com

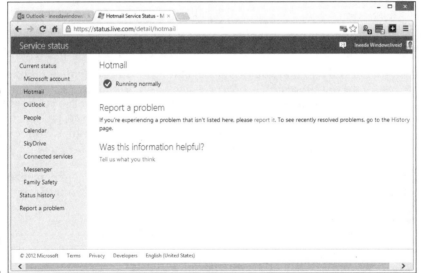

Figure 4-3: Microsoft's Hotmail Service Status site gives a very broad overview of current Outlook.com status.

✦ **downrightnow,** which isn't aligned with Microsoft, gives you a crowd-sourced consensus view of what's really happening with Outlook.com/ Hotmail. downrightnow (shown in Figure 4-4) not only actively solicits comments from people who visit the site, but also has a Twitter monitoring program that finds some (not all) of the tweeted complaints in real time. (`www.downrightnow.com/hotmail`)

Figure 4-4:
Compare
the
Microsoft
Party Line
with the
crowd-
sourced
downright-
now.

Importing Outlook.com Messages into Gmail

If you find that you prefer Gmail to Outlook.com, you don't have to give up your @hotmail.com or @live.com or @outlook.com e-mail address. Gmail gladly — I'm tempted to say "gleefully" — takes your Outlook.com mail, pulls it into Gmail and, if you reply to a message, tacks your @hotmail.com or @live.com or @outlook.com address onto it. Your correspondents won't know that you've switched e-mail providers.

Assuming you have both a Gmail and an Outlook.com e-mail address, here's how to set up Gmail so that you can read and respond to your Outlook.com mail via the Gmail interface:

1. **Fire up Gmail and log in with your account.**

2. **In Gmail, tap or click the gear settings icon and choose Settings.**

   The Settings page appears, as shown in Figure 4-5.

3. **At the top, tap or click Accounts and Import; then under the heading Check Mail from Other Accounts (Using POP3), tap or click Add a POP3 Mail Account You Own.**

   Gmail asks for the e-mail address.

Book X
Chapter 4

Using Hotmail and
Outlook.com

Figure 4-5:
The Gmail
Settings
page.

4. **Type your @hotmail.com or @live.com or @outlook.com e-mail
    address — the full address — and then tap or click Next Step.**

    Gmail fills in all the details for hooking into an Outlook.com (or Hotmail)
    account, as shown in Figure 4-6, and asks for your password.

Figure 4-6:
Enter the
details
for your
Outlook.com
account
here.

5. **Type your password, and then tap or click Add Account.**

   Gmail asks whether you want to be able to send e-mail using your `@hotmail.com` or `@live.com` or `@outlook.com` address.

6. **Choose Yes, I Want to Be Able to Send Mail, and then tap or click Next Step.**

7. **Accept the rest of the default responses.**

   Gmail sends a message to your Outlook.com account to make sure you own it.

8. **Tap or click the link in that e-mail message.**

   You're all set up.

Gmail's melding onto your Outlook.com account doesn't change anything inside Outlook.com: You still get your mail in Outlook.com, and can respond to it there, if you don't want to use Gmail.

Questions about Outlook.com? Go to `http://answers.microsoft.com`.

Weighing the Alternatives

In Book IV, Chapter 2 I talk about choosing an e-mail program. Hotmail, er, Outlook.com is just one of many, many e-mail programs. At this moment, Microsoft offers about a dozen different e-mail programs:

✦ The tiled Windows 8 Mail app (see Book IV, Chapter 2);

✦ Outlook.com, formerly Hotmail (this chapter);

✦ Outlook (many flavors in various versions of Office, some of them Exchange Server-based, some on Windows);

✦ The Outlook web App;

✦ The desktop program Windows Live Mail (see Book VI, Chapter 5);

✦ The nearly identical twins Outlook Express (for Windows XP) and Windows Mail (for Vista and Windows 7).

With the exception of Outlook Express and Windows Mail, and to a lesser extent the various versions of Office Outlook, no two Microsoft e-mail programs look even vaguely similar. In particular, Outlook.com doesn't look or act anything at all like Outlook.

Microsoft isn't the only e-mail game in town, of course. Yahoo! Mail still has a lot of users, especially in the U.S. Gmail's in the same league, although its appeal reaches worldwide. Microsoft's been trying to catch up with Gmail for years, and its latest switch to Outlook.com is widely viewed as an attempt to shore up Hotmail's rapidly declining market share.

In Chapter 3 of this minibook, I cover Gmail in some depth, and branch out to show you how Gmail, Google Drive, and Google Apps cooperate.

Outlook.com doesn't tie in with the other Microsoft apps the same way Gmail ties in with Google Apps. Microsoft's approach to an all-encompassing application solution, Office 365, uses Outlook and its variants for managing mail, not Outlook.com. (Confusing, yes, I know.) Although you can get your Outlook.com messages fed into Outlook, and you can coerce the Windows 8 tiled Mail program to grab your Outlook.com messages, Outlook.com isn't integrated into Microsoft's Grand Scheme. Yet.

**Book X
Chapter 4**

Using Hotmail and
Outlook.com

Chapter 5: Windows' Best Free Add-Ons

In This Chapter

✔ Finding out which Windows add-ons you must have

✔ Getting the lowdown on the best of the (free) rest

✔ Figuring out what software you don't need

Much as I love — and hate, and love to hate — Windows 8, it has a few glaring holes that can be fixed only by non-Microsoft software.

In this chapter, I step you through two different kinds of software. First come the (few) programs that you need to fix holes in Windows. Second is a much larger group of programs that just make Windows work better. Both of the collections have two things in common: They're absolutely free for personal use, and they all run on the desktop side of Windows 8.

As of this writing, Windows 8 tiled apps are in their infancy. A year or two from now, I hope to include many of them in this Hall of Cheap Charlie Honor.

At the end of this chapter, I turn to one of my favorite topics: Software that you *don't* need and should never pay one cent to acquire. There are a lot of snake oil salesmen out there. This chapter tells you why they're just blowing smoke.

Windows Apps You Absolutely Must Have

Depending on what kind of Windows machine you have, there's a short and sweet list of free software that you definitely need.

File History

It isn't an add-on. There, I fooled you to get your attention.

I don't know how Windows users miss this one, but File History (see Figure 5-1) is a fantastic backup application; it works very easily, and it's part of Windows. You already own it.

Microsoft's telemetry says that more than 80 percent of all Windows 7 users missed the analogous feature in the older version of Windows. Now you have no excuse. All it takes is a USB drive or a hard drive.

Figure 5-1:
File
History, the
Windows
version
of Time
Machine.

Think of File History as the Windows version of Apple's long-admired Time Machine. You get full backups, automatically, and it's easy to retrieve all the earlier copies of a file.

If you haven't yet turned on File History, drop everything, head over to Book VIII, Chapter 1, and turn it on.

I apologize for the deception. From this point on, I turn to add-ons.

VLC Media Player

Unless you paid to get Windows Pro Media Center Edition, Windows itself can't play DVD movies.

If your computer doesn't have a DVD drive, you can yawn right now and skip to the next topic. But if you have a DVD drive, you need to check something.

Find a DVD movie somewhere — if you don't have one, rent one . . . if you can find a place to rent them any more — and stick the DVD in your PC. A Windows notification appears and you can tap or click that notification and play the DVD. It ought to be like falling off a log.

Unfortunately, many Windows 8 PCs — brand spanking new machines — won't play DVD movies. Why? Microsoft decided that, even though it shipped the DVD-playing capability in previous versions of Windows, putting that capability in Windows 8 just cost too much. You can read the details on my blog at `www.infoworld.com/t/microsoft-windows/windows-8-wont-be-able-play-dvds-192567`.

Some PC makers step in and provide the DVD movie-playing software with their new machines, but they're under no obligation to do so. That's why I suggest you get a DVD movie and see whether it'll play.

If it won't play, a simple solution is the free VLC Media Player program. In fact, VLC is so good that I use it, and recommend it, for all media playing — music and movies. VLC includes the small translation programs (called *codecs*) that let you play just about any kind of music or video on your Windows 8 PC.

Another poster child for open source, VLC Media Player plays just about anything — including YouTube Flash FLV files — with no additional software, downloads, or headaches.

Unlike other media players, VLC sports simple, Spartan controls; built-in codecs for almost every file type imaginable; and a large, vocal online support community. VLC plays Internet streaming media with a click, records played media, converts between file types, and even supports individual-frame screenshots. VLC is well-known for tolerating incomplete or damaged media files. It will even start to play downloaded media before the download's finished.

Hop over to VLC (`www.videolan.org`) and install it (see Figure 5-2). Yeah, it's ugly. But it works very well indeed.

Figure 5-2:
VLC Media Player plays every song and video type imaginable, even your video DVDs.

PSI Inspector

Every system — absolutely every Windows system — should run Secunia's Personal Software Inspector (www.secunia.com/vulnerability_scanning/personal). It keeps track of all the software on your PC and alerts you when updates are needed. It'll even install those updates for you, if you let it.

The security intelligence company Secunia makes PSI available free to advertise its other services, just make sure you tell the PSI installer that it's for personal use.

Secunia PSI knows about thousands of programs (see Figure 5-3). It scans your computer and advises you on which ones need security patches, and then installs most of the updates automatically. Details in Book IX, Chapter 4.

Recuva

File undelete has been a mainstay PC utility since DOS. But there's never been an undeleter better than Recuva (pronounced "recover"), which is fast, thorough, and free. See Figure 5-4.

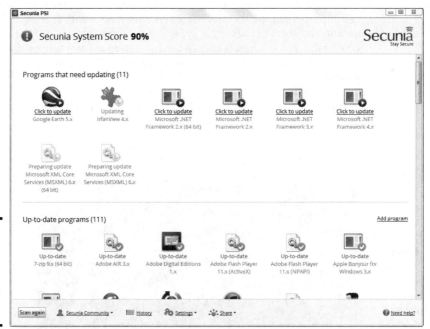

Figure 5-3:
Every
Windows
PC needs to
run Secunia
PSI.

Book X
Chapter 5

Windows' Best
Free Add-Ons

Figure 5-4:
Recuva
undeletes
files — even
on your
phone or
camera.

When you throw out the Windows Recycle Bin trash, the files aren't
destroyed; rather, the space they occupy is earmarked for new data.
Undelete routines scan the flotsam and jetsam and put the pieces back
together.

As long as you haven't added new data to a drive, undelete (almost) always
works; if you've added some data, there's still a good chance you can get
most of the deleted stuff back.

Recuva can also be used to undelete data on a USB drive, an SD card, and
many phones that can be attached to your PC.

Powerful stuff.

The Best of the Rest — All Free

Here are my recommendations for useful software that you may or may not
want, depending on your circumstances.

Hey, the price is right.

Revo Uninstaller

Revo Uninstaller (www.revouninstaller.com) well and truly uninstalls programs, and it does so in an unexpected way.

When you use Revo, it runs the program's uninstaller and watches while the uninstaller works, looking for the location of program files and for Registry keys that the uninstaller zaps. It then goes in and removes leftover pieces, based on the locations and keys that the program's uninstaller took out. Revo also consults its own internal database for commonly left-behind bits, and roots those out as well.

Revo gives you a great deal of flexibility in deciding just how much you want to clean, and what you want to save. For most programs, the recommended Moderate setting strikes a good balance between defenestrating problematic pieces and deleting things that really shouldn't be deleted.

The not-free Pro version monitors your system when you install a program, making removal easier and more complete. Pro will also uninstall remnants of programs that have already been uninstalled.

If you uninstall programs — whether to tidy up your system or to get rid of something that's bothering you — it's worth its weight in gold.

Paint.net

In Book VII, Chapter 6, I talk about the Microsoft Paint program, which can help you put together graphics in a pinch.

For powerful, easy-to-use photo editing, with layers, plugins, and all sorts of special effects, along with a compact and easily understood interface, I stick with Paint.net.

The program puts all the editing tools a non-professional might reasonably expect into a remarkably intuitive package.

Download it at www.getpaint.net and give it a try.

7Zip

Another venerable Windows utility, 7Zip (www.7-zip.org) still rates as a must-have, even though Windows supports the Zip format natively.

Why? Because some people of the Apple persuasion will send you RAR files from time to time, and 7Zip is the fast, easy, completely free way to handle them.

7Zip also creates self-extracting EXE files, which can come in handy (although heaven help you if you ever try to e-mail one — most e-mail scanners won't let an EXE file through). And it supports AES-256 bit encryption. The interface rates as clunky by modern standards (see Figure 5-5), but it gets the job done with Zip, RAR, CAB, ARJ, TAR, 7z, and many lesser-known formats. It even lets you extract files from ISO CD images.

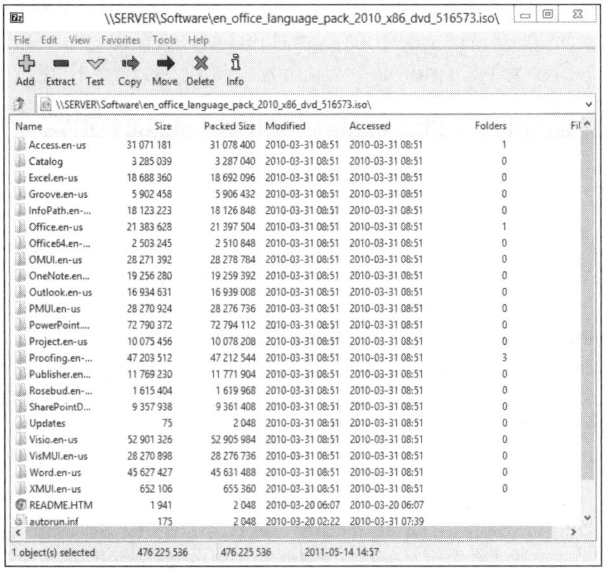

Figure 5-5:
7Zip may
not have
the greatest
interface,
but it's a
workhorse.

Another poster boy for the open-source community, 7Zip goes in easily, never nags, and wouldn't dream of dropping an unwanted toolbar on your system. Enlightened.

Dropbox, Google Drive, SkyDrive, or . . .

Even if the thought of putting your data on the Internet drives you nuts, sooner or later you're going to want a way to store data away from your main machine, and you're going to want an easy way to share data either with other people, or with other computers (desktops, laptops, tablets, and phones).

I give you an overview of the options available in Book IV, Chapter 4. There's no obvious winner — no cloud storage that's inherently better than any of the others. Just pick one and get it set up. Some day it'll save your tail.

You may not need to buy Microsoft Office

Maybe.

If your needs are simple and you don't have to edit fancy documents created in Word, Excel, or PowerPoint, you may be able to get by with Google Apps (which I discuss in Book X, Chapter 3) or LibreOffice.

Whenever somebody asks me, "Why do you recommend Office when OpenOffice does everything for free?" I have to cringe. It's true that Microsoft Office is enormously expensive. It's also true that good, but not great, alternatives exist — including Google Drive, or Google Apps (which I discuss in Chapter 3 of this minibook), among many others.

Here are two substantial problems:

✦ As much as I would love to recommend a free replacement for Word, Excel, or PowerPoint, the simple fact is that the free alternatives aren't 100-percent compatible. In fact, for anything except the simplest formatting, and most basic features, they aren't compatible at all. Even Microsoft's free Office Web Apps doesn't come close to the real Word, Excel, or PowerPoint. If your needs are modest, by all means, explore the alternatives. But if you have to edit a document that somebody else is going to use, and it has any unusual formatting, you may end up with an unusable mess.

✦ Many people don't realize it, but OpenOffice.org isn't the same organization it used to be. In fact, there's an ongoing debate about the superiority of the new OpenOffice.org (which now belongs to Apache) and the renegade offshoot LibreOffice (www.libreoffice.org). Basically, some feel that OpenOffice.org moved away from its open source roots when Oracle owned it, and so a new organization, LibreOffice, forked the code and have released several new versions that are not associated with OpenOffice.org or Oracle. So you're left with two organizations, slightly different products, and no clear indication of which version (if either) will be around for the long-term.

Don't Pay for Software You Don't Need!

If you've moved to Windows 8, there's a raft of software — entire *categories* of software — that you simply don't need.

Why pay for it?

Many people write to ask me for recommendations about antivirus software, utility programs, Registry cleaners, or backup programs. They cite comparative reviews — even articles that I wrote a few years ago — debating the merits and flaws of various packages.

Time and again, I have to tell them that all the information they know is wrong. On second thought, I guess the accumulated knowledge isn't so much wrong as obsolete.

The simple fact is, if you moved up to Windows 8, you wouldn't need a lot of that stuff — and the old reviews are just that. Old reviews.

In this, the last section of the last chapter of this book, I'm going to lay it on the line — point out what you don't need, in my considered opinion — and try to save you a bunch of money.

Windows 8 has all the antivirus software you need

Windows Defender works great. And it doesn't cost a cent.

I've railed against the big antivirus companies for years. And I'll rail once again. You don't need to pay a penny for antivirus, antispyware, anti-anything software, and you don't need a fancy outbound firewall, either.

I talk about Windows Defender and the Windows Firewall in Book IX, Chapter 3.

There are *other* security programs you need, however. I list those in Book IX, Chapter 4.

Windows 8 doesn't need a disk defragger

Because of the way Windows stores data on a drive and reclaims the areas left behind when deleting data, your drives can start to look like a patchwork quilt, with data scattered all over the place. *Defragmentation* reorganizes the data, plucking data off the drive and putting files back together again, ostensibly to speed up hard drive access.

Although it's true that horribly fragmented hard drives — many of them handcrafted by defrag software companies trying to prove their worth — run slower than defragged drives, in practice the differences aren't that remarkable, particularly if you defrag your hard drives every month or two or six. (Note that you should never defrag a Solid State Drive.) In practice, even moderately bad fragmentation doesn't make a noticeable difference in performance, although running a defrag every now and again helps.

With Windows 8, you don't need to run a defrag. Ever. Windows runs one for you, by default, one day every week at 1:00 a.m. You can check that your defrags are running properly by looking at the Task Scheduler, as I describe in Book VI, Chapter 4.

Windows 8 doesn't need a disk partitioner

I personally hate disk partitioning, but rather than get into a technical argument (yes, I know that dual-boot systems with a single hard drive need multiple partitions), I limit myself to extolling the virtues of Windows 8's partition manager.

No, Windows 8 doesn't have a full-fledged disk partition manager. But it does everything with partitions that most people need — and it gets the job done without messing up your hard drive. Which is more than I can say for some third-party disk partition managers.

For details, see Book VIII, Chapter 5.

Windows 8 doesn't need a Registry cleaner

I've never seen a real-world example of a Windows 8 machine that improved in any significant way after running a Registry cleaner. As with defraggers, Registry cleaners may have served a useful purpose for Windows XP, but nowadays, I think they're useless (correction: worse than useless). I've never found a single run of a single Registry cleaner that caused anything but grief.

There's a great quote that (as best I can tell) originated on the DSLReports forum in March 2005. A poster who goes by the handle Jabarnut states, "The Registry is an enormous database, and all this cleaning really doesn't amount to much . . . I've said this before, but I liken it to sweeping out one parking space in a parking lot the size of Montana." And that's the long and short of it.

Jabarnut is correct: The Registry is a giant database — a particularly simple one. As with all big databases, sooner or later some of the entries get stale; they refer to programs that have been deleted from the system or to settings for obsolete versions of programs. Sure, you can go in and clean up the pointers that lead nowhere, but why bother? Registry cleaners are notorious for messing up systems by cleaning things that shouldn't be touched.

Windows 8 doesn't need a backup program

The built-in backup options, which I discuss at length in Book VIII, Chapter 1, work very well.

Don't turn off services or hack your Registry

I just love it when someone writes to me, all excited because he's found a Windows service that he can turn off, with no apparent ill effect. Other people tell me about this really neat Windows pre-fetch hack they've found, in which a couple of flipped bits in the Registry can significantly speed up your computer. Before they changed, Windows boot times were sooooo slow. Now, with the hack, it's like having a new PC all over again!

Meh.

I call it the Registry Placebo Effect. If you find an article or a book or a YouTube video that shows you how to reach into the bowels of Windows to change something, and the article (book or video) says that this change makes your machine run faster, well — by golly — when you try it, your machine runs faster! I mean, just try it for yourself: Your machine will run *so* much better.

Yeah. Sure. Once upon a time, when dinosaurs walked the earth, it's possible that turning off a few Windows *services* (little Windows subprograms that run automatically every time you boot) might have added a minuscule performance boost to your daily Windows ME routine. Bob might have jumped up faster, or Clippy could have offered his helpful admonitions a fraction of a millisecond more quickly. But these days, turning off Windows services is just plain stupid. Why? The service you turn off may be needed, oh, once every year. If the service isn't there, your PC may crash or lock up or behave in some strange way. Services are tiny, low-overhead critters. Let them be.

That covers the high points. I hope this chapter alone paid for the book — and the rest is just gravy!

Index

F

X

Y

Z

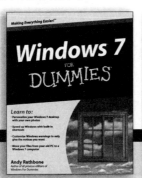

le wherever books are sold. For more information or to order direct: U.S. customers visit www.dummies.com or call 1-877-762-2974.
.K. customers visit www.wileyeurope.com or call (0) 1243 843291. Canadian customers visit www.wiley.ca or call 1-800-567-4797.

Connect with us online at www.facebook.com/fordummies or @fordummies

Math & Science

Algebra I For Dummies, 2nd Edition
978-0-470-55964-2

Biology For Dummies, 2nd Edition
978-0-470-59875-7

Chemistry For Dummies, 2nd Edition
978-1-1180-0730-3

Geometry For Dummies, 2nd Edition
978-0-470-08946-0

Pre-Algebra Essentials For Dummies
978-0-470-61838-7

Microsoft Office

Excel 2010 For Dummies
978-0-470-48953-6

Office 2010 All-in-One For Dummies
978-0-470-49748-7

Office 2011 for Mac For Dummies
978-0-470-87869-9

Word 2010 For Dummies
978-0-470-48772-3

Music

Guitar For Dummies, 2nd Edition
978-0-7645-9904-0

Clarinet For Dummies
978-0-470-58477-4

iPod & iTunes For Dummies, 9th Edition
978-1-118-13060-5

Pets

Cats For Dummies, 2nd Edition
978-0-7645-5275-5

Dogs All-in One For Dummies
978-0470-52978-2

Saltwater Aquariums For Dummies
978-0-470-06805-2

Religion & Inspiration

The Bible For Dummies
978-0-7645-5296-0

Catholicism For Dummies, 2nd Edition
978-1-118-07778-8

Spirituality For Dummies, 2nd Edition
978-0-470-19142-2

Self-Help & Relationships

Happiness For Dummies
978-0-470-28171-0

Overcoming Anxiety For Dummies, 2nd Edition
978-0-470-57441-6

Seniors

Crosswords For Seniors For Dummies
978-0-470-49157-7

iPad 2 For Seniors For Dummies, 3rd Edition
978-1-118-17678-8

Laptops & Tablets For Seniors For Dummies, 2nd Edition
978-1-118-09596-6

Smartphones & Tablets

BlackBerry For Dummies, 5th Edition
978-1-118-10035-6

Droid X2 For Dummies
978-1-118-14864-8

HTC ThunderBolt For Dummies
978-1-118-07601-9

MOTOROLA XOOM For Dummies
978-1-118-08835-7

Sports

Basketball For Dummies, 3rd Edition
978-1-118-07374-2

Football For Dummies, 2nd Edition
978-1-118-01261-1

Golf For Dummies, 4th Edition
978-0-470-88279-5

Test Prep

ACT For Dummies, 5th Edition
978-1-118-01259-8

ASVAB For Dummies, 3rd Edition
978-0-470-63760-9

The GRE Test For Dummies, 7th Edition
978-0-470-00919-2

Police Officer Exam For Dummies
978-0-470-88724-0

Series 7 Exam For Dummies
978-0-470-09932-2

Web Development

HTML, CSS, & XHTML For Dummies, 7th Editi
978-0-470-91659-9

Drupal For Dummies, 2nd Edition
978-1-118-08348-2

Windows 7

Windows 7 For Dummies
978-0-470-49743-2

Windows 7 For Dummies, Book + DVD Bundle
978-0-470-52398-8

Windows 7 All-in-One For Dummies
978-0-470-48763-1